Society and
Personality Disorders

by

S. KIRSON WEINBERG, Ph.D.

Roosevelt College

New York
PRENTICE-HALL, INC.
1952

PRENTICE-HALL SOCIOLOGY SERIES

Herbert Blumer, Editor

TO
CELIA KIRSON, M.D.

Preface

This book is intended as an integrated analysis of disordered behavior from social psychological and sociological viewpoints. It regards disordered behavior as a breakdown in social learning and as a result of obstructions in communication and in social participation. It views the disordered person as an emergent of his social relations within the cultural setting. Though the discussion of disordered behavior is limited mainly to the American setting, cross-cultural comparisons are also indicated. Its approach to the varied types of disorders is developmental and it deals with disordered behavior in sequential phases covering the processes which precede the disorder, the behavior during the disorder, and the readjustments after the disorder. Though these aspects of disordered behavior can not be described in elaborate detail within the scope of one volume, all of the more salient facts have been presented.

I am grateful to the following persons either for having read and commented on portions of the book or for illuminating discussions: Professor Herbert Blumer, Professor Ernest W. Burgess, Dr. Jerome Kavka, Mrs. Fannie Press, Professor David Shakow, Professor J. Sidney Slotkin, Dr. John Spiegel, and Dr. Morris Sklansky. I am especially grateful to Professor Blumer, editor of this series, for his interest in the manuscript, for having read the manuscript twice, and for offering constructive suggestions. Of course, these persons are in no way responsible for the way I have used their suggestions.

My thanks are extended to the Social Science Research Council for a grant-in-aid for a study of schizophrenia, parts of which were incorporated into Chapter Ten, and to Dr. D. Louis Steinberg, Superintendent of the Elgin State Hospital, for his co-operation with me in this study. Also, I wish to acknowledge the joint study with Professor H. Warren Dunham and Dr. J. Fremont Bateman, Superintendent of the Columbus State Hospital, on "Culture and Personality of the Mental Hospital." Sections of Chapter Seventeen were first written by me as chapters of that report but have since been elaborated considerably by further inquiry. Many materials from these and other inquiries which have been used for illustrative and documentary purposes are in the author's files. Hence their sources have not been acknowledged in the footnotes.

Mrs. Jane I. Perry, Miss Charlene Palman, and Miss Evelyn Schulgasser, who typed the manuscript, deserve my gratitude. And, for her patience and encouragement while the manuscript was being written, my wife, Mrs. Rita M. Weinberg, merits my deepest thanks.

S. Kirson Weinberg

Minneapolis, Minnesota

Contents

CONTENTS

Part IV. Care and Custody

Part V. Rehabilitation and Prevention

PART I

Approach and Theory

CHAPTER ONE

The Sociology of Personal Disorders

This book deals with the effects of social relations upon disordered behavior in contemporary American society. It covers the kinds of social relations and personality processes which lead to disordered behavior, and the social aspects of treating, caring for, and preventing disordered behavior. It emphasizes that disordered behavior is the result of personal conflicts.

Conflicts and Personal Disorganization. Personal conflicts arise from the social relations and experiences in the various groups in which one participates. In these groups, such as the family, peer group, school, church, and occupational group, the individual acquires his language, gestures, status, roles, aspirations, and conceptions of himself; he becomes socialized. But the way he becomes socialized depends in large part upon the way he handles his conflicts.

By conflict we mean any indecision, any fight, any inability to reconcile opposing attitudes, contradictory modes of activity, or discrepant goals. But, like a two-edged sword, conflict cuts in two directions. It can lead to personal growth and maturity or to personal retardation and disorder. The processes by which it leads in the former or latter direction depend upon whether or not the conflicts are solved. Many conflicts are worked through effortlessly, others are resolved after much searching and worry, and still others are not solved at all.

As the basis of personal disorganization, conflict is usually not pathological but is a constructive medium to personal reorganization and personal change, for every personal change involves a

3

transitory interlude of indecision. A person can end his indecision when he can face his alternatives of action, can make preferences, and can act upon the basis of his preferences. One's tastes, interests, infatuations, aspirations, and behavior continually change. Frequently, these personal changes occur so gradually that one hardly realizes the transition. For example, when does the girl stop playing with dolls, or the boy with marbles? When does the child disavow his belief in Santa Claus and the boy abandon his wish of becoming a cowboy?

Many conflicts are solved only after much distress. In this indecisive interim the disorganized person becomes anxious and restless. For example, a college student who was about to graduate was upset because his father wanted him to enter his business. The student realized that this step implied a loss of freedom and initiative. Besides, he had a distaste for his father's business and preferred to study law. But he did not want to hurt his father. Knowing his father's rages, he anticipated no financial aid if he embarked on a career different from that of his father's choosing. Pondering alternatives, he sought the advice of friends and could not study. Swayed by his girl friend and by a story he had read, he decided to leave home and to study law. When he entered law school, his routine became more taxing because he had to work as well as study. But he has been pleased with his decision and, despite outside employment, has become a better student.

When experiences are too painful, too humiliating, or too terrifying to face, one's resultant conflicts may not be solved at all. Unwittingly or deliberately, the person may try to escape from and to forget his predicament. Or, facing his stark predicament, he may find no satisfactory way of handling it. Without an alternative course for constructive action, his conflict and his disorganized condition will persist. We refer to this condition as disordered behavior because the person then becomes a problem to himself and is more or less incapacitated. Sometimes he may not realize or admit that he is in conflict. Troubled, he has to divert time and energy to manage his tensions which interfere with his social relations and with the performance of his duties. Under these handicaps, the disordered person's suffering can be as genuinely distressing as any physical illness.

For example, a child was treated with alternate tenderness and ridicule by his mother. When visitors were present or when she was "in the mood," she seemed very affectionate and pleasant to him. When they were alone, she either became indifferent or began to ridicule him. Her ridicule hurt him deeply because he craved her affection. In addition, he could not be sure when she would be kind or hostile to him. In his confusion he began to hate her because he did not know what responses to expect. But he felt that hating his mother was wrong. Besides, if he expressed hate, she would deny him the very affection he craved. He did not know how to cope with the situation. Although he disavowed his conflicts about loving and hating his mother, his conflicts did not disappear but were expressed in frightful dreams, in negativism, and in aggressions against younger children.

In another instance an adult who dreaded fires recalled that as a child she had been overcome by a fire in the home. She was asleep when it happened, and when she awoke she tried to run out, but the flames prevented her. Terrified, she started screaming wildly until she was rescued by a fireman who carried her to safety. Although she forgot the incident, her dread of fires persisted for a long time and she could never bear to watch one.

But dangerous experiences do not always create persistent conflicts; this depends upon the person's attitudes instead of upon the external danger alone. For example, a test pilot, while flying a newly designed airplane, found that some mechanism had broken and he could no longer control the vehicle. Despite strenuous efforts, he crashed and was taken to the hospital in a critical condition. He hovered between life and death for more than a month but eventually recovered. Undaunted by the accident, he insisted upon flying an airplane of the same design after its errors had been corrected. On the other hand, another test pilot who crash-landed was so unnerved by his experience that he refused to fly another airplane.

In brief, conflicts cause personal disorganization but lead to personal reorganization when they are solved. Conflicts may be solved effortlessly, or they may require anxious situational scrutiny and self-scrutiny. When conflicts, whether gross or subtle, cannot be faced, when personal disorganization recurs, the learning processes in the areas of these conflicts become arrested, and a mild or severe personal disorder sets in.

Personal Disorganization and Social Disorganization. Personal disorganization is closely tied in with social disorganization, but the two processes do not coincide. By social disorganization we mean the conflicts between two or more subgroups or conflicts among the members of a given group so that they cannot act toward common goals. But a disorganized society is not necessarily composed of disorganized persons. That is, a disorganized group cannot respond toward common goals because the participants may have disparate goals. At the same time, each participant may be organized in his own way.

Any given society is usually not totally disorganized. Certain institutions of the society may be in a transitional or chaotic state and may not fulfill the common needs of the participants, but other institutions and groups may be relatively organized. For example, many industries during war conversion may be disorganized, but other groups and institutions may be relatively organized. Although social disorganization may prevail in some segments of society, the individual may integrate his attitudes by his allegiance with a single group. For instance, during a strike two groups may be in conflict, but the individual striker may remain organized by his allegiance to the striking group. Thus, personal disorganization can be determined not by group disorganization in the society but by the way the individual participates in the group, what influences the group has upon him, and how he selects, internalizes, and integrates his group influences.

From this viewpoint the social groups in which one participates can provide the direction, content, and even the intensity of his personal conflicts. These conflicts may result from the contradictory demands of two or more groups, from the inconsistent demands of two dominant individuals in a single group, and from the unreasonable and inconsistent demands of one dominant person.

Some first-generation Americans of immigrant parents have felt conflicting influences between the family and peer group. Individuals in contradictory roles can experience irreconcilable conflicts, for example, the unfaithful spouse, the policeman who is in collusion with criminal interests, and the cultural hybrid who rejects one group and is not accepted by another.

When two dominant members of a single group have discordant goals, they can disorganize each other as well as the group members who depend upon them for guidance—for example, children whose parents place contradictory demands upon them or employees who must obey two conflicting superiors may not know which way to behave.

Personal disorganization may arise from the inconsistent demands of a single dominant person such as the oversolicitous and hostile parent who behaves in unpredictable ways can easily confuse the child.

But the individual, by leaving one group for more compatible associates, can avert worry and disorganization. The dependent individual who cannot leave, however, becomes vulnerable to recurrent conflicts and intense disorganization.

In brief, personal disorganization ties in with social disorganization on the level of inconsistent, discordant, and disrupted social relationships within the specific groups in which a given person participates. But the ways he participates in these groups influences the ways he internalizes and integrates the meanings of his social relationships.

Cultural Norms and Personal Conflict. But conflicting relations imply discordant norms of behavior. Generally, social norms consist of the common expectations and demands of the group. However, participants in the group may interpret norms differently. For example, if a Quaker husband and wife quarrel over the wife's failure to attend church, the norms of behavior in the husband's group would be those which make church attendance important. If an adolescent prefers to loaf rather than to attend school or work, his behavior is censured because the family has other expectations of his role in the group and of his norms of behavior. Thus, the deviant interpretations of the cultural norms by individuals in given groups create interpersonal conflicts. The interpersonal conflicts can become personal conflicts when the individual internalizes the expectations of the group and begins to judge himself as others do. A boy who feels guilty if he steals realizes that stealing is "bad" and is not expected of him.

Norms of behavior vary in different cultures and subcultures. What is proper in one culture may be improper in another culture. This discrepancy pertains especially to our fast-changing and heterogeneous society. Many subcultures juxtaposed side by side sanction discrepant forms of behavior. For instance, the conflicting norms between family and adolescent groups may create abiding conflicts in the adolescent.

Personality Disorders as a Category of Behavior. The persistently disorganized person who has no accessible means to solve his conflicts or who finds his conflicts too painful to face eventually becomes emotionally incapacitated in some way, whether he escapes from his troubles or broods over them. Usually, personality disorders have no demonstrable organic pathology, and they differ from organic disorders and from mental deficiency.

Organic disorders arise from demonstrable anatomical pathology such as infection of the central nervous system, poisoning, head injury, disturbances of the metabolism, glandular changes, or growths on the brain, among other conditions. Mental deficiency, or feeble-mindedness, does not necessarily result from conflict and emotional derangement only; it results also from heredity, from brain or sensory injury, from physiological deficiencies, or from lack of training.[1]

Although personality disorders, organic disorders, and mental deficiency are mutually exclusive disabilities with divergent sources, these disabilities may be mingled, and one handicap may overlie and influence the other. Psychosis may be mixed with feeble-mindedness, or brain injury with schizophrenia, or a brain injury may cause mental deficiency.

Types of Personality Disorders. Personality disorders vary in severity, types of symptoms, and course of development and range from simple maladjustments to deteriorated psychoses. We will limit our discussion, however, to (1) the neuroses, (2) the psychoses, and (3) acting-out disorders. These disorders have been selected because they are relatively clear-cut in personality organization, in development, and in symptom formation.

The Neuroses. Neurotic persons usually are mildly disordered. From encountering one or a series of threatening experiences, they become helpless and, in some measure, emotionally disabled. This helplessness is known as anxiety. Their other neurotic reactions, such as phobia, hysteria, and obsessive compulsion, arise as defensive mediums for warding off the anxiety. Sometimes these defenses

[1] See Mandel Sherman, *Intelligence and Its Deviations,* pp. 126–137 (New York: The Ronald Press Company, 1945).

are not successful and the reactions may be mingled into anxiety-hysteria, or anxiety phobia, or anxiety and obsession. Also, some neurotic reactions may combine more than one defense, such as hysteria and phobia or phobia and compulsiveness. But neurotics, despite their relatively disabled condition, are not disoriented, can communicate with others, can evaluate their behavior, and can usually abide by social controls. Usually able to retain their sense of social reality, neurotics can participate and remain socially accepted in society.

The Psychoses. Psychotic persons are severely disordered and are characterized chiefly by their disorientation to aspects of the culture and to themselves. The two broad psychotic types are schizophrenia and manic depression.

Schizophrenia, the most frequent of the disorders, is manifested by apathy, seclusiveness, emotional withdrawal, and by the substitution of private notions for socially shared ideas and feelings. Hence, the schizophrenics have lost touch with some phases of social reality.

Manic depression is a series of emotional disorders with either undue elation, as in mania, undue emotional retardation, as in depression, or in cycles of both. The manic person displays an unusual but forced buoyancy which is not founded on actual situations. His thinking and actions are scattered and nonpersevering, and he switches from one task to another. The depressive person has inverted his aggressions against himself and is so full of self-reproach that he becomes either agitated by his woes or overwhelmed and retarded in his acting, thinking, and feeling.

Psychotics usually have private ideas which are not accepted and often not tolerated by conventional persons. They harbor delusional beliefs and bizarre ideas, and frequently have hallucinations and peculiar body sensations. They are withdrawn, disturbed, queer, or hostile, and sometimes they have difficulty in adjusting and in controlling and caring for themselves. Whether agitated or unconventional, they are considered socially abnormal. Despite severe personal conflicts, some milder psychotics can communicate and, within limits, can participate in supervised groups.

Acting-out Disorders and Deviant Behavior. Acting-out and anti-social persons persistently deviate from the norms of a given society. Unable to conform to social demands, they tend to act out rather than to inhibit their conflicts and aggressions. But acting-out persons vary in their personality make-up and can be classified into the following types: (1) the true psychopath, (2) the acting-out neurotic, (3) the self-centered, indulged personality, and (4) the cultural deviant. Regardless of their personality differences, which we will describe in Chapter Twelve, all these types reveal a faulty personal development and/or a set of associations which makes them less responsive to conventional controls and which impels them to deviate from the norms of society.

Symptoms and Conflicts in Personal Disorders. Symptoms are end reactions and indicators of underlying personal conflicts and personal disorganization. These symptoms, which cluster into patterns or syndromes, generally present a static picture of a given personal disorder because the disorder can be understood best by the dynamics of the person's conflicts. Frequently, these symptoms are defined as "real" by the afflicted person or by the group, and the conflicts are overlooked. Thus, a child who has enuresis or who stammers is expressing symptoms of more basic conflicts. But the enuresis and stammering, instead of the conflicts, are the behavioral forms which hinder the child and disturb the mother.

Symptoms represent a partial solution to conflicts, but the solution works to the person's detriment. For example, a student who fears and refuses to take an examination may rationalize that the course isn't important anyway. In this way he resolves his conflict in part, but at his own expense. Frequently, symptoms represent self-defeating behavioral patterns. These patterns persist because disordered persons do not necessarily learn from experience. They commit and repeat errors to their disadvantage because they are motivated by conflicting attitudes which they cannot control and frequently cannot understand.

Many different disorders can be identified and classified by the symptoms. For example, symptoms which characterize anxiety behavior differ from symptoms which characterize schizophrenia; the subclasses of schizophrenia, such as catatonia and hebephrenia, also have different behavior patterns.

The static approach to disordered behavior involves the description, classification, and treatment of the given affliction in terms of the symptoms. The dynamic approach attempts to understand and to treat the disordered person in terms of the meanings and conflicts which create the symptoms.

Social Reactions to Disordered Behavior. The person who becomes disordered does not terminate his experiences at the time of breakdown. Depending upon the severity of his disorder, his experiences vary. The neurotic may seek out a psychotherapist in order to rid himself of his problems, or he may drift along in his neurotic manner. The psychotic who is committed to a mental hospital will experience a new if unpleasant role and new relationships with the clinical personnel, attendants, and other patients. If he improves and is discharged, he will be free to renew his former role in the larger society.

These experiences during the disorder comprise a phase of the person's life; this phase may be brief or prolonged and involves the reactions of society to the disordered person, for different societies react differently to disordered behavior.

In some nonliterate societies, disturbed and disordered persons may seek the tribal shaman or medicine man to banish their "evil spirits." In the early nineteenth century neurotics were ignored, mild psychotics were cared for at home, and agitated psychotics were treated very harshly. In many contemporary urban communities, disordered persons are generally treated as patients. These social reactions, as expressed by the institutional outlets and trained personnel, affect disordered "careers." Since social reactions vary among cultures, we have limited our discussion largely to the "careers" of disordered persons in American society.

Viewpoint of This Book. To orient the reader to the viewpoint of this book, we shall present the following broad formulations as a summarized view of the amplified discussions in the later chapters.

Disordered behavior arises in the socialization process within a cultural setting. By socialization we mean the kinds of social relations and personal processes which change a biological infant into a person and which develop and sustain his capacities for symbolic communication and social participation. In this socialization process most persons experience conflicts which they can handle successfully and remain more or less organized. Some persons, however, experience conflicts which they cannot handle successfully and thus become disorganized.

Disordered behavior arises when the person's inability to solve his conflicts leads to a helpless or incapacitated condition of varying degrees of severity. This helplessness results directly or indirectly from obstructions in social participation and in communication. It involves a breakdown in social learning, and it arrests or retards personal development within the area of conflict, for social learning means the ability to select an alternative of action in order to solve a problem.

Since the person is a biosocial unity, disordered behavior is affected by biological endowments and by biological injuries and crises. Seemingly, some individuals, because of their biological endowments, are more predisposed to disordered behavior than are other individuals. But those persons who are seemingly predisposed to disordered behavior do not inevitably become disordered until they experience distressing conflicts which incapacitate them.

Social relations during infancy and childhood decisively influence the formative bent of personality but do not determine all types of disordered behavior. Some disorders, such as chronic schizophrenia, recurrent manic depression, and "true" psychopathy, seem to be determined by early social relations. Other disorders, such as the milder neuroses and even the milder, temporary psychoses, may be influenced but not necessarily determined by early social relations, but by later experiences.

Within limits, different types of social relations may contribute to different types of disorders. For example, the contradictory and inconsistent relations which may contribute to neurotic anxiety vary from the indifferent and transitory relations which may contribute to psychopathic behavior.

But the types of social relations which the given person experiences do not invariably create specific kinds of conflicts or specific kinds of disorders. The given person's conflicts depend upon the meanings which he internalizes from these relations and upon his subsequent responses. Thus, two individuals may respond differently to somewhat similar relations, because each individual internalizes different meanings from them.

Since disordered behavior is defined and treated differently in different cultures, the disordered person will experience a different sequence of reactions from one culture to the next. The total sequence or "career" of disordered behavior covers the social relations and personality processes which lead to disordered behavior and to improvement or recovery. This "career" may be very brief or very prolonged, and it varies in different cultures.

Organization of Materials. Four of the five parts of this book describe the different phases of the "careers" of disordered persons in the contemporary American setting.

Part I covers the theoretical bases of disordered behavior. Part II encompasses the social factors and the different developmental processes which lead to neurotic, psychotic, and psychopathic disorders. The symptoms and dynamic processes which characterize the disorders will be presented first, the developmental processes which have led up to the disorders will be discussed next, and the relationship of the varied disorders to the culture context will be analyzed last. Part III includes the particular modes of relationships and personality processes in individual and group psychotherapy of neurotic disorders. Part IV deals with the treatment and care of psychotic or insane persons in mental hospitals, particularly in state mental hospitals. Part V covers (1) the patients' problems in post-hospital readjustment in the community and (2) the principles and measures taken to reduce or to prevent personal disorders.

Selected Readings

American Journal of Sociology, May, 1937, XLII:6.

Brown, L. Guy, "The Fields and Problems of Social Psychiatry," *The Fields and Methods of Sociology*, edited by L. L. Bernard, pp. 129–145 (New York: Ray Long and Richard R. Smith, Inc., 1934).

Committee on Social Issues of the Group for the Advancement of Psychiatry, "The Social Responsibility of Psychiatry: A Statement of Orientation," Report No. 13, July, 1950.

Dunham, H. Warren, "Social Psychiatry," *American Sociological Review*, April, 1948, XIII:2, pp. 183–197.

Folsom, Joseph K., "The Sources and Methods of Social Psychiatry," *The Fields and Methods of Sociology*, edited by L. L. Bernard, pp. 387–401 (New York: Ray Long and Richard R. Smith, Inc., 1934).

Krout, Maurice H., "The Province of Social Psychiatry," *Journal of Abnormal and Social Psychology*, 1933–1934, XVIII, pp. 155–159.

Mead, Margaret, "The Concept of Culture and the Psychosomatic Approach," *Personal Character and Cultural Milieu*, compiled by Douglas G. Harding (Syracuse, N.Y.: Syracuse University Press, 1949).

Mullahy, Patrick (editor), *A Study of Inter-Personal Relations* (New York: Hermitage Press, 1949).

Ruesch, Jurgen, and Gregory Bateson, *Communication: The Social Matrix of Psychiatry* (New York: W. W. Norton & Company, 1951).

Sullivan, Harry Stack, *Modern Conceptions of Psychiatry* (Washington, D.C.: The William Alanson White Psychiatric Foundation, 1945).

Witmer, Helen L. (editor), *Psychiatric Interviews with Children*, pp. 3–52 (New York: Commonwealth Fund, 1946).

CHAPTER TWO

Hereditary and Constitutional Approaches to Disordered Behavior

In the first chapter we described the scope and problems of the sociology of disordered behavior. This field of study is one among several specialties which deal with disordered behavior, including biology and psychology as well as social psychology and sociology.[1] Since the biological processes sometimes limit the social influences upon personal disorders, we shall discuss in this chapter the influences of heredity, constitution, and the organism generally upon disordered behavior.[2]

Heredity and Personal Disorders

Two claims have been made by students who regard personal disorders as hereditary: (1) The blood relatives of disordered persons have a far greater chance of becoming disordered than do persons in the general population. (2) The predisposition to a specific disorder is inherited. Our purpose is to evaluate the validity of these claims.

The hereditary influences upon personal disorders can be studied in three ways. The first way, the "pedigree method," traces family histories in order to find the number of disordered persons in the

[1] Adolph Meyer, "The Psychobiological Point of View," *The Problem of Mental Disorder,* edited by M. Bentley and E. V. Cowdrey (New York: McGraw-Hill Book Company, Inc., 1934).

[2] See Roy G. Hoskins, *The Biology of Schizophrenia* (New York: W. W. Norton & Company, 1946).

family line.[3] The second way compares the expected percentages of disorders among blood relatives of disordered persons with the expected percentages among the general population. The third and perhaps most definite way compares the percentages of disorders among identical twins and fraternal twins when one of the pair has experienced a breakdown. We will discuss the findings arrived at by these techniques in order to evaluate the influences of heredity upon schizophrenic, manic-depressive, neurotic, and "psychopathic" disorders.

Schizophrenia. Meyerson studied 97 families of schizophrenics. He found a greater number of psychotic parents for schizophrenics than for the general population, but the forebears usually did not have the same psychosis, nor did their psychoses occur at the same period of life.[4] In the first generation a psychosis usually developed in later life in senile or involutional form. In the second generation the psychosis occurred at an earlier period and in paranoid, manic-depressive, or schizophrenic form. Meyerson found also that those with paranoid conditions in the first generation had descendants who incurred paranoid or schizophrenic psychoses. He concluded that psychotic disorders resulted from damaged or disturbed germ plasm, which he called "blastophoria." By his conclusion he indirectly disagreed with the Mendelian theory which would regard the disorders as products of the genes.

Kallmann has made the most ambitious and definitive studies of the inheritance of schizophrenia.[5] In his first study he obtained the records of 1,087 hospitalized schizophrenics (called probands) who were under 40 years of age and who were committed to the Herzberge Hospital in Berlin during the years from 1893 to 1902. He selected his schizophrenic cases from 15,000 records and made his own diagnoses from (1) neurological and psychiatric findings, (2)

---

[3] See, for example, Henry H. Goddard, *The Kallikaks* (New York: The Macmillan Company, 1913); Richard L. Dugdale, *The Jukes* (New York: G. P. Putnam's Sons, 1877); Arthur H. Estabrook, *The Jukes in 1915* (Washington, D.C.: Carnegie Institution of Washington, 1916).

[4] Abraham Meyerson, *The Inheritance of Mental Disease* (Baltimore: The Williams & Wilkins Company, 1925); Abraham Meyerson, "The Relationship of Hereditary Factors to Mental Processes," *The Inter-relationship of Mind and Body* (Baltimore: The Williams & Wilkins Company, 1939).

[5] Franz J. Kallmann, *The Genetics of Schizophrenia*, pp. 106–115 (New York: J. J. Augustin, Inc., 1938).

onset and progress of the psychosis and, when possible, (3) findings in the autopsy. He also compiled information on the relatives of these probands and altogether accumulated data on 13,851 persons. From these data he computed the following expectancy figures for the blood kin of the schizophrenic probands. Children with two schizophrenic parents would be expected to become schizophrenic in 68.1 cases out of 100. Children with one or two schizophrenic parents would be expected to become schizophrenic in 16.4 per cent of the cases, or 19 times the expected figure for the general population (which was 0.85 per cent). Siblings—i.e., brothers and sisters—would be expected to become schizophrenic in 11.5 per cent of the cases; half siblings in 7.6 per cent; nephews and nieces, 3.9 per cent; and grandchildren in 4.3 per cent of the cases. Children of catatonic and hebephrenic parents—"nuclear schizophrenics"—would be expected to become schizophrenic about twice as frequently as children of paranoid and simple schizophrenic parents—"peripheral schizophrenics."

Pastore has questioned Kallmann's conclusions, because of defects in his methods.[6] Pastore chiefly criticized the following procedures: 1) Kallmann's diagnoses of the forebears of the schizophrenic probands seemed very unreliable. Many forebears were committed to mental hospitals during the middle of the nineteenth century and their records consisted chiefly of anecdotal materials. 2) Kallmann's sample of schizophrenics was not random because it included the most severe cases only. Had he included less severe cases, the expectancy figures for the offsprings probably would have been lower. 3) In computing the expectancy figures of offsprings of schizophrenics, Kallmann included 17 doubtful cases. Had these doubtful cases been excluded, the expectancy figures for offsprings would have been lower. Also, he counted 35 of 108 offsprings of the schizophrenic probands although they were not hospitalized. These 35 non-hospitalized offsprings might have been schizophrenics, but Kallmann's way of selecting them differed from his selection of the probands who were all hospitalized.

Pastore claims that, because of Kallmann's unreliable diagnostic procedures, unsound statistical treatment of data, inadequate sampling procedure, and the presence of uncontrolled variables, his

[6] See Nicholas Pastore, "The Genetics of Schizophrenia," *Psychological Bulletin,* July, 1949, 46:4, pp. 285–302.

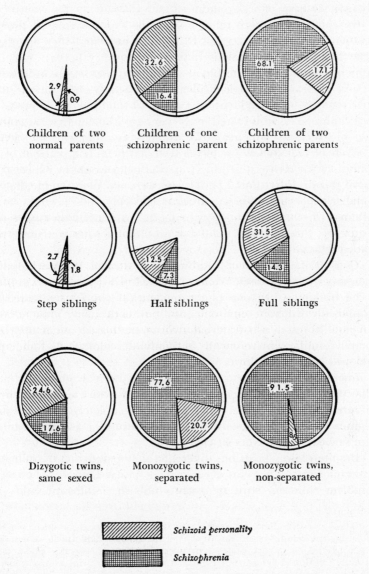

CHART 1

EXPECTANCY OF SCHIZOPHRENIA AND SCHIZOID PERSONALITY IN BLOOD RELATIVES OF
SCHIZOPHRENIC TWIN INDEX CASES.*

Children of two
normal parents

Children of one
schizophrenic parent

Children of two
schizophrenic parents

Step siblings

Half siblings

Full siblings

Dizygotic twins,
same sexed

Monozygotic twins,
separated

Monozygotic twins,
non-separated

Schizoid personality

Schizophrenia

* From Franz J. Kallmann, "The Genetic Theory of Schizophrenia," *American
Journal of Psychiatry*, 1946, 103, pp. 309–322.

inquiry did not provide "reliable information" for assessing the hereditary basis of schizophrenia.[7]

In a later and more reliable study of schizophrenia, Kallmann gathered information on 794 twin index cases and their families.[8] He found from his analysis that the expectancy figures of schizophrenia decreased as the blood relationship became more distant. Thus, when one of a pair of identical twins was schizophrenic, 85.8 per cent of the other identical twins also would be expected to be schizophrenic. Twins reared in the same environment had a percentage of 91.5, and twins reared in different environments had a percentage of 77.6. When one of the fraternal twins had schizophrenia, only 14.7 per cent of the other fraternal twins would be expected to have this disorder. Full siblings who were not twins had a slightly smaller expectancy figure than fraternal twins—14.3 per cent. Half siblings who had one common biological parent had an expectancy figure of schizophrenia of 7.3 per cent. Stepsiblings who were not blood relatives had an expectancy figure of 1.8 per cent.

Case Studies of Twins. Kallmann illustrated the workings of heredity by varied cases. We have selected two types of cases to illustrate his theory. In one case two identical twins were reared in supposedly different environments, but both twins broke down. In another case, two fraternal twins were reared in an approximately similar environment, but only the biologically underdeveloped twin broke down.

Identical twins: Kaete and Lisa were normal physically and difficult to tell apart.[9] Soon after birth each twin was adopted by a different maternal uncle. They grew up completely apart because the uncles lived in different cities, and during the first ten years of life saw each other very briefly.

Despite their separation, different foster parents, and "different environments," the twins developed in similar fashion. They were problem children, hard to teach, stubborn, indifferent, and cal-

[7] *Ibid.*

[8] These cases were obtained over a nine-year period from the resident population and new admissions in the New York mental hospitals which were supervised by the New York State Department of Mental Hygiene. These cases actually constituted 691 pairs of twins, but sometimes two twins who were index cases were counted. This accounted for 794 index cases.

[9] Franz J. Kallmann, *The Genetics of Schizophrenia,* pp. 207–209 (New York: J. J. Augustin, Inc., 1938).

loused. Physically, they were of the same size, had the same features, and were rather pretty.

After they left school their careers began to diverge. Kaete began to work in a factory, and Lisa became a domestic servant. At the age of 15 Kaete was seduced by a fellow worker and gave birth to a baby who was entrusted to an orphanage. After the birth Kaete became excited, disturbed, and full of anxiety, and then lapsed into a catatonic stupor. She was committed to a mental hospital, improved in about one year, and was discharged under family care. Within another year she had another catatonic breakdown and was returned to the hospital, where her condition became worse.

At about the time of Kaete's second breakdown, Lisa, who had been in a relatively protected environment as a domestic, began to show increasing helplessness and emotional indifference, and within a few months she too was entrusted to the same mental hospital as a catatonic. Lisa's condition, however, was never so severe as Kaete's.

Fraternal twins: These female fraternal twins were 2 years old when abandoned by a psychotic and alcoholic mother.[10] Reared in different charity homes until the age of 10, they were then returned to the father, an irresponsible alcoholic. They were maltreated by their father and by their stepmother who considered them incorrigible and mentally retarded and eventually deserted them. When 13 years old, they were incestuously assaulted by the father and were then entrusted to an institution. Although one twin began to manifest schizophrenic reactions, the other twin, who was 5 inches taller and about 30 pounds heavier than the first, developed normally.

Kallmann's Conclusions. Kallmann cited these cases to prove that the environment is not so crucial as the inherited constitution in the development of schizophrenia. In the case of the first set of twins, both girls were reared in different environments, had different experiences, and both became schizophrenic. Kallmann regarded this fact as evidence of a predispositional "taint" to schizophrenia. But certain reservations can be made about his conclusions. First, the environments were not so dissimilar as Kallmann emphasized, because each child was reared by different maternal uncles whom

[10] Franz J. Kallmann and S. Eugene Berrera, "The Heredoconstitutional Mechanisms of Predisposition and Resistance to Schizophrenia," *The American Journal of Psychiatry.* January, 1942, 98:4, p. 549.

Kallmann described as "eccentric borderline cases" or "schizoids." [11] Second, the twins' mode of rearing and their relationships with the foster parents were taken for granted, but these relationships might have been crucial in their subsequent breakdowns. Third, the disorder in each girl appeared benign rather than severe. In fact, Kallmann granted that had he not known that Kaete was a twin and that her sister had broken down, he would have called it a "symptomatic psychosis." Fourth, stress situations in each case were apparent, and were more apparent in the first twin than in the second. Consistently, the first twin had the more severe disorder.

In spite of these reservations, the important fact is that both twins reacted to adverse situations in a schizophrenic or quasi-schizophrenic manner. Perhaps this fact shows that the specificity of a schizophrenic reaction may be influenced if not determined by hereditary predispositions.

With reference to the second illustration we find that, despite similar environments, only the fraternal twin who was underdeveloped biologically broke down; the other did not. Since little is known of the social influences of these fraternal twins, seemingly these biological differences may have been crucial in precipitating the disorder of one twin and not of the other. Yet we need definite evidence to understand the meaningful reactions of the twins before we can definitely conclude that their inherited predispositions were decisively responsible for their different reactions.

Conclusions. Heredity and Schizophrenia. Blood relatives of schizophrenics have a higher proportion of schizophrenic disorders than does the general population. Identical twins have a significantly higher percentage of schizophrenics than fraternal twins, when one of the pair is affected. Kallmann, Rosanoff, and others conclude that a hereditary predisposition affects the specificity of the schizophrenic reaction when adverse and critical experiences occur. This does not mean that schizophrenia is inevitably inherited, but that, under given conditions of stress, the predisposed person may have a schizophrenic breakdown. But predisposition, as it has actually been studied, means that the closer one's blood relationship to a schizophrenic, the greater are his chances of breaking down.

Hence, schizophrenia is a result of many factors, including con-

[11] Franz J. Kallmann, *The Genetics of Schizophrenia,* p. 108 (New York: J. J. Augustin, Inc., 1938).

stitutional changes and personal reactions as well as innate predispositions. Since many "predisposed" individuals would not break down if they did not experience stress situations, the social experiences in effect are decisive in determing whether or not the breakdown will occur.

Kallmann did not claim a Mendelian ratio for his expectancy figures of schizophrenia. Also, he considered the workings of the inherited predisposition in schizophrenia to be autosomal—i.e., not sex linked—and recessive. He regarded the disorder as recessive because he found schizophrenic offspring so frequent among inbred marriages; this latter inference also requires certain qualifications, which are discussed in the section dealing with the influence of the "ingrown family" upon schizophrenia, in Chapter Nine, pages 188–199.

Manic Depression. Manic depression in some form occurs thirty times as frequently among close relatives of manic depressives as among unselected groups in the general population. In 60 to 80 per cent of the cases of manic depression, this disorder also appeared in some member in the direct family line.[12] Slater found that nearly 15 per cent of the parents and 13 per cent of the siblings of manic-depressive patients were similarly affected.[13] By contrast, only about 0.5 per cent of the general population would be expected to have close relatives with manic depression.[14] In a study of 23 pairs of identical twins and 35 pairs of fraternal twins, Rosanoff found that when manic depression occurred in one identical twin, it occurred in the other twin in 69.6 per cent of the cases. When one fraternal twin was manic-depressive, the other twin was affected in 16.4 per cent of the cases.[15]

As in schizophrenia many factors, such as heredity, personal experiences, and body changes, are responsible for the onset of manic

[12] A pedigree study of manic depression has been made by Abraham Myerson and Rosalie D. Boyle, "The Incidence of Manic-Depressive Psychoses in Certain Prominent Families," *The American Journal of Psychiatry,* July, 1941, 98:1, pp. 11–21. John M. Nielsen and G. N. Thompson, *The Engrammes of Psychiatry* (Springfield, Ill.: Charles C. Thomas, Publisher, 1947).

[13] E. Slater, "The Inheritance of Manic-Depressive Insanity," *Proceedings of the Royal Society of Medicine,* 1936, XXIX, pp. 981–990.

[14] James D. Page, *Abnormal Psychology* (New York: McGraw-Hill Book Company, Inc., 1947).

[15] A. J. Rosanoff, L. M. Handy, and I. R. Plesset, "The Etiology of Manic-depressive Syndromes with Special Reference to Their Occurrence in Twins," *The American Journal of Psychiatry,* 1935, 91, pp. 725–762.

depression. The hypothesis that a single dominant gene is responsible for manic depression appears very questionable.

There are a variety of manic-depressive predispositions. Although most of them may be inherited as dominant traits, social influences do affect the actual breakdown of manic depression. Also, the severity of this disorder varies among members in the same family, and sometimes a generation is skipped before this disorder may recur.

Neuroses. Neuroses, like psychoses, exist more frequently among members of the same family than among family members in the general population. Cobb, in a study of family lineage, found that of 73 persons with a neurocirculatory disorder—i.e., anxiety neurosis—47 per cent of their mothers had a similar disorder. In the control group of normals, only 4.9 per cent of the mothers were neurotic. Of the neurotics 20 per cent had neurotic fathers, but none of the fathers of the controls were neurotic; 12.4 per cent of the neurotics' siblings but none of the controls' siblings were neurotic.[16] Gillespie found that 20 per cent of the parents of neurotics had similar neuroses and that another 20 per cent of the parents were unstable in other ways.[17] Paskind found that 51 per cent of the parents of 890 neurotics were also neurotic.[18]

Although neurotics may appear frequently in the same family, whether parents and siblings or siblings only, this phenomenon alone does not mean that neuroses are hereditary. In fact, the hereditary aspects of neuroses are very difficult to investigate. Penrose has pointed out that, since most persons have some neurotic symptoms, the very investigations of the presence or absence of neurotic constitutions among family members are not very reliable. Cobb has also recognized that the incidence of a neurotic disorder in the same family does not prove that it is hereditary because social influences must also be considered.[19] Although emotional instability on the

[16] Stanley Cobb, "Integration of Medical and Psychiatric Problems," *Psychiatric Research: Harvard University Monograph in Medicine and Public Health*, No. 9, p. 60 (Cambridge, Mass.: Harvard University Press, 1947).

[17] R. D. Gillespie, *Psychological Effects of War* (New York: W. W. Norton & Company, 1942).

[18] Henry A. Paskind, "Heredity of Patients with Psychasthenia," *Archives of Neurology and Psychiatry*, 1933, 29, pp. 1305–1310.

[19] L. S. Penrose, "Heredity," *Personality and the Behavior Disorders*, edited by J. McV. Hunt, p. 519 (New York: The Ronald Press Co., 1944); Stanley Cobb, "Integration of Medical and Psychiatric Problems," *Psychiatric Research*, p. 60 (Cambridge, Mass.: Harvard University Press, 1947).

innate temperamental level may possibly be inherited, the early parent-child relationships and later experiences are far more decisive in influencing personal stability or personal instability.

Acting-out Disorders: Psychopathy and Criminality. Acting-out disorders cover the types of behavior which lead to criminality and to perverse and destructive behavior generally. But this category of personal disorders is so vaguely defined that the influence of heredity may be questioned at the outset.

Kallmann found that expected percentages of psychopathy did not follow nearness of blood kinship.[20] Children of psychopaths had a higher expected percentage, 17.0, than siblings, 10.7. Grandchildren and great-grandchildren also had higher percentages than the siblings—14.0 and 13.8, respectively. He attributed this increase among the children and grandchildren to the decline of family status after the psychopathic probands were committed to the hospital. Although this conclusion seems plausible, Kallmann's second conclusion seems very questionable. He maintained that, since the descendants declined in social status, their marriage partners in this new environment were somehow tainted with psychopathic tendencies.

Lange studied 30 pairs of twins in which one of each pair was a criminal.[21] Thirteen were identical twins and seventeen were fraternal twins. When one twin had a prison record, 77 per cent of the identical twins but only 12 per cent of the fraternal twins also had prison records. Though Lange showed that the similarity of criminality in identical twins was 6.4 times that of fraternal twins, other studies by the same methods get a 1.4 to 1 ratio.[22]

Lange's conclusions have been criticized for two main reasons. First, the number of cases used was small. Second, the classification of twins as identical or fraternal was frequently doubtful because evidence about birth seldom was available.

Sutherland also has shown that more identical twins than fraternal twins came from "bad families." [23] Since identical twins were

[20] Franz J. Kallmann, *The Genetics of Schizophrenia*, pp. 214–225.

[21] Johannes Lange, *Crime and Destiny*, translated by Charlotte Haldane (New York: C. Boni, 1930).

[22] See also Aaron J. Rosanoff *et al.*, "Criminality and Delinquency in Twins," *Journal of Criminal Law and Criminology*, January–February, 1934, 24:5 pp. 923–934.

[23] E. H. Sutherland, *Principles of Criminology*, pp. 103–119 (Philadelphia: J. B. Lippincott Company, 1947).

more likely to be treated the same way by other persons because they could not be told apart, they experienced a more similar social environment than did fraternal twins. In short, despite some attempts to find the hereditary bases of psychopathy and of criminality, the claims seem untenable.

The Constitution and Personal Disorders

The constitutional aspect of the personality has been regarded as the combination of innate tendencies and earliest life influences, but for our purposes we will equate this term with body type or physique. The pertinence of body types to personal disorders received attention initially from Kretchmer. In his studies Kretchmer related physique to character and body types to manic depression and schizophrenia.[24]

Using Swabian peasants as his subjects, Kretchmer amassed data to formulate such body types as the pyknic, athletic, and asthenic, besides the dysplastic, and sundry varieties of other body types. The pyknic is rotund, with well-developed body cavities in the stomach, breast, and head; he reaches his most typical body build between the ages of 30 and 40. His mood type is circular, alternating between gay and sad. When a pyknic breaks down, he usually becomes manic-depressive. By contrast, the asthenic is gaunt, narrowly built, has delicately boned hands, a narrow flat chest, and a stomach devoid of fat. He is sensitive and seclusive. When he breaks down, he tends to become schizophrenic. The athletic type is muscular and thickly built and also tends toward schizophrenia. Later, Kretchmer combined the asthenic and athletic types into one category which he called leptosomatic.

Studies based upon normal and psychotic subjects seem to challenge some of Kretchmer's findings. Though a relationship is observed between asthenia and schizophrenia, a corresponding relationship is not observed between the pyknic type and manic depression. The most serious objection to Kretchmer's results was the differential age levels of manic depressives and schizophrenics.[25]

[24] Ernest Kretchmer, *Physique and Character* (New York: Harcourt, Brace and Company, Inc., 1925).
[25] See M. L. Farber, "A Critique and an Investigation of Kretchmer's Theory," *Journal of Abnormal and Social Psychology*, 1938, XXXIII:4, pp. 398–404.

Apparently, Kretchmer claimed too much in his studies, but his general conclusion that the body type influences the direction of certain psychotic disorders may be plausible and has been pursued with greater empirical refinement by Sheldon and his associates.[26]

Sheldon found that anthropometric measurements were unsatisfactory in deriving body types. Instead, he used films of frontal, lateral, and dorsal positions of 4,000 college and noncollege subjects which were then arranged on a tridimensional scale of body build or somatotype. On the basis of 17 criteria with a 1 to 7 degree of intensity for each trait, Sheldon derived 76 different body types which he placed along a continuum.[27] The three large brackets of those types were the endomorph, which approximates the pyknic, the mesomorph, which resembles the athletic type, and the ectomorph, which approximates the asthenic.[28] In a later study Sheldon evolved prepotent temperamental types or trait clusters from these body types.[29] The fat endomorph centers his activity around the viscera, loves food and comfort, is sociable, and is called the visceratonic. The muscular mesomorph has vigorous body assertiveness, is energetic and aggressive, and is called the somatotonic. The thin ectomorph is seclusive, restrained, sociophobic, and inhibited, and is called the cerebrotonic.[30] In an analysis of two hundred cases, the correlations between physique and temperament seemingly substantiated his hypothesis, as can be seen in Table 1.

In relating body types and temperament types to psychotic dis-

[26] P. S. Cabot, "The Relationship between Characteristics of Personality and Physique in Adolescents," *Genetic Psychology Monographs,* 1938, XX, pp. 3–20; Otto Klineberg, S. E. Asch, and H. Block, "An Experimental Study of Constitutional Types," *Genetic Psychology Monographs,* 1934, XVI, pp. 145–221.

[27] William H. Sheldon, S. S. Stevens, and W. B. Tucker, *The Varieties of Human Physique* (New York: Harper & Brothers, 1940).

[28] William H. Sheldon and S. S. Stevens, *The Varieties of Temperament* (New York: Harper & Brothers, 1942).

[29] William H. Sheldon, S. S. Stevens, and W. B. Tucker, *The Varieties of Human Physique* (New York: Harper & Brothers, 1940).

[30] William H. Sheldon, "Constitutional Factors in Personality," *Personality and the Behavior Disorders,* edited by J. McV. Hunt, p. 544 (New York: The Ronald Press Co., 1944).

From a psychoanalytic viewpoint, the reverse influences may apply to body types. The person with intense oral desires becomes fat. The person with athletic interests becomes muscular. This criticism, however, does not necessarily affect the basic criteria which Sheldon used in devising his types. See Jules H. Masserman, *Principles of Dynamic Psychiatry,* p. 9 (Philadelphia: W. B. Saunders Company, 1946).

TABLE 1

	Viscera-tonia	Meso-morphy	Somato-tonia	Ecto-morphy	Cerebro-tonia
Endomorphy	+0.79	−0.29	−0.29	−0.41	−0.32
Visceratonia		−0.23	−0.34	−0.41	−0.37
Mesomorphy			+0.82	−0.63	−0.58
Somatotonia				−0.53	−0.62
Ectomorphy					+0.83

* From William H. Sheldon, "Constitutional Factors in Personality," *Personality and the Behavior Disorders*, edited by J. McV. Hunt, p. 544 (New York: The Ronald Press Co., 1944).

orders, Sheldon and his associates devised three psychotic components —affective, paranoid, and heboid. These psychotic components were given a 1- to 7-point rating ranging from a complete lack to a most extreme presence of the particular component. By correlating the type of psychotic behavior with the body type, Sheldon found that the affective patients seemed to be mesomorphic endomorphs, i.e., they had both muscle and viscera but lacked ectomorphic components. The paranoids tended toward mesomorphy. The heboids tended toward ectomorphy and lacked components of mesomorphy. These differences can be seen in Table 2.

TABLE 2

Body Type	Psychotic Reaction Affective	Paranoid	Heboid
Endomorphy	+0.509	−0.060	−0.302
Mesomorphy	+0.468	+0.536	−0.612
Ectomorphy	−0.638	−0.283	+0.542

* From Phyllis Wittman, William H. Sheldon, and Chas. J. Katz, "A Study of the Relationship between Constitutional Variations and Fundamental Psychotic Behavior Reactions," *Journal of Nervous and Mental Disease*, December, 1948, 108:6, p. 472.

From these 312 cases in Table 3 we see that, when temperament types were correlated with psychotic types, the correlations were higher, which indicates that factors other than body type influence temperament. These findings indicate, too, that temperament may have a real influence upon the direction of a given disorder.

TABLE 3

TEMPERAMENT TYPES AND PSYCHOTIC BEHAVIOR REACTIONS[*]

Temperament Type	Psychotic Reaction		
	Affective	Paranoid	Heboid
Visceratonic	+0.733	+0.197	−0.565
Somatotonic	+0.165	+0.688	−0.456
Cerebrotonic	−0.705	−0.554	+0.808

* From Phyllis Wittman, William H. Sheldon, and Chas. J. Katz, "A Study of the Relationship between Constitutional Variations and Fundamental Psychotic Behavior Reactions," *Journal of Nervous and Mental Disease*, December, 1948, 108:6, p. 472.

As a determinant of the "functional psychoses," the body type of the person may reveal the direction of a disorder when a breakdown occurs. Though body type or morphology may have some influence upon temperament, other factors apparently also contribute to the temperamental formation of the personality.

The Place of the Organism in Personal Disorders

We have described the extent to which heredity, body types, and temperament contribute to disordered behavior. The dynamic physiological processes involved in the specific disorder still require further clarification. To say that John Que became schizophrenic because his father was psychotic and because he was lean and physically weak does not tell us very much. In other words, we should know what organic processes made him less resistant to intolerable experiences so that he did break down, and what organic process contributed to his specific type of breakdown.

The personality behaves as a unity, and the segments of "mind" and "body" work as indivisible aspects of that unity. The person has certain physical endowments and acquired reactions which, in combination, contribute to his ordered or disordered condition. The physical aspects cover (1) inherited constitution, (2) birth injuries, and (3) diseases and injuries during childhood and later life. The social experiences cover (1) modes of family relationship,

(2) subsequent intimate relationships and experiences in marital, friendship, and neighborhood groups, and (3) subsequent impersonal relationships in business and in other social groups. All these aspects of the total personality influence each other.

The pertinent problems concerning organic features in personal disorders center about the fact that as yet no "causal" relationship has been established between organic pathology and personal disorders.

At one time it was thought that brain changes were responsible for personality disorders. For decades brain physiologists made autopsies of dead patients. This research has not been abandoned, but it has become more pertinent. The aim in the study of the brain is to find the effects and the correlative changes in the brain for given disorders instead of trying to discover the "causes." Schizophrenia and manic depression may involve disturbed brain functions, but this does not tell us whether the disturbed brain functions caused, accompanied, or resulted from the personality disorders.

The function of the glands in psychotic behavior, although a relatively dark continent, still has some bearing upon certain psychotic disorders. Generally, hyperthyroidism may create hyperactivity and conditions which resemble agitated depressions or manic behavior. Nielsen and Thompson report a case in which an individual took an overdose of thyroid extract and became intensely agitated and depressed. When the extract was not imbibed, he apparently improved. But it is not known why his hyperactivity assumed a depressed form. It is possible that the excess intake of the thyroid may have aggravated a depressed condition.[31]

The influence of vitamin deficiency upon disordered behavior has not been completely investigated, but it has been pointed out that the deficiency of vitamin B1 may lead to deranged behavior. A nutritional experiment was conducted on 12 patients who had a deficiency of vitamin B1. All the patients became irritable, combatative, unco-operative, fearful, and depressed; they had memory lapses, became confused, had headaches and backaches, and became very much irritated by loud noises.[32]

[31] John M. Nielsen and G. N. Thompson, *The Engrammes of Psychiatry,* pp. 359–362 (Springfield, Ill.: Charles C. Thomas, Publisher, 1947).

[32] R. M. Wilder, "Symptoms and Signs of Thiamine Deficiency," *Publications of the Association for Nervous and Mental Diseases* (Baltimore: The Williams & Wilkins Company, 1940).

The organism plays a part in the resistance or lack of resistance in resolving conflicts and hence in neurotic and psychotic breakdowns. In experiments on animals, such as on dogs and rats, it was found that sturdy animals resisted breakdowns more readily than did weaker animals.[33] Lewis has suggested that clumsy, awkward individuals who have difficulty in physical adjustments also may become predisposed to emotional disturbances and conflicts and may become psychotic.[34] Perhaps weaker individuals who become exhausted more easily than sturdy persons may also be more prone to given personality disorders.[35]

Specific defensive reactions and symptoms may be influenced by organic conditions as well as by social experiences. It is not known definitely whether one individual will respond to a series of intolerable experiences by a neurotic reaction, by a schizophrenic reaction, by a depressive reaction, or by a psychosomatic affliction. Very likely the organism, by somatic compliance, may play a part in these distinct reactions, but how and in what manner this is done has not been definitely ascertained.

Also, physical disturbances may affect the organism in ways somewhat similar to very disturbing emotional experiences. For example, anxiety frequently results from threatening social experiences, but an anxiety condition can be induced by outside physical means. Gerard has traced this sequence as follows:[36]

> . . . anxiety leads to overbreathing, extra carbon is washed out and the blood content lowered, low carbon dioxide induces constriction of cerebral vessels and inadequate nourishment of certain neurones, local metabolic disturbance evokes discharges. One can reproduce by controlling CO_2 in the inspired air, the full symptomatology of disordered action of the heart or neurocirculatory asthenia [i.e., anxiety].

In general, the increased knowledge of the physiological aspects of disordered behavior does not preclude the importance of the

[33] See Ivan Pavlov, *Conditioned Reflexes and Psychiatry*, translated by W. Horsely Gantt (New York: International Publishers Company, 1941).

[34] Nolan D. C. Lewis, *Constitutional Factors in Dementia Praecox* (Washington, D.C.: Nervous and Mental Disease Publishing Company, 1923).

[35] Franz J. Kallmann and S. Eugene Berrera, "The Heredoconstitutional Mechanisms of Predisposition and Resistance to Schizophrenia," *The American Journal of Psychiatry*, January, 1942, 98:4, pp. 544–550.

[36] Ralph W. Gerard, "Physiology and Psychiatry," *The American Journal of Psychiatry*, September, 1949, 106:3, p. 163.

social experiences of the individual. The physiological and social psychological are different dimensions of personality. The attempt to explain social psychological experiences by physiological mechanisms inevitably reduces one level of reality to another and can have only distorted consequences. We cannot explain life by analyzing the components of a cell. We cannot explain types of interactions or socialized meanings by the physiological workings of the body. Disordered behavior is influenced by physiological processes but it is also influenced by the types of social relations and meanings the person acquires in his series of groups. For this reason we turn now to the influences of social relations upon disordered behavior in order to present a more complete picture of disordered behavior.

Selected Readings

Burchard, E. M. L., "Physique and Psychoses," *Comparative Psychological Monographs*, 1936, 13:61.

Farber, M. L., "A Critique and an Investigation of Kretchmer's Theory," *Journal of Abnormal and Social Psychology*, 1938, 33:4, pp. 398–404.

Gerard, Ralph W., "Physiology and Psychiatry," *The American Journal of Psychiatry*, September, 1949, 106:3, pp. 163–165.

Hoskins, Roy G., *The Biology of Schizophrenia* (New York: W. W. Norton & Company, 1942).

Kallmann, Franz J., *The Genetics of Schizophrenia* (New York: J. J. Augustin, Inc., 1938).

———, "The Genetic Theory of Schizophrenia," *The American Journal of Psychiatry*, 1946, 103, pp. 309–322.

———, and S. Eugene Berrera, "Heredoconstitutional Mechanisms of Predisposition and Resistance to Schizophrenia," *The American Journal of Psychiatry*, January, 1942, 98:4, pp. 544–550.

Kretchmer, Ernest, *Physique and Character* (New York: Harcourt, Brace and Company, Inc., 1925).

Lange, Johannes, *Crime and Destiny*, translated by Charlotte Haldane (New York: C. Boni, 1930).

Meyerson, Abraham, "The Relationship of Hereditary Factors to Mental Processes," *The Inter-relationship of Mind and Body* (Baltimore: The Williams & Wilkins Company, 1939).

Pastore, Nicholas, "The Genetics of Schizophrenia," *Psychological Bulletin*, July, 1949, 46:4, pp. 285–302.

Penrose, L. S., "Heredity," *Personality and the Behavior Disorders*, edited by J. McV. Hunt, pp. 505–525 (New York: The Ronald Press Company, 1944).

Sheldon, William H., S. S. Stevens, and W. B. Tucker, *The Varieties of Human Physique* (New York: Harper & Brothers, 1940).
———, and S. S. Stevens, *The Varieties of Temperament* (New York: Harper & Brothers, 1942).
Wittman, Phyllis, William H. Sheldon, and Chas. J. Katz, "A Study of the Relationship between Constitutional Variations and Fundamental Psychotic Behavior Reactions," *Journal of Nervous and Mental Disease,* December, 1948, 108:6, pp. 470–476.

CHAPTER THREE

Social Relations as Perspective

In the first chapter we pointed out that this book aims to understand the influence of social relations upon disordered behavior. In the second chapter we described those organic processes which contribute to disordered behavior and which limit the favorable or adverse effects of social experiences. In this chapter we shall trace the spreading interest in social relations as a perspective to disordered behavior among several disciplines which deal with disordered behavior.

This interest in social relations spread to these fields because of (1) the unsuccessful efforts to understand some psychotic disorders on the basis of organic pathology only, (2) the efforts to find an intermediate area between impersonal cultural norms and the behavior of the biological individual, (3) the attempts to understand clearly and explicitly the patient-therapist relationship, and (4) the general recognition of the effects of social relations upon human behavior and motivation. Within the past three decades, particularly within the past ten years, the study of social relations has become increasingly important as a perspective or factor for understanding disordered behavior among such diverse disciplines as psychiatry, psychoanalysis, sociometry, psychiatric social work, psychology, sociology, and anthropology.

Psychiatry. Psychiatry as a branch of medicine deals with the diagnosis, understanding, and treatment of "mental disease." Through the years its conception of personality and of disordered

behavior has changed considerably.[1] Initially, psychiatrists confined
their practice to hospitalized psychotics and regarded them as ailing
organisms. Not until the twentieth century, when the influence of
psychobiology and psychoanalysis began to make headway against
powerful Kraepelinian or biological traditions, did psychiatrists
give more attention to the social and psychological phases of personality. The psychobiological psychiatrists recognized that the
patient was an active being in a total environment instead of a
static organism; hence they began to study the social aspects of
personality with other facets of behavior.[2]

In trying to understand the disordered person, especially the child,
psychiatrists had to recognize the influence of social relations upon
the patient's condition. For example, Bunker acknowledged that
it was very difficult to treat the child as an isolated unit instead of
as an integrated part of a group.[3]

This approach also became widespread among specialists in child
guidance, in mental hygiene, and among those psychiatrists who
were influenced directly by social sciences.[4] White, for example,
considered the understanding of social relations as the beginning
of a "social psychiatry which deals with man as a social being in his
relations to his fellows."[5] By 1934, Bentley was able to contrast the

[1] Before the Civil War some psychiatrists believed in the "moral" or social
causes of psychoses. This view was influenced by Pinel and Esquirol of France.
But with the rise of neurology after the Civil War and the influence of
Kraepelin in the late nineteenth and early twentieth centuries, the biological
approach dominated psychiatry until about the second quarter of the twentieth
century. See Gregory Zilboorg and G. W. Henry, *A History of Medical Psychology*
(New York: W. W. Norton & Company, 1941).

[2] Alfred Lief (editor), *The Commonsense Psychiatry of Dr. Adolph Meyer*
(New York: McGraw-Hill Book Company, Inc., 1948); W. Muncie, *Psychobiology and Psychiatry* (St. Louis: The C. V. Mosby Company, Medical Publishers, 1939).

[3] Henry Alden Bunker, "Psychiatry as a Specialty," *One Hundred Years of
American Psychiatry*, p. 497 (New York: Columbia University Press, 1944).

[4] Trigant A. Burrow, "So-called 'Normal' Social Relationships Expressed in the
Individual and the Group, and Their Bearing upon Neurotic Disharmonies,
Publications of the American Sociological Society, 1929, XXIV, pp. 285–286;
William A. White, "Psychiatry and the Social Sciences," *The American Journal
of Psychiatry*, March, 1928, VII:5, pp. 729–747; Herman Adler, "The Relation
between Psychiatry and the Social Sciences," *The American Journal of Psychiatry*, April, 1927, VI, pp. 661–670.

[5] Wm. A. White, *Forty Years of Psychiatry*, pp. 83–84 (Washington: Nervous
and Mental Disease Publishing Company, 1933).

psychiatric approach of the preceding generation with the approach of that time. One generation before, "the patient was an afflicted organism; now [1934] he is a disturbed, distorted and unadjusted member of a family and of a community . . . a disordered person." [6] Later, Plant systematized this tendency when he studied the disordered personality in life situations. In criticizing the medical or classical psychiatric approach to personal disorders, Plant stated:[7]

> The classical psychiatric approach—preoccupied with the structure of the individual in vacuo, thus seems to us inadequate to a situation facing frankly the sociological forces. . . . We are suspicious that psychiatric theory demands considerable reformulation after it has had a much more extensive experience with individuals actually adjusting to a certain milieu. As long as we center our interest in hospitals —and will study our patients at ten, twenty, or hundreds of miles away from their actual homes, psychiatric theory must suffer from a certain parochial sort of individualism that quite lacks realism.

Plant explicitly analyzed the influences of the social matrix upon the person and recognized the importance of social relationships within this matrix.

Sullivan was a psychoanalyst whose early interests were focused upon schizophrenics. He was among the first psychiatrists to recognize the effects of interpersonal relations upon personal disorders and, indeed, regarded this field as the essential subject matter of psychiatry. Perhaps more than any other psychiatrist, Sullivan was instrumental in giving currency to the term "interpersonal relationships." By emphasizing the effects of interaction above the sexual drive, as conceived by orthodox psychoanalysts, he began to explore the emergents of varying types of relationships such as meanings, language, and the self.[8] Also, he investigated the modes of relationships that contributed to the development of anxiety and other disorders, the interpersonal processes between patient and therapist, the influences of early personal relations upon personality

[6] Madison Bentley, "General and Experimental Psychology," *The Problem of Mental Disorder,* edited by Madison Bentley and E. V. Cowdrey, p. 294 (New York: McGraw-Hill Book Company, Inc., 1934). By permission.

[7] James S. Plant, *Personality and the Cultural Pattern,* p. 143 (New York: Commonwealth Fund, 1937).

[8] Harry Stack Sullivan, "Multidisciplined Coordination of Interpersonal Data," *Culture and Personality,* edited by S. Stansfeld Sargent and Marian W. Smith, pp. 175–194 (New York: Viking Fund, Inc., 1949); also, Harry Stack Sullivan, "The Study of Psychiatry," *Psychiatry,* 1947, 10, pp. 355–371.

development, and the use of varying approaches to the study of interpersonal relations.

Sullivan's followers and many other psychiatrists recognized the influence of interpersonal relationships upon personality develop-ment. Consequently, they explored many neglected facets of the disordered behavior such as the patient's whole constellation of re-lations before his breakdown, his unintelligible expressions, and his capacity for relating with other persons during and after his breakdown. This change in orientation also was evident in the spe-cialized field of psychoanalysis.

Psychoanalysis. Although psychoanalysis has become accepted completely or partially by many psychiatrists, it differs from psy-chiatry proper because it is chiefly concerned with neuroses rather than with psychoses and because it has formulated a distinct body of theory and psychotherapeutic method. Recently, it has extended its theory and psychotherapeutic method to cover psychoses and psychosomatic disorders.[9] In spite of its instinctual bias and its in-dividual genetic approach to culture, psychoanalysis has been chiefly concerned with psychodynamics.[10] From the outset, Freud recognized the effects of interpersonal relationships in the family upon personality, particularly in the form of the Oedipal complex. But the difficulty with this psychoanalytic emphasis was that it was rooted in biological sources and considered behavior in its universal aspect. The early psychoanalysts did not recognize the relativity of cultures and the variations in the socialization at the personality. Recently, however, the psychoanalysts have begun to attribute more importance to the varying culture contexts in which personality dynamisms are developed and expressed. Their shift in viewpoint was influenced by two sources: (1) the challenging questions offered by the social scientists, and (2) the increasing awareness of the interpersonal process between the therapist and the patient.

It is not surprising that women, notably Karen Horney and

[9] John N. Rosen, "The Treatment of Schizophrenic Psychosis by Direct Analytic Therapy," *Psychiatric Quarterly,* January, 1947, 21:1, pp. 1–37; Freida–Fromm–Reichmann, "Remarks on the Philosophy of Mental Disorder," *A Study of Interpersonal Relations,* edited by Patrick Mullahy, pp. 162–191 (New York: Hermitage Press, 1949).

[10] Sigmund Freud, "The History of the Psychoanalytic Movement," *The Basic Writings of Sigmund Freud,* translated and edited by A. A. Brill (New York: Random House, 1938).

Clara Thompson, were among the Neo-Freudians who rejected some of Freud's early formulations.[11] They rejected the notions of innate psychological differences between men and women and the seeming inferiority of women. They pointed out that many psychological differences between the sexes stemmed from their respective roles in society. They correctly maintained that Freud universalized the social position of women in middle and upper middle classes of the Victorian period. From this vantage point Horney, particularly, emphasized the modes of relationships within the culture as the bases for understanding disturbed and disordered persons and pursued a sociological instead of a physio-anatomical view of personality.

Horney, Fromm, Thompson, and others have attributed faulty early relationships as the developing sources of neurosis and have revised or disposed of many of the ontogenetic complexes in which many orthodox Freudians believed.[12] Fromm has scrutinized the relationships between the authority figure and the child, and in another study he has shown how the context of relationships has differentiated "modern man" from other historic types. Even the psychoanalysts who have not veered far from Freud have concentrated more attention upon the ego or the self and as such have attributed more importance to the sphere of interaction. For example, Alexander and his associates have come to regard neurosis as "the result of emotional experiences in human relations which the patient could not deal with adequately in the past."[13]

In reappraising patient-therapist relations, psychoanalysts have become more sharply aware of the intrinsic effects of the mode of interaction upon the patient's condition. Ferenczi and Rank were among the first to call attention to the fact that the "emotional experience of the patient in his relationships to the physician" was the main therapeutic factor and that the recall of forgotten events was

[11] Karen Horney, *New Ways in Psychoanalysis* (New York: W. W. Norton & Company, 1939); Clara Thompson, *Psychoanalysis: Evolution and Development* (New York: Hermitage House, Inc., 1950).

[12] Karen Horney, *Our Inner Conflicts* (New York: W. W. Norton & Company, 1945); Erich Fromm, "Individual and Social Origins of Neurosis," *American Sociological Review*, 1944, V, pp. 380–384.

[13] Franz Alexander, "Introduction," *Proceedings of the Third Psychoanalytic Council*, p. 13 (Chicago: Institute for Psychoanalysis, 1946). See also Paul Schilder, "The Sociological Implications of the Neuroses, *The Journal of Social Psychology*, 1942, XV, pp. 3–21.

not so essential to the treatment.[14] This notion has been developed by psychoanalysts in prolonged and in brief psychotherapy.[15] In addition, they recognized that clinical relationships are an integral segment of the total web of the patient's relationships. The relationships which the patient experienced between treatment sessions in the family, in the office, and among his friends could hinder or facilitate his improvement. The cautious therapist, therefore, became aware of the problems confronting the patient in his diverse spheres of contemporary activity. Because of this interest, he had to examine the patient's competitive associations which were on a somewhat different dimension than relationships encountered in the family. As a matter of fact, these competitive relationships of the impersonal community became a distinct means for interpreting our culture.

Horney and Sullivan, among others, reinterpreted the importance of the transference process in understanding and in treating neurotic behavior.[16] The knowledge of human psychology, Horney maintained, was essentially based upon understanding social relationships, and the therapist, by skillful use of these relationships, could make the treatment far more effective.[17]

In addition to sociometry, the two clinical disciplines related to psychiatry and psychoanalysis were psychology and psychiatric social work. The two research disciplines which collaborated with psychiatry and psychoanalysis were sociology and anthropology. These disciplines also began to implement or had implemented social relations as media for understanding personal disorders.

Sociometry and Psychodrama. Sociometry and psychodrama are

[14] Sander Ferenczi and Otto Rank, *The Development of Psychoanalysis,* translated by Caroline Newton, p. 21 (Washington, D.C.: Nervous and Mental Disease Publishing Company, 1925).

[15] *Proceedings of the Third Psychoanalytic Council* (Chicago: Institute for Psychoanalysis, 1946); also, Franz Alexander, *Our Age of Unreason* (Philadelphia: J. B. Lippincott Company, 1942).

[16] Karen Horney, *New Ways in Psychoanalysis,* pp. 34–35 (New York: W. W. Norton & Company, 1939).

[17] See Franz Alexander and Thomas M. French, *Psychoanalytic Therapy,* pp. 25–65 (New York: The Ronald Press Company, 1945); also, Harry Stack Sullivan, *Modern Conceptions of Psychiatry* (Washington, D.C.: The William Alanson White Psychiatric Foundation, 1940).

techniques devised by Moreno and refined by his associates.[18] These techniques have been adopted widely and have been incorporated into sociology and psychology. Sociometry represents a technique for ascertaining the informal organization of a given group based upon the preferences of the individual members. This informal organization can be delineated in diagram form by a device known as the sociogram. The sociogram can reveal what members of a given group have close or distant relationships, frequent or infrequent associations. Since it can discern the structure of social relationships in such groups as the classroom, the office, and the peer group among other groups, the sociogram becomes a relatively useful device for detecting what persons are isolated from or have low status in the group.[19]

The dynamic processes of interpersonal relations on the prescribed setting of a stage are expressed in a form of diagnosis and therapy known as psychodrama. In this setting the conflicts of ordered persons as well as disordered persons, when acted out, can be understood more clearly and hence diagnosed or treated. The subject who acts out his conflicts with other persons engages in role taking and in role playing. He may be asked to respond to imaginary persons whom he invents and with whom he fantasies a relationship to his own liking. Or he may participate with actors— "auxiliary egos"—who represent persons whom he knows in real life. Many techniques in psychodrama have been devised and have been applied for diagnostic and therapeutic purposes for neuroses, psychoses, delinquency, marital discord, and other problems of maladjustment.[20]

Psychodrama has been applied by psychologists in mental hospitals for treating disordered persons, and sociometric techniques have been used by sociologists for understanding group morale and the maladjusted persons in the group. Although not used very ex-

[18] J. L. Moreno, *Who Shall Survive?* (Washington, D.C.: Nervous and Mental Disease Publishing Company, 1943); Helen H. Jennings, *Leadership and Isolation* (New York: Longmans, Green & Co., Inc., 1943).

[19] Merl E. Bonney, *Popular and Unpopular Children* (New York: Beacon House, Inc., 1947); Mary L. Northway, "Outsiders: A Study of Personality Patterns of Children Least Acceptable to Their Age Mates," *Sociometry,* February, 1944, 7, pp. 10–25.

[20] J. L. Moreno, "Psychodramatic Shock Therapy: A Sociometric Approach to the Problem of Mental Disorder," *Sociometry,* 1939, 2:1, pp. 1–30; J. L. Moreno, "Psychodramatic Treatment of Psychoses," *Sociometry,* 1940, 3, pp. 115–132.

tensively by psychiatrists, these techniques and concepts have been useful for understanding the modes of relationships in artificially designated groups and in natural groups.

Psychiatric Social Work. Like psychiatry, psychiatric social work is an applied discipline. But it has been developing a rationale to supplement its techniques for treating and for preventing personal disorders.[21] The influences of social relationships upon personal disorders were more clearly discerned by the social workers when they shifted attention to the individual as an integral part of his social milieu.

This viewpoint became clearer during and after the economic depression, for then they recognized that social conditions, rather than the adequacy or inadequacy of the particular individual, were frequently responsible for disturbed and disordered behavior. Hence, the social workers often emphasized "the continued study of social factors in mental disease and social treatment." [22] As a matter of fact, psychiatric social workers, more than any other members of the clinical team, were entrusted with the "manipulation of the environment" and with changing the attitudes of these persons who were part of the patient's milieu. By visiting the patient's family or by interviewing them in the clinic or hospital, they had ample opportunities to see the patient's network of relationships and to determine the effects of these relationships upon the patient's condition.[23]

Within this general framework, certain constructive modes of therapy developed, as "relationship therapy," which was an outgrowth of Rank's "will therapy." [24] In this functional version of therapy the social worker refrained from projecting or imposing her

[21] "Psychiatric social work stands today as one such specialized area, with a developing body of knowledge and skill that is forming the basis of specialized training. It represents social work practiced in connection with psychiatry and mental hygiene in organizations that have for their primary purpose the study, treatment and prevention of mental and nervous disorders." Lois M. French, *Psychiatric Social Work*, p. 3 (New York: Commonwealth Fund, 1940). Quoted by permission of Harvard University Press.

[22] *Ibid.*, pp. 19–20.

[23] See Kimball Young,, "Social Psychology and Social Casework," *American Sociological Review*, February, 1951, 16:1, pp. 54–61; Jessie Taft, *The Dynamics of Therapy* (New York: The Macmillan Company, 1933).

[24] Lois M. French, *Psychiatric Social Work*, pp. 202, 203 (New York: Commonwealth Fund, 1940).

wishes upon the client or patient. Instead, by a detached sympathy and friendly interest, she helped him solve his own problems. This client-centered approach aimed to have the patient face his problems, understand his role in these difficulties, and, through a process of insight, work out a solution. By the very character of this approach the patient's social relations were stressed, and the role of the social worker to the client became more explicit.

Psychology. Early experimental psychology concentrated upon taste, vision, intelligence, reaction time, and other individualistic phenomena. But this individualistic approach presented an incomplete picture of personality. Wundt recognized this fact in the nineteenth century when he concerned himself with folk psychology. In the United States, James, Prince, Hall, Baldwin, and McDougall, among others, studied the influences of modes of interactions upon personality formation and behavior.[25] But the increasing recognition of the influence of social relationships and the socialization process upon personality formation and behavior came with (1) the repudiation of the instinct theory, (2) the application of the conditioning hypothesis to social relations, and (3) the influence of pragmatic philosophy and social psychology—especially by Dewey and Mead.[26]

In addition, the personalistic psychologists made empirical inquiries and general insights into personality development. J. F. Brown attempted to reconcile Freudian psychology, social psychology, and field theory. Neo-Freudians influenced psychologists by their analyses of the aberrant phases of personality in terms of social relationships. Gordon Allport and others emphasized and studied the unique development of the single person. Sears, Orlansky, and others assessed Freudian concepts in terms of their empirical validity. All these types of studies provided firmer theoretical bases

[25] William James, *Principles of Psychology* (New York: Longmans, Green & Co., Inc., 1890); Morton Prince, *The Unconscious* (New York: The Macmillan Company, 1924); G. Stanley Hall, *Adolescence* (New York: Appleton-Century-Crofts, Inc., 1905); James M. Baldwin, *Mental Development in the Child and the Race* (New York: The Macmillan Company, 1895); William McDougall, *Introduction to Social Psychology* (London: Methuen & Co., Ltd., 1908).
[26] John Dewey, *Human Nature and Conduct* (New York: Henry Holt and Company, Inc., 1922); George H. Mead, "Social Psychology as Counterpart to Physiological Psychology," *Psychological Bulletin*, 1909, VI, pp. 401–418.

for psychology generally and were increasingly influencing clinical and abnormal psychology.[27]

Early clinical psychologists devoted most of their attention to psychometric tests, or interpreted projective tests, such as the Rorschach Psychodiagnostic Ink-blot Test, from an individualistic viewpoint. Usually they took their cues of interpreting personality from the psychiatrists, but, with the added knowledge of the social aspects of personality, they were able to analyze personality from their own frames of reference.

The concepts of social interaction, role taking, the self, and other concepts were directly applied to disordered behavior for understanding client-counselor relationships and for understanding the examiner-testee relationships. The derivative concepts of social psychology were also used in interpreting the results of the Thematic Apperception Test and other projective tests. In part, this shift to social psychology enriched the interpretations of these tests. Although the social aspects of personality were more difficult to discern in the Rorschach Psychodiagnostic Test than in the Thematic Apperception Test, still the subject's conception of himself, his relationships with other persons, and his degree of self-tolerance and social tolerance could be discerned from his responses in both tests.[28]

Psychologists and anthropologists have collaborated in studying personalities in different cultural settings; for instance, the Bleulers found that the inhabitants of Morocco concentrated upon trivial details of the Rorschach cards, which would be considered indicative of schizophrenia among Western Europeans.[29] Moreover, their

[27] J. F. Brown, *Psychology and the Social Order* (New York: McGraw-Hill Book Company, Inc., 1937); see Theodore Newcomb, *Social Psychology* (New York: The Dryden Press, Inc., 1950); Gordon Allport, *Personality* (New York: Henry Holt and Company, Inc., 1937); Robert R. Sears, *Survey of Objective Studies of Psychoanalytic Concepts* (New York: Social Science Research Council, 1943); Harold Orlansky, "Infant Care and Personality," *Psychological Bulletin,* January, 1949, 46:1, pp. 1–48; David C. McClelland, *Personality* (New York: William Sloane Associates, 1951).

[28] See W. Joel, "The Interpersonal Equation in Projective Methods," *Rorschach Research Exchange and Journal of Protective Techniques,* December, 1949, 13, pp. 479–482.

[29] M. Bleuler and R. Bleuler, "Rorschach's Inkblot Test and Racial Psychology: Mental Peculiarities of Moroccans," *Character and Personality,* December, 1935, IV, pp. 97–114.

studies emphasized that the projective techniques could not reveal the developmental processes of the persons in different cultures and thus were limited to the terminal facets of personality development.[30]

The psychologists have attempted to correlate personal stability and opinions toward social issues such as race and religion. Despite the limitations of these studies, psychological interest has been centered upon the influence of disturbed and disordered behavior upon attitudes to specific minority groups.

In brief, psychology is applying increasingly the concepts and derivative meanings of social relations in the examiner-subject relations, in interpreting projective tests, in the counselor-client relations, in understanding personality types and modes of relationships in different cultures, and in understanding the relationship between personal instability and social ideologies.

Sociology. Sociologists and social psychologists developed and applied the concept of social interaction at an earlier time and perhaps more thoroughly than did specialists in other disciplines.[31] Their orientation, however, was directed to social relationships among normal persons and groups, instead of neurotics, psychotics, and other disordered deviants. Though aware of the studies of psychoanalysts and psychiatrists, they did not readily incorporate or restate these concepts into social psychological terms.[32] Two factors seemingly contributed to this lack of interest. Apparently, sociologists and social psychologists, as "academic outsiders," found some difficulty in gaining access to clinics and mental hospitals to study disordered persons. Also, social pressures within the discipline led to an avoidance of "tragic" and bizarre phenomena as subjects of inquiry.[33]

[30] Theodora Abel, "The Rorschach Test in the Study of Culture," *Rorschach Research Exchange and Journal of Projective Techniques,* 1948, 12, pp. 79–93.

[31] The "social psychologists" referred to here are those who have stemmed mainly from the sociologists and have been directly influenced by them.

[32] See Kimball Young, "The Contribution of Psychiatry to the Study of Group Conflict," *Publications of the American Sociological Society,* 1930, XXV:2, pp. 111–125; Wm. F. Ogburn, "The Contributions of Psychiatry to Social Psychology," *Publications of the American Sociological Society,* 1926, XXI, pp. 82–91.

[33] See Kurt H. Wolff, "Notes Toward a Sociocultural Interpretation of American Sociology," *American Sociological Review,* October, 1947, XI:5, pp. 550–551; also, C. Wright Mills, "The Professional Ideology of Social Pathologists," *American Journal of Sociology,* 1943, XLIX, pp. 165–180.

Nonetheless, by the second decade of the twentieth century, the sociologists had worked out the influence of interpersonal relations upon the socialization of the personality, both theoretically and in part by empirical research. Cooley, for example, considered human nature an outgrowth of intimate face-to-face contacts, a phase of the primary group and a product of fellowship, which "decays in isolation." [34] George Mead, a philosophical pragmatist, was also among the first social psychologists to analyze the dynamic quality of social interaction as a role-taking process and as a medium of self-control and social control.[35] He analyzed the social genesis of the self and showed how interaction led to common meanings and to concerted action between the interactants. His analysis of role taking superseded the inadequate explanation of communication and social learning by imitation and has similarities to Cooley's notion of sympathetic introspection, to Burgess' conception of empathy, and in some ways to Freud's mechanism of identification.[36] Though role taking was interpreted mainly as a symbolic process, it also could be used to interpret the transmission of latent attitudes and tensions by unwitting body gestures. In his analysis of the emergence of common meanings and "significant symbols" as products of interaction, Mead presented a dynamic conception of culture and placed culture within the scheme of interpersonal relations. It was this approach to culture which Sullivan and Sapir also described in attempting to find a mid-point between individual psychiatry and cultural anthropology.[37] In fact, by these concepts, Mead formulated the criterion of ordered behavior which Sullivan elaborated later as a criterion of improvement in therapy.

From this social psychological viewpoint Thomas, Park, Burgess, Faris, and Blumer, among others, made theoretical and empirical studies.[38] The specific application of interpersonal relations to per-

[34] Charles H. Cooley, *Human Nature and the Social Order* (New York: Charles Scribner's Sons, 1902).

[35] George H. Mead, *Mind, Self and Society* (Chicago: University of Chicago Press, 1934).

[36] Charles H. Cooley, *Human Nature and the Social Order* (New York: Charles Scribner's Sons, 1902); Ernest W. Burgess, "Discussion," *The Jackroller*, edited by Clifford R. Shaw (Chicago: University of Chicago Press, 1930).

[37] George H. Mead, *Mind, Self and Society*, p. 69 (Chicago: University of Chicago Press, 1934).

[38] William I. Thomas and Florian Znaniecki, *The Polish Peasant in Europe and America* (New York: Alfred A. Knopf, Inc., 1927); Robert E. Park, "Reflec-

sonal disorders arose from the general interests in social and personal disorganization, from the problems of the family, "mental hygiene," and from the general tie-in between personality and culture.[39]

The studies of mental hygiene, and of the psychoses, of the neuroses, and of psychopathy, particularly, laid the basis for an integrated area between sociology and psychiatry. The studies of the functional psychoses, particularly schizophrenia, were preceded by ecological studies, initiated by Faris and Dunham.[40] The schizophrenic, for example, was studied within the context of the local urban area. Burgess summarized the sociological importance of these studies as follows:[41]

> The sociological description and explanation of mental disorders may be concerned with hypotheses upon the role of communication in mental life and upon the effect of isolation upon mental breakdown. Mental disorder is interpreted as a phase of personal disorganization arising out of maladjustment in the social relations of the person.

Concomitant and subsequent studies were made of the social personality of the schizophrenic as an emergent of his social relationships.[42] The studies of the neuroses and of psychopathy which have occurred during and since the war years have also pursued this line of attack.[43]

tions on Communication and Culture," *American Journal of Sociology,* 1939, XLIV, pp. 182–205; Ernest W. Burgess, "The Study of the Delinquent as a Person," *American Journal of Sociology,* May, 1923, 28, pp. 657–680; Ellsworth Faris, *The Nature of Human Nature* (New York: McGraw-Hill Book Company, Inc., 1937); Herbert Blumer, *Critique of the Polish Peasant in Europe and America* (New York: Social Science Research Council, 1939); see Leonard S. Cottrell, Jr., and Ruth Gallagher, *Important Developments in American Social Psychology during the Past Decade* (Ithaca, N.Y.: Cornell University, 1940, mimeographed).

[39] Ernest W. Burgess, "A Unity of Interacting Personalities," *The Family,* pp. 141–150, edited by Ernest Byron Reuter and Jessie Ridgway Runner (New York: McGraw-Hill Book Company, Inc., 1931).

[40] Robert E. L. Faris and H. Warren Dunham, *Mental Disorders in Urban Areas* (Chicago: University of Chicago Press, 1939).

[41] Ernest W. Burgess, "Introduction," *Mental Disorders in Urban Areas,* Robert E. L. Faris and H. Warren Dunham, p. xiii (Chicago: University of Chicago Press, 1939).

[42] H. Warren Dunham, "The Social Personality of the Catatonic-Schizophrene," *American Journal of Sociology,* May, 1944, XLIX, pp. 508–518. Robert E. L. Faris, "Cultural Isolation and the Schizophrenic Personality," *American Journal of Sociology,* September, 1934, XL, pp. 155–164.

[43] S. Kirson Weinberg, "The Combat Neuroses," *American Journal of Sociology,* March, 1946, LI:5, pp. 465–478.

Finally, the mental hospital was analyzed in terms of interpersonal relationships.

In the general problem of personality and culture, psychiatrists and sociologists have emphasized different phases of personal development. The psychiatrists have emphasized the import of early relationships upon personal disorders, while the sociologists have stressed the juvenile, adolescent, and adult relationships upon these disorders.[44]

In brief, the sociologists, by extending their concepts to cover the individual variant, directed attention to the personal relationships and social experiences which affected the personal disorders. Usually they studied the variant within the neighborhood context. Since their studies were not limited to this neighborhood context, they were able to discern and to emphasize the importance of studying social relationships and types of disorders within different groups and culture contexts.

Social Anthropology. The anthropologists, who are mainly concerned with objective cultural patterns, practices, and functions of nonliterates, were almost "antipsychological" in their approach before 1920, and to a large extent many still remain so.[45] Some anthropologists published biographies and personal documents of nonliterates before that time, and some ethnologists were cognizant of certain types of abnormal behavior in their inquiries.[46] But their concerted use of psychiatric and psychoanalytic concepts in investigating nonliterate groups came after Freud's anthropological work, *Totem and Taboo*.[47]

The Freudians who were influenced by the English anthropologists adopted an evolutionary approach to society and tried to find a parallel in societal development for the stages of individual growth. Consequently, their views assumed a nonhistoric character and were founded on very doubtful evidence. Yet the criticism

[44] See Herbert Blumer, "Social and Individual Disorganization," *American Journal of Sociology*, May, 1937, XLII, p. 876.

[45] Sapir and Kluckhohn attribute this resistance to psychiatry in part to the particular types of personalities who are attracted to anthropology. Clyde Kluckhohn, "Psychiatry and Anthropology," *One Hundred Years of American Psychiatry* (New York: Columbia University Press, 1944).

[46] Alfred L. Kroeber in 1906, Paul Radin in 1913, and Elsie Clew Parsons in 1922 collected personalized sketches of nonliterates.

[47] Sigmund Freud, *Totem and Taboo* (New York: Dodd, Mead & Company, Inc., 1918).

by anthropologists at first had little if any impression upon them. In fact, both the psychoanalysts and the anthropologists talked past each other for some time. But in spite of the aloofness of the psychoanalysts, their provocative theories began to affect the views of some anthropologists.[48] For example, Kroeber, who castigated Freud's work for its flimsy and distorted evidence, nonetheless agreed that the work contained significant insights. Malinowski, Margaret Mead, and D. Eggan, among others, began to test or to apply certain Freudian hypotheses, such as the Oedipal attachment, in their field investigations of nonliterate societies.[49] The net effect of these inquiries was to direct attention to social relationships, particularly parent-child relationships, in other cultures. These studies emphasized also the relativity of intrafamily relations, and the effects of different roles upon parent-child attachments. This approach, in part, paved the way for discerning the nonliterate person as a dynamic individual rather than as a cultural automaton similar or identical to others in his homogeneous group.

From a theoretical line of attack, Sapir, who was familiar with anthropology, sociology, and psychiatry, tried to find a mid-point between individual psychiatry and cultural anthropology. This middle area resided within the field of social psychology and within the sphere of social relationships. In characterizing this culture-personality nexus, Sapir saw this area to consist of the emergent meanings of interpersonal relations, as Mead did earlier in social psychology. Sapir said:[50]

> The true locus of culture is in the interactions of specific individuals and in the subjective side of the world of meanings which each one of these individuals may unconsciously abstract for himself from his participations in these interactions. . . . The concept of culture as it is handled by the cultural anthropologist is necessarily something of a statistical fiction and it is easy to see that the social psychologist and the psychiatrist must eventually induce him to reconsider his terms.

[48] Alfred L. Kroeber, "Totem and Taboo: An Ethnologic Psychoanalysis," *American Anthropologist*, 1920, XX, pp. 48–55.
[49] Bronislaw Malinowski, *Sex and Repression in Savage Societies* (New York: Harcourt, Brace and Company, Inc., 1927); Margaret Mead, *Sex and Temperament in Three Primitive Societies* (New York: William Morrow & Company, Inc., 1935); Dorothy Eggan, "The General Problem of Hopi Adjustment," *American Anthropologist*, 1943, XLV, pp. 357–373.
[50] Edward Sapir, "Cultural Anthropology and Psychiatry," *Journal of Abnormal and Social Psychology*, 1932, XXVII, pp. 236–237. Quoted by permission of the American Psychological Association.

From this point of view the emergence of the distinct and unique personality became inevitable,[51] because of the unique as well as the common interpretations which each individual acquired in interpersonal relations.[52]

Though this approach was not always pursued in empirical inquiry of the personally disordered, there have been field researches by Cooper, Hallowell, and Landis who have shown that the meanings arising from personal relationships could contribute to disordered behavior.[53] Opler traced the therapeutic relationships between the shaman and the disordered person among the Apache.[54] Beaglehole has indicated how a gross superorganic view of culture complexity could be misleading in understanding the personal disorders.[55] From a cultural viewpoint Benedict, Fortune, and others have shown clearly the relativity of abnormality.[56]

Kardiner, Linton, and their associates, in an integration of psychoanalysis and cultural anthropology, have shown that the value systems within a given culture are patterns of interpersonal relationships.[57] By their studies of the effects of early parent-child relationships upon adult personality structure, they have shown how these early relationships create a typical or modal personality who

[51] Edward Sapir, "The Emergence of the Concept of Personality in the Study of Cultures," *The Journal of Social Psychology*, 1934, V, pp. 408–415.

[52] Ernest Beaglehole, "International Theory and Social Psychology," *A Study of Inter-personal Relations*, edited by Patrick Mullahy, pp. 50–79 (New York: Hermitage Press, 1949).

[53] John M. Cooper, "Mental Disease Situations in Certain Cultures," *Journal of Abnormal and Social Psychology*, April–June, 1934–1935, XXIX, pp. 1–9; A. Irving Hallowell, "Culture and Mental Disorder," *Journal of Abnormal and Social Psychology*, April–June, 1934–1935, XXIX; Ruth Landis, "The Abnormal among the Objiwa," *Journal of Abnormal and Social Psychology*, 1938, XXXIII, pp. 195–225.

[54] Edward M. Opler, "Some Points of Comparison and Contrast between the Treatment of Functional Disorders by Apache Shamans and Modern Psychiatric Practice," *The American Journal of Psychiatry*, 1930, XCII, pp. 1371–1387.

[55] Ernest Beaglehole, "Cultural Complexity and Psychological Problems," *Psychiatry*, August, 1940, III, pp. 335, 336.

[56] Ruth Benedict, *Patterns of Culture* (Boston: Houghton Mifflin Company, 1935); Reo Fortune, *The Sorcerers of Dobu* (Boston: Little, Brown & Company, 1932).

[57] Abram Kardiner *et al.*, *The Individual and His Society* (New York: Columbia University Press, 1939); Abram Kardiner *et al.*, *Psychological Frontiers of Society* (New York: Columbia University Press, 1945); Abram Kardiner and Lionel Ovesey, *The Mark of Oppression* (New York: W. W. Norton & Company, 1951).

tends to sustain the characteristic relationships within the culture. They have distinguished, however, between a typical or modal personality and the individual personality, and they also have investigated the neuroses in different cultures.

Davis, Warner, and their associates also studied the influence of human relations upon personality in the varied socioeconomic levels of contemporary society, and have described the deviant and aberrant persons in these positional groups.[58] Since personality differences were noted among the social classes, it could be inferred that the types of personal disorders might also vary, in frequency at least, among the social classes. As yet there have been no definitive studies of disordered behavior within the context of social strata, except possibly for the development of anxiety, which presumably concentrates among the middle class. As a point of fact, this class approach has one common point with the ecological approach to psychotic disorders. For these ecological distributions can be considered indices to the types of social relationships which obtain in areas of different income levels.

From an operational standpoint, Chapple has attempted to classify persons on the basis of their mode of interpersonal relations, and he has attempted to differentiate between types of communication among disordered and normal persons.[59]

In brief, many anthropologists have veered from a superpersonal approach to an interpersonal approach to culture. In this process they have devoted more attention to the unique personality. Their chief contributions have been to point out and to elaborate the relativity of social relations in diverse cultures and social classes, and to show the varying effects of these relationships in contributing to the onset of personal disorders.[60]

Social Relationships and Personal Disorders. From these varied contributions from the different disciplines, we can summarize our

[58] Allison Davis and Robert R. Havighurst, *Father of the Man* (Boston: Houghton Mifflin Company, 1948); W. Lloyd Warner, "The Society, the Individual and His Mental Disorders," *The American Journal of Psychiatry*, 1937, XCIV, pp. 275–284.

[59] Eliot D. Chapple and Carleton S. Coon, *Principles of Anthropology*, pp. 52–60 (New York: Henry Holt and Company, Inc., 1942).

[60] For a competent summary of the influence of social relations upon personality generally and disordered behavior particularly, see Jurgen Ruesch and Gregory Bateson, *Communication: The Social Matrix of Psychiatry* (New York: W. W. Norton & Company, 1951).

position with reference .to the pertinence of social relationships to
the study of personal disorders under the following headings: (1)
the nature of social relationships, (2) social relationships and the
culture context, and (3) social relationships and personal development.

The Nature of Social Relationships. Social relationships generally
refer to mutual influences between two or more persons. In a dynamic sense these relationships are midway between objective cultural patterns and biological individuals. Through social relationships individuals select and internalize the culture as symbols,
meanings, and patterns of responses. Social relationships, however,
involve more than symbolic interchange between the interactants,
for interactants often influence each other in unwitting and nonverbal ways; these forms of interaction often exert more influence
upon personality than the verbal forms of interaction, because the
interactants are unaware of and hence cannot control the effects of
these nonarticulate kinds of relationships.

Social relationships can lead to agreement or to disagreement.
Those social relationships which lead to agreement or consensus
create shared or common behavior patterns. Those social relationships which lead to disagreement or discord create unshared or
unique behavior patterns. Frequently, both shared and unshared
processes ensue between the interactants.

Social Relationships and the Culture Context. These modes of
interaction must be understood within the given cultural framework
in order to evaluate their effects upon the given individual. In a
composite heterogeneous culture such as exists in the United States,
social relationships differ by ethnic group, class position, and to
some extent by region. In this respect the frequencies of the different
disorders which occur among ethnic, class, or regional groups are
sociologically relevant, because these figures can be considered indices to different types of relationships within these given groups.
In the same sense, ecological studies of personality disorders in the
urban community are significant because these different residential
distributions reflect the social organization and the types of relationships among the inhabitants of different areas. Certainly, different
frequencies of disordered behavior may indicate biological differences, as do age, sex, and constitutional type. But if these studies
reflected only biological differences, they would be less relevant to

the sociologist and more relevant to the biologist. Since every person occupies a series of social positions in any given group, these social positions become important because they give him a perspective to the culture and to other persons about him, and affect the relationships of other persons toward him and his toward them. These social positions or roles are both formal and informal.

The person's formal role affects his official relationships with other persons. For example, a domestic would call out different sets of relationships than would an executive. A mother in a father-dominated family would have different relationships with other family members, particularly the father, than would a mother in an equalitarian family. The different frequencies of disorders among women or men, in terms of their respective roles, would reflect in part their different family and business relationships.

The informal relationships within an established role, however, cannot be overlooked in this respect because they reveal the person's qualities. For example, two people who occupy similar formal roles may call out different responses from others because of their varying personalities. Consequently, we can see why certain individuals in one formal role may have intense conflicts while other individuals in a relatively similar role may have few conflicts.

Since any individual actually has many roles, his inconsistent and contradictory roles also must be understood to understand his conflicts. This is especially true of persons who are marginal to two groups. These marginal persons, when in an isolated and precarious position, can experience such intense conflicts that they can become disturbed and even disordered.

These differences in informal roles and personal qualities point to the influence of interpersonal relationships upon self-esteem in personal development. By internalizing the attitudes of others, the person acquires not only certain conceptions of his role but also certain estimates of himself. In other words, the socialized individual is able to evaluate himself in the same way that he can evaluate others. This capacity for self-reference becomes crucial in the individual's behavior, for it influences the person's self-control, his definitions of situations, and his capacity to tolerate frustration and rejection. The way the individual internalizes his social relationships and evaluates himself affects his subsequent ways of accepting himself or rejecting himself. Our knowledge of these processes is essential in understanding ordered and disordered behavior.

Social Relationships and Personal Development. In the process of development the individual acquires common meanings which he can share with others and unique meanings which he cannot or does not share with others.

The sociologists have dealt with the socialized aspects of behavior and with the common meanings, attitudes, and practices which a person acquired in becoming an accepted member of a group, even of a variant group. The psychiatrists and other clinicians have dealt with distinct persons who were partly unsocialized or desocialized, and they have emphasized the unique, unshared, and individualized meanings which the person acquired in interpersonal relationships and which contributed to his retardation or breakdown, whether in neurotic, psychotic, or psychopathic form. They had to understand these processes to diagnose and treat these disordered persons.

Later, some psychiatrists slightly modified their points of view and saw the significance of the relationships in later years upon personal development. This revised perspective was necessary because many mild disorders could be traced to recent severely critical experiences, as in the war neuroses. The sociologists, on the other hand, who emphasized the relationships in the symbolic period of childhood and of subsequent years, began to recognize the significance of the early years of life in personality formation even though not as the locus of all personal disorders. In brief although the modes of relationships in the early years of life may be crucial to personality formation, these early relationships are not always the loci of mild disorders.

Occupational Roles and Divergent Disciplines. The concept of social relationships varies with the particular occupational role of the specialist and with the problems of his particular discipline. The psychiatrist and psychoanalyst, as therapists, are concerned with the use of social relationships and their derivative concepts to explain and to treat the patient's disorder. The psychiatric social worker is mainly concerned with the patient's relationships in the family, and in other groups, in order to understand and to ameliorate his condition. The sociometrist is mainly concerned with allocating the disordered person or maladjusted person in diverse groups, and in finding the types of static relationships among these groups; or, as psychodramatist, he is concerned with those interpersonal relation-

ships, in a therapeutically designated setting on a stage, which uncover his patient's conflicts.

The psychologist has devoted his attention chiefly to the use of
social psychological concepts for analyzing diagnostic tests, for understanding the relationship between the examiner and the tested
subject and between counselor and client. With the help of anthropologists, he is beginning to see that the norms of his tests may vary
in different cultures.

The sociologist is concerned with the influences of the different
social groups upon the disordered person and with the emergence of
disordered persons by their particular roles and types of relationships in the social structure. The anthropologist has been concerned
with the use of social relationships to understand the varying dynamic phases of disordered behavior in different cultures or in
different socioeconomic levels.

Thus, the various specialists apply the construct of social relationships and its derivative concepts for different purposes, but the
theory behind these applications may be consistent for the several
disciplines. Hence, each discipline adds to the knowledge of disordered behavior from a somewhat distinct point of view.

Selected Readings

Adler, Herman, "The Relation between Psychiatry and the Social Sciences,"
  The American Journal of Psychiatry, April, 1927, VI, pp. 661–670.
Alexander, Franz, and Thomas M. French, *Psychoanalytic Therapy* (New
  York: The Ronald Press Company, 1945).
American Journal of Sociology, May, 1937, XLII:6.
American Psychiatric Association, *One Hundred Years of Psychiatry: A
  Century of Psychiatric Research in America* (New York: Columbia Uni-
  versity Press, 1944).
Blumer, Herbert, *Critique of the Polish Peasant in Europe and America*
  (New York: Social Science Research Council, 1939).
Brown, J. F., *The Psychodynamics of Abnormal Behavior* (New York:
  McGraw-Hill Book Company, Inc., 1940).
Burgess, Ernest W., "The Study of the Delinquent as a Person," *American
  Journal of Sociology,* 1923, XXVII, pp. 657–680.
Cameron, Norman, *The Psychology of Behavior Disorders* (Boston: Hough-
  ton Mifflin Company, 1947).
Faris, Robert E. L., and H. Warren Dunham, *Mental Disorders in Urban
  Areas* (Chicago: University of Chicago Press, 1939).
French, Lois M., *Psychiatric Social Work* (New York: Commonwealth
  Fund, 1940).

Freud, Sigmund, "The History of the Psychoanalytic Movement," *The Basic Writings of Sigmund Freud,* translated and edited by A. A. Brill (New York: Random House, 1938).

Fromm, Erich, *Escape from Freedom* (New York: Rinehart & Company, Inc., 1941).

Haring, Douglas G. (compiler), *Personal Character and Cultural Milieu: A Collection of Readings* (Syracuse, N.Y.: Syracuse University Press, 1949).

Healy, William, and Augusta F. Bronner, *New Light on Delinquency and Its Treatment* (New Haven: Yale University Press, 1936).

Horney, Karen, *New Ways in Psychoanalysis,* Chaps. I and II (New York: W. W. Norton & Company, 1945).

————, *Neurosis and Growth* (New York: W. W. Norton & Company, 1950).

Hunt, J. McV. (editor), *Personality and Behavior Disorders,* 2 vols. (New York: The Ronald Press Company, 1944).

Kardiner, Abram, *et al., The Individual and His Society* (New York: Columbia University Press, 1939).

————, *et al., Psychological Frontiers of Society* (New York: Columbia University Press, 1945).

Kluckhohn, Clyde, and Henry E. Murray (editors), *Personality in Nature, Society and Culture* (New York: Alfred A. Knopf, Inc., 1949).

Mead, George H., *Mind, Self and Society* (Chicago: University of Chicago Press, 1934).

Ruesch, Jurgen, and Gregory Bateson, *Communication* (New York: W. W. Norton & Company, 1951).

Sapir, Edward, "Cultural Anthropology and Psychiatry," *Journal of Abnormal and Social Psychology,* 1932, 27, pp. 230–237.

Sears, Robert R., *Survey of Objective Studies of Psychoanalytic Concepts* (New York: Social Science Research Council, 1943).

CHAPTER FOUR

The Social Personality in Ordered and Disordered Behavior

In the preceding chapters we pointed out that social relations are ways of viewing and understanding disordered behavior. We implied that the person is the bearer and product of these relations. Our purpose in this chapter is to describe the personality processes that lead to ordered behavior or to disordered behavior. These processes cover four broad aspects of personality: (1) action and motivation, (2) role taking and social relations, (3) the self system, and (4) self-defenses.

The Nature of the Social Personality. The social personality emerges from social relations. In this socialization process the person acquires motives, aspirations, roles, self-evaluations, purposeful actions, and many other qualities. People of a given group have common behavior patterns which we characterize as "culture." This content phase of personality has been the basis for defining personality as the "subjective side of culture." [1] Although this definition is adequate for typical behavior, it is less adequate when we study atypical behavior. The constitutional disposition may influence one's unique behavior, but his specific relations may have even more bearing upon his unique personal organization.[2] The responses of

[1] This aspect of personality was emphasized first by W. I. Thomas. It was then used by Ellsworth Faris. See Ellsworth Faris, "The Concept of Social Attitudes," *Journal of Applied Sociology*, 1925, IX, pp. 404–409.

[2] Gardner Murphy, *Personality: A Biosocial Approach to Origins and Structure* (New York: Harper & Brothers, 1948).

others to him will influence his range of needs, but he will select different meanings from his relations and he will respond to them in a unique way. As an extreme instance, the psychotic interprets the culture in a manner which others neither share nor accept. But the psychotic expresses in exaggerated form what characterizes all persons, because all persons have unique and private views of their culture and communicate only a small portion of them. Hence, the person's inner life becomes a necessary object of inquiry, for his inner life reveals directly his conflicts and meanings which are the bases for understanding deviant behavior.

A second broad phase of the socialized person is his role and status in the group. The role that the individual plays in his group and the evaluations which the group has of his behavior—his status —determine his social position. This social position provides the basis for his perspective to himself and to his culture. But social position alone does not directly reveal the person's attitudes toward himself. Consequently, these attitudes become essential for understanding the meaning of his behavior. For example, the psychotic may be isolated from some groups in which he formerly participated. But his isolated position can be understood only when we know what his isolation means to him and how it arose from his past relations.

A definition of the social personality must cover the integration of the individual with his group and reveal his unique personality development and his organization of meanings and motives. By these criteria we can define the socialized aspect of personality as (1) emerging from social relationships (2) with unique and common motives (3) which influence his social position and (4) which affect his responses to himself and to his environment.

The Social Personality Is a Unity. The person is not a set of discrete and disconnected traits but a dynamic and integral unit.

First, his overt behavior is an outcome of inner motives. Some motives are conscious and others are beyond awareness.

Second, each motive has a developmental history which antedates and which is continuous with present behavior. The attempt to understand the present personality at any given time must consider the sequence of past relationships and past attitudes.

Third, motives and attitudes are interrelated. A given disorder, such as an attitude of dread toward certain objects, can be best understood within the total context of the social personality. Active motives are related to latent ones, and conscious intentions are related to unconscious purposes.

Fourth, the person can be understood most clearly by seeing him as a social participant within the orbit of his groups. Although the clinical analysis of personality may uncover many basic and generic reactions and experiences, the development and meanings of these reactions for the subject and for others can be understood more clearly in the context of his "natural habitats" or subcultures, such as the family, community, friends, and business associates.

The Action Theory of Behavior

Actions, Drives, and Motives. Activity is the most obvious fact about personality. From birth on, and even before, the human continually strives to satisfy his drives and to relieve his tensions. Basic drives, such as hunger, thirst, sex, and fatigue, among others, are biological in origin, but, as these drives acquire goals and purposes by social relationships, they become motives.

The infant's behavior has no concerted direction. It is random, aimless, and stirred by inner unrest. By relating with his parents and others, the infant slowly learns to channelize his amorphous tension-reducing behavior into socialized activity. He learns to differentiate objects which he wants and does not want. He learns to inhibit and to manage his drives in accord with parental expectations. He integrates his behavior within a symbolic scheme of self-control. This is possible because the infant is continually responded to by parents and by others who try to mold him to their expectations; they, in turn, are affected by his responses. Since alertness and intensity of drives, as well as the organism generally, differ for each individual, individuals exposed to relatively similar relationships will internalize different phases of the culture in these relationships. That is, each person will select and rework facets of the culture which satisfy his unique needs.

But personality also develops around the satisfaction or dissatisfaction of basic drives; for about these drives intimate human relationships revolve. In early development of body comfort, the feeding process as well as toilet training have much to do with personal organization. At this time, and especially later, the sexual drive looms in importance.

In the socialization process these drives become directed, inhibited, and managed. As such, socialized activity involves orientation for time and place. It involves checking and postponing behavior in order to conform to social expectations and in order to achieve specified goals. Socialized action, by the very fact of delay, involves the imaginative use of symbols for retrospection of past actions and for rehearsal of future actions. Inevitably, it becomes linked with meanings and intent. Tension reduction or drive relief among infants does not involve symbols or delay or a temporal perspective.

The function of social relationships in channelizing tension-reducing behavior into socialized activity can be illustrated by a fundamental drive—hunger. The appeasement of the infant's hunger is far more complex a problem than the mere ingestion of food. It is immersed in degrees of affection or hostility to the mother figure by the way the food is given, particularly when the child is breast-fed. In some cultures, as the Arapesh, the child is fondled, caressed, and allowed to linger in his feeding period. He associates eating with affection and regards the whole process as pleasurable. In other cultures, as the Mundugumor, the child associates eating with hostility and discipline.[3] These experiences not only affect feeding in the subsistence process but may affect his relations with other persons and his conception of himself. From being fed at any call of hunger, the child in the growth process learns to inhibit his feeding urges to specific intervals and, in time, to acquire tastes for specific foods. In time, these foods are associated with hunger appetites. Thus, the whole process of eating becomes enveloped in ritualized behavior at the table, in the use of food utensils, and in certain approved manners in eating.

In brief, the meanings of the drives rather than the unsocialized drives themselves create conflicts, unless certain basic drives are so frustrated that the individual concentrates only upon satiating these needs. For starving persons will concentrate upon eating at the expense of other needs. But in our culture these extreme organic deprivations are seldom crucial determinants of conflict and of disordered behavior. Instead, the meanings and purposes which arise

[3] Margaret Mead, "Sex and Temperament in Three Primitive Societies," *From the South Seas,* pp. 40–43, 195 (New York: William Morrow & Company, Inc., 1939).

in human relations become the motives of behavior and the sources of conflict. The drives or impulses which are biological resultants and which lead to tension reduction are aimless, goalless, and non-symbolic. Motives and actions which emerge in the socialization process have a direction and are symbolic and goal-oriented. To understand the person, whether organized or disorganized, the motives rather than the drives must be analyzed.

Biological and Social Phases of Personality. The person, however, is not disembodied. The organism is relevant to socialized behavior in these ways: First, the human infant has a biological constancy in "original nature," in the sense of possessing a brain and nervous system, larynx, thumb, biological plasticity, and so on, all of which enable him to become socialized. Second, his unique physiological structure and unlearned dispositions contribute to his individuality. Third, his disposition will be affected by illness, fatigue, malnutrition in its broadest sense, and by organic changes. Fourth, his biological organs become the mediums by which he attempts to fulfill his motives, whether in manipulating the environment or in communicating with others.

The first two aspects of the human organism are somewhat self-explanatory and well known.[4] The third aspect concerns physical illness and other physical manifestations which sometimes precede and are related to certain personal disorders. For example, sometimes influenza and pneumonia precede a psychotic breakdown. Although these illnesses may not have "caused" the breakdown, still they may have contributed to the breakdown. On the other hand, a person's self-recrimination and defeatism may so weaken his physical condition that he can become physically ill.

Fatigue is related to one's ability to adapt. Fatigue was considered by Janet and his followers as an outcome of differences in "psychic energy."[5] Although individuals differ in their endurance capacities, a term such as "exhaustion neuroses" often implies that

---

[4] See, for example, Kimball Young, *Social Psychology*, Chap. II (New York: Appleton-Century-Crofts, Inc., 1944); William F. Ogburn and Meyer F. Nimkoff, *Sociology*, Chap. XI (Boston: Houghton Mifflin Company, 1950). Read Bain, "Producing Marriageable Personalities," *Family Marriage and Parenthood*, edited by Howard Becker and Reuben Hill, pp. 174–178 (Boston: D. C. Heath and Company, 1948).

[5] See Pierre Janet, *Major Symptoms of Hysteria* (New York: The Macmillan Company, 1920).

the decisive factors are physical instead of emotional. Certainly overwork and intense physical strain do affect one's perspective, but so do "worry" and conflict. Sometimes a sick patient and an organically oriented doctor tend to concentrate chiefly upon organic characteristics. In some cases these physical signs may be symptoms rather than causes, but in other cases, they may directly contribute to the disorder. This can be evaluated best in a particular case, but it reveals the close and integral connection between the biological and social aspects of personality.

When a person experiences malnutrition and pathological changes, such as lesions or injuries, we are, of course, dealing with a different organism. For example, hypothroidism may lead to quick fatigue, which may be overcome by pills containing thyroid extracts.

The bodily organs are instruments for consummating motives. In this respect the organs are integral parts of the action system. On a conscious level the hands, larynx, and other organs are used to execute given attitudes. But organs beyond voluntary control are also involved in adjustments. This is evident in hysterical disorders, such as blindness or deafness, or even in psychosomatic disorders such as asthma. A frightened person may hold his breath, while an enraged person may breathe more rapidly; and these responses, which are stimulated by the situation, are usually spontaneous. In other words, meanings and purposes, however unwitting, affect the organism and the functioning of specific organs. When in conflict, the person's organism generally is affected.

Friedman has shown that in the concentration-camp situation many men became impotent and many women ceased to menstruate. Only after liberation did the women begin to menstruate again. The children also showed psychosexual retardation. The male adolescents were almost sexually inactive, and some females did not start to menstruate until they were 17 or 18 years old.[6] The inmates were concerned with staying alive, and the other functions seemingly were kept in abeyance.

Even a fundamental expression such as crying, especially in children, can be inhibited when it overwhelmingly threatens the subject. Consider the following case:[7]

[6] Paul Friedman, "Some Aspects of Concentration Camp Psychology," *The American Journal of Psychiatry*, February, 1949, 105:8, pp. 601–605.
[7] *Ibid.*, p. 602.

When [this girl] was 5 years old, the persecution of the Jews had started in her home town in the Ukraine. Her parents hoping to save her even if they themselves were captured, left her with neighboring peasants trusting that her blond hair and blue eyes would save her from the Nazis. Several days later when the child was in the meadow with cattle, she heard shots being fired, and a few hours later a boy came along with a card in his hand. She recognized her father's identity card. She asked where he had found it and the boy answered that it came from one of the men the Nazis had just killed. The child said that she wanted to cry but was afraid that he would recognize her as Jewish and deliver her to the Nazis. So she didn't cry. She didn't even cry when the boy took her by the hand and led her to a nearby wood, where lying in the ditch she saw her parents, her two brothers and many other Jews—all of them dead. Even then she did not cry, and when I saw her, 4½ years later, she was still incapable of crying.

Thus, physiological symptoms can become meaningful in ineffective responses to threatening situations. For example, sweating, tremors, tensions, and unrest which accompany confusion and loss of confidence are biological expressions of intense conflict and actually are ineffective preparations for response.

In brief, we respond to a situation by the way we define it. The voluntary and involuntary organs are involved in these responses and are affected by conflicts. Hence, the organism is the instrument for carrying out our intentions. When these intentions are in conflict, the organism will respond accordingly.[8] Consequently, action includes social and biological components which function as a unit.

The Act as a Unit of Analysis. The act consists of motivational and motor components. The motives consist of the orientations and directions to certain objects. The persistent and generalized motives are the attitudes. The attitudes, as generalized and durable predispositions to objects, subsume the motives which are specific but temporary orientations to given objects and can be satiated temporarily and renewed.[9] For example, one may have a favorable attitude to a friend but may not be motivated—i.e., wish—to see him when occupied with his duties.

The overt or motor expression of one's motives permits the group

[8] See section on Body Image and Self-conception, p. 77, for other relations between the biological and the social.
[9] See Abram Kardiner et al., The Psychological Frontiers of Society, p. 21 (New York: Columbia University Press, 1945).

to evaluate activity, while the subject, in turn, can reappraise and correct his behavior from their social judgments. Thus, overt behavior links the person to the group and permits socialization to develop.

A "simple" act denotes the process of satisfying a given motive. It involves a given intent, the execution of that intent, and subsequent satisfaction or dissatisfaction. Motives have to be expressed or executed in order to be satisfied even if the execution means a fleeting glance. The overt behavior is usually the end stage of the action process. No act is really "simple" except in a relative sense, for it involves motives, perceptions, feeling tone, ideas, images, and motor executions before it is completed. But each act is subsumed within acts of larger scope. Thus, the more complex acts include a series of related acts. Each act is subsumed within larger action patterns until the person's basic theme of behavior or general personal organization is encompassed.

For example, passing an examination is an action which is subsumed under the larger act of passing a course, which in turn is a phase of graduating from school. And graduation may be subordinate to the pursuit of a definite career. That is, each act is part of the integral personality, both inner and outer, as well as of past experiences and of future goals. But what happens when the act remains incomplete? For instance, the student who fails an examination may see this experience as part of a larger whole, namely receiving a low grade in the course, reducing his general scholastic average, and perhaps jeopardizing his career. In addition, he may begin to have doubts about his ability to do competent work. Thus, disordered behavior has its focus upon one's inability to resolve conflicts or to complete activity.

Action, Conflict, and Disorder. "Life is interruptions and recoveries," said Dewey. "Continuous interruption is not possible in the activities of an individual." But Dewey was referring to ordered persons and to "normal" activity.[10] The person who is faced with a threatening situation does not necessarily recover from interrupted actions. Instead, he may be "stuck," caught in a dilemma which he cannot resolve. Either he does not know how to face his predicament or he flees from it. Often he does both. Janet observed

[10] John Dewey, *Human Nature and Conduct*, p. 179 (New York: The Modern Library, 1930).

that many of his patients became exhausted by the difficulties of a complicated daily routine and became "stuck" by the obstacles they encountered. To disentangle some of his patients from their complicated situations, Janet had to manipulate their situations so that they were able to solve their problems by achieving their desired goals.[11]

Whatever one may think of Janet's supportive therapy, it is clear that his patients were unable to pursue and to complete their intended objectives. And why? Undoubtedly, they were involved in threatening situations. But not all situations create such conflicts. For example, a person who is undecided about whether to wear one garment or another, or who cannot make up his mind whether to go to a play or to a movie for recreation may not feel threatened. His temporary indecision may be quickly resolved. But a threatening conflict is essential to one's self-esteem. It does not become resolved very easily. For example, the death of a loved one is something very important to the person, but, whatever he does, the conflict lingers when he wants the person back. Hence, a threatening conflict is the inability to define a situation because no effective choice is available.[12] For example, a soldier is hemmed in by an enemy. If he flees he will be branded a "deserter" by his unit and will forfeit his self-respect. If he remains, death looms before him. He can only stay and fight it out. But with this dismal prospect he lacks confidence to fight. Or, to continue with the example of the student who fails an examination, we find that his mother, to whom he is very closely identified, will "disown" him if he does not attain his career goals. This prospect threatens him, and he cannot solve it.

Under such general circumstances the beginnings of persistent personal disorganization may set in and have the following characteristics: First, the subject becomes more preoccupied with himself rather than with the demands of the situation. His interest becomes inverted, and he consciously gives up trying to complete the action. Second, the situation remains a problem; his responses to it and his scheme of action become narrowed. Third, unconsciously he tries to resolve the conflict and to complete the activity. In

[11] Pierre Janet, *Principles of Psychotherapy*, pp. 228, 229 (New York: The Macmillan Company, 1928).

[12] See H. Maslow, "Conflict, Frustration and the Theory of Threat," *Journal of Abnormal and Social Psychology*, January, 1943, 38:1, pp. 81–86.

chronic and insidious disorders this unwitting activity may be less evident.

The person who meets a nonthreatening problem can be objective about solving it. But the person who is overwhelmed becomes stymied, and he begins to reassess himself as well as the situation. For example, two women hear a disturbance on the lower floor of their home. One is frightened but goes down to investigate; the other, overcome with anxiety, hides in a closet. The former acts in accordance with the demands of the situation; the latter is concerned primarily with escaping from the situation and with defending herself.

Freud, who dealt primarily with chronic neurotics, regarded behavior as essentially defensive. He began where social psychologists generally stop. His interest was with traumatic or critical reactions which could not be faced, let alone resolved. This mental flight or repression became the keystone of psychoanalytic theory. His interest was focused upon unconscious material and upon defensive behavior resulting from unsolved conflicts.[13]

On a neurotic level, incomplete and fixed behavior is expressed in ambivalent attitudes, in compulsive rituals, in hysterical paralyses, or in repeated attitudes of dread.[14] But some neurotics "act out" their conflicts; they do not solve their conflicts by this means but merely express them overtly, and, as such, repetitiously. Usually their "acting out" is irrational and self-compromising. For example, a delinquent boy who was undergoing treatment was persuaded to restrain himself from stealing. The boy exerted a great deal of effort to control his behavior for a few days, just to see what would happen. After a few days of no stealing, however, he developed marked feelings of anxiety. The therapist concluded that the stealing provided a defensive means against the anxiety.[15] When persons are taught to express their conflicts, as in some ethnic groups of the lower socioeconomic levels, they become involved in fights when they become hostile, although the expression of this hostility does

[13] *The Basic Writings of Sigmund Freud,* translated and edited by A. A. Brill, p. 939 (New York: Modern Library, Inc., 1938).

[14] Franz Alexander and Thomas French, *Psychoanalytic Therapy,* pp. 87, 88 (New York: The Ronald Press Company, 1945).

[15] See Hyman S. Lippman, "Difficulties Encountered in the Psychiatric Treatment of Chronic Juvenile Delinquents," *Searchlights on Delinquency,* edited by K. R. Eisler, p. 157 (New York: International Universities Press, Inc., 1949).

not eliminate the anxiety. It merely alleviates it or covers it up for the moment.

On a psychotic level this incompleted behavior is manifested in the indecision and the ritualistic gestures of the schizophrenic; in the unfinished, scattered, and abruptly diverting responses of the manic; and in the immobility of the depressive and of some cata-tonics. Furthermore, the psychotic distorts the demands of the group, invents goals which are satisfactory to him only, and drifts away from social expectations because, as Meyer points out, of the "ravages of habitually incomplete or directly inadequate and ill-adapted and ill-controlled reactions." [16] Sometimes the schizophrenic substitutes fantasy for action and regards ideas as representing their enacted equivalents.

Psychopaths act out their conflicts. The psychopath's inability to postpone his desires and to manage his aggressive tensions are one of the chief symptoms of his disorder.

In brief, ordered behavior means that conflicts can be met and resolved. In this reorganizing process, activity can be renewed and growth can occur. Disordered behavior means that conflicts cannot be met and resolved, that activity remains incomplete and fixed. Hence, disorganization persists and development is retarded.

The Unconscious and Repeated Behavior. In spite of fixed, de-fensive reactions, the person who has active conflicts often unwit-tingly strives to break through the impasse. Sometimes persons who are long bent upon solving problems suddenly come up with an answer. This applies not only to simple problems but also to intri-cate mathematical formulas.

A mathematician had been attempting to work on a problem that had puzzled him for over two years. He had made some halfhearted calculations on scraps of paper but nothing came of his efforts. One evening he attended a lecture on an entirely different subject, fol-lowed by an argument with a friend about the lecture. He then went to his room intending to read for the rest of the evening. Somehow, reading did not appeal to him. He then picked up some scraps of paper and with hardly a pause proceeded to write out the solution to his problem. Somehow or other he knew that something had been

---

[16] Adolph Meyer, *The Commonsense Psychiatry of Adolph Meyer,* edited by Alfred Lief, pp. 204–205 (New York: McGraw-Hill Book Company, Inc., 1948).

solved in the back of his mind but he had no idea of the solution until his pencil automatically wrote it out.[17]

Disturbed persons heighten their tendencies to resolve personal conflicts. Consequently, their unconscious efforts at conflict resolution, however painful, become intense and are repeated. This is evident in the recurrent dreams of traumatic neurotics; in the play therapy of children who act out and correct painful episodes according to their fantasies; in somnambulistic states during which a person may carry out acts which he inhibited while awake. Persons who have active unconscious conflicts often become tense and rigid and are readily fatigued by the strain.

Unconscious behavior, as it pertains to disordered behavior, consists of those experiences which the person cannot face or recall or speak about. It represents those experiences which arouse his helplessness and diffidence. Consequently, to forget his critical experiences he retrenches his activities in order to function at all. Thus repression, suppression, dissociation, inhibition, or denial of experiences are defensive reactions and cushions for the person. Despite these defenses, his conflicts press for a solution.

Hence, two types of behavior are repeated. One type consists of an unconscious pressure to solve one's conflicts. The other type consists of the defensive reactions which cover up or evade the conflicts. The unconscious conflicts are the bases for personal development; the defenses enable the person to function and prevent him from becoming more seriously threatened, but they tend also to arrest or restrict personality development.

The Unconscious in Personal Development. Earliest adverse experiences may possibly be the most critical because the infant is plastic, generally helpless, and unable to resolve his conflicts symbolically. These experiences, however, are not the only residue of the unconscious. The unconscious runs the gamut of one's life experiences which are pushed out of awareness. Orthodox Freudians are concerned mainly with repressed instinctual drives and infantile experiences. But the unconscious also includes distressing and painful experiences in adolescence and adulthood.

[17] Eliot Dole Hutchinson, "Varieties of Insight in Humans," *A Study of Inter-personal Relations*, edited by Patrick Mullahy, pp. 388–389 (New York: Hermitage Press, Inc., 1949).

Consequently, the "depth" of the inhibition varies. Some inhibited experiences which are relatively easy to recollect have been called the "foreconscious" by the Freudians. Other experiences can be recalled with great difficulty and only after sustained relationships with a skilled psychotherapist. The important fact in these recollections is that the person, by identifying with the psychotherapist, can get a strong enough self-conception so that he can re-evaluate his past critical experiences without succumbing to his former helpless condition. When the person cannot reappraise his experiences in this manner, he may possibly become "retraumatized"—i.e., relapse to his former condition. Even in dreams the person may so disguise the images and symbols that he will protect his self-esteem. This fact has been discovered by psychoanalysts, but it does not mean that the disguised symbolism necessarily has a sexual meaning.

In psychotic behavior the individual is unable to control his unconscious meanings, and often the voices, imagery, and visions that appear before him are not unlike the dreams of the ordered person. Although the psychotic's unconscious reactions outrun conscious control, still the psychotic may attempt to solve his conflicts and to reorganize his perspective. This is especially evident among agitated catatonics, who are striving to regain their self-esteem. Many agitated catatonics do not accept the lowered estimate of themselves but fight against it, and often their very delusions, however generalized and however misunderstood by others, may be the clues to the direction of their attempted personal reorganization. Boisen has referred to this process as a "fever" and healing process.

This unconscious effort at personal reorganization is a basic tendency in human behavior. It has been referred to as "homeostasis," and on a physical level means the equilibrium between the organism and the environment. Allport states:[18]

> The self-preserving, self-repairing, self-regulating processes of the body imply to them a root tendency to maintain wholeness. In the constant return of all psychophysical systems to a state of equilibrium, some see a "wisdom of the body," others a "state of vigilance." The more prosaic refer merely to "homeostasis." But whatever terms they employ these physiological doctrines all assume an inherent tendency of every organism to form itself into one intricate homogeneous system.

[18] From *Personality*, by Gordon W. Allport, p. 349. By permission of Henry Holt and Company, Inc., 1937.

The tendencies to action completion and conflict resolution on a meaningful level are highly integrated with the physiological tendencies toward reorganization and growth. For the personality, like the culture, strives for consistency. And this consistency is attained by resolving conflicts so that self-acceptance can be regained.[19] But persons who cling to fixed defensive reactions, as do certain psychotics, apparently strive less for personal reorganization, and the pressure of their conflicts ebbs to a minimal point.

Role Taking and Social Relationships

We have described the dynamics of action that influence ordered and disordered behavior. But channelized action results from social relationships, and the essential dynamism of social relationships is role taking.

The Processes of Role Taking. Role taking is an acquired capacity to shift and to share another's viewpoint, attitudes, and feelings. It enables two or more persons to evolve common meanings and to participate in concerted activity by attaining common goals. It involves an awareness of the viewpoint of other participants and a common frame of reference with them. Its mediums of expression are verbal and nonverbal gestures. For example, the adult does not use the same language and gestures toward a child that he would use toward another adult; he shifts his perspective to that of the child and expresses himself so that the child will understand him. The participants must have common bases of agreement or consensus—a universe of discourse. Without a universe of discourse, role taking and communication would be difficult if at all possible. For a universe of discourse does not only involve a shifting of one's point of view to that of another, it also means that in this process each interactant can foresee the ends of each other's action. Since they have common ends of action, their gestures, whether in words or in hand motions, become meaningful. If one beckons to another to come forward and he departs in the opposite direction, each is not shifting to the perspective of the other and each has interpreted the

[19] This fact has been accepted by a variety of investigators. See Anton Boisen, *The Exploration of the Inner World*, pp. 54–57 (Chicago: Willet, Clark & Co., 1936); Carl R. Rogers, *Counseling and Psychotherapy*, pp. 28–30, 221 (Boston: Houghton Mifflin Company, 1942). For a physiological explanation of this process, see Franz Alexander, *Psychosomatic Medicine: Its Principles and Applications*, pp. 75–80 (New York: W. W. Norton & Company, 1950).

gesture for different ends. Hence, we would not call this gesture meaningful or say that these individuals had a common universe of discourse, at least for that given action.

For example, a paranoid recounted an experience in which a neighbor ended a conversation with the informal farewell of, "I'll see you later." The paranoid pondered over and read dire meanings into this statement. "Why should he want to see me later? How late? About what?" She mulled over all the innuendos of threat which such a statement might imply. At night she bolted the door securely, pulled down all the shades, and could not sleep. Periodically she peeked out the window to see if the neighbor were coming. Clearly, this type of interaction did not have a common universe of discourse. Although the interactants knew the meaning of these words, their basic assumptions were so different that their interpretations of the words varied considerably.

Role taking involves prediction among the interactants in order to foresee the ends of communication. Within limits, each interactant can anticipate the effect of his conduct, for the interactant arouses in himself the type of responses which he expects from the other. If a teacher commands a class to be quiet, she expects her gestures will create silent attention from the class. If a parent brings a gift to a child, he can rehearse in his mind the child's pleasant reaction to the gift.

The extent to which one has developed a capacity for role taking indicates his degree of ordered behavior. The individual who can judge and respond to the actual attitudes of another person can also control and revise his conduct accordingly. His behavior is realistic because he responds to attitudes which actually exist in the other person and are not imagined. If the other person is friendly, hostile, indifferent, or exploiting, he can perceive these attitudes and respond accordingly. For example, one greets an acquaintance in a formal way, but the returned greeting is both friendly and warm. The first individual then changes his behavior to meet this gesture and becomes more informal himself. The two interactants, then, devise the type of relationship which is mutually acceptable.

Role taking, as an adjustive process, enables the individual to control his behavior in accordance with the demands and expectations of other persons.

Types of Role Taking. But role taking differs in closeness and intensity. Clearly, the conversation between two diplomats differs from the relations between mother and child. The casual greeting of two acquaintances varies from the spontaneous confidences of two friends. Sociologists have implied these distinct role-taking processes in their analyses of primary and secondary groups or in personal and impersonal relationships. The generic types of role taking that are consistent with these particular groups are: (1) role identification and (2) role evaluation.

Role Identification and Intimate Relationships. By role identification we mean that one interactant calls out and shares in himself approximately similar attitudes and feelings which the other person experiences. Role identification is a self-involving and self-extending process, because the other person is included within the orbit of one's self-esteem. Seemingly, one incorporates the attitudes and feelings of the other person. The mother who identifies with the child will feel sad or insulted if the child is sad or insulted. One will become happy when his friend is happy. Role identification is intimate, personal, spontaneous, informal, usually durable, involves a "we" feeling, and, within limits is nondefensive.

Role identification usually emerges from the institutionalized primary group, such as the family, but this is not inevitable. Marital partners may cordially dislike each other, brothers may be overcome by rivalry, and parents and children may be mutually hostile. As a matter of fact, some families may be more clearly characterized by familiarity, informality, and lack of restraint, instead of intimacy and identification. But familiarity does not necessarily inspire reciprocal identification. Consider the following illustration of family interaction.

There are five of us in the family. Two sisters, my mother and father, and me. My oldest sister don't talk to my father because she thinks he has no sense. My younger sister don't say much to my mother because she doesn't let her stay out late. When we're home together we start fighting about little things. Last time, for instance, my younger sister had her friends over to watch television. I came home from work and went to the radio to hear the results of the ball game. The girls couldn't hear the television so they said they would leave. I turned off the radio and got mad. Then my sister started at me, and called me a stupid pig, and I got mad and wanted to hit her. Then my mother chimed in and called me a louse. . . . My family is always getting in my way like that. . . . We've been fighting around for years and I hate them all.

Because many families do not have these mutually role-identifying relationships, disorder-creating situations can arise. For example, the ambivalent attitudes of parents to their children can have anxiety-creating effects upon the children.

The crucial fact of role identification in primary relationships is that the participants feel, express, and receive affection, loyalty, gratitude, or sympathy. Cooley regards this process as the essence of human nature and the basis of socialization.[20]

This capacity for role identification becomes an essential criterion for ordered behavior. Some neurotics are too hostile to identify with others and too fearful of being "found out" to become socially intimate. The psychotic who experiences emotional withdrawal usually is unable to share the feelings of others. The psychopath who cannot identify with others is condemned to a kind of emotional isolation.

Role Evaluation and Impersonal Relationships. By role evaluation we mean that one interactant understands but does not share the feelings of another. Instead, he considers the other interactant as a utilitarian means rather than as an end in himself. He considers him beyond the pale of self-identity. He evaluates the other in terms of his impersonal utilitarian role, whether as clerk or customer, employee or employer, competitor, or acquaintance. For example, in relationships between clerk and casual customer, it would be almost unseemly for one to inquire about the personal life of the other. And though informality and personal interests may creep into competitive relationships, these personal qualities soften but do not obviate the competitiveness.

The competitive character of the market place coupled with the anonymity and impersonality of urban life have accentuated a type of role taking in which interactants are considered utiltarian means for impersonal ends or are of such slight and casual concern that identification does not arise. Instead, relationships become socially distant, segmentalized, unemotional, and defensive. In this way the individual can meet many people and transact his affairs without becoming emotionally involved. In this way the impersonal institu-

[20] See Charles H. Cooley, *Human Nature and Conduct* (New York: Charles Scribner's Sons, 1922).

tional ends can be attained without the intrusion of personal considerations.

Yet the kinds of approvals which one obtains in his impersonal
careeristic relationships are necessary, even vital, for self-esteem,
because the prospect of failure can be so threatening. In fact, the
person in this milieu views not only others but also himself as a
utility. But these types of relationships which inhibit self-involving,
self-identifying forms of role taking become very frustrating and
tend to atomize the person into an isolated, lonely creature and
cannot easily sustain him. For example, rooming-house dwellers in
large cities may have many impersonal contacts, but they find these
relationships insufficient to sustain them. Consequently, in their
search for identifying relationships, they retreat to the movies or to
true-story magazines, or lavish their affection upon pets.[21]

The ordered person can differentiate effectively between his role-
identifying and role-evaluative relationships. This difference becomes indispensable for his adjustment in our society because of the
distinct gap between the types of social relations in the family and
in industry. The neurotic, on the other hand, may project personal
hostilities into his impersonal relationships, or he may become
unduly competitive and hostile in his personal relationships. The
psychotic may find this difference even more difficult to achieve
because he usually responds in terms of his disoriented projections
rather than in terms of the conventional requirements of the given
situation.

Projection and Role Taking. Although ordered persons can share
common meanings and thereby participate socially, each individual
also interprets the actions of others in a unique way. Since each person has a unique development and a unique framework of meanings, each person will project singular interpretations into his social
relationships. Thus, role taking between two or more persons does
not create identical interpretations but has individualized and unshared increments. For example, no two individuals interpret the
pictures of a Thematic Apperception Test alike, although persons
with approximately similar backgrounds may have superficially
common interpretations.

[21] Harvey W. Zorbaugh, "The Dweller in Furnished Rooms," *The Urban Community*, edited by Ernest W. Burgess, pp. 98–105 (Chicago: University of Chicago
Press, 1926).

But projection becomes acute when an individual experiences a relationship in which he is helpless. He then responds as he would when encountering obstacles from the physical environment. First, he becomes more concerned with maintaining his self-esteem than with understanding and coping with the other person. Second, his perspective becomes fixed and arrested and his role-taking facility less flexible. He tends, therefore, to project his defensive techniques which he has acquired from this disturbing experience into his subsequent relationships. Third, in this defensive process he becomes less able to evaluate and to share the viewpoints of other persons. His essential helplessness is vested in his lack of confidence to change the behavior of the other person toward him, or in his anticipation of intense disapproval or loss of affection. He resorts to defensive techniques because he has surrendered his confidence in coping with the other person. Since these attitudes persist, he projects them onto other persons.

For example, if an individual is persistently threatened by his parent and, as a result, becomes very hostile, he may respond to other authority figures in the same hostile manner, regardless of their attitudes. Although he can communicate and is aware of the other's formal role, in the area of conflict his role-taking facility becomes limited.[22] This projective process interferes with role taking among neurotics and disrupts role taking among psychotics.

Although neurotics project past fixed attitudes upon other persons, they can take the roles of others and can communicate. But their role-taking capacity tends to lack flexibility and reveals ambivalent attitudes toward other persons. On the one hand, they strive for approval and affection. On the other hand, they are too hostile to call out the approval of other persons. Since their behavior is fixed, they may be troubled by not having friends, or may wonder why they antagonize others. As a result, their self-corrective reactions also decline. By falsely evaluating other's responses, they reinforce their deceptive self-evaluations because they actually want

[22] Idealization of others is also a form of projection as may occur in a love relationship or in hero worship. Generally, this is a positive form of projection and an extension of role identification. However, in extreme cases, it is indicative of immaturity and sometimes may leave the person very vulnerable and suggestible. This type of idealization occurs in therapeutic relationships and is considered a positive type of transference. Presumably, the person imputes what he considers an idealized image onto the other person.

to shield their real estimates of themselves. As Horney points out:[23]

> If the psychic conditions of the neurotic person were what they frequently appear to himself to be, it ought to be easy for him to gain affection. If I may verbalize what he senses only dimly, his impressions are something like this: What he wants is so little, only that people should be kind to him, should give him advice, should appreciate that he is a poor, harmless, lonely soul, anxious to please, anxious not to hurt anyone's feelings. That is all he sees or feels. He does not recognize how much his sensitivities, his latent hostilities, his exacting demands interfere with his own relationships; nor is he able to judge the impression he makes on others or their reaction to him. Consequently he is at a loss to understand why his friendships, marriages, love affairs, professional relations are often so dissatisfactory. He tends to conclude that others are at fault, that they are inconsiderate, disloyal, abusive, or that for some unfathomable reason he lacks the gift of being popular.

Although mild psychotics can participate socially, they persistently feel threatened. For example, one female preschizophrenic belonged to many groups but always felt uneasy and became very anxious when others were quiet. Hence, she or someone else had to keep talking. In her past, when she misbehaved, her parents would purse their lips and put their fingers over them in awesome and forbidding silence. Their punitive gestures continued to her postadolescence when she left home. The intense disapproval associated with silence persisted in her future relationships. But insofar as the neurotic or the mild psychotic can shift his point of view so that he can anticipate the judgments of others, he is able to participate in society.

The most fixed and isolating type of relationship comes when projection supersedes role taking. For example, many paranoids visualize other persons as hostile figures, regardless of the others' intentions. Although these negative appraisals may not cover all persons, they include many. As in any conflict process, the paranoid does not only negate his enemies, but he often attributes an importance to himself which other persons consider bizarre and unacceptable.

Psychotics, then, become deprived of their role-taking facilities in the area of personal conflict. They are less able to communicate and

---

[23] Karen Horney, *The Neurotic Personality of Our Time*, p. 106 (New York: W. W. Norton & Company, 1937).

lose interest in the attitudes of others and become immersed in their own private attitudes. Hence, their words are not designed for communicative purposes but for expressing their own conflicts—as is evident by their neologisms or newly coined words. For example, the schizophrenic who has withdrawn emotionally from certain individuals may feel that they are "dead" and may respond as if they were "dead."

The psychopathic also cannot control his behavior because of his retarded role-taking facility. Self-centered, the psychopath cannot easily identify with others and cannot foresee the objections of others to his predatory behavior.

In brief, just as action completion involves conflict resolution, so does development in interaction involve the socialization of private conflicts and a flexibility in shifting one's perspectives. When the individual can take the roles of others in terms of their present intentions, his behavior becomes realistic. For in this condition he responds to existing attitudes rather than to imagined attitudes which were encountered in the past. He then can more easily anticipate the behavior of the other person, can modify his behavior in terms of the social expectations, and can acquire a realistic version of himself.

The Self System

The self is the most important phase of the social personality. It is dealt with in some form by nearly all disciplines that try to understand people. The anthropologist who is concerned with cultural patterns emphasizes such peripheral concepts as status and official role. The psychoanalyst who deals with biopsychological aspects of personality emphasizes the functions of the ego in adapting to reality. The sociologist and social psychologist who deal with symbolic aspects of behavior concentrate upon self-conception and self-aspiration as well as upon status and role.

The self is not a substantive thing. It cannot be located in the organism, but neither can love nor admiration nor other human expressions. The self is an acquired process; and it arises when the child internalizes the attitudes of others and can perceive and appraise himself as a distinct entity or object.

But the self is more than an object. As an indivisible unity, it combines (1) a responding subject or "active self," (2) an image or idea—a self-conception of this responding subject, and (3) an organization of social norms and images of other forms—an "organized other," [24] As such, self-esteem involves an inner interacting process in which one can evaluate himself in terms of his internalized norms and social expectations.

The Active Self and the Self-conception. The active self or responding subject is the ego or "I" of the personality. Of the many versions concerning this phase of the self we will consider two:

First, from a psychoanalytic viewpoint, the ego is an all-inclusive orientation to reality with an anatomicophysiological base. It is a process for organizing the inner and outer environment to satisfy one's attitudes and drives. When the ego fails to respond in an organized fashion, neurotic and psychotic behavior can result.[25] This version of the self parallels the action phase of personality; it involves the degree to which a given subject can organize and reorganize his behavior and his environment in his efforts at adaptation.

Second, from a social psychological viewpoint, the self is essentially a reference process, a form of internalized interaction and an outgrowth of role taking. The subject, by taking the role of another, can evaluate his behavior, his capacities, and his body image as he can evaluate these phenomena in others. The person can consciously appraise himself as an object in the same way that he can become aware of and appraise other objects. Thus, the two aspects of the self which are involved in identity include an evaluated object, symbol, or image, and a perceiving, orienting, and evaluating subject or agent. This evaluating subject is the active self; the appraised symbol is the self-conception, self-estimation, or self-esteem.

In this referring process all sorts of appraisals may arise. The person may accept himself if he is ordered; he may hate and condemn himself if he is depressed; he may be very uncertain of himself if he has anxiety; he may repress and dissociate one phase of himself if he is overcome by a fugue; he may even lack or lose this process of referring back to himself if he is severely psychotic.

[24] The "organized other" is adapted from the term "generalized other" as used by George H. Mead, *Mind, Self and Society,* pp. 152–158 (Chicago: University of Chicago Press, 1935).
[25] Franz Alexander and Thomas M. French, *Psychoanalytic Therapy,* p. viii (New York: The Ronald Press Company, 1945).

Generally, the person's self-evaluation results in part from his succession of self-images which he experienced in the past, and in part from his present role and status in groups in which he participates. For example, two persons may have similar roles of prestige in their occupations, but one may be bitterly discontent and the other may be relatively content. The first person may have been goaded from childhood to excel in all his activities. These perfectionistic cravings may so dominate his life that any position short of outstanding will be considered unacceptable by him. Further, he may feel that his rivals are ahead of him, and this may distress him further. On the other hand, the second person may have had lesser ambitions and other ideas about occupational success. Hence, he may feel that he has attained the goals to which he has aspired and be relatively content. A person may be relatively successful and have prestige in his present social position, but, because of a series of failures and humiliations in the past, he may still be uncertain of, and dissatisfied with, himself.

But if we confine self-esteem to the influences of the present, the individual who functions competently and/or in a socially approved manner enhances his confidence and self-esteem. When he behaves incompetently and/or in a socially disproved manner, his self-esteem may decline. One who anticipates severe self-criticism when he fails may be more hesitant in his responses. On the other hand, a person who takes failure lightly may be less hesitant in his responses. Thus, action is meaningful because it pertains to one's present and/or anticipated self-evaluations. Of course, not all actions affect the self in the same way. A scientist may be a poor baseball player, but his poor athletic prowess may not affect him very seriously. On the other hand, a professional baseball player may be seriously upset by one bad play. Thus, the activities and values which are directly related to one's self-esteem are sometimes called self-involving.[26] The norms of behavior by which one judges himself vary with one's past and present relationships, his roles and degree of success. It has been found by experimentation that successful activity leads to a raising and failure to a lowering of one's levels of aspiration. Failure in a pursuit may result in avoiding the

[26] See Muzafer Sherif and Hadley Cantril, *The Psychology of Ego Involvements* (New York: John Wiley & Sons, Inc., 1947).

setting up of a high level of aspiration.[27] Thus, goal aspiration also is related to one's expected conception of himself.

Body Image and Self-conception. The body image also has a definite effect upon one's self-conception. The physique, facial features, and other parts of the body are objects of social evaluation and directly influence one's self-evaluation. This is attested by the nicknames of children and adolescents. It is apparent in the efforts of women to look younger or slimmer. It is brought to continual awareness by the advertisements in newspapers, magazines, television, and radio. Often the physically underdeveloped boy may not be accepted completely by the peer group; and the fat adolescent girl may sacrifice her companionship with males. The blemishes or defects in the body type by adverse social definitions, which are expressed in ridicule, avoidance, social exclusion, or limited participation, can contribute to a devaluated self-conception. Consider the following self-appraisal of a twenty-year-old male student:

Has any person in this world suffered as much as I because of the lack of three inches in height? I do not think so. For ten years I have known this suffering. With each passing year my hopes have diminished. Now at the age of twenty-one, my hopes have all but vanished.

I have a picture, vividly burned in my mind, of the moment when I first felt this haunting desire to be taller. One summer day ten years ago, I was seated on a cement ash container, waiting for a friend to come outside to play ball. He came out and walked to where I was sitting. He stopped and I slid off the container. For the first time I had to look up to meet his eyes. He looked down at mine and simply said, "You're short." I said nothing, and we walked to play ball. From that time, not a day has passed that the words of that boy have not taunted me. They return virtually every time I walk into a restaurant and the hostess looks *down* at me and smiles. I imagine her to be smiling only because of my height. How ridiculous a thought, but so very painful. Everytime I see my uncles I hear those words, "You're too short." How many times when a child have I said to them, "You just wait till I grow up." They are still waiting. Boys whom I knew as little children now look either on an even level or down at me. I dare not accept a blind date. . . . I have tried high-heeled shoes; it was a total failure. I felt that I had committed a crime.

[27] See C. L. Child and John M. W. Whiting, "Determination of Level of Aspiration: Evidence from Everyday Life," *Journal of Abnormal and Social Psychology,* July, 1949, XLIV:3, pp. 306–308; Kurt Levin, Tamara Dembo, Leon Festinger, and Pauline S. Sears, "Level of Aspiration," *Personality and the Behavior Disorders,* edited by J. McV. Hunt, Vol. I (New York: The Ronald Press Company, 1944).

Another individual was harassed by his mother because he was "too short." She took him to the doctor to facilitate his growth. The physician prescribed something, but it did no good. After a few visits the doctor admitted that there was nothing that he could do to make the boy grow. The mother, in weird identification, began to chide and hit him because he was "so short." His schoolmates called him "shrimp" and would not let him play in football and baseball games. He developed intense inferiority feelings and compensated by excellent schoolwork. Only at the age of 16, when he grew slightly, did he begin to participate more frequently with boys and girls.

The self-evaluation may be influenced not only by physical appearance but also by different parts and movements of the body. For example, a girl had an unimportant accident which led to two superficial scars on her thumbs. She felt that life was not worth living. Long before the accident she regarded her hands as the most beautiful parts of her body.[28] The individual whose occupation depends on his hands, as a musician, or on his larynx, as a singer, or on his legs, as a dancer, can become very concerned about these parts of the body. Sometimes the clumsy individual becomes very self-conscious about his movements. In brief, in our body-conscious culture, one's effectiveness in social participation depends in part upon his appearance and movements. These facets of the body enter into the stream of social evaluations and, in the process, affect self-evaluations favorably or unfavorably.

Self-reference in Ordered and Disordered Behavior. What different processes in self-reference operate in ordered and disordered behavior? Let us consider ordered behavior first.

Since the ordered person can take the role of other persons in terms of their present intentions, he can also appraise himself in the same realistic way. By perceiving, judging, and correcting his faults he can also control, change, and develop himself within the limits of his social situation and his abilities. He can face himself in terms of his performances, appearance, and aspirations. Even when at odds with social demands, his conflicts are on a present, realistic level rather than carry-overs from past dissatisfactions. Consequently, he tends to be concerned with his problems and situa-

[28] Paul Schilder, "The Somato-Psyche in Psychiatry and Social Psychology," *Journal of Abnormal and Social Psychology,* October–December, 1934, 29:3, p. 318.

tions rather than with himself. He can be spontaneous and can express his deeper feelings, because he has a capacity for role-identifying relationships of love and friendship. Moreover, he shows balance or symmetry in his conception of his different formal and informal roles. He does not use one role to compensate for another. For example, a ditchdigger may be perfectly stable and ordered when he achieves some balance between his occupational, marital, and friendship roles.[29]

Although it would be difficult for one to express himself spontaneously in a hostile, highly competitive group, still his conflicts would be results of contemporary situations, rather than past hangovers.

The disordered person usually cannot face and accept himself as he is but, inevitably, has to retreat into deceptive self-images. Although he becomes more concerned with himself than with his problems, he cannot assess himself accurately. As Horney points out, he is in fear of being "unmasked" and "found out." Under his generosity is selfishness; under his efficiency is a fear of incompetence; beneath his intelligence might be gaps of ignorance. If people knew him too well they would be disappointed. His deceptive image then becomes a retreat and defense, but underneath stirs the anxiety of what he is really like; and he must flee from this image because it uncovers his weakness and helplessness. Hence, the neurotic creates a "front" to which he hangs on and which becomes vital to his self-esteem. Consequently, his self-conceptions are contradictory. One self-conception is a "front" and a retreat. The other self-conception reveals his weakness and diffidence.

Since the psychotic's capacity for role taking has been disrupted, he also tends to lack a capacity for internalized self-reference.

First, many psychotics have unshared and delusional conceptions of themselves which the social judgments of others cannot change.

[29] Fromm, in a suggestive study, contends that to be free is to be spontaneous. In many facets of our competitive society, spontaneity is difficult to achieve except within primary groups. Thus, the individual who is spontaneous in a hostile, suspicious group will change in time, although he will not necessarily become neurotic because his conflicts will be on a present level. The other alternative implies a revision of the social dynamics of an impersonal society. Fromm sees that an impersonal competitive society cannot function in such a manner which would permit this complete spontaneity. Eric Fromm, *Escape from Freedom*, pp. 262–265 (New York: Rinehart & Company, Inc., 1941).

For example, they may feel that they are made of wood or stone or are wasting away; they may ascribe undue importance to themselves—that they are God, an angel, the devil—and judge the activities of other persons on the basis of their self-conceptions. Thus, the paranoid may interpret a smile as an avowal of love, or people whispering as a dire plot. Second, many psychotics cannot attain identity in all spheres of behavior because they cannot control all their activities. For example, psychotics who hallucinate do not circumscribe this behavior as their own but attribute it to outside sources. Third, some psychotics may be unable to revise their self-conceptions because they have cut off their social ties. They judge themselves in terms of their private frames of reference. And psychotic depressives who internalize the social judgments of others in fierce self-condemnation often lack the strength to revise their self-estimates.

In short, the more a person can face, assess, and correct himself, the greater is his tendency toward ordered behavior and personal development. His behavior tends to become spontaneous, problem-centered, self-realizing, rather than self-inverted and distracted by helpless self-concern. On the other hand, the less one can accept himself, the more he has to hide behind illusional or delusional self-images and to obscure his "real self." He becomes less amenable to self-correction in terms of attainable aspirations and social demands and more fixed in his orientation to himself and to others.

The Organized Other and Social Expectations. The "organized other" consists of the internalized framework of behavioral norms and of personal images by which the given individual directs and controls his conduct.[30] It channelizes both permissible and forbidden behavior, limits the individual's activities, and provides the bases for self-judgments. In essence, it is the conscience.

It is derived from Mead's concept of the "generalized other" which reflects the internalized norms that are common to the members of a given community.[31] The "organized other" covers the unique as well as the common norms of each person. The "general-

[30] Freud's conception of the "superego" differs from the "organized other" because it is essentially a medium with repressed and suppressed instincts, early infantile complexes, and early images of the parents.

[31] George H. Mead, *Mind, Self and Society* (Chicago: University of Chicago Press, 1935).

ized other" is analyzed in terms of a temporal present and is tied in with the self-conception, or "me." But the norms and images by which one feels unworthy are distinct from the image of oneself. Also, the internalized norms of the individual may make for different types of self-control. One individual may censure himself and feel guilty because of his inner scruples, and he may do so when he is alone and after a given act is completed. This individual may judge himself adversely quite apart from the judgments of others, as we say, because of "principles." Another individual may feel shame for having been caught doing something scandalous. He may fear contemporary disapproval, but he may feel very little guilt when alone or after the incident. The first individual is responding to norms and images which he has internalized from the past. The other individual is responding to reactions in the present. Both are exerting self-control, but in entirely different ways.

Each person has unique norms both in content and in form, because each individual has acquired a unique set of aspirations and has internalized his norms of behavior in a unique way.[32]

Although Freud and others considered the moral demands in early childhood as most crucial, still adolescent and early adult experiences may so profoundly impress the person that these experiences can readily become the bases of his behavior. For example, the adolescent who is unacquainted with the techniques of social climbing may act out against authority as he did against his parents, but he may be repeatedly rebuffed. Thus, inhibiting his aggression against authority, wittingly or unwittingly, he may regard submissiveness as one of the prime norms of his behavior. Also, intense prohibitions, such as killing, can be modified in a matter of months by intensified group pressures, as occurs in the army and in subsequent combat.

The ordered person has internalized coherent images and norms which allow him to be "himself." He does not have to retreat into pretense about himself. Nor is he driven into a rigid, perfectionistic style of living. He can remain flexible because he does not strive for pseudo-perfectionism and can tolerate and abide by his moral demands. His internalized norms of behavior have not incapacitated

---

[32] See Jean Piaget, *The Moral Development of the Child* (Glencoe, Ill.: The Free Press, 1948).

him in his competitive relationships and in his identifying relationships.

The neurotic, on the other hand, has internalized ambivalent images, especially of his parents. On the one hand, he idealizes his parents. On the other hand, he sees them as they are. Thus, his conduct tends to be motivated by hostile, vague, and contradictory ends. Because the neurotic is driven by rigid internalized rules, he experiences intense guilt when disobeying these rules. And this self-reproach is a result of past demands and of the images associated with those demands. The neurotic cannot afford to be "himself." If a child has had it drummed into him by his parents that he is very talented and that any other estimate he has of himself leads to intense disapproval, he will of necessity operate under that façade, regardless of what he may feel underneath. Since his basic attitudes toward himself will be repressed, he will shift his real attitudes away from himself by behaving and conceiving himself as he feels his parents would have wanted him to.

The "organized other" of the psychotic varies. The depressive tends to internalize a demanding set of images which he directs toward himself in stark self-condemnation. This applies also for many schizophenics. But the schizophrenic tends to externalize his wishes through hallucinations so that he does not feel responsible for them. His expressions, which were hidebound by certain norms, no longer are restricted by them. The schizophrenic also may have delusions which vaguely indicate an attempt to pull away from his norms of conduct. The psychopath who does not identify with parental figures has few internal restraints and rarely feels guilty.

The Self-defenses and Disordered Behavior

Personal Organization and Self-defenses. The person who can remain organized and confident in critical situations has little need for pathologically defensive behavior. In many critical situations, however, this type of behavior can be only partly achieved. For example, Bettelheim, while he was an inmate in a concentration camp, tried to avert the usual intense personal disorganization by studying his fellow inmates. He described his experiences as follows:[33]

[33] Bruno Bettelheim, "Individual and Mass Behavior in Extreme Situations," *Journal of Abnormal and Social Psychology,* 1943, XXXVIII, pp. 417–452. By permission of American Psychological Association.

During the first days in the camp, the writer realized that he behaved differently from the way he used to. He observed, for instance, the split in his person into one who observes and one to whom things happen, a typical psychopathological phenomenon. He also observed that his fellow prisoners, who had been normal persons, now behaved like pathological liars, were unable to restrain themselves and to make objective evaluations. Thus the question arose, "How can I protect myself against disintegration?" The answer was: to find out what changes occurred in the prisoners and why they took place. By occupying myself with interviewing prisoners, by pondering my findings while forced to perform exhausting labor, I succeeded in killing the time in a way which seemed constructive. As the time went on, the enhancement of my self-respect due to my ability to continue to do meaningful work despite the contrary efforts of the Gestapo became even more important than the pastime.

Clearly, this type of personal organization was more integrative than that of the other inmates, but it is doubtful whether in this extreme situation he was able to face and to ward off the ever-pressing threats around him. Despite his organization, he had to resort to a kind of detachment which in less extreme situations would have been very defensive. Murphy regards this basic "defense" as "autistic self-stabilization." [34]

The whole problem of adaptability becomes a function of one's ability to organize and to handle past and present critical situations in terms of one's self-esteem. Horney refers to this basic stabilizing fact as a feeling of safety. Yet safety arises only when the individual can define and organize his situation. Hilgard has said:[35]

> The healthy self will achieve an integrative organization. Note that I say integrative and not integrated. It is the integrative personality which can handle the complexity of relationships with other persons in a culture like ours, a culture which makes plural demands.

Hilgard points out further that although the paranoid may be a very integrated personality because of his highly systematized delusions, he is not "integrative." [36] His capacity for organizing his environment within the framework of the culture is far less facile than that of ordered persons.

When the person cannot master a given set of experiences, he

[34] Gardner Murphy, *Personality: A Biosocial Approach to Origins and Structure*, p. 530 (New York: Harper & Brothers, 1947).

[35] Ernest R. Hilgard, "Human Motives and the Concept of the Self," *American Psychologist*, September, 1949, IV:9, pp. 379–380.

[36] *Ibid.*, p. 380.

becomes disorganized, incapacitated; it is then that the basic defenses arise. From a psychoanalytic viewpoint, Grinker and Speigel have shown from cases of soldiers in combat that as the pressure upon the ego or personality increases, the person's inhibitory and intellectual functions give way because anxiety is intensified.[37] This results in tremors, rapid heart beat, rapid breathing, and restlessness. When the anxiety is intensified further, the person becomes confused and cannot concentrate. He cannot differentiate between dangerous and secure situations because all situations appear dangerous to him. In this predicament the person, feeling that he has to get a grip on himself, often seizes the object nearest to him and squeezes it as if his very life depended on it.

Characteristics of the Defenses. As partial or incomplete adaptations to conflict, the defenses are static, repetitive, inhibit personal development, and restrict personal organization. The pathological degree of the defenses depends upon the severity of the person's conflicts and upon his general degree of stability. The defenses also seem to have some continuity, and they range from the techniques devised in mild neurotic behavior to the extreme private retreats of psychotic activity.

Neurotic defenses which avert attitudes of helplessness may also prevent the lapse into the more serious disturbances of psychosis. For when neurotic defenses fail, anxiety may become so intense that sometimes a psychosis may possibly result. At other times a psychosis may often develop without an intervening neurotic period. In other instances neurotic and psychotic defenses may be mingled. Psychotic disorders do not always imply that the defensive system has failed. For example, a paranoid who has a very tight logical delusional system may become a more severely disorganized hebephrenic if this delusional system is penetrated. On the other hand, an acute psychotic without a fixed defensive system may possibly reorient himself more quickly than the chronic neurotic whose defenses are very deep.

Defensive reactions are specific to the individual. Hence, we do not know what defensive structure a given person will develop. Under relatively similar conditions, two persons may respond by different defensive reactions. Each person has a defensive system

[37] Roy R. Grinker and John Spiegel, *Men Under Stress,* pp. 132, 133 (Philadelphia: The Blakiston Company, 1945).

peculiar to him because of his constitution and his unique sequence of experiences. The hypnotic experiments of Wolberg point up this phenomenon rather clearly.

Wolberg instructed three subjects, a conversion hysteric, an anxiety type, and one with psychosomatic symptoms, that each would see a chocolate bar and would have an irresistible desire to eat it.[38] By eating the chocolate he would simultaneously feel that he was doing something "very wrong and very bad." After awakening from the hypnotic trance each subject was to forget these suggestions but was to react to them.

The conversion hysteric saw everything else but the chocolate bar. His blindness for the object persisted for twenty minutes. After that he saw the candy but would not eat it.

The anxiety subject became dizzy, pale, had violent tremors, and was unable to walk. In fact he became so severely anxiety-ridden that he had to be rehypnotized in order to remove the conflict.

The third subject was composed and talked about eating and about food. He justified his attitudes by disclosing that visitors should eat food offered to them. He started to eat the chocolate but it tasted bitter. He complained of stomach pains and nausea, and went to the bathroom and vomited.

We see that each subject responded differently in an externally similar critical situation. Yet the anxiety-ridden person without a defensive scheme seemingly suffered the most. Unless we know the developmental history of a person we don't know what defenses he will summon in a critical situation. We do not know to what extent the defensive system is a function of constitutional proneness or of specific social influences. More research of developmental sequences as well as in experimental situations is necessary for a clearer understanding of this phase of personality.

Defenses and Disordered Behavior. Defensive reactions are usually unwitting and nondeliberate, but in some instances they may be amenable to control. Defensive behavior can arise from internal as well as external dangers. When the person cannot cope with external danger, he attempts to flee from it. Later, he tends to so organize his activity that he will not re-encounter the threat. In the same way the person attempts to flee from the recollection of a pain-

---

[38] Louis R. Wolberg, "Hypnotic Experiments in Psychosomatic Medicine," *Psychosomatic Medicine,* 1947, IX, pp. 337–342.

ful or distressing experience by repressing, suppressing, or denying it. This type of forgetting, as Freud early saw, constitutes a kind of internal flight, and in a sense is the basic defense in disordered behavior. Another type of defense averts self-reproach by imputing the blame to the environment, as in projection and rationalization. A third type redeems one's lowered self-estimate by redirected or substituted behavior, as in overcompensation, reaction formation. The fourth type, "withdrawal and externalization" which pertains to psychotic behavior, reveals a dissociation from self-controlled activity. But these generic defenses, which are among the multitude of specific defenses selected in the struggle for adaptation, also combine in unique patterns for each person. These defensive reactions will be elaborated in the specific discussions of the disorders.

Defensive Behavior and Social Relations. Horney has described defensive behavior in terms of social relationships. She has described the following three types of defenses which the neurotic implemented in his relationships with other persons: (1) moving toward people, (2) moving against people, and (3) moving away from people, or social detachment.[39]

Although neurotics may have all three defensive attitudes in some measure, they select one predominant defense as their life style. This is seemingly the mode of behavior by which they feel best organized and most secure. Although ordered persons also may have these attitudes, neurotics are driven to these relationships in an inflexible and rigid manner, even when this type of relationship is inappropriate for them. Without this defensive manner they become very insecure, and even panic-stricken. Further, these attitudes toward other people reflect their attitudes toward themselves. Thus, the individual who moves toward people by being very submissive also may be self-contemptuous. The individual who is hostile to others is also hostile to himself. The individual who withdraws from others also tends to become distant and estranged from himself and tries to look at himself with a detached interest.

Selected Reading

Alexander, Franz, and Thomas M. French, *Psychoanalytic Therapy* (New York: The Ronald Press Company, 1945).

[39] Karen Horney, *Our Inner Conflicts,* pp. 42–44 (New York: W. W. Norton & Company, 1945).

Allport, Gordon W., *Personality* (New York: Henry Holt and Company, Inc., 1937).

Cantril, Hadley, and Muzafer Sherif, *The Psychology of Ego-Involvements* (New York: John Wiley & Sons, Inc., 1947).

French, Thomas M., "Defense and Synthesis in the Function of the Ego," *Psychoanalytic Quarterly*, 1938, 7, pp. 537–541.

Fromm, Erich, *Escape From Freedom* (New York: Rinehart & Company, Inc., 1941).

Hilgard, Ernest R., "Human Motives and the Concept of the Self," *The American Psychologist*, September, 1949, IV:9, pp. 374–382.

Horney, Karen, *New Ways in Psychoanalysis* (New York: W. W. Norton & Company, 1939).

Hunt, Joseph McV., *Personality and the Behavior Disorders*, Chaps. I, III, IV, VI, IX, X, XI (New York: The Ronald Press Company, 1944).

Kluckhohn, Clyde, and Henry A. Murray (editors), *Personality: In Nature, Society and Culture*, Chaps. I, II (New York: Alfred A. Knopf, Inc., 1948).

McClelland, David C., *Personality* (New York: William Sloane Associates, 1951).

Mead, George H., *Mind Self and Society* (Chicago: University of Chicago Press, 1935).

Murphy, Gardner, *Personality*, Chaps. I, II (New York: Harper & Brothers, 1947).

Murray, Henry A., *et al.*, *Explorations of Personality*, Chaps. I, II (Cambridge, Mass.: Harvard University Press, 1938).

Newcomb, Theodore M., *Social Psychology* (New York: The Dryden Press, Inc., 1950).

CHAPTER FIVE

Abnormal Behavior, Personal Disorders, and Culture

In the preceding chapter we described the dynamics of the social personality and the changes that occur among disordered persons. But disordered persons emerge within a given society, and the members of that society define their behavior in certain ways. Some neurotics who are able to fulfill their responsibilities may be considered "normal" by the group. But psychotics, unable to fulfill their responsibilities, may be considered "abnormal." Also, behavior that is acceptable in one society may be reprehensible in another. Frequently, behavior cannot be interpreted as ordered or disordered unless its meaning in the given society is understood. In the attempt to sharpen the disparate concepts of disordered behavior and of social abnormality, and to show the importance of understanding these forms of behavior within the cultural context we shall discuss: (1) the individual and cultural views of abnormality, (2) the relationships between personal disorders and abnormality, (3) culture and disordered behavior, and (4) the social definitions of specific types and expressions of personal disorders in our culture.

Forms of Abnormal Behavior

Abnormal behavior has been defined in terms of the individual's performance and in terms of the group's definition of the individual's performance.

Personal Stability and Disordered Behavior; Individualistic Conceptions of Abnormality. The individualistic conceptions of "abnormality" or personal instability may be interpreted as: (1) the deviation from the usual performance of a given individual; (2) the deviation from a hypothetically ideal personal stability; and (3) the deviation from the average or mode of personal stability in a given group. These individualistic connotations of "abnormality" denote disturbed or disordered behavior.

Deviation from Usual Behavior. The individual whose performance or mood is not "up to par" or not characteristic of his usual demeanor is sometimes considered "abnormal." Some persons who experience critical situations such as bereavement, marital discord, or disappointment about a job may have interludes of atypical behavior. Temporarily disorganized as a result of these stress situations, they may behave in an unusual manner; after a respite they revert to their usual condition. Even when their behavior persists, their performance is often gauged by their usual behavior in the past.

Deviation from Ideal Personal Stability. The clinical conception of abnormality refers to the deviation from ideal personal stability. For example, if a random group of persons were tested, a large proportion of the sample might be found to be disturbed. Since few individuals realize the optimum development of their social capacities or are very well organized, few persons are "ideally normal." Also, in a society where the individual continually encounters frustration and conflict, ideal stability is difficult to attain. For instance, many people in our culture are insecure and have certain fears which cannot be overcome completely. Ideal personal stability has often been described by advocates of mental health, but relatively few people attain this ideal.[1] For example, the National Committee for Mental Health defines mental health as follows:[2]

> Mental Health clearly means that an individual has found a reasonable measure of peace within himself and with his environment—it means that an individual is able to pursue reasonable purposeful goals; may use his capacities and talents fruitfully; experiences a sense of security, of belonging, of being respected; has a knowledge

[1] See Chapter Nineteen, "Prevention: Personal Stability and Society."
[2] The National Health Assembly, *America's Health,* p. 302 (New York: Harper & Brothers, 1949). By permission.

that he is liked or loved and wanted; has self-respect and self-reliance; has a sense of achievement; has an opportunity for new experiences and adventure. Mental health also means that an individual has learned to respect others, to accept others, and to live with others.

How many persons in our society measure up to this omnibus definition of ideal personal stability is not known precisely, but very likely many do not. For example, 24 per cent of 4,828,000 men rejected for military duty in World War II had personal or organic disorders. This does not mean that the other soldiers who entered the Army were all stable.[3] In a comparative study of 100 psychiatric battle casualties and 100 noncasualties, 22.8 per cent of the former and 11.9 per cent of the latter group had unhappy childhoods, and 5.9 per cent of the former and 3.6 per cent of the latter group had some neurotic traits.[4] Since the huge group of potential inductees and soldiers were usually under 40 years old, and the majority under 30, it is apparent that a substantial proportion of the population in our society do not by any means achieve ideal stability or maturity.

Deviation from Modal Personal Stability. The third conception of abnormality is the deviation from the average or modal stability for a given group.[5] The difficulty with this attempt at definition is that the units of what constitutes normal stability are not readily amenable to quantification and even to definition. As yet we do not know the norms of behavior, mood, and orientation for children, adolescents, or young and old adults. In addition, the modal stability may vary by socioeconomic level, ethnic group, and even occupation. For example, the modal emotional stability for children in middle-

[3] William C. Menninger, *Psychiatry in a Troubled World,* p. 587 (New York: The Macmillan Company, 1948).

[4] W. A. Needles, "A Statistical Study of 100 Neuropsychiatric Casualties from the Normandy Campaign," *The American Journal of Psychiatry,* September, 1945, 102, pp. 214–221.

[5] Lundberg proposes that those within the lower 16 per cent of a group be considered within the abnormal category. Yet Lundberg bases his statistical average on behavioral expressions, and lumps together the lame, the blind, the feeble-minded, and the "insane," although it can be readily seen that the character of their deficient performances would vary in kind. A feeble-minded person would be unable to adjust because of his poor performance on a job. A paranoid, however, would probably be quite competent on his job but would be unable to get along with other persons. Obviously, this type of characterization of the abnormal has serious shortcomings by its overinclusive categorization of "abnormal." See George Lundberg, *Foundations of Sociology,* pp. 214–215 (New York: The Macmillan Company, 1939).

class Italian families, for lower-class Negroes and for upper-class white Americans very probably differs.

If we compare the average persons in other cultures the discrepancies become greater. The modal or average Alorese would probably be neurotic; the normal Dobuan would be very suspicious; the normal Mundugumor would be very hostile; the Zuñi would be relatively noncompetitive and the middle-class American very competitive. In short, the average person in one culture develops differently from the average person in another culture because of the technology, patterns of relationships, goals, social structure, and ethos in a given culture.

Horney has broadly sketched the normal person in the American urban culture as one who is inclined to become more reserved and less inclined to trust people as he reaches adulthood and is aware that people are not motivated by straightforward actions but are often prompted by expediency and cowardice.[6] Despite the recognition of these shortcomings in others and in himself, he does not become helpless in dealing with them. Moreover, he has some people with whom he can be friendly and to whom he can confide. This normal or healthy person presumably has experienced conflicts which he could usually integrate in contrast with the neurotic who has had traumatic experiences which he could not integrate, and thus has become predisposed to anxiety. But how characteristic this personality type is, is not known, because the sketch is thin and is a means of differentiating the supposedly stable person from the neurotic in our culture.

The so-called average or characteristic personality varies in different cultures. Since each culture, subculture, and perhaps even each historical epoch, may have a constant and recognizable personality type, it becomes misleading to expect the same kind of personality to emerge or to thrive in different cultures. For example, the noncompetitive Zuñi would be somewhat out of place in our competitive society, and the aggressive, climbing American "go-getter" would be in complete disfavor among the Zuñis.

Abnormality as Social Definition: the Cultural Approach. Abnormal behavior, as defined by the group, refers to the individual's

---

[6] Karen Horney, *The Neurotic Personality of Our Time*, p. 95 (New York: W. W. Norton & Company, 1937).

departure from the norms, standardized practices, and approved outlets for his specific roles. From this viewpoint the crucial point of abnormality is the group's evaluation of individual behavior rather than the degree of personal stability. Each society possesses and transmits a singular configuration of attitudes, gestures, and expressions. These constitute the social expectations and social definitions which members of that society have to observe and follow. These unique group definitions are used to determine whether or not a person is socially normal in that society. Two individuals in two distinct societies may behave in somewhat the same way, yet the behavior of each will have a widely divergent meaning in each society. Kroeber has described in striking fashion how collective superstitions can be mistaken for personal delusions.[7]

> . . . an elderly Neapolitan cobbler comes to a hospital clinic with a rambling story told in broken English. His account wanders from headaches and listlessness to an old woman who has made him sick. He is referred to the neuro-psychiatric department with the comment: "Question of psychosis." Examination brings out little more than irrelevant detail about the enemy and how long she wished him ill, and why, and how she makes his head hurt. There is all the more indication of a persecutory delusion. The man is told to come back with an interpreter. He returns with a fluent Italian-American who explains apologetically that the old man is illiterate and he believes the woman is a witch and has cast the evil eye on him. The apparent delusion dissolves into a bit of superstition typical of the lower orders of Neapolitan society. What is normal belief there, is a psychotic symptom in one of our hospitals . . . the norm of one culture is a sign of nervous pathology in the other.

What appeared as disoriented behavior to the psychiatrist in our culture was indicative of oriented and approved behavior in another society. For this significant reason behavior cannot be correctly evaluated unless we know how that behavior is defined by the given society or subsociety. This is true not only for what seems to be disoriented behavior in our culture but also for varied gestures.

For instance, although laughter may have many shades of meaning in American society, it is frequently associated with pleasant experiences. But among the Japanese of the nineteenth century,

[7] Alfred L. Kroeber, "Cultural Anthropology." By permission from *Problems of Mental Disorder,* edited by Madison Bentley and E. V. Cowdrey, p. 347. Copyright, 1934. McGraw-Hill Book Company, Inc.

laughter was not necessarily a reaction to amusement but frequently a social duty. The Japanese child was taught to smile just as he was taught to bow or to prostrate himself. He was taught to express a happy appearance so as not to impose his grief upon his friends. In this light, Klineberg, who used Hearn's materials among others for studying the Japanese, relates the following:[8]

> The story is told of a woman servant who smilingly asked her mistress if she might go to her husband's funeral. Later she returned with the ashes in a vase and said, actually laughing, "Here is my husband." Her mistress regarded her as a cynical creature; Hearn suggests that this might have been pure heroism.

The white mistress interpreted her servant's smile as one of joy rather than as a cover-up for the intense grief and sorrow that this servant might have felt. Yet the Japanese would have clearly understood her gesture as socially normal.

It is usually necessary, too, that behavior be accessible to group evaluation. An individual who silently harbors deviant private beliefs cannot be defined as socially abnormal if he does not allow his actions to be influenced markedly by his views. For example, some mild paranoids in our culture have enough situational insight to suspect that their grandiose ideas of themselves would be denounced by other persons. Consequently, they usually are silent about their private notions unless they feel completely confident in the other person. Sometimes they express their ideas in such a way that the listener is not sure whether they are serious or joking.

Sometimes "adherence to reality" is considered a criterion of social normality. But different societies have different versions of "reality." What may be "real" in one society may be clearly "false" in another society. "Reality" is a function of communication and agreement rather than of objectively demonstrated truths. It refers to the individual's ability to share and to evaluate the viewpoints of his immediate groups. Johnson has described this phenomenon in the case of the " 'Phantom Anesthetist' of Mattoon,"[9] and Cantril

[8] Otto Klineberg, *Race Differences*, p. 286 (New York: Harper & Brothers, 1935).
[9] D. M. Johnson, "The 'Phantom Anesthetist' of Mattoon; a Field Study of Mass Hysteria," *Journal of Abnormal and Social Psychology*, April, 1945, XL, pp. 175–186.

and his associates have done so in the analysis of *The Invasion from Mars*.[10]

In many parts of Western culture if one sees a religious miracle he may be believed and perhaps elevated in status. But if he claimed to have seen a fish walking on dry land or some other unlikely episode, his sanity would be questioned. At this writing (1950) 100,000 persons are waiting for a farm woman to behold a "heavenly" vision. This same process applies to other societies. For example, if a Saulteaux Indian saw a nonexistent great snake he would be believed, or at least tolerated, for these illusions are transmitted in the folklore and socially sanctioned. On the other hand, if he claimed to have seen a Jabberwocky he would be considered a liar, or a "madman."

Furthermore, what may be considered abnormal on one occasion may be sanctioned on other occasions. The antics to which some fraternity pledges submit, or the behavior of anonymous visitors during conventions in large cities would, on other occasions, be considered definitely abnormal. If a fraternity pledge is fishing in front of a theater he would be tolerated, but another person without this social role would probably be considered psychotic.

Abnormal behavior, then, has a specific group connotation. It challenges, disrupts, or threatens the group and contributes to its demoralization. From a functional point of view, abnormal behavior cannot be used by the society. From the interactional point of view it is activity which is collectively disapproved. Hence, the more threatening a given form of behavior, the more severely it is collectively disapproved and suppressed.

Disordered Behavior and Socially Abnormal Behavior

Disordered behavior is essentially a result of sustained personal conflict and personal disorganization. Socially abnormal behavior is a result of social definitions and social expectations. The extent to which an individual can reorganize his behavior is a criterion of his being ordered or "mentally healthy." But the extent to which an individual fulfills his social roles and abides by the dictates of the group determines the degree to which he is socially normal. Although personal disorders, especially the psychoses, the severe neuro-

[10] H. Cantril, H. Gaudet, and H. Hertzog, *The Invasion from Mars* (Princeton, N.J.: Princeton University Press, 1940).

ses, and the acting-out disorders, may usually be defined as socially abnormal, the two concepts do not necessarily coincide.

For example, in analyzing the personality structure of four people in a small town, i.e., Plainsville, Kardiner found that though three persons were severely neurotic, they were able to participate in the community and were considered "normal" by the other residents. Although Kardiner claims that "the distinction between normal and neurotic breaks down completely," [11] it is apparent that the two terms, i.e., normal and neurotic, denote distinct dimensions of behavior. From a clinical point of view these three individuals spoken of by Kardiner lacked personal stability. From the viewpoint of social definition they were normal because they were able to participate in the group within the range of the demands of their prescribed roles. Also, it is not known how far they veered from the empirical norm of stability within this particular community.

Many neurotic persons, who are troubled with severe conflicts, conform in their daily relationships and perform their duties satisfactorily. Some neurotics are more rigorously conformistic than stable persons because they are more easily threatened by self-assertion and more easily disturbed by social disapproval. Indeed, all their behavior is oriented around being socially accepted. Horney has referred to these neurotic persons as the "compliant type" because they resort to submission as a defense to allay their anxiety.

Fromm claims, however, that in our competitive society many normal persons who are well adapted and who can satisfactorily fulfill their social roles do so at the expense of their individuality. Insofar as they sacrifice what they want to do in order to be well adapted, these normal persons become emotionally crippled. For their compulsive social efficiency deprives them of the kind of self-realization which can make for optimum development and happiness.[12] Fromm maintains that some neurotics, on the other hand, have not completely surrendered their efforts at self-realization and individuality but strive for it through neurotic symptoms and in fantasy life.

People who cling to the letter of the rule are often highly uncer-

[11] Abram Kardiner et al., *Psychological Frontiers of Society*, p. 378 (New York: Columbia University Press, 1945).

[12] Erich Fromm, *Escape From Freedom*, pp. 138–141 (New York: Rinehart & Company, Inc., 1941).

tain of themselves and need external props to remain organized. Benedict regards the Puritans of New England, who persecuted others as "witches," as more disturbed than the people they persecuted. Yet they were the normal persons of their society. In fact,[13]

> Few prestige groups in any culture have been allowed such complete intellectual and emotional dictatorship as they were. They were the voice of God. Yet to a modern observer it is they, not the confused and tortured women they put to death as witches, who were the psychoneurotics of Puritan New England. A sense of guilt as extreme as they portrayed and demanded both in their own conversion experiences and in those of their converts is found in a slightly saner civilization only in institutions for mental diseases.

An extreme example which clearly points up the difference between disorder and abnormality was observed by the writer over a six-months period. This was in a group of psychotic persons in a hopeful ward of a mental hospital.[14] All these persons were disordered and some were severely disordered, and they were, of course, considered abnormal by conventional society. Nevertheless, in the process of collective participation they evolved standards of "normal" and "abnormal" behavior. The patients usually wanted to be released from the hospital and wanted to improve as a means of being released. Those few patients who claimed that they were content with the hospital or would never recover were considered atypical or abnormal by the other patients and were often avoided by them. This patient group, like any other group, had norms of approved behavior and strived to retain a collective morale. The few patients who disrupted this morale by their complaints were thus considered "abnormal." On the other hand, despite their disordered behavior, the patients were able to maintain a simple informal social organization and to create some value judgments within that organization.

Even certain types of behavior such as lack of self-management and self-care, which Gillin suggests as probable criteria of social abnormality in all cultures, would not apply if this type of behavior were collectively approved and had institutionalized outlets in the given society.[15] For instance, the shamans of Siberia, as Benedict has

[13] Ruth Benedict, *Patterns of Culture*, p. 255 (New York: Penguin Books, Inc., 1946). By permission of the authorized publishers, Houghton Mifflin Company.
[14] See Chapter Seventeen, The State Mental Hospital: The Patients.
[15] John P. Gillin, *The Ways of Men* (New York: Appleton-Century-Crofts, Inc., 1947).

shown, are able to rise to leadership despite their temporary inability for self-care.[16]

This feature in Siberian culture, however, is not characteristic. Seemingly low-grade mental defectives or paretics or other types who were not necessarily self-sufficient at least for survival purposes might be considered abnormal in most cultures. For it is difficult to see how a society could long survive which would place a premium on complete helplessness. Generally then, lack of self-care would be a cross-cultural criterion for abnormality unless in exceptional cases, as we have illustrated, it became institutionalized for specific persons.

Personality Patterns and the Dynamics of Disorders

But disordered behavior also cannot be judged apart from the cultural context. Sometimes individual behavior in two different cultures may appear alike, but one type may be ordered and the other disordered. We have shown that what appears as hallucinatory or delusional behavior to us may be accepted as socially normal in other cultures. But what personality dynamics distinguish disordered behavior in one culture from seemingly similar but ordered behavior in another culture? This point can be clarified by comparing the supposed "paranoidal" behavior of the Kwakiutl Indian with the behavior of the individual paranoid in an American urban society.

The motivational emphasis of the Kwakiutl Indians in the Pacific Northwest was bent upon vindication of insult and upon unrestrained self-glorification.[17] This intense emphasis upon personal superiority made the characteristic Kwakiutl Indian unable to tolerate an affront. The opponent had to be avenged, whether by killing him or by outdoing him in an institutionalized ceremony called the Potlatch. In this ceremonial contest the outraged person distributed gifts to his rival but at the same time glorified himself and berated his opponent. Although this unabated drive toward self-glorification and hypersensitivity to insult seems analogous to paranoidal behavior in our society, the two forms of behavior differ markedly.

The Kwakiutl brave learns his behavioral patterns in a normal

---

[16] Ruth Benedict, *Patterns of Culture*, p. 247 (New York: Penguin Books, Inc., 1946).

[17] See *Ibid.*, Chap. VI.

process of personal development. He responds as others expect him, and even compel him, to respond. He has no alternative but to fulfill his prescribed role. The chieftain, shaman, or whoever else in the tribe engages in these self-glorifiying practices can share the viewpoints of the group and can anticipate the censure of the group should he fail. When he does fail by being defeated in a Potlatch contest, or for some other reason, he may become psychotic, commit suicide, or kill his competitor. For example, a shaman was discovered by other members of the tribe to have performed a feat by a trick rather than by his supposedly supernatural powers. He "withdrew and went crazy within the year." [18]

Hence, this behavior of the Kwakiutl brave is socially normal and ordered in his social context because it fulfills the group's expectations. This does not mean that the Kwakiutl necessarily is a stable person; he may be rather unstable. But his seemingly "paranoidal" behavior is distinctly different from the symptoms of the paranoid in our society.

In our society the paranoid does not pursue an approved course of action but is responding to a defensive and distorted outgrowth of an individual conflict.[19] To retain his self-esteem the paranoid has selected individualized slants to the culture and to himself which others do not share. Only by his distorted evaluations can he retain his self-esteem. The paranoid usually violates the role prescribed by society. He is less amenable to self-control and to social control because he cannot share the views of other persons; and in this respect he isolates himself from the group. This criterion of disordered behavior obtains regardless of the institutionalized patterns within the culture. For example, were a Kwakiutl female to claim that she were a male she would probably be disordered. Moreover, the paranoid does not resolve his conflict by his distorted outlook and activities. On the other hand the Kwakiutl Indian, by resorting to the Potlatch or to some other compensatory means, tends to remove the feeling of being insulted and thus has resolved his conflict.

Cultural Determinants and Disordered Behavior. In discussing the disparate conceptions of personal disorders and of social abnor-

[18] *Ibid.*, p. 197.
[19] Henry J. Wegrocki, "A Critique of Cultural and Statistical Concepts of Abnormality," *Journal of Abnormal and Social Psychology*, 1939, 50, pp. 166–178.

mality, we pointed out that empirical norms of personal stability vary in different cultures. But what cultural determinants contribute to these different degrees of stability and, more specifically, contribute to disordered behavior? Some determinants which may have a direct bearing upon disordered behavior include the following: (1) degree of technology and rapidity of social change, (2) cultural heterogeneity and social contacts, (3) discipline and frustration of "original drives," such as sex, and (4) characteristic early mother-child relationships.

Technological Complexity and Social Change. One of the evils frequently blamed for disordered behavior is the increasing complexity and rapid tempo of modern civilization. It is believed that, as civilization becomes more complicated, conflicts multiply, and that some persons unavoidably weaken and break down.[20] On the other hand, some investigators maintain that disorders have not increased.[21] Goldhammer and Marshall, in a study of state hospital commitments for Massachusetts from 1840 to 1860 and for the United States as a whole during 1940, found that the rates of commitment did not increase for persons under 50 years of age.[22] The chief question with respect to this inference is whether Massachusetts at that time was less complex than many communities in contemporary United States as a whole. But the investigators leave this question open by positing two alternative conclusions. Either stress factors have not increased during the past century, or, if stress factors have increased, they are not as directly relevant to psychotic breakdowns as had been supposed.[23] It appears, however, that the

[20] See Mabel A. Elliott and Francis E. Merrill, *Social Disorganization*, p. 511 (New York: Harper & Brothers, 1941); Sigmund Freud, *Civilization and Its Discontents* (New York: Jonathan Cape and Harrison Smith, 1930).

[21] See Ernest Beaglehole, "Cultural Complexity and Psychological Problems," *Psychiatry*, August, 1940, III, pp. 330–332.

[22] Herbert Goldhammer and Andrew W. Marshall, *The Frequency of Mental Disease: Long-term Trends and Present Status* (Santa Monica, Calif.: The Rand Corporation, 1949).

[23] *Ibid.*, p. 50. (Some investigators who have studied shorter time periods and have found increases of mental disorders have attributed the rise to the greater availability of hospital facilities.) See Henry B. Elkind and Maurice Taylor, "The Alleged Increase in the Incidence of the Major Psychoses," *The American Journal of Psychiatry*, 1936, XCII, pp. 817–825; "The Epidemiology of Mental Disease: A Preliminary Discussion," *The American Journal of Psychiatry*, 1927, VI, pp. 623–640; Ellen Winston, "The Assumed Increase of Mental Disease," *American Journal of Sociology*, 1935, XL, pp. 427–439. (Other investigators of

differences in technological complexity and degree of social change during the two periods are not so great as would be supposed. Massachusetts was somewhat industrialized, prone to rapid social change, and had a large influx of immigrants. For a definitive comparison of the effects of technological complexity upon psychotic disorders, a more rural area would have to be considered. Yet a comparative analysis of this type is difficult, because in rural areas mildly psychotic persons can more easily be cared for at home.

The Hollow Folk. The past discussion pertained mainly to psychotic behavior. But what effects do technological complexity have upon neurotic behavior? The comparative study, by Sherman and Henry, of five communities in the Blue Ridge Mountains of Virginia may be pertinent in this respect because these communities varied in degrees of technological complexity, rapidity of social change, and social discipline.[24] Neuroses were supposedly more frequent in the more technologically complex communities of Oakton and Rigby than in the technologically simple communities of Colvin and Needles. Only 2 children in Colvin and Needles had nervous symptoms, such as nail biting and excessive blinking of the eyelids.[25] In Oakton and Rigby the investigators found 5 neurotic adults in addition to many children who had conflicts of insecurity and inferiority.

This analysis has been accepted by some sociologists as indicating the positive relationship between cultural complexity and the amount of mental disorder.[26] To be sure, few persons in Colvin had the nervous symptoms that we find in urban culture, but this does not mean that they were all stable persons and that few were disordered. They may have expressed their conflicts differently. They accepted sexual indulgence, stealing, and lying; they had slight guilt feelings and shallow, emotional relations. In general, they

---

trend studies believe that there has been an actual increase of psychotic disorders.) See Benjamin Malzberg, *Social and Biological Aspects of Mental Disease,* pp. 38–51 (Utica, N.Y.: State Hospital Press, 1940).

[24] Mandel Sherman and Thomas R. Henry, *Hollow Folk* (New York: The Thomas Y. Crowell Company, 1933).

[25] *Ibid.,* p. 204.

[26] See, for example, William F. Ogburn and Meyer F. Nimkoff, *Sociology,* pp. 263–264 (Boston: Houghton Mifflin Company, 1950).

revealed a stunted emotional development.[27] Their conflicts and hostilities would not have been inhibited as in the urban culture, but probably would have been expressed by stealing, lying, sulking, sexual escapades, fighting, and other acting-out activities. Since the authors searched for symptoms that characterize guilt-laden neurotic behavior in the disciplined urban cultures, they obviously found few persons with those symptoms in the technologically simple communities.

Thus we can infer from this particular study that neuroses which reflect inhibitions and which characterize neurotic persons in an urban community increase with cultural and technological complexity and with rapid social change. Or, conversely, we can infer that acting-out disorders which tend to psychopathy decrease with cultural and technological complexity and rapid social change. Inhabitants of simple communities studied were not more stable but expressed their neurotic aberrations differently from persons in more complex communities.

Of course we cannot infer from this study what degree or type of personal stability pervades other simple societies. In some simple nonliterate societies neuroses are markedly less frequent than in complex industrial societies. For example, Malinowski claimed that among the Trobriands not a single native had hysteria, nervous tics, compulsions, or obsessive notions.

Cultural Heterogeneity and Social Distance. The marginal individual who is on the limbo or margin of two cultures may experience acute conflicts and feelings of isolation which he may be unable to resolve. In the position of "outcast" his conflicts may become so severe that a neurosis or psychosis could emerge. Warner has shown that some aspiring Negroes who strive to rise into the white "caste-line" may become so severely disturbed that a disorder may result.[28]

Specific studies of nonliterate societies have tried to relate cultural heterogeneity and social distance to psychoses. Ellsworth Faris contends that cultural homogeneity and intimate social contacts deter

[27] Mandel Sherman and Thomas R. Henry, *Hollow Folk,* p. 298. The apparent decline in emotional complexity may also have reflected the inability of the investigators to reach emotionally and to communicate intimately with adolescents and adults.

[28] W. Lloyd Warner, "The Society, the Individual and His Mental Disorders," *The American Journal of Psychiatry,* 1937, 94, pp. 275–284.

or prevent the rise of psychotic behavior, especially schizophrenia. In his study of the Congo Forest Bantu in equatorial Africa he found that the natives never heard of anyone with schizophrenia or manic depression. He also visited four hospitals in the region and found no psychotics among these groups. He concluded that psychotic disorders in these tribes must be very rare.[29] Faris' conclusions, however, are based upon a search for symptomatic behavior rather than upon the dynamics of psychotic breakdown. In this society psychoses could have been expressed differently from those in Western societies. Also it is possible that psychotics could have been treated by shamans and/or cared for by the society rather than committed to mental hospitals.

Such investigators, as Devereux, Seligman, and Carothers (among others), also have claimed that nonliterate groups which have had minimal contacts with Western peoples rarely have psychotic members in their midst.

On the other hand, the same and other investigators, such as Seligman, Dhunjibhoy,[30] Carothers,[31] and Wulf-Sachs,[32] have shown that nonliterate groups which have had persistent contacts with European peoples do have disordered persons in their midst. Still other investigators claim that the psychoses are biological disorders and, as such, are universal, regardless of the simplicity or complexity of the culture. Further, Beaglehole claims that structural complexity is not an accurate indication of subjective complexity which can lead to personal conflicts and to personal disorders.[33] He contends that structural complexity is not the same as subjective complexity which consists of the range of meanings and conflicts that the individual internalizes from the culture. According to his view, participants in apparently simple nonliterate societies may experience as many conflicts and become as susceptible to neurotic and psychotic

[29] Ellsworth Faris, "Culture Among the Forest Bantu," The Nature of Human Nature, pp. 287–288 (New York: McGraw-Hill Book Company, Inc., 1937).

[30] C. G. Seligman, "Temperament, Conflict and Psychosis in a Stone Age Population," British Journal of Medical Psychology, 1929, IX, pp. 187–202; J. E. Dhunjibhoy, "A Brief Résumé of the Types of Insanity Commonly Peculiar to the Country," Journal of Mental Science, 1930, 76, p. 254.

[31] J. C. Carothers, "A Study of Mental Derangement in Africans and an Attempt to Explain Its Peculiarities," Psychiatry, February, 1948, 11, pp. 47–86.

[32] Wulf-Sachs, Black Hamlet (Boston: Little, Brown & Company, 1947).

[33] Ernest Beaglehole, "Cultural Complexity and Psychological Problems, Psychiatry, August, 1940, III, pp. 330–332.

disorders as participants in structurally more complicated societies.

Seemingly, the advocates who maintain that cultural hetero-geneity and distant social relationships are the bases for an increase in disordered behavior, especially schizophrenia, have provided more evidence than those investigators who maintain that psychoses are universal.[34] But the claims of the former group are not conclu-sive. Intensive inquiries, by a team of psychiatrists, social psycholo-gists, and anthropologists, of relatively isolated folk peoples who have had minimal contacts with industrialized Western groups might clarify whether or not psychotic breakdowns occur, what forms these psychoses assume if breakdowns do occur, and how the group responds to psychotic persons.

Cultural Suppression of "Original Drives." We have pointed out that all original drives become channelized into attitudes and motives. The basic attitudes which arise from the sex, hunger, or elementation drive may become laden with guilt. It has sometimes been said that the prohibition of sex attitudes may create repressions and conflicts which can contribute to disordered behavior. Hence, the society which prohibits and frustrates the expression of sex atti-tudes, by associating these expressions with intense guilt, may pro-vide the situations in which such intense conflicts may arise that disordered behavior on a neurotic level may possibly occur.

Although suppression of sexual attitudes may contribute to dis-ordered behavior, unrestricted sexual activity does not necessarily obviate disordered behavior. For example, Linton and Kardiner have shown that the Marquesan women, who are unrestricted sexually, nonetheless experience sexual frustrations because the sexual act is not accompanied by tenderness.[35] In this society men far outnumber the women. The women, as a result, are in the aggressive and dominant position in this area of activity. They initiate the sexual experience, and the men have to please them. Since the women are so completely outnumbered by the men, they play down their competitiveness for women and, instead, direct their hostility to them. The women, on the other hand, are very competitive in the sexual area. They regard pregnancy as a source

[34] See section on Schizophrenia and Culture, p. 228, for a more detailed discus-sion of cultural complexity and schizophrenia.

[35] Abram Kardiner *et al., The Individual and His Society,* pp. 227–234, 414–416 (New York: Columbia University Press, 1939).

of prestige because they place a high value upon children. Consequently, when they experience intense sexual conflicts, one of their neurotic outlets is pretended pregnancy. Thus Marquesan women do experience neurotic conflicts concerning sex despite their unrestricted sexual freedom.

This instance illustrates that social relationships governing the sex drive rather than the sex drive itself contribute to personal stability or personal instability.

Of course, the more fundamental drive of hunger is intimately bound up with personal stability. Those societies which have definite problems in attaining food and no sex problems will have their anxieties centered upon food. For example, the nomadic Siriono of Eastern Bolivia are very permissive in their sexual activities but have difficult food problems.[36] Thus, if a person is ill and loses his appetite, the Siriono consider this a sign of grave illness. When the person does not eat for several days, they regard this as a sure sign that he is going to die. Hence, the sick person never diets when he is ill, even though it hastens his death. This may indicate that the most intense forms of anxiety center around eating.

Mother-Child Relationships. The Freudians, Neo-Freudians, and some anthropologists have emphasized the influence of early relationships upon personality formation. In their comparative studies of peoples, they have pursued this emphasis. On this basis Margaret Mead, Kardiner, and Linton, among others, have attempted cross-cultural comparisons of personality types.

Kardiner and his associates, in a detailed and systematic inquiry, have maintained that the early mother-child relationships determine the "basic personality" or the characteristic personality of the particular culture. These mother-child relationships, in turn, are influenced by the socioeconomic organization of the group, and when the socioeconomic organization changes, these mother-child relationships are revised accordingly.[37] The "basic personality" presumably sustains the given culture by its behavior in adulthood.

Fromm has criticized Kardiner's interpretations on the grounds that Kardiner does not analyze mother-child relationships in terms

[36] Allan R. Holmberg, *Nomads of the Long Bow: The Siriono of Eastern Bolivia,* pp. 86–87 (Washington, D.C.: U.S. Government Printing Office, 1950).
[37] Abram Kardiner *et al., The Individual and His Society* (New York: Columbia University Press, 1939).

of feeling tones but tends to concentrate upon the constancy and consistency of mother-child relationships and the influence of these relationships upon erogenous-zone development, particularly in feeding and in toilet training.[38] In addition, the difficulty with appraising the method of mother-child relationships in another culture is that the feeling tones in these relationships are not easy to understand and that ethnocentric value judgments can be made. For example, Gorer and LaBarre have inferred that the compulsive behavior among the Japanese is in part a result of the severe toilet training and the overemphasis upon cleanliness.[39] Sikkema, on the other hand, has shown that what appears to be severe toilet training to the Western person does not reflect the mother's feelings to her child because the mother actually feels kindly disposed to the child. In fact, she found no indication of emotional upset in toilet training.[40]

Despite the shortcomings of this Neo-Freudian approach, parent-child relationships are crucial in personality formation. The characteristic early relationships in a particular society may provide significant clues for finding the comparative stability of the "average person" in different societies.

Disordered and Abnormal Behavior in American Society

But when persons in American society become disordered, how are they defined socially? Generally, the different disorders are not defined alike. In the broadest sense psychotics are usually considered socially abnormal; neurotics usually are not; and the psychopath

[38] Fromm maintains that no convincing relationship has been established between the economic organization and mother-child relationships, at least for the Alorese society. In this society the woman works the fields; hence, she has to desert the child two weeks after his birth, but the very fact that she deserts the child does not completely explain her inconsistent teasing and neglect of the child when she returns from the fields. Erich Fromm, "Psychoanalytic Characterology and Its Application to the Understanding of Culture," *Culture and Personality,* edited by S. Stansfeld Sargent and Marian W. Smith, p. 4 (New York: Viking Fund, 1949).

[39] Geoffrey Gorer, "Themes in Japanese Culture," *Transactions of New York Academy of Science,* 1943, 5, pp. 106–124; Weston LaBarre, "Some Observations on Character Structure in the Orient! The Japanese," *Psychiatry,* August, 1945, 8:3, pp. 319–342.

[40] Mildred Sikkema, "Observations of Japanese Early Child Training," *Personal Character and Cultural Milieu,* compiled by Douglas G. Haring, pp. 500–599 (Syracuse, N.Y.: Syracuse University Press, 1949).

and other deviants may be considered abnormal in one group but not in another. A rough index to this social deviation is the legal norm of insanity. Although the neurotics are far more numerous than psychotics, in 1946 they comprised 8.0 per cent of the hospital first admissions in contrast to schizophrenics and manic depressives who together comprised 28.8 per cent of the hospital first admissions. Psychopathic personalities without psychosis comprised 1.1 per cent of first admissions.[41] Of course, many neurotics seek outpatient treatment. Of 100 consecutive patients who went to psychiatrists, with the exception of those patients who were very depressed and cried easily, there was no way of distinguishing these patients from any other group of "theoretically normal citizens." [42]

Although psychotics usually are unable to conform to their social roles and are liable to commitment, mild psychotics may be able to function better in some jobs than in others. For example, one who works for himself may be able to perform his job despite his delusions. On the other hand, delusional behavior in the employ of others may be a definite sign for dismissal.

Although neurotics, as a rule, can conform to their prescribed roles, their conformity depends upon their defenses and upon the severity of their physical symptoms. Some hysterical persons who become sensorily incapacitated by blindness or who forget their identity obviously cannot conform. Psychopaths who persistently and flagrantly become destructive or perverted and who cannot fit into an industrial routine may also be considered abnormal.

Selected Readings

Beaglehole, Ernest, "Cultural Complexity and Psychological Problems," *Psychiatry,* August, 1940, III, pp. 330–332.

Benedict, Ruth, "Anthropology and the Abnormal," *The Journal of General Psychology,* 1934, X, pp. 59–82.

————, *The Patterns of Culture* (Boston: Houghton Mifflin Company, 1934).

Cooper, John M., "Mental Disease Situations in Certain Cultures—a New Field for Research," *Journal of Abnormal and Social Psychology,* April–June, 1934, XXIX:7, pp. 10–17.

[41] *Patients in Mental Institutions, 1946,* p. 18 (Washington, D.C.: Bureau of the Census, U.S. Department of Commerce, 1949).

[42] N. K. Rickles, J. J. Klein, and M. E. Bassan, "Who Goes to a Psychiatrist," *The American Journal of Psychiatry,* May, 1950, 106:11, p. 847.

Edwards, A. S., "A Theoretical and Clinical Study of So-Called Abnormality," *Journal of Abnormal and Social Psychology,* January-March, 1934, XXVIII:4, pp. 366–367.

Foley, John P., Jr., "Criterion of Abnormality," *Journal of Abnormal and Social Psychology,* April–June, 1935, XXX.

Hallowell, A. Irving, "Culture and Mental Disorder," *Journal of Abnormal and Social Psychology,* April–June, 1934, XXIX:7, pp. 1–9.

Kardiner, Abram, *et al., The Individual and His Society* (New York: Columbia University Press, 1939).

———, *et al., The Psychological Frontiers of Society* (New York. Columbia University Press, 1946).

Sapir, Edward, "Cultural Anthropology and Psychiatry," *Journal of Abnormal Psychology,* October–December, 1932, 27:2, pp. 229–242.

Sargent, S. Stansfeld, and Marian W. Smith (editors), *Culture and Personality* (New York: Viking Fund, Inc., 1949).

Skaggs, E. B., "The Meaning of the Term 'Abnormality' in Psychology," *Journal of Abnormal and Social Psychology,* July–September, 1933, XXVIII:2 pp. 113–118.

Wegrocki, Henry J., "A Critique of Cultural and Statistical Concepts of Abnormality," *Journal of Abnormal and Social Psychology,* 1939, XXXIV, pp. 166–178.

PART II

Disordered Behavior and the Social Process

CHAPTER SIX

Social Aspects of Anxiety Behavior

In the previous chapters we dealt with the theoretical bases of personal disorders. We covered the scope and problems of the sociology of personal disorders; the influence of heredity, body type, and temperament and of the organism generally upon disordered behavior; the use of social relationships as a means for viewing and understanding personal disorders among the several social and psychological sciences. We then described the social personality as an emergent of social relationships and pointed out the differences between ordered and disordered personalities. We next differentiated between disordered behavior which arises from conflict in contrast with socially abnormal behavior which grows out of one's inability to fulfill a prescribed social role as defined by the group.

In this section we will discuss the specific types of disorders. The first and basic disorder to be dealt with is anxiety. Anxiety is the keystone upon which the understanding of other neurotic and even psychotic disorders rests; for anxiety is the dynamic core from which other neuroses arise as defensive reactions.[1] Reactions such as dread or phobia, dissociated behavior, compulsivity, reassuring bodily gestures, as in psychasthenia, arise to prevent the anxiety from recurring. The types of defenses vary with the innate endowments and experiences of the person, but in all cases anxiety underlies the defensive reactions. Moreover, these defensive reactions do not always succeed in concealing the anxiety. Consequently, anxiety as a

[1] See Charles Berg, "Anxiety—the Foundation of Nervous Illness," *The Case Book of a Medical Psychologist,* p. 14 (New York: W. W. Norton & Company, 1948).

diagnostic category usually does not occur alone but often is mixed with other neurotic reactions.

In discussing the social aspects of anxiety we will consider: (1) the action pattern of anxiety, (2) types of anxiety, (3) the development of anxiety, (4) the effects of anxiety upon the self and thought, (5) anxiety and the class structure, and (6) the expression of anxiety in diverse social contexts, illustrated by a preliterate society, by mining communities in Great Britain, and by the combat unit.

The Action Pattern of Anxiety

Neurotic anxiety arises when the subject becomes involved in one or a series of threatening situations with which he strives to cope but is helplessly unable to do so. Beset with these threatening situations, he has the alternative of trying to flee from them or of attempting, however inadequately, to manipulate the situation. Since he cannot formulate a satisfactory response, he becomes increasingly disorganized and overwhelmed. Anxiety develops in this process of incompleted activity, and it involves an inability to define and to respond effectively to a threatening situation which then becomes problematic and leaves the residue of persistent conflict which harasses the subject in the future.

The onset of anxiety may occur quickly or slowly. When one is overcome by sustained physical danger, and/or by threatening social situations, the onset may be relatively quick. When self-confidence is whittled away by certain inconsistent interpersonal relationships which make the individual feel too inadequate to handle certain situations, the onset may be relatively slow. In either case the subject cannot respond effectively, successfully, and completely to a given set of goal-directed stimuli. The actual defensive responses in these given situations, of course, vary: Enforced immobility, flight or avoidance, or compulsive aggression are some alternatives. Whatever the response, the subject becomes defeated and helpless and cannot attain his desired objective or master the particular situation. His responses indicate shock and personal disorganization, persistent conflict, and apprehension.

Types of Anxiety

But not all anxiety is incapacitating. In some instances anxiety may not lead to neurosis. In these instances the anxiety is warranted by the outside danger, yet the subject can face the situation and can still manage his behavior without becoming helpless.[2] It is well known that soldiers entering combat are usually scared and apprehensive about prospective dangers. These attitudes may make them more alert and cautious about getting hurt, and, as long as they can respond effectively to protect themselves from the dangers, they can keep their anxiety under control and remain organized. But it is argued that these are fear reactions which differ from anxiety; for fear is directed toward an object or set of objects, while anxiety is a vague apprehension of varying intensities which is not limited to a specific object. Yet, in combat, some soldiers may have these vague apprehensions and gnawing doubts about being able to cope with the many and unknown perilous situations that they may face. Despite these attitudes they may still control their behavior, and when they are removed from the battle area their anxiety may disappear. Moreover, anxiety can even lead to constructive achievement.[3]

For example, in a study of adolescents, Symonds found that those adolescents who had anxiety fantasies were able to adjust favorably. He interpreted their favorable adjustment as a reaction against possible failure with its subsequent anxiety.[4] In short, persons in threatening and critical situations may become temporarily apprehensive, but insofar as they do not become defenseless in future threatening situations, their anxiety does not have neurotic consequences.

Neurotic anxiety which persists from past experiences is not warranted by the outside danger. It involves persistent conflicts, lack of confidence, a narrowing of activities and awareness, and the development of neurotic symptoms and defenses.[5]

Yet neurotic anxiety may vary in degrees of severity. This depends upon how severely threatened the individual feels, how vital the threat is to his self-esteem, and how severely disturbed and over-

[2] Rollo May, *The Meaning of Anxiety*, pp. 193–95 (New York: The Ronald Press Company, 1950). He regards normal anxiety as being proportionate to the outside danger even if it includes helplessness.

[3] Allison Davis and Robert Havighurst, *Father of the Man*, pp. 212–213 (Boston: Houghton Mifflin Company, 1947).

[4] Percival M. Symonds, *Adolescent Fantasy*, p. 174 (New York: Columbia University Press, 1949).

[5] Rollo May, *The Meaning of Anxiety*, p. 197 (New York: The Ronald Press Company, 1950).

whelmed he becomes. Anxiety may be mild or it may be so malignant and so fraught with intense panic that the individual, as it were, cannot control his behavior at all, feels completely helpless, and "goes to pieces."

Also, the period when anxiety is experienced may sometimes affect its severity. When an individual is predisposed to neurosis from early childhood and the anxiety becomes an integral part of his personality—sometimes called a character disorder—he would have more difficulty recovering from his anxiety than one who experienced anxiety later in life. This does not mean, however, that the stage of life alone determines the severity of anxiety. It also depends, as we have pointed out, upon the severity of the threat. Hence, an adolescent or an adult can become severely incapacitated by a series of sustained critical experiences.

The Development of Anxiety: Social Relationships

Developmentally, anxiety arises with the helplessness of the child. How does this helplessness arise? It may result from biological helplessness, but usually it is a function of social relations.

The shocks resulting from biological processes associated with breathing and food absorption are not quite the same as emotionally induced anxiety. It has been shown that sudden startle reactions, such as loss of balance, the crescendo of loud noises, sudden changes in temperature, or any other unexpected stimulus for which the infant is unprepared, may leave him shaky, tense, and with a reaction that has been labeled fearful. But these reactions, however similar to anxiety, are not quite the same. The infant's reaction is a conditioned fear, while the socialized person's reaction would be a symbolic, temporally oriented anxiety.

Of the two forms of relationships in the presymbolic period that may provide the basis for a protoanxiety for the child, one is the mother's intensified overattachment to the child who, in turn, becomes very dependent. The overdependent child finds it difficult to function without the presence of the mother, and this easily leads to conflict in the weaning process and in his general separation from the mother. The other and most pervasive type of protoanxiety-creating relationships inhere in the inconsistent, unstable, and unpredictable relationships between the parents and the child—especially between the mother and the child.[6]

These inconsistent relations become more meaningful to the child when he acquires symbols and self-awareness and when he can compare himself with others. Then his anxieties may arise from anticipated failure and consequent loss of status as defined by the parents.

Horney points to parental hypocrisy as a definite source for disturbed and disrupted relations with the child. These contradictory parental relationships create ambivalent attitudes and conflicts within the youngster who strives to cope with these relationships but often cannot. A wide variety of adverse parent-child relationships can create this helplessness. The parents, directly or indirectly, may dominate the child. They may be erratic or indifferent, or may ridicule the child. They may make him take sides in parental quarrels. The child, in turn, may become so harassed and so fearful that he cannot handle these relations. As a result, he develops improvised techniques and basic anxiety-ridden orientations to the parents and to other people. Horney has referred to these tendencies as neurotic trends.[7]

But these parent-child relationships lead to anxiety only when the child internalizes this ambivalence. For example, a child who sees his parents objectively may play one parent against the other and use each to his own advantage. A child with indifferent parents may cultivate attachments with other persons such as siblings or accessible relatives. Consequently, the child's meaning of parental relations becomes crucial.

The child who identifies with his parents so that his conception of himself is dependent upon their approval and affection cannot easily tolerate their rejection, ridicule, or disapproval. Sullivan has pointed out that the very anxious child does not see his parents as "bad." Instead he cannot decide whether they are "good" or "bad." [8]

---

[6] See Arthur T. Jersild, *Child Psychology* (New York: Prentice-Hall, Inc., 1940); also Margaret A. Ribble, "Anxiety in Infants," *Modern Trends in Child Psychiatry*, edited by Nolan D. C. Lewis and Bernhard L. Pacella, pp. 17–25 (New York: International Universities Press, Inc., 1945).

[7] Karen Horney, *Our Inner Conflicts*, pp. 41–42 (New York: W. W. Norton & Company, 1945).

[8] See in Rollo May, *The Meaning of Anxiety*, pp. 341, 342 (New York: The Ronald Press Company, 1950).

Fromm indicates that "irrational authority" which is unjust may leave a mark of self-defeat upon the child.[9] The child who is apprehensive about displeasing a parent has his conception of himself tied to the parent's attitude toward him. When his hostile attitudes to the parent do arise, his self-esteem becomes threatened because his hostile expressions will deprive him of the very parental approval by which he evaluates himself. He will tend, therefore, to inhibit his hostility. But, by being unable to "talk back," hit back, or otherwise defend himself, the child feels unprotected and, as we have emphasized, helpless. But this hostility does not disappear; rather, it takes a devious route in dreams and in other vicarious ways. By carrying this hostility the child may behave in antagonistic ways which he cannot control and cannot understand. As a result he may not "trust himself" because he does not know when these hostile attitudes will be expressed. This attitude, in turn, increases his anxiety because he has less confidence in his relationships.

In an intensive study of 13 unwed mothers, May found that nine subjects who experienced varying degrees of anxiety during childhood were involved in a dilemma between their idealized expectations of their parents and the realistic behavior of their parents.[10] They confused the real behavior of their parents with expectations of what the parents should have been or might have become. Since their attitudes toward the parents became internalized, they affected their attitudes toward themselves. It would seem that, by internalizing parental rejection, they began to reject themselves, and they needed and wanted the idealized expectations of their parents in order to accept themselves.

Apparently, the parental pretenses of love, approval, and admiration which are expressed to the child are a means of eliciting his affection and dependency. When these parental attitudes are combined with rejection, cruelty, or punitiveness, the child in turn assumes self-regarding attitudes of self-condemnation. In May's study subjects who were rejected outright by the parents and who did not internalize this rejection did not develop anxiety. Instead, they merely cultivated other relationships. It seems that with the

[9] Erich Fromm, "Individual and Social Origins of Neurosis," *American Sociological Review*, 1944, IX, pp. 380–384.

[10] Rollo May, *The Meaning of Anxiety*, pp. 340–343 (New York: The Ronald Press Company, 1950).

new relationships they began to evaluate themselves from the per-spectives of these more favorable relationships and thus could get an integrated and acceptable estimate of themselves.

In a comparative study of children of Polish immigrants and the children of middle-class American families, Green shows that, de-spite the beatings and harsh parental treatment, the immigrants' children did not become neurotic. These Polish children were accustomed to little parental affection and did not look upon their parents as role models. In a kind of defensive alliance, they avoided them when possible and tolerated or maliciously despised them. This lack of intimate identification, combined with personal and group defenses, deterred or prevented the children from evaluating themselves by their parents' attitudes. Parental beatings, beratings, and depreciation did not affect their self-esteem and did not create attitudes of helplessness with reference to their personal problems.[11]

In contrast, children from middle-class American families are first blanketed with affection. This affection is used by the parents as a lever of control when they threaten to withdraw it. Since these chil-dren become attached to the parents, their self-evaluation depends upon parental attitudes. Consequently, parental ridicule, humilia-tion, belittlement, and abject submission of the children can have an early and very marked effect in predisposing them to anxiety.

Moreover, as these children get older, the parents shift to contra-dictory demands. They may want implicit obedience in the family and assertive competitiveness outside the family. When these pa-rental relationships are intense enough, they form the typically inconsistent relationships which can predispose middle-class chil-dren to anxiety.[12] These children, particularly, are apprehensive that affection may be lost when they are unable to compete success-fully outside the family. The need for affection and prestige on the one hand and the need to compete successfully on the other hand constitute one of the typical anxiety conflicts among middle-class children. Since other influences may operate to offset parental de-mands, these parent-child relationships obtain only in a general sense. The effects of sibling rivalry cannot be discounted in this family context. The parental favoritism of one child over another,

---

[11] Arnold W. Green, "The Middle Class Male Child and Neurosis," *American Sociological Review*, February, 1946, XI:1, pp. 31–41.

[12] *Ibid.*

as the son over the daughter, the bright child over the dull child, can readily contribute to an anxiety-creating situation.

The Self in Anxiety

The anxiety-ridden person becomes less confident, more intensely preoccupied with himself, and more uncertain of himself. Since he feels unworthy, regards himself as a failure, is apprehensive about dealing with his problems, the self of this neurotic type as it were —if spatially conceived for clarity—contracts. He becomes a helpless and diffident figure whose self-defeatist attitudes are exemplified in such statements as: "I can't do it," "It's too much for me."

This retrenching of the self means less esteem and also a narrowing of self-awareness in order to avoid experiences to which he cannot respond effectively.[13]

But the self-recrimination of defeat is counteracted by an effort to regain a wanted and fancied self-prestige. Torn between these desires, the anxiety-ridden person's self-evaluating attitudes become ambivalent and problematic. On the one hand, he feels insignificant and threatened in an uncertain social world. For example, Horney relates that one patient drew a picture in which she was portrayed as a helpless, nude baby surrounded on all sides by human and animal monsters.[14]

On the other hand, the neurotically anxious person strives compulsively to attain his desired or imagined goals. He strives for reassurance and affection from others to bolster his confidence, but he is too self-concerned and often too hostile to reciprocate that affection. The anxiety-ridden person is essentially hostile—however deviously this unresolved hostility may be expressed.

His inconsistent attitudes to himself reflect the ambivalent expectations which he has internalized from his parents or from other persons. He is thus divided by a series of contradictory self-conceptions. Though lacking confidence, he has an idealized image of what he should be or might have been. His self-regarding attitudes are reflected in his relations with other persons. Dependent upon others,

[13] Patrick Mullahy, "A Theory of Interpersonal Relations and the Evolution of Personality," in Harry Stack Sullivan, *Conceptions of Modern Psychiatry*, p. 130 (Washington, D.C.: The William Alanson White Psychiatric Foundation, 1940).
[14] Karen Horney, *The Neurotic Personality of Our Time*, pp. 92–93 (New York: W. W. Norton & Company, 1937).

he is hostile too, because they do not recognize him for what he believes he should be or can become. These ambivalent attitudes are
described as follows by a 24-year-old male student:

> I want and need sympathy—someone to understand me and to love me.
> Yet when I think I have access to such persons, I turn them down, making
> all types of rationalizations to explain why I don't care for sympathy from
> them. Tonight I have taken several Benzedrine tablets in order to study
> and feel relaxed and alert, but they have had no effect on me. I'm nervous,
> too sorry for myself to get down to anything where I have to concentrate.
> I just can't concentrate.
>
> The other night I managed to sever all connections with a girl I was
> engaged to. At the time I felt elated and relieved—for I believed that I
> no longer loved her, and I didn't want to continue the farce any longer.
> But now my feelings are changed, and I want to call her and tell her what
> a fool I've been. I called, but she wasn't home. I'm afraid that if she ever
> comes back to me again, the same old story will repeat itself, and as soon
> as I'm sure of her, I'll lose all my feelings for her, and become bored with
> her company. I called up another girl, who I knew had at one time cared
> for me, but she was indifferent over the phone. This made me more de-
> pressed. In her case, too, when she responded, I shied away. When she
> became indifferent then I wanted her. So I'm afraid to accept defeat. I
> tell myself that I should leave her alone, but I know I'll call her up soon.
> When I go out with girls the same divided feelings arise. I try to force my-
> self on them—make them pet with me—but I get no feelings out of it
> except petty mastery. I fear and want women. I want to master them.
>
> The same feelings are with my friends. Because I need someone to talk
> with, I always center on my problems, and my friends are getting tired
> of my telling them my troubles. They must respect me less, but I want
> them to respect me more. I want to be the leader. When I go out stagging,
> I become tired, bored, and impatient. They see this boredom, and that
> makes them suspicious of me. I want to depend on people and yet I want
> to control them.
>
> It's the same way with a job. There is a fear that prevents me from
> going to ask for a job. Without a job I feel useless, unwanted, inferior.
> But I won't go looking for a job. I have that awful fear of being turned
> down by the manager; of having to approach him and then being turned
> away. It's worse when I have to go in alone. I want to be with somebody
> when I ask for a job. It seems easier, somehow. So when I think about
> looking for a job, I tell myself I need the time for studying, but I lie
> around on those free afternoons and don't study. Then I consider myself
> a failure, and I say I'll look for a job, and the whole thing starts all over
> again.
>
> And I have these feelings about my parents. I sometimes despise my
> father for not being rich and taking all these worries away from me. Then
> I turn around and try to be loyal to him. The doctor tells me that I want
> to succeed very much, and yet I don't want to because of the fear of sur-

passing my father. I curse my father and feel sorry for him. The whole thing puts me in a mess and makes me feel miserable.

On the one hand this student gauges himself by his aspirations; on the other hand by his specific attitudes of helplessness. But he cannot tolerate this helplessness. He flees from it and tries to suppress it. Yet he avoids, or becomes compulsively aggressive in, situations which might overwhelm or distress him. His aspirations impel him to strive to surpass others; yet by feeling helpless he becomes very dependent, especially upon those persons who, by accepting him, make him more acceptable to himself.

Thinking and Conflict. Thinking, in the case of the intensely anxious person, becomes suspended as a problem-solving medium in the area of conflict. Since the conflict persists, indecision and uncertainty become prominent components of his behavior. In acute forms of anxiety the contradictory alternatives are expressed by avoiding a threatening or distressing situation and by trying to cope with it. Thinking becomes both repetitive and circular because the conflict is not resolved. Although an anxiety-ridden person may know what he wants, he behaves in a way which defeats him. Usually, he escapes his real problems or resorts to autistic or self-oriented fantasies about what he should have done or might have done under different circumstances. This type of thinking provides him with rationalizations for avoiding his real problems.

Sometimes the anxious person escapes from his conflicts by retreating to generalities. This is frequently observed by therapists who are pressing near the source of the patient's conflicts. One person undergoing therapy said:

The most difficult part of the therapy has been in expressing emotions and feelings outside of an intellectual blueprint which I constantly have sought. He [the therapist] has pointed out that this is an attempt to meet the situation by intellectualizing.

It appears that the more the anxiety-ridden person organizes his environment, the more readily he can avoid his unconscious conflicts.

Yet, the anxiety conflict tends to distract him from immediate and objective problems at hand and also impedes his powers of retention, because of his preoccupation with himself and with matters other than those which require his present concentration. It makes him forget certain experiences and evade other problems by creating "blind spots" which he cannot face in himself.

In short, anxiety prevents the person from resolving his problems objectively; it narrows the range of thinking because the person is too concerned with defending himself from further anxiety by whatever means he can. Yet, his incompleted or nonintegrated experiences and conflicts subconsciously press for a solution and often emerge during dreams; for anxiety dreams often represent attempted solutions of his conflicts.

Anxiety Dreams. Although the content of anxiety dreams may have innumerable manifestations, the essential contradiction between the subconscious effort to resolve the conflict and the apparent helplessness of the person is evident in the dream. Yet the repeated attempts to complete satisfactory experiences in the dreams indicate a basic striving for personal growth. Simmel says:[15]

> From the very beginning my attention was captured by the characteristic dream life of my patients. I recognized that tendency to repeat the traumatic experiences and conceived that this must be a latent tendency at self-cure. . . . I learned to understand that their tonic-clonic muscle spasms signified a discharge of their rage in the form of uncoordinated movements. I became aware of this, by being able, under hypnosis, to lift the amnesia for these fits, or by getting contact with the individual even during his original state of unconsciousness. I concluded that I must make use of this self-curing tendency, manifesting itself during sleep.

In fact, when these conflicts are very active, these anxiety dreams may be repeated as many as five or six times a night.[16]

But lack of confidence and severe personal disorganization in handling the conflict situation lead to distressing, even catastrophic, endings in the dreams. This was particularly evident in the anxiety onset among combat men. Continually disturbed by battle dreams, they pictured themselves in the dreams as fleeing from some hazards certain to overtake them—being sprayed by machine-gun bullets from airplanes, seeing their friends killed, being nearly struck by a shell, or being chased by the enemy and about to be captured or killed. Many men in the air forces during World War II dreamed

[15] Ernest Simmel, "War Neuroses," *Psychoanalysis Today*, edited by Sandor Lorand, p. 243 (New York: International Universities Press, Inc., 1944).

[16] Abram Kardiner et al., *The Individual and His Society*, p. 437 (New York: Columbia University Press, 1939).

that they were shot down in flames. In all the dreams the person was completely helpless and unable to manage the situation.

In hazardous occupations such as mining, in which anxiety is repressed, distressing dreams also occurred.[17] The most frequent type was that of "falls." The earth or rubble collapsed and the men had to flee for safety. Another type was that of "runaway hutches." The buggies which ran on rails had become detached, and, since the rails were on an incline, the "buggies" sped uncontrollably and furiously down the slope and frequently caused injury. Another was "cage slipping," in which the elevator that took the men down to work slipped and fell. These dreams occurred usually after some accident. Since the collective pressure opposed the expression of anxiety, the men were reluctant to reveal these dreams. Those who did were usually ashamed of them. In contrast, the men who had pleasant dreams usually indicated that their thoughts about the mines usually concerned "the comradeship of the men."

In less traumatic or shocking experiences, anxiety dreams may be expressed by the person's feeling of insignificance in social affairs or in his relationships with other persons.

Anxiety and Diverse Social Contexts

We have described anxiety as a uniform type of personal reaction regardless of the social situation in which it occurs. Nonetheless, the modes of social relationships in the culture context can stimulate anxiety not only as an atypical response among a few individuals but also as a prevalent response among many group participants. For this purpose we shall describe the varied collective contexts in which anxiety can arise as an expected and even as a modal response: (1) Anxiety can arise when the participants in a given society feel isolated from and threatened by other participants, as is illustrated by the "failures" or "frustrated climbers" among certain social segments of the mobile, industrial, competitive society, and by the "sinners" in the Saulteaux Indian society. (2) It can arise when the basic values and purpose of a society begin to disintegrate, as is illustrated by the British mining communities during the 1930's. (3) It can arise in situations of external stress when personal interests are basically in conflict with group demands, or when

[17] James L. Halliday, *Psychosocial Medicine: A Study of the Sick Society*, p. 262 (New York: W. W. Norton & Company, 1947).

the group ceases to be a protective symbol, as is illustrated by the combat unit during battle. (4) Anxiety can become a pervasive form of behavior in a given culture as a developmental result of mother-child relationships, as is illustrated by the Alorese society.

Anxiety and the Class Structure

The scant research which pertains to anxiety and socioeconomic levels has shown that anxiety occurs more frequently in the middle socioeconomic income levels than in the lower socioeconomic levels. Green, as we have pointed out, maintained that the children of Polish immigrant groups did not become predisposed to anxiety, in contrast to the middle-class American.[18] May found that of his 13 cases, the 4 who were in the lower socioeconomic levels did not become predisposed to neurotic anxiety. On the other hand, of the other 9 cases who had become predisposed to anxiety, the majority were in middle socioeconomic levels.[19] Lemkau, Tietze, and Cooper found that the Negroes had more conduct problems but fewer cases of neuroses than the whites.[20] Jenkins and Hewitt found that Jewish children had more cases of neuroses than Negro children.[21] It is not known, however, whether this investigation included middle-class Negro groups. From a study in progress by the writer, it seems that Negro college students tend to exhibit the same anxiety-ridden tendencies found among students of other ethnic groups.[22]

These class differences have been explained by the ambivalent parent-child relations and by the intensified competitiveness and ambitious desires for climbing that pervade the middle classes.

Seemingly, parent-child relations are more ambivalent in middle than in lower classes. Not only is the middle-class child usually given affection, he also is driven to compete successfully. When he does

[18] Arnold W. Green, "The Middle Class Male Child and Neurosis," *American Sociological Review,* February, 1946, XI:1, pp. 31–42.

[19] Rollo May, *The Meaning of Anxiety,* pp. 344, 345 (New York: The Ronald Press Company, 1950).

[20] Paul Lemkau, Christopher Tietze, and Marcia Cooper, "Mental Hygiene Problems in an Urban District," *Mental Hygiene,* April, 1943, XXVII:2, pp. 28, 29.

[21] Robert L. Jenkins and L. Hewitt, "Types of Personality Structure Encountered in Child Guidance Clinics," *American Journal of Orthopsychiatry,* 1944, XIV:1, pp. 84–94.

[22] S. Kirson Weinberg, "Anxiety among College Students in Minority Groups." (Study in progress.)

not excel, his parents may withdraw or may threaten to withdraw their affection. These ambivalent attitudes are less intense in the lower classes because parental affection is not measured by the child's success. Also parental training in the middle class is such that the middle-class child inhibits his aggressions more effectively than does the lower-class child. Hence, the anxious middle-class child would have symptoms which would tend to reveal his inhibitions. The anxious lower-class child would tend to express his symptoms in fighting, stealing and in other forms of destructive behavior. Sometimes, the lower-class child, because of his acting out symptoms, is considered a "conduct problem" rather than a "neurotic."

Also, it may be likely that the motives which create anxiety may differ for these two social strata. Perhaps the middle-class children and adolescents, because of mobility aspirations, are more likely to become anxious when they face the prospect of failing or even not advancing in their careers. The lower-class children and adolescents, on the other hand, are more likely to become anxious because of economic insecurity and subsistence deprivation.

Anxiety and the Impersonal Society. We have pointed out how family relations may predispose the child to anxiety. But the impersonal and secondary society, in which competition, mobility, social climbing, and success are paramount goals, tends to stimulate anxiety. For success is relative to the social positions others hold. Each person who competes to climb feels surrounded by other competitors who can possibly deprive him of the thing he wants most—success. Thus, these other competitors express hostility, or at least uncertainty, toward each other. Their mutual hostility leads to estrangement and contributes to the feelings of loneliness and to the personal isolation of each one. Personal isolation, in turn, exaggerates apprehension and a feeling of powerlessness. The only means of overcoming this isolation is by the approval attained from being successful. Hence, the competitive individual who has not attained success continually renews his efforts to attain it. On the other hand, his self-esteem depends upon his success in a competitive market rather than upon his personal qualities. Hence, with ever-changing conditions his self-esteem is bound to remain shaky and insecure. This is the social mold of impersonal society, which participants experience in more or less degree and which creates the basis for apprehension, uncertainty, and the general feelings of helplessness that characterize anxiety.

Anxiety and Occupational Groups. These apprehensions are perhaps more prevalent among middle-class and upper middle-class groups who are most keenly bent upon social climbing than among lower socioeconomic levels. But these attitudes are increasingly pervading unskilled, manual occupational groups. Nonetheless, differences in opportunities for climbing prevail between the lower and middle classes.

White-collar workers who have individual aspirations of social climbing usually have the skills and opportunities for advancement. Manual workers in the mass industries may strive and have fantasies of advancement, such as going into business for themselves, but their opportunities for climbing depend more upon collective action in unions than upon individual efforts only. In addition, workers in mass industry are protected by their union. From an occupational standpoint, such extreme groups as traveling salesmen and coal miners would be in markedly different networks of competitive relationships, and these relationships would affect their behavior and their types of disorders.

The white-collar worker depends more upon the good graces of his employer for his economic security and advancement. He can become distraught and apprehensive by the disapproval and recrimination of that employer. For that employer can deprive him not only of his economic and social position but also of his essential economic security. If this person's situation is complicated by a nagging ambitious wife, as frequently happens, or by friends who are surpassing him, his resentment to this employer may become intensified. Moreover, his ideology is such that climbing is essential to his self-esteem so that not climbing may be equated with failure. But along with attitudes of aggression and hostility toward his employer, he is also very dependent upon him. This ambivalence can create helplessness and anxiety. When this conflict becomes unbearable, the individual may experience a relapse or may resort to varied neurotic defenses.

Ritualized Escapes from Anxiety. Characteristic socialized defenses arise as modes of escape from the conflicts occasioned by mobile aspirations.

The individual may renounce his mobile strivings by claiming that he does not want to aim too high, that he is "playing it safe," that he does not want to "stick his neck out." He withdraws from the competitive process by repressing or suppressing his competitive desires.[23]

Or he may renounce his aggressiveness and take recourse in intensified submission. If continually rebuffed whenever he is assertive, he may begin to distrust himself so much that individualized expression becomes tantamount to helplessness. Sometimes this submissive behavior may be his only resort when the employer is impatient, insecure, and irritable. In extreme instances he may hesitate to express an opinion, to take a stand, or to assert a point of view. He becomes completely noncommittal on any issue and remains completely neutral as far as this position is possible or feasible. Usually, he first sees how his superior will react, and in this way takes a clue as to how he should respond. This may protect him from the anxiety of being "caught out on a limb," of irritating others above him, of antagonizing persons that he feels he cannot afford to antagonize. This type of retreatism can lead to a kind of compulsive conformity which may be indispensable in some instances for emotional security, but which leaves the individual afraid of his own feelings and opinions and is based upon intense feelings of helplessness.

Yet the other means for escaping the apprehension of failure and emotional vulnerability is in the intensified driving, pushing, vindictive direction which centers primarily upon getting ahead, in moving against people, and in regarding people as utilities. When these intensified efforts are upset by trifles, this type can become anxiety-ridden or afflicted with psychosomatic symptoms.

The Saulteaux Indians. The normative anxiety toward careeristic failure among competitive personalities in Western industrial society has a parallel anxiety in the morbid appraisal of illness among the Saulteaux Indian tribe.[24] Among the traditions of the Saulteaux

[23] See Robert K. Merton, *Social Theory and Social Structure*, pp. 140–141 (Glencoe, Ill.: The Free Press, 1949).

[24] A. Irving Hallowell, "The Social Function of Anxiety in a Primitive Society," *American Sociological Review*, December, 1941, VI:6, pp. 869–881; also A. Irving Hallowell, "Fear and Anxiety as Cultural and Individual Variables in a Primitive Society, *The Journal of Social Psychology*, 1938, IX, pp. 25–47.

Indians are certain beliefs that severe illness or disease is a penalty for a misdeed.[25] Since the Saulteaux tribe are positively oriented toward health and long life, they invest disease with a meaningful fear beyond its actual physical threat to the afflicted person.

When a Saulteaux Indian does not readily recover from an illness or disease, he interprets his affliction as a penalty for some past misdeed. Not knowing the specific cause of his illness, he is faced with a definite crisis which frightens and overwhelms him. Since his definition of the illness exceeds the actual danger, his response becomes essentially "neurotic." This helpless reaction is evident, too, when his child, for whom he is responsible, becomes ill; for his child's illness is attributed to his transgression as a parent. His anxiety specifically begins to arise when medicinal treatment has failed and when the source of the illness remains unknown. Then he no longer regards the ailment as an impersonal, objective danger but as something personal and critical, and he interprets it as a probable retaliation for something he has done in the past.

This defenseless reaction to illness is typical among the Saulteaux because all members of the society are susceptible to it. It lies midway between objective fear, which is caused by natural dangers, and a unique neurotic anxiety, which is caused by the individual's singular upsetting experiences. Hallowell states:[26]

> . . . disease may arouse "normal" or objective anxiety, but among the Saulteaux, native theories of disease invest certain disease situations with a traumatic quality which is a function of the beliefs held rather than of the actual danger precipitated by the illness itself. The quality of the anxiety precipitated in the individual affected by such situations suggests neurotic rather than objective anxiety because the ultimate cause of the disease is attributed to the expression of dissocial impulses. The illness is viewed as a punishment for such acts and the anxiety is a danger signal that heralds the imminence of the penalty. Insofar as individuals are motivated to avoid dissocial acts because of the penalty anticipated, the pseudoneurotic anxiety aroused in disease situations has a positive social function. It is a psychic mechanism that acts as a reinforcing agent in upholding the social code.

In this predicament the Saulteaux has one recourse. He can confess his transgressions, almost always in public. Although very

[25] A. Irving Hallowell, "The Social Function of Anxiety in a Primitive Society," *American Sociological Review*, December, 1941, VI:6, pp. 869–881.

[26] *Ibid.*, p. 881.

reluctant to expose his "sins" in this way, he is confronted by the tribe who remain suspicious of anything held in privacy or secrecy; for secrecy carries the taint of potential magic or sorcery. Yet confession presumably relieves the individual of his guilt and reduces his feeling of isolation. Confession then paves the way, psychologically, for recovery from illness.

By these potential anxieties the Saulteaux Indian who places a high value on health and long life is deterred, although not prevented, from practicing forbidden activities. In a society where punitive controls are at a minimum, this anxietylike reaction to illness becomes an effective means of social control and of self-control.

The Collapse of Social Values: the British Mining Communities. The disintegration of group values in a community is exemplified by periods of mass unemployment. If a minority of individuals are unemployed, they can still believe in the basic values of the culture, despite their doubts about their abilities and despite their apprehensions about their security. But with mass unemployment the individual can no longer have faith in his basic institutions. In this mood of purposelessness he may, with others, be seized with panic, hostility, and helplessness.

These pervasive attitudes of anxiety with their neurotic consequences are clearly illustrated by Halliday in his description of British mining communities.

The Mining Communities in Great Britain. Until about 1916 the mining communities in Great Britain were relatively isolated and self-sufficient settlements.[27] The men dug coal by hand and worked in small cohesive units, which were composed of relatives and close friends. The practice of mining was a definite source of pride to the miner and was an integral part of family tradition. The father imparted to the sons the skills they needed in the mines. In addition, there was a continuity between the work situation and the community, which was culturally homogeneous by its long isolation. The workmates in the mines were friends outside the mines. Despite the many dangers in the pits, the miners knew and shared these dangers which intensified their solidarity and social purpose. Since work was done by hand, it afforded a certain personal satisfaction. After 1916 the mines began to be mechanized, and contacts with

---

[27] From James L. Halliday, *Psychosocial Medicine,* pp. 184–195 (New York: W. W. Norton & Company, 1948).

the outside world increased. Although this transition period stretched to 1936, it began to corrode the very social processes which made for personal stability without providing some means for a needed reorganization of such stability. The introduction of machinery for cutting and removing coal reduced the function of the miners "to shoveling coal only." The skills with which miners previously prided themselves were now of no importance. In addition, and perhaps more important, the teams of workers were broken up, and each miner worked alone. Also, many of the more personal phases of mining began to disappear; the miner began to feel himself part of a gigantic impersonal machine.

Before mechanization the miner could eat his meal in leisure and at his own pace. Now he had an allotted fifteen minutes of a seven-hour shift for eating. Before, the miner worked at his own time. Now he was compelled to become geared to the pace of the machinery. Before, he could detect impending danger by the noises from the cracking of the strata, because the mine was relatively quiet. Now the din of the machinery precluded such warnings. Before, he had the determination instilled by the example and support of the other miners who formed part of his work team. Now, as an isolated individual, he was without this collective determination, and the prospect of danger mounted by the very fact of his being alone. His work patterns became disrupted; his prestige derived from work skills was removed. These disruptive changes laid the bases for personal disorganization, which was aggravated by the culture conflicts in the community.

The advent of mechanized mediums of transportation, an acculturation process hastened by the miners who returned from the armies after World War I and by workers who lived in the community during the war period, and the economic depression with its consequent mass unemployment precipitated anxiety and other neuroses among many miners. The miners, of course, realized that the coal they produced was no longer wanted, but more significantly they realized that, as workers, they were no longer useful. Their quest for other types of employment was futile because of pervasive unemployment. In addition, their former status as workers and as providers was gone. They condemned themselves but also became hostile to the community. Some felt they could no longer give anything useful to the community. At the same time they became dependent upon the community for survival. Then dependency was coupled with feelings of hostility and aggression. They felt their self-respect was compromised by their very predicament. Another factor, however, lessened their desire for employment and provided a secondary gain for their neurotic behavior.

During the depths of the depression wages declined, but unemployment insurance, which was supplemented by local public assistance, went up, particularly for men who were ill. Occasionally some found it possible to receive more money while sick than while working. With the incentives for employment reduced, the unemployed miners began to influence those who were employed, by their emotional condition and by their lack of social purpose, for these miners were often relatives and members of the same household.

Under these social conditions anxiety and other neurotic expressions increased. With a decline in social purpose and in social cohesion, the members of the community became more individually isolated, and their conflicts and hostility to each other became more manifest. This paved the way for an increase in situational anxieties and in psychosomatic ailments.

Anxiety and the Combat Situation. The onset of anxiety in the battle situation in war reflects the types of interpersonal relations within the combat unit as well as the personality make-up of the individual combatants. Both contribute to the deterrence or acceleration of this anxiety experience.

The types of relationships within the combat unit are virtually opposite to those of the mining community which has just been discussed. To sustain itself, to prevent the onset and diffusion of anxiety and panic, the unit firmly and effectively encourages each member to repress anxiety-ridden expressions, and it is almost as intolerant of psychosomatic ailments. Since individual hardship and distress are commonplace and death usually imminent, the main protective force for the individual is the cohesion of the unit itself. By its social solidarity the platoon or company acquires a collective pride and determination, which instills a protective feeling into the individual and which prevents him from disturbing such feelings in others. This individual identification with the other members of the unit, especially with the leaders, anchors the self in the texture of stable relationships and reduces anxiety reactions. In fact, when pride and cohesion in the combat unit decline, neurotic cases correspondingly increase.[28] Thus, the group with high morale can effectively deter neurotic relapses.

In such cohesive units the neurotically anxious person is considered a deviant, although efforts are made to retrieve him into the group. The soldier is made to feel that the group is greater and more important than he, and that individual sacrifices are necessary for its continuance. His courage and resolve reflect the stimulated courage that develops from participating with others. When this solidarity and determination weaken, the soldier then becomes more concerned with himself; the group no longer provides the essential security which he seeks. Within this social situation, individual breakdowns are more likely to develop.[29]

The crux of the individual soldier's conflict is between his sense of attachment to his unit and his self-concern for safety within an orbit of danger. When the group is loosely integrated, this individualized self-concern mounts. In newly and hastily formed units more breakdowns usually occurred. Replacements who did not learn to fit into the unit organization also had higher rates of relapses.[30] And as has been mentioned, survivors of platoons or companies that suffered severe losses, despite withstanding past arduous ordeals, eventually became extremely anxious or suffered derivative neuroses.

But what soldiers did break down? Before entering combat nearly all soldiers were apprehensive and tense. Many were uncertain as to how they would respond under fire.[31] Though they became more confident after the first few successful battles, they seemed to lose this confidence as the campaign persisted. Some soldiers became fatigued more easily, lacked determination, and had to exert greater effort than formerly to keep pace with the combat unit. Their tensions mounted and they became more anxious and apprehensive. The combat unit tried unsuccessfully to suppress and to counteract these feelings. Inadvertently, these soldiers felt that they couldn't

[28] Morton C. Wyatt, "Psychoneurosis and Leadership," *Infantry Journal*, April, 1945, p. 29.

[29] Roy R. Grinker and John B. Spiegel, *Men Under Stress*, pp. 129–130 (Philadelphia: The Blakiston Company, 1945).

[30] Edwin Weinstein, "The Function of Interpersonal Relations in the Neurosis of Combat," *Psychiatry*, August, 1947, X:3, pp. 307–314.

[31] Herbert X. Spiegel, "Psychiatric Observations in the Tunisian Campaign," *American Journal of Orthopsychiatry*, 1943, XIV:3, p. 383.

"take it any more" and that their "number was up." They found obstacles more formidable than before and they became increasingly preoccupied with their own safety. They felt frightened and overcome by incidents. The unit then was unable to reach them emotionally or to restore their effective identification with the unit. Each potential "breakdownee" felt himself a discrete and isolated individual rather than a member of a combat unit, and his main concern was with his own safety. In this tense, irresolute and indecisive condition his main concern was with avoiding or fleeing from the combat situation. Weinstein said:[32]

> The main characteristic of the soldier with a combat induced neurosis is that he has become a frightened, lonely, helpless person whose inter-personal relationships have been disrupted. The nature of modern warfare is such that in order to survive in combat, the soldier must function as part of a group, and his resistance to the traumata of combat will vary with the ability to integrate himself with the group.

The Alorese: the Development of "Anxiety." [33] Whether the anxiety component is a common or average characteristic among the Alorese can be ascertained more clearly after we present a brief developmental picture of the Alorese personality.[34] This developmental pattern depends in large part upon the mother-child relationships.

After the first two weeks of maternal care the Alorese mother abruptly deserts her child and returns to work in the fields. Thereafter, her care of the child is inconsistent, sporadic, and unreliable. During the mother's absence the child is cared for by other persons, usually siblings. Consequently, the child does not have a sustained, consistent association with a single person. Weaning is consummated by pushing or slapping the child away. Or the child is teased in various ways—another child is deliberately taken to the breast, or food is promised but not given. In fact, teasing, deception, and inconsistent relationships are frequent adult responses to children.

[32] Edwin Weinstein, "The Function of Interpersonal Relations in the Neurosis of Combat," *Psychiatry*, August, 1947, X:3, pp. 307–314.

[33] See Abram Kardiner *et al.*, *Psychological Frontiers of Society*, pp. 146–258 (New York: Columbia University Press, 1945); also Cora DuBois, *The People of Alor* (Minneapolis: University of Minnesota Press, 1944).

[34] Alor is a small island in the Netherlands East Indies situated about six hundred miles east of Java and seven hundred miles west of New Guinea. The people described were settled in the small village of Atimelang of this island.

The children's intensified hostility and helpless rage find an outlet in unorganized temper tantrums. But these childish tantrums become rather futile because others remain indifferent to them and the children do not secure their desired objects, namely the systematic attention and care of the parents. Hence, from the very beginning of personal development and continuing into the symbolic period, the child's orbit of social relationships is such that he acquires a low estimate of himself and deep feelings of worthlessness. This attitude of personal inadequacy, however, is not accompanied by attitudes of self-condemnation and feelings of guilt as is characteristic in Western cultures. These latter feelings were comparatively weak. Consequently, depression and suicide were very rare.

The Alorese tends to have a low and somewhat hazy conception of himself. This confused self-conception is revealed in contradictory patterns of behavior which mark the anxiety of the Alorese behavior. This ambivalence seemingly is not as clear-cut as it might be in the Western culture.[35]

But to what extent are there the ambivalent components of hostility on the one hand and the need for affection on the other, as would be characteristic in American culture? The hostility among the members of the Alorese society leads to marked social distance between them and to lack of co-operation. The need for affection seems to be expressed indirectly. Apparently, the affection which the individual Alorese expects from others is very little. Whether the compensatory foraging for and stealing of food is symbolic of the search for affection can only be inferred indirectly. Presumably, relieving hunger may be associated with needed affection. This is also shown in the ritual among the wealthy of preparing a feast for the other villagers as a means of allaying envy.[36]

We thus get a picture of a group in which a protoneurotic anxiety may be the "common" or "average" form of behavior.[37] Yet the

[35] Abram Kardiner *et al.*, *Psychological Frontiers of Society*, pp. 225–226 (New York: Columbia University Press, 1945).

[36] *Ibid.*, pp. 229–230.

[37] Whether "anxiety" is an average behavioral pattern among the Alorese is a moot point. Oberholzer, on the basis of Rorschach tests, did find that the Alorese were suspicious, distrustful, fearful, apprehensive, insecure, and very careful, but had no neurotic anxiety and no neurotic attitudes of insecurity. Kardiner insists that the Alorese are neurotic because of their mode of development. Abram Kardiner, *et al.*, *Psychological Frontiers of Society*, pp. 240–246.

anxiety expressions of the Alorese, despite basic similarities, are different from those of, say, urbanized middle-class Americans.[38] Like the neurotic American, the Alorese have devalued self-estimates, are ambivalent, easily discouraged, "touchy," compensatory in their prestige-seeking ways, very competitive, apprehensive, and hostile in their relations with others but also dependent upon them. Finally, because of their tenuous and distant ties with others, they feel isolated and alone.

Unlike the neurotic American, the Alorese tend to acquire a rather vague self-image, a less organized inner life, less severe feelings of self-condemnation, less organized and satisfying patterns of aggression, less need for affection—although dependence upon the parents remains subconscious as is manifested in their dreams—and a general kind of self-control which functions more completely on a conscious level.

Anxiety and Social Organization. The four societies which we have described illustrate certain relations between individual anxiety and social organization.

The spread of anxiety weakens and disrupts group cohesion and tends to undermine collective determination and social purpose, particularly in critical situations. The individual members become more preoccupied with their own problems, become distrustful of and hostile to others, and less integrated within the group; hence, social relations become more distant and less satisfying. This was evident in the mining community during the depression. It was reflected in its low morale, loss of social purpose, and increase of illness. It was evident in the combat unit when anxiety spread and the unit became less effective in battle; the unit ceased to stimulate the individual to collective goals and ceased to be a symbol of protection. In its extreme, the unit disintegrated and each individual became concerned primarily with his own safety. Among the Alorese, the distrust, the tenuous social relationships, and social distance between the members is persistent. Each individual tended to be encysted almost as a discrete unit because of his distrust of the other members and because of their distrust of him. But among the Saulteaux this did not obtain. The Saulteaux dreaded being isolated

[38] Karen Horney, *The Neurotic Personality of Our Time,* pp. 13, 14, 95 (New York: W. W. Norton & Company, 1937).

from the group and anything held private or in secret was a source of suspicion.

From the opposite perspective, when the group strives to preserve its solidarity, anxiety behavior becomes a threat to the unit and the basis for social disapproval. The neurotic individual becomes a variant and is isolated from the group, and his anxiety is prevented from spreading. This was evident both in the combat unit and in the Saulteaux society. Since the mining community had been disorganized, the spread of anxiety could not be deterred. Among the Alorese, the social relations remained very tenuous, and anxiety activities had sanctioned outlets.

But when the unit is well organized and the members more effectively integrated within it, anxiety breakdowns decline. It seems that persons who acquire the support and approval of the group tend to become sustained. Highly integrated military units had less breakdowns than the loosely integrated units. The mining work units who were intimate and more solidified also had fewer neurotic breakdowns.[39] The participants of cohesive units are less likely to break down. They find that other participants bolster their self-confidence; they feel less isolated and more protected by identifying with the group; they can reintegrate their behavior more readily by the demonstrated example of others. The Saulteaux Indian who was helplessly isolated from the group had a powerful need to become reaccepted, and hence had to confess his "sins," however distasteful this practice might have been to him. Thus, the group used individual anxiety as a means for controlling him. On the other hand, the group in Alor had such a tenuous family organization and such distant social relationships that the anxiety reactions were perpetuated because the group could not counteract these reactions.

Summary

Anxiety, the core neurosis which creates the tensions from which other neuroses may be formed, arises when the subject is overwhelmed, threatened, or distressed by one or a series of situations to which he cannot respond completely and effectively. On the one

[39] James L. Halliday, *Psychosocial Medicine*, p. 269 (New York: W. W. Norton & Company, 1948).

hand, the subject may strive to flee from or avoid or react compulsively to the distressing situation. On the other hand, the effort to resolve the problematic situation persists, although it is manifested unconsciously, as in dreams. Not all anxiety has neurotic consequences. Normal anxiety does not lead to escapist behavior but leads often to dealing with the situation constructively. Neurotic anxiety, however, is a response that is not proportionate to the danger and results in escape from the danger by repression and by other neurotic defenses.

Neurotic anxiety develops when the child is subject to inconsistent and ambivalent relationships with the parents and siblings. Since the child in the usual American family identifies closely with his parents or siblings, he evaluates himself by their attitudes. When these responses are ambivalent and reduce the child's self-esteem, or when he is placed in an orbit of familial relations in which he becomes hostile toward and yet dependent upon the parents, he becomes unable to respond effectively to those situations and thus resolves the problematic relationship by improvising neurotic defenses. When the juvenile, however, does not rate himself by parental attitudes but builds up defenses by his alliance with the play group or with other persons, self-devaluation and helplessness tend to be avoided.

The self of the anxiety-ridden person is characterized by diffidence, often to the point of incapacitating helplessness and self-preoccupation. Since he is uncertain of his abilities and uncertain of the responses of others, self-evaluation becomes problematic and ambivalent for the intensely anxious person. He wants to gain or retrieve self-prestige, but he is unable to do so. These contradictory attitudes of the anxiety-ridden person reveal his conflicts and his need for his neurotic defenses.

Anxiety is acquired in divergent social contexts and tends to have somewhat similar effects upon the social personality. Anxiety also affects the social process and is antithetical to collective cohesion and collective purpose. When anxiety spreads in the group, the group tends to become loosened and "fragmented." Groups that retain their cohesion tend to isolate the neurotic type and to consider him a variant.

Selected Readings

Freud, Sigmund, *The Problem of Anxiety*, Translated by H. A. Bunker (New York: W. W. Norton & Company, 1936).

Fromm, Erich, *Escape From Freedom* (New York: Rinehart & Company, Inc., 1941).

———, "Individual and Social Origins of Neurosis," *American Sociological Review*, 1944, IX, pp. 380–384.

Green, Arnold W., "The Middle Class Male Child and Neurosis," *American Sociological Review*, XI:1, pp. 31–41.

Grinker, Roy R., and John P. Spiegel, *Men Under Stress* (Philadelphia: The Blakiston Company, 1945).

Halliday, James L., *Psychosocial Medicine* (New York: W. W. Norton & Company, 1948).

Hallowell, A. Irving, "Fear and Anxiety as Cultural and Individual Variables in a Primitive Society," *The Journal of Social Psychology*, 1938, IX, pp. 25–47.

———, "The Social Function of Anxiety in a Primitive Society," *American Sociological Review*, December, 1941, VI:6, pp. 869–881.

Hoch, Paul H., and Joseph Zubin (editors), "Anxiety," *Publications of the American Psychopathological Associations*, Vol. V (New York: Grune & Stratton, Inc., 1950).

Horney, Karen, *The Neurotic Personality of Our Time* (New York: W. W. Norton & Company, 1937).

Masserman, Jules H., *Behavior and Neuroses* (Chicago: University of Chicago Press, 1943).

May, Rollo, *The Meaning of Anxiety* (New York: The Ronald Press Company, 1950).

Weinberg, S. Kirson, "The Combat Neuroses," *American Journal of Sociology*, March, 1946, LI:5, pp. 456–478.

Weinstein, Edwin A., "The Function of Interpersonal Relations in the Neurosis of Combat," *Psychiatry*, August, 1947, X:3, pp. 307–314.

CHAPTER SEVEN

Dissociation, Phobia, and Compulsivity—
Forms of Neurosis

In the past chapter we have shown that anxiety is the core neurosis. Other neuroses develop as efforts to handle and to cover up the anxiety, its feelings of distress, and the conflicts which it represents. Such neuroses take the form of defensive symptoms or partial solutions to the anxiety. These neuroses, however, do not necessarily succeed in obliterating the anxiety or in preventing its recurrence. Instead, the anxiety usually becomes interwoven into the neuroses.

The general neurotic types which we shall describe in this chapter indicate how the anxiety is handled. These types are dissociation, phobia, and compulsive behavior. Frequently, the hysterical person absolves himself from anxiety by fleeing into another role or by physical incapacity. The phobic person binds his anxieties by circumscribing his activities to avoid dreaded situations. The compulsive person averts his anxiety by irresistibly impelling ideas or personalized rituals.

But neurotics also have common underlying characteristics. First, they have basic contradictory tendencies, whether expressed in hostility and dependency, submission and aggression, obedience and rebellion, destruction and guilt, competitiveness and noncompetitiveness, or in other specific forms. Second, their behavior has an insatiability which is reflected by their continual need to ward off anxiety. Hence, their behavior becomes repetitive when the same defenses are used. But those defenses do not resolve their conflicts and remain dissatisfying. Those persons who, out of irresistible guilt, continually wash their hands exemplify this behavior. Third, their behavior is indiscriminate insofar as it pervades all their activities. Neurotics express their hostility whether or not the situation warrants hostility. Fourth, they retrench or restrict their personal organization to avoid activities or situations which might call out anxiety. Fifth, despite secondary gains, they are basically self-defeating because their behavior represents a flight from rather than a solution of their conflicts.

Dissociated Behavior

Dissociated behavior is one type of hysterical behavior. In contrast to organic conversion such as paralysis, blindness, seizures, or prolonged sleep, dissociated behavior primarily affects the self.[1] Its simplest form, amnesia, involves the temporary loss of one's identity. Fugue or flight involves the identification with another self. In more complex forms, dissociated behavior involves identification with many discrete selves. These reactions represent compulsive flights from one's self-orientation into another role when experiences become too unbearable for the given person.

Dissociative Behavior and Ordered Behavior. Dissociated behavior is similar and yet is essentially different from ordered behavior. Ordered persons have unpleasant experiences which they cannot recall, play multiple roles, some of which may be contradictory, have latent systems of incompleted activity which are laden with hostility, and sometimes have fantasies that they are somebody else whom they admire. But ordered persons generally can control their behavior, can integrate their disparate roles, and can control their latent attitudes and fantasies.

Many persons who have blocked out keenly distressing experiences still can carry on their daily routines without losing sight of their real roles and their actual selves. Ordered persons also take many different roles, such as father, friend, businessman, athlete, which involve discrete attitude systems, roles, and self-estimates. Some of their roles may be almost contradictory. A hardheaded, cal-

---

[1] Freud claims that the "splitting of consciousness so striking in the familiar classical cases of double consciousness exits rudimentarily in every hysteria. . . ." Sigmund Freud, *Selected Papers on Hysteria and Other Psychoneuroses*, p. 8 (New York: Nervous and Mental Disease Publishing Company, 1909).

culating businessman may be an easygoing, credulous father, or a very submissive office worker may be a tyrant to his subordinates.

Some persons may simulate roles which contradict their true feelings, as, for example, those who pretend sympathy when they feel very hostile. Then again, many persons have repressed schemes of activity which are potentially active, which crave fulfillment, and which may be expressed in dreams and in surreptitious and vicarious activities. Some persons have stray and vagrant impulses which they do not associate with themselves, and some persons, perhaps, resort to antisocial behavior under hypnotic suggestion which they would refrain from doing while awake.

Further, some persons can engage in two disparate and even disconnected activities at the same time. They may absent-mindedly complete certain activities, or they may engage in automatic activities, such as automatic handwriting, without intervening conscious control. It is not surprising, then, that Murphy regarded dissociative disorders as exaggerations of normal behavior. "Perhaps the normal personality is more dissociable than we suspect," claimed Murphy, "and the pathologically dissociated is a bit played up, dramatized by the patient and the doctor alike." [2]

The Nature of Dissociative Behavior. But dissociative behavior, as neurotic behavior, is an overpowering escape from a severely critical situation which the person cannot endure. It absolves him from responsibility for his actions and relieves him from any guilt. The more complicated types of dissociation serve to act out certain latent and repressed attitudes. But this behavior enables the person to forget his identity so that the self becomes both a different subject and object with different attitudes, aspirations, and general patterns of behavior.

The hysterical person not only acts out dominant and unresolved impulses but also becomes involved in an uncontrollable and aberrant form of role taking—"hysterical identification." In this process he may identify with and simulate another person or even some role in his own past.

For example, a woman patient developed a hysterical form of tuberculosis similar to what her father had as a young man.[3] Dora,

---

[2] Gardner Murphy, *Personality: A Biosocial Approach to Origins and Structure*, p. 442 (New York: Harper & Brothers, 1947).

[3] Otto Fenichel, *The Psychoanalytic Theory of Neurosis*, pp. 221–223 (New York: W. W. Norton & Co., Inc., 1945).

one of Freud's patients, developed a cough like that of another woman, Mrs. K., whom she unwittingly considered a rival. Persons who have no direct relationship with others, as in social contagion, may get fainting spells or go into trances.

The person who expresses dissociated behavior may identify with many episodes of his past as well as with the roles of other persons as we shall see later. This aberrant form of identification may even result from fantasy. For instance, a hysterical girl felt an intense pain in her finger as if it had been cut with a knife. She was in love with a medical student who was in another city, and at the time she experienced the pain she imagined that he might have cut himself while dissecting some animals. This hysterical tendency involves the loss of control over one's latent attitudes and one's identity, as well as an identifying process with one or more persons whom one admires. This tendency is basic to dissociated behavior.

Amnesia and Fugue. In its simplest form, amnesia develops as a reaction to anxiety, in which the person forgets who he is and what his experiences have been. Frequently, neurotic soldiers at the onset of their anxiety become amnesic, as do persons who have awakened from a nightmare and cannot immediately shift their perspectives to their present roles. They then become temporarily oriented away from their surroundings and from themselves. Sometimes, persons who have these conflicts may enact them during their sleep as is evident in somnambulism. For example, a soldier who was given to somnambulism divulged his dual selves as follows:[4]

"I want to do my part, but this other man inside of me won't let me. I want to help out in this war, but there's this other fellow who has more influence over me than anybody. He is constantly in my dreams. He keeps telling me: 'You could do much better on the outside. You could be a great help in defense work.' But I keep telling him I want to help out—I have to help out—but he replies: 'My boy, you are lucky you are alive. I will help you out. I will get you out of this; if you stay in, you may never come back. Be sensible!'

"He makes me get up and walk around. He won't tell me where I am going. I wake up and I'm fighting him off, but he won't let me fight him off. He tells me I am just an ordinary person—that I am young. I still have a right to live in a free country. I tell him I have just as much freedom as anybody else."

4 Samuel A. Sandler, "Somnambulism in the Armed Forces," *Mental Hygiene,* 1945, 29, pp. 238–239.

Some persons who have very threatening experiences can retreat aimlessly because of a vague desire for emotional flight. In the process they become confused and can lose their identity. Other persons who have flight experiences, however, seem to have latent attitudes toward a goal. Despite loss of identity, the persons, during the fugue, behave as intelligently as during their normal condition.

For example, a sergeant, delivering a message on a dangerous sector of the front, was hurled down by a shell explosion.[5] Some hours later, he was pushing his motorcycle along the streets of a coastal town about one hundred miles away. In complete confusion he surrendered to the military police and could recall nothing of his trip. By hypnosis he pieced his experience together, remembering that he got up and headed for the coastal town, sought out signs, and even asked directions for the town. It was at this town that men embarked for home.

Fugues and Multiple Selves. But emotional flights from one's identity may lead to identification with one's past role or with another person. The new selves which evolve may be alternating or coexisting, and one self may or may not be aware of the other.

Reverend Bourne withdrew some money from the bank to pay some bills.[6] Two months later, as A. J. Brown, he opened and furnished a store in another town. Sometime later, he awoke in the middle of the night and asked people to tell him where he was. He knew nothing of the shopkeeper, A. J. Brown, but remembered only the name and the experiences of Ansel Bourne. His last recollection came with his withdrawing money from the bank. Later, he admitted that there was "trouble back home" and that he wanted a rest. Under hypnosis, his Brown memory was so well restored that he could not recall the Reverend and could not even recognize his wife. During the hypnotic condition he assumed all the features of Mr. Brown. His responses and competence seemed about the same, but his movements were somewhat slower. In spite of his efforts, James admittedly was unable to organize the two selves into one.

This fugue process may result in taking another person's role.

---

[5] William McDougal, *Outlines of Abnormal Psychology*, p. 258 (New York: Charles Scribner's Sons, 1926).

[6] William James, *Principles of Psychology,* pp. 391–393 (New York: Henry Holt and Company, Inc., 1910). See also L. H. Zeigler, "Hysterical Fugues," *Journal of the American Medical Association,* 1933, 101, pp. 571–576.

This flight is not deliberate "impersonation," because this hysterically identifying process is beyond the subject's control. For example, in one case a housewife, 42 years old, unwittingly assumed her friend's role for 4 years as a defense against an unbearable situation.[7]

Reared by fanatically religious but hypocritical parents, Bernice spent a lonely troubled childhood lightened only by her deep attachment to her sister. When Bernice was 17, her sister died and she was thrown into a severe depression. Recuperating, she was persuaded to attend college, where she met and became deeply attached to a roommate, Rose P., who stimulated her talents, introduced her to new interests, and continually befriended her. But Rose P., after this happy interlude, married and left. Depressed at her departure, Bernice improved enough to return to school and graduate. After graduation, she married at the behest of her parents a man whom she did not love. Together, they spent six unhappy years in missionary outposts in the Far East, then they settled in a Midwestern town where all her interests were stifled because of the town's rigid conservatism. In her lonely misery she reminisced continually about her happy life during college with Rose P. When her younger and favorite child died, she could tolerate no more. The next day, she disappeared, and eventually she showed up in her college town, where she claimed she was Rose P. In this new identity she taught piano and was so successful that she became assistant director of the conservatory. Losing her former identity as well as a knowledge of her past, she avoided persons who were too curious about her. She continued this routine until recognized by a common friend who knew both her and the real Rose P. Brought back to her home she steadfastly denied she was Bernice until intensive therapy was able to penetrate her amnesia and reveal her true identity.

The Development of Dissociated Behavior. But dissociated behavior has a long history and generally afflicts certain personality types. Whatever the constitutional tendencies of these persons, it seems that from childhood they have been neurotically predisposed, with the characteristic ambivalence toward one or both parents. Generally, this type is rigidly conformistic and obedient but has a repressed tendency toward divergent behavior. This becomes in-

[7] See Jules Masserman, *Principles of Dynamic Psychiatry,* pp. 33–34 (Philadelphia: W. B. Saunders Company, 1946).

creasingly manifested and is usually brought out by one or a series of critical situations which the subject cannot tolerate. These processes are illustrated in the case of John Roberts.[8]

The Case of John Roberts

John Roberts, age 37, while in the south of England, picked up a newspaper and read that a schoolmaster had been missing for three weeks from Ireland. From the description of the person in the paper, he felt that he must be that person. He reported to the police who wired his wife. She went to England, identified him, and brought him home. This had been the third time he had experienced memory lapses. The following history was gathered by hypnosis and by free-association interviews.

John was virtually an only child because another son died before John was born, and his sister died when he was 10. His mother was very devoted to him and never ceased telling him how bright he was and what an attractive career lay before him. His early life was dominated by his mother's whims.

At the age of 5 he abandoned his happy, spontaneous attitude and transformed into a "model boy." This change was a compulsive defense which began when he was playing in the garden and was throwing stones into an ornamental lake. Since he did some slight damage his mother pushed him into the house, put him to bed, and brought up his supper some time later, but refused to speak with him. He refused to eat the food. The next day silent hostility strained their relationship. Unable to endure his mother's disapproval, John began helping his mother with the household chores. By this submissive manner, he regained his mother's approval, but he lost his spontaneity. To keep his mother's approval he felt that he had to become a model boy.

But he wished to be like other boys. Frequently, he stood in front of the curtains, not daring to disarrange them and watching enviously the other boys running about with complete freedom. When permitted to leave the house, he fled in a dash, flinging into some wild game which symbolized freedom. Throughout his early life, he had the conflict between this model role, necessary to gain his mother's approval, and his hostility to her for curbing his spontaneity.

At school, John made friends easily and participated in the school's social life, although he never became a leader. At 18, he took the examinations for entering the University and passed by a very narrow margin. Immediately, he was acclaimed as the genius of the family. Pleased with his family's approval, he knew that they did not realize how near he came to failing. While he was regarded as a "genius" at home, he knew that in the University he was, at best, the "unpromising undergraduate." Also, he was disturbed by a personal conflict which had begun with his practice of masturbation. On the one hand, he was the bright and morally model son

[8] See E. A. Bennett, "Fugue States," *British Journal of Medical Psychology,* 1928, 8, pp. 143–149.

who was able to enter the University. On the other hand, he regarded himself as the unpromising student, who committed the extreme sin of masturbation. As more difficult examinations approached, he was seized with an intense anxiety that he might fail. His first fugue, which lasted 48 hours, occurred at that time.

He departed from college dressed in his best clothes and took a train to a seaside resort, where he had spent his previous holidays as a child. He traveled first class, which was beyond his means and contrary to his usual custom. He spent money freely on clothes and cigars, and dined at the best hotels. Later, he came into his own identity and returned to school.

Continuing his university course for two years, he decided to switch to a commercial course. At about that time World War I started. Enlisting, he joined the infantry battalion and saw action at the front. After demobilization, he went back to his academic career. He was then elected president of the leading undergraduate society, chiefly because of his war record.

Again, he became apprehensive that the examinations would show him up. Unable to endure this prospect, he began having fantasies about his freedom in the army. He got some money and lapsed into his second amnesia. He was found wandering in the deserted army camp where he had trained. His third amnesic period occurred eight years later.

By then he was a schoolmaster, married, the father of two children, and in sound physical health. Prior to his disappearance he was in deep conflict which had persisted for several years. Now it became very intense. The school in which he taught was sponsored by a religious denomination. Mr. Roberts, like all the teachers, was expected to be sympathetic to the theological doctrines and practices of the church. He implicitly observed these demands, and, in addition, participated in religious activities during his spare time. His social life, too, was beyond reproach and a "model" for others. In his private life, however, he engaged in moral misdemeanors, such as in petty thefts. During one of these thieving adventures, he was almost exposed. Filled with intense anxiety, he thought he would be exposed and disgraced. He had to explain certain events to a school committee which would have involved some exposure of his private life. He feared the impending interview. Indeed, a hysterical "sore throat" which developed postponed the meeting.

His marital life was not very happy. He and his wife never saw things the same way. His manner was strained and this was observed by others. At this time, he lapsed into various fantasies in which he visualized himself as an emissary carrying out religious and social work between different churches. This he believed would free him from his irksome routinized tasks. He also had depressive moods during which he contemplated suicide. He became determined to flee, and his fantasies involved escape from the restricting religious, social, and marital life.

These fantasies were realized during his fugue state. During the week in which the fugue occurred, he bought a ticket on Wednesday afternoon for London. He returned home, taught school the next day, and attended a social function in the evening. On Friday, he carried out some routine work, left home in the afternoon, and took a train to Belfast. From there he went to London. Though he left home on Friday, he could not recall what occurred after he purchased the tickets on Wednesday. His wife observed that, during this period, his behavior was rather unusual. After he arrived in London, he proceeded to Colchester where he had been stationed during his military training in 1914. He wandered about the town and talked to several persons about his training days. Discontent and restless, he went to Salisbury Plain where his army training had been concluded. The trip took several days and involved walking and getting lifts. After arriving at this place, he spent several hours throwing stones into a stream with marked enjoyment. Later, at the village in Salisbury Plain, he read in the newspaper of his disappearance.

The Process of Dissociated Behavior. Certain somewhat characteristic developmental processes are evident in this case.

First, the subject conforms rigorously externally but secretly resents his conformity. His conformism tends to be compulsive and is done so as not to lose the affection or approval of authority figures. The person tends to abide by his role with a kind of tenacity, but he chafes in his role and finds it very dissatisfying. In consequence, certain countering aggressive tendencies arise about which the person becomes guilty but which he cannot control. Second, he builds up and harbors an unconscious competing system of attitudes early in life which he wants to express. Though repressed as a competing system, these attitudes seem to become independent and operate automatically. These attitudes are outside the focus of personal consciousness, seem to split off, and go on by themselves.[9] Whether this developmental process, as Piaget has pointed out, results from an ineffective integration of the self at an early age is not definitely known, although it may exist in some cases. Third, the subject who resents his present role and his present self-conception longs for another role, reminisces about it, and may express this desired role by petty hostile acts, by depression, and by somnambulism. Fourth, the dissociation and hysterical identification occur after a critical situation in which the subject experiences unbearable conflicts. Fifth, during the dissociation, the person seems to forget all persons whom he might have known as well as himself. Despite this amnesia, the victim's behavior often is highly consistent within the range of his new role. Like other types of hysteria, by this escapist

[9] Morton Prince, *The Unconscious*, pp. 558–559 (New York: The Macmillan Company, 1914).

role taking, the afflicted person absolves himself from anxiety. Hence, the hysterical role of the victim is less guilt-ridden and less inhibited than is his usual role.

The Problem of "Multiple" Selves. Although investigators in the past have claimed that hysterical persons have dissociated themselves into three, four, five, or more selves, very few if any cases have been recorded recently. There have been cases in which persons have had an unsuspected "self" which seemed to behave beyond conscious control, but the other types of dissociation seem to require further evidence for additional substantiation. Although it seems possible that such multiple dissociation may occur, it is likely, however, that the hypnotic procedures may have had some influence upon some cases of "dissociated selves."

Phobic Behavior

Phobic behavior is an irrational dread or morbid aversion to an object, act, or situation. This behavior is illustrated by the woman who becomes terrified by a bug, or by the man who becomes panic-stricken in a closet. Sometimes phobia becomes fixed at its source, as in the case of the flyer who dreaded to go up in a plane because he had been shot down and had saved himself by bailing out in a parachute. More frequently, the phobia is neutrally displaced to an object which will not arouse the anxiety so easily, as the child who dreads dogs but actually fears his father.

Phobia and Rational Fears. Phobia results from past anxieties which may or may not correspond to actual danger situations. For example, some people who have cancer phobias may or may not have cancer. The fact that they have cancer does not reduce the neurotic aspect of their phobia. Phobia usually disables the person because it becomes one of his central considerations. For example, one woman could not stand a door closed behind her. When she entered a room she saw to it that the door remained open. Even at home she could not tolerate a closed door. But she also was afraid of other closed places, such as tunnels or even public halls. When she went to a public hall she had to remain as close to the exit as possible so that she would not become panic-stricken.

Phobia is usually individualized, private, and differs from shared fears of a given group. In most cultures children acquire fears which are transmitted by their elders as mediums of social control. These fears are transmitted in nonliterate groups by legends and folklore, and in contemporary culture by ghost stories and demonstrated examples.[10] These shared fears may influence the choice of feared objects. The individual who experiences anxiety may bind the anxiety to a socially feared object. Thus, the person not only neutralizes the source of his anxiety, but he also acquires a way of behavior to defend himself against anxiety.

Phobias which emerge from actual danger frequently are tied in with a general neurotic condition. During World War II in England, when the air raids were widely feared, some persons became afflicted with air-raid phobia and experienced acute anxiety reactions when the air-raid sirens were sounded. These persons did not have the attacks in the open country, even when planes were flying overhead. On the other hand, their phobias persisted in the city even though air raids had ceased for some time. Their phobias seemingly were extensions of mild peacetime agoraphobias and claustrophobias. Generally, these critical experiences, which were coupled with unfavorable emotional relationships with their nearest relatives, led to their phobic reactions.[11]

The Processes of Phobic Behavior. When phobia is bound up with the actual anxiety-creating situation which presents actual danger, the removal of the individual from the situation may abate the phobia. The phobia may still linger but not spread. On the other hand, displaced types of phobia may spread and become generalized from a single object to a category of objects. A person who fears one dog, in time may begin to fear all dogs, then all animals of a certain size.

When a phobic object or action is encountered, the subject becomes panic-stricken and helpless. This can be illustrated by the experiences of William Ellery Leonard, the sensitive poet and professor of English.[12] Leonard had an overpowering fear of locomotives. Later, he also became dreadfully afraid of water, and even afraid to stay near shore, though he had formerly been an able swimmer. Still later his condition was aggravated by his wife's

[10] John Gillin, "Magical Fright," *Psychiatry*, November, 1948, XI, pp. 389–400.
[11] E. Stengel, "Air-Raid Phobia," *British Journal of Medical Psychology*, 1944, 20:2, pp. 135–143.
[12] William Ellery Leonard, *The Locomotive God*, pp. 304–307 (New York: Appleton-Century-Crofts, Inc., 1927).

suicide, for which her family blamed Leonard. Shortly after, while on a stroll with a friend, he dropped into a roadhouse for a beer. Near the table he saw a map with a train.

> Through the center of the gaudy map, a passenger train was depicted as dashing head-on down a track, as if bursting out of Wisconsin. . . . Head on. Right at me. Hideously hostile . . . huge . . . God . . . death. . . . To destroy me for my guilt, as myself the destroyer of my wife. . . . Here again was the old split in the personality, creating this split in the objective world: the picture, to the eye an old map on a tavern wall; to the feel, a horrible alien monster.[13]

In time, Leonard was unable to venture far from home unless accompanied by his mother or father. When he remarried, three years later, his wife always had to be near him. Basic to Leonard's feelings was the intense dread of being left alone, and the locomotive seemed to symbolize this loneliness. But Leonard seemed to have a secondary gain from the presence of other people upon whom he could depend.

The phobic person generally is basically afraid of loneliness and personal isolation. Without confidence to solve this problem himself, he can do so indirectly through his neurotic symptoms. The phobic person tends to be hostile to himself and to others. These hostilities become displaced upon animals, inanimate objects, or restricted movements.

Since phobic behavior is more prevalent in children than any other neurotic disorder, it reveals an intense emotional dependency which the phobic person does not outgrow. The so-called separation anxiety is a conspicuous basis of phobic behavior, despite the varied objects upon which the phobic fastens his anxiety.

Compulsive Disorders

Compulsive disorders arise from irresistible attitudes which compel a given person to feel, to think, or to act in a given way. Obsessives have irresistibly persistent ideas of destruction, of sex, of aggression, which they seldom act out. On the other hand, compulsives have irresistible tendencies to act out their ideas and impulses and usually cannot inhibit them. Frequently, the two forms are mixed.

[13] William Ellery Leonard, *The Locomotive God*, p. 61 (New York: Appleton-Century-Crofts, Inc., 1927).

Compulsive Behavior and Compulsive Disorders. Compulsive behavior is not necessarily disordered behavior. In fact, compulsive behavior is very prevalent in our society. Punctuality, orderliness, cleanliness, and prescribed routines create compulsive attitudes among many persons who are not disordered. Their attitudes are shared and socially approved and frequently are mediums to economic security and social advancement. In fact, many compulsive persons who feel compelled to be on time or to be perfectionistic in their work and in their dress are well adjusted.

Compulsively disordered persons, however, are emotionally disabled. They are completely preoccupied by irresistibly destructive notions, sexual ideas, or other untoward aggressions. As a result of their compulsive ideas or actions, they devote much time trying to control them. For example, a cook felt that he might unknowingly poison the customers of the hotel by the varied chemicals that he used in the kitchen. Consequently, he spent hours during the day and night washing and scrubbing the pots and pans, and still he was in continual torment that he might poison the customers.[14]

The compulsive neurotic is continually trying to control his rebelliousness, his unwitting emotions, and his peculiar impulses. In the obsessive condition he may be plagued with these impulses and doubts, but he will not act them out. He may, however, try to undo these impulses by a compulsive ritual of doing the opposite. The overt compulsive, despite his attempts at self-control, may still irresistibly find himself acting out.

For example, a young woman was continually obsessed with worry over trivial as well as significant matters.[15] She was so overcome by worry that every problem which preoccupied her had to be examined continually and relentlessly. When she worried about losing her job, the obsession became so unbearable that she resigned her job to eliminate the problem. Despite her efforts at self-control, she could not stop worrying. In addition, she felt compelled to confess everything to her mother.

Her compulsion to confess began when she was 15 years old. She started to have persistent sexual fantasies, became alarmed, and

---

[14] Edward Weiss and O. Spurgeon English, *Psychosomatic Medicine,* p. 556 (Philadelphia: W. B. Saunders Company, 1943).

[15] Charles Berg, *The Case Book of a Medical Psychologist,* pp. 84–89 (New York: W. W. Norton & Company, 1948).

tried in vain to shut them out. Finally, her obsession became so distressing that she told her mother all her thoughts which she had been bottling up since the age of 12. From that time on she examined her thoughts in great detail and then compulsively confessed them to her mother. At first she tried to dispel any thought of a sexual act by confessing it; then to confess anything pertaining to sex. Finally she had to confess her worries about nonsexual matters.

The obsessive strives to defend himself against his hostile impulses by bringing them to awareness and organizing them ideationally. This intellectual mode of self-organization becomes a defense against his anxiety; thus the obsessive keeps himself in check. Sometimes, his impulses become so forceful that the very thought of doing something arouses so much guilt that it seems almost equivalent to its overt enactment.

Dynamic Differences of Neurotic Types

Not only do hysterics and compulsives differ symptomatically; they also are different personality types.

The hysteric is highly suggestible, prone to aberrant role taking or "hysterical identification," and not necessarily solidly grounded in reality. He may even drift off into disorientation such as by suggested hallucinations. Highly suggestible, the hysteric can have his symptoms eliminated or new symptoms introduced by hypnosis. This could hardly occur among compulsives. The hysteric finds more difficulty in conceptualizing his conflicts and intellectualizing his difficulties than the compulsive does.

The compulsive does not resort to "hysterical role taking," and often has insight into his emotions. Not necessarily suggestible, he tends to conceptualize his conflicts. The obsessive can recount many facts and experiences which have led to his breakdown and the agonies which he has endured during his disorder. The obsessive then is an "overresponsible," overscrupulous individual who is plagued and preoccupied by indecision. His disorder does not have a defined beginning or ending as does the hysteric, whose attack is precipitous.[16]

Neuroses and Culture. Neurotic types may vary in frequency by historic period, by social class, and by culture. Seemingly, hysteria was the pervasive neurotic disorder of the feudal and early indus-

[16] Pierre Janet, *Les Neuroses*, pp. 16–17 (Paris: Ernest Flammarion, 1909).

trial period. Compulsivity and psychosomatic disorders are the prevalent disorders of modern life.

Has Hysteria Declined? Psychosomatic disorders differ from conversion hysterias, because the psychosomatic disorders affect the vegetative and visceral organs (such as the stomach, the intestines, colon, lungs, and heart) among other internal organs and are referred to as "vegetative neuroses." [17] Hysterical disorders affect the voluntary muscles and sensory organs such as the limbs, eyes, or ears, and often are expressed in paralysis or in uncontrollable movements such as laughing or weeping. The psychosomatic disorders result from given bodily conditions in times of crisis. Thus continually suppressed, silent rage may heighten the blood pressure which may contribute to hypertension. The hysterical disorders are the symbolic conversions of the anxiety tensions into bodily symptoms. For example, a student who has intense anxiety over an examination may develop a paralyzed hand and become absolved from taking the examination.

Even within the past century or past quarter of a century, the frequency of hysteria seemingly has declined. Janet noted in his later years that the incidence of hysteria had notably diminished, and Freud observed this change as far back as when he returned to Vienna after studying in France.[18] Hysteria was far more frequent among British and American soldiers during World War I than during World War II. Grinker and Spiegel claimed that conversion hysteria was rare among American soldiers during World War II.[19] Other psychiatrists who claimed that hysteria was prevalent during World War II seemed to confuse hysterical with psychosomatic disorders. Menninger, in evaluating varied reports of the incidence of neurotic reactions among soldiers, claimed that the incidence of hysteria was 10 to 25 per cent of the total neurotic casualties, while 44 to 70 per cent were anxiety reactions, and the other neurotic reactions comprised phobia, depression, and compulsivity. Com-

[17] See Franz Alexander, *Psychosomatic Medicine,* pp. 41–43 (New York: W. W. Norton & Company, 1950).

[18] Elton Mayo, *Some Notes on the Psychology of Pierre Janet,* p. 67 (Cambridge, Mass: Harvard University Press, 1948).

[19] Roy R. Grinker and John P. Spiegel, "The Management of Neuropsychiatric Casualties in the Zone of Combat," *Manual of Military Psychiatry,* p. 526 (Philadelphia: W. B. Saunders Company, 1944).

pulsive behavior, however, usually was incurred before the soldiers went into the service.[20]

The Increase of Psychosomatic Disorders. Seemingly, psychosomatic disorders have increased in the past fifty years; and psychosomatic disorders are related closely to obsessive disorders.[21]

In World War I, 709 British soldiers were discharged from the services because of psychosomatic disorders, but in World War II, 23,754 British soldiers were discharged because of these disorders. In the American Army during World War I the annual rate of peptic ulcers was 0.71 per 1,000 soldiers; during World War II the rate was 2.75 per 1,000 soldiers, almost four times as many.[22] In fact, during World War II, gastric disorders were the most prevalent complaint in the Army.

Although these studies do not provide conclusive evidence of the increase of psychosomatic disabilities, they do provide suggestive leads for further exploration of this trend.

Neuroses and the Social Structure. Hysteria may occur more frequently than compulsive disorders among persons in the lower socioeconomic levels, and compulsive disorders may occur more frequently than hysteria among the higher socioeconomic levels. Janet noted that obsessive disorders were encountered more frequently in private hospitals than in public hospitals, and that educated persons were most frequently afflicted with compulsive disorders.[23] In Britain, hysteria among males was most pervasive among workers in dangerous occupations, such as underground miners, steeple jacks, and workers with explosives. Hysteria among females was most pervasive among nurses and domestic servants. Also, hysteria was relatively frequent among mental defectives, uneducated persons, and persons reared in orphanages.[24] This

[20] William C. Menninger, *Psychiatry in a Troubled World*, pp. 128–129 (New York: The Macmillan Company, 1948).

[21] James L. Halliday, *Psychosocial Medicine*, p. 107. Halliday relates an incident in which an observer who investigated many patients with peptic ulcer found that few had obvious anxiety conditions, but at the same time found a "significantly high prevalence" of obsessive tendencies among the patients.

[22] William C. Menninger, *Psychiatry in a Troubled World*, p. 160.

[23] Elton Mayo, *Some Notes on the Psychology of Pierre Janet*, p. 68 (Cambridge. Mass.: Harvard University Press, 1948).

[24] James L. Halliday, *Psychosocial Medicine*, p. 61 (New York: W. W. Norton & Company, 1948); Grinker and Spiegel have noted that relatively pure hysteria

writer has observed that soldiers in the Army who were prone to hysteria were those from backward rural areas and from the lower socioeconomic levels in the city. Generally, hysteria was more frequent among enlisted men than among officers. But we do not know definitely the distribution of these disorders in the social structure of the United States. On the basis of impression, it would seem that hysteria occurs more frequently in the lower socioeconomic levels than among the higher socioeconomic levels and more among the isolated rural groups than among the urban groups, but this problem awaits further inquiry for a more conclusive answer.

Neuroses and Nonliterate Societies. Donnison and others have pointed out that psychosomatic disorders are far less frequent among many isolated nonliterate and folk societies than among modern societies.[25] We can infer tentatively that psychosomatic disorders are rare in some nonliterate societies. On the other hand, hysterical disorders prevail among both simple, nonliterate groups and complex, industrial societies. Carothers found no individual cases of obsessive compulsion among East Africans, but he did find three men with hysteria, such as fugue, deafness, and inability to speak; these symptoms are similar to those found among Europeans.[26]

Among the Yakuts in Siberia, during episodes of panic, hysterical persons may repeat uncontrollably, because of hysterical role taking, the words or statements spoken by another (echolalia) or may imitate the gestures and movements of another (echopraxia). They may fall into trances, howl, and become convulsive. The Yakuts consider this behavior pathological and believe that it results from evil spirits who have entered the bodies of the afflicted persons.[27]

Among the Eskimos of Greenland, the women, when hysterical, tear off their clothes, cry, scream, jump into the ice-cold water, or

---

existed among paratroopers who did not express their anxieties because of the intense group solidarity. Consequently, their anxiety was completely repressed. See R. Grinker and J. Spiegel, *Men Under Stress* (Philadelphia: The Blakiston Company, 1945).

[25] C. P. Donnison, *Civilization and Disease* (Baltimore: Williams & Wilkins, 1937).

[26] J. C. Carothers, "A Study of African Derangement," *Psychiatry,* February, 1948, 2:1, pp. 69–71.

[27] M. A. Czaplicka, *Aboriginal Siberia,* pp. 727–729 (New York: Oxford University Press, 1914).

wander away into the hills.[28] Among the Malayans, women servants and others in subordinate positions who are prone to hysteria become very suggestible and very imitative, after some critical experience, and verbalize their repressed desires. When teased and frightened they begin to imitate their persecutors.[29] In short, as Cooper points out, hysteria is no respecter of cultures and may occur in nonliterate as well as in modern societies. Psychosomatic disorders, on the other hand, seem to be far more prevalent in industrial, urbanized societies than in nonliterate societies.[30]

Tentative Explanations. How can we account for this changing incidence of neurotic types? One contributing factor may be the influence of early rearing. The other contributing factor may be the influence of the adult impersonal society. .

Halliday suggests that differences in rearing children have contributed to these different disorders. Psychosomatic disorders, which are connected with the gastrointestinal functions, are influenced by the frustrations endured during the first six months of life. Hysteria may be influenced by the frustrations endured from six months to the first year of life when the infant is disorganized in locomotor activity and voluntary muscles. Halliday suggests that the predisposition to compulsive and psychosomatic disorders may be formed earlier in life than hysterical defenses, although the two disorders may be mixed. The greater prevalence of psychosomatic disorders, then, would be the changed kinds of mother-child relationships during the first six months of life.[31]

Although early predisposition may influence hysterical and compulsive disorders, a more definitive inquiry into this phase of com-

[28] A. A. Brill, "Piblokto or Hysteria Among Peary's Eskimos," *Journal of Nervous and Mental Disease*, 1913, 40, pp. 514–521. See also E. Saindon, "Mental Disorders among the James Bay Cree," *Primitive Man*, 1933, VI, pp. 1–12. Saindon has observed that about 85 per cent of the natives were hysterically predisposed.

[29] F. H. G. VanLoon, "Protopathic-Instinctive Phenomena in Normal and Pathological Life," *British Journal of Medical Psychology*, 1927, 8, pp. 264–279. Also see Kimball Young, *Personality and Problems of Adjustment*, pp. 727–730 (New York: Appleton-Century-Crofts, Inc., 1947).

[30] See Bronislaw Malinowski, *Sex and Repression in Savage Society*, pp. 85–90 (London: Routledge and Kegan Paul, Ltd., 1927).

[31] James L. Halliday, *Psychosocial Medicine* (New York: W. W. Norton & Company, 1948).

parative rearing is necessary, and its direct bearing upon the psychosomatic disorders requires far more evidence.

In terms of adult participation, compulsive and competitive striving for success in contemporary society is more prevalent than in most nonliterate groups. In fact, peptic ulcer has been called a "disease of modern civilization," a "businessman's disease." Biological as well as social factors contribute to the increase of peptic ulcers.[32] But the socially contributing processes inhere in the urban, mobile, and competitive society. In this cultural orbit have emerged certain specific types of disorders which are consistent with the types of social relationships in the given culture. This culture reflects the discrepant and discontinuous social relationships between primary and secondary groups. Thus, the individual who emerges from the family as a dependent person may acquire the hard-driving, indirectly aggressive way of life from his secondary groups. The contradiction between these two sets of relationships is perhaps the basis of many of our disorders. In the feudal and early industrial periods there may have been greater continuity between primary and secondary groups. The individual participant was more suggestible, perhaps more docile, and perhaps more amenable to the disorder of suggestion, namely hysteria.

Neurotic Expressions and Cultural Rituals. Neurotic defenses and cultural rituals differ in their dimensions of reality. A neurotic defense is the individualized result of an anxiety-ridden conflict. Ritualistic behavior is a learned type of social conformity. Even on a collective level a neurotic experience, as expressed by social contagion, differs from culturally stylized rituals. Since hysterical persons are suggestible and can imitate other persons, their hysterical outbursts can be precipitated by the hysterical reactions of other persons. Consider the following incident of "social contagion" which occurred during the early period of industrialization in England:

> At a cotton manufactory at Hodden Bridge, in Lancashire, a girl, on the fifteenth of February, 1787, put a mouse in the bosom of another girl, who had a great dread of mice. The girl was immediately thrown into a fit, and continued in it with the most violent convulsions for 24 hours. On the following day, three more girls were seized

[32] See Franz Alexander, *Fundamentals of Psychoanalysis* (New York: W. W. Norton & Company, 1948); Franz Alexander, *Psychosomatic Medicine,* pp. 101–111 (New York: W. W. Norton & Company, 1950).

in the same manner; and on the seventeenth, six more. By this time the alarm was so great that the whole work, in which 200 or 300 were employed, was totally stopped and the idea prevailed that a particular disease had been introduced by a bag of cotton opened in the house. On Sunday, the eighteenth, Dr. St. Clare was sent for from Preston; before he arrived three more were seized, and during the night and the morning of the nineteenth, eleven more, making in all 24. Of these, 21 were young women, two were girls of about ten years of age, and one man who had been much fatigued with holding the girls.[33]

Some girls lived away from the mill and did not even see the other girls, but were completely overcome by what they heard. They believed that a plague spread from the cotton. These convulsions, which revealed intense anxiety, were so fierce that four or five persons had to prevent some girls from tearing their hair or dashing their heads against the floors or walls. The fits lasted from fifteen minutes to twenty-four hours. This social contagion was eventually stopped by the doctor who had a portable electric machine and induced electrical shocks into the patients. Also, when the group heard that the symptoms were "merely nervous" and were not introduced by the cotton and were easily cured, no new persons were affected. To dissipate the disorder still further, they were given a "cheerful glass" and joined in a dance. On the twentieth of February they danced, and the next day all were at work except for two or three who were weakened by their fits.

From this description, not all persons who saw the seizures became convulsive. In addition, the spread of these seizures was not culturally sanctioned and was not stylized into ritualistic behavior. Those persons who were neurotically predisposed were most influenced in this social-contagion process and thus responded in this imitative manner.

Cultural rituals which superficially resemble hysterical seizures differ basically from them. For example, among African and South American Negro groups, the participants in certain magicoreligious rites may roll on the ground, mutter meaningless phrases, or assume a totally immobile posture. But these trancelike conditions and seizures are learned and stylized in the particular group. The ritualistic behavior is limited to specific deities. The periods when the

[33] *Gentlemen's Magazine*, March, 1787, p. 268. Quoted in Robert E. Park and Ernest W. Burgess, *Introduction to the Science of Sociology*, pp. 878–879 (Chicago: University of Chicago Press, 1924).

individual performs these rituals are designated by others in the tribe. The participants in these rites comprise all types of persons of the particular society. Moreover, the persons who are never possessed seem to be far less adjusted than those persons who do participate in these ceremonies.[34]

> . . . such designations as hysteria, autohypnosis, compulsion have come to rest easily on the tongue. Employed solely as descriptive terms, their use in technical analysis of the possession phenomenon may be of some utility. But the connotation they carry of psychic instability, emotional imbalance, departure from normality recommends the use of other words that do not invite such a distortion of cultural reality. For in these Negro societies the interpretation given behavior under possession . . . falls entirely in the realm of understandable, predictable, normal behavior. This behavior is known and recognized by all members as something which may come to any one of them, and is to be welcomed not only for the psychological security that derives from assurance of oneness with the powers of the universe it affords, but also for the status, economic gain, esthetic expression and emotional release it vouchsafes the devotee.

This type of confused thinking which attempts to explain group phenomena on an individual level is called "reductionism." It is evident in the attempt to characterize the Japanese people as compulsive neurotics because of their fondness for bathing and cleanliness, or to liken ritualistic taboos to individualized phobias.[35] Cultural dynamics and personality dynamics may have analogous features but are on different dimensions. Hence group practices which are shared and collectively approved cannot be analyzed in the same way as individual aberrations.

Summary

Hysteria, phobia, and compulsivity comprise three neurotic defenses which arise to ward off anxiety. Since these defenses do not necessarily succeed in covering the anxiety, the neurosis is frequently mingled with anxiety. These neurotic forms have certain basic similarities, such as an insatiability of behavior which is necessary for managing tensions created by anxiety, repetitive behavior, and a retrenched personal organization.

[34] Melville J. Herskovits, *Man and His Works,* pp. 66–68 (New York: Alfred A. Knopf, Inc., 1948).
[35] Hermann M. Spitzer, "Psychoanalytic Approaches to the Japanese Character," *Psychoanalysis and the Social Sciences,* edited by Geza Roheim, pp. 131–156 (New York: International Universities Press, Inc., 1947).

Developmental and dynamic differences are evident in these disorders. The hysteric tends to be more suggestible, less disposed to conceptualize his conflicts, and has a weaker hold on himself than the compulsive.

Hysteria and psychosomatic disorders, which are related to obsession compulsion, vary in frequency by historic period, social class, and culture. Hysterical disorders seem to have been more prevalent during the pre-industrial era, but psychosomatic and obsessive disorders seem to be more prevalent during the contemporary industrial period, especially among the urban dwellers.

Selected Readings

Abeles, M., and Paul Schilder, "A Psychogenic Loss of Personal Identity," *Archives of Neurology and Psychiatry*, 1935, 34, pp. 587–604.

Brill, A. A., "Piblokto or Hysteria Among Peary's Eskimos," *Journal of Nervous and Mental Disease*, 1913, 40, pp. 514–521.

Cooper, John, "Mental Disease Situations in Certain Cultures," *Journal of Abnormal and Social Psychology*, 1934, XXIX, pp. 10–17.

Despert, J. Louise, "Anxiety, Phobias and Fears in Young Children," *The Nervous Child*, January, 1946, 5:1, pp. 8–24.

Halliday, James, *Psychosocial Medicine* (New York: W. W. Norton & Company, 1948).

Janet, Pierre, *Major Symptoms of Hysteria* (New York: The Macmillan Company, 1907).

Jersild, Arthur J., *Child Psychology*, Chap. VIII, *Feeling, Emotion, and Fear* (New York: Prentice-Hall, Inc., 1947).

Leonard, William Ellery, *The Locomotive God* (New York: Appleton-Century-Crofts, Inc., 1927).

Masserman, Jules H., *Principles of Dynamic Psychiatry*, pp. 32–35 (Philadelphia: W. B. Saunders Company, 1946).

Peck, M. W., "A Case of Multiple Personality: Hysteria or Dementia Praecox," *Journal of Abnormal and Social Psychology*, April–March, 1922–1923, XVII, pp. 274–291.

Prince, Morton, *The Dissociation of a Personality* (New York: Longmans, Green & Co., Inc., 1906).

———, "The Theory of Psychogenesis of Multiple Personality," *Journal of Abnormal Psychology*, 1920–1921, XV, pp. 67–135.

Stengel, S. E., "On the Etiology of the Fugue States," *Journal of Mental Science*, 1949, 87, pp. 572–599.

Young, Kimball, *Personality and Problems of Adjustment* (New York: Appleton-Century-Crofts, Inc., 1947).

Ziegler, L. H., "Hysterical Fugues," *Journal of the American Medical Association*, 1933, 101, pp. 571–576.

CHAPTER EIGHT

Social Characteristics of the Psychoses

Schizophrenia (sometimes called dementia praecox) and manic depression are the two most frequent psychoses which involve personality changes without definite organic pathology. Schizophrenia usually denotes disorientation, emotional apathy, and social withdrawal. Manic depression usually denotes a mood disorder, whether of unwarranted elation, dejection, or of cycles of both. These two disorders differ markedly too in their social characteristics. Different rates exist for size of community, for types of concentration in urban areas, for age and sex, and for socioeconomic status and occupation, as well as for race, ethnic group, nativity, and marital status.[1]

Urban-Rural Differences. What influence does type of community have upon schizophrenic and manic-depressive psychoses? We must remember that the commitment of a psychotic to a mental hospital cannot be considered apart from the judgments of the family and community and apart from the accessible hospital facilities. The disordered person may function more easily and may be more tolerated in a rural area than in a metropolitan area, and is less likely to be committed to a mental hospital. Perhaps this factor may contribute in some measure to the higher rates of disordered behavior in the urban area, particularly for schizophrenics. But these differences do not apply to the distribution of manic depressives.

The standardized rates for schizophrenia during 1933, based upon the 1930 population, show 1.92 times more schizophrenics committed from urban than from rural areas. These differences apply

[1] See Chapter Two for differences of body type and temperament as related to schizophrenia and manic depression.

for the sexes separately. The urban males had 1.79 and the urban females had 2.07 times as many commitments as their rural counterparts.[2] In short, about twice as many urban as rural schizophrenics had been committed to hospital care.

The manic depressives show a far smaller difference. Manic depressives are committed 1.28 times more frequently from urban than from rural settlements. This discrepancy also applies for the sexes separately. The urban groups had 1.15 times as many males and 1.43 times as many females as the rural group.[3]

This difference between the two major psychoses is shown even more clearly when size of city is considered. Pollack found that for the years 1915 to 1920 the rates of schizophrenics (8,518 cases) in New York increased with size of city. The rates varied from 11.7 per 100,000 inhabitants in cities between 20,000 and 50,000, to 21 in New York City. Landis and Page found that the rates of schizophrenia increased as the size of the city increased. On one extreme, the metropolis of New York City had 28.7 patients per 100,000 of the general population, while the rural communities of 2,500 or less people had 14.8 patients. The manic depressives, on the other hand, had 13.3 patients per 100,000 population in urban areas and 10.0 in rural areas. About one third as many manic depressives come from the metropolitan as from the rural areas. In fact, for the manic depressives, the highest proportion of hospital commitments, 14.1, is in cities between 100,000 and 200,000 people.[4]

On the basis of the evidence presented, it seems that schizophrenics are more frequently hospitalized than manic depressives in more densely populated areas. These differences in rates may be indices of actual breakdown and are rates of hospital commitments.

Urban Areas and Psychotic Disorders. Although no convincing studies have been made of the residential distributions of neurotics, many investigations have traced the residential patterns of psychotics, such as schizophrenics and manic depressives. Faris and Dunham initiated ecological studies of these disordered types for Chicago and Providence, R.I.[5] Their conclusions have been cor-

[2] Carney Landis and James D. Page, *Society and Mental Disease*, p. 164 (New York: Rinehart & Company, Inc., 1938).

[3] *Ibid.*

[4] *Ibid.*

[5] Robert E. L. Faris and H. Warren Dunham, *Mental Disorders in Urban Areas* (Chicago: University of Chicago Press, 1938).

roborated, with slight variations, by other investigators for such cities as St. Louis, Cleveland, Omaha, Kansas City, Milwaukee, and Peoria.[6] The patterns of residential distributions of schizophrenia and manic depression in the urban community differ, and the differences will be analyzed in terms of the social factors which might have contributed to the breakdown.

TABLE 4

AVERAGE ANNUAL STANDARDIZED RATES PER 100,000 GENERAL POPULATION OF FIRST ADMISSIONS TO THE NEW YORK STATE HOSPITALS (1929–1931) BY PSYCHOSIS AND SIZE OF CITY.[*]

Diagnosis	Total Urban	New York City	Size of City				
			100,000–200,000	25,000–100,000	10,000–25,000	2,500–10,000	2,500 or Less
Schizophrenia	27.0	28.7	22.6	21.3	19.7	20.1	14.8
Manic depression	12.8	13.3	14.1	11.7	11.3	12.7	10.0
Total	39.8	42.0	36.7	33.0	31.0	32.8	24.8

[*] Data taken from Carney Landis and James D. Page, *Modern Society and Mental Disease*, p. 164 (New York: Rinehart & Company, Inc., 1938).

Schizophrenia. The rates for schizophrenia vary in different areas of the city. They are highest in those communities adjacent to the center of the city and progressively decline with distance from the center of the city. (See Map 1.) On the basis of zonal patterns, Faris and Dunham found, from a study of 10,575 cases, that the rates vary from 102.3 per 100,000 residents in Zone I to 15.8 per 100,000 residents in the northern periphery of Zone VI. This residential pattern of decreasing rates of schizophrenia includes the cases from both state and private hospitals. It conforms to the residential scatter of all psychoses and to the pattern of other indices of personal disorganization, such as delinquency, adult crime, prostitution, drug addiction, and families on relief. The main fact is that schizophrenia is

[6] Stuart A. Queen, "The Ecological Study of Mental Disorder," *American Sociological Review*, April, 1940, V, pp. 201–209; Howard W. Green, *Persons Admitted to the Cleveland State Hospital, 1928–1937* (Cleveland: Cleveland Health Council, 1939); Clarence W. Schroeder, "Mental Disorders in Cities," *American Journal of Sociology*, July, 1942, XLVIII, pp. 40–47.

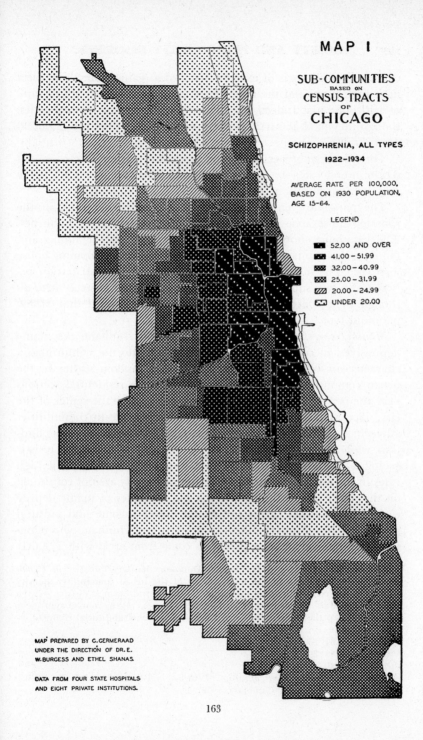

MAP I

SUB-COMMUNITIES
BASED ON
CENSUS TRACTS
OF
CHICAGO

SCHIZOPHRENIA, ALL TYPES
1922-1934

AVERAGE RATE PER 100,000,
BASED ON 1930 POPULATION,
AGE 15-64.

LEGEND

52.00 AND OVER
41.00 - 51.99
32.00 - 40.99
25.00 - 31.99
20.00 - 24.99
UNDER 20.00

MAP PREPARED BY G. GERMERAAD
UNDER THE DIRECTION OF DR. E.
W. BURGESS AND ETHEL SHANAS.

DATA FROM FOUR STATE HOSPITALS
AND EIGHT PRIVATE INSTITUTIONS.

163

concentrated in areas of extreme social disorganization; these areas have high rates, and the majority of areas have relatively low rates of schizophrenia. Indeed the higher fourth of these communities, though they have about 24 per cent of the population, had about 40 per cent of the cases.[7]

Though the subtypes follow the residential pattern of the general schizophrenic category, some distinct differences are noted in specific areas of concentration.

The paranoids (2,154 cases) tend to have higher rates in the rooming-house areas than in the near-by residential communities. The catatonics, however (1,360 cases), cluster in the immigrant-family areas and have a comparatively low rate in the rooming-house districts.[8] The hebephrenics have an intermediate distribution between the two subtypes in areas adjacent to the city's center, although their concentration inclines somewhat toward that of the paranoid type.[9]

Manic Depression. According to Faris and Dunham, the manic depressives, in contrast to the schizophrenics, do not conform to a characteristic ecological pattern but have a random scatter in the urban community. High rates prevail in some residential sections near the periphery as well as in some sections near the center of the city. (See Map 2.) The highest rates, however, are in communities adjacent to or near the center of the city.[10] Mowrer, however, finds that while the manic depressives do not follow the characteristic ecological pattern, the scatter is not completely random. The high rates in the areas adjacent to the center of the city are not continued on the south side of the city, which has low rates of manic depression, although these areas are in the lower income and cultural groups.[11] Thus, Mowrer differs from Faris and Dunham who maintain that manic-depressive psychoses come from areas with a "fairly

[7] Robert E. L. Faris and H. Warren Dunham, *Mental Disorders in Urban Areas*, p. 48. According to the zonal theory of the urban community, the city consists of five concentric zones including (1) the central business district, (2) the zone of transition, (3) the zone of workingmen's homes, (4) the zone of apartment houses, and (5) the commuters' zone. Indices of personal and social disorganization concentrate in the zone of transition.

[8] *Ibid.*, pp. 84, 85, 92, 93.

[9] *Ibid.*, pp. 88, 89.

[10] *Ibid.*, p. 66.

[11] Ernest R. Mowrer, *Disorganization: Personal and Social*, pp. 419–421 (Philadelphia: J. B. Lippincott Company, 1942).

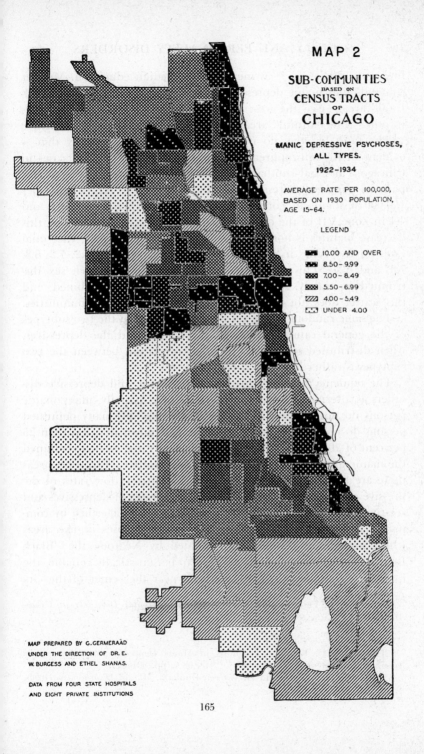

MAP 2

SUB-COMMUNITIES
BASED ON
CENSUS TRACTS
OF
CHICAGO

MANIC DEPRESSIVE PSYCHOSES,
ALL TYPES.

1922-1934

AVERAGE RATE PER 100,000,
BASED ON 1930 POPULATION,
AGE 15-64.

LEGEND

10.00 AND OVER
8.50 - 9.99
7.00 - 8.49
5.50 - 6.99
4.00 - 5.49
UNDER 4.00

MAP PREPARED BY G. GERMERAÅD
UNDER THE DIRECTION OF DR. E.
W. BURGESS AND ETHEL SHANAS.

DATA FROM FOUR STATE HOSPITALS
AND EIGHT PRIVATE INSTITUTIONS

165

high cultural level," [12] as measured by median education. Mowrer contends that manic depressives have high rates in some "low cultural" areas—e.g., the west and northwest sections—and low rates in other "low cultural" areas—e.g., the south section of Chicago.

The rates by zone do not show the range of disparity that is evident in the schizophrenic group. On the basis of 2,311 cases in Chicago, Faris and Dunham found that the zonal range is from 13.2 patients per 100,000 residents in the first zone to 9.2 patients per 100,000 residents in Zone VI in the city's northern periphery and 4.4 in Zone VII of the city's southern periphery. What is more, this decrease in rates is not always continuous. For instance, the zonal rates for five zones in the northwestern direction are 13.2, 7.2, 6.8, 7.0, and 6.3[13] This unsystematic scatter applies for each sex distributed separately, for private and state hospitals combined, and this scatter does not concentrate in the disorganized communities.

The same random ecological design is evident in the two subtypes of the general category, namely, the manics and the depressives, when distributed separately. But the correlation between the two subtypes is rather low, 104 ± 0.09.[14]

The tendency has been to regard the manic and depressive disorders as alternating phases of one disorder. Actually, many manic persons do not necessarily become depressed, and many depressed persons do not become manic. Rennie has shown that less than 25 per cent of 208 cases of the manic-depressive category had combined the manic and depressive features of the disorders.[15] In some areas there are high rates of manic cases but relatively low rates of depressive cases; in other areas there are high rates of depressives and relatively low rates of manics.[16] This point can be clarified by comparing the rates of manic and depressive psychoses in five areas which are almost completely populated by Negroes, the "Black Belt." Although the cases are too few to be statistically reliable, the rates for manic psychoses decline from near the center of the city

[12] Robert E. L. Faris and H. Warren Dunham, *Mental Disorders in Urban Areas*, p. 78.

[13] *Ibid.*, p. 72.

[14] *Ibid.*, p. 76.

[15] Thomas A. C. Rennie, "Prognosis in Manic Depressive Psychoses," *The American Journal of Psychiatry*, May, 1942, 98:6, pp. 801–814.

[16] See Robert E. L. Faris and H. Warren Dunham, *Mental Disorders in Urban Areas*, pp. 68–71.

to the areas away from the center. The rates for the depressive psychoses, however, tend to increase very slightly in the areas away from the center of the city.

Interpretation of the Distributions. These findings can be viewed (1) as reflecting the results of urban ecological processes and (2) as indices of the influences affecting the onset of these disorders.[17] Our concern is with the latter problem.

The advocates of the constitutional approach to disorders maintain that persons predisposed to schizophrenia remain in or gravitate to areas adjacent to the center of the city. From their assumption the lower socioeconomic levels would have a greater proportion of persons predisposed to schizophrenia. On the other hand, manic depression, which is distributed randomly among the socioeconomic strata, would tend to occur in similar proportions among all socioeconomic groups. Attempts to probe more deeply from the perspective of constitutional predisposition have not been very illuminating.[18]

Krout, from a psychoanalytic viewpoint, has read into these distributions, differences of childhood training.[19] The schizophrenics, who predominated in the lower socioeconomic levels, had an arrested development at the oral stage of infancy because of feeding difficulties. But the manic depressives, who more frequently come from the higher socioeconomic levels, had an arrested development in the anal stage of growth because of defective toilet training. First, it has not been ascertained empirically that these respective differences in feeding and toilet training hold for the lower and higher socioeconomic levels, respectively. Second, there is no definite evidence that frustrations in these different erogenous zones of the body are causally correlated with schizophrenia and manic repression, respectively. In short, this contention seems untenable.

Another interpretation is that some schizophrenics drift or remain

---

[17] There have been some criticisms of the validity of these findings. One criticism has been that the number of cases initially used for the manic-depressive group were too few. The second criticism is that the differences between the rates in the communities were due to chance and were not significant.

[18] For an analysis of the present status of the ecological approach to personal disorders, see H. Warren Dunham, "Current Status of Ecological Research in Mental Disorder," *Social Forces*, March, 1947, XXV:3, pp. 321–326.

[19] Maurice H. Krout, "A Note on Dunham's Contribution to the Ecology of the Psychoses," *American Sociological Review*, April, 1938, III, pp. 209–212.

in or near the center of the city and thus are a selected group. This interpretation implies indirectly that foreign-born white and Negro groups would have a greater tendency to schizophrenic disorders than native groups. Faris and Dunham, however, have pointed out that the rates for the foreign-born populations divided by the total foreign-born population are distributed similarly to the rates for all cases.[20] Rates for Negroes are high in areas not populated entirely by Negroes but low in areas inhabited predominantly or entirely by Negroes.[21] Although this evidence is not sufficient to invalidate the drift hypothesis, it makes the validity of the hypothesis unlikely.

The other problem concerns the downward mobility of some schizophrenics and the upward mobility of some manic depressives, particularly manics.[22] As we have pointed out, the schizophrenics most likely to drift downward would be the paranoids and hebephrenics who inhabit the "hobohemian" sections of the city. But these "hobohemian" areas comprise only a small proportion of the total cases. In addition, some schizophrenics have been born and reared in family slum areas adjacent to the central business district and were influenced apparently by the local neighborhood. Hence, this "drift" hypothesis does not explain the allocation of schizophrenia by a selective process resulting from economic maladjustment.

The other side of the coin emphasizes the influences inherent within the community. There are those who claim that communities with high rates of mobility tend to have high rates of disordered persons.[23] This may mean that the more mobile persons are

[20] Robert E. L. Faris and H. Warren Dunham, *Mental Disorders in Urban Areas*, p. 169.

[21] *Ibid.*, pp. 164–169. Faris and Dunham studied catatonics and paranoids separately between 15 and 29 and those 30 and over. They found that the younger cases of paranoids, who did not have time to drift, were concentrated in central areas as were the older cases. The younger catatonic cases had a slightly different distribution than the older cases. Seemingly, the catatonics showed a tendency to drift from the slum residential areas to the hobo areas. See Robert E. L. Faris, *Social Disorganization*, p. 231, footnote (New York: The Ronald Press Company, 1948).

[22] See Morris S. Schwartz, "The Economic and Spatial Mobility of Paranoid Schizophrenics and Manic Depressives" (University of Chicago: unpublished master's thesis, August, 1946).

[23] Christopher Tietze, Paul Lemkau, and Marcia Cooper, "Personal Disorders and Spatial Mobility," *American Journal of Sociology*, July, 1942, XLIII, pp. 29–39.

more likely to be predisposed to psychotic disorders than are the less mobile. On the one hand, it can be argued that excessive personal mobility may create personal instability which may contribute to an eventual breakdown. On the other hand, it may be contended that, in areas of very marked mobility, the anonymity and isolation among the residents would deprive each person of those intimate social relations which are necessary for sustaining an ordered condition.

Also in "family" slum neighborhoods competitive relationships are claimed to be harsh. Since social relationships are presumably more harsh than in other areas, the individual resident adjusts with difficulty. In part, this may be true, but it is not known whether this factor is crucial. Indeed, before they break down, prepsychotic persons from the lower income groups have experiences in different groups through their job experiences. Hence, a psychotic breakdown cannot be attributed merely to the social relationships within the community, at least not for all cases. The catatonics who are committed at a relatively early age may be influenced by the play patterns and by the modes of relationships with juvenile and adolescent groups who may contribute to the onset of their personal disorders.[24] Nonetheless, despite the harsh relationships among lower income groups, these groups do not always practice exclusion as intensely as do the same age groups in upper-middle socioeconomic levels.[25]

The different value judgments and the reasons for committing disordered persons to mental institutions in different communities may also affect the ecological distributions. Are there uniform criteria in this commitment process in all types of communities? Owen maintains that certain types of disorders may lead to commitment in one community but not in another.[26] Faris contends that the persons committed to mental hospitals are so "extremely insane" that few families would be wealthy enough to care for them outside the

---

[24] H. Warren Dunham, "The Social Personality of the Catatonic-Schizophrenic," *American Journal of Sociology*, May, 1944, 49, pp. 508–518.

[25] Based on case studies from these areas.

[26] Mary Bess Owen, "Alternative Hypotheses for the Explanation of Some of Faris' and Dunham's Results," *American Journal of Sociology*, July, 1941, 47, pp. 48–51.

hospital.[27] Very likely most schizophrenics and manic depressives may be committed to mental hospitals, but it is also known that some cases are reported long after the breakdown has occurred, or they may not be reported at all.[28]

Lemkau, Tietze, and Cooper, in a survey of a Baltimore community, found that 367 psychotics were hospitalized and that 73 psychotics were not hospitalized. Age and sex seemed to influence the commitment of psychotics in this community. Nonhospitalized patients were somewhat older than the hospitalized—median age, 51 against 43—and were more often females—59 per cent against 46 per cent. The racial distribution was the same for both groups.[29]

In general, ecological distributions are significant in showing the communities where the varied disorders are concentrated and where the disorders are sparse. From these facts, we can analyze more intensively the social influences upon the persons within these communities. The disparate concentrations of these disorders in different communities, however, are only indices to the whole universe of personal relationships which disordered persons experienced until they broke down and were then committed by others to mental hospitals.

Age and Sex. Schizophrenics and manic depressives showed considerable, almost contrasting, variations by age and by sex. More male than female schizophrenics were committed to hospitals for permanent care; the respective rates were 55.6 and 44.4 per cent. But far fewer male than female manic depressives were committed; the respective percentages were 36.6 and 63.4.[30]

Schizophrenics were hospitalized at a younger age than were manic-depressive groups. Schizophrenics had a younger median age (30.0 years) than manic depressives (40.1 years). The vast majority of schizophrenics were admitted *before* 35 (67.2 per cent of all first admissions), but the majority of manic depressives were admitted *after* 35 (63.2 per cent of all first admissions).

[27] Robert E. L. Faris, *Social Disorganization,* pp. 230, 231 (New York: The Ronald Press Company, 1948).

[28] Robert W. White, *The Abnormal Personality,* pp. 564, 565 (New York: The Ronald Press Company, 1948).

[29] Paul Lemkau, Christopher Tietze, and Marcia Cooper, "Mental Hygiene Problems in an Urban District," *Mental Hygiene,* 1942, 26, pp. 275–288.

[30] *Patients in Mental Institutions, 1946,* p. 21 (Washington, D.C.: Bureau of the Census, U.S. Department of Commerce, 1949). All the following figures in this section are for 1946.

The male schizophrenics had a younger median-age onset (28.5 years) than the females (32.2 years), but the manic-depressive males had a slightly older median-age onset (41.2 years) than the females (39.6 years).

Of the subtypes of schizophrenia, the catatonics had the youngest average age at the time of breakdown (28.5 years), the paranoids the oldest average age (38.6 years), and the hebephrenic and simple types were in between (32.5).[31]

Sex. The comparative ratios of the different disorders reveal that more men than women become schizophrenic—the ratio is 1 to 0.87—but that more women than men become manic-depressive—the ratio being 1.25 to 1.

Economic Status. The economic status of manic depressives averages higher than that of schizophrenics. The criteria for this difference include residential location, which has been discussed, rentals, admissions to private hospitals, and occupation.

Faris and Dunham have found that manic depressives come from higher economic and social levels than do schizophrenics. Manic depressives came from communities in which the median rental was $61.68 per month. Schizophrenics came from communities in which the median rental was $33.45 per month. Even when the private-hospital cases were eliminated, the median rental of the manic-depressives' communities was $43.44 or above.[32]

Schizophrenics have far higher rates of admission to state hospitals, but manic depressives have higher rates to private hospitals. This difference obtains particularly for females.[33]

Occupation. Since schizophrenics cluster in lower socioeconomic areas, we might expect that they would come from the less skilled occupations.[34] In a study of 3,332 white male schizophrenics between the ages of 20 and 49 from the Chicago area, Clark found that the

---

[31] Computed from data taken from Robert E. L. Faris and H. Warren Dunham, *Mental Disorders in Urban Areas*, pp. 85, 89, 93.

[32] *Ibid.*, p. 79.

[33] The female rates for manic depression were usually higher than for schizophrenia in the private hospitals. Some investigators contend that the psychiatrists give the more hopeful diagnosis of manic depression to patients in private hospitals. Nonetheless, it is also possible that, despite this inclination in diagnosis in private hospitals, the different percentages of manic depression in state mental hospitals and in private mental hospitals may be true differences.

[34] See Franz J. Kallman, *The Genetics of Schizophrenia*, p. 31 (New York: J. J. Augustin, Inc., 1938).

TABLE 5

| | State Hospitals | | Private Hospitals* | |
Year	Schizophrenics	Manic Depressives	Schizophrenics	Manic Depressives
1939	20.5	9.6	15.1	15.1
1941	21.0	8.4	16.1	15.8
1942	20.8	9.0	15.6	14.7
1943	19.8	7.9	14.9	14.5
1944	20.0	8.6	14.8	15.8
1945	19.4	8.3	13.6	14.4

* Data taken from *Patients in Mental Institutions* (Washington, D. C.: Bureau of the Census, U.S. Department of Commerce, 1939, 1941, 1942, 1943, 1944, 1945).

schizophrenia increased as the occupations declined in prestige and in income.[35] The occupational groups with rates of admission below the average for the total group studied included large proprietors, professionals, major salesmen, small tradesmen, the clergy, teachers, engineers, subexecutives, office workers, and salesmen. Those occupational groups with higher rates than the average included skilled workers, domestics, semiskilled and unskilled workers, as well as minor governmental employees, peddlers, errand boys, and office boys.[36] In brief, persons in high-income and prestige occupations were less likely to be hospitalized as schizophrenics than were those from the lower occupational groups. The correlation between schizophrenic rates and occupational prestige groups was −81.

Clark inferred from his study that the schizophrenics are hindered by their personality difficulties from securing more responsible jobs. Initially, they came from the lower socioeconomic levels but apparently were unable to rise vocationally. Secondly, they derived slight job satisfaction. Those in more highly paid jobs may have derived greater job satisfaction than did those in the lower-paid jobs. Those in lower-paid jobs with less prestige may have been continually harassed by a sense of failure because of their inability to achieve a better occupation.

[35] Robert E. Clark, "The Relationship of Schizophrenia to Occupational Income and Occupational Prestige," *American Sociological Review*, June, 1948, 13, pp. 325–330.

[36] *Ibid.*, pp. 325–330. The age factor also affected the differences.

With reference to regularity of employment among schizophrenics, Pollock and his associates found that 51.2 per cent worked regularly and 46.3 per cent worked irregularly, that the attitudes of the patients toward their employers were predominantly favorable (85.6 per cent), and that antagonistic relationships were in the distinct minority (10.6 per cent). These same attitudes presumably prevailed toward the fellow employees.

Manic Depression. Even though the occupational levels of the manic depressives tend to be higher than those of schizophrenics there are no definite relationships between manic depression and type of occupation, either by prestige or by income. The manic depressives vary from the conventional patterns of occupational correlations in the same manner that they do in the ecological distributions. This can be seen in the comparative rank-order correlations of the following psychoses, in Table 6.

TABLE 6

RANK-ORDER COEFFICIENTS OF CORRELATION CALCULATED OVER SEVENTEEN OCCUPATIONAL GROUPS BETWEEN VARIOUS PSYCHOSES, RATES FOR WHITE MALES. FIRST ADMISSIONS AND THE OCCUPATIONAL FACTORS OF INCOME AND PRESTIGE [*]

Type of Psychoses	Occupational Income	Prestige Factors
Schizophrenia: all types	−0.71	−0.81
Manic depression	−0.02	−0.01
Senile psychoses and psychoses with arteriosclerosis	−0.57	−0.50
Alcoholic psychoses	−0.78	−0.92
General paralysis	−0.75	−0.73
Other psychoses	−0.53	−0.63
All psychoses	−0.75	−0.83

[*] Data from Robert E. Clark, "Psychoses, Income and Occupational Prestige," *American Journal of Sociology,* 1949, LIV:5, p. 440.

Clark found that engineers, small tradesmen, domestic employees, and office workers had rates of manic depression which were significantly below the rates of all occupations, but salesmen, subexecutives, waiters, the clergy, teachers, and errand boys had rates which were significantly higher than the rates for all occupations.[37] It is

[37] Robert E. Clark, "The Relationship of Occupation and Various Psychoses" (University of Chicago: unpublished Ph.D. thesis, 1947).

apparent that there is no clear relationship between occupational income and prestige and manic depression, and that those in higher occupations are as susceptible to manic depression as are those in lower occupations.

Ethnic and Nativity Groups. Are certain races or ethnic groups more susceptible to schizophrenia and manic depression than others?

Schizophrenia. It appears that rates of schizophrenia are higher among Negroes than they are among whites. In a comparative study of the rates of first admission of the two groups for New York State for the years 1929 to 1931, Malzberg found that the standardized rates for Negroes were 51.1 per 100,000 and that those for whites were 25.7 per 100,000—which constitutes a ratio of approximately 2 to 1.[38]

Dayton computed the rates for schizophrenia in Massachusetts in the period from 1917 to 1933. He found that, although the Negroes comprised 2.83 per cent of the admissions, they represented only 1.2 per cent of the general population.[39] These higher rates of schizophrenia among Negroes are believed to be resultants of their greater poverty, younger age composition, and greater concentration in large cities, because all these factors correlate positively with schizophrenia.[40]

Pollock found that the foreign-born whites had rates twice as high as the native-born whites—30.2 to 15.2 for 100,000 of their respective populations—with native-born of foreign-born parents having intermediate rates—18.5 per 100,000 population.[41] The respective rates for native-born whites, natives of foreign-born parents, and the foreign born were 22.2, 26.4, and 32.8 per 100,000 of the same nativity group. From these figures it appears that as a group assimilates, the probability of breakdown declines. Since the assimilated groups correlate positively with higher socioeconomic levels, the

---

[38] Benjamin Malzberg, "Mental Disease Among Negroes in New York State," *Human Biology,* December, 1935, VII, p. 486.

[39] Neil A. Dayton, *New Facts on Mental Disorders,* p. 357 (Springfield, Ill.: Charles C. Thomas, Publisher, 1940).

[40] S. P. Rosenthal, "Racial Differences in the Incidence of Mental Disease," *Journal of Negro Education,* July, 1934, p. 490.

[41] Horatio Pollock, "Prevalence of Manic-Depressive Psychoses in Relation to Sex, Age, Environment, Nativity and Race," *Manic-Depressive Psychoses: Association for Research in Nervous and Mental Disease* (Baltimore: The Williams & Wilkins Company, 1931).

rates for those in the higher socioeconomic levels also would be lower.

In a study of selected communities in Chicago, Faris and Dunham found that though the foreign born comprised 35.3 per cent of the population, they had 61.6, 59.6, and 56.8 per cent, respectively, of the paranoid, hebephrenic, and catatonic commitments.[42] The native-born whites, who comprised 60.3 per cent of the population, had 32.3, 33.7, and 36.8 per cent, respectively, of the paranoid, hebephrenic, and catatonic disorders. The Negroes, who constituted 4.4 per cent of the population, had 3.7, 5.7, and 6.4 per cent, respectively, of the paranoid, hebephrenic, and catatonics committed.

Manic Depression. As among schizophrenics, rates of first admissions to state mental hospitals of manic depressives are higher among Negroes than among whites. In New York State the Negroes had a 1.7 times higher crude rate than whites and a 1.5 times higher standardized rate. The average annual rates of first admissions in New York State hospitals from 1929 to 1931 were 20.0 Negro manic depressives per 100,000 of the same general population 15 years of age and over, and 13.3 whites per 100,000 of the same general population 15 years of age and over.[43]

In a study of first admissions to New York State Civil Hospitals for the period 1918 to 1920, Pollock found that the standardized rates for manic depressives were 6.5 per 100,000 of the population for white males and 11.5 for white females, while the rates for Negro males and females were 8.8 and 20.8, respectively. Generally, it would seem that the Negroes, particularly female Negroes, are more disposed to manic-depressive disorders, or at least to being hospitalized for manic-depressive disorders, than are the whites.

However, when the category of manic depression is subdivided into manic and depressive subtypes, it seems that the concentration of cases among the Negroes is in the manic rather than in the depressive subtype.[44]

[42] Robert E. L. Faris and H. Warren Dunham, *Mental Disorders in Urban Areas,* pp. 104, 105.

[43] Benjamin Malzberg, *Social and Biological Aspects of Mental Disease,* p. 252 (Utica, N.Y.: State Hospitals Press, 1940). See also Benjamin Malzberg, "Mental Disease Among Negroes in New York State," *Human Biology,* December, 1935, VII, p. 486.

[44] Horatio Pollock, "Prevalence of Manic-Depressive Psychoses in Relation to Sex, Age, Environment, Nativity and Race," *Manic-Depressive Psychoses: Association for Research in Nervous and Mental Disease,* p. 762 (Baltimore: The Williams & Wilkins Company, 1931).

The early observations by O'Malley, Green, and Lewis and Hubbard maintained that manic depression was relatively infrequent and that depressive psychosis was rare among the Negroes.[45] The rates of manic depression which we have presented for New York State would seem to refute the notion about the low rates of manic depression generally among Negroes, unless the influence of the urban community may have contributed to this increase.

Faris and Dunham have presented the percentages of subtypes of manic depressives admitted to mental hospitals from the Chicago area. Although the number of cases is relatively small, still these differences may be clues. They found that the foreign-born white and the native white of foreign or mixed parents had higher percentages for depressive psychosis than for manic psychosis; the native white of native parents had the highest percentage for mixed, i.e., manic and depressive psychosis, and the lowest percentage for depressive. The Negroes had the highest percentage among the manics and the lowest rate among the depressives.

The different rates for manic and depressive psychoses are confirmed by data from two state hospitals in Alabama. In the Searcy State Mental Hospital only Negroes were patients. In the Bryce State Mental Hospital, only whites comprised the first admissions. In the Searcy hospital there were far fewer depressives than manics. In Bryce hospital the difference was not so marked. Although the higher rates of manics among Negro patients may possibly have been complicated by the fact that some catatonics might have been diagnosed as manics, still this does not explain away the wide discrepancy between the two disorders.[46]

Depressive Negroes in the South may be tolerated in their culture to a greater than manics. That is, the depressives may be quiet and may not affect others, but the manics may act out and become threatening. But even apart from social definition of the

[45] Mary K. O'Malley, "Psychosis in the Colored Race," *American Journal of Insanity*, 1914, 71, pp. 309–337; E. M. Green, "Manic Depressive Psychoses in the Negro," *American Journal of Insanity*, 1917, 73, pp. 619–626; Nolan D. C. Lewis and Lois D. Hubbard, "Manic Depressive Reactions in Negroes," *Manic Depressive Psychoses*, pp. 779–817 (Washington, D.C.: Nervous and Mental Disease Publishing Company, 1928).

[46] Nolan D. C. Lewis and Lois Hubbard, "Manic Depressive Reactions in Negroes," *Manic Depressive Psychoses*, pp. 779–817 (Washington, D.C.: Nervous and Mental Disease Publishing Company, 1928).

disorders, it appears that there may be some aspect of the culture which leads to these reactions. For when the proportions of these two disorders among Negroes are compared with the proportions among whites, most of whom are native-born, the Negroes have a far lower percentage of depressives.

With regard to nativity, the foreign born had higher crude rates than the native born by about 82 per cent. The respective rates were 14.9 and 8.2 per 100,000 of the respective populations. The native born of native parents had the lowest rates (7.6), but their rate did not differ significantly from the rates of native children of foreign born (8.4) or from natives of mixed parents (9.9).[47]

When these nativity rates are compared by age groups, however, the foreign born had higher rates than the natives of native parents before the age of 50 but had lower rates after the age of 50. Although the natives of foreign-born parents had lower rates than the foreign born before the age of 45, after the age of 45 they had higher rates. The native born of mixed parents had the highest rates of manic depression after 45.[48]

However, when the rates of manic depression are standardized by sex, age, and environment, the foreign-born males and the native-born males had about identical rates, namely 10.7 and 10.1, respectively. The higher rates among the foreign born were for females, the manic-depressive rate being 19.0 for foreign-born females and 14.4 for native-born females.[49]

Marital Status. On the basis of Malzberg's study of first admissions to New York State civil hospitals, schizophrenic single persons had the highest standardized rates of first admissions but manic-depressive divorced persons had the highest rates of first admissions.[50] From Table 7 it is also apparent that both male and female manic depressives had higher first admission rates among single than among married persons, but the difference between single and mar-

[47] Benjamin Malzberg, *Social and Biological Aspects of Mental Disease*, pp. 164, 165 (Utica, N.Y.: State Hospitals Press, 1940).

[48] *Ibid.*, pp. 204–205.

[49] *Ibid.*, p. 171.

[50] *Ibid.* Landis and Page found that the divorced group had the highest rates among the schizophrenics. Their rates for divorced male and female schizophrenics were 4.1 and 4.4 as against the respective rates in the general population of 1.2 and 1.3. Carney Landis and James D. Page, *Modern Society and Mental Disease*, p. 166 (New York: Rinehart & Co., Inc., 1938).

ried females is not very great, 19.5 to 15.7. However, female schizophrenics had over twice as many single as married persons, while the male schizophrenics had nearly six times as many single as married persons.

TABLE 7

COMPARATIVE STANDARDIZED AVERAGE ANNUAL RATES OF FIRST ADMISSIONS OF
MANIC DEPRESSIVES AND SCHIZOPHRENICS TO ALL INSTITUTIONS FOR MENTAL DISEASE
IN NEW YORK STATE, 1929–31, BY MARITAL STATUS*

Marital Status†	Schizophrenia			Manic-Depression		
	Male	Female	Total	Male	Female	Total
Single	64.9 ± 1.3	46.9 ± 1.2	55.4 ± 0.9	15.3 ± 0.6	19.5 ± 0.8	17.2 ± 0.5
Married	11.9 ± 0.4	19.3 ± 0.6	15.4 ± 0.4	7.7 ± 0.4	15.7 ± 0.5	11.7 ± 0.3
Widowed	43.1 ± 3.2	26.2 ± 1.5	34.4 ± 1.5	24.3 ± 2.4	15.1 ± 1.1	19.5 ± 1.1
Divorced	49.0 ± 10.0	54.6 ± 9.0	51.3 ± 6.7	27.0 ± 7.5	42.8 ± 8.0	34.8 ± 5.5

* Data from Benjamin Malzberg, *Social and Biological Aspects of Mental Disease*, pp. 127, 128 (Utica, New York: State Hospitals Press, 1940).

† By standardized rate is meant the proportion per 100,000 of the general population of the same marital status 15 years of age and over.

In general, if we would discount the age factor, it would seem that schizophrenics tend to remain single in far greater proportions than do manic depressives. But since schizophrenics break down at an earlier age than do manic depressives the discrepancy in rates would probably be lower if age were held constant. On the other hand, a greater proportion of single male than single female schizophrenics are admitted to mental hospitals. Seemingly, many male schizophrenics come from the lower socioeconomic levels, are hindered in the courtship process by their seclusive ways, and find it hard to keep a job or advance in a job; these factors may deter or prevent marriage.

Whether marriage tends to reduce the number of schizophrenic breakdowns is still an unsettled point. Hamilton and Wall found that 49 out of 100 schizophrenic females were married and that 32 had children. Out of 32 cases, 25 became psychotic within one year after a pregnancy, abortion, or childbirth.[51] This may mean that

[51] Donald M. Hamilton and James H. Wall, "The Hospital Treatment of Dementia Praecox," *The American Journal of Psychiatry*, November, 1948, 105:5, pp. 347–348.

bearing children may precipitate a schizophrenic disorder among the predisposed women. Marital discord, as evidenced by the high proportions of divorced schizophrenics and manic depressives, may contribute to the breakdown of those who are predisposed. But the function of the spouse in this breakdown process awaits further inquiry.

Concerning the types of schizophrenics, Faris and Dunham found that male hebephrenics had the highest proportion of single persons admitted, 73.6 per cent; the catatonics were next with 68.2 per cent, and the paranoids last with 56.9 per cent. For these same categories the females had the respective percentages of 37.9, 23.1, and 29.7.[52] Since marital status is influenced by age, this would account for the least percentage of single persons among paranoids who break down at a later age than do the other two schizophrenic subtypes. But the catatonics who break down at an earlier age than hebephrenics had a higher percentage of married persons. This discrepancy may be a rough clue that hebephrenics are more disorganized before the breakdown than are the catatonics.

Summary

Schizophrenia is the most frequent of all psychotic disorders, organic and personal. It tends to be more sensitive to social characteristics than does manic depression. It occurs more frequently in younger age groups. It predominates in more densely settled areas, among lower occupational and educational levels. The rates for this disorder are high in the center of the city and decrease as one moves to the city's circumference. The rates are higher among foreign-born and Negro groups than among native white groups, but rates for given nativity groups increase in areas in which the groups are in the minority. It occurs more frequently among men than women, and occurs predominantly between the ages of 20 and 35. In proportion to the same marital status in the general population, single persons have the highest rates and married persons the lowest, although married women are more prone to schizophrenia than are married men.

Manic depression seems relatively unaffected by size of commu-

---

[52] Robert E. L. Faris and H. Warren Dunham, *Mental Disorders in Urban Areas*, p. 242. The years for which these differences are shown were 1922 to 1934.

nity, has a random scatter in the urban community, is more frequent or as frequent among native white as among foreign-born white groups, is not confined to the lower occupational and educational levels, tends in fact to occur among higher socioeconomic levels, occurs at a later age than schizophrenia, is more frequent among women than men, and has a relatively high incidence among married persons.

In general, these factors indicate under what common conditions the incidence of schizophrenia and manic depression would be highest. These factors are only rough indices to the types of interpersonal relationships, attitudes, meanings, and defenses which these persons experienced before the breakdown.

Selected Readings

Clark, Robert E., "The Relationship of Schizophrenia to Occupational Income and Occupational Prestige," *American Sociological Review*, June, 1948, pp. 325–330.

———, "Psychoses Income and Occupational Prestige," *American Journal of Sociology*, 1949, 54:5, p. 44.

Dayton, Neil A., *New Facts on Mental Disorders* (Springfield, Ill.: Charles C. Thomas, Publisher, 1940).

Dunham, H. Warren, "The Ecology of the Functional Psychoses in Chicago," *American Sociological Review*, 1937, 2, pp. 467–479.

———, "Current Status of Ecological Research in Mental Disorders," *Social Forces*, March, 1947, 25:3, pp. 321–326.

Faris, Robert E. L., "Ecological Factors in Human Behavior," *Personality and the Behavior Disorders*, edited by J. McV. Hunt (New York: The Ronald Press Company, 1944).

———, and H. Warren Dunham, *Mental Disorders in Urban Areas* (Chicago: University of Chicago Press, 1939).

Green, Howard W., *Persons Admitted to the Cleveland State Hospital: 1928–1937* (Cleveland: Cleveland Health Council, 1939).

Landis, Carney, and James D. Page, *Society and Mental Disease* (New York: Rinehart & Company, Inc., 1938).

Lemkau, Paul, Christopher Tietze, and Marcia Cooper, "Mental Hygiene Problems in an Urban Area," *Mental Hygiene*, 1942, 26, pp. 275–288.

Malzberg, Benjamin, *Social and Biological Factors in Mental Disease* (Utica, N.Y.: State Hospitals Press, 1940).

Mowrer, Ernest R., *Disorganization: Personal and Social* (Philadelphia: J. B. Lippincott Company, 1942).

Owen, Mary Bess, "Alternative Hypotheses for the Explanation of Some of Faris' and Dunham's Results," *American Journal of Sociology*, July, 1941, 47, pp. 48–51.

Queen, Stuart A., "The Ecological Study of Mental Disorders," *American Sociological Review*, April, 1940, V, pp. 201–209.

Schroeder, Clarence W., "Mental Disorders in Cities," *American Journal of Sociology*, July, 1942, 48, pp. 40–47.

Sherman, Mandel, and Irene C. Sherman, "Psychosis and Cultural Background," *The Problem of Mental Disorder*, edited by Madison Bentley and E. V. Cowdrey (New York: McGraw-Hill Book Company, Inc., 1934).

Tietze, Christopher, Paul Lemkau, and Marcia Cooper, "Personal Disorders and Spatial Mobility," *American Journal of Sociology*, July, 1942, 43, pp. 29–39.

CHAPTER NINE

Social Aspects of Schizophrenia: Development

Schizophrenia is a very puzzling and widespread psychotic disorder. Since so many schizophrenics do not respond favorably to treatment, they are largely responsible for the crowded conditions in our mental hospitals. In our time, this disorder has become a grave social problem which has interfered with personal careers and has broken up families.

The social experiences of schizophrenics at one time were considered of peripheral importance in contributing to this breakdown. Since schizophrenia has been studied developmentally, however, the social side of this disorder has become more centrally important. But the social side of schizophrenia means more than the coexistence of certain social variables, such as residential area, socioeconomic levels, age, sex, ethnic group, and marital status, with rates of schizophrenia, as we have described in the preceding chapter. The more vital social side of schizophrenia refers to the relationships, attitudes, and meanings which contribute to the eventual breakdown.

From this viewpoint, in this chapter, we shall (1) define schizophrenia, (2) describe and evaluate the behavioral patterns or symptoms of the static subtypes of schizophrenia, and (3) analyze the influences and personality processes during childhood and adolescence which contribute to this disorder. In the next chapter we shall (1) classify subtypes of schizophrenia in terms of patterns of personality development, (2) present a sociological hypothesis of the rise of schizophrenia as a general personality disorder, and (3) show the relationship between schizophrenia and culture.

What Is Schizophrenia?

Schizophrenia is a very inclusive term. In fact, schizophrenics react in such a variety of ways that some investigators claim it is more than one disorder.[1] Some schizophrenics hear voices; others do not. Some are listless; others are agitated. Some recover quickly; many others become progressively worse. What common components characterize schizophrenia?

Schizophrenia in the broadest sense is a type of disorder in which a person loses interest in some phases of "reality" and substitutes his own private attitudes. By "reality" we mean the shared attitudes, interests, and expectations of the groups in which he participates.

First, although the schizophrenic retains many of the qualities of ordered persons, he does not share the "reality" of others in the sphere of his conflicts. In this conflict area he is unable to shift his perspective to that of others because his facility for role taking has been disrupted; hence, he cannot share the attitudes of others, and he remains disoriented. He may feel his body is made of wood, or that the world is square, or that his mother is an enemy in disguise. By retreating into a realm of unshared fantasies of himself and of his environment, he becomes less amenable to social control because his capacity for self-control is disrupted. In extreme instances he becomes so severely disorganized that he loses his socialized attitudes and cannot care for himself.

Second, the schizophrenic has blunted or perverse emotional reactions. He seems incapable of investing many situations or relationships with conventionally expected feelings. He may become disinterested in these outer situations because he concentrates upon his fantasies. He may become so immersed in his conflicts that he is unable to attend to immediate matters and to responses of persons.

Third, the schizophrenic, along with his disrupted role-taking facility, also has disturbed thought processes. His thinking becomes oriented around himself rather than socially oriented. Frequently, he shows a cleavage in his thought processes. He may be rational in some areas of his behavior but is highly irrational in other areas. His delusional or disoriented ideas and imagined and deceptive perceptions or hallucinations, which he cannot control, intrude

[1] See L. J. Meduna and Warren S. McCulloch, "The Modern Concept of Schizophrenia," *Clinics of North America,* January, 1948, 29, pp. 147–164.

upon and interfere with his rational thinking. These hallucinations
emerge because of the upsurge of unconscious attitudes, ideas, and
perceptions. For this reason, the behavior of schizophrenics is comparable to the dreams of ordered persons. The schizophrenic feels
compelled to behave by "forces" which seem uncontrollable. For
example, one schizophrenic summarized her condition as follows:
"I'm not really crazy. I'm just controlled." These "outside forces"
are especially represented by hallucinations which can be of the
hearing, seeing, or feeling type.

✱Thus, schizophrenia may be defined as a personal disorder which
results in the substitution of private attitudes for shared attitudes,
in blunted or perverse emotional reactions, and in the disturbance
of thought processes.

Types of Schizophrenia by Behavior Patterns

The different clusters of behavior patterns of schizophrenia are
categorized into the (1) catatonic, (2) paranoid, (3) hebephrenic,
(4) simple, and (5) undetermined types. These types represent the
particular defenses and the severity of the disorganization of the
particular schizophrenic. The catatonic tends to withdraw but frequently struggles to regain his self-esteem. The paranoid repudiates
the judgment of others, rationalizes his social position, and projects
his hostilities and faults upon his social situation. The hebephrenic
seems to revert to a less responsible role and becomes severely disorganized. The simple schizophrenic tries to drift into situations
which he can manipulate more readily and withdraws from others
without a vigorous effort to regain his self-esteem. Since more than
one type of defense is built up by a particular patient, these schizophrenic categories merely mean the predominance of certain behavior patterns. For example, other schizophrenic types, like the
paranoid, are very suspicious. Some hebephrenics assume the stuporous posture of catatonics. Sometimes the patterns are mixed or do
not fit into any particular category. Often, it is difficult to decide
into what particular category a schizophrenic belongs, as is amply
shown by the diverse views of psychiatrists during staff meetings in
state mental hospitals.

Catatonic Type. The catatonic experiences periods of excitement
and stupor, usually mixed with delusions and hallucinations. The
excited periods are usually brief and frequently occur at the begin-

ning of the disorder. During this agitated period the catatonic makes an intense but futile and random bid to resolve his conflicts or to restore his self-esteem. In this process he becomes agitated and is even capable of homicide or suicide. After the excited period the catatonic may then experience one of two patterns of reactions.

He may become stuporous, negativistic, stereotyped in his attitudes and actions, and generally retarded in his responses. He may sit without stirring for days on end and, in extreme cases, abandon all self-care. Despite this immobile stance and an apparent disinterest in his surroundings, he is often alert emotionally and mentally to what is going on. When some catatonics improve, they are able to recount the happenings during these stuporous periods.

In the second sequence of reactions the catatonic becomes increasingly less excited until his behavior approximates his prepsychotic condition. He then begins to approach the ordered state and is on the road to recovery.

Paranoid Type. The paranoid generally has delusions or beliefs of persecution and frequently of undue self-importance. His delusions are of such a character that he attributes hostile intentions to other persons and to the environment. To sustain himself, he projects the blame for his difficulties upon others or upon his situation. His system of rationalizations becomes his delusional defense system.

The paranoid schizophrenic differs from the true paranoiac because his delusions may pervade his general behavior. The true paranoiac, in contrast, has a few fixed delusions, does not hallucinate, and may participate acceptably in other spheres of activity. His incased private and unshared beliefs do not interfere markedly with his orientation in other conventional matters. The paranoid schizophrenic may deteriorate. Theoretically, the paranoiac does not.

Hebephrenic Type. The hebephrenic's cluster of reactions denotes a very severe and profound personality disorganization. His symptoms consist of silly and inappropriate smiling and laughing, incoherent talk, and incoherent scattered thinking, delusions, and hallucinations. Often, he experiences fragmentation of behavior and a completely shattered self-conception. The hebephrenic is more disoriented than the paranoid. Frequently, he loses self-control and finds it very difficult to conform to socialized demands. Like other schizophrenics, in the process of becoming desocialized, he cannot anchor himself onto others by meaningful communication. Usually more disorganized than either the catatonic or the paranoid, his disorganization is more tenacious because he does not struggle so vigorously to regain his self-esteem but tends, rather, to accept the social verdict of others and to revert to a past, immature role. The hebephrenic is least responsive to treatment, and it is quite likely that he tends to be more biologically predisposed to his disorder than are the other schizophrenic types.

The Simple Types. Simple schizophrenia is the least frequent of the categories mentioned. The chief symptom of the simple schizophrenic tends to be emotional apathy. He expresses slight emotional enthusiasm and seems to be overcome by a series of emotional blockings. Usually avoiding the more demanding and complex facets of the culture, he drifts to a simple and nondemanding periphery of the culture. His apathy is not accompanied by hallucinations and delusions.

Some schizophrenics, who are diagnosed early as "simple," later acquire delusions and hallucinations. Few schizophrenics retain these disinterested attitudes and apparent lack of empathy without acquiring some delusions or hallucinations.

The Undetermined Type. The undetermined or unclassified type consists of the mixed or combined symptoms of any of the four types which have been described. This type also covers those disorders which are in the borderland of two disorders, such as schizophrenia and manic depression, or neurosis and schizophrenia. The assumption is that with the passage of time the patient's disorder becomes more amenable to classification.

Limits of the Classificatory Approach. This classification of subtypes of schizophrenia provides a short cut for understanding the defenses of the particular person and can be used as a beginning for more dynamic and developmental analyses. But in a more fundamental sense its use is limited. First, as end products of a disorder, these subtypes do not necessarily add to the understanding of the process leading to schizophrenia. Second, these categories contribute to the danger of forming a stereotype around the patient so that the patient is known by his diagnosis rather than by his personality —the latter being an essential beginning for understanding his conflicts and his experiences that have contributed to his breakdown.

Third, no specific therapy has been derived from these particular diagnostic types, with the possible exception that the paranoids may be given insulin shock to a greater extent than the other types, and that some diagnostic types—e.g., catatonic—usually have better chances for recovery than other types—e.g., hebephrenic or simple. This classification has limited value for psychotherapy, with the exception that catatonics and undetermined types recover more readily than others.

The logic of symptom analysis means that the symptoms reveal a more basic disease for which specific therapies can be prescribed.[2] This practice, however, does not work with the subtypes of schizophrenics. Although these diagnostic subtypes may provide a short cut for getting an over-all view of the patient, still the diagnostic subtype may change in some instances, i.e., some simple or catatonic schizophrenics may become hebephrenic.

The most feasible way of understanding the schizophrenic is by his social development and by certain expressions of his behavior which reflect his personality organization, something which is not always apparent in a static diagnosis. This developmental approach is becoming increasingly accepted by clinicians and researchers.

The Development of Schizophrenia

Since schizophrenia is the end product of a long developmental process, we will describe in the following sections the social influences and the personality processes which contribute to a schizophrenic breakdown.

Family Relationships. The family, more than any other social unit, provides the basic attitudes and orientations in personality development, especially during childhood. Since the family fashions personality, it can stifle personal growth and it can limit or distort social participation, both of which are necessary for personal stability and maturity. To understand the development of schizophrenia, we must understand the family relationships which provide the setting that so often contributes to a schizophrenic onset.

[2] "Not only have we fallen victim to the fallacies involved in artificial experimentation; we have also become so entranced with technical procedures that we have lost sight of the patient himself, the individual person who is subjected to so many of these laboratory tests." Ian Stevenson, "Why Medicine Is Not a Science," *Harper's Magazine*, April, 1949, 198, p. 37.

No single pattern of family relationships predetermines schizophrenia. The many patterns, at best, are traced and ascertained after the disorder has occurred. The modes of family relations that obtain for schizophrenia are also found in the families of other disorders. Generally, the family may contribute to the breakdown of its members by diminishing self-confidence, by intensifying and prolonging emotional dependency, by encouraging distorted views, by hindering or preventing association with persons outside the family, and by creating irreconcilable conflicts. There is no single, definite social path to schizophrenia because the innate biological endowments among schizophrenics vary. Except for extreme cases, it is often difficult to predict that given family relationships will create schizophrenia among the members. For schizophrenia combines a series of influences which must be understood as a configuration. This will be seen in the following discussion of (1) the ingrown family, (2) parent-child relations, (3) the preschizophrenic's position in the family, and (4) *folie à deux*.

The Ingrown Family. In the "ingrown family" the members' relationships and attachments are confined to the family. More or less isolated socially, they become estranged from the practices and expectations of the community. They, in turn, are considered "queer" or "different" by the neighbors.

Within this "ingrown family" the dominant and significant parent, usually the mother, subjugates the rest of the family and forbids them to cultivate outside relationships. Children experience extreme difficulty in transitional adjustment to the outside community. At this juncture they are personally retarded and cannot cultivate outside relations. In brief, the families which approximate this type contribute to personal immaturity, and possibly lay the basis for schizophrenic reactions, especially among the children. This process will be illustrated later in the case of the Carrington family.

Parent-Child Relationships. To understand the interacting process between parents and preschizophrenic children, two considerations must be stressed. First, the relationships are a dynamic continuous sequence rather than a static and terminal affair; hence, all participants are affected. Second, the unwitting and unconscious aspects of the interacting process are usually as effective, if not more so, in influencing the children than the overt and direct types of expressions because these former modes of interaction are less understood by the participants and are more difficult to revise. In general, parental relationships with preschizophrenic children tend to be conflict-creating at an earlier age than with neurotics, and to be more intense in their effects upon lowered self-evaluation of the preschizophrenic, although some schizophrenics seem outwardly "normal" during childhood. Hence, as indices or pointers to understanding parent-child relations, the personalities of the parents become quite crucial because they initiate and, in part, determine the relationships with their children.

Despite the variety of personality differences among the parents of schizophrenics, the two characteristics of instability and harsh or subtle domination stand out as being most significant. Lidz and Lidz found that only 5 out of 50 schizophrenics came from reasonably stable families in which the parents were relatively balanced and compatible. The parents of the other 45 were unstable or incompatible.[3]

The mother usually is the more influential parent, but this does not always follow. Friedlander found that the parents were markedly inconsistent in their relations with their children. The fathers were austere and strict, while the mothers were indulgent.[4] Despert found that in 19 out of 29 cases the mothers were aggressive, oversolicitous, and overanxious about the children, but the fathers were docile and understanding.[5] Wittman and Huffman found that though the mothers were unstable, oversolicitous, and overprotective, the fathers were more or less normal.[6] In a study of 100 schizophrenics, Terry found that 58 mothers or mother substitutes were domineering, possessive, oversolicitous, overindulgent, neurotic, eccentric, or psychotic. She found that many mothers and fathers fell into the roles demanded by the children who eventually broke

[3] Ruth W. Lidz and Theodore Lidz, "The Family Environment of Schizophrenic Patients," *The American Journal of Psychiatry*, November, 1949, 106:5, p. 343.

[4] Dorothy Friedlander, "Personality Development of 27 Children Who Later Became Psychotic," *Journal of Abnormal and Social Psychology*, 1945, 40, pp. 330–335.

[5] Louise J. Despert, "Schizophrenia in Children," *Psychiatric Quarterly*, 1938, 12, pp. 366–371.

[6] M. Phyllis Wittman and A. V. Huffman, "A Comparative Study of Developmental Adjusted Teen Aged Youths," *Elgin State Hospital Papers*, December, 1944, 5, pp. 228–237.

down.[7] During adolescence and adulthood, the offspring retained intense attachments to and dependency upon the parents, especially the mothers. Sometimes, the children's behavior aggravated the parents' instability because they did not turn out as the parents had hoped.

In comparing the parental reactions of schizophrenic, neurotic, and normal subjects whose ages were over 12 and under 32 years, McKeown found that the parents of the schizophrenic children were more "demanding-antagonistic" and more "discouraging" than were the parents of normal children, but that their reactions were somewhat similar to the parents of neurotic children.[8]

Despite the variations in personalities, the parents seemed to make the children very dependent upon them, to suppress their initiative, and to impose their own distorted goals upon their children. Hence, many preschizophrenic children seemed to live for their parents and could not evaluate themselves in terms of their own needs. When the children did not measure up to parental demands, the children were frequently taunted, ridiculed, or made to feel very guilty.

Many parents encouraged immaturity in the children. One schizophrenic recalled that when she got into difficulty with her father and went into a tantrum, the father would "forgive and forget." When she tried to behave maturely by accepting responsibility after some mistake, the father became ruthless in his reprimands and persisted in nagging allusions weeks after the incident occurred. Consequently, she continued with these tantrums until late adolescence because that was the only way she could absolve herself from difficulties.

In a study of 25 mothers of schizophrenics, Tietze found that almost all of the mothers were domineering, but that their techniques of domination were of two general kinds—open and subtle. Of the two types, the subtle domination was more harmful because the mother's activity was not clear to the children and hence did not lead to open defiance and rebellion. For example, one mother subtly dominated her three daughters, two of whom became schizo-

---

[7] Described in Leo Kanner, *Child Psychiatry*, p. 492 (Springfield, Ill.: Charles C. Thomas, Publisher, 1942).

[8] James Edward McKeown, "The Behavior of Parents of Schizophrenic, Neurotic, and Normal Children," *American Journal of Sociology*, September, 1950, 56:2, pp. 175–179. Since the neurotic subjects in this study were children, it is possible that these children may incur a schizophrenic disorder in later life.

phrenic and one of whom was afflicted with ulcerative colitis. When displeased or angry, this mother would not shout or raise her voice, but cried, had headaches and fainting spells, and eventually took to bed when these sick spells came on. Conveniently enough, her sick spells occurred when her daughters wanted to go to a party or have "some fun." The mother then insisted that the daughters stay home and care for her. Consequently, the daughters despaired of planning for "any fun." [9]

The most harmful types of parent-child relationships were those in which the children were rejected very early in life. In these instances, the children, feeling unwanted, unloved, and despised, often despaired of obtaining affection from other persons. In a gesture of protective avoidance they turned inward and became distant and isolated from others. These extremely rejecting relationships occurred in few cases, but many other parents expressed unwitting feelings of rejection and hostility; then they tried to cover up these attitudes and to compensate for them by oversolicitousness for which they expected the gratitude of the children.

Finally, the parents seemed to contribute to the psychosexual retardation of the preschizophrenic children. They instilled deep feelings of guilt concerning masturbation and relationships with the opposite sex. In general these parental influences led to the preschizophrenics' isolation from the conventional patterns of the peer group, to a denial of their sexual roles as demanded by the peer group and to a lowering of their self-esteem.

Family Position. It is thought sometimes that the eldest child is most susceptible to schizophrenia. For example, one study found that the eldest children were most prone to paranoid schizophrenia.[10] More intensive studies, however, do not substantiate this finding. In a study of 549 schizophrenics, Malzberg found the first-born children were no more susceptible to schizophrenia than the later born.[11] Patterson and Ziegler arrived at similar conclusions

---

[9] Trude Tietze, "A Study of Mothers of Schizophrenic Patients," *Psychiatry*, February, 1949, 12, pp. 55–65. See also Joseph Kasanin, E. Knight, and P. Sage, "The Parent-Child Relationship in Schizophrenia," *Journal of Nervous and Mental Disease*, 1940, 79, pp. 249–263.

[10] Edgar A. Schuler, "The Relationship of Birth Order and Fraternal Position to Incidence of Insanity," *American Journal of Sociology*, 1930, 36, pp. 28–40.

[11] Benjamin Malzberg, "Is Birth Order Related to the Incidence of Mental Disease?" *American Journal of Physical Anthropology*, 1937, 24:1, pp. 91–103.

from a comparative study of 442 schizophrenics and 495 admissions to the hospitals who were selected at random. In their study, twins were eliminated. They found that the middle children had a higher percentage in the schizophrenic group than in the control group.[12] "Only children," however, had a higher percentage in the control group than in the schizophrenic group. The eldest and youngest children also had higher proportions in the control group as is shown in Table 8.

TABLE 8

POSITIONAL DISTRIBUTION OF SCHIZOPHRENIC AND CONTROL SUBJECTS*

Position	Control		Schizophrenic	
	Number	Per Cent	Number	Per Cent
Oldest child	127	25.7	98	22.2
Middle child	222	44.8	238	53.8
Youngest child	101	20.4	83	15.8
Only child	45	9.1	23	5.2
Total	495	100.0	442	100.0

* From R. M. Patterson and T. W. Ziegler, "Ordinal Position and Schizophrenia," *The American Journal of Psychiatry*, November 1941, 98:3, p. 456.

From this study it appears that "only children" may be less susceptible to schizophrenic disorders. That middle children are more prone to schizophrenia than children in other ordinal positions is not confirmed by other studies.[13] It has also been shown that among normal children the subjects in middle ordinal positions are as well adjusted as are those in other positions. Hug-Hellmuth points out, however, that the middle ordinal position is subject to heavy stress and strain.[14] From these studies it can be said that the influence of ordinal position upon schizophrenia is as yet inconclusive.

Although birth order is not definitely related to schizophrenia, the preschizophrenic often was isolated in the family. Terry found that 61 per cent of her cases had such a solitary family position.[15]

[12] Ralph M. Patterson and Thornton W. Ziegler, "Ordinal Position and Schizophrenia," *The American Journal of Psychiatry*, November, 1941, 98:3, pp. 455–458.
[13] Benjamin Malzberg, "Is Birth Order Related to the Incidence of Mental Disease?" *American Journal of Physical Anthropology*, 1937, 24:12, pp. 91–103.
[14] Hans V. Hug-Hellmuth, "Mittleren Kinde," *Imago*, 1921, 7, p. 93.
[15] Described in Leo Kanner, *Child Psychiatry*, p. 492 (Springfield, Ill.: Charles C. Thomas, Publisher, 1942).

The preschizophrenic may have been the youngest or eldest sibling, the only boy, or only girl. He may have been estranged from other family members because of age, differential ability, or physical condition. Sometimes his isolation from other family members intensified his attachment to the mother.[16]

Folie à Deux: "Disorder of Two." By *folie à deux,* we mean that one person who becomes disordered is influenced by intimate relationships with another person who is disordered or disturbed. This disorder is not necessarily confined to two persons only, but may extend to three persons, *folie à trois,* or to four persons, *folie à quatre.* Though occurring chiefly among family members, this disorder sometimes is found among intimate friends.[17] Gralnick, in an intensive review of the literature, classifies these disorders, chiefly by mode of relationships and by mode of onset, into four types: (1) simultaneous, (2) communicated, (3) imposed, and (4) induced.[18]

The simultaneous type refers to identical psychotic conditions of two or more family members at the same time. The communicated type means that one person, despite his resistance, acquires the delusional ideas of another. The imposed type refers to the acquisition of similar delusions and mannerisms by a person, who may be ordered, but who is submissive and dependent upon a domineering disordered person. When the two persons are separated, the submissive person tends to improve. The induced type refers to the acquisition of new delusions by a disordered person who is influenced by another disordered person.

All these disorders result from direct learning by at least one of the disordered persons. Although these disordered expressions may vary, the paranoid schizophrenic form is the most frequent. Of the types of *folie à deux,* the "imposed" form is the most frequently occurring. Among the schizophrenics, Gralnick found that 38 cases were imposed, 18 communicated, 3 simultaneous, and 1 was induced. Of the family combinations, 17 were sister combinations, 13 mother-child, 15 husband-wife, 5 brother, 1 father-daugh-

[16] Nicholas J. Demerath, "Adolescent Status Demands and the Student Experiences of 20 Schizophrenics," *American Sociological Review,* 1943, 8, pp. 513–518.
[17] Alexander Gralnick, *"Folie à Deux*—The Psychosis of Association: A Review of 103 Cases and the Entire English Literature," *Psychiatric Quarterly,* April, 1942, 16:2, pp. 491–520.
[18] *Ibid.,* p. 3.

ter, 1 sister-brother, and 1 was between two friends. Two cases involved three sisters.[19]

Since these types of breakdown are influenced directly or indirectly by family relationships, many important phases of family life can be illuminated by the extreme character of the cases. In the following instance of the Carrington family, compiled by Gralnick, the entire family of four broke down, but at different times. The mother, Anne, was the initially disordered person, a paranoid, and the dominant member of the family. Because of her influence the husband and the two children also became psychotic. Her influence is especially evident upon her two children.[20]

The Carrington Family

Mother's Attitudes to Edith

Edith, a full-term, nine-pound baby, was remembered by her father as a "jolly and lively child" and as "always laughing and full of energy." Anne devoted herself completely to her child. She dressed her so well that people commented favorably on her good appearance. Anne was overprotective to the child, and carried her about a great deal. Edith grew into a healthy, normal child. She walked at the age of 9 months and began to talk at 15 months. She was playful about the house and expressed particular affection for her father. At 4, Edith surprised him by reading a few words in the newspaper. Her only mishap occurred when she was 2 years old. Falling against a bedpost, she lacerated her forehead. Shortly thereafter her eyes began to squint, but Anne refused to have them examined. At 5, Edith began to wear glasses. She was finally operated upon when she was 7.

Since her suspicions of people increased, Anne never let Edith out alone or let her play with the other children unless it was in her presence. When Edith was scratched in the face by a child, Anne forbade her to play outside and kept her indoors. She even deterred Edith from entering school until her ninth year, when a truant officer had threatened her with court action unless the child went to school. Anne relented and, inconsistently enough, placed her in a Catholic school.

Anne escorted Edith to and from school. Placed in the 2B grade, Edith adjusted very well and was a bright pupil. On one occasion Edith was struck over the head by one of the teachers. This incident started a quarrel between Anne and the nuns. Anne became convinced that the nuns were antagonizing other children against Edith and were telling them that Edith was "crazy" because she had no religion. When a child pushed Edith

[19] *Ibid.*, pp. 4–7.
[20] Alexander Gralnick, "The Carrington Family: A Psychiatric and Social Study Illustrating the Psychoses of Association or *Folie à Deux*," *Psychiatric Quarterly*, April, 1943, 17, p. 32.

down the stairs, breaking one of her teeth, Anne promptly withdrew her from school.

Removed from parochial school, Edith began to believe that the Catholic Church was against her. When she and her mother walked outdoors, they imagined that the other children smirked at them. Edith was told by her mother that this was done at the behest of the Church. Despite peculiarities, Edith adjusted well in the public school where Anne later transferred her. She studied hard, and, though she often asked her father for help, her homework was "always right." Considered very bright by the school principal, he regarded her as "peculiar and dominated by her mother." Since Anne persisted in accompanying her to school and refused to let her associate with other children, Edith was isolated. But the mother also began to estrange Edith from her father.

Edith was continually reminded by Anne that it was her father who had sent her to the Catholic school. When Anne forbade her to speak to her father, Edith became so upset that, in a "high-spirited and resentful outburst," she threatened to leave home. In time, she became subdued by her mother. Her only social outlets were her mother and, to some extent, her brother.

At 14, after graduation from grade school, Edith entered high school the following semester. The quality of her work began to decline. At 15 her father was committed to a mental hospital for reasons which will soon be discussed. She was removed from school and taken in search of employment by her mother. When Edith's religion was asked at the employment agency, her mother said she had none. When Anne was advised that employment would be facilitated if she had a faith, the mother countered that she would rather starve than admit having a religion. Edith returned to school and for the next year did so poorly that she did not wish to return. The mother apparently agreed, and Edith was "discharged as being over seventeen years of age." Edith never sought work but remained at home, despite the fact that the family was aided by charity.

Edith never had a friend, and of course, no sexual indiscretions. She was influenced by her mother to wish never to marry. Subject to a rigid routine at home, she displayed little affection to her parents and received none. In time, Edith became a shy, seclusive, diffident, suspicious person, who was completely dominated by her mother.

Mother's Attitudes to Cameron

After John's birth, Cameron believed that Anne's condition became worse. When people stopped in front of their door to talk, she thought they were spying on her and sent them away with abuse. She allowed no one to enter the apartment. She compelled her husband to whisper or be quiet for fear the neighbors would overhear them.

Cameron had been working at an express company, and, a few months before his resignation, he thought he was being followed. It seemed to him that the "same man would turn up frequently." Later, Anne told him that a detective had come to the house and had inquired about some missing valuables. Angered by this visit, Cameron went to the company's offices, showed his receipts to prove his innocence, and resigned. With satisfaction he read later that a company employee had been jailed for robbery.

After working in several places, Cameron found a job in a pickle factory. When he started work there, he was told that he should be careful because some things were stolen from his orders, and he began to worry.

In contrast to Anne's behavior, Cameron noted the gay manner of the girls in the factory. He claimed that Anne was driving him "nutty." He began to hear the singing voices of the girls while at home. At night, he heard the neighbors' daughter singing and dancing upstairs and thought they watched him. During the day, he thought that they talked and laughed —at him. At times, he would cry without any reason. He heard voices threatening his wife and him. He told a physician: "The gang that is after me is trying to burn out my sexual organs with rays coming through the ceiling. I woke up and found my glands all heated up." He heard voices say, "Shoot him." Cameron, of course, thought the voices were real. Had not Anne told him that people always talked about them? Had she not frequently gone to the door to see if people were eavesdropping? When he asked why she did this, she never replied, only told him to be quiet. Finally, Cameron became so fearful and anxious that he was hospitalized.

In the hospital Cameron adjusted well and began to improve rather quickly. He realized that the "voices" were imaginary and claimed that Anne's behavior caused his worries. After 13 months he was released on conditional discharge, and after another year, he was discharged outright.

Mother's Attitudes to John

John was a normal bright child, who was responsive and well behaved. He entered school at 6 and graduated at 13½. Entering high school, he graduated three years later with excellent ratings in "reliability, leadership, civic spirit, industry, and good manners." His grades were very high, his I.Q. was 123, and he was regarded as having an excellent personal appearance. His English teacher, however, observed that although a very capable student, he was obviously suffering from some inner disturbance "which was expressed in extreme shyness and sensitivity." His history record stated: "The boy has such an inferiority complex that he makes a poor impression in spite of his ability."

Like his sister, John was forbidden to talk about sexual matters. At the age of 13, he said that he would never marry or have children. He promised to remain with his sister and take care of her when she grew older. He disliked the frequent quarrels that took place in the home but sided with his father. He had a growing hostility toward his mother, and when she tried to pat him as she helped him with his coat, he shrank away. His mother considered him "stubborn and self-willed." Her attempts to restrict him made him very angry. Anne watched his moves, never allowed him out to play with boys his age, and had him sleep with her until shortly before his eighteenth year. John was unable to do anything independently. With no other way to turn, he became a "bookworm." But his resentment toward his mother became deep and lasting. Unable to understand why he could not speak to his own father, he objected vigorously. But she succeeded in making her domination complete, and John, learning from his father, surrendered to her will, and obeyed.

When his father was rehospitalized, it was more than John could bear. He sat most of the day and refused to go out. Refusing food, he became steadily weaker. When not sitting, he paced up and down the room which his mother regarded as exercise.

Seized with abdominal pains, he vomited and believed his heart was bad. His hostility toward his mother increased. Frequently, he chased her out into the hall, slamming the door after her. A neighbor once observed a "wild look in his eyes" and his arms waving over his head as if he were in a frenzy. The mother explained to the neighbor that he had tried to beat her, and explained that his outbursts were brought about because he was born under Taurus and this gave him "the temper of a bull." A social worker, during a visit, characterized him as a "morbid, silent boy, who barely said yes or no," and who was "ill of starvation." Over his mother's protests, the social worker called a doctor who recommended that John be sent to the hospital, on May 2, 1939. The physical examination was generally negative, except for some minor physical defects. He was diagnosed as having "mixed hysterical pyschoneurosis."

During one visit to the hospital, the mother read John's palm in the presence of Edith. She said that his life line was broken and he might not live. Seeing the "sign of death" in his hand, Anne decided to have him returned home. Impassively, she said that it was too bad that John had to die. The investigators who heard this felt that the mother wanted her son to die. Despite their objections, the doctors had to release him, at the mother's insistent demand, 17 days later. A social worker who visited the home shortly afterward described the setting as one in which John was "lying on a pile of rags on one of the bedsprings. The dirt and grime was so thick on his body that it could have been scraped off of him." Despite the mother's signs, John remained alive, even gained weight, ate better, and exercised. He recovered sufficiently to make biweekly visits to the City Hospital Neurological Clinic.

John complained of abdominal pains and severe constipation, but his physical examination was negative. Encephalitis was regarded as a possible diagnosis, and bromides and chloral were prescribed for him from August to December, 1939.

During the last few weeks of his life, John remained at home without venturing out. He ate little and said almost nothing. His mother once described his behavior to the janitress, saying, "My boy is crazy. He's lying on the floor. He and his father are both mad." Since the mother bought no coal, the house was cold, and the boy, who refused to wear his coat and hat in the house as his mother and sister did, became weaker and weaker from exposure. Four days before his death, he went to bed, and for two days did not eat, nor drink any water. On the third day, he ate one egg and two pieces of bread. He arose only to go to the toilet; otherwise, he remained silent and immobile. When asked to eat he said, "No, go away and don't bother me." Some time later when Edith was in the mental hospital she said that he resembled the patients in the hospital who were diagnosed as catatonic schizophrenic. She then observed that her brother should have been force fed. At times, the mother and daughter remained undecided as to whether to send him to the hospital or not. At one instance they even dressed him for the ambulance, but then desisted. Was the mother thinking of the broken life line? The night preceding his death, his breathing became heavy and forced. His mother and sister sat by his bedside all night, even slept in this position with blankets over their heads and shoulders. Although Anne, the mother, knew the son was dying, she would not look at him, although his breathing became shorter and weaker. In the early morning his breathing ceased. His sister, at the mother's request, held her hand over his mouth and felt no breath. The mother said simply, "He must be dead." She did not cry, although Edith shed a few tears.

Edith missed her brother with the shallow feelings of which she was capable. She felt that she "didn't have much interest in living any longer." She ate little, lost weight, and ceased menstruating. Like John after the removal of his father to the mental hospital, she began to decline rapidly. In this condition her dependency upon her mother was complete. The social workers feared that Edith would go the way of John.

Since the mother was able to make a favorable impression by hiding her symptoms and was a rather clever woman, a plan was decided upon. The mother was persuaded to accompany her daughter to the Bellevue Hospital but did not know that she, too, was to be kept there. Later she blamed the Catholic Church for detaining her.

After a few weeks in the hospital they were transferred to a ward for co-operative patients. They constantly occupied the same chairs from which they could get a view of the corridors. When a person in authority approached, they became apprehensive, and Anne would usually rise and hide in the hallway. When Anne was questioned about her behavior, she offered unconvincing excuses. The outstanding feature observed by all who had contact with the two women was the mother's domination of the daughter. Such random statements as "Edith never talks when her mother is around," and "Edith doesn't think for herself," characterized this view.

Anne remained seclusive and suspicious. She continued to believe that the attendants and the others who caused her difficulty were Catholics. She usually spoke softly so that no one would overhear. When her husband visited her, she accused him of being an "enemy" and of wanting her hanged.

Edith, however, changed markedly after her separation from Anne. In six months she said that she had more confidence in herself, cultivated several friends, and regarded her former behavior as follows: "It all seems so silly. I am not shy now. I have more confidence now and carry out a conversation better." Although Edith still missed her mother, she showed more initiative in her work. She said, "I am not a child. I am old enough to get along." In the meantime, she incurred a neurological illness, which grew progressively worse and was diagnosed as "multiple sclerosis." She was forced to give up working in the kitchen, because her vision was blurred and she dropped objects. In spite of her physical condition she continued to improve and to become more sociable. She summarized this personal improvement by the following attitude about herself: "I can face the world now. I don't let people step all over me the way I used to." She remains concerned about her physical condition and sometimes wonders whether her neurological handicap will be a permanent disorder.

Interpretation. The social dynamics among the family members made some kind of disordered behavior of the children almost inevitable, regardless of what their constitutional endowments might have been.

1. Both Edith and John apparently were "normal" children. They were normal and probably above average in intelligence. Affectionate, they responded to affection. They played together and, from the fragmentary evidence in the case, were able to associate with other children.

2. The family was isolated from neighborhood contacts. The children were most profoundly influenced by the family and particularly by the mother, whose paranoid delusions and general behavior isolated both John and Edith by restraining and forbidding them to associate with other children, and who influenced Edith to become very suspicious and submissive.

3. The mother did not permit the children to become emotionally independent and to acquire the cultural skills and conventional behavior patterns, the social give-and-take, which usually are acquired by ordered children.

4. The effect of conflict was evident in the profound sense of failure and submission which John felt by being "broken" by his mother. Undoubtedly, he suffered from his mother's intense hostility, and his breakdown was hastened by his father's removal. His breakdown, which seemed to be an acute schizophrenic episode, resembled in its later stages catatonic schizophrenia.

5. The father's breakdown resulted in part from his isolation in the family, his lack of friends, and his wife's domination. His recovery when away from home leads us to suspect that his disorder was influenced by his wife's behavior and by extra familial difficulties.

6. Malnutrition and the general physical hardships from the stricken condition of the family contributed to the disorder of the boy, particularly. But these factors were hardly as crucial as the retarded personal growth, diffident self-conceptions, anxieties, and conflicts created by the domineering mother who kept the children away from the peer group and from other normal relationships.

The Family and Schizophrenia. Thus, the modes of socialization among preschizophrenic children are definitely affected by parents (especially the mother) who tend to be unstable, domineering, and demanding. These parents try to control the lives of their children and to retard their development and emotional independence and try to isolate them from the peer group. Although schizophrenia is not definitely related to order of birth among the children, the preschizophrenic tends to be isolated from the other siblings either because of age or physique, or because of his general personality which makes him more dependent upon the parents. The ingrown family tends to influence children in this direction, and the presence of an irrational, domineering parent can create the phenomenon of *folie à deux* in which more than one person in the family becomes afflicted.

Although these familial influences are predominant, there is no single type of family from which schizophrenia arises. The family types are many, as are the parental types, and these family and parental types require more definitive analysis. Moreover, it appears that little is known of the siblings of schizophrenics. A study of this type would add to the knowledge of the family life of the schizophrenic and indicate why one sibling breaks down and others do not.

Childhood. Although behavior may be influenced by constitutional and hereditary predisposition, these reactions also are defensive resultants of family expectations and relationships. In this light we will discuss the preschizophrenic child in terms of his sociability or lack of sociability.

The withdrawn child who pursues a solitary routine, who is asocial, and who finds communication to be difficult has been pointed to as the most frequent preschizophrenic type. This shut-in personality has been described by Hoch, as reticent, shy, seclusive, sensitive, stubborn, almost uncommunicative, and steeped in fantasies.[21] He regarded this type as having particular constitutional deficiencies. Bowman characterized the typical schizophrenic as a conformistic and model child, who is solitary, has few friends, feels superior, and is closemouthed and uncommunicative. He found also that he is not "oversensitive and daydreams less than the normal." [22] In general, Hoch, Wittman, and Steinberg, Maslow and Mittleman, Sheldon, and others stress that the shut-in or seclusive type of personality is most frequent—i.e., from 50 to 70 per cent of the cases— among the preschizophrenics.[23]

Faris examined 100 consecutive records of schizophrenics. Of the 48 cases for which he could find full information, he noted that 27, as against 21, were sociable during childhood.[24] Wittman also found, by comparing two groups of 66 each, that one group of schizophrenics were behavior problems during childhood and that another group were not. Since she limited her subjects to those who did and to those who did not have records of behavior difficulties in agencies, very likely those schizophrenics who did not have official records of behavior difficulties may have had more subtle behavior problems which did not arouse the parents to disciplinary or treatment action.[25]

Another frequent childhood type which is found in schizophrenic histories, however, is the conscientious or "model" child who is also somewhat peculiar.

Hamilton and Wall found that 60 out of 100 schizophrenic girls were described by their parents as "model" children. The parents considered them as "good babies," "never giving any trouble," or

[21] August Hoch, "On Some of the Mental Mechanisms in Dementia Praecox," *Journal of Abnormal Psychology*, December, 1910, 5, pp. 255–273.

[22] Karl Bowman, "A Study of the Pre-psychotic Personality in Certain Disorders," *The Biology of the Individual* (Washington, D.C.: Association for Nervous and Mental Disease, 1934).

[23] August Hoch, "On Some of the Mental Mechanisms in Dementia Praecox"; M. Phyllis Wittman and D. Louis Steinberg, "A Study of Prodromal Factors in Mental Illness with Special Reference to Schizophrenia," *The American Journal of Psychiatry*, May, 1944, 100:7, pp. 811–816.

[24] Robert L. Faris, *Social Disorganization*, p. 234 (New York: The Ronald Press Company, 1948).

[25] M. Phyllis Wittman, "Diagnostic and Prognostic Significance of the Shut-in Personality as a Prodromal Factor in Schizophrenia," *Journal of Clinical Psychology*, April, 1948, 4, pp. 211–214.

"never crying." [26] Of the others for whom data could be obtained, 20 were stubborn, restless, and overactive, and 12 had perverse and traumatic sexual experiences imposed upon them by adults. In a study of 42 catatonics Dunham found that the mothers always appraised the boys as "very good boys" who were quiet, dependent, seclusive, and who usually remained at home.[27]

Frequently, adored and overprotected children were not accepted by the play group, as Faris found in 29 out of 54 cases.[28] Their social isolation became more clearly apparent during adolescence, when more was expected of them. Many preschizophrenics showed little insight into their personalities and into the influences which they were acquiring from the family and from the play group. Both the seclusive and the model children often considered themselves "different," inferior, or rejected. Also, both types of children, if dominated and overprotected, lacked confidence and the skills to defend themselves in competitive participation.

The concept "model childhood" is vague. Model children do not necessarily become schizophrenic. We do not know how many stable adults have been model children, but presumably many have been. Indeed, "model childhood" is relative to the attitudes and relationships in the particular family. When the parents are stable and happy, a model child may be quite stable. When the parents are unstable and disorganized, a model child may be quite disorganized. Hence, "model childhood" is not so indicative of the child's stability as it is of the preconceptions of his parents. Moreover, an emotionally unstable child can mature without breaking down.[29] Although the isolated child, except for extreme cases, does not invariably become schizophrenic, the child who accepts his social isolation, who begins to despair of receiving affection, and who becomes preoccupied with solitary fantasies at the expense of social relationships and a need for people, may tend to be more predisposed to a schizophrenic disorder than other children.

[26] Donald M. Hamilton and James H. Wall, "The Hospital Treatment of Dementia Praecox," *The American Journal of Psychiatry,* November, 1948, 105:5, p. 346.

[27] H. Warren Dunham, "The Social Personality of the Catatonic-Schizophrene," *American Journal of Sociology,* May, 1944, 49, p. 514.

[28] Robert L. Faris, *Social Disorganization,* p. 235 (New York: The Ronald Press Company, 1948).

[29] See Leo Kanner, "Early Behavior Problems as Signposts to Later Maladjustment," *The American Journal of Psychiatry,* May, 1941, 97, pp. 1261–1271.

It is still not known definitely to what extent the differences between the seclusive child and the model child reflect parental and sibling attitudes as well as constitutional tendencies. Yet the isolated or perverse child seemed to react more sensitively to family rejection and hostility. The model child who seemed to encounter these hostile attitudes outside the family depended more upon the parents but was not necessarily isolated in the family.

Adolescence. Interpersonal relations during adolescence generally become more difficult and more complicated. The majority of preschizophrenics showed greater personal backwardness during this period than during childhood. An increasing social dependency upon or "loyalty" to the family group became more apparent. Or an attempted revolt and an inability to cultivate intimate social relationships outside the family also were prevalent. Most preschizophrenics were unable to cultivate sustained informal social relations with persons of their own age groups, particularly with the opposite sex.

Whether or not their views were bizarre or necessarily impractical, they usually were not accepted in the peer group; hence, their feelings of inferiority, of self-reproach, or of being different became intensified. They reacted by withdrawing and by anxiety. Though some schizophrenics, especially the undetermined, the catatonics, and the paranoids, strived to improve themselves, they lacked the facility and the techniques to do so through social participation.

Harold was a normal adolescent who made splendid progress in school and during high school was at the head of the class. Although he was somewhat retiring in his manner, he made friends without effort and seemingly was popular and liked by his friends. He was unusually careful about his personal appearance and was very sensitive about any social slight. Though he was not very interested in girls, he did not avoid them.

He was very friendly to his sister's friends who came to the home and occasionally took a girl to a social gathering. For about ten weeks he was especially attentive to one girl, but she would not become serious with him, although he was very fond of her. Though upset by this rejection, he did not show any outward signs of it to his friends. But he became more solitary in his pursuits, read more, and became more religious.

When Harold attended the college in his town, he adjusted well at first; then his work declined. He believed that because he lived in the same town, and the others came from other cities, they looked down on him. Hence, he failed to attend classes or came very late. He could not concentrate and failed in his examinations. Since he thought he was avoided by the other students, he refused to go to school and remained at home.

Finally, he left school and home and sought employment. Soon after, he had a catatonic breakdown while employed as a laborer.

As we have indicated in Chapter Eight some adolescents were hindered in social participation by the neighborhood in which they lived. For example, some minority-group members in the culturally heterogeneous sections of the city could not or would not associate with those in the majority group. The divergent practices and opinions between the family and the neighborhood served to estrange them further. But even among those of similar ethnic groups, as in high-rate delinquency areas, for example, the precatatonics were the nondelinquents. Their attitudes and values were harmonious with those of the larger society but were incongruous with the attitudes and aspirations of the peer group and with the persons in the immediate neighborhood. In this particular situation, the male catatonics approached their problems in an awkward and clumsy manner and seemed unable to acquire a feel for social relationships, as did the other persons of their milieu.[30] This affected their conception of themselves and placed them in a position whereby they could not participate in the informal aspects of community life. In a study of 20 preschizophrenic persons, Demerath found that the schizophrenics did not participate with their peers, were intensely interested in their studies and in adult values, and consequently were rejected as companions.[31]

The female group, too, were unable to cultivate informal and socially intimate interpersonal relationships, particularly with the opposite sex. Many females who were competent intellectually and who were well adjusted in school and at work lacked the personal independence for the competitive interpersonal relationships of their own age groups. As a result, they became estranged from the common meanings and practices which emerged from these informal types of relationships. Hamilton and Wall state:[32]

> In general, emotional maturity lagged far behind intellectual growth. Interest in profound philosophical and religious subjects

[30] H. Warren Dunham, "The Social Personality of the Catatonic-Schizophrenic," *American Journal of Sociology*, May, 1944, 49, p. 514.
[31] N. J. Demerath, "Adolescent Status Demands and the Student Experiences of Twenty Schizophrenics," *American Sociological Review*, October, 1943, 8, pp. 513–518.
[32] Donald M. Hamilton and James H. Wall, "The Hospital Treatment of Dementia Praecox," *The American Journal of Psychiatry*, November, 1948, 105:5, p. 349. (Italics mine.)

often preceded by some years direct attempts to manage the *realities of interpersonal relationships, particularly with the opposite sex.* Some, because of the nature of their psycho-sexual immaturity, remained on an adolescent level, centering their lives around groups of their own sex who had esoteric interests. One middle-aged patient relied in great part upon an organization known as the "Serious Thinkers." They often clung to emotionally dependent relationships with one woman friend. Others in an early adolescent attitude sought the companionships of older men and women, who as parent figures, were the object of their hero worship and their dependency. Unconscious fantasy played a large role in such relationships. Among the patients who responded least well to treatment were a few who never developed the capacity to make close friends outside the home.

Many adolescent preschizophrenics strived to rise in status. But they resorted to solitary pursuits, which increasingly isolated them from their immediate milieus. Some read about self-improvement or strived to increase their knowledge, but they did not improve their social capacities and did not experience emotional growth. Some were uncertain about their goals, or placed their goals too high, or did not know how to attain the goals they had formulated. Frequently, their aspirations were enmeshed in fantasy rather than in plans of action. Even those who were more outgoing, who participated in sports and in other activities, resorted to them as kinds of compulsive escape, rather than as mediums of self-expression.

The preschizophrenics had conflicts about themselves—especially their sexual roles—and their social world which they could not resolve, and frequently these conflicts came sharply into focus during adolescence. Their lack of confidence in dealing with their peers exaggerated a tendency to fantasy which was not corrected by social participation. In their isolated state they tended to become emotionally dependent and to become removed from the accepted patterns of the immediate peer group. They tended, then, either to retreat further into fantasy or to make a random bid for social acceptance to bolster an ever-weakening self-esteem.

In the following case we see the impact of contradictory values between the family and play group upon the personality of a 17-year-old sensitive adolescent. To retain his parents' approval he became very docile and limited his play-group activities. Consequently, he did not acquire the play skills for coping with the neighborhood boys and was rejected by them. During his breakdown he revealed his acute awareness of the activities necessary for peer-group acceptance and for enhancing his self-esteem by regaining an approved male role.

Allen had been living with his father, bedridden mother, and spastic brother. He had always been restricted because his father did not want an accident to befall him. His younger brother being spastic, his father dreaded having anything happen to Allen, too. His actions were carefully surveyed by the parents, and any "rough" activities were frowned upon. Sheltered from other boys and encouraged to play with girls, he remained relatively ignorant and fearful of boys' activities. In addition, he resided in a neighborhood where mischief and some measure of violence were esteemed. Because he was thin, he became very self-conscious of his appearance and felt that people were looking at him critically. Since he would not engage in any rough sports and would refuse to fight when challenged, he was called "chicken," "mousie," and "sissy" by the other boys. On the other hand, he avidly sought the affection of his parents, particularly his mother, by implicit obedience. Even the father became disgusted at the way his mother and aunt would repeatedly send him to exchange articles from the store. At times, the father hoped that he would tell them to exchange the articles themselves or at least refuse to go back. Fearing parental disapproval, he avoided the rough games of the play group. He said: "I couldn't play games with the boys because I thought I would get hurt. My parents told me I might get hurt and I saw some boys get hurt." On some occasions the boys teased and molested him to the point where his father had to come out and rescue him. Among girls, he lacked the confidence to start a conversation because, "I didn't know what to talk about."

When he was 16, his mother was sent to a sanitarium because of tuberculosis. Her departure, he claimed, "broke me up inside," and he couldn't think as he formerly did. He missed her very much, although he was glad to have her go to the hospital because she was cross with him on many occasions. He lost interest in his schoolwork and failed in two subjects, but he made some friends and quit Sunday school because he was the only boy in the class. During one class session in high school he got up and claimed that now he was strong and had friends and would never be without them again; that the others did not know what it was to play with girls all one's life. The teacher removed him from the class, but he begged to be returned. When she let him come back, he stated again that he was very glad that now he would act differently, that he would study hard and wanted to stay in school. Later he stated: "It's my mission to make everyone happy. I'm the type now that things change for. Now I can go out for sports and things like that."

Conflict and the Peer Group. Although many preschizophrenics had been isolated from the peer group, Hunt has described a peer group in which conflicting activities contributed to schizophrenia as well as to other disorders.[33] Of 15 boys in the peer group, 4 were committed to a mental hospital for personality psychoses, another was committed for paresis, and still another died on the streets from a "stuporous depression complicated by alcohol."

The boys had a hangout near a slaughterhouse and barns where race horses were kept for the winter. There they were introduced into sexual perversions by the laborers. Near by was a Pentacostal church where emotional revivals were often held. The 5 boys who regularly practiced sex perversions and who regularly attended church revivals broke down.

The other boys who practiced perversions, but who did not participate fervently in religious revivals, did not break down. They were not so intensely affected by the conflicting activities. Though the age of onset and the type of psychosis differed among the 5 boys, the important fact is that these intensely contradictory factors seemed to contribute to their eventual breakdowns.

Summary

Although no single set of family relationships and no single personality type fit all preschizophrenics during childhood and adolescence, certain definite patterns can be discerned for many preschizophrenics. From their relations with their parents, especially with the mother, preschizophrenics tend to become emotionally dependent, to perceive themselves in terms of their parents' needs rather than in terms of their own needs, to lack the knowledge of peer group patterns of behavior and to lack the skills for competitive participation and for cultivating friends. Frequently rejected by the peer group, they experience a low self-conception and resort to solitary pursuits and to fantasy both as retreats from social participation and as devious means for lifting their status. Hence their goals and pursuits seem to lack a realistic quality.

During adolescence, many are unable to relate effectively with members of the opposite sex; for they seem to lack the self-confidence, the requisite social skills and the knowledge of conventional peer

[33] J. McV. Hunt, "An Instance of the Social Origin of Conflict Resulting in Psychoses," *American Journal of Orthopsychiatry*, 1938, 8, pp. 158–164; also in *Personality in Nature, Society and Culture*, pp. 367–374 (New York: Alfred A. Knopf, Inc., 1949).

group behavior. Unable to anchor themselves into the social reality of their age-grade associates, they do not know how to correct their behavior and cannot lift their self-esteem by social participation. Further they become deprived of the satisfactions which come from fulfilling the social aspects of their sexual roles. In retreat or compensation, they become further involved in their private fantasies and private aspirations.

But the intensity of these personality trends vary as we shall see in the next chapter. On the one extreme, many preschizophrenics are severely disorganized and isolated throughout their lives and seem to be relatively resigned to their isolation and content with their private pursuits. On the other extreme, some schizophrenics seem to be relatively well-adjusted, if conformistic and passive. Between these two extremes are persons who combine the characteristics of both or who incline toward one extreme or the other.

Selected Readings

Boisen, Anton T., *Exploration of the Inner World* (Chicago: Willet, Clark & Co., 1936).

Demerath, N. J., "Adolescent Status Demands and the Student Experiences of Twenty Schizophrenics," *American Sociological Review,* 1943, 8, pp. 513–518.

Dunham, H. Warren, "The Social Personality of the Catatonic Schizophrene," *American Journal of Sociology,* May, 1944, 49, pp. 508–518.

Ellison, Alden, and Donald Hamilton, "The Hospital Treatment of Dementia Praecox," *The American Journal of Psychiatry,* December, 1949, 106, pp. 454–461.

Faris, Robert E. L., "Cultural Isolation and Schizophrenia," *American Journal of Sociology,* 1934, 40, pp. 155–169.

Gralnick, Alexander, "*Folie à Deux*—The Psychosis of Association: A Review of 103 Cases and the Entire English Literature," *Psychiatric Quarterly,* April, 1942, 16, pp. 491–520.

———, "The Carrington Family: A Psychiatric and Social Study Illustrating the Psychoses of Association or *Folie à Deux,*" *Psychiatric Quarterly,* April, 1943, 17, pp. 1–33.

Hunt, J. McV., "An Instance of the Social Origin of Conflict Resulting in Psychoses," *American Journal of Orthopsychiatry,* 1938, 8, pp. 158–164.

Kasanin, Joseph S. (editor), *Language and Thought in Schizophrenia* (Berkeley: University of California Press, 1944).

Miller, Wilbur R., "Relationship between Early Schizophrenia and Neuroses," *The American Journal of Psychiatry,* January, 1940, 96, pp. 889–896.

Patterson, Ralph M., and Thornton W. Ziegler, "Ordinal Position and Schizophrenia," *The American Journal of Psychiatry*, November, 1941, 98, pp. 455–458.

Raphael, Theophile, and L. E. Himmler, "Schizophrenia and Paranoid Psychoses among College Students," *The American Journal of Psychiatry*, January, 1944, 100, pp. 443–446.

Sullivan, Harry Stack, *Conceptions of Modern Psychiatry* (Washington, D.C.: The William Alanson White Psychiatric Foundation, 1945).

Tietz, Trude, "A Study of Mothers of Schizophrenic Patients," *Psychiatry*, February, 1949, 12, pp. 55–65.

Weinberg, S. Kirson, "A Sociological Analysis of a Schizophrenic Type," *American Sociological Review*, October, 1950, 15, pp. 600–610.

Wittman, Phyllis, and D. Louis Steinberg, "A Study of Prodromal Factors in Mental Illness with Special Reference to Schizophrenia," *The American Journal of Psychiatry*, May, 1944, 100, pp. 811–816.

CHAPTER TEN

Social Aspects of Schizophrenia: Types

The Problem of Types of Schizophrenia. We have pointed out in the preceding chapter that a static typology of schizophrenia, based upon symptoms, has definite limitations. This static classification was initiated and elaborated by Kraepelin.[1] He believed that "dementia praecox" occurred relatively early in life, usually after puberty, had a poor chance for recovery, and resulted from a metabolic disturbance. Later, Bleuler differentiated between this classical type of dementia praecox and schizophrenia.[2] He thought that schizophrenia occurred later in life, had a relatively good prognosis, and presumably involved a separation between the mental and emotional reactions. Although Bleuler pointed out some dynamic processes in schizophrenia, he believed that schizophrenia was a result of brain pathology. Freud, Jung, and Adolph Meyer gave a more dynamic interpretation of this disorder. For example, Meyer maintained that it was primarily a result of failure in adjustment and of habit deficiency.[3]

Since Meyer's time there have been varied classifications of schizophrenia. Meduna and McCulloch have differentiated between schizophrenia and oneirophrenia on the bases of mode of onset and biological differences.[4] The schizophrenic presumably had a clear

[1] Emil Kraepelin, *Dementia Praecox and Paraphrenia*, translated by R. Mary Barclay (Edinburgh: E. and S. Livingstone, 1919).

[2] Emil Bleuler, *Textbook of Psychiatry*, translated by A. A. Brill, pp. 1–35 (New York: The Macmillan Company, 1934).

[3] Adolph Meyer, *The Commonsense Psychiatry of Adolph Meyer*, edited by Alfred Lief, pp. 184–206 (New York: McGraw-Hill Book Company, Inc., 1949).

[4] L. J. Meduna and Warren S. McCulloch, "The Modern Concept of Schizophrenia," *Clinics of North America*, January, 1948, 29, pp. 147–164.

outlook at the time of the disorder; the oneirophrenic had a cloudy or confused outlook at the time of the disorder. Langfeldt has differentiated between the schizophrenic and the schizophreniform. The schizophrenic apparently is one who does not recover from his disorder, but the schizophreniform has a temporary disorder and does improve or recover.[5] Bellak has considered the biological and psychological factors in classifying schizophrenia into three types which could be placed along a psychosomatic continuum: (1) classical constitutionally determined schizophrenia, (2) psychogenically determined schizophrenia, and (3) acute, brief schizophrenia which resembles hysteria.[6]

These varied classifications, however, have not refuted the classical dementia praecox type which Kraepelin described and which does characterize an extreme type of schizophrenia. But many schizophrenics do not fit Kraepelin's classical description. Some schizophrenics do not break down in adolescence or early adulthood, many improve or recover, and some do not seem biologically predisposed to this disorder. Hence, a classificatory scheme of schizophrenia must consider (1) the mode of personality development, (2) the mode of onset, and (3) the course of the disorder—some indices of which are the length of the disorder and the degree of agitation during the disorder. Since the duration can be determined only when the person improves, it is necessary at the time of onset to consider only the first two criteria.

The mode of personality development covers the person's general adjustment or maladjustment before the onset. This developmental process includes the biological as well as the social component because the ways the individual internalizes his experiences and reworks his social influences and conflicts are, in part, influenced by the organism.

The mode of onset is important. At the one extreme there is the slow insidious type of breakdown without any visible external stress to precipitate the disorder. At the other extreme, there is the quick stormy conflictful type of breakdown which reveals heightened agitation and which occurs in one or a series of very critical situations.

[5] Georg Langfeldt, *The Schizophreniform States* (New York: Oxford University Press, 1939).
[6] Leopold Bellak, *Dementia Praecox,* p. 447 (New York: Grune & Stratton, Inc., 1948).

Concerning the duration of the disorder, we find that some schizophrenics do not improve and that others improve rather quickly. For example, in a five-year follow-up study of 177 schizophrenics, Malamud and Render found that 14 per cent recovered, 8 per cent had a social recovery, 3 per cent improved markedly and 7 per cent improved slightly, 10 per cent died, and 58 per cent did not improve.[7] Langfeldt found that 66 per cent of those whom he regarded as schizophreniforms recovered without appreciable treatment.[8] Bellak, who summarized a variety of studies, found that over-all improvement ranged from 22 per cent to 53.6 per cent, with the majority of studies showing a fluctuation around 40 per cent.[9]

The schizophrenic's experiences during the disorder cannot be discounted and do affect his chances of improvement. Some schizophrenics have become worse because they were slighted by their doctors, betrayed by their relatives, or punished without just cause. The schizophrenic's outlook, whether clear and apathetic or confused and agitated, also influences his chances of improvement. Some schizophrenics who have a clear but apathetic outlook may have less chance for improvement than other schizophrenics who are confused, emotional, and full of conflict.

Chronic Schizophrenics and Transient Schizophrenics

On the basis of these criteria, then, two general schizophrenic types emerge—the chronic and the transient. These types represent opposite extremes, usually are approximated in actual cases, and can be referred to as "ideal types."

The Chronic Schizophrenic. Developmentally, the chronic schizophrenic is usually a seclusive, shy, somewhat sensitized person who accepts his seclusiveness. Whether conformistic or perverse, he tends to withdraw socially and to be a shut-in personality. He does not cultivate friends, and generally he is awkward in his relationships with others. Because of his lowered self-esteem and his difficulties in social participation, he accepts fantasy and isolated pursuits more readily as a refuge. Not infrequently, he is considered queer or

---

[7] William Malamud and N. Render, "Course and Prognosis in Schizophrenia," *The American Journal of Psychiatry*, March, 1939, 95, pp. 1039–1057.

[8] Georg Langfeldt, *The Schizophreniform States* (New York: Oxford University Press, 1939).

[9] Leopold Bellak, *Dementia Praecox*, p. 402.

somehow different from other children because his personality difficulties are observed at an early age and become increasingly accentuated during adolescence and early adulthood. He has pronounced difficulties in fostering relationships with the opposite sex and generally tends to be retarded psychosexually.

His disorder develops slowly and insidiously and seems to bind itself into his personality so that the actual onset is sometimes hard to detect until he has been psychotic for a definite period. Moreover, he does not necessarily become psychotic as a result of perceptible external stress but tends to drift into his disorder. In other words, since the chronic schizophrenic is responding to some internalized conflicts which he cannot resolve, he becomes disordered despite the relatively mild external stress which precipitates the disorder.

There are many schizophrenics, however, who express agitation and conflict of varying intensities during the breakdown. This type, despite an adverse background, may improve slightly when removed from the conflict situation. When this conflictful onset occurs in a situation of great stress, this type combines features of the chronic and transient schizophrenic. The duration and outcome of his disorder then would result, of course, from his past development and general personality structure. When the onset has been very slow, or when it is accompanied by a flicker of agitation, as the culminating process of a seclusive, withdrawn development, the chronic schizophrenic tends to settle into the psychosis by intensifying his private attitudes and accepting his lowered self-esteem.

In a study of 100 schizophrenics, Sullivan found that the onset was slow and insidious in 22 cases. These 22 cases became gradually more and more peculiar until the disorder was recognized. Of these 22 patients, 7 persons, or 32 per cent, improved, and of the 7 only 2 were able to attain a condition that was equal to that of the general population. In 78 patients the onset was acute and abrupt. Of these 78 patients, 48, or 61 per cent, improved markedly, and many in this improved group recovered.[10] Thus, the person with an abrupt onset seems to have more favorable chances for recovery. Nonetheless, 30 patients with abrupt onsets did not improve. Even

[10] Harry Stack Sullivan, "The Relation of Onset to Outcome in Schizophrenia," *Schizophrenia: Association for Research in Nervous and Mental Disease,* pp. 110–115 (Baltimore: The Williams & Wilkins Company, 1929).

if we consider that some may have been affected adversely after the disorder occurred, their personal backgrounds may also have hindered recovery.

The chronic schizophrenics who have a maladjusted background and reveal an arrested development, may be divided into two types —those schizophrenics who have an insidious slow breakdown, and those schizophrenics who have an agitated, abrupt, and stormy breakdown.

The following case of John Alfred illustrates the development, onset, and course of the disorder in a chronic schizophrenic whose breakdown showed some conflict but which was neither intense nor prolonged.

When John, diagnosed a hebephrenic, was interviewed, he had been in the chronic ward of a mental hospital for seven years and was unable to work. Silently and limply he sat in his chair, disinterested in the others beside him. He was able to carry on a conversation of a simple sort, but he seemed indifferent and sometimes answered irrelevantly. Often he stopped and paused in silence.

John's father, who owned a 150-acre farm, was a hard-working and diligent farmer. His mother was devoted to the home and to her 7 children, of whom only John incurred a breakdown. John, the sixth of seven children, appeared quieter than the other children. His birth was normal, as were his first few years. Very obedient, he tried to do what he was told, but was very slow. Having little initiative, he waited for orders. To his parents, especially after the birth of his younger sister, he became more quiet, unemotional, and withdrawn. "He was never seen to shed a tear," as his parents put it. The parents favored the youngest child, a bright and friendly girl.

John entered Catholic school at 7; he had difficulty adjusting because of his marked shyness and his dislike for his teacher. He did so poorly that he had to repeat the first grade, but thereafter he did well in school. When in the fourth grade, at the age of 10, he began doing light chores on the farm. Thereafter, he spent most of his time doing his homework and working on the farm. Afraid he would fail in his studies, he devoted an unusual amount of time to them. Frail, tiring easily, he was not always pressed by his parents for help. Usually they pressed him less than his brothers. Obedient, he was presented to others as a "good boy."

But John felt neglected. He resented being called a "good boy." He was very sensitive and stayed out of the way of others because he was so easily offended. Whenever his brothers kidded him, he withdrew. In his teens he became even more drawn into himself. He was unable to defend himself in an argument and resorted to a passive kind of anger. He demanded very little for himself and usually wore his clothes to "shreds," unless his parents insisted that he change.

He made one acquaintance during his grammar-school days. He was very dependent upon him. The two went to ball games and visited back and forth. When the family moved to another farm, he was unable to cultivate other friends. Though not unusually bashful with girls, he seemed indifferent to them. He never had a date, never was friendly with a girl, and did not care to become friendly with girls. He spent a great deal of time reading magazines like *Popular Mechanics* and felt that he might become a great inventor. His reactions were recorded in a small diary, which he kept secret. Occasionally he listened to the radio, and he spent much time at the movies, alone. He seemed most content when he was alone, and not bothered by others.

Becoming more and more seclusive, he reached a point where he could not concentrate. He studied harder but could not grasp what he was studying. He then would stop, completely fatigued. He began to fail in his studies. Keenly disappointed, he withheld the information from his parents. He did not want them to scold or despise him. At times his father kidded him with his being a failure. Often they contrasted him with the sister who excelled in school and who was so popular. He felt that he was a failure.

At this time, 1942, the draft for 18-year-olds came up, but he neglected to register. He wanted to join up like the other boys and get away from his family, but his father had him deferred on the claim that he was needed badly on the farm. The patient seemed to agree, passively. Later, when asked by his father if he preferred going to the Army, he said, "Yes." He kept to himself even more, would not confide in the family, and remained in his room when the family was together or when visitors came. Especially hostile to the father, he felt he wanted to "go out and see the world."

As graduation day approached, his schoolwork fell off in some subjects. When asked by his parents whether he would graduate, John admitted that he would not. He was stung and disheartened by having to confess this to his parents, and they intensified his bitterness by admitting their disappointment and then ridiculing him. A few days later the patient returned home from school and demanded the car for a "trip." When his father asked him where he was going, he refused to say. Again the father asked. The patient then blurted out, "Shut up"—his first real outburst. Angered, the father consented that he should leave home. He volunteered to take him to the train, with the understanding that John thereafter would be "on his own."

Six days later he was found wandering in the streets of P——, He had amnesia and could not remember what had happened during the past six days. He had traveled to P—— after his father left him at the station. After he had taken the train to P——, he was filled with remorse at having spoken so rudely to his father. He began to feel lost and depressed. In P—— he went to a cheap hotel, then thought of seeking work. Because of his draft age, he could not get employment at the one place he tried. Despondent, he was afraid to return home. He did not know what to do with himself and started to walk aimlessly about the town. At this time he incurred his amnesia and was wandering the streets when he was picked up by the police. The family was notified and he was sent to a sanitarium where he received electroshock treatment, improved, and returned home.

Again he was very obedient but very withdrawn and forgetful, and he said that his head felt as if it were "blank." After a few months he was returned to the state hospital. He was hyperactive, giggled, and made manneristic movements with his hands and eyes. But basically he was indifferent, and he admitted having auditory hallucinations. Since 1943 he has remained in the state hospital continually, relatively out of contact with others and somewhat fearful of the world outside the hospital. He was able to converse about various matters concerning his past, but his whole demeanor and manner of conversation revealed a silliness and a kind of apathy, although he became slightly defensive when the possibility occurred that his family may have been responsible for his breakdown. He has been given 22 electroshock and some insulin shock treatments without any positive effects.

Interpretation. This person fits the chronic type of schizophrenia because of his personal background, onset, and the course of the disorder.

His development reveals a seclusive, shy, shut-in person who was awkward in his relations with others, easily offended, unable to endure strain, somewhat resigned to his isolation, and more or less content with his fantasy and solitary pursuits. Although conformistic and rather dependent upon his family, he was also hostile and withdrawn from them. He had almost no friends, did not know how to make friends, and was disinterested in girls. His school adjustment was fair until he seemingly had a breakdown when he failed in his courses.

He expressed some agitation during the onset of his disorder, but this agitation was neither intense nor prolonged. Furthermore, it seemed to be the culminating point of a disorder that had probably occurred before and went more or less unnoticed. Yet his agitation was somewhat consistent with his temporary improvement. That is, he was able to retrieve his prepsychotic condition, but he could not retain it, because of his rather poor personality organization. Although he encountered a stress situation before the breakdown, when viewed externally it would not have been of dire distress to the average person. He tried to emancipate himself from the family but did not have the confidence, social skills, or self-reliance to do so successfully. Thus what ordinarily would have been a growth process for the normal person became the precipitating situation of his disorder.

Since his return to the hospital, his chances for improvement have been decidedly unfavorable. His disorder, which has persisted for about seven years, reveals no signs of improvement.

The Transient Schizophrenic. Transient schizophrenia, as we have indicated, occurs among "fairly well adjusted" persons in situations of severe stress, as in combat, prison, or in the duress of civilian life generally. Often this type of psychosis is preceded by a neurosis and after some treatment, even as much as removal from the situation of stress, leads to improvement. The most extreme form which was noted in combat was so temporary that Braceland and Rome referred to it as "three-day schizophrenia," a term devised by Halloran.[11] Porter, the Malamuds, Parsons, and Menninger reported acute psychotic reactions, many of which resembled schizophrenia, among the combat participants.[12] Porter has observed that among these soldiers recovery started almost as soon as they were hospitalized with no particular therapy having been administered. Their improvement resulted from the belief or rationalization that they were to be removed from the situation of danger or that they were to be discharged.[13]

In a study of 67 cases of schizophrenia from Army camps, Klow pointed out that 13 were really transient schizophrenic types because they were well adjusted socially and had an abrupt and conflictful onset. Their disorders were of brief duration and terminated quickly.[14]

Grinker and Speigel have observed that, during extreme stress in combat, some soldiers lost their capacity to make discriminatory

[11] Francis J. Braceland and Howard P. Rome, "Problems in Naval Psychiatry," *War Medicine*, Oct., 1944, 6:4, pp. 217–220.

[12] See William C. Menninger, *Psychiatry in a Troubled World*, p. 168, footnote (New York: The Macmillan Company, 1948); William C. Porter, "Psychiatry in the Army," *Psychiatry and War*, edited by F. J. Sladen (Springfield, Ill.: Charles C. Thomas, Publisher, 1943). William and Irene Malamud, "Socio-Psychiatric Investigation of Schizophrenia Occurring in the Armed Forces," *Psychosomatic Medicine*, October, 1943, 5:4, pp. 364–375. E. H. Parsons, "Military Neuropsychiatry in the Present War," *Annals Internal Medicine*, 18, pp. 935–940. William C. Menninger, *Psychiatry in a Troubled World*, pp. 167–169.

[13] William C. Porter, "Psychiatry in the Army," *Psychiatry and War*, edited by F. J. Sladen, p. 245 (Springfield, Ill.: Charles C. Thomas, Publisher, 1943).

[14] Sidney D. Klow, "Acute Psychoses in Selectees," *Elgin State Hospital Papers*, December, 1944, 5, pp. 128–134.

judgments, expressed extremely peculiar behavior, and generally lost self-control. They laughed uncontrollably, wept, ran about aimlessly, or fell down and were unable to rise because of weakness.[15] This type of breakdown generally occurred from severe anxiety and panic for which the individual could muster no effective response.

Thus, the onset among transient schizophrenics is abrupt, agitated, stormy, and full of conflict. These schizophrenics, unable to resolve their conflicts, made a vigorous but random bid to reorganize themselves and to regain their self-esteem.[16]

Among the transient schizophrenics, however, there are two patterns of development. The first shows a conformistic, striving, but somewhat passive personality who seems to be fairly adjusted externally; the second consists of acting out perverse behavior. Both types tend to be neurotic or highly disturbed before the schizophrenic onset.

Conformist Type. In a study of 53 cases of transient schizophrenics between the ages of 20 and 35, who were selected from about 335 cases of schizophrenics in two state mental hospitals, the following somewhat typical developmental patterns were noted:[17] As among parents of chronic schizophrenics, the parental figures, especially the mothers, sometimes were unstable and domineering and sometimes overprotective. They instilled a marked dependency into the children and yet incurred their hostility by suppressive tactics. Usually the fathers seemed to be passive, indifferent, or removed figures. Nonetheless, the preschizophrenic children appeared normal to the parents and to others. They were not noticeably seclusive, queer, or unruly. Some subjects were even characterized as bright and happy children, and slightly mischievous. Despite their ability to adjust outwardly, they were unsure of themselves and had a low tolerance for rejection. The subjects usually had friends and many seemed to mingle well, although some subjects were isolated from others of their age because of family mobility or geographic distance. Moreover, the subjects seemed to adjust well in school, and some were exceptionally competent. But in their peer-group

[15] Roy R. Grinker and John Speigel, *Men Under Stress*, p. 130 (Philadelphia: The Blakiston Company, 1945).

[16] Anton T. Boisen, "The Form and Content of Schizophrenic Thinking," *Psychiatry*, February, 1942, 5:1, pp. 23–33.

[17] S. Kirson Weinberg, "Sociological Analysis of a Schizophrenic Type," *American Sociological Review*, October, 1950, 15:5, pp. 600–610.

relationships they were either passive followers or operated on the periphery of the group. Usually, they were unable to emancipate themselves from their parental and/or familial attachments, and their most crucial weakness resided in the sphere of heterosexual relationships.

Almost all the subjects had difficulties in fostering intimate social relationships of a durable kind with the opposite sex. The women subjects, who especially had difficulties in learning courtship skills or in defending themselves with men, were exploited, abused, or jilted. In fact, some female subjects broke down as a result of a disrupted "love affair" or an unhappy marriage. The male subjects had similar difficulties and were also very dependent upon the females with whom they did associate. In the exceptional instance of a somewhat mature love relationship, the mother opposed the relationship and tried to break it up. In fact, this type of experience directly contributed to the breakdown of two subjects.

Since the subjects incorporated parental aspirations, they were conscientious and ambitious. They were able to retain jobs, but they lacked social facility and found it difficult to advance occupationally. Their inability to advance occupationally was often interpreted as an intolerable personal rejection.

Prior to the onset, 7 subjects had definite neurotic breakdowns in which there were high components of anxiety, "hysteria," and depression. The others were also definitely agitated and disturbed on a neurotic level before the schizophrenic onset. Seemingly, their additional crises upset their life schemes and penetrated their neurotic defenses. Before and during the onset the subjects had nobody to whom they could confide their conflicts. This reticence, in part, concerning their condition resulted from intrafamily hostility and social distance, and from the death or departure of a family member to whom the subject was very attached. In the agitated and often panic-stricken condition which resulted at the time of the breakdown, it was sometimes difficult to distinguish whether the person was in a neurotic or a psychotic condition.

The Case of Alma Reeves

Alma was 23 when she broke down. In a fit of despair she tried suicide by swallowing bits of glass, but she vomited and lived. She then became so disordered that her admission into the state hospital was necessary. There she was diagnosed as "schizophrenia undetermined." She was dirty, careless, and disheveled in appearance and was completely out of contact with others. Usually she sat and stared into space as if intently preoccupied. She spoke continually of suicide. Once she asked whether jumping from the third-story window would kill her. She had the oppressive delusion that her father would lose his job. After four months in the hospital she recovered, for over five years has maintained her recovery, and with psychotherapy has even surpassed her prepsychotic condition.

The youngest of three sisters, Alma disappointed the wish of her father for a boy. Ten years younger than her next sibling, she was truly the "baby of the family."

"But after a while, still in my early childhood, I recall that there were things that made me feel unhappy, and I would be unhappy without knowing why. I was so dependent upon everyone because everyone seemed so adult to me. All through grammar school in the small town, X, New York, I played alone most of the time. We moved from the neighborhood in one part of X, and I didn't get to know the new kids who lived there. I didn't get experience in dealing with other kids, and this was part of my trouble in getting on later with the kids in school. For a while, I was with a little in-group of girls there, and occasionally we asked each other to parties.

"I didn't dress as well as the other girls and that made me feel inferior. One blond girl, I can picture her, was always dressed so neatly and I was a mess. I told Mom about it, but Mom had little interest in clothes. More than once, she told me that she'd have been a better mother for a boy than for a girl. She likes the outdoors so much—to walk and to camp—as a scout girl or something. The other kids had families who kept up with the Joneses. Mine didn't, but we were as well off as any of the other families because we owned property. This caused me to feel insecure and different from the other kids and made me have a passionate need to conform. I was so good and quiet, I almost never got into mischief.

"When I was ten, the family moved from New York to Y, Iowa, where father got a better job. But we had all new friends to make. After two years in Iowa, father got in a squabble with his office manager and was given notice to leave. We were afraid we would be reduced to poverty. Then he got a job as a salesman for lower pay and this made him very unhappy. He was easily irritated and would go into fits of anger for no reason at all. There was tension in the house and I considered my family unhappy.

"Father loves children, but when they get older he loses interest and sympathy for them. That's what he's done with me. He played with me a lot because I was the youngest, but then he changed. He wanted all us girls to be docile, submissive, and helpful, and he hoped that we would all get married when we grew up. He became more insecure because of his change in jobs, and he didn't give us money for clothes. Still I wasn't supposed to be independent. I never worked, not even on vacation. My only thought of becoming independent was by getting married when I grew older.

"I used to think that getting married was an escape from home and Dad. The world seemed like such a terrifying place to go. Of the children, Dad liked my second sister Alice the best. She was cheerful, industrious, and docile and made excellent grades in school. She got her degree, then got married and is very happy. I tried to be like her so Dad would give me some attention and praise me for a change. But I wasn't good in school. I tried hard, but I was babyish in many ways. I wanted to be in activities, but was always absent-minded, late, and messed things up. I wanted to be real important and popular, but I fouled up everything I tried. When I graduated from high school, I was in the second half of the class, which was worse than my sisters.

"When I was 15, I was keen on getting to know a man. I was on vacation with my family and a man ten years older than I was there. He took me on an automobile ride and promised to marry me, then he forced me to have sex relations with him. That so terrified me that I drew into myself, and imagined when anyone referred to me that this was involved. And I felt very guilty and inferior.

"Dad wanted me to go to a college in New York. I got in and couldn't get along well. Through a mix-up I got pledged late in the sorority. And I didn't get acquainted with the other pledges for some time. This college was a sad place for me. I didn't know how to get acquainted with the other girls, and I didn't know how to strike up and keep a conversation with the boys. I didn't feel the other girls liked me. I was about the only one who didn't go out with someone. I was really relieved when I was called home because Mother got sick.

"I was frightfully unrealistic at 18. I used to have such impossible ideals for myself. I always wanted to be beautiful, popular, and brilliant. But I didn't work to get this way. I wouldn't even try too hard because I'd fail anyway. I generally didn't do well in the things I tried, so I used to make up for it by daydreaming about these ideals. I was nervous and unhappy and very timid. I was afraid to try anything because I was afraid I would fail. I wore a worried look on my face. My doctor once told me that I was so strained in my expression, I looked as if I were afraid to do anything. I couldn't seem to be good at anything. I tried to get dates by fixing myself up and trying to get more boy friends. I got asked out by some boys, but they wouldn't stick and I wound up without any that I really liked. My family was still full of conflict, with the women lined up against my father.

"During summer I decided to go to a different college. I went to an Eastern college and liked it so well that I didn't want to come home. I made one girl's acquaintance and we had a very enjoyable time together.

"It didn't go well in this college. I flunked a couple of exams. I had a difficult time in the sciences and changed to psychology because I did much better. This switch in majors helped my morale. I didn't want to flunk out and go to work. Working scared me. But lots of things scared me! My courses! My father and what he thought! Not getting boy friends! Other girls had boy friends. Going out East to this college would· change everything—I had hoped.

"In school I met some swell girls. My roommate, Jane, was easy to get along with and she was one of the reasons that I wanted to stay in school. I tried to get into some sororities, was invited to two functions, and then dropped. This saddened me very much; I felt confident about getting in. It was about that time, I met Tom.

"Tom was a soldier who was attending one of the Army training school programs, and we met at the U.S.O. He was so angry about being washed out of the Air Corps. He told me I was cute and kept coming to see me. I was very happy. Sometimes I was afraid he'd change his mind, but he didn't. When he left me to go back to school, I was in the depths. When he wrote, I was very happy. When he didn't, I was in agony. But I kept writing to him, asking him to write to me.

"My confidence went up and I passed all my courses. I felt better and though I didn't have many dates like the other girls, it was an achievement for me to have a boy friend. Dad and Mom had always wanted me to get married since I was 16. Now I was 22 and before I met Tom I worried whether I ever would get married. I went back home for the summer, and Tom wrote he would like to meet me in Indianapolis."

After her parents gave permission, she met him and they became engaged.

"I wrote a letter to my parents telling them. I loved Tom, but I was afraid of sex, because of the experience I had before. I still was worried I might not be able to hold him.

"When I returned to school, I showed the girls my ring and some were impressed. When they asked me when we would be married, I hoped I could have said a definite date for the marriage. That would have impressed them more. I kept feeling afraid he'd jilt me and with all the boys off to war, I thought I'd never get another chance. I knocked myself out to please Tom, but he didn't go out of his way to please me. Sometimes he acted as though he did me a favor by writing to me.

"Things at the house began to get worse. I had gotten along well with the girls in the house, and felt secure with my roommate, Jane. I looked up to her because she had good grades and had many boy friends. Nobody ran after me but Tom, and I wasn't real sure of him. But I liked the engagement ring. At that time, Jane and another girl in the dormitory, Edith, quarreled. Everybody took sides, and I was in the middle. Edith told me that she could get me into a sorority if I quit speaking to Jane. Tom had criticized me and said I was introvertish. He said that I had to go out and do things. I wanted to join a sorority so very much, to keep Tom. Tom meant self-respect, because he proved I was worthy of love. I began to speak with Edith to get into the sorority. When Jane found out, she and my other friends stopped speaking to me. Jane said that I was a social climber and would do anything to climb. It was awful. The only people, my friends, whom I'd known well, couldn't stand me now. I couldn't sleep. I was miserable. It was on my mind when I tried to study and I couldn't study. I became more than ever dependent upon Tom. Before I wrote cheerful letters to him. After this fight I wrote him everything—like a diary. Then I learned that Edith and her friends wouldn't take me into a sorority. I became so upset and I didn't know to whom to turn.

"The other girls and I had to move from the house. I moved in with new and strange girls. They were cliquish and not friendly at all. Jane and my other friends lived together in another house. I was very lonesome, and turned more to Tom. As the semester nearly ended I wanted to see him. I asked him if we could meet. He wrote back: 'Darling, I think you'd be much happier going home.' At the beginning I was relieved because it wouldn't bring up the matter of sex. Then I was very, very miserable because he didn't want to see me. Where was all his love that he threw around in his letters? I had feeling that he might be going with some other girl, and I was ready for the brush-off. But I hoped against it. Then he typed a short note without all the endearing pet names. I became a nervous wreck from it all. I was without a friend in the world. Those sex relations came to my mind and made me feel degraded and guilty. I thought that his love for me and my love for him justified these sex relations. Now I was no good. I couldn't keep my boy friend and my girl friends. I hated to think what my father would say that a definite day had not been set for the wedding.

"I came home and my misery showed on my face. I told my mother about it, but not the real things that bothered me—just that Tom didn't write, and I didn't know what was the matter. I kept the affair with the girls and about sex to myself. I was very depressed. I moped during the summer.

"In school, things didn't get better. The other girls were unfriendly to me. I was very lonesome, and left out that I wasn't in a sorority. I felt awful about Tom not writing. I called him long distance and asked him why. He said it was hard to say over the phone, and he would write to me. I waited anxiously for the letter; it came special delivery the next day. He had found a girl whom he cared for more than he did me. Our engagement was off. I burst into tears. I couldn't talk, I couldn't eat, I couldn't think. I went over to the girls who used to be my friends and asked them what I should do. They told me to send his ring back but to keep the presents.

"I had the feeling that I'd never get married. I was a failure and nobody had any use for me. I put on a brave front, but it didn't work. I cried nearly all the time. I was afraid to tell my parents and my father especially. He had been nicer to me since I was engaged, and he liked Tom. Now he would become unpleasant, nasty, and would tease me in his way that made me feel I would be a burden on him for the rest of my life.

"I became more nervous, depressed, and mixed up. I kept thinking 'I wish I were dead.' When I studied, I kept thinking, 'I wish I were dead.' There was a water glass in the washroom, and I looked at the water glass, and the thought came to me: 'I could eat a little of that glass and be out of this world where I always failed at everything.' I couldn't stand being so miserable. I went into the washroom, and threw the glass on the floor, and ate a few splinters. I began feeling panicky and I vomited. I rushed to a girl seated in another room, and told her I had broken a glass. She looked at me disgusted and gave me a brush to clean it up. I cleaned it up, and high-tailed it to a doctor. He became disgusted and said that I couldn't stay in school. The idea of not staying in school made me feel like escaping from hanging. I was so unhappy there. I packed my things, and the doctor told me I could become a volunteer patient in a near-by hospital. Through all my feelings of hating myself, I was shocked when the door shut and I realized that I was in a hospital for the mentally ill."

Interpretation. This schizophrenic breakdown had a transient character for the following reasons: First, the subject approximated the conformistic model child instead of the perverse or isolated child. Her isolation from other children denoted not a shut-in personality but a situational isolation, which was brought on by family mobility and by deficits in social learning. During college she cultivated the companionship of other girls, although she remained a passive follower. She was also able to cultivate relations with the opposite sex despite her inadequate knowledge of courtship relations and lack of confidence. Second, her psychotic episode was preceded by a neurotic depression which meant that she lacked the requisite defenses for coping with her situation. Third, the onset of her disorder was abrupt and fraught with conflict, and was a result of perceptible stress. Fourth, her psychosis represented a desperate effort to reorient herself and to resolve her conflicts. It thus signifies a drastic attempt at social learning and personal growth. As French and Kasanin put it: ". . . an acute psychosis may be a transitional episode in the process of emancipation from an old method of adjustment and 'learning' a new one." [18] This is fully represented by the emancipation of Alma from her parents after her recovery, her ability to adjust in the business world, and her successful marriage.

Acting-out Perverse Type. Acting-out perverse persons may become either chronic or transient schizophrenics. That they can become chronic schizophrenics may not be surprising, but it is also evident that they can experience acute temporary breakdowns and recover. These developmental types are infrequent. Of 175 cases, Boisen found 6 boys who belonged to antisocial groups and who acted as "toughs." Of these 6 boys, only 1 developed an acute schizophrenic reaction.[19]

In a study of the opinions of 30 psychiatrists concerning the

[18] Thomas M. French and Joseph Kasanin, "A Psychodynamic Study of the Recovery of Two Schizophrenic Cases," *Psychoanalytic Quarterly,* January, 1941, X:1, p. 21; also in *Contemporary Psychopathology,* edited by Sylvanus S. Tomkins, pp. 355–370 (Cambridge, Mass.: Harvard University Press, 1947).

[19] Anton T. Boisen, *Exploration of the Inner World,* p. 50 (Chicago: Willet & Clark, 1936).

"psychotic psychopath," Cruvant and Yochelson found that the majority felt that the concept was valid. These psychiatrists emphasized the transient character of the disorder, which in some instances resembled schizophrenia. This type had a background of acting-out, antisocial behavior and had a sudden explosive onset and relatively rapid improvement or recovery.[20]

Among prisoners, Paskind and Brown noted psychotic disorders which were similar to schizophrenia. These prisoners had defects of attention, hallucinations, delusions, impairments of judgment, dullness, apathy, lessening of volitional impulses, and a decline of spontaneous speech and mannerisms. These disorders differed from chronic schizophrenia because of constant emotional conflict, very rapid onset, tendency to recover, and general inability of the persons to recall the psychotic episode after recovery. Since similar symptoms resulted because the same dynamics were present in both types of disorders, they suggested such names as "shock psychoses" or "situation psychoses" to characterize this type of disorder. This type is illustrated in the following case:[21]

A 35-year-old attorney and Certified Public Accountant, who had no nervous or mental disorder, was jailed because of charges of obtaining $160,000 fraudulently from clients seeking home loans. Since boyhood, he claimed that he had been irritable, stubborn, suspicious and depressed. Soon after his arrest, he showed marked personality changes. He became apathetic, dull, and careless in his appearance. He didn't associate with other inmates and remained in the same position all day. Frequently he refused to eat or to participate in activities. He developed hallucinations and delusions that men entered his room at night and tried to murder him . . . "these men have lions' bodies where women keep springing out—these women have knives and guns as well as hatchets." They threatened "to chop his head off." He claimed that at night 100 men and 100 women visited him in jail and that he had received a little over two million dollars from these visitors, that 2,000 women entered his cell at night in groups of from two to ten, to have sex relations

[20] Bernard A. Cruvant and Leon Yochelson, "The Psychiatrist and the Psychotic Psychopath," *The American Journal of Psychiatry*, February, 1950, 106:8, pp. 594–598.

[21] See Henry A. Paskind and Meyer Brown, "Psychoses Resembling Schizophrenia Occurring with Emotional Stress and Ending in Recovery," *The American Journal of Psychiatry*, 1940, 96:2, pp. 1379–1388.

with him because they had heard that his genitals were so large. He boasted of possessing fifty properties, ten checking accounts, four wives, and one-half million diamonds. Finally he claimed that God tells him to be a "good boy."

During the examination, his attention wandered. He was completely disoriented for time and place. He gave irrelevant responses to general knowledge tests. During the examination his head would jerk sharply to the left. He had no neurological difficulties or syphilis, but five years before admission he had diabetes, which went untreated. He was sent to a Security Hospital and recovered in six months. Then, he worked around the hospital. One year after admission, he was returned to jail and reexamined. He had no signs of disorder in mood, speech or appearance, gave a detailed coherent history, had no hallucinations, was perfectly oriented from general knowledge tests, showed superior ability, and expressed interest in his future. He recalled being in jail once before, but didn't remember being transferred to a Security Hospital or his experiences there; and he could not recall his hallucinations and delusions during his disordered episode.

Hypotheses of Schizophrenia

What sociological and social psychological hypothesis best explains the rise of schizophrenia? Although some hypotheses may fit the chronic schizophrenic, these hypotheses do not necessarily fit the transient schizophrenic. Can a hypothesis cover both of these types? [22]

A Sociological Hypothesis of Schizophrenia. The sociological hypotheses of schizophrenia concentrate primarily upon personal isolation and disorientation. According to one version, schizophrenia results from "any form of isolation which cuts the person off from intimate social relationships for an extended period of

[22] J. N. Nielsen and George N. Thompson, *The Engrammes of Psychiatry* (Springfield, Ill.: Charles C. Thomas, Publisher, 1947). "[In] one group of cases . . . the removal of frustration results in a rapid clearing of symptoms with no other treatment necessary," p. 216. Hoskins, in a more eclectic discussion which concentrates on the biopathology of schizophrenia, also recognizes the two types. See Roy G. Hoskins, *The Biology of Schizophrenia*, pp. 72, 73 (New York: W. W. Norton & Company, 1946); George Devereaux, "A Sociological Theory of Schizophrenia," *Psychoanalytic Review*, 1939, 26, pp. 315–342.

time." [23] The bizarre behavior emerges after the individual fails to establish intimate relationships. Although isolated behavior sets the necessary framework in which schizophrenia occurs, it is not sufficient as an explanation of the disorder.

Although many chronic schizophrenics were shut-in, seclusive types, other schizophrenics were not isolated from their peer groups, although they may not have acquired the cultural skills and role-taking facilities in those areas of behavior in which their conflicts became most intense. In addition, some participated with intimate groups until the very onset of the disorder. In fact, some schizophrenics became more compulsively sociable before the breakdown. Hence, it is not the isolation itself, but the meaning and reaction to isolation that pertained most directly to the eventual schizophrenic breakdown. This isolation pertained especially to the disruption of intimate contacts such as courtship and marriage. Hence, the feeling of isolation becomes significant only as it is reflected upon the preschizophrenic's self-involving, unbearable conflicts, and it could not be understood without these conflicts.

In fact, schizophrenics had such unbearable conflicts that they regarded themselves as failures and completely lost confidence in their ability to manipulate their environment.[24] Some schizophrenics who attempted suicide exemplified this effort to destroy a reproachful self-image. Other schizophrenics, who acted out in random aggression against their relatives, spouses, and against other persons, made futile bids for regaining their self-esteem. On the other hand, those schizophrenics who expressed slight agitation at the time of the breakdown were too overwhelmed to resist their lowered self-esteem. Perhaps they did not have the kind of personality organization which could resist such severe conflicts and self-depreciation.

[23] Robert E. L. Faris, "Cultural Isolation and the Schizophrenic Personality," *American Journal of Sociology*, 1934–1935, XL, p. 456. Faris has since modified and amplified his version of schizophrenia so as to include the inner reactions to isolation. See Robert E. L. Faris, *Social Psychology*, pp. 352–361 (New York: The Ronald Press Co., 1952).

[24] Boisen has pointed out that of the causative factors in schizophrenia the primary factor resides in the realm of social relationships. From their social relationships, schizophrenics become imbued with a sense of personal failure. They internalize and accept this social judgment of personal failure and hence, they experience an "intolerable loss of self-respect." Anton T. Boisen, *Exploration of the Inner World*, p. 28 (Chicago: Willet & Clark, 1936).

The onset of schizophrenia, which frequently may begin in social isolation or social estrangement, then, resides in the following unified sequence of reactions: (1) the rejection of the self-image and the intense or feeble striving for self-acceptance and social acceptance, (2) the inability to communicate one's conflicts or the inaccessibility of others to whom these conflicts could be communicated, and (3) the recourse to withdrawal as a medium of self-defense.

This withdrawal process is essentially a disrupted role-taking process in which the schizophrenic is spared the ordeal of interpreting the evaluations of others, and thereby of evaluating himself. This cutting off of role taking and self-reference in the spheres of conflict creates the defense of disoriented behavior. But this disoriented behavior is a result of the inability to shift and to share the perspectives of others. Thus, the schizophrenic pays the price of aggravating his conflicts by disrupting or losing the essential capacity for communication which binds him to the group.

Schizophrenia and Culture

Is schizophrenia universal or is it limited to certain cultures? On the basis of analyses in the United States, it has been shown that the rates of hospitalization of schizophrenics increase as the size of the community increases. Also, it has been pointed out that within the urban community the ethnic groups which are minorities in certain areas have higher rates of schizophrenia than the majority groups in this setting. But this problem can be examined more thoroughly by knowing to what extent schizophrenia exists among nonliterate societies. From past studies it appears that three positions concerning this problem have been taken: (1) Schizophrenia and other personality psychoses are very rare or do not exist among some nonliterate peoples. (2) Psychotic disorders, particularly schizophrenia, exist among those nonliterate peoples who have had contacts with Western cultures. (3) Schizophrenia exists among nonliterate as well as among Western peoples.

Robert Faris, Cooper, Devereaux, and Seligman, among others, maintain that schizophrenia is rare or nonexistent in homogeneous nonliterate societies which have had minimal contacts with Western cultures.[25] Ellsworth Faris, as we have pointed out, attributes the

[25] Robert E. L. Faris, "Some Observations on the Incidence of Schizophrenia in Primitive Society," *Journal of Abnormal and Social Psychology*, April–June,

absence of schizophrenia among the Bantu of the Congo Forest to their intimate relationships.[26] Devereaux attributes the relative absence of schizophrenia among some nonliterate groups to their "one-answer" universe or to their consistent value system in the culture.[27] This cultural consistency seemingly would preclude the kinds of personal disorientation that lead to schizophrenia.

On the other hand, on the basis of M. Mead's data, Winston suggests that a high incidence of psychosis exists among certain groups of nonliterates.[28] Mead maintains that, because of exogamic marriages, the husbands who enter a different clan as strangers become so involved in conflict that some may experience a schizophrenic breakdown. She also implies that the constitutional and temperamental variants may also have a schizophrenic lapse. An example of a so-called schizophrenic type, whom Mead observed for a few days, is a 14-year-old boy.[29]

> He was at the time when I saw him definitely demented, giving an external picture of catatonic dementia praecox. He took those attitudes which were urged upon him, at times, becoming violent and unmanageable. The relatives insisted that he had always been stupid but only recently became demented.

Patently, such an observation would not be conclusive for a diagnosis of catatonia in our culture, and it becomes increasingly difficult to make such a diagnosis in a completely different culture. But it does seem that feeble-minded persons in preliterate societies (from this study and other studies) are the ones likely to become psychotic.

Seligman, on the basis of researches in New Guinea, and Dhunji-

---

1934, XXIX, pp. 30–31; John Cooper, "Mental Disease Situations in Certain Cultures," *Journal of Abnormal and Social Psychology*, April–June, 1934, XXIX, pp. 10–17; George Devereaux, "A Sociological Theory of Schizophrenia," *Psychoanalytic Review*, 1939, XXVI, pp. 315–342; C. G. Seligman, "Temperament, Conflict and Psychosis in a Stone Age Population," *British Journal of Medical Psychology*, 1929, IX, pp. 187–202; B. F. J. Laubscher, *Sex, Custom and Psychopathology* (New York: Robert M. McBride & Company, 1938).

[26] Ellsworth Faris, "Culture among the Forest Bantu," *The Nature of Human Nature*, pp. 278–288 (New York: McGraw-Hill Book Company, Inc., 1937).

[27] George Devereaux, "A Sociological Theory of Schizophrenia," *Psychoanalytic Review*, 1939, XXVI, pp. 315–342.

[28] Ellen Winston, "The Assumed Increase of Mental Disease," *American Journal of Sociology*, 1935, XL, pp. 427–440.

[29] Margaret Mead, "Coming of Age in Samoa," *From the South Seas*, p. 279 (New York: William Morrow & Company, Inc., 1939).

bhoy, on the basis of studies in sections of India, claim that psychoses
are manifest among those nonliterate or folk groups who have had
persistent contact with Europeans.[30] Carothers, on the basis of
seven years' experience in a mental hospital in Kenya, Africa, found
174 cases of schizophrenia, of which 122 patients were Bantu. He
found further that 63 natives, or 41 per cent, became "detribalized."
These natives had left their tribes to secure employment and, upon
their return, were unable to readjust and eventually broke down.
He thus shows that schizophrenia can occur particularly among
nonliterate peoples who have had contacts with Western cultures.[31]
Wulf Sachs' *Black Hamlet* observes that those confined in the
psychotics' asylum of South Africa were seemingly more prone to
psychotic disorders when they accepted European culture. He
says:[32]

> I hear so much silly talk when these people think they are God, Jesus
> Christ or Satan. But I have not heard a single one imagine to be a
> Mwari or a Midzimu. . . . The Christian religion makes trouble in
> the native brain.

Investigators have maintained that schizophrenia is universal for
two reasons. One reason is that when nonliterate cultures are studied intensively, intense personal conflicts among the members
become apparent and that disordered and psychotic behavior may
also become discernible. Another reason is that schizophrenia is
considered a biological disorder and as such can occur in any culture.

From the first viewpoint, the emphasis is upon the manner in
which the individual participant acquires and reshapes the culture
to satisfy his personal needs. Presumably, the individual participant
in even the simplest-structured culture is no automaton but an
agent who must make discriminatory and often conflicting judg-

---

[30] C. G. Seligman, "Temperament, Conflict and Psychosis in a Stone Age Population," *British Journal of Medical Psychology*, IX, 1929, pp. 187–202; J. E.
Dhunjibhoy, "A Brief Résumé of the Types of Insanity Commonly Met with in
India, with a Full Description of 'Indian Hemp Insanity' Peculiar to the Country," *Journal of Mental Science*, 76, 1930, pp. 254–64. (Dhunjibhoy maintains, too,
that only Hindus who have been overseas or who have lived in strongly western-
ized Indian communities develop schizophrenia.)

[31] James C. Carothers, "A Study of the Mental Derangement in Africans and
an Attempt to Explain Its Peculiarities More Especially in Relation to the
African Attitude to Life," *Psychiatry*, February, 1948, XI, pp. 47–86.

[32] Wulf Sachs, *Black Hamlet*, p. 185 (Boston: Little, Brown & Company, 1947).

ments. When he becomes enmeshed in profound and sustained conflicts, he may become so completely upset that the bases for a schizophrenic disorder may arise.[33]

The second view emphasizes the "constitutional" or innately temperamental variations of those who may break down. In explaining the frequency of schizophrenia in rural China, which has been only slightly influenced by Western culture, Kao and his associates maintain that the onset can only be satisfactorily explained in terms of the constitution of the patients. They state:[34] "Although not final these results are compatible with the concept that the ubiquitous schizophrenias are deeply rooted biological disorders, and not mere psychogenic reactions to social or cultural conditions."

Kardiner, Nielsen, and Thompson also maintain that schizophrenia is a constitutional disorder and would exist probably in all cultures.[35] There is, however, no definite and complete evidence to support their assertions. Even though schizophrenics are found in some nonliterate societies, this does not mean that their disorders resulted from biological predispositions only. A profound knowledge of the motivational facets of each culture would be required to verify this point.

On the basis of evidence, it appears that schizophrenics exist in those nonliterate societies which have had contacts with Western culture. Schizophrenics seldom appear in some nonliterate societies which are isolated from Western culture and in which intimate contacts prevail. Psychoses, and perhaps schizophrenia, may exist in

[33] Ernest Beaglehole, "Cultural Complexity and Psychological Problems," *Psychiatry*, August, 1940, III, pp. 330–332. See N. J. Demerath, "Schizophrenia among Primitives: Present Status of Sociologic Research," *The American Journal of Psychiatry*, 1942, 93, pp. 703–707.

[34] R. S. Lyman, *et al.* (editors), *Neuropsychiatry in China*, p. 363 (Peking: Henry Vetch, 1939).

[35] "Even in the endogenous psychoses, manic depression and schizophrenia, some equivalents of which are probably universal, the content shows up the basic personality." Abram Kardiner *et al.*, *Psychological Frontiers of Society*, p. 431 (New York: Columbia University Press, 1945). "The disease (schizophrenia) is known among all races and is the most frequent functional psychosis found in the Negro and Oriental races. Similarly the American Indian is susceptible and not even primitive peoples seem to be exempt. The writers have also seen cases among the Eskimo, Asiatics, Polynesians and Virgin Islands." J. N. Nielsen and George N. Thompson, *The Engrammes of Psychiatry*, p. 210 (Springfield, Ill.: Charles C Thomas, Publisher, 1947). The authors do not indicate, however, under what conditions their observations were made and present no evidence for their assertions.

those nonliterate societies which are isolated from Western culture but in which hostile relationships prevail. Those societies where schizophrenia was rare either had group forms of tolerance, which deterred the complete breakdown of the individual members, or provided institutionalized outlets for disordered persons which were not discerned by the investigators of these societies. Also, the content of schizophrenia in nonliterate societies differs from the content of schizophrenia in Western societies.

Schizophrenia and the Social Structure

This leads to the general problem of the relationship between social structure in our culture and schizophrenia. Clearly, the modes of rearing children, the areas of anxiety, and the modes of personal expression vary among the social classes; hence, the development and expression of schizophrenia in different social strata would also vary. For example, schizophrenics who are in the upper socioeconomic levels and have had few subsistence anxieties could be compared with schizophrenics who are in the lower socioeconomic levels and have had intense subsistence anxieties.

The "Ambulatory Schizophrenic" and Culture. The "ambulatory schizophrenic" refers to a person who has no emotionally close relationships with other persons and who seems unable to foster such relationships. Presumably, he can adjust vocationally, can relate with others on an intellectual or on an impersonal level but seemingly cannot foster a close rapport with others on an emotional level. If this criterion of schizophrenia is taken as a norm of psychosis, then the pervasiveness of this personality type is apparent in an impersonal society and requires far more elucidation. For many people, some of whom are very successful, may have many business "contacts," casual "friends," but few, if any, intimate friends, and cannot cultivate such relationships.

Summary

The static approach to the classification of schizophrenics is in process of being supplanted by developmental and dynamic approaches to a classificatory scheme. These developmental criteria for classifying schizophrenics consist of (1) degree of personal stability, (2) mode of breakdown, and (3) duration of the disorder.

From these criteria, two broad types of schizophrenics emerge—the chronic and the transient.

The chronic schizophrenic is unstable and withdrawn during childhood, and definitely unstable during adolescence. He drifts slowly into his disorder and tends to settle into his psychosis. Hence, his chances for improvement tend to be slight.

The transient schizophrenic tends to be relatively more stable and sociable during childhood and adolescence, experiences an agitated and stormy breakdown, and tends to improve or recover from his disorder.

Regardless of type, the schizophrenic is usually socially isolated or socially estranged and experiences the following sequence of reactions prior to the breakdown: (1) He rejects himself but strives intensely or feebly for self-acceptance and social acceptance. (2) He is unable to communicate his conflicts or cannot find persons to whom he can communicate his conflicts. (3) He resorts to withdrawal as a means of defense. (4) He becomes disoriented in this process.

Although disagreement exists concerning the universality of schizophrenia, it appears that schizophrenia is less frequent in cultures which are homogeneous and have intimate contacts than in cultures which are heterogeneous and have impersonal and hostile contacts.

Selected Readings

Bellak, Leopold, *Dementia Praecox* (New York: Grune & Stratton, Inc., 1948).

Caldwell, John M., Jr., "Schizophrenic Psychoses: 100 Cases in U.S. Army," *The American Journal of Psychiatry,* March, 1941, 97:5, pp. 1061–1072.

Collins, R. T., "Affect in Schizophrenic Reaction Types," *Journal of Mental Science,* 89, pp. 21–41.

Devereaux, George, "A Sociological Theory of Schizophrenia," *Psychoanalytic Review,* 1939, 26, pp. 315–342.

Duval, A. M., and Jay L. Hoffman, "Dementia Praecox in Military Life as Compared with Civil Life," *War Medical Institute,* pp. 854–862.

Kant, Otto, "Comparative Study of Recovered and Schizophrenic Patients," *Journal of Nervous and Mental Disease,* 93, 1941, pp. 616–624.

Kraepelin, Emil, *Dementia Praecox and Paraphrenia,* translated by R. Mary Barclay (Edinburgh: E. & S. Livingstone, 1919).

Langfeldt, George, *Schizophreniform States* (New York: Oxford University Press, 1939).

Lewis, Nolan L. C., and E. Blanchard, "Clinical Findings in 'Recovered' Cases of Schizophrenia," *The American Journal of Psychiatry,* November, 1931.

Malamud, William, and Irene Malamud, "A Socio-Psychiatric Investigation of Schizophrenia Occurring in the Armed Forces," *Psychosomatic Medicine,* 1943, 5:4, pp. 364–375.

Meduna, L. J., and Warren S. McCulloch, "The Modern Concept of Schizophrenia," *Clinics of North America,* January, 1948, 29, pp. 147–164.

Paskind, Henry A., and Meyer Brown, "Psychoses Resembling Schizophrenia Occurring with Emotional Stress and Ending in Recovery," *The American Journal of Psychiatry,* 1940, 96, pp. 1379–1388.

Stengel, E., "Significance of Compulsive Neurotic Personality in Schizophrenia," *The American Journal of Psychiatry,* 1950, 106, pp. 590–603.

Sullivan, Harry Stack, "Schizophrenia: Its Conservative and Malignant Features," *The American Journal of Psychiatry,* July, 1924, IV, pp. 77–91.

Wall, Conrad, "Some Prognostic Criteria for the Response of Schizophrenia Patients to Insulin Treatment," *The American Journal of Psychiatry,* May, 1941, 97, pp. 1397–1399.

Washburne, Annette, and Ed. R. Hodgson, "Regression Neurosis and Schizophrenia," *The American Journal of Psychiatry,* March, 1941, 97, pp. 1073–1076.

Weinberg, S. Kirson, "A Sociological Analysis of a Schizophrenic Type," *American Sociological Review,* October, 1951, 15:5, pp. 600–610.

CHAPTER ELEVEN ·

Social Aspects of Manic Depression and Allied States

Manic depression and schizophrenia comprise the two large categories of personality psychoses. But manic depression, in contrast to schizophrenia, more frequently afflicts persons over 35, some of whom have reached the prime of their careers. Manic depression seems less sensitized than schizophrenia and other forms of personal disorganization to broad urban processes. It is an atypical form of personal disorganization. It affects in somewhat similar proportions the rich and poor, the educated and uneducated, the married and single, the rural and urban. In fact, manic depression seems to hit many persons who are favored by wealth, rank, and ability, and who are sociable, outgoing, and externally adjusted. Consequently, manic depression has been considered by some investigators as an almost inevitable hereditary disorder. But, as is quite likely, this disorder may result from more subtle and not easily discernible social influences. In contrast to chronic schizophrenia, manic depression usually responds favorably to treatment. Manic depression usually is a very recurrent disorder. Manic depressives, especially depressives, frequently try to commit suicide. Although not so pervasive or pressing a social problem as schizophrenia, manic depression remains a more puzzling personality problem.

In this chapter our purpose is to describe manic depression as a category of behavior, to differentiate between manic depression and schizophrenia, to discuss the developmental processes and the precipitating experiences among manic depressives, and to indicate the effects of divergent cultural influences upon this category of disorders.

What Is Manic Depression?

Manic depression, in its most restricted sense, is a disorder of mood and selfhood without evident organic pathology. It includes manic, depressive, and circular subtypes, among other variations.[1] Apparently, most persons afflicted with the manic-depressive disorder experience only the manic or depressive reaction and not both reactions. As we have pointed out, in a study of 208 cases Rennie found that less than 25 per cent of the cases had both manic and depressive reactions, although 80 per cent of the cases had one or more recurrences of their disorders.[2]

Allied to manic depression are other types of depression such as involutional melancholia, which resembles an agitated depression, schizophrenia with depressive features, and the neurotic depressions.[3] Sometimes these depressed conditions are included with manic depression.

Manic Behavior. Manic behavior is a flight from conflict into hyperactivity, exaggerated enthusiasm, intensified but compulsive sociability, and open display of formerly inhibited feelings. Despite apparent buoyancy, the manic runs away from himself, and underneath his apparent elation he usually is depressed and uneasy. One manic described his behavior as follows: "When I am still, I feel badly. I have to keep going, to get excited about something in order to feel good."

The manic is preoccupied with intensified activity toward ever-changing goals. His flights into activity are means of evading reflection and self-reference. Hence, he is distractible and is not readily amenable to self-control and to social control. His compulsive, outgoing overactivity disrupts the role-taking process because he be-

---

[1] The other classified subtypes include agitated depression, perplexed, manic stupor, and unclassified.

[2] Thomas A. C. Rennie, "Prognosis in Manic-Depressive Psychosis," *The American Journal of Psychiatry*, May, 1942, 98:6, pp. 801–814.

[3] See Adolph Meyer, *The Commonsense Psychiatry of Adolph Meyer*, edited by Alfred Lief, pp. 147, 164, 165 (New York: McGraw-Hill Book Company, Inc., 1948); also Harry Stack Sullivan, *Conceptions of Modern Psychiatry*, pp. 50, 51 (Washington, D.C.: The William Alanson White Psychiatric Foundation, 1945).

comes less capable of logical reflection and of sharing the attitudes of others. Unable to tolerate interference with his plans and activities, he ruthlessly brushes it aside.

The manic reaction varies in intensity and includes mild mania, acute mania, and intense delirious hypermania. These states reveal the degree of overactivity and the intensity of the disordered state. Also, many manics seem to be vindictively hostile, with underlying paranoid features. Few manics seem to be elated and without any discernible hostility.

The hostile and agitated manic can become intensely destructive.[4] The few manics who do not express hostility seem generous and enthusiastic. One intelligent and fluent manic described his exhilarated condition as one in which he had an abnormal desire for beginning enterprises and for accomplishing things. He had an unusual feeling of adequacy, and, despite various side schemes and ambitions, he had an intense desire for intellectual activity and organization, which became wearying because of his simultaneous restlessness and powerful mental delirium. He compared his sheer good feeling to an ordered person who is deeply in love. He felt so intensely kind and generous toward other people that it embarrassed him.[5]

In most instances the manic reaction tends to spend itself, and the person improves. Rennie found that 93 per cent of manics improved, but recurrences usually follow, although few manics remain permanently disordered.

Depressive Behavior. Depressive behavior is characterized by self-reproach, dejection, and psychomotor retardation. The depressive feels worthless, inadequate, guilt-ridden, and self-depreciative. He does not have the confidence or resolve to engage in any new task and is overcome by his stark hopelessness and self-reproach. One typical depressive stated: "I am hopelessly bad, wicked, forever and ever. I do not deserve to live. I should be destroyed, for once and always." With this preoccupied state of self-reproach, the psychotic

[4] Rennie found 8 manics had paranoid content. Thomas A. C. Rennie, "Prognosis in Manic-Depressive Psychosis," *The American Journal of Psychiatry,* May, 1942, 98:6, pp. 801–814.
[5] See James T. MacCurdy, *The Psychology of Emotion,* pp. 298, 299 (New York: Harcourt, Brace and Company, Inc., 1925).

depressive usually tries to commit suicide.[6] In fact, psychotic depressives are all potential suicides.

The psychotic depressive whose thinking, activity, and feeling have slowed down considerably feels an inner emptiness and lack of purpose. Sometimes his self-reproach is so intense that he cannot talk or eat, is insomniac, and cannot care for himself. He differs from the oriented neurotic depressive, who usually can care for himself, and from the depressive schizophrenic, whose depression is not so intense and is one symptom among other symptoms.

According to one author, the depressive schizophrenic has transient self-reproaches and relatively slight motor retardation.[7] The depressive manic-depressive person continually depreciates himself and has marked motor retardation. The schizophrenic, in the early stages, may have some insight into his condition. The true depressive cannot introspect enough to complain of his depression and merely echoes his worthlessness or sinfulness. The schizophrenic depressive has other symptoms which may accompany the depression, nearly always expresses hostility and paranoidal ideas to others as well as to himself, and frequently hallucinates. The depressive seldom expresses paranoidal ideas and seldom hallucinates. The depressive schizophrenic may have experienced anxiety and other neurotic and psychotic features. The depressive has the essential expression of continual and marked self-reproach and may or may not have other symptoms.

Despite the differences between the types, depressives who incline to schizophrenia are frequently diagnosed as manic depressives. Moreover, the dynamic processes of depression are common to all these types despite their personality variations, insofar as it involves self-reproach and self-condemnation. Consequently, the prepsychotic background will include depressives who are regarded by some investigators as depressive schizophrenics.

Depressives do not recover as frequently as do manics. Lundquist found that 172, or 79.6 per cent, of 216 depressives recovered, but 95, or 92.2 per cent, of 102 manics recovered. But depressives are

---

[6] See R. E. Fairbank, "Suicide," *Journal of the American Medical Association,* 1932, 98, pp. 1711–1714; G. K. Jamieson, "Suicide and Mental Disease," *Archives of Neurology and Psychiatry,* 1936, 36, pp. 1–12; J. H. Wall, "The Psychological Problem of Suicide," *The American Journal of Psychiatry,* 1944, 101.

[7] See Rankine Good, "Depression," *British Journal of Medical Psychology,* December, 1946, 20:4, pp. 355–356.

less prone than manics to have recurrences. For example, Lundquist found that about 66 per cent of 216 depressives had no recurrent disorders.[8]

Circular Behavior: Manic and Depressive. The circular type of mood swing from manic to depressive and back again may or may not have an intervening normal state. This circular mood condition reveals certain dual thought processes and unintegrated personality perspectives.[9] For example, an individual who had these recurrent attacks believed he had died and, during the manic state, felt that he was an angel in heaven. He was jolly, mixed with others, and experienced a pressure of activity for doing things for others. When he was depressive he felt that he was unworthy of being in heaven, shrunk to one corner, and would not talk to anybody for fear they would discover him.

Some investigators maintain that sometimes this rhythmic change from mania to depression occurs with a periodicity that seems independent of outside events and results from physiological changes. In one instance a man, aged 55, had these alternating moods for twenty years with calendarlike regularity.[10] He would become manic about October, and become increasingly active until February or March, at which time he became depressed in a few days. His depression would last for about three or four months and then he would experience a period of conventional behavior for about two months.

But this periodic kind of reaction may be influenced by recurring conflicts which are subconscious and are not easily observable or even understood by the subject. Generally, persons with circular disorders do not recover as quickly or for the lengths of time that manics or depressives do.

Manic Depression and Schizophrenia

How does manic depression differ from schizophrenia? By comparing the extreme cases of the chronic schizophrenic and of manic depressives, these differences become clear.

[8] Gunnar Lundquist, "Prognosis and Course in Manic-Depressive Psychosis," *Acta Psychiatrica et Neurologica*, Supplement No. 35 (Copenhagen: Einar Munksgaard, 1945).
[9] See, for example, Samuel J. Beck, *Rorschach's Test: II. A Variety of Personality Pictures*, pp. 350–361 (New York: Grune & Stratton, Inc., 1945).
[10] J. M. Nielsen and George N. Thompson, *The Engrammes of Psychiatry*, p. 254 (Springfield, Ill.: Charles C Thomas, Publisher, 1947).

The schizophrenic is a seclusive and shy person. The manic depressive is a sociable person and likes people. The schizophrenic's emotional reactions are perverse or blunted. The manic depressive's reactions are exaggerated in terms of seeming elation or of actual depression. Within his emotional state the manic depressive tends to be oriented. The manic has accelerated thought processes; the depressive has retarded thought processes. The schizophrenic tends to become highly disoriented. The schizophrenic usually expresses his uncontrolled wishes by fantasy, hallucinations, and delusions, and has a weak hold on social reality. The manic usually expresses his uncontrolled wishes by action and sociability; the depressive by self-reproach. The manic depressive has a stronger hold on social reality than does the schizophrenic. The manic depressive has greater skills in role taking and seemingly a greater capacity for empathizing with other persons and thereby sharing their perspectives, which accounts for his stronger hold on social reality. Another fact is that the manic depressive, especially the manic, tends to have recurrent disorders which a schizophrenic does not experience. That is, a manic may be severely disturbed for a brief period and even behave like a schizophrenic; then he may suddenly improve for a short time and have another recurrence. This cycle may be continued indefinitely.

Since these general differences obtain only for extreme cases, it must be stressed that some transient schizophrenics are hard to differentiate from manic depressives. This writer has seen many cases of manic depression, especially of the depressed type, who were strikingly similar to transient schizophrenics in personality development, in mode of onset, and in reactions during onset. In addition, some persons who are first diagnosed as manic depressive later turn out, after the disorder has begun to settle, to be schizophrenic, whether undetermined, catatonic, or paranoid.[11] For instance, one person was successively diagnosed as obsessive neurosis, depression, manic depression, schizophrenia, and catatonic schizophrenia. In one sample of 5,779 subjects, 415 who were eventually diagnosed as schizophrenic had been diagnosed as manic depressives for the

[11] See Alfred H. Stanton and Morris S. Schwartz, "Observations on Dissociation as Social Participation," *Psychiatry*, November, 1949, 12:4, pp. 340–342. They describe some difficulties in diagnosing some patients as manic depressive or schizophrenic.

first five years.[12] As we have pointed out, whether these types are depressed schizophrenics or depressed manic depressives is still in a stage of controversy that has not been settled.

Some seeming manic depressives do change and deteriorate into an unmistakable schizophrenia. For example, a 45-year-old married woman, a tailor by occupation, was diagnosed as an undifferentiated depressive. From her history she had had a depression when she was 14 years old and attempted suicide, and she was afflicted again at the age of 43 during her menopause. She also felt that people were talking about her, heard voices, smelled disagreeable odors, was self-accusatory, and had ideas of being persecuted. She also attempted suicide by hanging. After twenty months in the hospital, where she was diagnosed as having involutional melancholia, she improved and was discharged. At the age of 54 she was readmitted, was diagnosed as hebephrenic, and remained in the hospital until her death at the age of.61. Toward the latter part of her hospital stay she was indifferent, negativistic, hallucinated continually, had memory defects, and was paranoid. Her behavior alternated between a state resembling an ordered condition and silly manneristic episodes.[13]

From 1936 to 1946, the percentage of manic depressives admitted to state mental hospitals declined from 14.0 to 10.0 per cent of the total admissions. This decline may have resulted in part from the increase of other disorders—especially psychoses of old age—and in part from the changed criteria of manic depression and schizophrenia. Some psychotics who were formerly diagnosed as manic depressives are now diagnosed as schizophrenics.[14]

[12] See Gunnar Lundquist, "Prognosis and Course in Manic-Depressive Psychosis," *Acta Psychiatrica et Neurologica*, Supplement No. 35, pp. 18–19 (Copenhagen: Einar Munksgaard, 1945).

[13] Thomas A. C. Rennie, "Prognosis in Manic-Depressive Psychosis," *The American Journal of Psychiatry*, May, 1942, 98:6, p. 808.

[14] Mowrer contends that from 1917 to 1932 in some state hospitals, there has been a consistent tendency to place most of the doubtfully diagnosed psychotic cases in the manic-depressive instead of in the schizophrenic category. See Ernest R. Mowrer, *Disorganization: Personal and Social*, p. 442 (Philadelphia: J. B. Lippincott Company, 1942). The tendency to which Mowrer refers has not been true in other state mental hospitals. Hoch and Rachlin found that in the Manhattan State Mental Hospital the manic depressives comprised 15.7 per cent of the total admissions in 1928 and 3.1 per cent of the total admissions in 1938. Schizophrenic admissions went down slightly for these years, from 19.6 to 12.5 per cent of the total admissions. The authors found this tendency to obtain for

Development of Manic Depression

We have pointed out that manic depression is an atypical form of personal disorganization because many manic depressives in the prepsychotic condition are adjusted in their jobs and in their general social relations; their conflicts are covert and not easily observable. On the other hand, some manic depressives are maladjusted and reveal personality difficulties which are frequently evident among schizophrenics. The important end to be observed is what precedes the mood disorder as it affects self-esteem and motivation.

With this end in view, the family background, personality configurations, and the personality processes among adult manic and depressive behaviors will be described. Although an inherent predisposition to manic depression is evident, the social relationships and personal reactions leading to these conditions become crucial, because the predisposition itself does not necessarily make the disorder inevitable. Nonetheless, the hereditary predisposition may possibly contribute to the intensity of the manic or depressive reaction.

The Family. There are no decisive external indications of family disorganization during the childhood of manic depressives. Malzberg, Pollock, and Fuller found that 78.1 per cent of 155 manic depressives came from families in which the parents were living together, and that 72.4 per cent of 154 manic-depressive subjects experienced no family dissension during childhood.[15] Of 145 subjects, 131 were affectionate and 14 were antagonistic to the father, and 139 were affectionate and 6 were antagonistic to the mother. Of 155 manic depressives, 111 did not experience any major family crises during childhood.

Nonetheless, the types of family organization and disrupted family relationships which contribute to schizophrenia and which may also contribute to manic depression, such as birth order, parent-child relationships, and the ingrown family, are expressed in more

New York State generally as well as for California. They attribute the decline of manic depression to "a change in viewpoint in evaluating the clinical picture." See Paul Hoch and H. L. Rachlin, "An Evaluation of Manic-Depressive Psychosis in the Light of Follow-Up Studies," *The American Journal of Psychiatry*, January, 1941, 97:4, pp. 833, 834.

[15] Benjamin Malzberg, Horatio Pollock, and Raymond Fuller, *Hereditary and Environmental Factors in the Causation of Manic-Depressive Psychosis and Dementia Praecox*, pp. 185–186 (Utica, N.Y.: State Hospitals Press, 1939).

subtle ways. But no single external family process, at least, obtains for all manic depressives.

Parent-Child Relationships. Instability is evident among some but not among other parents of manic depressives. In a study of 100 manic depressives—63 women and 37 men—Bonner found that in 30 cases there was strong hereditary influence and in 20 cases mild hereditary influence. In 44 cases hereditary causes were negative and in 6 cases unknown.[16] In a study of 40 depressive subjects, Anthonisen found that 10 parents were definitely depressive, that 17 other parents were nervous, high-strung, intolerant, domineering, or easily hurt, and that the parental condition of the other 13 subjects was not clear.[17] Pollock, Malzberg, and Fuller found that the social relationships of the majority of parents were confined to the immediate family, relatives, friends, and neighbors, and that relatively few—30 fathers and 2 mothers out of 155 fathers and 155 mothers—belonged to formal social organizations.[18] Whether this characteristic reflects the mode of social life in mid-New York State, where this survey was taken, or whether it is peculiar to manic-depressive families cannot be inferred from this study. Smalldon found that of 68 manic depressives 30 had strong family attachments, 35 had slight family attachments, and 3 had no family attachments.[19]

But on a more subtle emotional level the parents and children had ambivalent attitudes and relationships. By identifying with the parents, the children internalized the ambivalent viewpoints of the parents toward themselves. Thus, the premanic-depressive children acquired self-regarding conceptions of aggression and of intense guilt.

Some subjects had many parental figures who shared responsibility for them during infancy and childhood, but these subjects could not relate intimately and meaningfully with any single adult.

[16] Clarence A. Bonner, "Psychogenic Factors as Causative Agents in Manic-Depressive Psychoses," *Manic Depression: Association for Research in Nervous and Mental Disease* (Baltimore: The Williams & Wilkins Company, 1931).

[17] Niels L. Anthonisen, "Depression as a Part of Life Experience," *Journal of the American Medical Association,* July–December, 1935, 105, pp. 1249–1251.

[18] Horatio Pollock, Benjamin Malzberg, and Raymond G. Fuller, *Hereditary and Environmental Factors in the Causation of Manic-Depressive Psychosis and Dementia Praecox,* pp. 178–180 (Utica, N.Y.: State Hospitals Press, 1939).

[19] John L. Smalldon, "The Prepsychotic Personality of the Manic-Depressive," *Psychiatric Quarterly,* January, 1934, 8:1, pp. 144–146.

The adults did not seem interested in the subjects for themselves. Frequently, the adults imposed burdens upon the subjects and held them responsible for these burdens. Although the subjects assumed the desired responsibility, they resented parental impositions. Feeling guilty over their hate for their parents, the subjects became intensely ambivalent to their parents and to themselves. Insofar as they were intimately bound to their parents, they internalized parental values and thus remained oriented. But they found it difficult to accept criticism or ridicule because their self-esteem was weak. Often, their behavior was impeded by their difficulty in managing their hostilities to their parents. Seemingly, they internalized these hostilities toward themselves.

Birth Order and Social Position in the Family. Birth order and manic depression are unrelated, but the more subtle aspects of sibling rivalry may contribute to the emotional vulnerability of manic depressives. That is, there is no significant difference among the proportions of first-born, middle-born and last-born children who are manic depressive, but the abrupt displacement of one sibling by another may contribute to emotional instability. Berman, in a study of birth order among 100 manic-depressive cases in the St. Lawrence State Hospital, found that 48 cases were first-born, 15 second, 10 each were third and fourth, and 17 were fifth or later. Since 10 of his subjects were only children, the first-born children in families with two or more children comprised 42.2 per cent of the total cases.[20] Yet these conclusions obtain for this sample only and are not decisive. Pollock, Malzberg, and Fuller found, in a study of 155 cases, that 39.7 per cent were first-born and 29.7 per cent were second-born in the family.[21] In a more definitive study, Malzberg found no relationship between birth order and manic depression. Katz arrived at a similar conclusion.[22]

Yet the spacing of children and the displacement of one child by another possibly may have some indirect effect upon personal

[20] Harold H. Berman, "Order of Birth in Manic-Depressive Reactions," *Psychiatric Quarterly,* January, 1933, 12:1, pp. 430–435.

[21] Horatio M. Pollock, Benjamin Malzberg, and Raymond G. Fuller, *Hereditary and Environmental Factors in the Causation of Manic-Depressive Psychosis and Dementia Praecox,* p. 48 (Utica, N.Y.: State Hospitals Press, 1939).

[22] See Benjamin Malzberg, "Is Birth Order Related to Incidence of Mental Disease," *American Journal of Physical Anthropology,* 1937, 24:1, pp. 91–104; Siegfried E. Katz, "The Family Constellation as a Predisposing Factor in Psychosis," *Psychiatric Quarterly,* January, 1934, 8:1, pp. 121–128.

stability or instability and may adversely influence a person with a manic-depressive predisposition. It is not known whether the child who is followed very soon by another sibling who replaces him in the affection of the parents is more prone to manic depression than the one who has been the center of attention for a relatively longer time. The pattern of sibling relationships is such that the manic depressive, as the displaced sibling, becomes hostile to the other person, but in order to get parental favor identifies with the sibling or tries to be like him. This dependent identification with the other sibling, however, is mingled with repressed hostility. Or he may drive himself in order to regain this parental affection. This constellation of sibling relationships does not pertain to manic depression only but also to a general instability. It may, in some instances, intensify the instability of a person who is already predisposed to manic depression because of hereditary and parental influences.

Childhood and Adolescence. In general, manic depressives are usually more sociable, more adjusted, and better oriented than schizophrenics. Of the three subtypes, the manics tend to be the most outgoing and sociable, the depressives the least sociable, and the circular types are intermediate between these two categories.

In a comparative study of 73 manic depressives, 125 schizophrenics, and 96 women social workers who were used as normals, Bowman found that the manic depressives had the same percentage of model children as the schizophrenics, but they had more friends, were more likely to be leaders, participated more readily in recreative activities, were more sympathetic, more ambitious and energetic, and daydreamed less than schizophrenics.[23]

Titley found that agitated depressives were model children— earnest, overconscientious, stubborn, meticulous, anxiety-ridden, diligent, and often unvaryingly honest.[24] Frequently, they expected a lot from themselves and blamed themselves rather than their environments or blamed both. On the other hand, Anthonisen found that, of 40 depressives, 31 had difficulties in socializing and were shy, awkward, and sensitive. Some had practically no associates outside

[23] Karl M. Bowman, "A Study of the Pre-psychotic Personality in Certain Disorders," *The Biology of the Individual*, pp. 652–660 (Washington, D.C.: Association for Research in Nervous and Mental Disease, 1934).

[24] W. B. Titley, "The Pre-psychotic Personality of Patients with Agitated Depressions," *Archives of Neurology and Psychiatry*, February, 1938, 39:2, p. 335.

of the family circle and other subjects; although others were good mixers, they felt lonely, unpopular, and very dependent upon favorable circumstances.[25]

Pollock, Malzberg, and Fuller found that, out of 58 males, 54 were normal in their childhood and only 4 were seclusive. Of 94 females, 81 participated in normal play activities, but the other 13 were either seclusive or could not play at all because they had to work. During adolescence, 33 out of 59 males were good social mixers with both sexes; 10 associated with boys only, and 16 were poor mixers. By contrast, they found that of 91 male schizophrenics, 34 were good mixers, with both sexes, 27 associated with boys only, and 30 were poor mixers. Of 94 female manic depressives, 67 were good mixers with both sexes, 8 associated with girls only, and 19 were poor mixers. By contrast, they found that, of 80 female schizophrenics, 37 were good mixers with both sexes, 1 associated with boys only, 6 associated with girls only, and 36 were poor mixers.[26] From this study more premanic depressives participated in normal play activities and were sociable than was true of schizophrenics. On the other hand, some preschizophrenics were more sociable than some premanic depressives.

Smalldon found that, of 75 manic depressives, 41 had many friends, 31 had few friends, and 3 had no friends. Forty-seven manic depressives were open and frank in their relationships with people and 28 were reserved and reticent; 40 were demonstrative, and 22 were stolid in their relationships. Thus, it is difficult to tell from external sociability whether the person will become manic-depressive or not. The simple fact is that many persons who become manic-depressive, especially depressive, are not sociable and outgoing. These external indications can be better understood, however, when the person's self-regarding attitudes and reactions to his relationships are understood.

For example, one prevalent developmental sequence among depressives is their somewhat socially isolated and emotionally dependent childhood and early adolescence. During adolescence

[25] Niels L. Anthonisen, "Depression as a Part of Life Experience," *Journal of the American Medical Association,* July–December, 1935, 105, pp. 1249–1251.

[26] Horatio Pollock, Benjamin Malzberg, and Raymond G. Fuller, *Hereditary and Environmental Factors in the Causation of Manic-Depressive Psychosis and Dementia Praecox,* pp. 192–194 (Utica, N.Y.: State Hospitals Press, 1939).

they apparently "grow out" of this condition and start to participate successfully. They then become socially outgoing and appear
rather stable. Their sociability obscures but does not eliminate their
emotional vulnerability and dependent attitudes. Thus, a highly
critical experience with an intimate person, especially a parent, can
upset them completely. This is illustrated in the following case:[27]

The subject was one of two children, who had always been devoted to his
family. When young, he was afflicted with a succession of illnesses which
kept him close to home, and was always nursed by his mother. When he
attended preparatory school he was homesick, had no friends, and felt
lonely and unhappy. The school felt like prison to him; and he looked
forward to his vacations as a happy release. Since his mother's marital life
was unhappy she devoted a lot of time to him. He recognized his mother's
marital difficulties and felt deeply bound to her, but this did not detract
from his affection and admiration for his father. Since he had been with
adults so much of the time, he was hindered in his relationships with his
peers and felt himself a "sissy" when he was with other boys; he felt more
comfortable with adults.

The summer before he was to enter college, his mother left his father and
went to England. This disillusioned him and intensified his attachment to
his father and sister, which was a substitute for his attachment to his
mother. He admired his father and wanted to be successful like him. But
he became alienated from his father when the father remarried. Both he
and his sister resented the remarriage and he opposed it bitterly and would
not be reconciled to his father and his new stepmother.

When he knew he was going to college, he resolved to be accepted by the
right "crowd" and to be successful. During his first year he realized his
resolution. He was socially active; his friends were among the outstanding
students; he was a member of a prominent fraternity and he was well
known on the campus. He appeared as an out-going, happy-go-lucky person
who seemed to enjoy his college life. Although upset by his mother's departure, he became completely overcome by his father's remarriage. He felt
that he no longer wished to be successful because he no longer identified
with and admired his father. In fact, he considered himself worthless. He
remarked that he had felt inferior for a long time, that he felt inferior
when he was a child and in preparatory school. His social acceptance and
prominence at Yale had obscured but had not done away with his feelings
of inferiority and of dependency.

He had gastro-intestinal symptoms, vomited, was slow in his movements,
tearful, upset and depressed. He became fearful and nervous, felt everything was hopeless, wanted to die and thought he was becoming insane.
Discouraged and no longer ambitious, he became distressed by the thought

[27] Adapted from Clements C. Fry, *Mental Health in College*, pp. 323–325 (New
York: Commonwealth Fund, 1942). For a somewhat similar case, see Marianne
Weber, *Max Weber: Ein Lebensbild* (Tubingen, 1926).

of work. He wanted to return home and hoped then that things would be all right. He remained depressed for a few months, received intensive therapy, and remained out of school for one year, then returned to complete his work.

Prepsychotic Personality Types among Manic Depressives. The prepsychotic personalities of manics, depressives, and circular types differ and can be characterized as follows:[28]

The premanic is talkative, overactive, energetic, and has fits of overactivity at the start of certain enterprises, but he tends to disperse his interests and cannot devote enough time to any single interest. He is matter-of-fact about his duties and sometimes can get things done. He is sociable, friendly, cheerful, and optimistic, but also is inclined to be stubborn, is somewhat self-centered, and is determined to have his own way. Light-hearted and optimistic, he tends to inspire confidence in others and as a result can become a leader. On the other hand, the premanic is frequently sensitive and faultfinding. Frank and at ease with people, he tends to be adjusted in his heterosexual relationships, although he does experience marital difficulties. In some instances the premanic becomes very interested in projects which he starts but cannot finish. Losing interest, he abandons the project and in time starts new projects only to abandon them also. His enthusiastic interest and subsequent disinterest continues until his breakdown. In some instances the predepressive follows this pattern.

The predepressive may be introverted or extroverted, but he is quieter, less energetic, less active, and has narrower but more intense interests than the premanic. Very conscientious, which is one of his outstanding characteristics, he is less practical, less matter-of-fact, and more visionary than the premanic. Less demonstrative in his affections than the premanic, he is also more shy and dependent in his social relations, has fewer friends, and has deeper feelings of inferiority. Since he is emotionally dependent and pessimistic, he is also less inclined to become a leader than is the premanic.

The circular type is inclined to periods of overactivity and inactivity, is less cheerful and lighthearted than the premanic, but is not so worrisome as the depressive. He is less facile in making

[28] See John L. Smalldon, "Prepsychotic Personality of Manic Depressive Disorders," *Psychiatric Quarterly*, January, 1934, 8:1, pp. 144–146.

friends than is the premanic, but is more so than the depressive. He is more adjusted heterosexually and less inclined to be visionary than is the depressive. In brief, his personality is somewhat intermediate between the two other types.

Good, who has differentiated between the manic depressive, depressive, and schizophrenic depressive, describes an extreme type of manic-depressive depressive.[29] He is characterized by an oppressive overconscientiousness and is self-punitive and very devoted to humdrum, restricting duties. Self-denying and self-sacrificing, he can endure without complaint circumstances against which the ordinary person would immediately protest. He tends to take the blame for his mistakes and anticipates detection and punishment for his errors. Ready to help the underdog, he defends the failings and shortcomings of other people. He does not boast, sometimes even depreciates himself. Very honest, he cannot tell a white lie in a convincing manner and is preoccupied with the gloomier and pessimistic aspects of life. Continually aware of how other persons feel, he is keenly sensitive about not hurting other people, and his aggressions are in defense of other people. He cannot genuinely enjoy himself, but he is not a supine person because he may espouse and fight very hard for causes—even lost causes.

The manic depressive usually does not relinquish his interest in and capacity for social relationships. Usually he tends to have friends and to retain his social interests, and he has a relatively strong hold on social reality. Despite his sociability, he is acutely self-conscious because of his inner demands upon himself. Sensitive and emotionally dependent in his intimate relationships, he is very vulnerable to rejection and disappointment, and as a result of these crises, when depressive he turns his aggressions against himself, but when manic he flees from his self-reproach. The following case of John illustrates the development of a depressive.[30]

Case of John

John was 27 when he developed a pronounced depression and expressed

[29] Rankine Good, "Depression," *British Journal of Medical Psychology*, December, 1946, 20:4, pp. 343–367.

[30] Adapted from Leland E. Hinsie, "Successful Socialization and Compensation in Manic-Depressive Psychoses," *Manic-Depressive Psychoses*, pp. 141–160 (Baltimore: The Williams & Wilkins Company, 1931).

a desire for suicide. He was hospitalized, and he improved and later married and has maintained a good adjustment. The relevant points of his family relationships and personality development include the following:

When John was three his mother died. His father, a docile, passive individual, was a steady worker who provided moderately well for the family. The father remarried a woman who had been reared and chafed under a forbidding and disciplinary mother. She had been married before, not so much because she loved her husband as because she hated her own mother. She found little satisfaction from her first marriage and after a son was born she was divorced. Later she married John's father. John competed with his stepbrother for his stepmother's affection and won out. His stepbrother was entrusted to a grandmother's care.

John's relationship with his stepmother was mingled with love and hate. The stepmother admitted that she couldn't get the love from her own son that she received from John, who often appeared to her like a sentimental, sensitive little girl. She liked him very much even though he looked "so sissy-like." Her interest in him made life fuller for her. Although able to develop emotionally, John's identification was primarily with strong women. He developed a strong attachment for a teacher who in his estimation was like a mother to him, and he felt like a son to her. He even failed a grade to remain in her classes longer.

When John was eight years old his stepmother gave birth to a girl. His sister's arrival definitely changed John. Perhaps he feared that the half-sister would displace him in the favors of his stepmother. But instead of resenting his sister, he identified with her so completely that he ignored others in the family and lavished attention upon her. In time both John and his stepmother were competing for the attention of his sister. Since the sister developed normally during adolescence, she wanted to go out with boys. She encouraged John to adjust without her and to go with girls. Despite John's objections she went with boys and eventually announced her love for a man. Since John had concentrated his social relationships upon his sister and mother, he had few girl friends. He was generally suspicious of girls because the stepmother warned him that girls were prostitutes who would infect him and deprive him of his manhood.

After his sister's announcement of her engagement he began keeping company with a girl. His stepmother, however, reacted adversely to his relationship with the girl. She became highly disturbed and showed paranoid tendencies. John, on the other hand, also began to be suspicious of the girl and began accusing her of being unfaithful to him. He had tried to keep sex out of the affair with her but was unsuccessful. When the two did have sex relations he developed intense guilt feelings. As a result of the continual bickering with the girl the relationship collapsed and he was thrown into a deep depression, because he was so fond of her. He said that she was just the girl for him, that he had always longed for her and that it was heaven when he was with her.

Precipitating Experiences and Onset

The precipitating experiences of manic depressives which culminate a general personality trend may be severely critical or very trivial. But these experiences do not differ for the subtypes of manic depressives. Most manic depressives have had mild episodes of mania or depression before the psychotic breakdown, but some manic depressives have not had these previous adverse reactions. Regardless of past outbursts, many manic depressives do feel emotionally insecure and uneasy for long periods before the breakdown.

For example, a 47-year-old carpenter who had made friends easily, who was devoted to his wife, and who had been a cheerful, sociable person, became severely depressed and attempted suicide when he lost his job and could not find work. He was always a very capable worker, but because of an economic depression his search for a job was of no avail. He worried continually and became disheartened and pessimistic. He tried to hang himself but relented because he felt so devoted to his wife. For the past four years, he had become increasingly restless, irritable, and discontented because he still owed money on his property, despite his frugality and steady work. He became more dejected when he realized that he did not have enough money to tide him over during his unemployed period. His wife, who was a demanding but irresponsible woman, spent money recklessly and underwent many operations. When he chided or scolded her about her reckless spending, she taunted him about his stinginess. In addition, her sexual frigidity made him react with intense rage. Sometimes he thought about leaving her or about going out with more passionate women, but he never carried out his fantasies because he was so dependent upon her. Furthermore, he felt very guilty when he had these thoughts. His ambivalent reactions of hostility and guilt toward his wife continued until the time of his breakdown.

On the other hand, a depressive reaction may arise rather suddenly and the subject may not recall having had such an experience before. For example, a beauty-parlor operator who was 42 years old, who was outgoing, friendly, and ambitious, and who had married for the second time, helped her husband become established in her business. She encouraged him to learn this occupation, which he did. After he familiarized himself with the business, she discovered that he was going out with other women, some of whom were her customers. When she confronted him with these facts he coldly admitted it and implied that he would not stop. Very upset, she threatened to "get rid" of him. But he reminded her that when they married she had given him a partnership in her business. The next day, she felt "down in the dumps," every move became an effort, and she seemed to have lost interest in everything. She could not understand her mood, never having felt this way before. She lingered in this despondent state until she attempted suicide by drinking poison. She was stopped and brought to the hospital.

These critical experiences, which result in the loss of a love object, can also create manic behavior when the predisposition is present. For example, a businessman about 48 years old had been running himself ragged with overwork and overplay.[31] Impulsive, erratic, restless, he was forcibly gay and drank excessively. Formerly he had been a sober, somewhat sedate, and reserved person. Very much in love with his wife, who was much younger than he, he became severely upset when he learned that she had wearied of their marriage and had become unfaithful. To avoid the scandal of a second divorce, he asked her to take a trip and to postpone her decision until she returned. In addition to this difficulty, he also had intense fears that his executive position was being threatened by younger, better-trained, and energetic men. He found it necessary to become very progressive and to engage in athletics, drinking, and stag parties which he did not really enjoy. His wife, whom he had won away from more youthful suitors, symbolized his own renewed youth to him. But in their sex relations he sometimes was impotent, and he responded to this with outbursts of anger and envy. During his wife's absence, he was filled with suspense and became jealous and angry. He had little interest in his work and began to lose sleep. At someone's advice, he began to enjoy himself, began to overwork and overplay until he was fetched by a business associate to the hospital for a general checkup.

This person, as well as other persons who become mildly manic, did so by compulsively conforming to norms of behavior which he considered socially acceptable and which in large part are socially

---

[31] Jules H. Masserman, *Principles of Dynamic Psychiatry*, pp. 60, 61 (Philadelphia: W. B. Saunders Company, 1946).

acceptable. Had he been somewhat younger, his disturbed condition might have been even less noticed and less within the range of the socially abnormal. In fact, when he went to the hospital for a physical checkup and rest, he was not even considered within the bounds of a mild psychosis.

Generally, the culminating point in a depressive or manic reaction is a disrupted outcome of an intimate and dependent relationship, which calls out the person's inner ambivalence toward himself. This relationship may be with the spouse, parents, friends, or fiancé. The relationship may terminate by the death or separation of the loved person, or by the sudden or gradual hostility of the loved person. Those persons who become manic or depressed because of loss of finances, a job, or from disgrace not only experience loss of status but also internalize the attitudes of others toward themselves and become fiercely self-depreciative or flee from this self-reproach by distractible activities.

In judging the process of the manic-depressive breakdown, we must consider the intensity and persistence of the critical experiences. Some clinicians maintain that the intensity of the manic-depressive reaction to a crisis is the result of a biological predisposition rather than of early experiences. Although constitutional predisposition may possibly mean the difference between a psychotic depression or a neurotic depression, nonetheless the influences of early experiences may be just as significant in calling out the more profound psychotic defenses. Hence, as a result of precipitating situations, the depression would be deeper. There are, however, few if any decisive studies which can definitely show the influence of biological predisposition to the exclusion of early experiences.

Provisions for a Hypothesis of Manic Depression. Manic depression may be rooted in a hereditary predisposition, but this does not eliminate the need to explain the peculiar types of role taking and self-regarding attitudes which result in manic depression; for the predisposition to a given disorder does not mean that the disorder is inevitable. Hence, the personal experiences and reactions become crucial in explaining the onset of the disorder.

In contrast to schizophrenia, which begins with personal isolation and emotional withdrawal, manic depression can be understood best by the process of identification. The premanic depressive resorts to identification with others as a defensive reaction against his own anxiety and guilt. This defensive reaction, which may make him sociable and outgoing in his relationships with others, does not obliterate his intense feelings of guilt and his precarious estimate of himself; for the manic depressive is essentially very dependent, very ambivalent in his intimate social relationships, and also very ambivalent to himself. This ambivalence is acquired and internalized from his early family relationships, particularly with his parents, in which he acquires the parental attitudes of love and hate, of guilt and aggression, and directs these attitudes toward himself. But he defends himself against his aggression to himself by identifying with other people. Thus, his very sociability may precipitate his breakdown. By identifying with people who are ambivalent to him, he internalizes and directs these attitudes to himself in his subsequent relationships.

Thus, a person who has these role-taking qualities and self-regarding attitudes and who experiences one or a series of crises—or the recall of crises—becomes severely upset by the loss of a love object or by the sudden or gradual loss of self-esteem. When he becomes depressive, he assumes the ambivalent attitudes of the lost loved person toward himself. By turning these attitudes toward himself, he becomes involved in profound self-reproach.[32] In fact, he becomes so overwhelmed by self-reproach that he becomes incapable of new identifications with other persons. Thus, the depression disrupts his role-identifying capacities for new love objects and in extreme instances disrupts his capacity for role taking generally.

On the other hand, the manic flees from his self-reproach by becoming preoccupied with transient activities and with transient social relationships. By these outward, distractible activities, the manic evades sustained self-evaluation. Indeed, should the manic become involved in a sustained relationship, he would inevitably have to take the role of the other and also resort to self-evaluation which could drive him into a depression.

Since the manic and the depressive usually have had well-developed role-taking skills and since their role-taking capacities have

[32] Some psychoanalysts claim that this hostile aggression is directed to the internalized image of the lost love object, of whom the subject has been deprived by separation or hostility. See Otto Fenichel, *The Psychoanalytic Theory of Neurosis*, pp. 390–393 (New York: W. W. Norton & Co., 1945).

not been lost, they can usually regain the capacity for sharing the viewpoints of others and thereby can regain their hold on social reality. Hence, the manic and the depressive usually improve or recover, and they do so more readily than does the characteristic schizophrenic.

These tentative inferences do not explain, however, the shift from one condition to another—i.e., from mania to depression or from depression to mania. This problem requires further inquiry.

Manic Depression and Culture

Since manic-depressive behavior is regarded as a constitutional disorder, does it follow that this disorder should be universal? If the disorder does not exist in some cultures, is it a result of constitutional differences or of social influences? In other cultures manic disorders may be present, but depressive disorders may be very rare.

Depression and Culture. Among the Alorese, depression and suicide do not exist. The absence of this disorder was explained by the socially distant mother-child relationships and by the child's inability to organize his aggressions and to get a clear conception of himself. To cite Kardiner:[33]

> The earliest relations of the child to the mother prevent formation of constellations normal to Western man—the strong attachment to the mother, the capacity to idealize her, the capacity to introject her and the formation of strong and organized aggression patterns. In Alor, none of these are well developed. Hence, the aggressions directed against the mother do not ricochet back on the child in masochistic form. For this reason there is no depression and no suicide. The whole mechanism is related to superego formation, limited idealization, and disorganized aggression. However, in place of these mechanisms we find in Western man which form the constituents essential for the depressive mechanism, we find passivity and surrender, spinal rages (tantrums) and all kinds of devices for indirect aggression.

Among the natives of Kenya, East Africa, who were hospitalized, Carothers found no cases of depression but did find cases of mania. Among these native groups, self-regarding attitudes of worthlessness, sinfulness, and guilt were lacking. Many natives, when disturbed, would be characterized by Westerners as resembling "psychopaths." This characterization was used by Kardiner in categoriz-

[33] Abram Kardiner, *Psychological Frontiers of Society*, pp. 246, 247 (New York: Columbia University Press, 1945).

ing the psychotics among the Alorese society. Carothers attributed the manic behavior among the Kenyans to the weak, repressing, and inhibiting features of the culture.[34]

Laubscher found that manic depression did not exist among the Tembu, although schizophrenia was prevalent among them.[35] He attributed the absence of this disorder to the "particular temperament of the people." He found the reason to be "in those characteristics of free play of instinctive energy similar to that attributed to the Latin." Since Laubscher did not attempt to relate motivation to early childhood development, the so-called "instinctive energy" could very well have been derived from the culture. The Tembu were outgoing, optimistic persons, who expressed their feelings freely and uninhibitedly.

Fisher arrived at a similar conclusion from a study of Indians and Negroes in Central America. He found that the descendants of Negroes, Indians, and whites had a higher proportion of manic symptoms than the Mestizos who were relatively free from Negro ancestry. He found, on the other hand, that the depressive symptoms were relatively shallow.[36]

Depression, Suicide, and Culture. Individualized suicide, which is so closely related to depression, may provide a relatively good index to the existence of depression in a given society. The pervasiveness of depression in a given society may parallel the collective attitudes to individualized suicide.

Depression may be rare among those peoples who cannot grasp the meaning of suicide because it is so alien to their customary practices. For example, a native of the Caroline Islands in the South Pacific, when asked about suicide, at first could not grasp its meaning. When it was explained to him, he claimed that he had never heard of anything so ridiculous.[37] The Zuñis also consider suicide an incredible type of behavior. Very likely, depression is also rare

[34] James C. Carothers, "A Study of Mental Derangement in Africans and an Attempt to Explain Its Peculiarities More Especially in Relation to the African Attitude to Life," *Psychiatry*, February, 1948, XI, pp. 47–86.

[35] B. F. J. Laubscher, *Sex, Customs and Psychopathology* (London: Routledge and Kegan Paul, Ltd., 1937).

[36] S. Fisher, "The Influence of Indian and Negro Blood on the Manic-Depressive Psychoses," *Journal of Nervous and Mental Disease*, 1943, 97, pp. 409–420.

[37] Louis I. Dublin and Bessie Bunzel, *To Be or Not To Be*, pp. 138–141 (New York: Harrison Smith and Robert Hass, 1933). See also S. R. Steinmetz, "Suicide Among Primitive Peoples," *American Anthropologist*, January, 1894, 7, pp. 53–60.

among these peoples. Depression may be more frequent among those societies who stigmatize suicide as sinful, cowardly, or ignoble and rigorously forbid it. The very fact that they forbid suicide is an index that their efforts are aimed to thwart the occurrence of suicide. For example, the Karens in Burma consider suicide as cowardly and deny the suicidal victim an honorable burial. Depression may be most frequent among those societies who tolerate, condone, accept, or institutionalize suicide. For example, the Kamchadals of Siberia, who do not penalize the suicide, frequently resort to suicide. The consistent tendencies in cultures would show a relationship between these phenomena. Thus, it would be of interest to investigate more thoroughly the relationship between depression and suicide within given cultures.[38]

The same apparent connection between suicide and depression also exists among different ethnic groups. The Negroes in southern rural United States tend to have relatively low rates of depression and relatively low rates of suicide. The Negroes in northern urban United States tend to have higher rates of depression and higher rates of suicide. Other ethnic groups, such as the Jewish groups, have relatively high rates of depression and high rates of suicide. Despite this apparent relationship between depression and suicide, no definite cross-cultural studies of these phenomena have been made.

Manic Behavior and Culture. It appears that, of the varied disorders, the mild manic disorder is most consistent with the demands of contemporary society. The premanic or mild manic who is not seriously disturbed and is outgoing, active, sociable, expansive, and cheerful can more readily become accepted and is hardly susceptible to being regarded as abnormal. Moreover, the mild manic is a matter-of-fact and practical person whose behavior is also consistent with our culture. But the mild manic among the dreamy Balinese or among the introverted Hindus would be regarded as too outgoing. Among the Ojibwa, his enthusiastic outgoing behavior could be considered a threat to the shaman, who would demand that persons be more dependent and reserved.

[38] For examples, J. and Z. Henry found that among the Pilaga Indians the dynamisms of self-accusation and self-reproach were weak and that consistently only one case of suicide was known. This case was more or less forced upon the doer and was not a result of internalized guilt. See J. and Z. Henry, *Doll Play among the Pilaga Indians* (New York: J. J. Augustin, Inc., 1939).

Mild manic behavior would also vary in social acceptability by type of occupation. It would be more acceptable among salesmen than among physical scientists. It would be more tolerated and even more acceptable among actors and entertainers, whose eccentric outgoing behavior is condoned, than among stenographers or waitresses. Thus, some hypomanics can find an acceptable, successful niche in our society by their occupations and would not necessarily be socially abnormal. Moreover, the hypomanic reaction is perhaps far more acceptable in the urban culture of the United States than in other societies. The emphasis upon "having fun" assumes so compulsive a character that some individuals who are not inclined to behave this way do so in order to remain accepted.

On a cultural level the festival represents an institutionalized release for inhibited behavior which at best is analogous to the individualized behavior of the manic, for the types of acting-out uninhibited behavior are more readily tolerated than during the rest of the year. According to Freud, the festival usually follows a period of repentance. This sequence tends to follow in many cultures. Freud regarded this emotional respite as a biological necessity to account for the periodic change of moods among normal persons. The important fact which we wish to emphasize is that the individual who behaves in an outgoing, friendly, and uninhibited manner during a festival is, of course, operating within culturally sanctioned bounds and on a different level than the individual manic.

Of course, uninhibited behavior and elated behavior is more permissive in some cultures than in others. The Puritans frowned on most forms of levity. At the present, we tend to sanction "fun" and out-going activities in avocational relationships. As yet, this area of manic behavior and culture remains a problem for further inquiry.

Selected Readings

Abraham, Karl, *Selected Papers* (London: Hogarth Press, 1927).

Anthonisen, Niels L., "Depression as a Part of Life Experience," *Journal of the American Medical Association,* 1935, 105, pp. 1249–1252.

Blalock, J. R., "A Case of Mental Mechanisms in Depression," *Psychiatric Quarterly,* 1940, 14, p. 412.

Bowman, Karl M., "A Study of Pre-Psychotic Personality in Certain Disorders," *The Biology of the Individual,* pp. 652–660 (Washington, D.C.: Association for Research in Nervous and Mental Disease, 1934).

English, O. Spurgeon, "Observations of Trends in Manic Depressive Psychoses," *Psychiatry,* 1949, 12, pp. 125–133.

Freud, Sigmund, "Mourning and Melancholia," *Collected Papers,* Vol. IV (London: Hogarth Press, 1924).

Fromm-Reichmann, Frieda, "Intensive Psychotherapy of Manic-depressives," *Confinia Neurologica,* 1949, 9, pp. 158–165.

Garma, Angel, "Melancholia and Related Depressions," *Psychiatric Inventory of the Yearbook of Psychiatry,* 1947, II, p. 75.

Good, Rankine, "Depression," *British Journal of Medical Psychology,* December, 1946, 20:4, pp. 345–367.

Hillyer, Jane, *Reluctantly Told* (New York: The Macmillan Company, 1927).

Isreali, Nathan, "Outlook of a Depressed Patient, Interested in Planned Gambling, Before and After His Attempt at Suicide," *American Journal of Orthopsychiatry,* January, 1935, V:1, pp. 57–63.

Krauch, Elsa, *A Mind Restored* (New York: G. P. Putnam's Sons, 1937).

Laubscher, B. F. J., *Sex, Custom and Psychopathology* (London: Routledge and Kegan Paul, Ltd., 1937).

Lewis, Aubrey J., "Melancholia," *Journal of Mental Science,* 1934, 80, p. 277.

Masserman, Jules H., *Dynamic Psychiatry,* pp. 200–209 (Philadelphia: W. B. Saunders Company, 1946).

Meyer, Adolph, *The Commonsense Psychiatry of Adolph Meyer,* edited by Alfred Lief (New York: McGraw-Hill Book Company, Inc., 1948).

Pollock, Horatio, Benjamin Malzberg, and Raymond G. Fuller, *Hereditary and Environmental Factors in the Causation of Manic Depressive Psychosis and Dementia Praecox* (Utica, N.Y.: State Hospitals Press, 1939).

Rennie, Thomas A. C., "Prognosis in Manic-Depressive Psychosis," *The American Journal of Psychiatry,* May, 1942, 98:6, pp. 801–814.

Smalldon, John L., "Prepsychotic Personality of Manic-Depressive Patients," *Psychiatric Quarterly,* January, 1934, 8:1, pp. 129–146.

Titley, W. B., "Prepsychotic Personality of Patients with Agitated Depressions," *Archives of Neurology and Psychiatry,* February, 1938, 39:2, pp. 333–342.

Zilboorg, Gregory, "Differential Diagnostic Types of Suicide," *Archives of Neurology and Psychiatry,* February, 1936, 35:2, pp. 270–291.

CHAPTER TWELVE

Acting-out Disorders: Psychopathy and Deviant Behavior

In the past chapters we described neurotic and psychotic persons who, as the result of inhibited conflicts and inward distress, eventually became overwhelmed and incapacitated. In contrast to these disordered persons we turn now to psychopaths, who act out their conflicts in an antisocial manner; for psychopathy is not based upon anxiety, as characterizes the neuroses, and it is not based upon a retreat into private attitudes, as characterizes the psychoses. As we shall see, psychopathy is essentially a result of emotional immaturity and an arrested capacity for intimate role taking. Yet, the term "psychopathy" has many meanings for different clinicians. As a matter of fact, the lack of agreement concerning these disorders is so prevalent that one of our purposes is to point out and to clarify the sources of this confusion. We shall then describe the types of persons who are classified under the category of psychopathy.

Investigators often confuse behavior which is acquired in a deviant subculture with behavior which results from psychopathic immaturity. For example, many delinquents who violate the norms of the larger society acquire their behavior in the particular subculture in which they are reared and participate. These delinquents conform to their criminal norms in the same way that conventional persons abide by conventional norms. Nevertheless, these delinquents also may experience guilt feelings and cultivate lasting intimate relationships. Yet, when delinquents are ·evaluated in terms of the implicit moral norms of the particular clinician, they may be considered psychopathic. Also, some anti-social persons are diagnosed psychopathic because they express very slight guilt feelings, but others who may be guilt-laden after persistent misbehavior also are considered psychopathic. Then again, some investigators contend that psychopaths cannot change; other investigators report psychopaths who have improved.[1] It is not surprising, then, that the category of "psychopathy" is fraught with disagreement and inconsistency.

At the present time, since psychopathy combines a series of loosely related disorders centering about overt, antisocial, or "inadequate" behavior, we refer to this anomalous category as "acting-out disorders." Statistics on psychopathy reflect this inconsistency. For example, Sutherland shows that more than 75 per cent of the inmates of Illinois state prisons were categorized as psychopathic, but only 10 per cent of the inmates in New York and Massachusetts were so diagnosed.[2] Clearly, this discrepancy resulted from different preconceptions among the psychiatrists rather than from differences in the types of criminals. In a survey of a district in Baltimore, Lemkau found that in 1933, 13 per 10,000 of the population were considered psychopathic. In 1936 only 5.2 per 10,000 of the population were so diagnosed. The figure was revised downward because many unemployed who were considered "psychopathic" in 1933 were not so regarded in 1936 when the lack of job opportunities during the economic depression was considered.[3]

Since the criteria of psychopathy are inconsistent, symptomatic behavior and social evaluations in addition to personality dynamics are usually regarded as the bases for categorizing psychopathy.[4] Yet these very behavioral reactions and social evaluations can be misleading. By this we mean that psychopathy cannot be ascertained merely by symptomatic reactions such as explosive or eccentric behavior. It cannot be ascertained by traits which characterize pre-

---

[1] See Robert M. Lindner, *Rebel without a Cause* (New York: Grune & Stratton, Inc., 1944).

[2] Edwin H. Sutherland, *Principles of Criminology*, p. 110 (Philadelphia: J. B. Lippincott Company, 1947).

[3] Paul Lemkau, *Mental Hygiene and Public Health*, p. 335 (New York: McGraw-Hill Book Company, Inc., 1949).

[4] See George E. Partridge, "Current Conceptions of Psychopathic Personality," *The American Journal of Psychiatry*, 1930, X, pp. 53–99.

psychotic and psychotic persons as schizoid or paranoid.[5] It cannot
be ascertained by using the norms of the urban, middle-class subculture for gauging the behavior of persons in another subculture
with such labels as "inadequate," or "criminal." Indeed, "psychopathic personality" can be ascertained chiefly by the personality
structure; and the personality .structure can be understood best
when traced developmentally.

Approach to Acting-out Personalities. Sociologists have been interested in acting-out behavior from a developmental viewpoint
because of its bearing upon crime. But they have been chiefly concerned with the types of associations and with the subculture which
have contributed to criminal behavior and less interested .in personality differences among delinquents. Although they have traced
the processes by which delinquents and criminals assimilate their
deviate forms, they have not pursued the process to .its logical
extreme by relating defective forms of socialization to criminal
behavior. Sutherland and others have studied the relationship
between psychopathy and crime,[6] while Burgess and others have
studied the personality structure of delinquents and criminals.[7]

On the other hand, psychoanalysts have emphasized personality
differences and the divergent courses of development among individual criminals. Although they often have confused acting-out and
antisocial behavior with criminality and have understated the
social influences of peer groups upon criminal activity, still they

[5] For example, consider the categories of thinking in the diagnosis of psychopathy in the following: On the basis of the Rorschach tests, Lindner found that
psychopaths were qualitatively related to the hebephrenics and the neurotics.
Batcheller found a neurotic condition superimposed on "a basic schizophrenic or
latent schizoid condition." Kisher and Michael have designated this condition .as
a "schizoneurosis." Obviously, the substitution of one label for another does not
explain anything about psychopathy; it merely leads to confusion. See Robert M.
Lindner, "The Rorschach Test and the Diagnosis of Psychopathic Personality,"
Journal of Criminal Psychopathology, July, 1943, V:2, p. 69; Samuel J. Beck,
"Introduction to the Rorschach Method," *Research Monographs*, No. 1 (Menasha,
Wis.: American Orthopsychiatric Association, 1937); the other citations in W.
Rottersman, "The Guardhouse .Inmate," *War Medicine*, May, 1944, V:5, p. 276.
It must be emphasized, however, that some paranoid persons and some very
seclusive persons act out their behavior, but these psychotic tendencies are on a
different vector than their acting-out behavior.

[6] Edwin H. Sutherland, *Principles of Criminology*, pp. 103–117 (Philadelphia:
J. B. Lippincott Company, 1948).

[7] Ernest W. Burgess, "The Individual Delinquent as a Person," *American
Journal of Sociology*, May, 1923, 28, pp. 657–680.

have been foremost in trying to classify acting-out persons on a dynamic and developmental level.[8]

In constructing a scheme of acting-out antisocial types which are mutually exclusive we must consider the criteria of personality organization, personality development, and the influence of the subculture. We must omit, however, the so-called "part psychopaths" who have minimal guilt feelings about one particular form of behavior, whether it be stealing, certain sex perversions, or other idiosyncracies; for these behavioral reactions are usually symptoms or expressions of more profound personality differences which often vary with the individual case.

Types of Acting-out Disorders. From this vantage point we can classify the varied acting-out disorders into the following types: (1) the "true" psychopath, (2) the acting-out neurotic, (3) the self-centered indulged personality, and (4) the subcultural deviant.

Since these types are ideal, particular cases only approximate them, and some acting-out persons may have components of two types. For example, a subcultural deviant, a delinquent, may have certain neurotic characteristics which intensify his acting-out behavior. An acting-out neurotic may be so incorrigible that, despite intense feelings of guilt, he may approximate the "true" psychopath in his hostile behavior, in his distorted social relationships, and in his resistance to treatment.[9] Certain psychopaths may have guilt feelings about certain matters, and thus be marginal to the "true" psychopath and the acting-out neurotic. Certain immature personalities who have been neglected, then overindulged, in early life may appear as "true" psychopaths by their lack of guilt and resistance to personal change. The vicissitudes of family constellations, parent-child relationships, and personal development are so varied and so complex that marginal and mixed types inevitably arise. The advantage of a classificatory scheme of ideal types is its

[8] Franz Alexander and Hugo Staub, *The Criminal, the Judge and the Public*, pp. 145–152 (New York: The Macmillan Company, 1931); Otto Fenichel, *The Psychoanalytic Theory of Neurosis*, pp. 117–139, 324–386, 466–492 (New York: W. W. Norton & Company, 1945); Walter Bromberg, *Crime and the Mind*, pp. 54, 55 (Philadelphia: J. B. Lippincott Company, 1948).

[9] See, for example, Margaret S. Mahler, "Ego Psychology Applied to Behavior Problems," *Modern Trends in Child Psychiatry*, edited by Nolan D. C. Lewis and Bernard L. Pacella, pp. 53–56 (New York: International Universities Press, Inc., 1945).

use as a guide in understanding the personality formation and structure of these types.

The "True" Psychopath

"True" psychopaths are relatively few. Even those state-mental-hospital patients who are diagnosed as psychopaths and who represent about 2.6 per cent of the total admissions are not all "true" psychopaths;[10] and the number of "true" psychopaths in prisons cannot be determined accurately because of the different preconceptions among clinicians concerning psychopathy.

The "true" psychopath is one who lacks the capacity for self-restraint and self-condemnation that comprise the makings of a conscience. He is emotionally incapable of abiding, for any long period, by the expectations of other persons, and he has evidently been incorrigible from early childhood. Seemingly, he has been deprived of a capacity for intimate social relationships and for internalizing the social norms which these intimate attachments represent. The psychopath feels slightly guilty about his wayward behavior. In undisciplined fashion, he concentrates primarily upon gratifying his urgent appetites.

Though the psychopath cannot sustain intimate relationships, he can get along with others on a casual level. He is not considered necessarily "queer" or bizarre. In fact, he may be quite adept in his impersonal relationships. Frequently "verbal" and charming, he may create a very favorable first impression, but, lacking perseverance, he soon becomes impatient and irritated. Usually, his relations turn out to be utilitarian, exploiting, and irresponsible. Since he lacks close or intimate relations he may become an isolate who is so set upon appeasing his desires that he needs no intimate company. Karpman describes the condition of a psychopath as follows:[11]

> A striking feature of this man's personality is his almost complete lack of social feeling. . . . He has never had any friends, let alone intimates. He never shared or felt the need to share his problems and confidences with anyone. He would associate with one or more men for the purpose of committing a crime; but this done, the loot secured, and the need satisfied, he would leave them and go by himself. As

[10] See *Patients in Mental Institutions, 1946* (Washington, D.C.: Bureau of the Census, U.S. Department of Commerce, 1949).

[11] Ben Karpman, "Passive Parasitic Psychopathy," *Psychoanalytic Review*, April, 1947, 34:2, p. 210.

he joined other men for the purpose of committing a crime, so he would seek the company of a woman for the purpose of satisfying his sexual needs. That done, he had little use for her; but he knew the sexual need would soon reassert itself, and this knowledge frequently made him stick to women for a considerable period of time. He is . . . the original isolationist, only more than the lone wolf. . . .

Along with the psychopath's inability to foster primary relationships is his inability to postpone immediate gratifications for more distant goals. In a sense, both identification with others and delayed behavior require inhibition and some capacity for suppression and reflection in order to guide activity into social channels. By empathizing with others, the ordered person can ·check his immediate actions in order to select alternative behavior which fits within the expectations of other persons. The psychopath, however, is so concerned with immediate self-gratification that he disregards or is unable to delay his behavior for any sustained period unless under external compulsion. The psychopath's desires override his self-restraint and ability for intimate role identification.

Since he lacks foresight, the psychopath lives in and for the present. He carries out his desires without concern for, sometimes without understanding, the consequences. He is unable to project himself into the future and to foresee the results of his activities or the objections of others, especially when he begins his actions. And he does not grieve about the past, except to stimulate or express "lip-service" grief in order to impress others. Although he may plan immediate activities, his plans are not integrated within a larger scheme or a total career; he has no life plan. Frequently, even his immediate behavior lacks any plan and is an impulsive and repetitive action, for he cannot tolerate tensions and must express them in order to achieve personal balance.[12] Sometimes this personal balance means exhausted satiation. Frequently, the psychopath's imperious demands are revealed in his sexual attitudes, for the true psychopath is far less inhibited sexually than the ordered person, or even than the neurotic or psychotic. Manson describes his sexual adventures as follows:[13]

[12] Ben Karpman, "The Principles and Aims of Criminal Psychopathology," *Journal of Criminal Psychopathology*, January, 1940, 1:3, pp. 200–201.
[13] Ben Karpman, "The Case of Walter Manson," *Case Studies in the Psychopathology of Crime*, p. 35, Vol. II (Baltimore: Medical Science Press, 1944).

I seemed to have gone woman crazy and the more I indulged in them, the more I wanted to indulge. It got so that I thought of taking the money that this fellow too intrusted in my care, and of going to these houses 'til I couldn't stand it any more. I wanted to live with them day and night and just indulge in sexual relations with them until I was completely satisfied.

The psychopath is self-centered. He continually seeks to satisfy his own interests, regardless of the pain, abuse, or sacrifices he causes other people. He cannot be considerate because he cannot feel the suffering of others. He is concerned mainly with the way he can use people to satisfy his desires, by whatever means and however unscrupulous.[14]

But the psychopath's self-centeredness reflects his shallow social relations; and his social relations are one means for benefiting himself, because his interests, attention, and strivings are circumscribed about his momentary desires.[15]

Furthermore, his self-centeredness reflects a limited capacity for self-reference. By not getting emotionally close to people, he does not see himself as a love object. Actually, in his avid, random pursuits, he abuses himself as he does others. Indeed, he has little insight into his behavior. Sometimes his behavior, because of its random waywardness, baffles him. Manson states the following about his sprees:[16]

Many times I have spent good money imagining that I was having a good time. Instead of investing the money I was throwing it away and many bitter lessons I have learned from this. . . . Not once but over a dozen times I have done this. I would wonder what made me doodle the money away and do this over and over again.

The psychopath's limited self-criticism and self-reproach result from this lack of identification and hence of conscience. By not taking the role of others and then evaluating his behavior, except for the present, the psychopath can experience shame but slight guilt. He may feel "humiliation" in public, but this merely creates

[14] Ben Karpman, "The Principles and Aims of Criminal Psychopathology," *Journal of Criminal Psychopathology*, January, 1940, I:3, pp. 200–207.

[15] Ben Karpman, "The Case of Walter Manson," *Case Studies in the Psychopathology of Crime*, Vol. II, p. 18.

[16] Ben Karpman, "The Case of Walter Manson," *Case Studies in the Psychopathology of Crime*, Vol. II, p. 79. See Harrison G. Gough, "A Sociological Theory of Psychopathy," *American Journal of Sociology*, March, 1948, XLIII, pp. 359–360.

resentment against others rather than an internalization of the shame and its consequent self-condemnation and self-control. On the contrary, he projects the blame upon others who frustrate him, regardless of the injury he has caused them. His hostility and vindictiveness are usually simple and direct. Since the psychopath blames the environment, he is often confused with the paranoid. But the two types are markedly different. The paranoid projects his hostility within a logical scheme of sustained delusions. The psychopath has transitory feelings of hostility toward those persons who thwart his wishes, but when his wishes are gratified or new wishes arise, his projections and rationalizations seem to pass away.

Usually in difficulty, the psychopath seems to regret his past deeds. But he does not feel what he says or, at best, feels it only for the moment; his behavior does not change. Instead, he renews his misadventures when the opportunities arise. His closest approximations to identifying relationships are his ingratiating technques, his demands for social attention, and his attraction for a sex object.

The psychopath uses ingratiating techniques for manipulating other people. Frequently, his ingratiating relations are mistaken for intimate relations. It is then that he takes advantage of other persons. In addition, he may indiscriminately demand social attention, whether he is praised and approved or chided and rebuked, and he becomes envious of those persons who do get this attention. Since the psychopath may become attracted to a sex object, he may strive to sustain this relationship. And the relationship may seem to have some characteristics of a primary relationship. The change comes about, however, when the sex attraction wears off or is supplanted by another sex object.

Frequently, it appears that the psychopath places a singular interpretation upon words and their meanings. If one can picture a person discussing "love," "gratitude," or "career" without that person being able to feel love or gratitude, or without having the foresight of a career, he would know what these terms might mean to the psychopath.

But the psychopath is not necessarily feeble-minded. His intelligence level may range even from normal to superior, and his intellectual abilities do not deteriorate. Yet he would express defective judgments in foresight, in planning, in sizing up social situations, and in sustained concentration. His judgment would become even more defective when aroused or when he is about to gratify his wishes.

The psychopath does understand social reality. He can communicate with others, as he does know the difference between right and wrong. He shuns ridicule and responds to external restraints. But he does not incorporate these restraints and does not control most of his future behavior in terms of these forms of social control. Yet he is aware of them and can avoid the external semblance of deviation. A psychopath states the following about looking for a new job:[17]

> There were many times when I would be self-conscious when walking on the street, and when I would see people looking at me I would imagine there was something wrong with my attire that made them amused or something else that made them look so much.

The psychopath sometimes seeks approval in the same way that he seeks to satisfy his other desires; and he conforms for a short time to obtain this approval. But this conformity cannot last because he is carried away either by his imperious desires or, when frustrated, by his direct hostility. Hence, the "true" psychopath's behavior is usually self-defeating simply because he is unable to sustain a relationship, and as such he becomes involved in difficulties from which he often cannot extricate himself. But his self-defeating behavior is not a result of guilt or a wish for self-punishment; his behavior is self-defeating because it contradicts and threatens the characteristic expectations of the group. Eventually, his behavior becomes intolerable to the group, and he is restrained or punished.

Conscience in the Psychopath. Although the psychopath frequently projects blame for his activities upon other persons and external situations, this does not mean that he has no guilt feelings. Were he without guilt feelings, he would not be human. His guilt feelings, though arrested, assume these forms. First, he does internalize in mild or marked degree such elementary restraints as incest, murder of his parents, cannibalism, and dress. These restraints are often expressed by disgust and aversion.

Second, he responds to intellectualized self-censure. Even though he may not reproach himself very deeply and he may not be de-

---

[17] Ben Karpman, "The Case of Walter Manson," *Case Studies in the Psychopathology of Crime*, Vol. II, p. 71.

terred by this self-censure in future misadventures, his self-reproach in superficial intellectualized form is evident.

Third, the psychopath frequently seeks other persons to limit his random aggressions. Hence, he behaves as if he seeks punishment. Actually, he too is puzzled by his waywardness and unwittingly may want to put limits to his random, appetite-fulfilling and destructive behavior.

Fourth, he may become somewhat depressed when his aggressions or his desires are thwarted. Even though he projects the blame for his activities upon others, he still may invert his aggression and become dejected. Furthermore, he may be unable to tolerate frustration, and then he may be prompted to momentary self-censure.

In brief, the psychopath is incompletely socialized and his capacity for self-reproach is limited. Hence, his conscience is less developed than that of an ordered person or than that of a neurotic or a psychotic.

Can the Psychopath Change? Since the psychopath's behavior can be noted in early childhood, and since the psychopath learns very little from experience, many investigators maintain that he is not amenable to personal change. Though the psychopath may resolve to conform or to restrain himself for a short period, seemingly he cannot achieve this disciplined redirection for very long. His undisciplined personality which becomes fixed, say in the first six years of life, becomes extremely difficult to modify.

Studies of the treatment of psychopaths are few, except for reports of individual cases. On the one hand, it appears doubtful that the few investigators who report improvements of psychopaths are even referring to the same personality type. On the other hand, other psychiatrists, such as Chornyak, Henderson, and Nielsen and Thompson, regard psychopathy to be a result of brain damage and consider treatment to be futile.[18] Karpman maintains that the psychopath is not amenable to change, that he seemingly cannot learn, and that experience teaches him nothing. Other therapists who dealt with psychopaths present similar accounts of failure.

[18] John Chornyak, "Some Remarks on the Diagnosis of the Psychopathic Delinquent," *The American Journal of Psychiatry,* May, 1941, 97:6, pp. 1326–1335; Donald K. Henderson, *Psychopathic States* (New York: W. W. Norton & Company, 1939); John M. Nielsen and George N. Thompson, *The Engrammes of Psychiatry,* pp. 206–207 (Springfield, Ill.: Charles C. Thomas, Publisher, 1948).

Heaver reports that of 40 acting-out patients whom he treated, 3 could not be helped because they were "adamant in their attitudes of negativism." From earliest years they were extremely stubborn, utterly selfish, self-centered, vicious, sadistic, had temper tantrums, and showed a total inability to postpone gratifications.[19] Since the psychopath can adjust to newly established relationships, Gough has suggested as a therapeutic medium that he be shifted from one set of relationships to another before he can act up.[20] Although this technique has not been tried, it is hard to see how it would modify the psychopath's personality to any appreciable extent. Johnson indicates that she was not successful with the very self-centered, anti-social persons whom she treated.[21]

In brief, it seems that the psychopath whose behavior is fixed at an early age is not likely to be amenable to change, and that those deviants who respond to treatment are either "acting-out neurotics" or immature persons whose antisocial behavior was recognized during late childhood or during adolescence. Moreover, the extent to which the "true" psychopath can change depends upon "the causes" of his disordered condition.

"Causes" of Psychopathy. The "causes" of psychopathy, whether biological or developmental, are still inconclusive because no definite research has decisively shown whether the biological or the developmental influence alone is crucial.

Biological Explanations. The biological explanation maintains that brain damage or disturbance, whether inherited or acquired through injury, is the "cause" of psychopathy. It has been shown that persons with varied types of brain injuries, brain growths, and spinal lesions become much less responsive to social pressures and to social control. Many children afflicted with such diseases as encephalitis or chorea later become delinquents.[22] But these subjects show demonstrable organic pathology and, hence, differ from

[19] W. Lynwood Heaver, "A Study of 40 Male Psychopathic Personalities Before, During and After Hospitalization," *The American Journal of Psychiatry*, November, 1943, 100:3, p. 343.

[20] Harrison G. Gough, "Sociological Theory of Psychopathy," *American Journal of Sociology*, March, 1948, 53, pp. 359–366.

[21] Adelaide M. Johnson, "Sanctions for Superego Lacunae of Adolescents," *Searchlights on Delinquency*, edited by K. R. Eisler, p. 235 (New York: International Universities Press, Inc., 1949).

[22] M. Molitch, "Chronic Post-Encephalitic Behavior Problems," *The American Journal of Psychiatry*, January, 1935, 91, pp. 843–861.

those "psychopaths" about whom organic damage is merely inferred.

Eliasberg, Chornyak, Henderson, and Nielsen and Thompson, among others, contend that the onset of psychopathy results from brain damage, and that this damage is frequently hereditary.[23]

Nielsen and Thompson, for example, maintain that, as a consequence of damage to the brain or to the anterior thalamus nucleus, control of the self-concept and of the concept of time diminishes. This damage may result from hereditary, or congenital—i.e., the fetal—influences, as well as from birth injuries or childhood infections.[24]

Nielsen and Thompson, in fact, claim that normal as well as psychopathic children are reared in adverse familial settings, such as broken homes, and adverse neighborhoods and schools, but that the normal children do not become psychopathic.[25] In short, these investigators attribute slight importance to social and developmental influences.

Yet, the hypothesis of psychopathy as a unique constitutional disorder seems to be a negative inference unless definitive evidence is found. Sometimes it implies that, since psychopathic behavior cannot be explained by influences from early and later social relationships, there must be something different about the psychopath's constitution. Yet it might also mean that the early social relationships of the psychopath have not been examined closely enough or completely. It is largely for this reason, as we have pointed out, that the hypotheses concerning causation in psychopathy are still inconclusive. The disagreement may result from the fact that some psychopaths have definite brain damage or are underdeveloped in certain areas, particularly the frontal lobes,[26] and that other psychopaths may be the victims of immature development.

[23] W. G. Eliasberg, "Psychopathy or Neurosis," *Journal of Clinical Psychopathology*, October, 1946, VIII:2, pp. 274–275; John Chornyak, "Some Remarks on the Diagnosis of the Psychopathic Delinquent," *The American Journal of Psychiatry*, May, 1941, 97:6, pp. 1326–1335; D. K. Henderson, *Psychopathic States* (New York: W. W. Norton & Company, 1939); J. M. Nielsen and George N. Thompson, *The Engrammes of Psychiatry*, pp. 168–176 (Springfield, Ill.: Charles C Thomas, Publisher, 1947).

[24] J. M. Nielsen and George N. Thompson, *The Engrammes of Psychiatry*, pp. 168–176.

[25] *Ibid.*, p. 176.

[26] Walter Freeman and James W. Watts, "The Frontal Lobes and the Consciousness of the Self," *Contemporary Psychopathology*, edited by S. Sylvanus Tomkins, pp. 290–301 (Cambridge, Mass.: Harvard University Press, 1947).

272 SOCIETY AND PERSONALITY DISORDERS

In this connection the theory upon which prefrontal lobotomies rests is relevant to our discussion because in this operation the connections between the prefrontal lobes and the thalamus are severed. As a result, the emotional energy and tone in the ideation of the patients becomes lowered.[27] It is in this frontal-lobe region where the true psychopath is supposedly defective, either through damage or through underdevelopment. Hence, these prefrontal operations can be illuminating by demonstrating the personality changes in the patients. Freeman and Watts found that their patients who had prefrontal lobotomies became less responsive to social controls, were less inhibited and self-conscious, and had less emotional intensity and foresight in their behavior.[28] They state:[29]

> While the operated patient may be able to function at a high level of efficiency in the matters of business, art, law, mechanics, and the like, nevertheless, there is a certain disturbance in the relationship of the individual with himself that permits certain characteristics to appear—characteristics which may or may not be offensive to others, but about which the individual is either unaware or unconcerned . . . he is either obtuse or indifferent to the effect that he himself is about to produce on other people. He is greatly lacking in what is termed self-consciousness.

Obviously, the role-taking facility of the individual changes, for the individual is less able to identify with others and evaluate himself from their perspectives. Moreover, the individual is less concerned about himself and is less able to project himself in the future and to see the consequences of his behavior. As a result, the prefrontal lobotomy reduces the emotional tone of the attitudes towards the image of the self.[30]

Yet physiological pathology can have effects similar to those of arrested personality development. This arrested personality development would result from a fixation in role taking by which the person

[27] Walter Freeman and James W. Watts, "Prefrontal Lobotomy: The Problem of Schizophrenia," *The American Journal of Psychiatry*, May, 1945, 6:1, p. 742.

[28] Walter Freeman and James W. Watts, "The Frontal oLbes and the Consciousness of the Self," *Contemporary Psychopathology*, edited by S. Sylvanus Tomkins.

[29] *Ibid.*, p. 292. Quoted by permission of Harvard University Press and *Psychosomatic Medicine*.

[30] *Ibid.*, p. 298. See Warren T. Brown and Charles I. Solomon, "Delinquency and the Electroencephalogram," *The American Journal of Psychiatry*, January, 1942, 98:4, pp. 499–503.

would be less able to identify with other persons and less able to be controlled by these identifications.

The Development of Psychopathy. Some psychopaths are victims of faulty development, and their development shows that they have been emotionally deprived of intimate relationships with parent figures from infancy or early childhood. Because of this deprivation they become retarded in their facility for intimate role taking and become less responsive to social control. When parent figures have been shifted in early life, and when the children have not had the opportunity to identify with and become attached to any parent figure, their deprivation becomes intensified. Because of these shifting and emotionally scant relationships with adults, they become restless, impulsive, sometimes intensely curious children. They lack foresight and other mental capacities; they have shallow relationships with other persons, and they are hard to restrain and hard to change. These developmental characteristics have been observed among children in nonfamilial institutions and have been noted in the histories of psychopaths.

Parent-Child Relationships. Since the kinds of relationships that a given child may have with his parents or with other members of the family are so varied, a representation of a static family constellation or of given parental characteristics is not enough to explain the development of psychopathy. The important influences consist of ways in which the child and parents relate to each other and of the way in which the child internalizes the meanings of these relationships. Even if a child is neglected by his parents, he may still cultivate binding, intimate relationships with the siblings or with other family members. Schachtel and Levi have shown that the children in a loveless family can still cultivate intimate relationships with other persons.[31] Moreover, if the child is deprived by the parents, he still may remain organized and may be able to abide by the social norms, although he may remain emotionally cold and indifferent to the feelings of others.[32] Hence, no definite and conclusive personality inevitably emerges from a given set of parent-child rela-

---

[31] Anna Hartoch Schachtel and Majorie B. Levi, "Character Structure of Day Nursery Children as Seen through the Rorschach," *American Journal of Orthopsychiatry,* April, 1945, XV:2, pp. 213–222.

[32] *Ibid.*

tionships. Yet within this type of family situation, the child may so develop that he may be unable to cultivate close attachments and conform to social controls.

The shift of parent figures, then, is as crucial as emotional deprivation in the formation of the psychopathic personality. The shifted child cannot form enduring primary relationships, especially when he lacks affection and tender care. Among the settings in which this type of personality may very likely emerge are child institutions such as nurseries or foundling homes and, sometimes, foster families.

Although these forms of parent-child relationships may contribute to psychopathic behavior, the content of the interaction cannot be overlooked. Some parents may be so undisciplined emotionally or so perverse sexually that the child, having no other role models, may identify with them and then internalize their perverse forms of behavior. Having received parental sanction from their behavior, he accepts their criteria of right and wrong and he may imitate their behavior with little or no guilt feelings.

These parent-child relationships combine one or more of these features in the developmental processes of "true" psychopaths.

Personality Development. The psychopath who emerges from these shifting relationships is a deprived child who tends to differ from the rejected child.[33] The deprived child's relationships with adults are usually very meager, barren, and distant. His emotions reflecting these thin relationships are shallow, simple, and direct, for he does not have the opportunity to acquire and to cultivate intense or complex feelings toward other persons. He does not experience the subtle, continual feelings that come with close attachments to one adult figure, and he does not learn to associate affection with the delights of tactual contact with the mother. The rejected child, on the other hand, is in continual interaction with his parents, and his emotional development centers about his not being wanted, or being despised. His emotions become complex, indirect, and intense, for he comes to identify with his rejecting parents who may have mixed feelings toward him. He sees them as anchor points with which to interpret his world and himself. In fact, by identifying with his parents in the process of socializa-

[33] William Goldfarb, "Effects of Early Institutional Care on Adolescent Personality," *Journal of Experimental Education,* 1943, 12, pp. 106, 129.

tion, he internalizes their viewpoints about himself and thus may become disturbed and even disordered. The deprived child does not have any adult figures with whom to identify and to regard as anchor points in interpreting his world and himself; hence, his estimate of himself is somewhat confused and is fixed around body gratification.

By not acquiring gratification from close and binding parental relationships, the deprived child becomes fixated upon his body for satisfaction, whether in thumb sucking or in masturbatory pleasures. Though he may want attention, he is also apathetic to other persons and more concerned with bodily pleasures.[34]

He becomes less threatened by the withdrawal and removal of affection because he has not experienced affection sufficiently as a means of self-control. For example, as Goldfarb points out, deprived children who were shifted or who were threatened with being shifted to other families took the change calmly and without any display of emotion.[35] In addition, the child's estimation of himself is not bound to any single parental figure who can control him. It is therefore questionable whether the deprived child who eventually develops into a psychopath sees himself as a love object and can express affection, for he has not internalized the images of sustained parent figures who see him as a love object. In addition, he has not had the opportunity to cultivate the capacity for intimate role taking in order to reciprocate a love relationship.

In this condition the deprived child frequently bids for attention. He may revert to negativistic displays such as temper tantrums, illness, or other devices. His bid for attention is indiscriminate and is even displayed to strangers, for whom he shows slight fear. As Fenichel points out, ingratiating devices for obtaining affection or attention may be a compensatory means for showing oneself that he can be loved or that he can master his interpersonal situations.

Moreover, the deprived child does not become disciplined, although he may adjust to a routine if external pressure is intense enough. Yet, basically, he finds no purposive rewards that are bound up with postponing and delaying behavior. His delayed behavior would have to be bound up with the approvals and disapprovals of

[34] William Goldfarb, "Psychological Privation in Infancy and Subsequent Adjustment," *American Journal of Orthopsychiatry*, April, 1945, XV:2, pp. 254, 255.
[35] *Ibid.*

those identifying images who represent the right and wrong of his behavior. But by not internalizing the images of parent figures completely, his norms of approval and disapproval are weak. Although this characterization is extreme, because no child is completely deprived else he would not be human, yet this tendency is the forerunner of a lack of self-restraint and of a stunted conscience. Anna Freud and Burlingham, who studied "infants without families," have made these observations about this developmental process:[36]

> In the beginning of life the child is ruled merely by its own desires. It next learns to renounce gratifications for the sake of the parents. Derrick, three and one-half, said about his family mother: "If Sara loves me, she can't love me wet." In the next phase it begins to share the parent's valuations. Bridget, two years and three months, when placed on the lavatory after an accident during the last stage of her habit training, said with sudden relief: "No more weewee on the floor. Mummy does not like it. Jean (her family mother) does not like it, Bridget does not like it." The educational task is completed in each particular respect when the child stands firm in its newly acquired attitudes, without further need to invoke the images of the people for whose sake this reversal of all inner values has been undertaken. It has then established within itself a moral centre—conscience, superego —which contains the values, commands and prohibitions which were originally introduced into its life by the parents and which now regulate its further actions more or less independently from within. . . .
>
> It is at this point that the institutional child is at its gravest disadvantage. An infant in a residential nursery may acquire the rough and ready methods of social adaptation which are induced by the atmosphere of the toddler's room; methods of attack and defense, of giving in and sharing, swapping, etc.; it may further acquire conventions and behavior patterns in obedience to the nursery routine and in imitation of its elders. But neither of these processes, though adding to the growth of the child's personality, will lead to the embodiment of moral values which is described above. Identification of this kind takes place under one condition only: as the result and residue of emotional attachment to people who are the real and living personifications of the demands which every civilized society upholds. . . . Where love objects of this kind are missing, the infant is deprived of an all important opportunity to identify with these demands.

Freud and Burlingham point out further that, in this nursery situation, if the adult or parent figures remain distant and imper-

---

[36] Anna Freud and Dorothy Burlingham, *Infants without Families,* pp. 124, 125 (New York: International Universities Press, Inc., 1944).

sonal, or if the adults are changed frequently, the children will then show defects in their personality structure and will "be exposed to the danger of all kinds of dissocial development." [37]

It is not surprising, then, that a child with less inner restraints may become restless, randomly hyperactive, and unusually curious. Fenichel calls attention to the fact that for these persons, "the environment is only an arena in which to stage their conflicts. The patients appear as restless, hyperactive personalities. . . ." [38] Healy and Bronner found that 53 delinquents exhibited these overactive tendencies in childhood or adolescence, and 25 were overactive and uninhibited before school age and a "few were overactive even in infancy." [39] However, Healy and Bronner do not specify what these thwartings and frustrations are, because the neurotic as well as the psychopathic child can be restless. [40]

In a more definitive study of emotional privation, Goldfarb investigated the development of 15 children who, from infancy, were reared in an institution until about the age of 3 when they were placed in foster homes. He compared these institutional children with children who had been reared by foster parents from early infancy. He found that the institutionalized children showed emotional and mental deficiencies which the foster-family children did not display. [41]

The institutional children were emotionally passive, even impoverished, and lacked the characteristic inhibitory qualities that characterized foster-home children. Of the 15 cases, 14 were unmanageable in their classes. Many were subject to temper tantrums, and some were enuretic through the late juvenile and adolescent periods. Frequently, their behavior was random, distractible, and nonpersevering. Their extreme curiosity resulted from an inability to grasp the meaning of their social situations, which left them continually dissatisfied; hence, they were continually moved to test and

[37] *Ibid.*, p. 126.

[38] Otto Fenichel, *Psychoanalytic Theory of Neuroses*, p. 374 (New York: W. W. Norton & Company, 1945).

[39] William Healy and Augusta F. Bronner, *New Light on Delinquency and Its Treatment*, p. 45 (New Haven: Yale University Press, 1936).

[40] *Ibid.*

[41] William Goldfarb, "Psychological Privation in Infancy and Subsequent Adjustment," *American Journal of Orthopsychiatry*, April, 1945, XV:2, p. 249.

to try out situations on a trial-and-error basis rather than on a re-
flective sizing-up process.[42]

Although they were emotionally passive, they continually demanded affection and attention. Their demands for affection were
on a physical and sensual level, by continual hugging and kissing.
Nonetheless, they could not reciprocate these relationships. Despite
their insatiable demand for attention, they did not enrich their
capacities to form social ties. During adolescence, they were emotionally isolated, socially removed, and cold. They were not responsive to "normal motivation" and could not be appealed to conform,
as could other children.

Their capacity for abstraction was also retarded, particularly
in terms of time and space. They had difficulty envisioning the
consequences of their wayward actions. Because of their poor conception of time, they would come home from school hours late.
Although repeatedly warned against such behavior, because of
spatial deficiencies, they would run off sidewalks or wander away.
Their lessened ability in foresight and their inability to appraise
a total situation made them repeat their mistakes over and over
again. Moreover, their meager emotional reactions were supplemented by the virtual absence of anxiety after acts of cruelty,
aggression, or hostility. They were unmoved by failing in school,
which sometimes bewildered their foster parents who did not know
how to motivate them. Even severe punishment and parental
threats of removal from the home were of no avail.[43] Seemingly
true psychopathy is formed in early life, perhaps before the age
of three, or at the latest by the age of five.

Spitz found marked developmental differences in the first years
of life between deprived children in a foundling home and illegitimate children of delinquent minors in a nursery.[44] Although the
children in the foundling home apparently had better-endowed
parents, they did not have a mother or a substitute mother, but
each shared the attentions of a nurse with seven other children. The
nursery children received far greater attention from their mothers,

[42] William Goldfarb, "Psychological Privation in Infancy and Subsequent Adjustment," *American Journal of Orthopsychiatry*, April, 1945, XV:2, p. 252.
[43] *Ibid.*, pp. 252, 253.
[44] Rene A. Spitz, "Hospitalism: An Inquiry into the Genesis of Psychiatric
Conditions in Early Childhood," *The Psychoanalytic Study of the Child*, pp. 53–
74 (New York: International Universities Press, Inc., 1945).

each of whom was in constant competition with the others in caring for her child. The effect of these differential mother-child relationships was that the foundling-home children became retarded and even declined in their development and that the nursery children remained normal.[45] The significance of these early primary relationships explains in large part why such children as Anna and the Wild Boy of Aveyron were regarded as feeble-minded and why they could not be successfully socialized.[46] It reveals, too, why psychopathic behavior can be so readily attributed to "constitutional" factors.

Although Walter Manson, who was so elaborately described by Karpman, was removed from his family at the age of 6, he was even at that time unaware of a primary relationship. Since Manson wrote his autobiography at the age of 36, when he was an opiate addict and had been psychotic, it is difficult to say what transpired during his early life; for he goes back only as far as his fourth year, and discusses this period very briefly and vaguely. Karpman indicates, however, that Manson's difficulties arose after his departure from the family, although these difficulties were somewhat in evidence before.

In brief, the psychopath develops within a matrix of distant and impersonal parent-child relationships, and especially amidst changing and emotionally depriving parent figures. Although this absence of primary relationships occurs in early life, it cannot be said definitely how early, although the evidence often points to the period before the age of 3. Presumably, this deprivation may lead to psychopathy when it occurs after the symbolic period, namely, from 2 to about 5, although the arrested development should not be so severe. Another significant fact is that faulty development may lead to behavior which is somewhat similar to brain injury or underdevelopment. In both instances, not only is behavior disorganized and the capacity for self-reference impaired, but also such mental conditions as lack of foresight and inability to concentrate are evident. This developmental process can be further illustrated in the following case of Channing Nogg.

[45] *Ibid.* See also Rene A. Spitz, "The Role of Ecological Factors in Emotional Development in Infancy," *Child Development,* 1949, 20, pp. 145–156.

[46] Kingsley Davis, "Extreme Social Isolation of a Child," *American Journal of Sociology,* January, 1940, XLV, pp. 554–565; J. M. G. Itard, *The Wild Boy of Aveyron* (New York: Appleton-Century-Crofts, Inc., 1932).

f Channing Nogg

is a 9-year-old white boy who was referred for treatment
us destructive and incorrigible behavior. Among other deeds,
from his foster parents, set fire to bedding, and to waste-
baskets, and recently tried to set fire to a shack by pouring gasoline over it
because it "thrilled" him. He had broken windows and caused such other
damage to the neighbors' property that they complained repeatedly. Very
curious and intense about sex, he masturbated persistently and had engaged in sex play with other children in the neighborhood. Attempts to
correct his curiosity were in vain. A persistent liar, he did not become
disturbed when his lies were proved to be impossible. He had stolen money
or small articles from his foster parents. Once he threw a rock at a small
child who irritated him, causing a wound which required stitches; he
killed two pets that belonged to another family, had broken the neighbors' windows, and tried to damage a hothouse plant near his foster home.
When confronted with his depredations, he seemed unashamed and unmoved.

Channing has no physical defects, is attractive in appearance, glib and
ingratiating, and above average in intelligence. The Thematic Apperception Test revealed few if any signs of self-reproach or anxiety. His responses
to the test did show self-centeredness, little or no fear of adults, the portrait
of a social world as cold and impersonal, and a need for acting out his
aggressions.

Channing Nogg is the illegitimate son of a borderline feeble-minded
mother who had a mental age of about 9 and a father who was of borderline intelligence. His maternal grandmother was committed to the Kanka-
kee State Hospital, then released; his maternal grandparent was epileptic.
His grandparents were married after the grandfather served six months
in jail. His mother had four illegitimate children from different men, was
an intermittent prostitute and a beggar, and was eventually committed to
an institution for the feeble-minded. His father, who was a ne'er-do-well
with an I.Q. of 88, disappeared soon after Channing was born.

By the age of 1 year, Channing was entrusted to a home-finding society
by the juvenile court because his mother was declared "unfit" when she
was apprehended soliciting on the streets. By the age of 3 he had been
moved to three foster families, because his foster parents complained of
illness in the family, because of his overactivity and problem behavior, and
because of his difficulty with toilet training. He was enuretic until 4. By
the age of 9, he had been transferred to ten different families, and every
foster parent commented upon his intransigent and destructive behavior.
His more recent foster parents reported the following pattern of his behavior. He tried to win his way into their affections; then, after he was
certain that they liked him, he became destructive. Though he seemed to
listen to their instructions, he did as he pleased afterward. When he did
anything wrong, no matter how serious, he was unaffected. When caught
lying, he persisted in his story. Some of his foster parents explained at

length to him that they knew he was lying, but to no avail. For instance, he once spilled some nail polish on his hands. When asked what he had on his hands, he replied solemnly: "There is nothing on my hands. I don't know what you are talking about." He looked his foster mother squarely in the eye as he spoke.

In his last foster home, he had been liked but had remained uncontrollable. The foster parents claimed that they were very affectionate to him and that he seemed to return their affection in a superficial manner, until things did not go his way. Then he became hostile, impulsive, and destructive. Once he threw a rock at his foster mother because she did not want to go in the direction he wanted to go. Although he got along with other children, he did not make any close friends, and at times fought with his playmates. He fought with them whenever they frustrated him. Despite this difficulty, he was accepted by other children.

At the time of the interview he was in the third grade on trial promotion, but in the past he had failed the second grade and had to repeat it. Very inattentive in class, he seemed to daydream and to be very restless. Expressing no interest in school, he could not understand why he had to attend school. Consequently, he truanted at every opportunity. When he escaped from a detention home where he was sometimes committed, he had no fear in approaching a stranger and asking him for shelter for the night. In bidding for sympathy he would say that he had no father or mother. When his tales were found to be untrue, he expressed no remorse and no shame.

Despite repeated assurances that he would conform and behave, he continued to indulge in hostile, irresponsible, and destructive behavior. At times he seemed sincere about changing his ways, but he also claimed that he had to receive attention from adults even if he had to misbehave to do it. He felt that he was at his best only when he received attention, whether favorable or punitive.

The Acting-out Neurotic

The acting-out neurotic is often confused with the "true" psychopath because his external behavior seems so similar. Yet the personalities of the two types differ markedly. First, the acting-out neurotic does experience feelings of guilt and has the makings of a conscience. As such, he may feel a subconscious need to be punished for his misdeeds. The psychopath, on the other hand, projects blame onto others and rarely feels guilty. Second, the acting-out neurotic can establish primary relationships, perhaps to a lesser degree than the ordered person but far more so than the psychopath. Third, the acting-out neurotic resorts to his hostile behavior as a compensatory defense against anxiety; the psychopath experiences a minimum of anxiety. The style of life of the acting-out neurotic is such that he moves against people and organizes his behavior around overt hostility. Because of his hostility he tends to feel isolated, and this isolation may make him extremely self-centered or self-concerned. Moreover, this may deter him from getting close to people. The psychopath has little need for people except to use them. Fourth, the acting-out neurotic, who can identify with others, may then become amenable to change, particularly under certain conditions of intense identification with the therapist. The "true" psychopath, who cannot identify with others, seems impervious to change or to treatment, at least under present-day techniques.

Yet both have much in common. They are continually in trouble and are maladjusted. Both seem to have no life plan or integrated goals and live for the impulsive moment. Both tend to concentrate upon the present, although the acting-out neurotic may possibly grieve about his past. Both seem to behave in a manner which is essentially self-defeating and erratic. Both may exercise poor judgment, seem not to learn from experience, and seem completely undependable and often irresponsible.

The Development of the Acting-out Neurotic. The development of the acting-out neurotic is characterized by a very permissive parent, usually the mother, and by a distant or hostile parent, usually the father. The parental constellation occurs in these cases again and again. Greenacre found that the parental constellation consisted of a "stern, respected, and often obsessional father who is remote, preoccupied, and fear-inspiring in relation to his children, and an indulgent, pleasure-loving, frequently pretty mother who is often tacitly contemptuous of her husband's importance." [47] Generally, Greenacre found a definite discrepancy between the parental attitudes concerning their children's experiences.[48] Though Greenacre's subjects were from upper middle classes, this family constellation is also evident in lower classes.

Generally, the child is either tacitly or overtly approved in his predatory or variant activities, and as a result he feels slight guilt

[47] Phyllis Greenacre, "Conscience in the Psychopath," *American Journal of Orthopsychiatry*, July, 1945, 15:3, p. 498.
[48] *Ibid.*

concerning it.[49] "In no instance in which adequate psychiatric therapeutic study of both parent and child has been possible," says Szurek, "has it been difficult to obtain sufficient evidence to reconstruct the chief dynamics of the situation." Frequently, the mother, although the father also is involved in some way, unwittingly encourages the "anti-social behavior of the child." [50] Johnson indicates that the therapy of acting-out children was difficult because the attitudes of guilt developed toward the therapist were counteracted by the unwitting permission of the parents. Consequently, the child became confused, then more fearful of the therapist, and eventually stopped going for treatment to avoid further confusion. Even mild "acting-out" cases could be treated only when the important parent, whether mother or father, was also treated.[51] Some children did not measure up to the perfectionist expectations and hopes of one or both parents. To escape from their anxieties about ever achieving these goals, they reacted by hostile and destructive behavior. Some responded this way, too, as a result of shocking experiences in early life.

The neurotic is supposed to limit his aggressions to fantasy. Hence, the "acting-out" neurotic seems to be an anomaly. Actually, however, the neurotic who acts out his hostility has many similarities to the neurotic who limits his aggressions to fantasy. Both react to anxiety; both are overcome by guilt feelings; and, in the last analysis, both are self-defeating in their behavior. The differences are symptomatic rather than basic, and they indicate the kinds of defenses to which different neurotics may resort. In addition, the different social definitions of their symptoms may give them different roles in society, and these divergent roles may affect their self-conceptions and their relationships with other persons.

Why one neurotic expresses his hostility overtly and another neurotic expresses his hostility in fantasy is still not completely

[49] See Margaret S. Mahler, "Ego Psychology Applied to Behavior Problems," *Modern Trends in Child Psychiatry,* edited by Nolan D. C. Lewis and Bernard L. Pacella, pp. 52–56 (New York: International Universities Press, Inc., 1945).

[50] Stanislaus Szurek, "Genesis of Psychopathic Personality Trends," *Psychiatry,* February, 1942, V:1, p. 6.

[51] Adelaide M. Johnson, "Sanctions for Superego Lacunae of Adolescents," *Searchlights on Delinquency,* edited by K. R. Eisler, pp. 234, 235 (New York: International Universities Press, Inc., 1949).

known. It seems that some types of neurotics, particularly obsessives, are incapable of acting out their hostile fantasies. As a result, they seldom become acting-out neurotics. Janet has pointed out the following relevant observations:[52]

> It is not strange that in so many observations of criminal obsessions bearing upon more than two hundred patients and collected during a dozen years, I could not observe a single real accident? I have never seen any crimes committed, any suicide accomplished by one of these obsessives. It cannot be due only to chance. It must be that in these obsessives, the tendency to act out is very weak.

In some instances the types of approval which the neurotic gets may stimulate him to act out his behavior. The overt hostility may become a compensatory means for social approval from his associates, which he does not get from his parents. It indicates, too, that the neurotic as well as the ordered or stable person, can be introduced into delinquent activities. Another important fact concerns the attitudes of one or both of the parents. In some instances one parent may have such hostility to the other parent that, tacitly, either may want the child to act out his aggressions although he or she may not say so directly. The child may respond to hurt his oppressive parent, whether his father or his mother, by his self-defeating and disgraceful behavior. Thus, the whole problem of the individual's acting out his behavior is involved in a developmental process.

Healy and Bronner, in their comparative study of delinquents and nondelinquents, have described a case in which this acting-out behavior was a direct reaction against the parents.[53] In contrast to his brother, the delinquent subject, who was the youngest child in the family, was healthier and more intelligent. But the control's behavior was uneventful both at home and in school. The delinquent was a difficult problem even in his first year in school. He was hard to control, spoiled, and wanted his own way. By the age of 10 he was studied at the clinic because he displayed many nervous habits and fears. By the age of 14, he had engaged in a long line of delinquencies, some of which were very serious. He admitted that

[52] Pierre Janet, *Les Observations and La Psychasthenie*, p. 78, Vol. I [Paris: Alcan (Librairie, Felix), 1903].

[53] William Healy and Augusta F. Bronner, *New Light on Delinquency and Its Treatment*, pp. 81–83 (New Haven, Yale University Press, 1936).

he began his delinquencies at the age of 8. Moreover, he ran away from home at least ten times.

The parents were immigrants who had a shop in front of a house that they owned. The father was a stubborn, tense individual who often got drunk and was very harsh to the boy during his juvenile period. When the subject was 11, the father devoted much of his time in trying "to manage" him. Apparently, because of the father's previous harsh and repressive tactics, an intense antagonism arose between father and son. Although the mother was forgiving and rarely scolded the subject, she was somewhat rejective of him. The older brother also took a hand in punishing him.

The curious result of these parent-child relationships was that the subject could not stand praise. When he was praised, he became uncontrollable; yet when he was punished he engaged in further delinquencies. But, as Healy and Bronner emphasize, he seemed to ask for punishment. At one time he gave himself up to a policeman. At other times he claimed that he would have to punish himself if nobody else did, or that he would have to be sent to a reform school. He dreamed frequently of being involved in some disaster. He claimed that he resorted to his delinquencies out of an uncontrollable compulsion.

Although many features of this history are omitted by Healy and Bronner, such as the family constellation and parent-child relationships, the neurotic reactions and self-chastisement indicate the pattern of development of the acting-out neurotic. When he was 18 years old, the subject began to be treated; he also began to behave much better, although his final outcome is not revealed.

The Self-centered, Overindulged Person

Another acting-out personality is the self-centered, overindulged person who closely resembles the psychopath. Yet he differs from the psychopath because his difficulties may emerge during adolescence. He may be quite attached to one of the parents, is a rather overprotected, spoiled child, who seems to expect and to demand a lot from his parents, and he continues his demanding ways from persons outside the family. Nonetheless, under certain conditions he is amenable to personal change.

The spoiled immature type usually does not have intense anxieties and does not have intense feelings of guilt, as the acting-out neurotic does. His hostility does not result from intense anxiety but from immaturity, although he appears to approximate the neurotic to a greater degree than does the "true" psychopath. Aichhorn considered this type to be a product of the excess of love. He stated:[54]

> This type of delinquency develops because the mother, or in some instances, the father, is not equal to the task of rearing the child. . . . Since such a mother is ready to do anything to keep her darling from suffering the slightest discomfort, she is unable to subject him to any denials. Punishment upsets her more than it does the child. Weighed down by cares for him, she worries continually about his welfare and cannot demand from him any postponement of renunciation of pleasure. She clears out of his way all disappointments and obstacles which the child must learn to face and overcome in later life and thus she robs the child of initiative. . . . Any criticism of him is as painful as a personal insult. The child's playmates are very severely criticized if they offer resistance to his having his own way. The child is the center of interest and lives without restraint. . . .

Hence, this child is encouraged to remain immature, to expect things from others, to concentrate upon gratifying his own desires, and to be averse to postpone or to delay his basic wants.

Levy, in his studies of maternal overprotection, differentiates between the acting-out type who emerges from parental deprivation and the acting-out type who emerges from parental overindulgence. The "true" psychopath seemingly is unable to cultivate identifying relationships. The overindulged person can cultivate warm social relationships, but he too exploits them for his own advantage.[55] This type is very self-centered, parasitic, cannot keep a job, and is seemingly unaffected by training or experience. Of Levy's cases, one led a criminal career and another lived off his wife's earnings. This type expects uncritical maternal support and devotion as the central focus of his life scheme. Levy has described such a child in his study of overprotected children.[56] The subject was the only criminal in Levy's series of cases.

[54] From *Wayward Youth* by August Aichhorn, p. 201, reprinted by permission of The Viking Press, Inc., New York.
[55] David M. Levy, "Maternal Overprotection," *Modern Trends in Child Psychiatry*, edited by Nolan D. C. Lewis and Bernard D. Pacella, p. 32 (New York: International Universities Press, Inc., 1945).
[56] Case adapted from David M. Levy, *Maternal Overprotection*, pp. 221, 390 (New York: Columbia University Press, 1943).

Robert: an Overindulged and Deprived Personality

By the age of 25, the subject had spent ten years either inside prisons or on parole. His delinquent career started before his fourteenth year when he was first referred to the clinic for treatment. The subject was glib and charming in conversation, and his intelligence level was in the "high-average" category.

His development differed from the other subjects in this series because he experienced both overprotected indulgence and deprivation. Since the mother had to help support the family, she was unable to supervise her son's schoolwork and his social life. Consequently, she was unable to stabilize his school life and deter him from delinquent influences. His early delinquencies apparently began when his school assignments became hard for him and he began to truant from school. It is not unlikely, however, that the other delinquents may have influenced him to be truant.

When the mother was with Robert she was always overindulgent and insisted on rearing the boy as she wished, regardless of her husband's attitude. When the stepfather wanted to punish him during infancy, she interceded and warned him that she would leave home if he ever touched him. "Robert is my life," she claimed. As a result, the stepfather not only never punished the boy but, on the contrary, gave in to the subject's wishes. Moreover, the stepfather had little to say about Robert's rearing, and though he disagreed with the tactics of the mother, he allowed her to rear the subject as she pleased.

Robert was allowed to keep his own hours, had no home responsibilities, was permitted to attend the movies when he wished, and was given a one-dollar allowance per day. When he returned home from outdoors his meals were usually ready for him. On the other hand, Robert disobeyed his mother, did pretty much as he pleased, stayed up late and got up late, and went out to play when his mother asked him to stay at home. He was boastful, overly familiar, and had an exaggerated ease of manner.

He was considered a sissy by the peer group and had been nicknamed "Mary." His irresponsibility was demonstrated on a camping trip when he let his companions and the group worker do all the work. He was careless with things and even insisted on discarding a campfire grate because he did not want to help take it home.

In school he was retarded four terms. Though good in English, he was very poor in arithmetic, yet he seemed unconcerned. He truanted, was boisterous, left his seat to look out the window, and appeared bored in school because he claimed "the work is too easy." He wore sneakers to school although expressly forbidden to do so. He masturbated in the classroom, and, in one instance, exposed his genitals to girls. Despite his mischief and misbehavior, "his parents do nothing about it."

The mother was so attached to him that it was difficult for her to think of losing him, and at one time she claimed that she "would like to hang on to him until he is about 30 or 35."

The Cultural Deviant

The cultural deviant is a product of a particular subculture which sanctions activities that are considered antisocial or inadequate by the larger society. Despite this behavior the cultural deviant may have feelings of guilt, can conform to social controls, is capable of identifying with others in his immediate groups, and can modify his behavior. Yet his antisocial behavior, because it is sanctioned, usually does not create guilt feelings. When two widely disparate cultures exist side by side, this deviant behavior is not unlikely. Carothers calls attention to the fact that the natives of Kenya, when judged by Western standards, would be considered "psychopathic." [57] Some habitual delinquents in our culture exemplify this deviant type. Though considered antisocial by the larger society, stealing is sanctioned in some subcultures, and the individual participant acquires his behavior patterns by participating in these deviant groups. Yet too often this cultural component is overlooked in differentiating between the cultural deviant and the psychopath. The essential problem, then, is one of differentiating between the acquired norms of a subculture and the personality components of the particular deviant. The following case of James Martin describes a person who was a habitual delinquent and who was labeled as a "psychopathic personality" by the prison psychiatrist.[58] This psychopathic label is not unusual in view of the fact that many clinicians regard habitual criminals as psychopaths.[59]

The Case of James Martin

His four brothers were delinquents and criminals. Yet, when he and his brothers were provided with economic opportunities and were treated in a "friendly, informal and confidential" way, they responded to this treatment and became reoriented to conventional and useful pursuits.

At the age of 21, when James wrote his autobiography, he had spent one half of his life in reform schools, jails, prisons, and other state penal

[57] James Carothers, "A Study of Mental Derangement in Africans and an Attempt to Explain Its Peculiarities, More Especially in Relation to the African Attitude to Life," *Psychiatry,* February, 1948, XI:1, pp. 47–86.

[58] Clifford R. Shaw *et al.* (editors), *Brothers in Crime,* pp. 220–255 (Chicago: University of Chicago Press, 1938).

[59] L. Kolb states: "Habitual criminals are psychopaths and psychopaths are abnormal individuals. . . ." L. Kolb, "Types and Characteristics of Drug Addicts," *Mental Hygiene,* 1935, IX, p. 301.

institutions. His difficulties with enforcement officers began from the time he was slightly older than 6, and lasted until he was 24.

His parents, Polish immigrants, settled in a typical first-settlement zone near a factory district. As far as is known, none of his ancestors was psychotic or had been committed to a mental hospital.

His father, an unskilled laborer, intermittently worked at odd jobs, but being an alcoholic he dissipated a large share of his salary in drinking. But alcoholism was prevalent among men in the community. Most of the men who worked in the near-by railroad yards and factories customarily gathered in the corner saloon on paydays to squander their money.

James' mother, however, was a hard-working woman who was prudent enough to save what money her husband did earn to bridge the lean days of unemployment and drinking. Pious, self-effacing, she devoted her life to her family and to her children. In retrospect James said, "As I think of all the hardships and troubles my mother went through when I was a small child, I feel ashamed of myself for causing her more trouble by being the kind of boy I was. . . . She was kind to me when I was small. Way back, since I can remember, she was always working, washing clothes, cleaning house, administering to our needs. . . . About the only diversion she took was to go to church." The father, however, was an indifferent figure who seemed too concerned with his own difficulties to bother with the children. Hence, he seemed somewhat distant to the children and they did not become attached to him.

At the age of 6 James began to help the family in obtaining the sheer necessities of life, such as food, clothes, and rent. In fact, begging was a family pattern in which all members at different times participated. When begging with his brother, James' practice was to beg if the residents were at home, but if they were out, he and his brothers would break into the house and steal.

Delinquency was both a family pattern and a neighborhood pattern. The neighborhood boys stole from local fruit stands and from the counters of large department stores. By the age of 8, when James was arrested for burglary, his two older brothers had already been committed to penal institutions. By the age of 9 he had been persuaded by his brother and a friend to help them break into a barbershop.

Conforming to this deviant pattern, he became a truant as well as a thief. When the school reported his chronic truancy to his parents, he lied about his absences. Slightly scared when his mother threatened to spank him, he "wanted to go back to school and behave, but the older fellows always taunted me saying I was a sissy. . . . Then I would go with them to do 'jobs.' " His begging and depredations were mainly from rich people and seldom from poor people. In fact, he seemed to identify with the poor and helpless and considered almsgiving a token of good luck.

By the age of 10, after being arrested for burglary, he was sentenced to St. Charles for three years, at his own request, in order to be with his brother, Michael. In the three years he became much tougher and began to hate the authority he met. After his release he continued burglarizing and stealing cars. But again he was caught and sentenced to St. Charles. While there, his father died, and James was permitted to attend the funeral; but, seemingly, he felt little attachment for his father.

Paroled to a farmer, James escaped and returned to his former associates and to stealing. Caught again, he was returned to St. Charles. Thereafter, he tried to escape at every opportunity. Finally, he was made an officer of a cottage and conformed to the routine.

At this time he had his first sex experience, but he abstained from "gangshags" in which a group of boys would successively have sex relations with a single girl, though it was not uncommon in the neighborhood. After being in and out of St. Charles a few times, he was finally released. Unable to become interested in or to hold a job for long, he worked intermittently. When unemployed, he loafed around the parks, and when the idleness irked him he and some neighborhood companions began stealing cars which they sold to a "fence." A confirmed automobile thief, he finally was caught and sentenced to the Illinois State Reformatory, where he was at the time he wrote his autobiography.

Throughout his life, from childhood to late adolescence, he was embittered and hostile to adult authority figures. ". . . the maltreatments in city and state institutions where I spent most of my childhood, induced me to avenge myself against the city and state officials."

On the other hand, his need for association with other boys and adolescents, and the influence and censure which they exerted, had a sustained effect upon his criminal career. Actually, his intimate friends did not regard him as a successful thief.

"To put it all in one statement, I didn't want to steal or take any chances in stealing but I did it anyway. Down in my heart I hated to go out and steal with other fellows, but I went with them to avoid 'ridicule.' " [60]

Comparison of the Four Types

The representative four acting-out types, which we have described, were all delinquents and were also diagnosed as psychopathic personalities.[61] Yet, upon closer inspection, we noted that despite certain similarities there were distinct personality differ-

[60] Clifford R. Shaw et al., Brothers in Crime, p. 250 (Chicago: University of Chicago Press, 1938). The psychiatrist who examined Martin concluded as follows: "This case raises serious questions with regard to the validity of the psychiatric classification of prison inmates and of the still somewhat prevalent belief that only an intrinsically abnormal individual can exhibit criminal behavior. The writer's recent examination of James did not reveal any evidence of psychopathic personality or mental abnormality." Ibid., p. 323.

[61] See Paul William Preu, "The Concept of Psychopathic Personality," Personality and the Behavior Disorders, edited by J. McV. Hunt, p. 928 (New York: The Ronald Press Company, 1944).

ences among them. These differences provided the bases for a more consistent classification, which included (1) the "true" psychopath, (2) the acting-out neurotic, (3) the self-centered indulged person, and (4) the cultural deviant.

Basic Differences. The "true" psychopath tends to be unable to identify with others, has minimal feelings of guilt or anxiety about his misadventures, lives in and for the present, has shallow emotional feelings toward other persons, and is very self-centered because of his indifference to others and because he concentrates upon satisfying his immediate wants. Yet the "true" psychopath does understand the difference between right and wrong, can adjust to others on an impersonal or casual level, and does respond to adverse reprimands for the moment. The basic causes of psychopathy may be either damage to the brain, especially to the frontal lobes, or emotional deprivation in early life, which comes about either from very negligent and/or shifting parent figures. The psychopath who is a victim of emotionally deprived parental relationships tends to be restless and uninhibited even as a child. Hence, this early fixation may make the "true" psychopath impervious to personality change.

The acting-out neurotic does experience feelings of guilt, does have intense feelings of anxiety about his depredations, is ambivalent about his attitudes toward other persons, and may have intense attitudes of hostility toward others. Though self-centered, he is self-preoccupied and fundamentally tends to have a low conception of himself. The acting-out neurotic may have a capacity for identifying with others, but this capacity is usually obscured by his hostility and self-reproach. The acting-out neurotic tends to emerge from a family constellation in which he has a very permissive mother and an aloof and/or hostile father. Under certain conditions of expert therapy, the acting-out neurotic may be amenable to personal change.

The self-centered immature type is primarily a product of excessive permissiveness and of lack of restraint by the parents. The overindulgent fulfillment of his demands and the parental attempts to create a social center around him, result in a spoiled, demanding, irresponsible person who shirks his obligations and who becomes and remains very immature. Since he does not experience intense proscriptions from his parents, who deliberately or unwittingly sanction his behavior, he tends also to develop a weak conscience. The extent of this type's immaturity would affect his capacity to change. When the immaturity is not too deeply rooted, personal change can come about. In other instances personal change is more difficult.

The cultural deviant tends to be a normal and accepted person within his immediate milieu. This cultural deviant may be a stable and even mature personality whose norms of behavior differ from those of conventional people. On the one hand, his behavior does not indicate psychopathic immaturity because he can cultivate intimate relations with others and does feel guilty about matters which are considered reprehensible by his immediate group. Like the other acting-out types, he tends to express his hostilities overtly. On the other hand, he is not overcome by undue anxiety and by feelings of guilt. This is manifested in his relationships with the mother and with the father. When the cultural deviant, as in the case of James Martin, feels a definite attachment to the mother and not an undue hostility to the father, the parent-child relations may not create the neurotic constellation that we see in the acting-out neurotic. Hence, under given conditions, the cultural deviant is amenable to personal change.

Similarities and Differences in Delinquent Behavior. Though all the types we described were delinquents, they acquired their delinquent attitudes and activities in different ways. Walter Manson, the "true" psychopath, stole as an impulsive means of getting what he wanted, even during childhood. Later, however, Manson consorted with different delinquents and criminals and was introduced into a criminal subculture. James Martin, on the other extreme, resorted to crime by conforming to accepted cultural practices in the family and the neighborhood. It was taught to him by his brothers, and by his companions, from a very early age. Robert seemingly resorted to delinquency as a means of being accepted socially by his peers. The acting-out neurotic got the social approval in the delinquent group which compensated for the intense ridicule and disapproval which he received from his father. Robert resorted to his truancies and crimes as a means of least resistance and from the influence of other delinquents in order to avert more difficult and responsible behavior in school.

Other similarities in their activities show a general hostility to persons or to "society," an inability to orient themselves around conventional activities, to conform to routine, to work out a life plan that would receive conventional approval. All four types were continually in trouble and continually placing society on the defensive, with respect to their behavior.

Psychopathy and Drug Addiction. It is often claimed by psychiatrists that drug addicts and alcoholic addicts are psychopathic. Some investigators have claimed that only psychopaths become addicts.[62] Yet the causes of addiction and the behavior of the addicted are different.

While it is true that some psychopaths become drug addicts, it is also true that ordered persons also become drug addicts. The cause of the addiction does not reside in the personality type. It resides in linking the distressing withdrawal symptoms to the opiates, and thereby creating an ineradicable cause-effect sequence from which the addicts can seldom liberate themselves permanently. Hence, persons who take to drugs for medical reasons can as readily become addicted as those who operate on the limbo of society and who can meet, associate, and be induced to imbibe the drug.

Whether psychopaths more readily seek out or succumb to drug addiction is not known. What is known is that the psychopathy per se is not the cause of the addiction. Rather, it seems that in the search for pleasure, it is possible that they may come to use drugs. The "true" psychopath, Walter Manson, interestingly enough, was a drug addict. The other acting-out types we described were not addicts. In large part, it seems that the associates whom the psychopaths select may contribute to their becoming addicted. In fact, as Lindesmith points out, no controlled studies have been made to show that a higher proportion of psychopaths are among drug addicts than nonaddicts; that the term "psychopathy" is loosely defined, as it very obviously is by these investigators; that none of the studies which link addiction to psychopathy was made before the addiction occurred; and that criminality is sometimes used as evidence that the subject is a psychopath, although, as we have shown, criminality is not necessarily an outgrowth of psychopathy.

Yet, after the addiction has taken root, then the particular person so reorients his behavior that securing the drug becomes the central

[62] See Alfred R. Lindesmith, *Opiate Addiction*, pp. 141–145 (Bloomington, Ind.: Principia Press, Inc., 1947).

aspiration of his life. In this condition the addict may behave as if he were a psychopath; for no long-range goals, no sustained relationships, no feelings of self-condemnation may be able to deter him from further addiction. His strategies of life may change, his sense of values shift, and his modes of relationships be revised. But this change results from the very strong craving for the opiate. The external behavior as well as the attitudinal changes do not, however, mean that drug addicts are necessarily psychopathic before they became addicted, although they may behave like psychopaths after the addiction has taken hold.

Antisocial Personalities and Society. Conventional society is usually hostile to the antisocial person. Such a person is considered a menace, and conventional society responds to him in a manner which frequently compels him to remain· hostile. The usual conventional attitude is exemplified in the notion that the antisocial person, commonly called "the psychopath," cannot change, is not amenable to treatment, and hence should be either punished or segregated. In a characteristic case which appeared in the newspaper, an individual who may very well have been a "true" psychopath was convicted for slaying a 16-year-old girl. He had been arrested previously for robbery. After a prolonged examination at that time, the prognosis of the case was that he was not treatable because the diagnosis showed that he was a "psychopathic person," immature and with "anti-social trends." [63] His history showed difficulties from early childhood. From the time he started school, he was a truant, was arrested many times, and was usually in trouble. Despite his record, he was not considered "treatable" by the court and no help was given. In this instance a psychopathic disorder was recognized but the clinicians as well as the court were relatively helpless because society does not provide institutions for this specific type of disorder.

Since the judicial institutions gauge antisociality in terms of the character of the offense rather than in terms of the personality and since the past offenses of this individual happened to be light, he went free. Obviously a more concerted approach for handling this type of person is necessary. As yet there are few if any facilities or institutions for dealing with this type. Research, apart from that of diagnostic differences, has also been scattered.

[63] *Chicago Daily News,* June 9, 1950, p. 1.

The more important fact is, however, that other acting-out personalities who may be amenable to therapy are confused with the psychopath and, as such, are ignored. Bromberg reports that, while in the Navy, he attempted to treat a patient diagnosed as "psychopathic personality" but who was very likely an acting-out neurotic. Bromberg met open resistance from the other naval officers who felt that there was "no use" trying to modify psychopathic behavior. He paraphrased their attitudes as follows: "You cannot cure criminals. Don't try it. They require punishment." [64] Despite their opposition, he persisted in treating this person and with some success. But treatment stopped when Bromberg left the Navy.

It is only recently that definite, concerted efforts have been made to treat acting-out behavior, and as these attempts continue, clinicians are becoming more encouraged to proceed further in their treatment of these acting-out personalities. But these treatment techniques are confined largely to children with behavior problems and to adults who can afford private treatment. As yet, little work of this kind is done in institutions where it is most needed.

Summary

The category of disorders known as "psychopathy" is fraught with confusion and inconsistency. The confusion is so great that the term "psychopathy" denotes a series of loosely related disorders and has been relegated to a "wastebasket" category. This confusion has been the result of applying symptomatic criteria and social evaluations as well as personality dynamics in analyzing and diagnosing acting-out personalities. The psychopath is often diagnosed on the basis of such prepsychotic traits as schizoid and cycloid, or of such reactions as eccentric or explosive, or by such subcultural labels as prostitute or criminal. Consequently, persons who become deviant because of the influence of a subculture, persons who manifest definite handicaps in their role-taking facilities and who feel no guilt, and persons who are overburdened with guilt and self-reproach are lumped together. This inconsistency becomes further complicated when the term "psychopath" is used as a derivative of psychopathological behavior and as a synonym for markedly abnormal

---

[64] W. Bromberg, "Dynamic Aspects of Psychopathic Personality," *Psychoanalytic Quarterly*, 1948, 17, pp. 58–70.

behavior.[65] Sometimes, "psychopathy" is applied to marginal cases which do not fit the standard psychotic and neurotic categories. In view of this confusion and in order to arrive at a sharper and clearer concept of "true" psychopathy, the concept had to be differentiated from other acting-out disorders. By analyzing the personality dynamics and by tracing the sources of arrested development of these acting-out personality types, we found that typological differences emerge.

Selected Readings

Aichhorn, August, *Wayward Youth* (New York: The Viking Press, Inc., 1935).

Alexander, Franz, and Hugo Staub, *The Criminal, The Judge and the Public* (New York: The Macmillan Company, 1931).

Bromberg, Walter, *Crime and the Mind* (Philadelphia: J. B. Lippincott Company, 1948).

Cleckley, Harvey, *The Mask of Sanity* (St. Louis: The C. V. Mosby Company, Medical Publishers, 1950).

Freud, Anna, and Dorothy Burlingham, *Infants without Families* (New York: International Universities Press, Inc., 1944).

Goldfarb, William, "Effects of Early Institutional Care on Adolescent Personality," *Journal of Experimental Education,* 1943, 12, pp. 106–129.

———, "Psychological Privation in Infancy and Subsequent Adjustment," *American Journal of Orthopsychiatry,* April, 1945, 15:2, pp. 254–257.

Gough, Harrison G., "A Sociological Theory of Psychopathy," *American Journal of Sociology,* March, 1948, 43, pp. 359–360.

Greenacre, Phyllis, "Conscience in the Psychopath," *American Journal of Orthopsychiatry,* July, 1945, 15:3, pp. 495–498.

Healy, William, and Augusta F. Bronner, *New Light On Delinquency and Its Treatment* (New Haven: Yale University Press, 1936).

Heaver, W. Lynwood, "A Study of 40 Male Psychopathic Personalities Before, During and After Hospitalization," *The American Journal of Psychiatry,* November, 1943, 100, p. 343.

Henderson, Donald K., *Psychopathic States* (New York: W. W. Norton & Company, 1939).

Johnson, Adelaide M., "Sanctions for Superego Lacunae of Adolescents," *Searchlights on Delinquency,* edited by K. L. Eisler (New York: International Universities Press, Inc., 1949).

Karpman, Ben, "The Principles and Aims of Criminal Psychopathology," *Journal of Criminal Psychopathology,* January, 1940, 1:3, pp. 200–207.

---

[65] See Richard T. LaPiere and Paul R. Farnsworth, *Social Psychology,* p. 360 (New York: McGraw-Hill Book Company, Inc., 1949).

Karpman, Ben, "The Case of Walter Manson," *Case Studies in the Psychopathology of Crime,* Vol. II (Baltimore: Medical Science Press, 1944).

————, "Passive Parasitic Psychopath," *Psychoanalytic Review,* April, 1947, 34:2, pp. 210–215.

Partridge, George E., "Current Conceptions of Psychopathic Personality," *The American Journal of Psychiatry,* 1930, X, pp. 53–59.

Shaw, Clifford R., Henry McKay, and James MacDonald, *Brothers in Crime* (Chicago: University of Chicago Press, 1938).

Spitz, Rene A., "Hospitalism: An Inquiry into the Genesis of Psychiatric Conditions in Early Childhood," *The Psychoanalytic Study of the Child,* pp. 53–74 (New York: International Universities Press, Inc., 1945).

————, "The Role of Ecological Factors in Emotional Development in Infancy," *Child Development,* 1949, 20.

Sutherland, Edwin H., *Principles of Criminology,* pp. 103–117 (Philadelphia: J. B. Lippincott Company, 1947).

PART III

Treatment

CHAPTER THIRTEEN

Psychotherapy as a Function of Social Relationships

In dealing with the dynamics and development of various types of personal disorders in the past section, we described how certain social situations and social relationships contributed to and often caused disordered behavior. We turn now to the treatment of the milder disorders, the neuroses, by social relationships.

Disturbed and neurotic persons who have persistent, unresolved conflicts are frequently faced with the prospect of seeking psychotherapy. Some feel no stigma in such a procedure and do so readily; others are more cautious and request the advice of friends or relatives; and a third group are persuaded or cajoled into accepting treatment. Whatever motive the person has in seeking a psychotherapist, he inevitably enters into a somewhat singular interpersonal relationship, and his attitude toward seeking therapy affects that relationship.

Frequently, patients expect their relationships with the therapist to be similar to that of a physically ill person with a doctor. After divulging their difficulties, they anticipate that the therapist or counselor will offer advice, in much the same way that a doctor prescribes medicine. Many therapists do give advice, but frequently the patient-therapist relationships are far more complicated. To describe what happens in this treatment process, we will discuss: (1) the common attributes of the therapeutic relationship, (2) the modes of therapeutic communication and (3) the disparate types of relationships as practiced by some contemporary schools of psychotherapy.

Psychotherapy Defined. Psychotherapy may be defined broadly as a therapist-patient relationship, which is designed specifically for the patient's improvement or recovery.[1] Whatever the therapeutic method, all modes of psychotherapy—except, perhaps play therapy—have the common features of role taking and verbalization. Whether the relational aspect is implicit or explicit in the rationale of the therapist, whether it is exhortatory or nondirective in form, whether it deals with present conscious experiences or past subconscious fantasies, the therapist, by his formally dominant role, can structure the relationship in accordance with his specific theories. He even can give up his dominant position. Of course, these roles vary with the mode of psychotherapy, with the condition of the patients, and with the length and intensity of the interaction. Some types of neurotics, for example, assign certain roles to the therapist, as occurs in transference,[2] but a transference relationship would not occur, perhaps, in certain types of brief therapy which can last for one or two sessions. Also, some types of counseling, such as nondirectivism, try to avoid this transference. Some types of psychotherapy, psychoanalysis, for instance, are very intensive and prolonged; other types may be less intensive and brief. Children have to be treated differently from adults. Persons with self-condemnatory attitudes have to be handled differently from those who can accept distressing truths.

To clarify this treatment process as a distinct type of interpersonal reciprocity, it is necessary to find out what its common features are.

---

[1] Wm. U. Snyder, who omits "educational procedures" in his definition of psychotherapeutic counseling, states that it is: "a face-to-face relationship in which a psychologically trained individual is consciously attempting by verbal means to assist another person or persons to modify emotional attitudes that are socially maladjusted and in which the subject is relatively aware of the personality reorganization through which he is going." "The Present Status of Psychotherapeutic Counseling," *Psychological Bulletin*, July, 1947, XLIV:4, p. 298. Allen regards this therapeutic process as "a unique growth experience created by one person seeking and needing help from another who accepts the responsibility of offering it." Frederick H. Allen, *Psychotherapy with Children*, p. 45 (New York: W. W. Norton & Company, 1942).

[2] See section on Psychoanalysis and Transference Relationships, p. 315.

Common Attributes of the Therapeutic Relationship

In every formally structured relationship, a person has an official role which is part of his profession, and an informal role which results from his behavior in specific interaction with others.[3] Every therapeutic session has some kind of formal structure. Within this formal structure a very important feature is the "stranger" role of the therapist, who combines the socially intimate with the socially distant. This makes the therapeutic relationship intimate in form but utilitarian in objective. It involves the intimate and very personal experiences of the patient, but a definite social distance by the therapist. For both therapist and patient have the specific expedient of using these very personal experiences for helping the patient to improve rather than to create a friendship. The patient is not praised or blamed by the conventional criteria of right and wrong but is judged in terms of the motives which prompted his behavior. The therapist is interested in the patient as a person with a problem and accepts him on that level. The patient, on the other hand, must want to trust and confide in the therapist. When the patient starts to improve or recover, he begins to reorganize his present personality conflicts and to resocialize his present relationships.

The Therapist and the "Stranger Role." Simmel, the German sociologist, defined "the stranger" as one who combines the personal with the impersonal, the socially intimate with the socially distant.[4] This description aptly characterizes the therapist's role. He is a professional confidant who is admitted, or who gains admittance into, the private, intimate experiences and feelings of the patient for utilitarian ends—the improvement of the patient and earning a living. In retaining a measure of objectivity, he does not distort his therapeutic perspective by overidentifying with the patient. These treatment interviews, by being set within specific time limits, become further formalized. Furthermore, the therapist may find it inadvisable to exchange confidences with the patient; the reasons for this vary—the patient may lose confidence in the thera-

[3] See Leonard S. Cottrell, Jr., "Roles and Marital Adjustment," *Publications of the American Sociological Society*, 1933, XXVII, pp. 107–115.

[4] George Simmel, "The Sociological Significance of the 'Stranger'" in Robert E. Park and Ernest W. Burgess, *An Introduction to the Sciences of Sociology*, pp. 372–377 (Chicago: University of Chicago Press, 1924).

pist, the therapist's problem may become more interesting to the patient than his own, or, as in psychoanalysis, the eventual transference may be loosened and even disrupted.

For some forms of therapy it means the exclusion of close friends and relatives as patients. Freud long ago cautioned against taking patients who were relatives or who were too socially intimate with the therapist. When the therapist did so, he admonished that it was at the cost of friendship, regardless of the outcome.[5] Rogers advocated a neutral, professional role for the counselor, and cautioned against participating in the outside social life of the client.[6] Allen maintained that the therapist should adhere to his own integrity and identity.[7] Though Horney and her associates advocated a more intimate treatment relationship with the patient, they definitely distinguished it from a friendship.[8] However close the relationship, the therapist usually tries to avoid self-involvement, overidentification, or the mutuality and spontaneity of a friendship, in order to proceed as a therapist, though this may have exceptions in supportive therapy. In addition, the therapist's interpretations of the patient's experiences prevent a completely spontaneous interchange, for his interpretations often impel the patient to face and to reflect upon experiences which are painful and fraught with anxiety. This cannot be the case in friendship in which mutual interests are ends in themselves. Should acquaintanceship develop which resembles the treatment relationship, it would be an informal, unsystematic proto-treatment affair which would miss many features of genuinely spontaneous friendship. Jung maintains that the doctor-patient relationship remains personal within an impersonal professional framework, but that both patient and therapist experience certain personality changes in the relational process.[9] As such, the therapeutic relationship is unique for the patient. It is very personal and yet utilitarian.

[5] Sigmund Freud, *Collected Works*, translated by Joan Riviere, Vol. II, p. 345, (London: Hogarth Press, 1924).

[6] Carl R. Rogers and John L. Wallen, *Counseling with Returned Servicemen* (New York: McGraw-Hill Book Company, Inc., 1946).

[7] Frederick Allen, *Psychotherapy with Children*, p. 60 (New York: W. W. Norton & Company, 1942).

[8] Karen Horney (editor), *Are You Considering Psychoanalysis?* (New York: W. W. Norton & Company, 1946).

[9] Carl Jung, *Modern Man in Search of a Soul*, pp. 56–58 (New York: Harcourt, Brace and Company, Inc., 1934).

The Therapeutic Relationship Is Utilitarian. However intimate the relationships between patient and therapist, the ends are directed toward the improvement and recovery of the patient. This is the objective toward which both therapist and patient strive. However warm and genuinely interested the therapist is in the patient, he knows that these attitudes are expedients to the goal of improvement. Although he accepts the patient as a person in difficulty, the therapist gives of himself to the patient only insofar as it will help, not please, him. Since one chief function of the therapist usually is to retain his professional identity and personal integrity regardless of the roles assigned to him by the patient, his reciprocity is limited.

First, he usually limits the relationships to the clinic or office. In fact, he would be unwise, as experience has demonstrated, to mingle socially with the patient in extraclinical relationships. The therapist usually does not become involved in the patient's problems outside the office, unless these outside problems are defeating the therapeutic process.

Second, he designs the relationship so that it will have a terminating point, although the terminating point may be indefinite. In other words, the success of the relationship depends upon ending it by the patient's improvement. Subsequent associations may be fostered, but these would not be on a patient-therapist level, unless the patient seeks further therapy.

Third, the therapist cannot recite his troubles and difficulties to the patient. Should the therapist have personal problems, he himself can submit or resubmit to therapy, and assume a patient's role. The psychoanalysts and their derivative schools emphasize this fact, and it is not uncommon for a psychoanalyst to go back into therapy as a patient. Indeed, the patient does not usually anticipate or even want such reciprocity. For he is the "sick" one, the one in difficulty, and the one dependent upon the therapist for help. One patient stated:

I was going to a therapist who had some difficulty with her husband. We became quite close and I thought she was excellent. One day, she drove to my house and was rather drunk and began to talk about her domestic difficulties. I consoled her, but I could not get myself to go back to her and sought out another therapist.

Yet, as Jung pointed out, imponderable factors arise in any treatment relationship, and the more stable and stronger personality will have the greater influence. Jung claimed to have seen many instances in which the patient proved stronger than the doctor, despite the doctor's intention and despite the doctor's rationalizing theory. He arrived at these conclusions of interpersonal influence during his very extensive practice of more than twenty-five years. He claimed further that for this reason, among others, Freud was justified in demanding that the analyst himself resort to analysis before becoming a practitioner.[10] Hence, this necessity for a one-sided but structured intimacy is another reason for the rather unique character of the therapeutic relationship.

The Therapeutic Relationship Is "Amoral" and Accepting. To ensure the uninhibited expression of the patient's personal feelings, the therapeutic relationship is, within limits, "amoral," noncondemnatory, and accepting. The therapist cannot assign conventional value judgments to patients' remarks; he must allow him, even "reward" him, to verbalize his feelings freely by accepting them as mediums to the patients' improvement. This degree of freedom may vary somewhat with the type of therapy and with the limits specified by the therapist.[11] In certain types of supportive and suggestive therapy, after the initial cathartic experiences of the patient, the therapist becomes the one who talks and advises the patient. But in the "uncovering" forms of therapy, an accepting attitude frequently is indispensable to the continuation of the interview. Whether the therapist assumes an impersonal, objective role or whether he assumes a more personalized role, the necessary and common factor in therapeutic interaction is to accept the patient as he is—as a person with a problem. The initial expression of this acceptance definitely impresses the patient and may influence his present and subsequent relationships with the therapist. One patient described his initial psychotherapeutic relationship as follows:

[10] Carl Jung, *Modern Man in Search of a Soul,* p. 58.

[11] Rank, for example, claimed that Freud attributed a "moral judgment" to the resistance of the patient. He maintained that this Freudian judgment was in a sense interfering with the therapeutic process, because the dynamics of the patient's behavior rather than the content was important and revealing. See Otto Rank, *Will Therapy and Truth and Reality* (New York: Alfred A. Knopf, Inc., 1936).

Before going to see a psychiatrist, I sought advice, unfortunately from one of my close friends. She told me just what to expect, and the methods that would be used to alleviate my state. As a result, I went with certain expectations as to the manner in which the consultation would be conducted. Everything went amiss from the beginning I went into his office. The psychiatrist arose, introduced himself, and in a cold, matter-of-fact approach, asked me what I had on my mind. I had intended to relate all of the intimate details leading to my visit. I wanted to describe the difficulties I experienced in adjusting, about my divorce, school, and anything else that I thought bothered me. But his abrupt, cold manner confused and antagonized me. So for an hour he tried to prod pertinent details out of me, but I couldn't divulge anything that was really personal. Finally he acknowledged the hopelessness of the interview. I waited a while after that and looked for somebody else.

Does the Patient Trust and Confide in the Therapist? Fundamental to any therapeutic procedure is the patient's desire to be helped and his desire to confide in the particular therapist. When this confidence is absent or minimized, it seems difficult, sometimes improbable, that the therapy can proceed satisfactorily. For this reason, much ·difficulty is encountered in treating psychopathic or certain psychotic types who are either unco-operative or who cannot be reached emotionally. For example, the Freudians may maintain preanalytic sessions so that some measure of rapport can be established when the patient is doubtful about the benefits of psychoanalysis. At worst, the Freudians ask for an attitude of "benevolent skepticism." The initial trust of the patient for the therapist, according to the Freudians, is, however, no criterion of his deeper resistances and of facilitating the transference process.

Freud has maintained that the initial expectations of the patient are neither crucial to the success of the therapy nor indicative of his eventual trust of the therapist. Although one type of patient may believe deeply in the treatment potential of psychoanalysis, his treatment may not be easier than that of another patient who is skeptical, for the preliminary beliefs or disbeliefs concerning the validity of psychoanalysis are quite mild compared to the defenses which constitute his neurotic condition. The initial co-operation of the patient may be easily disrupted by his resistances when his neurotic defenses are threatened. The initial distrust of the other type of patient is a symptom like his other symptoms, for, according to Freud, he is often not in a position to form a reliable judgment about the treatment process.[12] The patient's estimate of psycho-analysis may not be pertinent, but his attitudes to the particular therapist will obviously affect the therapy. If he distrusts and dislikes the therapist, he will resist confiding in him, or he may bring out the adverse attitudes which he has had to people whom he had disliked in the past.

Coleman has pointed out that the patient's trust or distrust of the therapist can be observed by the extent to which the patient begins to discuss his anxiety-inducing experiences.[13] But when the patient continues to question the treatment process, persists in asking for advice and suggestions, clings to the organic explanation of his symptoms, he is afraid to surrender himself to the therapist. The patient may view the therapeutic relationship as a possible trap and may need time to reassure himself before he can reveal his difficulties safely. In these instances the therapist must identify the patient's fears and distrust, and then help the patient to overcome them.

Of course, treatment which involves free association is far deeper than treatment in which the patient asks for counsel. The degree of surrender to the therapist differs because, when the patient freely associates, he lets himself go to a much greater extent than in the more rational type of therapy. Yet, even for similar types of therapy, the personality of the therapist must be considered. When a patient fiercely dislikes a particular therapist, the time involved in clearing up this hatred could be avoided if he begins treatment with a therapist whom he likes and trusts.

The Patient Is Involved in a "Reorganizing Relationship." In most types of therapy and counseling, with the exceptions of "symptom-removal" therapy, the patient is involved in a relationship of learning, of personal growth and re-education in which action is released and redirected toward constructive ends. This hypothesis of personal growth or personal reorganization depends upon removing the patient's neurotic symptoms by freeing him from his anxiety. The neurotic's behavior is usually self-defeating and self-perpetuating. The essence of therapy, that is of uncovering therapy, is to enable the patient to reorganize his behavior so that

---

[12] Sigmund Freud, *Collected Papers*, Vol. II, p. 245.
[13] Jules V. Coleman, "Patient-Physician Relationship in Psychotherapy," *The American Journal of Psychiatry*, April, 1948, 104:10, p. 638.

his self-defeating neurotic behavior is reorganized into more mature and constructive patterns.[14] Schoben states:[15]

> The goal of psychotherapy regardless of the therapist's theoretical leanings is to eliminate the anxiety and thereby to do away with the symptomatic persistent, nonintegrative behavior. To accomplish this goal, all therapists use the device of conversing with the patient about his anxiety and the situations calling it forth both currently and historically, and forming a unique therapeutic relationship . . . since psychotherapy seems to be a process whereby a patient learns to modify his emotional reactions and his overt behavior, it is hypothesized that therapy may be conceptualized from the point of view of general psychology as a problem in learning theory.

This emphasis upon personal reorganization and growth is more explicit in some forms of therapy than in others. For example, the Neo-Freudian group, and the adherents of Rank, explicitly accentuate this principle. The Freudians also pursue this principle but may interpret it differently. Nonetheless, they consider an essential outcome of the therapeutic relationship to be one in which the patient matures.[16] The Freudian concept of psychosexual development, of lifting subconscious conflicts to a conscious level, and of resolving personal conflict involves a process of personal development, which is expressed particularly in the patient's understanding of the transference.[17] Jung avers that his psychotherapeutic aim is to have the patient begin in "a state of fluidity, change and growth" in which he feels no longer fixed and "hopelessly petrified." [18] Adler indicates that in resolving the conflicts between inferiority and masculine protest, on the one hand, and social reality, on the other hand, the personality differentiates and matures.[19] Alexander and French emphasize that every personality change facilitates new adaptations,

---

[14] Edward J. Schoben, Jr., "Psychotherapy as a Problem in Learning Theory," *Psychological Bulletin*, September, 1949, 46:5, pp. 366–392.

[15] *Ibid.*, pp. 375, 376. Quoted by permission of the American Psychological Association.

[16] Karen Horney (editor), *Are You Considering Psychoanalysis?* (New York: W. W. Norton & Company, 1946).

[17] Sigmund Freud, *A General Introduction to Psychoanalysis*, p. 377. Garden City, N.Y.: Garden City Publishing Co., Inc., 1943.

[18] Carl Jung, *Modern Man in Search of a Soul*, p. 58 (New York: Harcourt, Brace and Company, Inc., 1934).

[19] See J. F. Brown, *Psychodynamics of Abnormal Behavior*, pp. 254, 255 (New York: McGraw-Hill Book Company, Inc., 1940).

and that psychotherapy involves corrective emotional experiences.[20] Sullivan stresses that the individual who learns to deal with his anxiety tends to expand the range of self activity, and this widening of the self is indicative of a significant growth process, particularly in the sphere of social relationships.[21]

The Patient Is Involved in a "Resocializing" Relationship. Many patients seek some form of psychotherapy because they feel something amiss in their social relationships. Their wish for personal change may be one of the chief reasons for visiting the therapist. They hope that the therapy will improve their relationships with others, whether family members, friends, or business associates. How is this resocialization achieved in therapeutic interaction? Of course, approaches differ, but certain common features nonetheless exist.

In the first or cathartic phase of therapy, the patient is encouraged to verbalize his formerly inhibited feelings and ideas. By sharing his individualized feelings and ideas with the therapist and by the therapist's permissive reaction to these expressed attitudes, the patient may begin to see himself and his experiences from a different vantage point. For example, the patient may be very self-condemnatory, and, because of the therapist's accepting attitude, the patient may begin to feel less guilty. This cathartic process may reduce the sharpness of his emotionally toned feelings, and, in daily living, it may obviate his need for fragmentary confessions to competing persons from whom he expects reassurance but who frequently may judge him adversely. As such, the confessional or catharsis expressions in a therapeutic relationship gives the patient some form of temporary relief. But catharsis may or may not be helpful in other relationships.

The second and more important phase arises when the patient has achieved insight into his own behavior and into the behavior of those about him. He gets a new perspective toward himself and toward others, for in the course of a therapeutic relationship, when denied his wishes or given unpleasant truths, the patient introduces into his responses to the therapist the hostilities and the humilia-

[20] Franz Alexander and Thomas M. French, *Psychoanalytic Therapy*, p. 104. New York: The Ronald Press Co., 1946.

[21] Harry Stack Sullivan, *Conceptions of Modern Psychiatry*, p. 92 (Washington, D.C.: William Alanson White Psychiatric Foundation, 1947).

tions that he has experienced with others, and reacts accordingly to him. These interacting responses become the raw materials for the patient's insight, which is achieved by the therapist's interpretations or by his helping the patient to clarify and to understand his own feelings.

This insight opens a trend to personal maturity, as a result of which the patient can eliminate or minimize immature reactions and can start on a path of resocializing his relationships on a more mature level. One criterion of improvement involves the person's ability to relate with persons in terms of their present and actual conduct. It means that he has acquired a realistic role-taking ability. It means that he is less prone to project his past hostilities, suspicions, and dependencies onto other persons, or feel that they, too, are hostile or suspicious. Instead, he can respond to them in terms of their actual behavior. In this sense, his behavior becomes rational because the person can more effectively shift and share the perspectives of other persons without projecting his own feelings and images onto them. But rationality, even for the mature person, has limits. Just as man has certain convictions and basic assumptions which he cannot explain away but by which he must live, so in his intimate and primary relationships, he may retain certain idealized images of his child, of his wife, or of his friend which are irrational insofar as the individual cannot rationally explain why he has these images and attachments. But he may do so on a more independent and mature level. Although therapy may revise the immature bases of these idealizations, it cannot eliminate the idealizations because it cannot make man completely rational, whether on an interpersonal or on an action level. Yet, within limits, this change can be achieved. In this connection, Sullivan has said:[22]

> One achieves mental health to the extent that one becomes aware of one's inter-personal relations; this is the general statement that is always expressed to patients. Every one of my patients with whom I have had more than a consultative relationship has received this reply to many different questions, asked throughout the greater part of the work. This is the essential element in replying to the questions, "What ails me?", "How can I get better?", "What good will the treatment accomplish?", "Why can't I overcome this or that habit?", "What shall I do about my hatefulness—my hostility—my ugly disposition—my

[22] Harry Stack Sullivan, *Conceptions of Modern Psychiatry*, pp. 102, 103 (Washington, D.C., The William Alanson White Psychiatric Foundation, 1947).

dependency—my domineering—my sensitivity—my suspiciousness—my uncertainty?" It is part of the framework that supports all explanations of what is going on, what might be going on, and what will presently be going on. It is one of the factual bases for interpreting unfortunate developments, unfavorable changes that are discouraging the patient. It is *the* necessary formula to which everything must be assimilable, if it is therapy.

. . . The processes of psychiatric cure include the maturation of personality; that is, the evolution of capacity for adult inter-personal relations.

Theory and Practice in Psychotherapy

But these norms of patient-therapist interaction are ideal. Not all therapists achieve these relationships with their patients. The capacity to deal with patients in this manner depends upon the knowledge and the personality of the therapist.

The therapist may overidentify with the patient. It is not rare to have a therapist like his patient; and it is not rare for a therapist to mingle socially with a particular patient. In a few instances, therapists marry their patients. The important fact in this treatment process is that the mode of interaction also depends upon the patient. Some patients, despite their neuroses, may be quite clever and demanding and strong in their social relationships. Obviously, they will affect the therapist. Some patients may deceive their therapists. The therapist is by no means omniscient.

To be sure, Freud and others cautioned about becoming involved with, or drawn in by, the patient. But Freud also advocated an aloof, unemotional, and impassive attitude for the therapist. Since the contemporary therapist is much less formal and aloof, the therapist is also more exposed to the wiles, whims, and tricks of the patient. There are all kinds of innuendoes and subtle means that particular patients may use to draw the therapist from his therapeutic role; and not all therapists have perfected the techniques to retain the therapeutic role. Moreover, not all therapists are so skilled that this can always be avoided. Hence, the therapy may deviate from its course and not always succeed.

The therapist may have ambivalent attitudes to his patients which he has not resolved. This may affect the course of the therapy. In some instances, as a result of the therapist's ambivalent attitudes, the therapy may reach an impasse, a stalemate, and the relationship may even deteriorate. In other words, there are instances when the therapist cannot completely control the situation, because the therapist himself has certain attitudes which he cannot completely control, and these attitudes enter and influence the therapeutic process.

As with all people, therapists have their failings and their merits. Their personalities inevitably affect their therapeutic relationships. Since we do not know as yet all the subtleties that ensue in the therapeutic process, the reasons for the failings of some therapists for certain cases await more definite research.

The therapist may be threatened emotionally by the patient. The patient may be in a position where he is more successful than the therapist, or where his strivings are akin to those of the therapist and he is outdoing the therapist. Clearly, the therapeutic relationship can be disturbed by some problems which the therapist has. This threat is a present, recurring, realistic situation, in which the therapist is a competitor in the outside world as well as the patient, and which he must resolve.

The therapist may dislike certain types of patients. He may or may not know why he dislikes them. It may be that the patient comes from another stratum of society which the therapist disapproves. It may be that the patient entertains certain beliefs which the therapist finds distasteful. The argument that the therapist is objective is really an exhortatory statement and implies merely that the therapist *should be* objective. Whether the therapist can be so objective with respect to his feelings is often questionable and requires more empirical study.

Values in Psychotherapy. Insofar as psychotherapy is an integral part of the social process, values inevitably arise.

First, the therapist has the implicit values of his own personal organization and subculture.[23] The psychoanalyst who has been in analysis himself has had many of these values reassessed in the process of reorganizing himself, and undoubtedly this process has reduced the emotional tone of his attitudes and the extent of his projections onto the patient. Yet it is doubtful whether he or any other therapist can detach himself completely from his own values. This is especially true with reference to his subculture, in which he is a participant like other participants. Yet, within definite limits,

[23] See Sol. W. Ginsberg, "Values and the Psychiatrist," *American Journal of Orthopsychiatry*, July, 1950, 20:3, pp. 466–478.

the psychoanalytic therapist is not concerned with the conventional value judgments in appraising the condition of his patient. Since other types of therapists have not been analyzed themselves, it is still not known to what extent they introduce their value judgments into the therapy. Since empirical knowledge in this area is so scant, a study of this type would cast light on a significant problem.

Another value which may be implicit or explicit in the therapy is the therapist's conception of an improved patient. Does he mean a person who has improved his interpersonal relationships? One who has come to terms with and can conform to the pressures of his environment? Or one who has worked out his individual integrity regardless of what the norms of his culture may be? For example, if an individual comes from a very competitive grouping of our society, should he improve his relationships with others in this competitive process? Should he learn to compete more effectively? Or should he disregard this competitive process and do what he really wants, apart from the values of other persons about him?

Closely related to this reference is the implicit criterion of when the therapy should end. This ending of the therapy is usually up to the judgment of the therapist, although for some types of counseling, such as nondirectivism, the patients may break off the therapy of their own accord. What degree of stability should the patient achieve? Should he reach a condition where he is able to make a social adjustment although his conflicts have not been resolved? Should he achieve a condition in which he can tolerate his conflicts? Should he achieve a condition in which most of his conflicts are resolved? For example, among middle-aged persons whose situational resources do not permit complete conflict resolution, it would probably be harmful to reopen certain conflicts. This decision implies a judgment of preference by the therapist.

Some patients regard psychotherapy as an "investment" which should "pay off" in their occupational and social life. For example, if a spinster succeeds in getting married or an ambitious man gets a desirable job or a promotion in his work, she and he may feel that treatment is no longer necessary. The therapist may or may not share this feeling depending upon his theory of personality. On the contrary, a patient may improve without a marked change in his social adjustment, and the therapist may have to face the complaints of the patient and of his relatives. These interpretations of personality improvement by the patient and the therapist enter into and affect the therapeutic relationship.

A third value concerns the intrinsic therapeutic relationships. All institutionalized relationships have a set of mores. These mores forbid behavior which disrupt or threaten the continuation of these relationships. For example, if the patient is continually defiant of the therapist, if he hits the therapist or destroys furniture, he prevents the therapy from continuing. When carried further, does it mean that the patient's resistance is in a sense immoral insofar as it may hinder the continuation of the therapy? This of course depends upon the modes of interaction permitted by the therapist.

Fourth, the particular form of therapy becomes a value or set of values. When a type of therapy is successful, the patient usually makes it one of his affirmative faiths. The writer has seen any number of patients who swear by the particular type of therapy by which they have been treated. Perhaps this belief in the effectiveness of the therapy is essential for the patient's improvement. Whether the mode of therapy is standard psychoanalysis, Adlerian therapy, or even a form of counseling, the particular patient usually becomes "loyal" to his school of therapy. This loyalty, in large part, arises from his role in the therapeutic process and his attachment to the therapist. Seemingly, this confidence is essential in helping the patient change himself. In fact, the patient incorporates the perspective of the therapist in getting well or in changing his behavior.

Fifth, the attitude toward personal stability or mental health becomes a value. Both the therapist and the patient have this objective in mind. By the very fact that the patient seeks out a therapist, he regards mental health as a significant value, and his preference may or may not be explicitly accentuated by the therapist. Generally, this value is important. The improved person usually feels more comfortable, because his conflicts are less intense; he can relate more effectively with other persons; and he can undertake more constructive pursuits with greater ease. In addition, many self-driving men who are easily threatened may in the long run become happier and generally healthier persons. In fact, this reorientation is very significant for persons approaching the age of retirement. On the other hand, when personal stability is overemphasized, it may become self-defeating.

For example, it may lead to a self-centered concern with one's feelings. By analogy, the individual who is concerned with having a beautiful body may avoid unduly heavy tasks or may avoid arduous pursuits which may retard his advancement. In the same way, the individual who becomes concerned with his "emotions" may not want to engage in taxing pursuits which will make him "worry" unduly. For example, a student who had deprived himself financially in order to save money to be therapized, broke off an engagement with his fiancée because she refused to be treated. He could not see himself marrying a girl who might be "neurotic" after he had gone to such trouble to become "healthy." This attitude is not characteristic of patients, but it reveals that the whole problem of personal stability as a value is implicit in the therapeutic process. As yet, we have little systematic knowledge of this area.

Sixth, the therapist's evaluation of the position of the patient in the social structure may influence the therapeutic process. Is the patient an important or unimportant person? Is he admirable or contemptible? Is he intelligent or unintelligent? Clearly, these views may possibly affect the therapy because of the cultural role of the therapist as well as the patient.

The therapist is usually a medical man or a psychologist who has a given role in his profession. Moreover, he acquires the values and attitudes of those in his groove, which means that he does not escape the middle-class competitive attitudes. He seeks and looks up to success and very likely has the characteristic attitudes about failure. Moreover, if he is in private practice, he reaches a type of patient or client who is substantially in the same social position and subculture that he is in. And he assumes many of the attitudes of those in his socioeconomic group.

In addition, psychotherapy has taken on many of the specialized characters of other professions. Therapists tend to become known for handling specific types of cases, whether children, adolescent boys, adolescent girls, middle-aged women, or old persons. Hence, the cultural scope of the psychotherapist becomes narrowed rather than broadened, however intensive his knowledge is in these spheres. This means further that, implicitly or explicitly, he is acquiring some of the collated meanings and values, the subculture, of these specific age groups, and sometimes of these age and sex groups. But insofar as the therapist may meet people from diverse ethnic groups, diverse socioeconomic strata, diverse age groups, and both sexes, his impartiality to the cultural scheme inevitably enters the therapeutic picture.

Cross-cultural Knowledge and the Therapist. The therapist who deals with diverse groups generally encounters diverse norms of behavior. Insofar as he is aware of the norms of his own culture, he will tend to impute these norms to the varied persons whom he encounters as patients. Although he may understand the dynamics of his patient's difficulties, there may be some phases of the cultural context which he may completely overlook because of his lack of knowledge concerning this segment of the culture.

In addition, the therapist may intrude his own values into the therapy, and this will also affect the patient. Hence, the more widely versed the therapist is in the varied subcultures with which he deals, the more emancipated he is from the sheer ethnocentrism of his social class and his ethnic group. Also, he will not view the dynamics from the bias of his own social grouping, and he will become more tolerant of the norms of other groups.

Disparate Features in Psychotherapeutic Relationships

The disparate types of relationships in the forms of psychotherapy emerge in part from the respective theories of human behavior. These categories of interaction will be applied to those forms of therapy which are considered "modern" and have become more or less accepted and used in clinics. First, we will begin with the essential Freudian contribution of transference, then we will cover also Neo-Freudian types and one of two derivative groups of Rank's therapeutic method, relationship therapy and nondirective counseling. In these types of therapy, only two persons are involved in the relationship. The multilateral relationships in group therapy will be discussed in the following chapter. These forms of therapy are among the chief groups in the legions of different therapy types. But even among these "therapies" every therapist forms a unique type of relationship with the patient, based upon the predilections of his personality and upon the patient's personality. In addition, some therapists have become somewhat eclectic in their techniques and in their theory, because they base the therapy upon the peculiar needs of the individual patient.

Psychoanalysis and Transference Relationships. Before Freud departed from cathartic hypnosis as a therapeutic method he noted

318 SOCIETY AND PERSONALITY DISORDERS

that hypnotic "cures" were usually of short duration and depended upon the attitudes of the patient to the therapist. When the therapist-patient relationships were favorable, the improvement of the patient was sustained; when these relationships were unfavorable, the improvement did not endure. In one case, when he had completely removed a severe condition by a short hypnotic treatment, it returned unchanged after the patient (a woman) had developed ill feeling against him without just cause. After a reconciliation he was able to affect its disappearance again and this time more thoroughly, but it reappeared when she again became hostile to him.[24] Freud also objected to the suggestive and tyrannic character of the hypnotic therapy. He observed: "I can remember even then [1889] a feeling of gloomy antagonisms against this tyranny of suggestion." [25]

During the first period when Freud practiced hypnosis, he found it necessary to inquire into the source and character of both the therapist's and patient's roles in suggestion. Since he wanted the patient to face consciously the conflicts which he had been unable to face and had to repress, Freud attempted a "waking suggestion" method as a therapeutic medium. He believed that the patient could recall his past conflicts if he tried hard enough. Freud learned, however, that suggestion alone was not enough to have the patient recollect past conflictful experiences.[26] In his third transition he resorted to free association in which the patient had the freedom, indeed was encouraged, to tell whatever came to his mind. In this therapeutic relationship the patient became more free and a more active conversationalist. It was during this free association method that Freud hit upon the phenomenon of transference in patient-therapist interaction. He found that it was essentially a reproduction of past irrational attachments and was repeated or re-enacted onto the therapist.[27] At first, Freud had difficulty understanding the

[24] Sigmund Freud, *A General Introduction to Psychoanalysis*, p. 391 (Garden City, N.Y.: Garden City Publishing Company, Inc., 1943).

[25] *The Basic Writings of Sigmund Freud*, translated and edited by A. A. Brill, p. 9 (New York: Random House, 1938).

[26] Franz Alexander and Thomas M. French, *Psychoanalytic Therapy*, pp. 3–16 (New York: The Ronald Press Co., 1946).

[27] Sigmund Freud, *A General Introduction to Psychoanalysis*, p. 385, published by the Liveright Publishing Corporation, New York City. Copyright: 1935, Edward L. Bernays, 1948, Susie Hach.

meaning of these relationships. He found that the patient, who should have thought only of solving his conflicts, instead became preoccupied with the therapist. He found that this phenomenon occurred in each new case, and existed even among elderly women in relation to elderly men when no temptations existed. Consequently, he could not attribute the attachment to a disturbing accident, but only to the disorder itself. He said:[28]

> The new fact which we are thus unwillingly compelled to recognize we call transference. By this we mean a transference of feeling on to the person of the physician because we do not believe that the situation in the treatment can account for the origin of such feelings.

Although hypnosis implied a kind of transference, this relationship was not analyzed by the therapist or understood by the patient. In psychoanalysis, however, the emphasis was in trying to understand the dynamics of the relationship between the patient and the therapist. The therapist's crucial role then centered in interpreting the dynamics of the patient's resistance and transference to him. And the transference relationship was used to uncover the patient's neurotic symptoms which were acted out on the therapist. The patient's resistance denoted the dynamics of repression; positive transference helped to uncover this repression. In hypnotic therapy these resistances were covered up, because the patient was not given sufficient freedom to participate in the interview because the therapist began to control the patient's behavior through suggestion. To overcome these resistances, Freud and others found justifiable reasons for revising the therapeutic relationship.

As Freud's theory developed and became more refined, it converged upon repression, repetition compulsion, infantile sexuality, and dream symbolism as conceptual tools. In its relational sphere which structured the interview sessions, the transference became one of the cardinal features. Freud says:

> The decisive part of the work is carried through by creating—in the relationship to the physician, in the "transference"—new editions of those early conflicts in which the patient strives to behave as he originally behaved, while one calls upon all available forces in his soul to bring him to another decision. The transference is thus the battlefield where all contending forces must meet.[29]

[28] *Ibid.*, pp. 383–384.
[29] *Ibid.*, p. 395.

The importance of this transference relationship, as Alexander later pointed out, was that it enabled the patient to recollect past critical experiences. Although the standard psychoanalysts were usually concerned with filling in the memory gaps of the patient's past, Rank, Ferenczi, Alexander, and others have shown that the relationship to the therapist was more important than retrieving these forgotten episodes.[30] There was much experimentation done in this area.

From one point of view, Rank and Ferenczi viewed the therapeutic relationship as a means of releasing the will of the patient. That is, the more the patient asserted himself, the more likely he was to free himself from his inhibitions and to find his "real self." At times, the therapist resorted to irritating the patient rather than resolving his conflicts. From another point of view, Ferenczi in his later period considered that the object of therapy was to provide the love that the patient missed in his early life. As such, the therapist became partially involved with the patient in order to give this love; but the difficulty was that the patient could not necessarily return this affection because of his neurotic defenses, and because the neurotic adult had other uses for love than the child, such as concealing his hostility, or taking advantage of another person. In short, the neurotic adult was incapable of reciprocating the love relationship, as Ferenczi had hoped.

Thus, the initial phase of the therapeutic sessions was to prepare and to guide the patient into a state of transference. This condition was a function of the basic neurotic's condition rather than of the therapeutic relationship itself. The neurotic projects a role onto the therapist so that he represents some person in the patient's previous experiences. In standard psychoanalysis the patient reverts to a childhood and even a babyhood role to verbalize his past conflicts and invests the therapist, at least initially, with the role of parent substitute.

Freud believed that the patient's transference relationship had its basis in the unresolved Oedipal relationship. Consequently, he believed that the patient had to relive these experiences in order to

[30] Franz Alexander and Thomas M. French, *Psychoanalytic Therapy*, pp. 21–23; Otto Rank and Sandor Ferenczi, *The Development of Psychoanalysis*, translated by Caroline Newton (New York: Nervous and Mental Disease Publishing Company, 1925).

understand and to reorient himself before definite improvement could be achieved.[31]

Subsequent Developments of the Transference. Although Freud identified the transference phenomenon and explained its negative and positive phases, this relationship had even broader and more complex meanings as therapists have subsequently discovered.

First, it was found that the transference relationship did not always revert back to early childhood and replace only the mother and father figures, but it also included subsequent persons in the subject's experiences, such as siblings, friends, and teachers. Second, aspects of the transference varied with the personality of the therapist. One therapist, at least initially, might call out hostile reactions from a given patient; another therapist might call out friendly feelings. Since therapists, by their appearance, manner, and general personality, called out different types of irrational reactions, the personality of the therapist was regarded as increasingly important in this essential relationship with the patient. Consequently, personality differences among therapists became increasingly important. Third, as we have pointed out before, it was necessary to differentiate between an irrational and repetitive attachment which was denoted by transference and so-called rational but realistic attachments. For the therapist had both types of roles. He was a professional, on the one hand, and had the roles assigned to him by the patient, on the other hand. Fourth, although many therapists began to recognize the importance of the present problems of the patients, they did not deny the extreme importance of resolving early conflicts. As an exception, however, Horney maintained that the past experiences are contained in the patient's present personality difficulties.

Horney revised the interpretation of the transference. The transference was not merely a repetitive relationship of the past but was a result of the patient's anxiety in the present. Because the patient's anxiety was aroused in the therapy, he had to cling more fiercely to the therapist. Hence, her aim was to point out the patient's personality trends which called out this dependent attachment. These personality trends were called out when the individual's defenses could no longer hide them. For example, the individual who was unduly

[31] For example, see the orthodox analytic sessions described by Charles Berg, *Deep Analysis* (New York: W. W. Norton & Company, 1947).

modest in order to conceal grasping and competitive tendencies
might become quite hostile to the therapist when these underlying
tendencies were called out, and he would have some anxiety about
them.[32]

In brief, the transference relationship has become a very useful
therapeutic tool. Although the emphases in the transference, as we
have seen, vary, these interpretations have common elements. First,
many therapists agree that the patient's irrational reactions arise
from past experiences, are enacted upon the therapist, and have
therapeutic significance. Second, many therapists agree that these
reactions and attachments represent or hide unconscious tendencies
of which the patient is unaware. Third, therapists recognize that the
patient's insight into these relationships may help free him from his
anxieties.

The interpretations of the transference vary in terms of the
patient's present and past behavior. The orthodox psychoanalysts
interpret the present behavior of the patient in terms of past
infantile and early childhood conflicts.[33] The Horney school attempts to interpret the past in the light of the patient's present
personality structure.[34] Other schools of psychoanalysis, for example, the Washington School of Psychiatry, tend to take an intermediate position. Although they recognize the importance of interpreting the present personality structure of the patient, they also
feel that early childhood experiences have to be relived and resolved.[35]

Other Changes. Another important development arose in part
from the changing family structure and the culture. With the decline of the authoritarian family in the second quarter of the
twentieth century, the relationship between the patient and the
therapist also had to be revised. The domineering father was less
apparent, particularly among middle- and upper middle-class per-

[32] Karen Horney, *New Ways in Psychoanalysis*, pp. 154–167 (New York: W. W.
Norton & Company, 1939).

[33] Otto Fenichel, *The Psychoanalytic Theory of Neuroses*, pp. 29, 30 (New
York: W. W. Norton & Company, 1945).

[34] Karen Horney, *New Ways in Psychoanalysis*, pp. 163, 164 (New York: W. W.
Norton & Company, 1939).

[35] See Frieda Fromm-Reichmann, "Recent Advances in Psychoanalytic Therapy,"
The Study of Inter-personal Relations, edited by Patrick Mullahy, p. 127 (New
York: Hermitage Press, Inc., 1949).

sons who came from relatively equalitarian families and who viewed authority somewhat differently from those persons in similar classes in the past. The therapist who had to represent these authority figures also had to take a more democratic role. No longer was he the aloof, distant, and impassive figure, the blank or mirror, but he became a more personable individual. Although this change was made intrinsically because the personality equation of the therapist was felt to be more important, the change in the family structure indirectly played its part in affecting this revised relationship.

Second, the problems of the women were interpreted in terms of her social role rather than in terms of biological differences. This emphasis upon the social •role of the woman was a result of the clear differences between the role of the woman in the Victorian period and her role during the present time.

Third, the place of sex as a ubiquitous motive for explaining many conflicts began to assume a more modest position. This change in the all-important emphasis upon sex was not only a result of a more lucid knowledge of motivation; it occurred also because the patients with intense sex repressions became less frequent. Sex, however important a motive, was one motive among many.

Fourth, the place of the individual in the culture or in the impersonal society had to be considered. Consistent with his period, Freud emphasized the subordination of the individual to the social pressures. He tried to make the individual come to terms with society and to do so by accepting and conforming to the culture.[36] Subsequent investigators did not see the conflict as the individual versus society, but the individual as an emergent of the society. Hence, they began to stress the function of the individual's integrity, because it was recognized that society had fundamental weaknesses, which precluded the individual's complete conformity.[37] Fromm emphasized that the individual, as a product of society, became a competitive and empty person, and that in the drive for status he had lost his freedom. The problem, then, was one of restoring his integrity and spontaneity. Others, however, indicated that this

[36] Clara Thompson, *Psychoanalysis: Its Evolution and Development* (New York: Hermitage House, Inc., 1950).

[37] Erich Fromm, *Escape from Freedom* (New York: Rinehart & Company, Inc., 1941). Fromm, too, has worked out a scheme for dream interpretation which is based upon but which varies from Freud's. See Erich Fromm, *The Forgotten Language* (New York: Rinehart & Company, Inc., 1951).

spontaneity could not work well in a bureaucratic society and emphasized more realistic goals.[38]

The Rise of Flexible Techniques. Since some psychoanalysts have become more empirical in their inquiries, they also have become more flexible in their therapeutic techniques. Brief psychotherapy, which represents one flexible approach, attempts to adjust treatment techniques to the needs of the particular patient.[39] First, it was found that some personality difficulties did not arise in early childhood but were acquired during adolescence or adulthood. Consequently, it was found neither feasible nor necessary to revert to the patient's earliest experiences. This revised notion of the conception of the milder neuroses became integrated with a treatment procedure and veered from the rigid procedures of the orthodox psychoanalysts. Second, it was found that therapists who were facile in treating some persons were not so adept in treating other persons. Consequently, it was necessary to see whether the patient "took to" the therapist. Third, it was necessary to find out why the patient sought therapy. For example, if the patient were sent to the therapist against his will, the therapist might become identified with the relatives who sent the patient, and an artificial and "unreal" relationship could develop. Fourth, it became more expedient to try to plan the therapy rather than improvise for each session. By planning the therapy, the therapist could anticipate difficulties and problems in future sessions and be prepared to deal with them although this planning was not always successful. Fifth, in addition to the manipulation of the transference relationship when it arose, the therapist found that the frequency of the interviews and the frequency of the interpretations could affect the therapeutic process. For example, when the patient used the therapy as a retreat from his actual problems so that his actual problems declined in intensity, the frequency of the interviews could be decreased. In the longer intervals the patient would have to face his problems alone, and his conflicts could become intensified. In addition, he would have to solve these problems by his own resources. When the patient was very self-condemnatory or when interpretations created anxiety, the

[38] Erich Fromm, *Escape from Freedom* (New York: Rinehart & Company, Inc., 1941). See also Arnold Green, "Social Values and Psychotherapy," *Journal of Personality,* March, 1946, 14, pp. 199–228.

[39] Franz Alexander and Thomas M. French, *Psychoanalytic Therapy,* pp. 25–65.

interpretations were withheld or given infrequently until the patient could accept the interpretations. In short, the therapist used varied aspects of his relationship with the patient in order to anticipate and to work out the patient's difficulties. In this way the therapist controlled the interview for the patient's particular needs, and he did so on an empirical level by devices which he could test and manipulate.

Perhaps these therapeutic changes represent the influences of the American society? The brief-therapy procedures are congenial to the temper of the American people for getting things done quickly. The wish to test and manipulate the therapeutic process is influenced by the pressures of the social sciences and psychological sciences of the universities. The whole therapeutic process with its intimate and distant phases parallels the pervasive tendency toward "psychologizing" about persons on the one hand, and the recourse to a financial transaction for "buying" health as a means to success on the other hand.[40]

Neo-Freudian Therapy. The departure from a rigid psychoanalytic technique by contemporary therapists has created many changes in the psychoanalytic techniques, as we have pointed out. Sullivan, Alexander and French, Fromm, Thompson, and Horney, among others, have contributed to these changes. In these modes of therapy the co-operative process between two persons was emphasized. We shall illustrate this process by a somewhat extreme departure from the orthodox Freudian position, as is represented by Horney and her associates.

The Role of the Therapist. In defining the procedure to the patient, the therapist does not only become the object of the irrational feelings and responses which the patient will eventually transfer to him, but he also has a present role as a person in his own right which the patient will have to countenance. The therapist does not have the patient assume an infantile or childhood role. Instead, he emphasizes the patient's present character structure which has emerged from disturbed social relationships. This gives

---

[40] See Jurgen Ruesch and Gregory Bateson, *Communication: The Social Matrix of Psychiatry* (New York: W. W. Norton & Company, 1951). For a criticism of this position, see K. R. Eissler, "The Chicago Institute of Psychoanalysis and the Sixth Period of the Development of Psychoanalytic Technique," *The Journal of General Psychology,* 1950, 42, pp. 103–157.

the patient more responsibility in solving his problems, because the patient's present personality trends have to be understood.

By creating an atmosphere of a present reality in the situation, the therapist provides the setting within which the patient can look back at his personality from the perspective of the analyst and thus confront his "real self." In the process of coming to face his real self, he is in a relationship which is both accepting and tolerant. This fact reduces the necessity of self-condemnation, which many patients have, and reduces the intensity of his personal defenses and thereby his resistances. Not only does the therapist help the patient in getting at his conflicts; he also tries to overcome the resistance which the patient may have in facing his conflicts.

The therapist responds to the patient not on an impersonal or intellectual level but on a personal level. He does so with a therapeutic intent and not with the intent of friendship or of mutuality. The therapist deters the patient from placing his responsibilities upon him and demanding "all the answers" from him. Despite this initiative in the analysis, still the therapist has a large share of responsibility. He sets the lead by his interpretations and questions; steers the patient from dead ends to more fruitful lanes; stimulates the patient to persist in solving problems when the patient might want to stop. The recovery of the patient is largely a function of the therapist's conduct and role in the relationship.

The Role of the Patient. Although the patient, at the outset, may want the therapist to assume complete responsibility for his improvement, he soon learns that this responsibility is a shared process and that he has to participate more actively and more concertedly in his own improvement.[41] The patient may feel stiff, apprehensive, tense, or uncertain about the imminent therapy. Unless his uncertainty passes and rapport grows as the therapy proceeds, the therapy may actually terminate.

Since the patient presents his problem from his present perspective, his transference to the analyst will be expressed by dependency rather than by reversion to a childhood or infantile role. Kilpatrick states:[42]

[41] Karen Horney (editor), *Are You Considering Psychoanalysis?* p. 160 (New York: W. W. Norton & Company, 1946).
[42] In *Ibid.,* p. 202.

When I speak of general human help, I mean the way the analyst helps the patient—not through his interpretation but through his attitude toward the patient. This includes his willingness to understand, his unflagging interest in the patient's growth, his faith in the patient's existing potentialities, his firmness that permits him to view the patient's sufferings with concern without letting himself be crushed by them, to remain unswayed by the patient's admiration and undaunted by the patient's aggressive demands or hostile attacks. The value of such an attitude is underrated by some and overrated by others. Freud undertook the task of the analyst as primarily an intellectual one. The less the analyst's personality was involved the more effective the therapy would be. The advice he gave on this score was in negative terms: the analyst should not be condemnatory; the analyst should not yield to the patient's neurotic demands. At the other extreme are some modern analysts who contend that the very friendship the analyst extends to the patient is essential in curing him of his disturbances in human relationships. Such notions, while flattering to the analyst and pleasing to the patient, may blur the fundamental issue, namely that patient and analyst come together in order to do work.

When the transference becomes intensified, it means that the anxiety has been aroused in the relationship with the therapist, and that the attachment tends to act as a prop for the patient who has become more dependent. Masochistic persons, for example, have deep need to hang on to other people, particularly when their anxiety is aroused. This dynamism, which is expressed by an emotional dependence upon the analyst, can work as directly from the upset caused by the reopening of previous anxiety experiences as by the need for a repetition of a previous attachment. It would seem that the attachment flows as much from the loss caused by the anxiety as from the repetition of a previous relationship. Horney points out three dangers which may result from stressing the transference relationship as merely a repetitious relationship. First, it leaves the underlying anxiety untouched, and, therefore, the patient's attachment to the analyst remains. Second, it may make the analysis unproductive, because the past experiences of humiliation may not be connected with the transference. The contributing factors in the personality structure which have led to humiliating or painful experiences are not sufficiently analyzed. Third, the person's present personality trends must be understood before they can be related to past experiences. Horney also questions whether a transference relationship can be distinguished from a genuine love relationship. She feels that this can be ascertained only by analyzing the actual personality structure and the character trends. She indicates further that the impersonal attitudes of the therapist to the patient cannot always be achieved, .that the analyst does have personal attitudes to the patient, and the best understanding of his own personal attitudes can arise not from attributing his reactions to infantile experiences but from a knowledge of his own character trends.[43]

Counseling. Another representative trend in psychological treatment has been the reaction against directive procedures in counseling.[44] Counseling generally deals with the milder disorders and is used chiefly by psychologists rather than by psychiatrists.

Nondirective Counseling. Nondirective counseling or nondirective play therapy is nonauthoritarian, noncoercive, and nonsuggestive and does not encourage a transference relationship.[45] It, too, initiates the therapeutic relationship by a warm acceptance of the patient, but it uses the relationship for different ends. It allows the patient to direct the interview within the structured limits set by the counselor and is extreme in its insistence that the patient have complete responsibility for solving his problems. By affording the client uninhibited freedom of expression, it relies upon ·the tremendous capacity for growth inherent in the personality as the medium for self-therapy.

This relationship is based upon the premise that the condition of development comes from within the person and not from the advice, suggestions of, or obligation to the counselor. It differs·from the status-competing relationships in daily life, whether of teacher to pupil, of friends, of co-workers, or of physician to patient. This

[43] Karen Horney, *New Ways In Psychoanalysis,* pp. 158–167 (New York: W. W. Norton & Company, 1939).

[44] See Carl R. Rogers, *Counseling and Psychotherapy* (Boston: Houghton Mifflin Company, 1942); Virginia Axline, *Play Therapy* (Boston: Houghton Mifflin Company, 1947); William U. Snyder, *Case Studies in Counseling* (Boston: Houghton Mifflin Company, 1947); Carl R. Rogers, *Client-Centered Therapy* (Boston: Houghton Mifflin Company, 1950).

[45] A somewhat related therapeutic procedure is "relationship therapy" which is used by psychiatrists. See Frederick Allen, *Psychotherapy with Children* (New York: W. W. Norton & Company, 1942).

Both nondirective counseling and relationship therapy stem from Otto Rank's therapeutic procedures.

relationship has three phases: (1) defining the respective role of counselor and client; (2) the statement and development of the client's problem; and (3) the acquisition of insight, self-understanding, and the achievement of new goals by the client.[46]

Role of the Counselor. As in relationship therapy, the counselor's function is to structure the relationship.

First he defines the client's freedoms, either by his behavior or verbally, but he limits the time intervals of the interview. He defines his "responsibility" for the client's problems and actions and prevents the client from indiscriminate aggression whether in harming others or in damaging property. Finally, he avoids becoming over-involved with the client, avoids transference, and avoids any resentments or dependencies from the patient. Within these limits he encourages a maximum of freedom to the client. The definition of these roles comes after the subject has stated his problem. Then the counselor indicates what the respective functions are in solving the client's problems. Rogers has pointed out that after a client states his problems, he waits for the counselor to advise him, to ask him questions or to lead the conversation in some way. For he expects the counselor to assume responsibility for managing the client's problems. At this juncture, the counselor presents:[47]

> a brief and partial explanation of the counseling situation, leaving the responsibility to the student, but nevertheless making plain that it is a joint enterprise mentioning the fact that the problem will not be solved for him, but giving him a way of proceeding.

Since this explanation may not be understood completely at the outset by the client, the counselor will reinforce the role of the client throughout the interview series. From the empirical studies made, it seems that the necessity for defining the client's role to him declines as the therapeutic process ensues.[48]

Second, he expresses attitudes of understanding and permission which enable the client to verbalize all his forbidden, humiliating, private, and inhibited reactions. By his responsiveness to these feelings, he enables the client to drop his "front" which shields him from any verbal appraisal of his conventional relationships. By not

<hr>

[46] Carl R. Rogers, *Counseling and Psychotherapy,* p. 80 (Boston: Houghton Mifflin Company, 1942).

[47] *Ibid.,* p. 93.

[48] *Ibid.,* p. 95–108.

projecting his own attitudes or feelings into the relationship, the counselor keeps the interview free of conventional values.

The third chief function of the counselor's role is to clarify and to reflect, to mirror and to verbalize the feelings in the patient's statements. He strives to see the problems from the patient's viewpoint rather than to assess the intellectual content of his statements. In this way he fosters a deeper emotional relationship within which the client acquires insight for his behavior. But though he becomes partially involved, he retains his main identity as professional counselor and as a neutral person. He avoids becoming involved in his social life and accordingly serves best in his restricted capacity as counselor.

Though he clarifies the feelings of the client, the counselor does not guide or necessarily anticipate his statements, for he may throw the client's feelings off the track and may even frustrate his further expressions of emotionally toned attitudes. He further helps the client to verbalize and to face latent reactions and unresolved conflicts and, eventually, to face his real "self."

Role of the Client. The client is a person in need of help who has the responsibility of utilizing a therapeutic time interval for personal development by resolving his conflicts. Within the limits mentioned, he can talk or be silent; he can speak of relevant or irrelevant matters. But, by definition, nondirective counseling is limited to persons who have responsibility for their behavior and who presumably want to solve their problems. The client finds that he cannot shift responsibility to or become dependent upon the counselor. He is free to express himself with no criticism and with a minimum of interference, except to have clarified the feelings implicit in his remarks. But the price of his freedom is the responsibility to resolve his conflicts.

The client leads and sets the course of the discussion. He may turn to the problems which disturb him. In successful sessions he must experience a growth process in the relationship, for, from this viewpoint, this need for personal growth is presumably deep. He must feel the fruition of this therapy, and he must want to come.

When the counseling relationship is successful, the client progressively becomes more independent and confident as his problems become resolved, until the session when he feels satisfied and confident enough to terminate the therapeutic relationship of his own accord.

Limitations of Therapy. There are, however, definite limits to some types of therapeutic relationships. These limits emerge from the situation within which a therapeutic relationship is fostered. Apparently, any therapist-patient contact which leads to uncovering therapy cannot go on in an authoritarian social context, particularly if there may be punitive consequences. This was apparent in the Army. Cobb has pointed out that psychoanalytic techniques were not used in his work-up of patients because such techniques would have failed anyway. The normal relationship between a doctor and patient was not evident.

> . . . the men looked on the doctor as a superior officer who would or might report what they told him for "the record." Free association in most instances would have been impossible. Suggestion was tried to some extent.[49]

A second limitation is the emotional involvement of the therapist and the patient. When the therapist and patient compete for status in daily life or are overinvolved, it is obvious that therapy cannot be effective. Apparently, a family or very friendly relationship would have to be changed, sometimes drastically, in order to create a relationship in which uncovering modes of therapy could be initiated. According to the analysts, these therapeutic relationships would be complicated by the extratherapeutic attachments or resentments of the patient to the therapist. Freud indicated that such therapeutic help should be given only when no other therapist is available, but that the analyst does so at the peril of sacrificing the previous friendship relationship.[50]

It is quite likely that the therapist may be able to persuade, suggest, and support the patient just as close friends may share secrets and may confide in each other. Though this type of relationship may be therapeutically effective, it is generally fragmentary and without the systematic or the profound character of the therapeutic analysis. Yet a sustaining relationship may have the implicit traits

---

[49] Stanley Cobb, "Integration of Medical and Psychiatric Problems: A Report of Progress," *Psychiatric Research: Harvard University Monograph in Medicine and Public Health,* No. 9, p. 58 (Cambridge, Mass.: Harvard University Press, 1947).

[50] Sigmund Freud, *Collected Papers,* Vol. II, p. 345.

of a transference, and improvement by this informal relationship may occur.

A third limitation resides in the personality of the patient. The intensely egocentric or narcissistic type is one who may be unable to enter into a therapeutic relationship. From the psychoanalytic viewpoint, he would be unable to affect a transference to the psychoanalyst, and, as such, the essentials of the psychoanalytic relationships could not be maintained, for these resistances would deter or prevent a relationship of confidence which permits rapport and an uncovering process to ensue. Also, a feeble-minded person could not be psychoanalyzed. In other words, some measure of communication and of an emotional relationship are vital to begin and sustain the therapeutic process.

The patient must submit to some degree of control by the analyst. When the patient refuses, as might occur with an intensely egocentric type, this therapeutic essential would be manifestly improbable. Fenichel says that when the patient is not co-operative, when he lacks "a reasonable ego," psychoanalysis cannot be applied. The difficulty, at times, in establishing rapport with these types is so great that it may be insolvable.[51]

He also points out, however, that co-operation can sometimes be established by nonanalytic methods in a preanalytic period, from which a sufficient transference may occur to provide the basis for subsequent psychoanalysis. Some acting-out neurotics, through a process of re-education, may be made ready for co-operation; stubborn persons, if convinced that they are unable rather than unwilling to co-operate, may become interested or concerned with this "inability" and thus respond to psychoanalytic therapy. Also, some seclusive or schizoid persons may be provoked into a psychosis if analyzed.[52]

A fourth factor resides in the negative reaction to the therapist's personality by certain patients. When the patient may not like working with the particular therapist, certain resistances may be called out which would impede therapy. Sometimes this resistance itself can be analyzed away. At other times it may be insurmountable.

[51] Otto Fenichel, *The Psychoanalytic Theory of Neurosis*, p. 578 (New York: W. W. Norton & Company, 1945).
[52] *Ibid.*, p. 579.

Some therapists may work better with some types of persons than with others. Fenichel believes that this may be the result of a disappointment on the part of the therapist because the patient does not fulfill his anticipations.

Differentiated Relationships for Different Types of Patients. It cannot be said that one type of therapy is best suited to all types of patients. The condition of the particular subject determines the best therapeutic relationships to apply. The contrast may be illustrated between the Freudian type of therapy, which evolved out of the treatment of neurotics, and relationship therapy or nondirective counseling, which evolved out of the treatment of problem children.

It is apparent that in children the unconscious life is less readily controlled, behavior is less disguised, and projection is more facile; the freedom afforded in the self-directive therapies enables the child to project his wishes outward and to arrive at his true feelings. Also, the child in our culture is more or less smothered by his parental relationships. The process of differentiation and self-distinction, by its very character, becomes therapeutic to these children. This process, of course, is not so readily arrived at when dealing with adults. The adult is more restrained and has more resistance in divulging buried conflicts which he may or may not be able to understand. This is particularly true for basic neurotics, who have to be helped in getting at their basic and intricate conflicts which may be too painful for them to lift to consciousness and to reach to self-awareness. Freud early realized that the sudden emergence of a painful and critical experience may lead to a relapse if the patient is unable to tolerate the experience. It was one reason among others that he turned to dreams as the "royal road to the unconscious."

Personality of the Psychotherapist. What type of person becomes a psychotherapist, or, specifically, a psychiatrist or psychoanalyst? Are there any personality requisites by which to determine more accurately who will and who will not become a helpful and capable therapist? The psychoanalysts, of course, use psychoanalysis itself as a means of determining whether the potential therapist will be admitted into their fold. Presumably, those who do not complete the analysis themselves are automatically excluded. Sullivan suggests that certain personality types who are puzzled by novelty or

who have to impress others as being omniscient do not have the requisite qualities for becoming therapists.[53]

Certainly those persons who have not been able to resolve their
hostility against others and who derive a kind of gratification in
hearing about the ills of other persons would not necessarily have
a positive attitude toward therapy. Another suggestion is that the
training therapist work with a clinical team in order to improve his
therapeutic skill and to become familiar with the childhood processes which he meets daily in the clinic.[54] To enhance the importance of this training, it would be advisable that psychotherapists
also have systematic training in the cultural processes and in the different norms of behavior among varied groups. This type of training
would equip the therapist to see the patient as a person within a
social setting and not as an isolated individual in a clinic.

In addition to the personality make-up of the therapist, there is
also an increasing emphasis upon knowing the cultural diversities
of a heterogeneous society. Would persons who are prejudiced
against minority groups be qualified to deal with these groups? It
seems that the psychiatrist generally should know enough about the
culture of his patients so that a group norm will not be mistaken
for a perverse individual trait. There is a need for more organized
and systematic knowledge concerning the prejudices as well as the
personality components of the therapists, as these bear upon the
therapeutic relationship. One phenomenon of interest concerns
the type of persons who enter the psychotherapeutic professions.
Presumably, the attraction of status and standard of living that go
with psychiatry and psychotherapy may be broad cultural influences,
but it would be of more definite value to find the type of persons
that enter this profession. This would challenge a frequently heard
stereotype concerning the personality of the psychotherapist. These
studies could also be done comparatively with other professions. It
would also be of interest to find what changes occur among those
persons who have entered the psychotherapeutic professions.

[53] Harry Stack Sullivan, *Conceptions of Modern Psychiatry*, p. 93, footnote
(Washington, D.C.: The William Alanson White Psychiatric Foundation, 1940
and 1945); Hans Sachs, "Observations of a Training Analyst," *Psychoanalytic
Quarterly*, April, 1947, 16, pp. 157–168.

[54] Jules V. Coleman, "Patient-Physician Relationship in Psychotherapy, *The
American Journal of Psychiatry*, April, 1948, 104:10, pp. 638, 639.

Comparative Studies of Psychotherapeutic Relationships. Experienced therapists realize that in some therapeutic situations everything seemingly goes right, and yet the patient does not progress markedly. Conversely, other relationships are not so well understood, but the patient makes definite progress. What function does the patient-therapist relationship have in these failures, as well as in these successes?

In prolonged therapy the majority of patients are in the middle and upper classes. By their participation in the culture of these strata, the therapists can understand more readily many of their problems. In our stratified society complicated by ethnic differences, additional knowledge is required for comparing the disorders among those in the lower income groups, who cannot afford psychotherapy, with those in the middle- and upper-class levels, to whom psychotherapy is largely confined. Kubie, in summarizing the results of a survey of a group of psychoanalysts, found that the fee per hour was about $15. Patently, this type of fee is beyond the means of most persons in our culture. Hence, a limited segment of our society benefits from psychoanalysis and, in another sense, a limited segment in our society encounters the psychoanalyst. An effort to reach more persons has been made, however, since World War II, when veterans of all strata were being treated.

It would be well to apply the varied types of psychotherapeutic procedures to patients with somewhat similarly disordered conditions in order to get comparable results. As yet, this knowledge is very scanty. Published studies are few but are increasing in number. A sharper and clearer definition of what constitutes improvement and recovery must be derived, for these therapeutic goals provide the objectives of the social psychological dynamics of the patients and clients as these dynamics are set in motion by the therapeutic relationship.

Fiedler factor-analyzed the therapeutic relationships created by two psychoanalytic, two nondirective, and one Adlerian expert therapist and by two psychoanalytic, two nondirective, and one Adlerian nonexpert therapist. Ten electrically recorded therapeutic interviews were assessed by one psychoanalytically, one nondirectively, and one untrained judge and one judge who had some psychoanalytic and some nondirective training. These judges listened independently to the interviews and evaluated them in terms of seventy-five traits. The results showed that there were no factors which clearly differentiated the therapists of one school from those of another school, but there were certain factors which differentiated the experts from the nonexperts. These differences included the therapist's ability to understand the patient's feelings, to be more secure, and to respond in an emotionally neutral way. The communicative aspects of the therapeutic interaction seemed to be more important than the particular technique used by the therapist.[55] Many therapists are recognizing increasingly the importance of the personality in the treatment process, as well as the modes of interaction which ensue in this process, and some therapists and counselors are publishing accounts of their interviews.[56]

Finally, it would be pertinent to discover why one therapist, rather than two or three therapists together, provides a more effective treatment situation. Does the therapist, as an anchored figure who interprets the patient to himself, lose his effectiveness when another person, as therapist, also interprets the same patient's behavior? As yet, we have little systematic knowledge of this area of psychotherapy.

Psychotherapy and Society. The patient undergoing psychotherapy still has to participate in and remain influenced by the social order. When this structure is highly unstable, he will still experience many conflicts, some of which may remain quite threatening to him. How does the given social organization affect the person who has been treated? Some investigators take the extreme position and claim that in an unstable society psychotherapy can-

[55] Fred E. Fiedler, "Factor Analyses of Psychoanalytic, Nondirective and Adlerian Therapeutic Relationships," *Journal of Consulting Psychology*, February, 1951, 15:1, pp. 32–38; Fred E. Fiedler, "A Comparison of Therapeutic Relationships in Psychoanalytic, Nondirective and Adlerian Therapy," *Journal of Consulting Psychology*, 1950, 14, pp. 436–445. Despite this research, it seems that the mode of therapy does play a role in the therapeutic process. It seems that whether or not the therapist interprets the patient's conflicts will affect the therapy. Seemingly, Fiedler did not probe deeply enough into the modes of interaction between patient and therapist.

[56] See Franz Alexander and Thomas M. French, *Psychoanalytic Therapy* (New York: The Ronald Press Company, 1946); Charles Berg, *Deep Analysis* (New York: W. W. Norton & Company, 1947); Charles Berg, *The Case Book of a Medical Psychologist* (New York: W. W. Norton & Company, 1948); William U. Snyder, *Case Studies in Counseling* (Boston: Houghton Mifflin Company, 1947).

not be effective for prolonged periods. Others take the very opposite position and maintain that psychotherapy can have the maximum benefit upon the person regardless of the social organization. The truth is somewhere between these extremes.

Clearly, the person who has had many of his problems resolved can devote more time to constructive pursuits without being troubled by these problems, but this treatment will not by any means immunize him from further intense conflicts, and it will not immunize him from recurrent disordered behavior. Even among relatively stable persons, persistent problems can easily arise. Thus, therapy is not a constant and ever-enduring process but varies with one's subsequent experiences.

The person who continually engages in new experiences involving risk and uncertainty and whose social relationships are generally hostile may re-experience anxiety anew, if, perhaps, with less intensity. Successful therapy can lessen these recurrent anxieties because the individual will handle his environment more effectively. He will so limit his experiences and so change his needs that he will select companions, a marital partner, and other friends who will be more beneficial to his personal development and personal organization. Nonetheless, situational influences inevitably enter into the process of therapy and obviously involve social implications. The woman past 35 who must reconcile herself to spinsterhood and loneliness, the male who must resign himself to a lesser role although he sees his brothers and friends ahead of him, the man who is uncertain about his business or about his job, or the individual who finds it hard to make ends meet—all clearly face recurrent problems of a threatening character which cannot be wished away. Presumably, these problems are "realistic" insofar as they are present, objective situations; still, their persistence and tenacity can make for continued instability. In brief, the effectiveness of therapy is contingent upon the series of roles and groups and aspirations of the individual. Consequently, the sustained effectiveness of therapy is limited in part by the external social conditions of the given individual.

In addition, sustained therapeutic effectiveness cannot be judged only by the insights which the person achieves during the therapy or by his acting out of these insights while he is dependent upon

the therapist. Instead, it depends upon his ability to handle subsequent crises and to integrate difficult situations, as well as upon
his general external adjustment.

Summary

In summarizing the forms of relationships developed by the different schools of psychotherapy presented in this chapter, we discern the following trends and common features among them. First,
with the shift from amelioration of symptoms by suggestion to the
search for "causes" of behavior problems, a greater degree of patient
participation as well as a greater freedom of patient expression has
resulted. Second, a need has arisen to understand explicitly the
nature of the patient-therapist relationship, particularly the transference, because the relationship itself has been recognized as an
integral component of the therapeutic process. Third, the therapist
has tended to abandon his extremely impersonal attitude and has
become more personal and more flexible in his relationships with
the patient. Fourth, there is a greater tendency to view the patient
as he is in the present and to work with him in this way rather than
to revert his career to a past infantile role. Fifth, because the dynamics of the therapeutic relationships have become more explicit,
there has been greater facility in understanding and in controlling
the relationships. Sixth, the neurotic patients tend to become dependent upon the therapist in a process of transference, although
the interpretation of the transference varies. This, in part, is discernible even in nondirective counseling, despite the claims against
its occurrence; for, as is apparent, the transference does not emerge
from the character of the relationship but arises from the condition
of the patient.

Selected Readings

Alexander, Franz, and Thomas M. French, *Psychoanalytic Therapy* (New
York: The Ronald Press Co., 1946).

Allen, Frederick, *Psychotherapy with Children* (New York: W. W. Norton
& Company, 1942).

Fenichel, Otto, *Psychoanalytic Theory of Neuroses* (New York: W. W.
Norton & Company, 1945).

Freud, Sigmund, *A General Introduction to Psychoanalysis,* translated by
Joan Riviere (Garden City, N.Y.: Garden City Publishing Company,
Inc., 1943).

Fromm-Reichmann, Frieda, *Principles of Intensive Psychotherapy* (Chicago: University of Chicago Press, 1950).

Ginsberg, Sol W., "Values and the Psychiatrist," *American Journal of Orthopsychiatry*, July, 1950, 20:3, pp. 466–478.

Green, Arnold W., "Social Values and Psychotherapy," *Journal of Personality*, March, 1946, 14, pp. 199–228.

Hinsie, Leland E., *Concepts and Problems of Psychotherapy* (New York: Columbia University Press, 1937).

Horney, Karen, *New Ways in Psychoanalysis* (New York: W. W. Norton & Company, 1939).

——— (editor), *Are You Considering Psychoanalysis?* (New York: W. W. Norton & Company, 1946).

Jung, Carl G., *Modern Man in Search of a Soul*, translated by W. S. Dill and Cary F. Baynes (New York: Harcourt, Brace and Company, Inc., 1934).

Kubie, Lawrence S., *Practical and Theoretical Aspects of Psychoanalysis* (New York: International Universities Press, Inc., 1950).

Law, Stanley G., *Therapy through Interview* (New York: McGraw-Hill Book Company, Inc., 1948).

Levy, David M., Sandor Rado, and Lauretta Bender, "The Relationship of Patient to Therapist: A Symposium," *American Journal of Orthopsychiatry*, 1942, XII, pp. 541–544.

Rogers, Carl R., *Counseling and Psychotherapy* (Boston: Houghton Mifflin Company, 1942).

———, *Client-Centered Therapy* (Boston: Houghton Mifflin Company, 1950).

Slavson, S. R., "Types of Relationship and Their Application to Psychotherapy," *American Journal of Orthopsychiatry*, 1945, XV, pp. 267–277.

Snyder, William U., "The Present Status of Psychotherapeutic Counseling," *Psychological Bulletin*, July, 1947, 44:4, pp. 297–386.

Sullivan, Harry Stack, *Conceptions of Modern Psychiatry* (Washington, D.C.: The William Alanson White Psychiatric Foundation, 1945).

Thompson, Clara, *Psychoanalysis: Evolution and Development* (New York: Hermitage House, Inc., 1950).

Witmer, Helen Leland (editor), *Psychiatric Interviews with Children* (New York: Commonwealth Fund, 1946).

CHAPTER FOURTEEN

Group Psychotherapy and the Social Process

Individual psychotherapy has been described in the preceding chapter as a unique patient-therapist relationship designed for the patient's improvement by revising his self-conception and by modifying his action patterns. Yet individual treatment usually takes a long time and cannot be offered to many persons. Group psychotherapy, which had been tried initially with hospitalized patients, children, and alcoholics, as well as with neurotics, became widespread during World War II, primarily as a timesaving expedient.[1] The many neurotic and psychotic casualties of the war could not possibly be treated individually. From this treatment of groups many principles and techniques began to evolve, and one conclusive feature was that the group itself played an integral part in the therapeutic process, which made it distinct from individual therapy.[2]

Despite this and other common features of group therapy, there are also many variations. It may occur inside or outside of an institutional setting. It may be expressed in play and activity, or in discussion and analysis. It may be confined to a few individuals

---

[1] Group psychotherapy in some form was recognized as early as 1906. For some early studies, see John H. Pratt, "The Home Sanatorium Treatment of Consumption," *Bulletin of the Johns Hopkins Hospital*, 1906, XVII, pp. 140–158; also John H. Pratt, "The Principles of Class Treatment and Their Application to Various Chronic Diseases," *Hospital Social Service*, 1922, VI, pp. 401–405; L. C. Marsh, "Group Treatment of Psychoses by the Psychological Equivalent of Revival," *Mental Hygiene*, April, 1931, XV:2, pp. 328–349.

[2] See Louis Wender, "Group Psychotherapy: A Study of Its Application," *Psychiatric Quarterly*, October, 1940, XIV, pp. 715–718.

or extended to a large group. The group may be closed to new members, or new members may enter and improved members may leave. It may provide the participants with new goals without attempting to resolve their conflicts, or it may emphasize conflict resolution. It may or may not be combined with individual therapy. The therapist's role may be relatively passive or very active, depending upon the mode of therapy.

To analyze the differences and similarities of various types of group therapy, our discussion in this chapter will cover: (1) the definition of group psychotherapy, (2) the differences between individual and group treatment, (3) the roles of the therapist, (4) the function of the group, and (5) the importance of group psychotherapy in our culture.

Definition of Group Psychotherapy

Group psychotherapy, as currently practiced, has a very loose meaning. It includes within its scope, lectures to mass audiences and intensified applications of psychoanalytic techniques.[3] Yet these procedures differ because the former is a superficial form and the latter a more profound form of social relationships. In fact, the relationships can be so superficial that the term "group psychotherapy" can be abused.

For example, if a doctor cheerfully greets his patients on the ward and receives a hearty response or if a teacher "peps up" his students by a talk, presumably these relationships, in a loose sense, can be called "therapeutic." But this "therapy" is superficial, and does not correspond to a systematic conception of group psychotherapy, however intrinsically desirable and possibly beneficial these relationships may be. Though "therapeutic" results may occur in a religious revival or in other tolerant social settings, the significant difference between these forms of collective behavior and group psychotherapy resides in the explicit principles and techniques which are implemented in group psychotherapy.

By group psychotherapy we mean a controlled social process be-

[3] See Robert G. McCarthy, "Group Therapy in Alcoholism," *Quarterly Journal of Studies on Alcohol,* June, 1949, XVI, pp. 63–108; L. C. Marsh, "Group Treatment of Psychoses by Psychological Equivalent of the Revival," *Mental Hygiene,* April, 1931, XV:2, pp. 328–349; Florence Powdermaker and Jerome D. Frank, "Group Psychotherapy with Neurotics," *The American Journal of Psychiatry,* 1948, 105:6, pp. 449–456.

tween one or more therapists and two or more patients, in which the group processes are utilized to improve the conditions of the participating patients, either on a symptom or on a conflict level.[4] The therapist has explicit knowledge and techniques by which he organizes and manipulates the group or allows the group to manipulate itself for these purposes. The therapeutic processes must be known to the therapist in order for him partially or completely to guide the group. To affect this control for the more intense types of therapy, he should know something about the particular problems, conflicts, and anxiety tolerance of the members. In their more superficial forms he must know something about his role and the group dynamics which lead to improvement. But, invariably, some methods and techniques are applied for manipulating the group and for guiding the specified functions and role of the therapist. For this reason the size of the group becomes important. Though Schilder limited his group to eight persons, and others have had many more persons, about twenty members would tend to approach the limit for intensive therapy when one therapist is present. In general, it would seem that the larger the group the more superficial the therapy would tend to become, because the group dynamics could not be controlled so readily.

Individual and Group Psychotherapy

Individual and group psychotherapy differ, but in many ways they supplement each other.

The participant has a different experience when he verbalizes his problem in a group than when he communicates with a single person. The atmosphere of secrecy and privacy declines. Usually he has to inhibit his attitudes to a greater degree than when with one individual. He does not receive the exclusive attention of the therapist but must compete with others for his attention. But by competing and yet feeling accepted in this milieu, he experiences the usual types of social relationships because a variety of persons are judging and responding to his behavior. The group thus provides a "social reality" to his participation. His desires become socialized into

[4] Bruno Solby regards group psychotherapy as a "psychotherapeutic process which results from group interaction." Bruno Solby, "Group Psychotherapy and Psychodramatic Method," *Group Psychotherapy*, edited by J. L. Moreno, p. 248 (New York: Beacon House, Inc., 1948).

group norms and into common standards by his interaction with other members. This is more difficult to achieve with an individual therapist.

The individual therapist usually has to create a certain social distance between himself and the patient. Though he may understand the patient's difficulties, he does not reveal his own. In the group, many participants discuss their personal problems. Each individual finds that he shares some things in common with many persons: all want to be accepted; all have personal problems which they want to understand; and all usually want to improve. Some find that their problems are similar to others', and, in discovering this emotional kinship, their self-reproach and feelings of isolation decline.[5] Because of these permissive and mutually identifying relationships, each member finds a social setting in which he is encouraged, even stimulated, to become more expansive and communicative. The more timid and more inhibited participants become encouraged by the more aggressive ones to express themselves. They become less hesitant and less reluctant to reveal personal conflicts after one or more persons have divulged their problems.[6]

The participant's self-condemnation and lack of confidence are counteracted by the group and by the leader therapist.[7] Should an individual member express misgivings about his prospects of improvement, or about the need of resolving his problems, or about the worth of the group itself, he will be resisted by other members, for any group that strives to survive evolves a set of objectives and a morale to justify and to sustain its existence, however unwitting this process may be. In effective group psychotherapy the identity of the collectivity and its survival center around the improvement of the members. Individuals who have been partially or completely stigmatized and isolated by the community, whether for alcoholism, for personal disorders, for physical handicaps, or for other reasons, intensify a "social hunger" for acceptance.[8] When accepted and

[5] Schilder says: "In a group, the patients realize with astonishment that the thoughts which have seemed to isolate them are common to all of them." Paul Schilder, "Results and Problems of Group Psychotherapy in Severe Neuroses," *Mental Hygiene,* 1939, XXXII, p. 91.

[6] J. W. Klapman, *Group Psychotherapy: Theory and Practice,* p. 138.

[7] *Ibid.,* pp. 87, 88.

[8] The term "social hunger" has been used mainly by Slavson. See S. R. Slavson, *An Introduction to Group Therapy,* p. 15 (New York: Commonwealth Fund, 1943).

able to express themselves in a tolerant social setting, they acquire a feeling of "belonging" to a real group.[9] The group becomes an outlet of prime importance. It reduces the loneliness, the isolation, and the self-consciousness which so many of those going into group psychotherapy feel. It strengthens their tolerance because it lifts their conceptions of themselves.

Though acceptance and tolerance operate in individual psychotherapy too, these processes are not as informal or as convincing as in groups. Moreover, the therapeutic context becomes more academic and artificial with a single person, because the patient has to assign a variety of roles to him. In the group the variety of roles of many individuals are expressed in actual social relationships by the approval or disapproval, the encouragement or discouragement of the other participants. For example, no matter how well a child or adolescent may interact with a single therapist, this relationship is only a substitute or a preparation for actual relationship with his peers. In other words, the individual participant has living models whose images he can internalize in the process of socializing in the group, and whose images can replace the former images he has had of other persons.

In the group, each member participates in these ways: (1) He describes his experiences, (2) he hears problems somewhat similar to his own discussed (Moreno has referred to this phenomenon as "spectator therapy"), and (3) he may provide solutions to the problems of others; by so doing, he may detect faults in others which are similar to his own. Moreover, the impetus of the group is greater in its effect upon the individual than in the relationship with a single therapist. Menninger points out:[10]

> There were certain advantages in group psychotherapy which were not obtainable in individual therapy. The social factor could be capitalized upon when selection considered distinctive types of behavior or symptomatology. A group, if effective, developed a unit morale, an identification of the members with each other. Often a

[9] As Schilder points out, the similarity of attitudes among the group which are called out by the expressions of a particular individual differentiate group psychotherapy from individual therapy and make it closer to real social living. "Results and Problems of Group Psychotherapy in Severe Neuroses," *Mental Hygiene*, p. 91.

[10] William C. Menninger, *Psychiatry in a Troubled World*, p. 316 (New York: The Macmillan Company, 1948). Reprinted by permission.

patient might be able to see symptomatic behavior similar to his own with more objectivity when it was presented by a fellow patient in a group discussion. . . . The opinion of the entire group often molded the point of view of its individual members toward that same problem in themselves.

Thus, group psychotherapy can be a resocializing and relearning, and a growth process like individual therapy. Since patients develop mutually identifying rather than mere utilitarian relationships, they can become more confident in developing friendships or love attachments. For example, it was found that friendships which had begun in hospital therapy sessions were retained in posthospital friendships.[11]

Group psychotherapy, however, as presently administered, usually does not resolve profound personal conflicts as effectively as does individual therapy. Perhaps under given conditions a type of group can be organized to cope with these problems, as we shall discuss later. Yet, as group psychotherapy usually is conducted, this is not evident. Friend and Sullivan, Klapman, Slavson, and Menninger have found that group psychotherapy did not deal successfully with profound personal conflicts.[12]

Thus, the two modes of therapy can supplement each other. In the group the therapist can select those persons who require intensive individual treatment. Those persons who require individual attention reveal these behavior patterns: they become very anxious when revealing their own experiences or when hearing the experiences of others; they become very shamed or panicky by the therapist's interpretations, or cannot tolerate the therapist's interpretations of other members' problems because these problems are too close to their own.[13]

[11] J. W. Klapman, Group Psychotherapy: Theory and Practice, pp. 88, 89.
[12] Maurice Friend and Walter F. Sullivan, "Group Psychotherapy in an Army General Hospital Relating to Civilian Readjustment," American Journal of Orthopsychiatry, April, 1947, XVII:2, p. 257; J. W. Klapman, Group Psychotherapy: Theory and Practice, pp. 134, 199, 200; S. R. Slavson, Introduction to Group Therapy, pp. 173–175 (New York: Commonwealth Fund, 1930); S. R. Slavson, "Differential Dynamics of Activity and Interview Group Therapy," American Journal of Orthopsychiatry, April, 1947, XVII:2, p. 300; William C. Menninger, Psychiatry in a Troubled World, pp. 316–317.
[13] S. R. Slavson, "Differential Dynamics of Activity and Interview Group Therapy," p. 299.

Role of the Therapist

Usually the therapist is the social catalyst of the group, as well as the leader and authority symbol. His attitudes and relationships with the group set the stage for the general conditions which prevail in the group matrix, both in formation and in process. Though the therapist may not form the type of group he precisely desires, he can influence its goals, modes of relationships, and degree of solidarity. His chief function usually is to set the group processes in motion. As a permissive figure he can encourage the members to feel accepted, to participate socially, and to verbalize their problems. Yet he can resist undue aggression, hostility, and intensified self-centeredness, which disrupt the therapeutic function of the group.

His control over the members, in addition to his official role, resides in knowing their personal problems and their anxiety tolerance. By leading the discussions he can stimulate the group to develop eventually a mode of indigenous participation.

Psychiatrists who are individually oriented tend to apply the dynamics of individual psychotherapy into the group by emphasizing transference to the leader.[14] This psychoanalytic take-off in therapy, however necessary, sometimes can restrain constructive group processes, for bilateral relationships between therapist and patient may merely mean individual therapy in a group setting. Also, some psychiatrists do not find group psychotherapy appealing because their roles are not as absolute as with a single individual.[15] Moreover, medical and psychiatric traditions are such that problems are kept secret rather than shared in a group.[16] On the other hand, it may be that psychiatrists who are expansive with groups are less sensitized to individual feelings.[17]

[14] A basic reference for many group therapists is Sigmund Freud, Group Psychology and the Analysis of the Ego (London: International Press, 1922).

[15] Schilder maintains that the patient does not surrender and submit as completely in group psychotherapy as he does in individual psychotherapy. See Paul Schilder, "Results and Problems of Group Psychotherapy in Severe Neuroses," Mental Hygiene, pp. 88, 89. See Giles W. Thomas, "Group Psychotherapy: A Review of the Recent Literature," Psychosomatic Medicine, April, 1943, V:2, pp. 166–180.

[16] Giles W. Thomas, "Group Psychotherapy: A Review of the Recent Literature," p. 166.

[17] Roy R. Grinker and John P. Spiegel, Men Under Stress, p. 385 (Philadelphia: The Blakiston Company, 1945); also Pauline Rosenthal, "The Death of the Leader in Group Psychotherapy," American Journal of Orthopsychiatry, April, 1947, XVII:2, p. 266.

Although therapists usually start the therapeutic process, they have no uniform procedure, because treatment aims differ and because group therapy is still in a fluid state. Some discuss the purposes with the members individually, and others with the whole group. The topics for discussion vary with the types of patients. There is, however, some agreement about the initial approach and the topics of discussion for neurotic patients.[18] The therapist may present the function of the defenses in human behavior, or show the connection between biological symptoms and personal conflicts, which may be important. Generally, he reaches for common and essential problems.[19]

Therapeutic roles, however, differ with the mode of therapy and with the types of patients. On the one extreme, in activity groups for children the therapist's contact with the group is personal but indirect, "because the greatest therapeutic value is derived from the children's contact with each other." [20] In discussion groups with adolescents and adults the therapist has to enter actively into the network of relations. Frequently the leader in discussions, he becomes appraised more as a real person who agrees, disagrees, and points the ways to solution. On the other extreme, with severe neurotics, the therapist's role becomes vital and very active.[21] Powdermaker and Frank maintain that in these instances the therapist is the most important single person in the group, and that the therapeutic process revolves about him.[22] For his aim is to resolve deep anxiety conflicts. Yet this type of role, as well as the integrational processes of the group, is built up slowly, sometimes during more than ninety sessions. Group therapy of this type is no parsimonious timesaver but becomes a distinct mode of treatment. As in individual therapy, the therapist must be aware of his short-

[18] Klapman maintains that despite different procedures in group psychotherapy, they tend to approach a certain uniformity. Group Psychotherapy: Theory and Practice, p. 151.

[19] Maurice Friend and Walter F. Sullivan, "Group Psychotherapy in an Army General Hospital Relating to Civilian Readjustment," pp. 258, 259.

[20] S. R. Slavson, Introduction to Group Psychotherapy, p. 175; Fritz Redl, "Group Psychological Elements in Discipline Problems," American Journal of Orthopsychiatry, 1943, XIII, pp. 77–80, found it desirable to make interpretations to the children on the spot.

[21] Paul Schilder, "Introductory Remarks on Groups," Journal of Social Psychology, 1940, XII, p. 83.

[22] Florence Powdermaker and Jerome D. Frank, "Group Psychotherapy with Neurotics," The American Journal of Psychiatry, December, 1948, 105:6, p. 451.

comings and his anxieties and must achieve an emotional independence from the group.[23]

With children as well as with adolescents, the therapist also serves as a role model. This is especially true when the child or adolescent has been rejected by his own parents and needs a parental figure with whom to identify. As Slavson said, of one typical case: "Although Ivor did not express it in so many words, the group therapist was a major factor in his life. . . . The image of a man who was kind and calm counteracted his phantasy that masculinity was evil, destructive, and something to fear and reject." [24] But there may be competition among some members "to possess" the therapist for himself, or to get his exclusive attention, or to create some nonverbal understandings. Though this is especially evident among children, it also exists among adolescents and adults. Little and Konopka point out that, under such circumstances, the therapist should encourage closer ties between the child and other group members.[25] Powdermaker and Frank state that patients may try to cultivate an illusory understanding with the therapist by trying to catch his eye. Should the participants elicit responses which they can interpret as revealing a special bond, the group can become disrupted.[26]

In brief, although the therapist's role has certain common features, his role varies with the objectives of therapy and with the type of patients. When the aim is to get the patients to participate socially, the therapist may provide a permissive setting and then retire into the background. When concerted discussion occurs, the therapist becomes more active, but even then his role differs with the intensity and depth of the interpretations. When participants express traumatic and anxious experiences, the therapist must exert more active control and deliberate intercession, for his interpretations become more profound and can arouse more easily the anxieties of the other members. Hence, the participants must identify more closely with him and with each other and must feel secure enough to want to express their conflicts.

[23] *Ibid.*, p. 451.

[24] S. R. Slavson, *Introduction to Group Psychotherapy*, p. 272.

[25] Harry M. Little and Gisela Konopka, "Group Therapy in a Child Guidance Center," *American Journal of Orthopsychiatry*, April, 1947, XVII:2, p. 309.

[26] Florence Powdermaker and Jerome D. Frank, "Group Psychotherapy with Neurotics," p. 452.

Functions of the Group

As distinct from the spontaneously organized group, the therapeutic group controls and orients its social relationships around treatment purposes. Competition and hostility decrease; group permissiveness is augmented to encourage self-confidence and insight among the members. These ends are attained by (1) group homogeneity, (2) group socialization, and (3) re-education through interpretation and example.

Collective homogeneity is attained both by the therapist's screening process and by the self-elimination of some members. Before the group is formed, prospective members are usually interviewed for selective purposes.[27] In most groups the participants thus have some problems in common. For example, if neurotics are to be treated, settled psychotics who have deeper problems or psychopaths who would disrupt the group are eliminated. Some members who find the discussions unsatisfactory drop out. The more homogeneous the members, the more likely it is that they will be able to share their experiences. Solby gives three criteria for likeness of the members: (1) symptoms, (2) social status, and (3) formulated goals.[28] If the group is not very homogeneous, it may break up into informal subgroups and cliques which may accentuate intragroup hostility and disrupt the collective solidarity; for an informal organization grows up within a formal social structure, and this informal organization may lack therapeutic effectiveness. This principle is especially applicable when the therapist's intercession is not very frequent and when the group is the chief treatment agent. Slavson cautions:[29]

A therapy group stands or falls on the insight and skill in grouping. Essentially, the group must consist of children who potentially have therapeutic value to one another. Obviously, a beaten down and rejected child would only be traumatized if he were assigned to a group where he would be beaten and persecuted. A frightened, withdrawn and sensitive child becomes only more frightened and withdrawn in a tumultuous and aggressive environment. If these children are each

[27] See S. R. Slavson, *An Introduction to Group Therapy*, pp. 119–136.
[28] Bruno Solby, "Group Psychotherapy and the Psychodramatic Method," *Group Psychotherapy*, edited by J. L. Moreno, p. 289 (New York: Beacon House, Inc., 1948).
[29] S. R. Slavson, "Group Therapy: Principles and Dynamics," *American Journal of Orthopsychiatry*, 1943, XIII, p. 654.

to be helped to make better social adaptations and overcome their personality problems they must have an environment in which their particular difficulties are counteracted and their needs are met. This is accomplished through a planned group in which interpersonal relations have in the long run positive values for every participant.

Since the therapeutic group usually fulfills a companionship need, it becomes emotionally supportive, because the members have a mutual need for each other. It calls out a desired tendency among the members that they "belong." It awakens a personal determination which the isolated individual ordinarily lacks. It makes individual behavior more meaningful because each person acquires approved goals to which he can aspire. The channels of companionship seem to be the common denominator of group psychotherapy and must be achieved in a group rather than with a single therapist. The anxieties and fears about being rejected by other persons tend to fade with social participation; the individual derives a different image of himself—one that is more acceptable because it is approved by others. Schilder points out that "social neurotics" who benefited from group participation were not responsive to individual treatment.[30]

The group provides the pragmatic testing ground for personality changes,[31] for the individual can respond to criticism and to hostility of others and can express his own feelings to a variety of persons who are judging him differently. The fact that the individual participant can act out his attitudes in a group context gives them a "reality," because his behavior acquires a social meaning by the responses of the other members. In brief, the most important effect of this permissive atmosphere is upon the self. First, it creates the tolerant attitudes which enable the individual participant to become more free in his expression. Second, the social approval tends to raise his self-conception. Third, the individual revises his images and expectations of other persons and hence feels less restrained in participating with them.[32]

By re-education the group participant acquires those tendencies

[30] Paul Schilder, "Results and Problems of Group Psychotherapy in Severe Neuroses," *Mental Hygiene,* 1939, p. 96. "Many of the cases treated in this group could not have been treated individually. They reacted only in the group. . . . This is especially true of the social neuroses."

[31] *Ibid.,* p. 96.

[32] George H. Mead, *Mind, Self and Society,* p. 213 (Chicago: University of Chicago Press, 1934).

to comport himself acceptably, and sometimes more aggressively, with others. The participant learns how to co-operate and becomes more amenable to self-correction and enhances the estimate of his self-worth. To this point the therapeutic process would reside in increasing one's favorable self-estimate, or what Thomas calls "repressive-inspirational" therapy.[33] Most types of group psychotherapy aspire to this objective. There is the relief that comes with expressing one's conflicts, in getting one's troubles off one's chest, and in finding new goals. Though superficial insight may result, still this procedure does not plumb deeply enough for the individual to resolve his conflicts.

In "insight therapy," re-education is more profound. The group would have to be smaller and more cohesive in order to control the discussions more effectively and to cope with the resurgence of anxiety. The social intimacy is greater; personal and "embarrassing" experiences are revealed and become part of the conversations and of the interpretations; sometimes it is quite difficult for an individual to withstand such personal interpretations in a group. The patient demands more emotional support to endure his anxiety. Should hostility prevail, the individual may hesitate, or be unable, to divulge upsetting intimate experiences. In addition, if the group members are hostile, the particular member either will not accept the interpretations or will become demoralized in the process. But by overidentifying with other members, the others may not discern their difficulties. The optimum type of social distance lies somewhere between these extremes. Powdermaker and Frank maintain that disturbing materials can be best handled by the therapist who should become more accepting. This can help the group to withstand the disturbing experiences and can reduce individual anxiety and guilt. When hostility between two individuals becomes intense, the therapist may encourage them to analyze the meaning of their hostility.[34] On occasion it may be necessary for the therapist to divert the hostility to himself.

[33] Giles W. Thomas, "Group Psychotherapy: A Review of the Recent Literature," *Psychosomatic Medicine,* April, 1943, V:2. "The general trend in repressive-inspirational psychotherapy is to urge the patient to control himself, to suppress asocial or worrisome thoughts or wishes, and to find an interest or inspiration in life, work, the community, religion, etc."

[34] Florence Powdermaker and Jerome D. Frank, "Group Psychotherapy with Neurotics," p. 452.

When the revelation of emotional and personal problems becomes the medium for improvement, improvement becomes the competitive basis for status. Certain practices are accepted in which interpretation becomes permissive. This pooled "reality testing" of ascertaining ways of adjusting more adequately becomes the content in the discussion of the group.

Some groups practiced the method of demonstrated example. A recovered patient revealed his particular problem and experiences and then showed how he benefited from the group. The new members became more optimistic about their own chances for improvement. This was found to be especially effective in group psychotherapy with discharged mental patients as well as with alcoholics.[35] Though not attempted very extensively with neurotics, its effect upon group morale and upon the individual participant probably would be beneficial, for such statements raise group morale and intensify the individual's determination for improvement.

Group Psychotherapy and Culture

Group psychotherapy is particularly applicable to the urban society. First, many persons are isolated and feel socially excluded. Second, because of the heterogeneous values, many persons become confused and feel life is purposeless.[36] Third, many can become depressed or anxious because of intensified competition. These aspects of the social process are so pervasive that group psychotherapy becomes peculiarly congenial to offset this process. By contrast, the intimate homogeneous folk society would have no need for this type of therapy. Moreover, the varied religious rituals in the intimate sacred society provide outlets for these needs. In the secular, impersonal urban society there are few such concerted outlets.

The chief importance of group psychotherapy pertains to the reincorporation of isolated individuals into the group. In this

[35] Abraham A. Low, "The Combined System of Group Psychotherapy and Self Help as Practiced by Recovery, Inc.," *Group Psychotherapy*, edited by J. L. Moreno (New York: Beacon House, Inc., 1948).

[36] See Paul Schilder, "Social Organization and Psychotherapy," *American Journal of Orthopsychiatry*, 1940, X:4, pp. 911, 912; also "The Analysis of Ideologies as a Psychotherapeutic Method, Especially in Group Treatment," *American Journal of Orthopsychiatry*, 1936, 93, pp. 601–604.

respect it has a singular function in our culture. This group incorporation is significant for the many isolated and rejected children; for the many "socially neurotic" adults; for socially ostracized persons such as the discharged mental-hospital patient, the alcoholic, the convict, and the ex-convict. Although we have confined our discussion to the group treatment of neurotics and mild psychotics, it is apparent that its application to other types of persons usually has been successful. The group practices of Recovery Inc. and of Alcoholics Anonymous have been rather successful despite the relatively elementary techniques used.[37] This success in large part has been due to the need of the participants for having social relationships and acquiring purposive goals. The extension of these techniques to convicts and ex-convicts has not been attempted, although its pertinence to their specific problems cannot be doubted, for some criminals as well as ex-convicts are isolated persons who have different outlooks and values and who are more or less excluded from conventional groups. The kinds of friendly associations that can be fostered, and that in the process lead to revised outlooks concerning themselves and their social positions, may be of definite importance to their rehabilitation.[38]

The aged are also in a position in which they have to learn to redefine their roles in the family and in the society at large. Group psychotherapy would not only provide this re-educative facet; it would also lead to mutually identifying relationships among the aged and thus pave the way for post-therapy friendships.

Results of Group Psychotherapy. The results of group therapy have been appraised rather loosely. The terms "improved," "benefited," "recovered," and "cured" have varying meanings for different therapists and are often based upon the version of the particular therapist. Yet the therapists generally report favorable results. Slavson found that many children in activity groups improved.[39] In a follow-up study of 105 children Lowrey found that 74 improved and 27 did not.[40] Schilder reports that of 31 neurotic

---

[37] Abraham A. Low, "The Combined System of Group Psychotherapy and Self Help as Practiced by Recovery, Inc.," *Group Psychotherapy*, edited by J. L. Moreno, pp. 94–99.

[38] Moreno has suggested this possibility.

[39] S. R. Slavson, "Group Therapy: Principles and Dynamics," *American Journal of Orthopsychiatry*, 1943, XIII, p. 202.

[40] Lawson G. Lowrey, "Group Therapy: Special Section Meetings," *American Journal of Orthopsychiatry*, 1943, pp. 648–691.

patients whom he treated, 9 were "cured," 15 "improved," and 6 were "unimproved," and 1 stopped treatment.[41]

Bierer found that 87 per cent of a group of 70 neurotics and recent psychotics were sufficiently recovered to be discharged from the hospital. But his therapy consisted mainly of individual therapy and an activity program.[42] It is not known, however, whether these patients would have improved spontaneously.

Lazell followed up several hundred patients who received group psychotherapy in a hospital for ten to twelve years. Many maintained a social adjustment consistent with their abilities and social status.[43]

Olnick and Friend, by means of "indirect group therapy" for neurotic soldiers with the intent of raising the "efficiency security and satisfaction," found that improvement varied between 50 and 58 per cent of the cases; however, they made no claim for "cure."[44]

Klopfer measured by the Rorschach Test the change of soldiers diagnosed as anxiety-ridden. He found that after three weeks of daily sessions, 3 improved markedly but 6 showed slight improvement.[45] Rashkis and Shaskan, by using the Minnesota Multiphasic Test prior to and after therapy on 22 battle casualties, found that they improved in all the nine categories of the test except psychopathic deviate.[46]

From the results of these diverse types of group therapy, it appears that many participants benefited—particularly those who had been rejected by or excluded from "natural" groups. The extent of the improvement varies with the types of therapy and with the types of subjects. As yet, these facts have not been precisely determined. More intensive research is necessary to ascertain which modes of therapy are effective with what types of patients, why

[41] Paul Schilder, "Results and Problems of Group Psychotherapy in Severe Neuroses," *Mental Hygiene,* 1939, 23, p. 97.

[42] J. Bierer, "Group Psychotherapy," *British Medical Journal,* 1942, I, pp. 214–217.

[43] E. W. Lazell, "The Group Treatment of Dementia Praecox by Mental Re-education," *U.S. Veteran's Bureau Medical Bulletin,* 1930, VI, pp. 733–747.

[44] Stanley L. Olnick and Maurice R. Friend, "Indirect Group Therapy of Psychoneurotic Soldiers," *Psychiatry,* 1945, VIII, pp. 147–153.

[45] W. G. Klopfer, "The Efficacy of Group Therapy as Indicated by Group Rorschach Records," *Rorschach Research Exchange,* 1945, IX, pp. 207–209.

[46] H. A. Rashkis and Donald A. Shaskan, "The Effects of Group Psychotherapy on Personality Inventory Scores," *American Journal of Orthopsychiatry,* 1946, XVI, pp. 345–349.

certain patients drop out, and why certain patients are not helped by the particular mode of group therapy.

Group Psychotherapy as an Area of Research. Group psychotherapy has usually been handled by psychiatrists and by clinicians. It is not surprising that the research has had a psychiatric emphasis. Yet the study of group phenomena has been the hub of sociological endeavor. The functions of group psychotherapy thus provide an apt meeting ground for joint sociological and psychiatric exploration and research.

A joint research study, in which the psychiatrist would investigate the effects of group therapy upon the individual member and in which the sociologist noted the sequential changes in the group processes, would be extremely profitable. Clinard has called attention to the effects of the group upon personality reorganization.[47] Since sociologists and social psychologists have studied the interactional processes of small groups, this knowledge may become increasingly helpful for studying group therapeutic processes.[48] Since the psychiatrist and clinician are concerned with the therapeutic outcome of the individual, their interests are primarily normative. The sociologists would be concerned with the collective and the individual processes that go on in group therapy. For example, they would be concerned with the differential social processes in supportive group therapy and in analytical group therapy, with the kinds of common meanings among children's groups as over against adolescent and adult groups, and with the individuals who respond favorably and those who respond unfavorably in treatment groups.

It would be of interest to know how the individual participant's self-conception is affected by his diverse modes of participation. The participant's self-conception may be affected merely by allowing him to confess his conflicts. His self-conception may be affected by collective approval and by his subsequent identification with the group. His self-conception may be raised by identifying with the therapist. To what extent do these identifications carry over after the individual has left the group? How do actual learning skills in group psychotherapy affect the participants' capacity in initiating

[47] Marshall B. Clinard, "The Group Approach to Social Reintegration," *American Sociological Review,* April, 1949, XIV, pp. 257–262; Karl Mannheim, *Diagnosis of Our Time,* pp. 73–94 (London: Routledge and Kegan Paul, Ltd., 1943).

[48] Robert F. Bales, *Interaction Process Analysis* (Cambridge, Mass.: Addison-Wesley Press, Inc., 1950).

and in sustaining relationships outside the therapy group? In brief, the individual-group nexus as a source of therapy has not been sufficiently explored by sociologists.

Another allied but peripheral interest to group therapy concerns the effects of spontaneous groups upon personal reorganization. Although the emphasis of group therapy is upon its concerted and explicit principles and practices, still there are inherent therapeutic processes in spontaneously formed groups. Though the therapeutic potentialities of various spontaneously formed groups have been mentioned, they have not been very thoroughly explored.[49] In redirecting the objectives and practices of delinquents, it has been found feasible to work with groups by influencing the so-called natural leaders, and by having the others follow the leader's pattern. Certainly, revivals and other forms of collective behavior create mutually accepting attitudes among the participants. Thus far, personality changes which occur in group revivals and in sectarian movements have not been studied intensively. Yet these social movements provide outlets and sources of satisfaction for certain basic needs of the participants. Furthermore, the individual, by selecting groups to satisfy his basic personal needs, is unwittingly searching for a type of companionship which will offset his self-consciousness and facilitate his personal development, for these specific groups provide meanings and purposes which the individual frequently cannot achieve alone. In the urban community the alternatives for selection of different groups is much greater than among other types of settlements. This area of inquiry, however peripheral to direct group therapy, certainly would cast light upon the informal social processes which facilitate or retard personal development. A joint sociological and psychiatric study of this type would very likely yield profitable findings concerning the processes of personality change.

Summary

Group psychotherapy is a distinct treatment process in which the group and the therapist are the treatment agents. In contrast to individual therapy, secrecy and privacy diminish. The individual has to compete with others for attention of the therapist and be-

[49] See Nathan W. Ackerman, "Dynamic Patterns in Group Psychotherapy," *Psychiatry*, November, 1944, 7:4, pp. 341–348.

comes responsive to a variety of persons. He finds that other persons have problems somewhat similar to his own, that all want to be socially accepted, and that all want to improve. The collective morale and identity that emerge encourage the isolated and timid person to increase his confidence, to become more socially active, and to feel that the therapeutic context is more real than in individual therapy. Through the hastening of individual-therapist attachment because of the group impetus, the more profound problems that require individual therapy can be selected from the group.

Though the therapist aims to place the therapeutic processes in motion, his role differs with the treatment aims, with the methods used, and with the types of patients. The function of the group can be gauged by its homogeneity, by its permissiveness by which the individual feels accepted, by its re-educative procedures in discussion of personal problems, and by demonstrated examples of improved patients. Research in group psychotherapy is scant. The methods and techniques of group psychotherapy are relatively indefinite as compared with individual therapy, and they are not so effective for profound personal problems. Nonetheless, the application of group therapy is peculiarly congenial for ameliorating the condition of the many isolated persons in our society.

Selected Readings

Abrahams, J., and Lloyd W. McCorkle, "Group Psychotherapy of Military Offenders," *American Journal of Sociology*, March, 1946, LI:5, pp. 455–464.

Ackerman, Nathan W., "The Psychiatric Viewpoint in Group Therapy," *American Journal of Orthopsychiatry*, 1943, XIII, pp. 678–687.

Clinard, Marshall B., "The Group Approach to Social Reintegration," *American Sociological Review*, April, 1949, 14, pp. 257–262.

Friend, Maurice R., and Stanley L. Olnick, "Therapy through a Group of Neurotic Soldiers in an Experimental Military Setting," *American Journal of Orthopsychiatry*, 1945, 15, pp. 483–488.

Hadden, S. B., "Group Psychotherapy: A Superior Method of Treating Larger Numbers of Neurotic Patients," *The American Journal of Psychiatry*, July, 1944, 101, pp. 68, 69.

Harms, Ernest, "Group Therapy—Farce, Fashion or Sociologically Sound," *The Nervous Child*, April, 1945, IV:3, pp. 186–195.

Klapman, J. W., *Group Psychotherapy: Theory and Practice* (New York: Grune & Stratton, Inc., 1946).

McCarthy, Raymond G., "Group Therapy in Alcoholism," *Quarterly Journal of Studies on Alcohol,* June, 1949, X:1, pp. 63–108.

Moreno, L. J. (editor), *Group Psychotherapy: A Symposium* (New York: Beacon House, Inc., 1948).

Paster, Samuel, "Group Psychotherapy in an Army General Hospital," *Mental Hygiene,* October, 1944, XXVIII:4, pp. 1–8.

Powdermaker, Florence, and Jerome D. Frank, "Group Psychotherapy with Neurotics," *The American Journal of Psychiatry,* December, 1948, 105:6, pp. 449–456.

Schilder, Paul, *Psychotherapy* (New York: W. W. Norton & Company, 1938).

———, "Results and Problems of Group Psychotherapy in Severe Neuroses," *Mental Hygiene,* January, 1939, XXIII:I, pp. 87–99.

———, "Social Organization and Psychotherapy," *American Journal of Orthopsychiatry,* 1940, X:4, pp. 911–915.

Schwartz, L. A., "Group Psychotherapy in the War Neuroses," *The American Journal of Psychiatry,* 1945, 101, pp. 498–500.

Shaskan, Donald A., "Must Individual and Group Psychotherapy Be Opposed?" *American Journal of Orthopsychiatry,* April, 1947, XVII:2, pp. 290–292.

Slavson, S. R., *An Introduction to Group Therapy* (New York: Commonwealth Fund, 1943).

———, "Differential Dynamics of Activity and Interview Group Therapy," *American Journal of Orthopsychiatry,* April, 1947, XVII:2, pp. 293–302.

Thomas, Giles W., "Group Psychotherapy: A Review of the Recent Literature," *Psychosomatic Medicine,* April, 1943, V:2, pp. 166–180.

Wender, Louis, "The Dynamics of Group Therapy and Its Applications," *Journal of Nervous and Mental Disease,* July, 1936, 84:1, pp. 715–718.

PART IV

Care and Custody

CHAPTER FIFTEEN

The Mental Hospital

In the past section we have described the modes of treatment relationships among persons who have been able to participate in the community. In this section our concern is with those persons who have become so emotionally disabled by their disorders that they are no longer able to participate in the community and hence have to be removed to the more protected environment of the mental hospital.

Scope of the Problem

The problem of caring for disordered persons of this type is not a small one. In sheer numbers it is greater than cancer, tuberculosis, and infantile paralysis combined. More than 200,000 new patients enter mental hospitals yearly.[1] Mental illness, in personal or organic form, strikes about 1 in 5 families, and about 1 in 13 people during the course of a lifetime. Out of 263 persons, 1 is in a mental hospital.[2] According to some estimates, more than 1,000,000 people will require mental hospital care in the next ten years.[3] Over 45 per cent of this number will be committed for personality disorders. Obviously, the task of caring for and treating so vast a group is enormous. Yet the group of disordered persons who require hospitalization is not static and fixed but continually changing. We can perhaps get a clearer conception of the direction and scope of this

[1] *Group for the Advancement of Psychiatry*, Report No. 7, March, 1949, p. 2.

[2] Illinois Department of Finance, *A Budget Survey of State Mental Hospitals*, p. 23.

[3] John Appel, "Our State Hospitals: What We Can Do to Improve Them," *Round Table, The University of Chicago*, No. 496, September 21, 1947, p. 2.

problem by answering the following queries: To what extent are first admissions increasing in mental hospitals? In what proportions are the disordered types committed to public and private hospitals? Why are resident patients in state mental hospitals increasing? What effect does this increase have upon the care of patients? How in general does the hospital help or hinder the patients' improvement?

The Increase of First Admissions. The first admissions of persons to mental hospitals for permanent care increased by almost 112.5 per cent in twenty-four years. In 1922 there were 71,993 first admissions; in 1946 there were 153,025 first admissions. During and since World War II, the sharpest increases have been in the veterans hospitals. The state hospitals, however, have shown a slow but continual increase through the years.

TABLE 9

FIRST ADMISSIONS TO MENTAL HOSPITALS FOR PERMANENT CARE, BY TYPE OF HOSPITAL, 1922 TO 1946 *

Year	Total	State	Veterans	City and County	Private
1946	153,025	89,299	30,136	3,018	30,572
1941	113,181	84,201	5,320	6,968	16,692
1936	105,994	76,309	3,565	7,908	18,212
1933	94,689	69,368			
1922	71,993	52,472			

* Data from *Patients in Mental Institutions* (Washington, D.C.: Bureau of the Census, U.S. Department of Commerce, 1949).

From 1936 to 1946 the total admissions to mental hospitals increased by almost 50 per cent: The state mental hospitals, which have the preponderant number of first admissions, increased by 17.0 per cent; the veterans hospitals, as a result of World War II and its aftermath, increased in first admissions more than ninefold; the private hospitals about doubled their first admissions. But the city and county hospitals declined in numbers of first admissions by more than one half. Although those seeking private care and treatment are increasing, the care and treatment of disordered persons generally is a state and Federal matter, rather than a local affair. In the long-run period, it may become largely a state matter. The present rise of admissions in veterans hospitals is an early aftermath of World War II, and it remains to be seen whether or not this trend will continue in the future.

First Admissions to Hospitals by Diagnostic Types. During the past twelve years, schizophrenic and aged psychotics—i.e., senile psychotics and arteriosclerotics—have been entering the mental hospitals in increasing proportions. During this time, paretics, whose psychotic behavior has resulted from syphilis, and manic depressives

TABLE 10

DIAGNOSIS OF FIRST ADMISSIONS WITH PSYCHOSIS TO HOSPITALS FOR PERMANENT CARE OF PSYCHIATRIC PATIENTS, FOR THE UNITED STATES, 1936 TO 1946, BY PER CENT DISTRIBUTION[*]

Psychosis	1946	1945	1944	1943	1942	1941	1940	1939	1938	1937	1936
Dementia praecox (schizophrenia)	24.6	26.1	26.1	24.4	23.0	22.8	22.5	22.4	22.7	22.2	21.8
With cerebral arteriosclerosis	13.0	13.4	13.6	14.0	14.2	13.8	13.5	13.5	12.8	12.4	12.0
Senile	11.2	11.1	11.5	11.7	11.1	10.1	9.6	9.0	9.2	9.1	9.4
Manic-depressive	10.0	10.8	10.6	10.3	11.2	10.8	11.5	11.9	13.1	13.5	14.0
Psychoneurosis	9.7	6.3	5.2	4.7	4.5	4.7	4.9	4.5	4.5	4.1	4.0
Involutional psychoses	5.7	5.0	4.7	4.7	4.9	4.8	5.0	4.5	4.1	3.9	3.5
General paresis	5.0	5.7	5.9	6.6	7.4	7.7	7.9	8.6	8.4	8.1	8.3
Alcoholic	4.7	4.2	3.5	4.9	5.1	5.5	5.3	5.1	5.3	6.0	5.8
Other	16.1	17.4	18.9	18.5	18.6	19.8	19.8	20.4	19.9	20.6	21.2

[*] Data taken from *Patients in Mental Institutions*, p. 20, 1945; p. 19, 1946 (Washington, D.C.: Bureau of the Census, U.S. Department of Commerce).

have remained the same or are seemingly decreasing in proportion.[4] In 1936 the proportion of schizophrenics entering mental hospitals was 21.8 per cent of the total commitments. In 1946 they constituted 24.6 per cent. In 1936 the combined percentage of senile psychotics and arteriosclerotics was 21.4, and in 1946 it was 24.2. The manic-depressive admissions declined during these years from 14.0 to 10.0 per cent, and general paretics also declined from 8.3 to 4.0 per cent of the total admissions. As we shall see, the increase has been predominantly among patients over 65 years of age.

[4] For an analysis of this trend by diagnostic types in New York state hospitals, which is the same as for the nation, see Benjamin Malzberg, "Patients in the New York Civil State Hospitals," *Psychiatric Quarterly*, 1948, 22:3, pp. 495–515.

Admission to State Mental-Hospitals by Age. The most conspicuous fact about patients admitted into mental hospitals is the increase of persons over 65 years of age. This trend is consistent with the general increase of aged people in the United States. In 1920, persons 65 years of age and over comprised 4.7 per cent of the total population, but in 1940 they comprised 7.9 per cent of the total population.[5] In 1933, persons 65 years of age and over comprised 16.7 per cent of the total first admissions in all mental hospitals. In 1946 this age group comprised 26.2 per cent of the total first admissions to the state mental hospitals.[6]

Since the number of people 65 years of age and over will continue to rise, it may be expected that their proportions in the state mental hospitals will also continue to rise. On the other hand, the proportions of the younger age groups admitted to mental hospitals has decreased. Persons under 35 years of age who were admitted into the state mental hospitals from 1927 to 1946 declined in proportions from about 35 per cent to 25.2 per cent of total first admissions.

Persons between the ages of 35 and 64, who comprise the largest age group to enter mental hospitals, have declined from 49.9 per cent in 1922 to 44.4 per cent in 1946. Johnson found somewhat similar results in a study of the Warren State Mental Hospital in Pennsylvania. The age group 65 and over comprised 11.6 per cent of the first admissions from 1910 to 1914, but 24.9 per cent of the total admissions from 1940 to 1944. This increase in first admissions by this aged group occurred during a general increase of first admissions by 77.2 per cent or from 1,587 patients in 1910 to 1914 to 2,813 patients in 1940 to 1944.[7]

Does the Increase of Patients in Mental Hospitals Mean an Actual Increase in Disordered Behavior? Since the number of patients in state mental hospitals and in other mental hospitals has increased so rapidly, does this increase denote an actual increase in psychoses? Those who claim that an actual increase in disordered

[5] Paul H. Landis, *Population Problems: A Cultural Interpretation,* p. 278 (New York: American Book Company, 1943).

[6] *Patients in Mental Institutions, 1933,* p. 30 (Washington, D.C.: Bureau of the Census, U.S. Department of Commerce, 1935); *Patients in Mental Institutions, 1946,* p. 81 (Washington, D.C.: Bureau of the Census, U.S. Department of Commerce, 1948).

[7] Nelson A. Johnson, "The Growing Problem of Old Age Psychoses: An Analysis of the Trend in One State Hospital from 1910 to 1944," *Mental Hygiene,* July, 1946, 30:3, pp. 431–449.

behavior has occurred have pointed to the rise of cities and to the increasing complexity of society as contributing factors.[8] On the other hand, the arguments which militate against this point of view are the following: First, the increase of urban communities and smaller homes makes it more difficult for relatives to keep the psychotic persons outside the hospital. Queer, awkward, or bizarre persons are more exposed to the judgment of others and can more likely become intolerable to their relatives and neighbors. Second, mental-hospital facilities have expanded and can accommodate more persons than before. The effects of hospital facilities upon the increased rates of admission can be shown by the differential rates among the varied sections of the country. For example, during 1943, admissions per 100,000 of the general population were higher in New England (93.4), Middle Atlantic (79.7), and Pacific (81.6) states than in the East South Central states (47.8) or the West South Central states (49.8).[9] Third, the dread and stigma of mental hospitals have lost some of their former sting, and relatives are less hesitant about committing disordered persons to state mental hospitals.

The only actual rise in disordered persons is among the aged. Although there has been a rise in the number of aged persons, there has also been an increasing unwillingness on the part of the children and other relatives to care for their disordered aged at home. Since institutions for the aged are relatively few, many aged are committed to state mental hospitals by their relatives as an easy way out. In addition, but of no less importance, is the fact that many disorders of old age are organic and not responsive to treatment.

Goldhammer and Marshall found that there was no long-time increase during the past century for the personal psychoses for persons under 50 years of age.[10] They based their conclusions upon age-specified rates of first admissions to state mental hospitals in

[8] See John Lewis Gillin, *Social Pathology*, 3rd ed., p. 137 (New York: Appleton-Century-Crofts, Inc., 1946). Mabel A. Elliott and Francis E. Merrill, *Social Disorganization*, p. 511 (New York: Harper & Brothers, 1941).

[9] *Patients in Mental Institutions, 1943*, p. 12 (Washington, D.C.: Bureau of the Census, U.S. Department of Commerce, 1946).

[10] Herbert Goldhammer and Andrew W. Marshall, *The Frequency of Mental Disease: Long Term Trends and Present Status* (Santa Monica, Calif.: The Rand Corporation, 1949).

Massachusetts. They report an increase of aged patients, which they believe is a result partly of a true increase in arteriosclerosis and largely of expanded hospital facilities.

To What Institutions Do Patients Go? More than 80 out of every 100 patients are committed to public mental hospitals and chiefly to state mental hospitals. Before the end of World War II, this rate ranged from 82 to 85 patients for every 100 patients hospitalized. Before the war, over 70 per cent of the patients went to state hospitals. Since the end of the war, and with the expansion of veterans hospitals, about 78 per cent of the patients are admitted into state and veterans hospitals. County and city hospitals—which are located mainly in the Middle West, particularly in Wisconsin and Iowa—declined in the total proportion of first admissions from 7.8 per cent in 1937 to 2.0 per cent in 1946. The care of mental patients, then, is primarily a public responsibility, because patients are entrusted mainly to state and to Federal institutions.

TABLE 11

PERCENTAGES OF FIRST ADMISSIONS TO HOSPITALS FOR PERMANENT CARE
IN THE UNITED STATES, 1936 TO 1946*

| Year | Public Hospitals Per Cent of Total | | | | Private Hospitals |
	State Hospitals	Veterans Hospitals	County and City Hospitals	Total Public Hospitals	
1946	58.4	19.6	2.0	80.0	20.0
1945	60.3	18.8	2.5	81.6	18.4
1944	65.2	16.3	2.4	83.9	16.1
1943	69.8	10.2	2.5	82.5	17.5
1942	74.4	5.4	3.0	82.8	17.2
1941	74.4	4.7	6.2	85.3	14.7
1940	74.4	5.3	5.3	85.0	14.6
1939	73.7	5.5	6.1	85.3	14.7
1938	72.0	5.6	7.4	85.0	15.1
1937	71.0	4.0	7.8	82.9	17.1
1936	72.0	3.4	7.5	82.9	17.1

* Data taken from *Patients in Mental Institutions*, p. 12, 1945; p. 12, 1946 (Washington, D.C.: Bureau of the Census, U.S. Department of Commerce).

The Increase of Resident Patients. The rapid increase of resident mental patients in hospitals is one of the unnoticed features of the past century. In the past sixty to seventy years, the patient population in state mental hospitals has increased five times as fast as the general population. In 1883 there were about 63 patients for every 100,000 persons in the general population. In 1946 there were about 345 patients for every 100,000 in the general population. Although more hospital facilities for care of mental patients may in part account for this increase, this rise reflects largely the number of patients who are admitted to state hospitals, and, more significantly, who are piling up as resident patients in these institutions.

Why Do Patients Pile Up in Hospitals? Although about 80 out of every 100 patients are committed to public institutions, over 97 per cent of the resident patients are in public institutions, as can be seen in Table 12. With the increase of the aged in our population, it is perhaps not surprising that their numbers have increased.

TABLE 12

PERCENTAGES OF RESIDENT PATIENTS IN MENTAL HOSPITALS FOR PERMANENT CARE IN THE UNITED STATES, 1937 TO 1946*

| Year | State Hospitals | Per Cent of Total Public Hospitals | | Total Public Hospitals | Private Hospitals | Total |
		Veterans Hospitals	County and City Hospitals			
1946	84.2	9.1	4.4	97.7	2.3	100.0
1945	84.7	8.1	4.6	97.4	2.5	100.0
1944	85.8	7.6	4.2	97.6	2.4	100.0
1943	86.1	7.2	4.2	97.5	2.5	100.0
1942	86.9	6.5	4.3	97.7	2.4	100.0
1941	85.1	6.2	6.5	97.8	2.2	100.0
1940	85.4	6.2	6.2	97.8	2.2	100.0
1939	84.7	6.1	6.9	97.7	2.4	100.0
1938	84.0	5.8	7.9	97.6	2.4	100.0
1937	84.0	5.5	7.9	97.4	2.6	100.0
1936	84.3	5.1	8.0	97.4	2.6	100.0

* Data taken from *Patients in Mental Institutions, 1946*, p. 11, 1945; p. 11, 1948 (Washington, D.C.: Bureau of the Census, U.S. Department of Commerce, 1949).

But the ones who accumulate most are the schizophrenics. This can be indicated by the length of stay of the different diagnostic types. One study found that 28.5 per cent of the schizophrenics had been hospitalized 2 years or longer, but that only 11.9 per cent of the manic depressives, 9.2 per cent of the alcoholics, and 13.8 per cent of all other diagnostic types had been hospitalized 2 years or longer. Further, 13.0 per cent of the schizophrenics, 3.4 per cent of the manic depressives, 2.8 per cent of the alcoholics, and 4.4 per cent of all other diagnostic types had been hospitalized 5 or more years.[11]

The schizophrenics also have the longest number of median years of hospital stay for patients who die in the hospitals. During 1943 the median lengths of stay for the disordered patients who died were: schizophrenics, 14.6 years; manic-depressives, 5.8 years; alcoholic psychotics, 3.9 years; and all psychotics, 1.5 years.[12]

Of the different schizophrenic types it seems that the catatonics remain in the hospital for the shortest period, while the hebephrenics remain the longest, with the paranoids having intermediate lengths of stay. Although these generalizations apply for these diagnostic types as a whole, they do not necessarily reflect upon the individual case, because factors other than the diagnosis itself contribute to length of stay in the hospital.[13]

The increase of schizophrenics in sheer numbers has almost doubled. The schizophrenics comprise about 45 per cent of the resident population.

This general accumulation of patients in state mental hospitals has resulted in overcrowdedness, in a shortage of personnel, and in a pressure to discharge patients prematurely in order to make room for new patients. It means, too, that the very care of patients is hampered, while its effects upon treatment could hardly be favorable. The state mental hospitals have felt these effects more sharply than have other types of mental hospitals. In private hospitals, the rates of discharge in 1946, for example, were very high, about 29.0 per cent of discharges for all mental hospitals, although the resident population was about 2.3 per cent. The veterans hospitals, by expanding their facilities and by recruiting more personnel, have been able to accommodate a larger number of patients; these hospitals

[11] Raymond G. Fuller and M. Johnston, "The Duration of Hospital Life for Mental Patients," *Psychiatric Quarterly*, 1935, IX, pp. 95–104.

[12] *Patients in Mental Institutions, 1943*, p. 29, 1946.

[13] See Leopold Bellak, *Dementia Praecox*, pp. 383, 406 (New York: Grune and Stratton, 1948); also H. Warren Dunham and Bernard Meltzer, "Predicting Length of Hospitalization of Mental Patients," *American Journal of Sociology*, September, 1946, 52:2, pp. 123–131.

tend to discharge more patients than are admitted. The county and city hospitals have also decreased their number of resident patients. The major burden of the care and treatment, as well as the accumulation of patients, then, converges upon the state mental hospitals, which have lagged behind in their rates of discharge.

TABLE 13

PER CENT OF ADMISSIONS, DISCHARGES, AND RESIDENT PATIENTS IN PERMANENT-CARE HOSPITALS, BY TYPE OF HOSPITALS, 1946 *

	State	Veterans	County and City	Private	Total
First admissions	58.4	19.6	2.0	20.0	100.0
Discharges	44.0	26.0	1.0	29.0	100.0
Residents	84.2	9.1	4.4	2.3	100.0

* Data from *Patients in Mental Institutions, 1946*, pp. 11, 12, 13 (Washington, D.C.: Bureau of the Census, U.S. Department of Commerce, 1949).

Differences of Length of Hospitalization in State and Private Hospitals. Although the difference in type of care and treatment contribute to the relatively large proportion of discharges in private hospitals and the relatively small proportion of discharges in state hospitals, the discrepant composition of the patients in the two types of hospitals and the attitudes of the relatives may also affect the length of hospitalization.

A large proportion of the patients in state hospitals require custody and are more resistant to treatment than the patients in private hospitals. For example, in 1946 the nonpsychotic alcoholics comprised 14.4 per cent of the first admissions in private hospitals but only 4.2 per cent in state hospitals. The neurotics comprised 11.2 per cent of the total first admissions in private hospitals and only 3.3 per cent in state mental hospitals. These two disorders usually can improve quickly, if temporarily, and can be discharged rather quickly. On the other hand, the disorders which are less amenable to therapy and which require custody are far more prevalent in the state hospitals. For example, in 1946 the old-age psychoses—cerebral arteriosclerosis and senile dementia—comprised 28.0 per cent of the total first admissions in state hospitals but 8.8 per cent in private hospitals. The schizophrenics, many of whom have an unfavorable chance for recovery, comprised 18.9 per cent of the first admissions in state mental hospitals but 14.1 per cent in private hospitals.[14]

Another difference shows that state mental hospitals have less readmissions than private hospitals. For example, in 1943 the readmissions constituted 22.5 per cent of all admissions in the state mental hospitals, but the readmissions in private mental hospitals comprised 33.6 per cent of all admissions.[15]

A third reason for the more rapid discharge of patients in private hospitals is that the relatives of patients have to spend large fees for their treatment. It is to their advantage to have them released as soon as possible. On the other hand, relatives of patients in state mental hospitals without this financial burden are frequently less concerned about having the patients released.

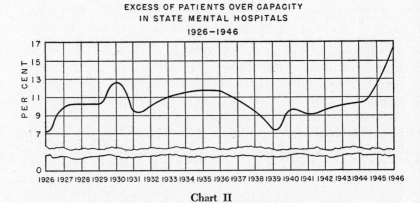

EXCESS OF PATIENTS OVER CAPACITY
IN STATE MENTAL HOSPITALS
1926–1946

Chart II

Overcrowdedness. Resident patients have increased so rapidly that, despite the building of more state-hospital facilities, over-crowdedness grows. In 1926 the normal capacity for resident patients was about 232,000, but the number of resident patients was about 248,000. In 1946 the normal hospital capacity had beds for 382,000 patients, but the number of patients had risen to about 444,000. In 1926 the excess of patients over capacity was 7.1 per

[14] *Patients in Mental Institutions, 1946,* p. 18 (Washington, D.C.: Bureau of the Census, U.S. Department of Commerce, 1948).

[15] *Patients in Mental Hospitals, 1943,* p. 11 (Washington, D.C.: Bureau of the Census, U.S. Department of Commerce, 1946).

cent. In 1946 the excess of patients over capacity was 16.3 per cent.[16] In short, the hospital capacity increased by 64.7 per cent, but the patient population increased by 79.0 per cent.

Before and during World War II, the excess of population over capacity fluctuated about the 10.0 per cent figure. After the war, it has continued to rise, until it is estimated that there is over 16.0 per cent excess population.

For example, in Rockland State Mental Hospital in New York, which is one of the better state hospitals in the country, there was an overcrowding of 30 per cent.

> . . . Some wards looked like seas of beds, with scarcely any aisle room. Beds lined dormitories. They spilled over into dayrooms originally intended for recreation and into the tub rooms from which therapeutic equipment had been removed to make space for sleeping quarters.[17]

In Pennsylvania, at the Bybeery State Hospital, the resident population was 75 per cent over its normal capacity of 3,400 patients. At the Cleveland State Hospital there was an overcrowding of 25 per cent over its normal capacity of 2,200. The minimum space for patients, according to the standards of the American Hospital Association, are 80 square feet per bed in four-bed rooms; 125 square feet in a single-bed room.[18]

More Resident Patients Are Older. Another result of the piling-up process in the state mental hospitals is that more of the patients are older. In a study of the age distribution of the resident patients for different time intervals from 1915 to 1947 in the New York state mental hospitals, Malzberg found that the mean age went up from 48.0 years in 1915 to 52.4 years of age in 1947.[19] The percentage of resident patients 65 years of age and over went up from 13.5 per cent of total resident patients to 23.1 per cent. On the other hand, the percentage of patients under 35 years of age went down from 20.6 to 15.4. The age group between 35 and 65 declined

[16] *Patients in Mental Institutions, 1946,* p. 25 (Washington, D.C.: Bureau of the Census, U.S. Department of Commerce, 1946).

[17] Albert Deutch, *Shame of the States,* p. 85 (New York: Harcourt, Brace and Company, Inc., 1948).

[18] *Group for the Advancement of Psychiatry,* Report No. 7, March, 1949, p. 2.

[19] Benjamin Malzberg, "Patients in the New York Civil State Hospitals," *Psychiatry Quarterly,* 1948, 22:3, p. 499.

slightly from 65.2 per cent to 61.2 per cent of the total resident patients.[20]

In comparing the percentages of resident patients of the different age groups from 1924 to 1944, Johnson found the most pronounced increase for the age group over 65 and the most pronounced decrease for the age group between 31 and 56.[21]

Expenditures per Patient. The per capita expenditure on patients in state mental hospitals is rising; in fact, the average expenditure per patient per year has risen by about 53 per cent. Yet it is still below the minimum required. The requirements of the American Psychiatric Association are $2.50 a day for long-term care and $5 a day for short-term care. In 1946 the state mental hospitals expended, on the average, $1.19 a day for the maintenance of each mental patient. By contrast, the private hospitals expended about $8 a day for each mental patient. The state with the lowest provisions spent about 60 cents per day. The state with the highest provisions, New York, spent about $1.55 per day.

Although the national average per capita expenditure in 1946 was about $436.72 or $1.19 per day, 35 states had less than the national average. In general, the Northeastern states had the highest per capita expenditures and the Southeastern states the lowest. Wisconsin had the highest per capita expenditure for patients in state mental hospitals, but most of her patients are committed to hospitals controlled by the counties.

The average per capita expenditure for state, county, and city hospitals in 1947 was about one fifth of that of private hospitals and about one fourth that of veterans hospitals.[22]

Premature Discharges and Waiting Lists. Because of the long waiting lists in some state mental hospitals, some patients may be discharged before their condition warrants such release. If the patient seems mild in his demeanor, somewhat communicative, has no obvious delusions, and does not harbor any detectable homicidal tendencies, the patient will in time be considered for conditional

[20] *Ibid.*

[21] Nelson A. Johnson, "The Growing Problem of Old Age Psychoses: An Analysis of the Trend in One State Hospital from 1910 to 1944," *Mental Hygiene*, July, 1946, 30:3, pp. 431–449.

[22] The average annual per capita expenditures for the respective hospitals are as follows: state, county, and city hospitals, $549; veterans hospitals, $2,133; private hospitals, $2,500. The American Psychiatric Association standard was $1,825.

release. This is often necessary in order to make room for new patients. There is no precise way of measuring the extent of this practice, except by a survey of the conditions of the ex-patients who are discharged. But the practice of discharging patients who would possibly remain longer is often admitted by hospital superintendents. As we shall see later, the patient is usually pleased with this practice.

On the other hand, a psychotic patient may require treatment but may not gain admission into the mental hospital because there is no room for him. Overcrowdedness thus becomes a destructive two-edged sword. It leaves the hospital the undesirable alternatives of discharging patients prematurely or of excluding patients who need treatment and/or care. In a study of 104 state mental hospitals by the National Committee for Mental Hygiene in 1934, 27 state mental hospitals found it necessary to bar new admissions. In 1 state, for example, there was a waiting list of 2,543 persons who had been legally committed to mental hospitals but who were denied admission; this state already had 3,383 patients beyond capacity. Moreover, in some states, some patients were being confined in jails for long periods because there was no room for them in the state mental hospitals.[23] Since 1934, as we have pointed out, overcrowdedness has increased rather than diminished in many states, and thus the situation for the committed and potential patients has become aggravated.

Summary

Schizophrenics and "old-age" psychotics are entering the mental hospitals in increasing numbers and represent a serious problem to society because so many do not respond to treatment. Thus, they pile up in the hospital, especially in state mental hospitals which bear the brunt of caring for these patients. These hospitals frequently do not have the facilities to accommodate them. In consequence, overcrowding, shortage of personnel, and the pressure to discharge patients prematurely have become prevalent. Increased appropriations to the state mental hospitals are essential to improve these custodial accommodations. But, as we shall see in the next chapter, these appropriations are also necessary for improving the

[23] Albert Deutch, *The Mentally Ill in America*, p. 449 (New York: Doubleday & Company, Inc., 1937).

caliber of the staff who are recruited and who remain in the mental hospital, for the effectiveness of state mental hospitals rests ultimately upon the attitudes among the personnel and their relationships with the patients.

Selected Readings

Deutch, Albert, *The Mentally Ill in America* (New York: Doubleday & Company, Inc., 1937).

———, *Shame of the States* (New York: Harcourt, Brace and Company, Inc., 1948).

Dorn, Harold F., "The Incidence and Future Expectancy of Mental Disease," *United States Public Health Service,* Public Health Reports, 1938, 53:45, pp. 1991–2004.

Dunham, H. Warren, and Bernard Meltzer, "Predicting Length of Hospitalization of Mental Patients," *American Journal of Sociology,* September, 1946, 52:2, pp. 123–131.

Elkind, Henry B., and Maurice Taylor, "The Alleged Increase in the Incidence of the Major Psychoses," *The American Journal of Psychiatry,* 1936, 42, pp. 817–825.

Fuller, Raymond G., and M. Johnston, "The Duration of Hospital Life for Mental Patients," *Psychiatric Quarterly,* 1935, 9, pp. 95–104.

Goldhammer, Herbert, and Andrew W. Marshall, *The Frequency of Mental Disease: Long Term Trends and Present Status* (Santa Monica, Calif. The Rand Corporation, 1949).

Group for the Advancement of Psychiatry, Report No. 7, March, 1949.

Johnson, Nelson A., "The Growing Problem of Old Age Psychoses: An Analysis of the Trend in One State Hospital from 1910 to 1944," *Mental Hygiene,* July, 1946, 30:3, pp. 431–449.

Malzberg, Benjamin, *Social and Biological Aspects of Mental Disease* (Utica, N.Y.: State Hospitals Press, 1940).

———, "Patients in the New York Civil State Hospitals," *Psychiatric Quarterly,* 1948, 22:3, pp. 495–515.

Patients in Mental Institutions, 1946 (Washington, D.C.: Bureau of the Census, U.S. Department of Commerce, 1948).

CHAPTER SIXTEEN

The State Mental Hospital: Functions and Personnel

The Mental Hospital as a Social Community

The patient who is admitted into a state mental hospital does not merely enter into a group of separate individuals who are placed together in the same building or buildings. Instead, he enters a social community, with traditions and fixed roles for the hospital staff and for the patients. These status positions have explicit and definite rules and, through the years, have become reinforced by traditions, rituals, and institutionalized ways of doing things. Also, the mental hospital is a relatively self-contained and isolated community. Like any other isolated community, it changes slowly. Innovations are suspect, and disruptions in the patterned routines are often opposed. The way of life in the hospital is such that the personnel who are recruited and who remain reinforce these traditional routines. These observations point to the need of understanding the mental hospital as a social setting for the mental patient.

Social Structure. Employees of the mental hospital set themselves apart from the patients and come to form the upper level of a castelike social structure. All social processes in the hospital revolve around this principle of staff dominance and patient subservience. These status lines are so inflexible that the primary kinds of competition which patients experienced in the outside community are absent in the hospital. Sullivan has expressed this point as follows:[1]

[1] Harry Stack Sullivan, *Conceptions of Modern Psychiatry*, p. 112 (Washington, D.C.: The William Alanson White Psychiatric Foundation, 1947).

The mental hospital is a sub-community strikingly different from the larger social system in which it is embedded. It is primarily a social system made up of fixed castes, which does not permit any vertical mobility. Moreover it is a social organization autocratically maintained in conformity to a relatively small number of simple, explicit, rules—in great contrast to the larger society with its however feebly democratic authority, coupled with complex, mostly implicit, often contradictory, demands that are variously and often inequably enforced by public opinion, group prejudice, the church, and the police powers of the community.

Among the two groups of personnel and patients a more mobile structure exists. Among the staff, the superintendent and professional staff are at the apex, followed by the clerical staff, and then the attendants and utility workers. Among the patients, (1) the hopeful or "curable" patients are on top, (2) the chronic patients are next, and (3) agitated patients are at the bottom. This latter arrangement results from the staff's attitudes toward the patients as well as from the patients' judgments of each other.

The Purpose of Dominance. Status arrangements have an intrinsic logic and are supported by a set of rationalizations by the dominant group. The dominant group uses and justifies its control of the subordinate group whether to exploit, to care for, or to help the patients. Frequently, the dominant group does all these things.[2] For example, in a general hospital physically ill patients are subordinate to the doctors and nurses who strive to facilitate the patients' improvement and recovery. With this rationale of therapy the doctors can prescribe what the patients should or should not do.

The relationships between the staff and the patients in the mental hospitals can be analyzed and assessed in the same manner, namely, by the ways the staff use their dominance in dealing with the patients.[3]

Functions of the Hospital

The hospital staff controls the patients for these purposes: (1) to protect the public and the patients; (2) to afford custody, care, and

[2] Allison Davis, Burleigh B. Gardner, and Mary R. Gardner, *Deep South*, pp. 15–20 (Chicago: University of Chicago Press, 1941).

[3] *Better Care in Mental Hospitals: Proceedings of the First Mental Hospital Institute,* edited by Daniel Blain, pp. 89–160 (Washington, D.C.: American Psychiatric Association, 1949).

work; and (3) to treat the patients. They combine these purposes in varying degrees for different patients. The hospital staff, by their attitudes toward the practice of therapy as well as to custody and care, will enable us to judge to what extent the hospital helps or retards the patients' improvement. These facets of hospital life can be clarified further by the modes of relationships among the staff and by the relationships between the staff and the patients.

Protection of the Public and the Patients. The hospital excels in its function of segregating psychotic persons, a minority of whom are harmful, from conventional society. Relatively few patients escape from the hospital, and, as far as can be determined, few patients commit suicide or homicide.

Patients who are potential suicides are closely watched, and all sharp instruments are removed from their possession. In one instance, a patient attempted to commit suicide while working in the kitchen. She was about to stab herself when another patient saw her, struggled with her, and succeeded in wresting the knife away. Thereafter the patient was carefully watched and lost her privileges, which included permission to walk in the grounds.

Patients who have potential homicidal tendencies are generally placed in an agitated ward in order to minimize their opportunities for escape. Indications of their homicidal attitudes are recorded on their charts, and these notations minimize their chances for eventual release. For example, a patient who was diagnosed as a paranoid schizophrenic was granted a week-end trial visit. While he was out, his wife claimed that he tried to kill her with a hammer. After this episode he was placed in an acutely agitated ward, and his file record indicated that he was "dangerous." Unaware of this notation, the patient still hoped to be released. He believed that were a former doctor still employed in the hospital, he would have been released, and he attributed his detention to the indifference of the present doctors.

The mechanical restraint of patients also has an administratively protective function. Often, agitated or violent patients can be potentially homicidal or suicidal. Since many state hospitals do not have enough qualified personnel to supervise these patients, restraint becomes a convenient, if harsh, recourse. For example, a catatonic schizophrenic, who was combative and agitated, managed to wriggle out of restraint, then attacked a patient near by. The assaulted patient was so severely injured that he was in bed for a few weeks.

The Custody of the Patients. Many state hospitals have so meager a budget that maintaining their institutions becomes an important, even trying, problem. This problem has become intensified by overcrowded conditions and by the maintenance of large buildings.[4]

The overcrowded conditions of the state mental hospitals make the patients increasingly uncomfortable and prevent privacy. Sometimes hopeful patients get better custodial care then either chronic or agitated patients because the hopeful patients are most frequently visited by relatives. Also, the hospitals can make a favorable impression upon the public by a few "dressed-up" wards.

Yet these custodial features of hospital life within limits have many favorable aspects. In progressive hospitals the wards are usually clean, and the patients are usually kept clean, although in less progressive hospitals this does not obtain. When possible, patients are provided with entertainment, such as motion pictures, dances, or outside entertainers. Untidy patients who cannot care for themselves are helped by attendants; the aged and the patients with organic disorders are given proper custody, especially when the budget of the hospital can include proper care. Periodic celebrations during holidays cut the pressing monotony of hospital life. Often, when these custodial features are not present, the low budget for hospital maintenance and hospital treatment may, in part, be responsible. The low budget affects other custodial aspects of the hospital.

The per capita expenditure on purchased provisions, including food, is low. Though rising, in 1946 it was 27 cents per day. This national average of expenditures, however, is not indicative of the amount of food consumed, because of the fluctuating prices and because a large share of the food is produced on hospital farms. Yet it gives us some rough notion about the quality and amount of provisions received. In addition, some state hospitals have separate menus for the staff and patients. The patients' food is often inferior to that of the staff. For instance, one improvement in a new program in Minnesota was to provide the same menu for patients and staff.

[4] See Albert Deutch, *Shame of the States* (New York: Harcourt, Brace and Company, Inc., 1948).

TABLE 14

AVERAGE PER CAPITA EXPENDITURES ON PURCHASED PROVISIONS IN STATE MENTAL
HOSPITALS AND IN PSYCHOPATHIC HOSPITALS, PER YEAR AND PER DAY*

| | State | | Psychopathic | |
Year	Annual Expenditures	Daily Expenditures	Annual Expenditures	Daily Expenditures
1946	$97.40	$0.27	$272.17	$0.75
1945	86.39	0.23	399.48	1.09
1944	85.33	0.23	361.32	0.99
1943	81.99	0.22	355.54	0.97
1942	76.61	0.21	429.23	1.18
1941	65.46	0.18		
1940	62.25	0.17		
1939	62.62	0.17		
1938	65.72	0.18		

* Data taken from *Patients in Mental Institutions* (Washington, D.C.: Bureau of the Census, U.S. Department of Commerce, 1946).

In a survey of 45 state mental hospitals by a group of 32 observers, the following results were obtained:[5] Of the hospitals, 95 per cent were overcrowded, some of them by 50 per cent. The Group for the Advancement of Psychiatry estimates that the range of overcrowdedness in state mental hospitals was from 20 to 74 per cent over capacity.[6] Of the state mental hospitals, 45 per cent did not supply sufficient bed sheets, and 35 per cent did not provide enough clothing. For example, it was not unusual to see women patients dressed with short cotton dresses and long white stockings so that they looked like overgrown children. Seventy per cent of these hospitals did not provide games and reading material; 20 per cent served unsanitary food, and 50 per cent served food poorly. In 35 per cent of the hospitals tubercular patients were not properly isolated from the other patients.[7] Many hospitals were inadequately built, and some were downright dilapidated.

The custodial function in many state mental hospitals is, indeed, inadequate; yet each hospital is a distinct institution and a distinct

[5] Frank L. Wright, Jr., *Out of Sight, Out of Mind*, pp. 127–128 (Philadelphia: National Mental Health Foundation, Inc., 1947).

[6] National Health Assembly, *America's Health*, p. 315 (New York: Harper & Brothers, 1949).

[7] Frank L. Wright, Jr., *Out of Sight, Out of Mind*, p. 128.

organization. The defects in any hospital may be counterbalanced by commendable qualities. Yet, whatever custodial shortcomings exist in the state hospitals, the attitudes of the staff to the patients are more important and their attitudes are influenced by the patients' roles in the state hospital. In this respect the attitudes of the staff are influenced by the work the patients do in the hospital, however beneficial some types of work may be for the patients.

State hospitals attempt to supplement inadequate appropriations by putting patients to work; this practice is traditional in nearly all state hospitals. Presumably, work benefits the patients when it keeps them occupied on constructive and useful projects. But the beneficial effects are often coincidental rather than deliberately planned by the staff. Frequently, patients work simply to maintain the hospital.

For example, in one typical state hospital 520 patients, or 20.8 per cent of 2,494 patients, were employed in some capacity. Of the employed patients, 101 received some stipend which totaled $261 per month. Seventy-six patients, or 3 out of 4 workers, received $2 monthly, 10 received $3 monthly, and 1 patient received $25 monthly. The other 14 patients received between $4 and $10 per month. In another hospital in the deep South, out of a total of 4,390 patients, 2,460, or 56.0 per cent, were employed in some maintenance capacity about the hospital. It is not known whether these patients received any stipend. In some state mental hospitals rewards for working are limited to "privileges."

Obviously, the larger the funds allocated for hospital care, the less the need for patient employment. When funds are low, the employment of the patients becomes an end rather than a means to lighten their monotony or to provide treatment for them. This aspect of hospital policy differs with the particular hospital. In one state hospital a patient who refused to work was placed in the agitated ward. In another state hospital a patient who said he would not work without pay was left alone, but the suspicion was that he might be psychopathic. In the former case the custodial and traditional aspects of the hospital were stressed. In the latter instance the therapeutic phase was considered, which is a departure from the usual state-mental-hospital procedure and is rather infrequent. Moreover, patients are supervised by maintenance and administrative workers.[8] These supervisors have little if any connection with the medical staff and are not concerned with the workers' treatment but with their usefulness in getting the chores done.

For example, one patient was assigned to help clean some rooms. The doctor told her that this was a kind of therapy, although he recognized that the type of work—cleaning rooms—was not in keeping with her college education. Convinced by his explanation, the patient worked one week, then quit and returned to the ward. She claimed that the person in charge insulted her, called her "stupid," "dumb," and other derogatory names. Though understanding this situation, the doctor also realized that his control of the situation was limited. When he spoke to the supervisor she informed him that her job was to see that the work was done and not "to baby the patients."

The hospital as a semiautonomous unit virtually requires many patients to work. Some patients claim that they benefit from this work, but it is not known to what extent they are benefited. Others feel that they are merely being exploited. In extreme situations this is the case. Sometimes hopeful patients hesitate about accepting certain hospital jobs, because they suspect these jobs will delay their discharges. In part, their suspicions are justified. They may be off the ward when the physician makes his rounds and thus not attract his attention by their improved condition. Their particular supervisors or the attendants may not want to lose their services or skills and may try to keep the patients in the hospital for longer periods.

In a study of the Chicago State Hospital, 1930 to 1932, Worthington found that, of 290 persons, the conditional release of 132 men was not encouraged because they were useful workers.[9] Since that time conditions have improved in the more progressive state hospitals. For example, the staff of progressive hospitals review the patients at least once every three months and discharge those patients who are improved, regardless of their jobs. However, other hospitals still retain this work-centered policy.

Treatment of the Patients. The treatment of the patients is one

[8] In a survey of 45 hospitals, 90 per cent of these hospitals "used patients in a work-centered rather than a patient-centered manner." *Ibid.*

[9] Florence P. Worthington, "Suggested Community Resources for an Extensive Parole System for Mental Patients in Illinois," *Smith College Studies in Social Work,* June, 1933.

of the more important functions of the hospital and many times is incongruous to its custodial functions. Ostensibly, all state mental hospitals have some forms of therapy. Our chief consideration is to see how certain representative types of therapy fit within the total patterns of the hospital community rather than to assess these forms of therapy *in vacuo,* for the way the therapy is defined by the staff and by the patients will determine its actual function in the hospital. In this light we shall evaluate (1) occupational therapy, (2) hydrotherapy, (3) electroshock and insulin therapies, and (4) psychotherapy.

Occupational Therapy. In contrast to the work done by patients in maintaining the hospital, occupational therapy is designed to help the patients. As yet, in some state mental hospitals this program is not very encompassing. In other hospitals it does not exist or at best functions on a token basis. In a few progressive hospitals it functions well. The principles of occupational therapy should be applied in such a way that the type of work proves helpful to the particular patient in terms of his individual attitudes and conflicts. Yet this consideration becomes secondary. Instead, the products made by the patients become primary. These products may be sold or displayed to the public, but the therapeutic effects upon the patients are not considered.

Occupational therapy, of course, is far preferable to idleness and to indiscriminate work. Yet occupational therapy and other forms of therapy serve to illustrate how a specific function within the hospital is diverted from its intended purpose and is made to fit consistently with the traditional practices of the hospital. Consequently, in many hospitals occupational therapy becomes a means for turning out materials either for hospital use or for sale to the public. For example, in one state hospital the occupational-therapy section became like a small factory which produced small articles needed by the staff. What was intended as a means became an end, and the original end—the improvement of the patients—lost its intended importance.

In some progressive state mental hospitals occupational therapy is designed primarily for the patients' benefit. The patients are assigned by psychiatrists to designated occupations according to their individual needs, and they are followed up in order to determine whether they are being benefited. In addition, the psychiatrists retain contact with the department heads and with the industrial activities of the hospital to know where the patients can best be assigned.

In an optimum situation the occupational therapist, in co-operation with the head nurse, trains the patient in a prevocational shop for hospital industry. After she has secured pertinent information about patient and industry, she refers this information to the psychiatrist, who assumes responsibility for placing the patient properly. Then the occupational therapist provides the patient with prevocational training, introduces the patient to his job, and then gives the industrial therapist all the information available about the personality and skills of the patient. The occupational therapist acts in a liaison capacity between the psychiatrist and the other hospital departments. It is apparent that such a program would create an atmosphere of industry throughout the hospital and would be sanctioned by the patients themselves. The patients would not be driven but led.[10] Their needs would be considered by regular rest periods, and by teachers who would stimulate the depressed, hold back the excitable, try to socialize the withdrawn, and encourage the discouraged.

Another practical consideration of occupational therapy is to link the type of work which the individual patient does in the hospital with his potentialities for outside employment. Since many jobs in many state mental hospitals are menial, this connection cannot be made. Yet hospital vocational training for posthospital adjustment would benefit the patients immensely. For this purpose vocational classes would help. This vocational training would be successful, however, when the hospital's attitudes toward the patients' work changed from a hospital-centered to a patient-centered orientation. When this occurs, the patients would be placed in jobs befitting their personality needs and skills. Occupational therapy and industrial therapy would then become the co-ordinated aims of state mental hospitals. This practice is being attempted in some progressive state mental hospitals.[11]

Hydrotherapy. In part, the same is true of hydrotherapy. Hydro-

[10] See William A. Bryan, *Administrative Psychiatry*, pp. 203–206 (New York: W. W. Norton & Company, 1936).

[11] See Thomas A. C. Rennie, Temple Burling, and Luther E. Woodward, *Vocational Rehabilitation of Psychiatric Patients*, pp. 6–9 (New York: Commonwealth Fund, 1950).

therapy is the use of warm baths to help quiet disturbed patients. As a form of sedation in some hospitals, the treatment has become twisted from its original purpose into a form of quasi punishment. For it has become defined by the patients as punitive, and some attendants may use it to warn patients against becoming disobedient. Nonetheless, hydrotherapy is a necessary treatment aid in the hospital, but the social meanings which become attached to it stray far from its specific intention.[12]

Electroshock and Insulin Therapy. Electroshock and insulin shock therapies have been instituted in many state mental hospitals during the past fifteen years. Shock therapy generally is peculiarly congenial to hospital traditions. Shock treatment can be administered in a simple way to many patients in a relatively short time and in an impersonal manner; it does not disrupt the custodial relationships between staff and patients; it tends to reinforce the biological approach to psychotic disorders. In the absence of systematic psychotherapy, these forms of physical treatment have been a boon to the state hospitals, because they represented actual therapy. Claims of recovery were very high in the first years, though more recently the claims of recovery have been more modest. Although in this section we will not appraise the results of these forms of therapy, we will concentrate on the way these therapies fit into or have changed the hospital traditions.

Generally, the shock therapies changed the routine of some hopeful patients and awakened hope among the staff that formerly difficult patients might now improve. But the general attitudes of the staff toward the patients have not changed. Some patients merely conformed to a new routine. Usually, they were not oriented to these new treatment mediums; the staff made scant efforts to understand why the patients improved or did not improve; improvement and nonimprovement were merely accepted as empirical facts. In some hospitals doctors did not make follow-ups of these physical therapies by systematic psychotherapy. A general lack of postshock psychotherapy resulted because of the social distance between the doctors and the patients and because of the shortage of doctors.

---

[12] Wright reports that one state hospital had the most modern hydrotherapy equipment for over two years, but the equipment was never used because "none of the doctors know how to use it and none of them will learn." See Frank L. Wright, *Out of Sight, Out of Mind,* pp. 63, 64 (Philadelphia: National Mental Health Foundation, Inc., 1947).

Since the patients were left in the dark concerning these forms of treatment and were not oriented to them, many became frightened by the shock and did not realize its worth.

The crucial meaning of these physical forms of therapy arises from the staff's control of the patients. This staff attitude bears especially upon the use of therapy for agitated patients. These patients may feel that they are being punished because of their agitation. In other words, when the staff have essentially custodial rather than therapeutic attitudes to the patients, they define physical therapy consistently with their general orientation. As a result the patients, left to themselves, define these devices in their own groping ways and often consider the physical therapy as punitive. Despite this fact, as we shall see in the next chapter, many improve and even recover, at least temporarily, with the help of shock therapy.

Psychotherapy. Although psychotherapy is not widespread in state mental hospitals, it has been used, as far as is feasible within the established routine, in some state institutions. This is true not only for the interview techniques used by doctors but also for the occasional practice of group psychotherapy. Marsh attempted to apply a vague kind of "group psychotherapy" to mental patients by a technique somewhat similar to the religious revival. His aim was "to make" the patients more sociable and outgoing.[13] Lazell and Klapman also have reported their experiences of group psychotherapy for hospitalized patients.[14] Generally, their group psychotherapy has consisted mainly of lectures. It is not known to what extent these lectures have proved successful. Lazell indicated that he was able, through the lectures, to help a hallucinating patient to improve, although he thought that his lectures had no effect upon the patient at the time.

As a result of the use of group psychotherapy during World War II, as we have pointed out, a greater understanding has been gained of the processes and techniques helpful to improvement. Such treatment practices as group psychotherapy and psychodrama, when

[13] L. C. Marsh, "Group Treatment of Psychoses by the Psychological Equivalent of the Revival," *Mental Hygiene,* April, 1931, 15, pp. 328–349.
[14] E. W. Lazell, "The Group Treatment of Dementia Praecox by Mental Re-Education," *U.S. Veterans Bureau Medical Bulletin,* 1930, VI, pp. 733–747; John W. Klapman, *Group Psychotherapy: Theory and Practice,* Chap. X, New York: Grune & Stratton, Inc., 1946.

supervised by competent persons, could facilitate the patients' improvement.

Klapman points out the effects of group therapy upon a group of patients who had been treated by insulin shock. He says:

> Often even a quite dilipidated patient who joins class will show marked changes in behavior and deportment after some class attendance. In the hurly-burly of the usual institutional practices it has often happened that for one reason or another a patient is transferred to a different ward and can no longer attend class. His behavior gradually lapses into its former character.
>
> On a certain ward where group therapy was given in conjunction with insulin shock therapy, but where any patient who desired it was admitted, a fine *esprit de corps* grew up between class members. They elected officers. They went for walks together, and if a patient developed secondary coma while on the grounds they solicitously looked after him and immediately supplied him with candy. Owing to the various changes necessitated by the shifting conditions of the institutional practices, group therapy was discontinued on that ward. The nurse reported a striking change in the class members. Many walked around as if lost, and repeatedly inquired whether they would have class again. The ward gradually became more noisy and its patients more bellicose. Injuries increased.[15]

In short, though treatment techniques are known, these techniques are hard to introduce and to sustain in state mental hospitals. The inertia of tradition tends to distort the intended functions of treatment. In fact, the types of therapy are made to conform to custodial patterns; for innovations create a disruption in the routines of the long-time staff members, throw them off balance, and make them insecure. Consequently, the staff members resist the changes which psychotherapy requires, or try to fit them as closely as possible into the established routine of the hospital. These immobile and inflexible routines in the state mental hospitals have their subjective counterparts in the attitudes and relationships among the hospital personnel.

The Hospital Personnel

Informal Organization. The hospital staff are an organized group, with many features of village life. Many employees live in the hospital and frequently confine their activities to the hospital during off hours. Permanent residents of a town generally suspect state

[15] *Ibid.*, pp. 283–284.

employees as transient sojourners and are often reluctant to accept them. Their suspicion about mental-hospital employees is heightened because of the transiency of the staff and because of their preconceptions and prejudices concerning the patients in the mental hospital as well as the mental hospital itself.

Consequently, the employees become an in-group who are restricted largely in their associations to other hospital employees. Gossip, rumor, and small talk prevail among them; persons become readily typed; each knows or tries to know something about the others. Enough mingling and gossip or "hospital grapevine" exist so that every member becomes known in some manner to a large segment of the hospital personnel. To avoid becoming the object of gossip, every employee is somewhat guarded about his nonofficial activities. Within this social setting distrust, hostility, and intrigue among the employees can magnify and personalize conflicts. The viewpoint one assumes in fulfilling his official role is shaped by the type of rewards and modes of approval given by other staff members. These attitudes among hospital personnel in the state mental hospitals are important because they are similar to the attitudes and relationships among personnel in many institutions, and, as we shall see, because they bear upon the staff's relationships with the patients.

The Doctors. The superintendent and the doctors are at the top of the hospital hierarchy. They have prime responsibility for the patients' improvement. In keeping with their position, they have the choice of dwellings in the hospitals, eat in the "professional" dining room, which is separated from the attendants' dining room, and may have one or more patients clean their apartments. Generally, they limit their associations to other professionals. The competence and qualifications of the doctors in state mental hospitals have been in a state of flux since World War II, because the added stress on psychiatric work has introduced more incentives for working in state mental hospitals. Nonetheless, in past years and largely at the present time, the doctors can be classified into two broad categories.

One group consists of those physicians who for varied reasons have become unsuccessful in or dissatisfied with private practice and have gone into hospital work as a means of economic security. The other group is composed of younger doctors who use their hospital experiences as a training interlude and eventually intend to enter private practice in psychiatry; sometimes these younger doctors do not enter private practice because they have become content with hospital work. Since the first group of doctors have been in the hospital for a longer period, they are generally in strategic positions and can control hospital policy. Not infrequently, the psychotherapeutic ideas of the younger doctors are considered threats to the positions of the older doctors and increase their insecurities.

Duties of the Doctors. The doctor has his duties laid out for him. He makes his morning rounds, interviews patients, writes progress notes of the patients, leaves instructions for the attendants concerning the patients, may perform shock therapy, attends staff meetings, sees visitors, and has other miscellaneous duties. The way the doctor fulfills these functions is the basis for his social rating by others in the hospital. Better-trained doctors, i.e., by education and types of experience, are often assigned to the hopeful wards; lesser-trained doctors are usually assigned to the chronic wards. Sometimes these assignments are made on the basis of seniority.

One of the most persistent complaints of hospital superintendents is shortage of doctors. In fact, the proportion of doctors to patients declined during World War II and is at present only catching up to the prewar rate. Estimates at present range from 1 doctor for 255 patients to 1 doctor for 275 patients.[16] This is less than one sixth of the minimum standard recommended by the American Psychiatric Association.

Because of the shortage of doctors and the emphasis on therapy in the hopeful wards, more doctors per patient are assigned to the hopeful wards and fewer doctors per patient are assigned to the chronic and agitated wards. In one state hospital 3 doctors had charge of 334 hopeful patients, but 4 doctors had charge of 1,907 chronic and agitated patients. In the hopeful wards the doctor-to-patient ratio was 1 to 111. In the chronic wards it was 1 to 477.[17]

In adjusting to the hospital routine, the doctor acquires certain

[16] The National Health Assembly, *America's Health,* p. 306 (New York: Harper & Brothers, 1949).

[17] In some hospitals the ratio is obviously higher. Although we have pointed out that the average doctor-patient ratio is about 1 to 255, Maisel reports that 1 doctor at Rhode Island state hospital had responsibility for 550 patients as well as 200 inmates in a prison. Albert Q. Maisel, "Our Mental Hospitals: a National Disgrace," *Life,* May 6, 1946.

TABLE 15

PATIENT RATIO PER PHYSICIAN—FULL TIME—IN STATE MENTAL HOSPITALS
IN THE UNITED STATES*

Year	Number of Patients per Doctor†	Number of Patients per Staff Physician‡	Number of Doctors per 1,000 Patients	Number of Staff Physicians per 1,000 Patients
1946	255.7	372.6	3.9	2.6
1945	295.4	432.1	3.4	2.3
1944	295.0	444.0	3.4	2.3
1943	279.8	379.8	3.6	2.6
1942	263.1	400.0	3.8	2.5
1941	224.4	328.6	4.5	3.0
1940	217.0	312.5	4.6	3.2
1939	221.0		4.5	
1938	216.6		4.6	

* Data taken from *Patients in Mental Institutions, 1945*, p. 27, 1942; p. 123, 1946; p. 28, 1948 (Washington, D.C.: Bureau of the Census, U.S. Department of Commerce).

† Doctors include all medical practitioners, specialists, and consultants associated with the state mental hospitals.

‡ Staff physicians are the doctors assigned to the wards or to special services and do not include the superintendent, assistant superintendent, and clinical director.

attitudes toward patients which are required for fulfilling a pre-established impersonal role. Though certain personality leeways exist in exercising this role, the role also has definite limits.

One of the prime functions of this role is diagnosing the patients. The diagnosis of personal and organic disorders is certainly important and obviously necessary. In the state mental hospital, however, it often reaches a point where the diagnosis virtually becomes a ritualized end rather than a means to treatment.

The diagnosis provides (1) a means for determining whether the person is disordered; (2) a differentiation between organic and personal disorders; (3) a short cut to categorizing the patient by giving him a diagnostic label; (4) a beginning for prognosis as, for example, in distinguishing between a hebephrenic and a manic patient; and (5) a basis for possible psychotherapy for personality psychoses.

There is neither time nor staff to provide the proper psychotherapy, which is usually prolonged and often requires individual attention. The diagnostic procedure for personal psychoses becomes, then, a symbolic ritual, because it loses its intended function of being a prelude to therapy.[18]

Doctors disagree about the value of psychotherapy. One group of doctors, usually the majority, maintains that personal disorders result from organic causes and should be treated medically. Another group of doctors, usually the minority, contends that, since no organic pathology is evident, personal experiences are most important. Since the organic approach predominates in many, perhaps most, state hospitals, systematic psychotherapy is usually given minor consideration. In some hospitals, however, psychotherapeutic interview sessions are held with those patients who have become communicative after shock therapy.

Obstacles to Psychotherapy. An incoming doctor who favors the use of psychotherapy will usually meet obstacles. First, he will find so many patients and so many other duties that he will be unable to devote enough attention to any particular patient without neglecting others. Second, he will learn from other doctors that a certain routine is maintained, that "five o'clock is quitting time," and that the condition of the patient is taken for granted and is not the subject of profound concern. Third, he will discover that he cannot always delegate instructions to the attendants who either may not understand these instructions or may have other ideas about their relationships to the patients. Fourth, he will find that in varying degrees the physician-patient relationship may be incidental rather than essential to his acceptance by and status with other staff members. As long as he inquires about the patient's welfare; does not manifestly abuse him; treats him for physical ailments and prescribes drugs, shock therapy, or hydrotherapy; sees that the patient does not escape, or returns after a week-end leave, he has done his duty. Fifth, should he be assigned to a chronic ward or an intermediary ward, he will learn that when some patients improve these patients will be transferred to another ward and to another doctor. Whatever attachments, whatever transference relationships he may have created with the patient can be undone. Sixth, he will find that although the patients are flattered and pleased by his interest in them, they usually will be more concerned with being dis-

[18] See Albert Graves. *The Eclipse of a Mind*, p. 565 (New York: The Medical Journal Press, 1942).

charged than with becoming improved and will consider improvement chiefly as a way to leave the hospital. Seventh, he will find that hospital routine goes on amidst a kind of repressed futility. This futility results from the difficulties involved in helping patients improve or recover; the staff find it easier to pursue an impersonal, fixed routine.

The almost contradictory roles of the patient are seemingly unavoidable in their effects upon the doctors. On the one hand, the patient is presumably an object of treatment or custody. On the other hand, he is a custodial charge of low status. By doing the menial work as well as other chores in the hospital, the patient is a worker who is responsible to utilitarian orders. The doctor who continually sees the patient in a subordinate work role, whether as a house cleaner or waitress or storekeeper, may in time regard the patient as a worker rather than as an object of therapy. His worker's role then may obscure his role as a patient.

Thus, the doctor who is placed in a social context has his discretionary relationships to the patients limited by an established impersonal role. By being compelled to fulfill this role, the doctor sees the patient as a custodial charge and as a worker as well as an object of therapy. Despite this fact, doctors respond differently to the patients.

Individual Differences. Some doctors work tirelessly on behalf of the patients; others seem indifferent and are content to follow routine; a third group may actually be a menace to the patients. This last group find in the patients convenient objects upon whom to work out their aggressions.[19] Some doctors, within limits, will do everything possible to help the patients and will derive a genuine satisfaction in seeing their patients improve or recover. Most doctors do their routine duties and, as such, may help some patients in this routine process but may neglect others who may need more help than the routine requires. A few doctors, however, who have intense aggressions, may express these aggressions toward patients whom they may dislike. According to Wright, these few may be capable of baiting persons in minority groups, or forcing some to needless cruelties.[20] Generally, little is known about the actual personality

[19] See section on Doctor-patient Relationships, p. 423.
[20] Frank L. Wright, Jr., *Out of Sight, Out of Mind,* p. 129 (Philadelphia: National Mental Health Foundation, 1947).

differences of state-hospital doctors except the broad differences mentioned. In some respects the patients are protected by the rules of the hospital, but an analysis of the personalities of the doctors would help clarify the doctor-patient relationships. In spite of the shortage of doctors, which is very great in some state mental hospitals, the question often arises whether the doctors make the best use of their time. It is not known to what extent the doctors' time could be saved from burdensome clerical duties, paper work, and other sundry chores so that they could be free to devote themselves to the treatment of their patients. For example, in a study of psychiatric clinics in New York City, it was found that the time of the doctors and the psychiatrists could have been used more profitably for the treatment of the patients.[21] The routine of doctors in state mental hospitals could be profitably studied in terms of this criterion.

The Social Workers and Psychologists. The social workers and psychologists are two other important professional groups who, with the psychiatrists, constitute the clinical teams which have been found effective in Army hospitals and clinics and which have been used increasingly in state mental hospitals.[22]

Social Workers. Since social workers have been in state hospitals for a longer period than psychologists, they are more established in the traditional scheme of the hospital social structure and routine. Yet not all hospitals have social workers on their staff. In 1947, 9 states had no social and field workers. (See Map 3.) Furthermore, if the American Psychiatric Association standard of 1 trained social worker for every 100 admissions is a measure, only 1 state, New Jersey, fulfilled this requirement. (See Map 4.) In 1946 and 1947 the average rate of social workers for the United States was 0.39 and 0.47 per 100 admissions, respectively.

The duties of the social workers are to provide a liaison between the patient and the outside community. They take the patient's history before his breakdown. They offer in this manner a crucial supplement to the psychiatric and psychological examinations. Often these histories are taken from the patient's family; the social workers can see more readily the type of family from which the

---

[21] *The New York Times,* April 12, 1950, p. 24.
[22] See Harold A. Greenberg, *The Clinic and the Community* (New York: G. P. Putnam's Sons, 1951).

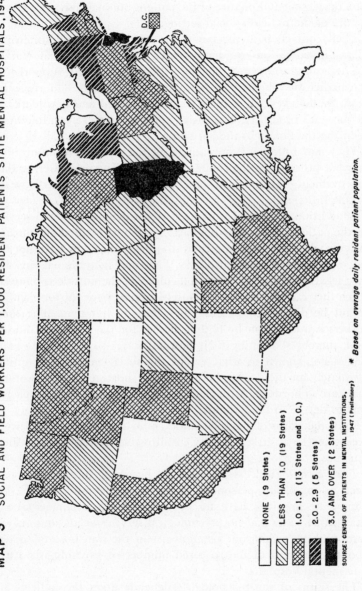

MAP 3 SOCIAL AND FIELD WORKERS PER 1,000 RESIDENT PATIENTS* STATE MENTAL HOSPITALS, 1947

D.C.

NONE (9 States)

LESS THAN 1.0 (19 States)

1.0 - 1.9 (13 States and D.C.)

2.0 - 2.9 (5 States)

3.0 AND OVER (2 States)

SOURCE: CENSUS OF PATIENTS IN MENTAL INSTITUTIONS, 1947 (Preliminary)

Based on average daily resident patient population.

patient comes. Thus, the psychiatric social workers not only can get a developmental picture of the patient but may also get a clearer picture of the patient's social setting.

Their contacts with the family are of added importance in pre-release investigations of the patient's family. The social workers can determine whether or not the patient's family will support him, or whether they benefit or harm him emotionally. On the other hand, the family itself may be slightly confused and bewildered by the patient's condition. The social workers can serve as a liaison for orienting the family to the patients.

They may follow up the patients in the outside community and see what processes in the community are helping or hindering their improvement,[23] although in some states community clinics have this specific function.

In addition, the social workers perform definite personal services for the patients. They may help arrange the personal affairs of those patients who have been admitted so quickly that they have not had time to straighten out their affairs. They may help the patients who have legal difficulties or other difficulties in the outside community which they cannot attend to themselves. Some patients, for example, cannot be discharged because they have no relatives. The social workers can aid them by finding homes for them outside the hospital, thereby shortening their hospital stay.

It is not known to what extent the social workers are trained adequately for these tasks. Because of the shortage of social workers, many are so burdened with clerical duties that they have insufficient time to devote to the patients.

Since the status of the social workers in the hospital is relatively fixed, they have little difficulty in adjusting to the hospital social structure.

The Psychologists. Psychologists are becoming increasingly recognized as important personnel in the state mental hospitals. Yet, many state hospitals have no psychologists. In 1945, mental hospitals in 31 states had no psychological services at all, and only 12 states had more than one psychologist in the state-hospital system. About 8 per cent of the required number of psychologists are in state mental hospitals.

The status of the psychologists depends upon the policies and

_____
[23] See Chapter Eighteen, "The Patient and the Community."

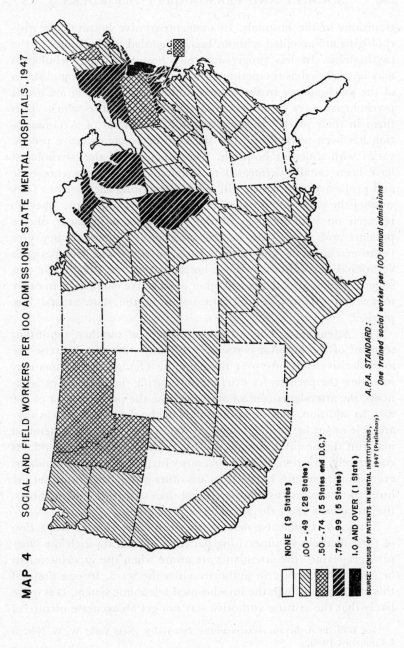

MAP 4 SOCIAL AND FIELD WORKERS PER 100 ADMISSIONS STATE MENTAL HOSPITALS, 1947

NONE (9 States)

.00 - .49 (28 States)

.50 - .74 (5 States and D.C.)

.75 - .99 (5 States)

1.0 AND OVER (1 State)

SOURCE: CENSUS OF PATIENTS IN MENTAL INSTITUTIONS, 1947 (Preliminary)

A.P.A. STANDARD:
One trained social worker per 100 annual admissions

traditions in the hospitals. In some progressive hospitals the psychologists are accepted without being regarded as challenges to the psychiatrists. In less progressive state hospitals the psychologists may be regarded as competitors who threaten the professional status of the psychiatrists. In these areas conflict and suspicion are great; psychologists may be subject to a type of acceptance which "puts them in their place." In most hospitals some kind of accommodation has been worked out, but the kind of accommodative process varies with different hospitals. The functions of the psychologist have been usually delineated as follows: They give psychometric and projective tests which will aid in diagnosing the patient. They counsel the patient and sometimes assist in psychotherapy. They do research on varied phases of the personality adjustment of the patients and participate in staff meetings. Sometimes they give vocational-aptitude and interest tests to determine the patient's vocational possibilities. In some hospitals they test prospective personnel, such as attendants and other prospective employees, in order to ascertain their potential adjustment in the state mental hospitals.[24]

The Attendants. The attendants comprise another significant segment of the hospital personnel. In many ways they exercise the most decisive influence over the patients. Though the doctors may interview the patients for brief periods during the morning or afternoon, the attendants control and supervise the patients most of the day. In addition, they carry out many of the doctors' orders as they are able or see fit. As one attendant phrased it, "the superintendent may run the hospital, but we run the patients." For the attendants collectively, this remark has a measure of truth. Since the attendants are with the patients longer than any other group, they interpret the hospital to the patients. Perhaps more than any other staff members, the attendants affect the attitudes of the patients.

By a kind of collective defense, they can offset also the inspection of their methods of supervising patients. Indeed, through the "hospital grapevine" the attendants are aware when the superintendent or some other person in authority visits the ward. In one hospital this was done through the intrahospital telephone system. It is quite likely that the visiting authority may not get an accurate picture of

---

[24] See William A. Bryan, *Administrative Psychiatry* (New York: W. W. Norton & Company, 1936).

the attendant-patient relations on the ward. One patient evaluated this situation as follows:

Truly I believe that officials do not know a lot that exists on the wards. For I notice that when officials come on the wards, the attendants are ready for them and are very careful that all things take on a vastly different appearance. I think that some men who are employed here do not always know the whole truth.

An attendant remarked:

An authority that starts making the rounds, attendant on the first ward may not know it, but those on other wards sure do. It gets around like magic.

Attendants are usually recruited from marginal occupational groups. The majority are unskilled workers and seek this employment because of personal reasons rather than because of any genuine interest in the patients. The job incentives are few: the pay is low, the hours are long—in some states twelve hours daily—and the company of disordered inmates is not especially pleasant. Often, they have too many inmates to supervise. The number of patients per attendant in state mental hospitals is over twice the ratio in veterans hospitals and psychopathic hospitals. We can get some idea of the difference from Table 16.

TABLE 16

RATIO OF RESIDENT PATIENTS PER ATTENDANT [*]

Year	State Hospitals	Veterans Hospitals	Psychopathic Hospitals
1946	11.5		1.9
1945	13.0	5.5	1.9
1944	13.4	7.4	1.6
1943	13.0	6.7	1.6
1942	11.6	6.0	1.7
1941	10.0	5.5	
1940	10.3	5.3	

[*] Data taken and computed from *Patients in Mental Institutions*, p. 27, 1942; p. 32, 1943; p. 28, 1945; p. 27, 1946 (Washington, D.C.: Bureau of the Census, U.S. Department of Commerce, 1948).

Although the number of patients per attendant may seem low at first glance, we must recall that attendants must be with patients twenty-four hours daily. Since this ratio includes all attendants and since attendants are distributed on a two-shift or three-shift basis, the ratio of patients per attendant would certainly be higher. On the average, over 22 patients per attendant per each shift would be a rough estimate. Generally, the ratio is even higher, because some persons who are hired as attendants are assigned to other jobs. The A.P.A. standards prescribe one attendant for 6 to 8 patients.[25]

It is apparent that the attendant's job is so unattractive that in periods of prosperity when other jobs are available, there are about 20 per cent to 25 per cent of the jobs vacant.[26] Some even encounter discrimination in the outside community because of their occupation.[27]

Many attendants are too old or too unsure of themselves to work at other jobs and come to the mental hospital as a kind of economic haven. Others are too unstable to last long at any job; even as attendants, they float from hospital to hospital. Among these "floaters" many are alcoholics or misfits. They find these jobs congenial because they have outlets for their aggressions and because they have few responsibilities. Moreover, the low pay discourages married men from accepting jobs as attendants. Many state mental hospitals do not have living quarters for attendants and their families. Married men who might otherwise consider these jobs find they cannot afford to live outside the hospital on their salaries. Because of this enforced celibacy, either unstable persons who may be averse to marriage or those who view the hospital work as temporary are attracted. Thus, the type of personnel selected and the large turnover of those attendants who seek other jobs tend to lower the morale of the hospital. Usually, the more prosperous the period the more rapid the turnover.

Maisel, in a 1946 article in *Life* Magazine, states:[28]

. . . the correlation between mistreatment and brutality on the one hand and low pay, long hours and overcrowding on the other hand is immediately apparent.

Maisel continues:[29]

[25] National Health Assembly, *America's Health,* p. 315 (New York: Harper & Brothers, 1949).

[26] See *Patients in Mental Institutions, 1946* (Washington, D.C.: Bureau of the Census, U.S. Department of Commerce, 1949).

[27] Frank Olmstead, "They Asked for a Hard Job," *Fellowship,* November, 1943.

[28] Albert Q. Maisel, "Our Mental Hospitals: A National Disgrace," *Life,* May 6, 1946. © Time Inc.

[29] *Ibid.*

Attendants in Pennsylvania state hospitals start at the magnificent pay of less than $900 a year [1945] plus maintenance. By contrast the state pays its guards off at $1,950 a year plus maintenance, although the psychiatric attendant's job is more dangerous and certainly far less pleasant than that of the prison guard.

Nor is Pennsylvania by any means the worst among states. At the state hospital at Howard, R.I. there were approximately 200 vacancies among attendants on December 13, 1945. The starting wage for attendants was $55.00 a month and maintenance.

At times the actual tutelage for attendants is negligible. The attendant "picks up" his information by bits and gradually learns what he can do and what he cannot do. One attendant said:

When I first came to the hospital, the superintendent and the charge attendant told me that I ought not leave the keys around, because once the patients get the keys they might all escape. They didn't tell me anything to the point at that time. I had to pick it up by myself. I would be told what to do at certain times, where to take the patients, and when to bring them back. I learned a lot from the old patients who had been on the ward a long time. The other attendants were either too busy trying to amuse themselves or seeing that the necessary work was done. I learned that the patients had to get the work done and the attendant had to supervise. There was nothing told me about trying to help the patients in their condition. That was up to the doctors only.

Because attendants have continual contact with patients, their predominant effort is to control them. But their control has chiefly a custodial purpose. As "keeper of the keys," they strive to retain their status and authority over the patients, but their dominance sometimes becomes an end in itself. Their way of acting toward patients is largely governed by what they learn from the tutelage of other attendants and from the reactions of the other personnel, especially physicians. Their duties are prescribed for them. The attendants must see that the ward is clean, that the patients do not escape, and that they remain tractable. To achieve these purposes they remain socially distant rather than intimate or informal with the patients. By remaining socially distant, many feel that it is easier to order the patients around.

Their tutelage, when it comes, often is enforced more directly by the attendant in charge of the ward. One attendant recalled his initial experiences as follows:[30]

When I first came to the hospital, I would occasionally ask a patient to come into the office and have a chat with me. I wanted to learn more about

[30] From an interview with the author.

patients, what they were like, and what seemed to bother them. One day, when I was talking to one of the patients a charge attendant came in, and instantly ordered the patient to stand up, to question his right of sitting in the office. When the patient left at my suggestion, he started after me, saying: "Don't you know familiarity breeds contempt. These are insane people you're dealing with. They're not like you or me." I said, "Look, this patient was acting all right until you came in. He didn't do a single thing that was out of the way." And he answered, "If you want to stay here, you'll treat the patients the way I tell you, and that means not calling them into the office."

This does not mean that the attendants are necessarily brutal, although in extreme cases some may be. Rather, many tend to regard the patients in stereotyped fashion, as inferiors who outnumber them, who may get out of hand, and who can create a disturbance. Ignorant of the whole process of organic and personal disorders, they can have few constructive relationships with the patients, which makes the relationships all the more dissatisfying for them as well as for the patients. Olmstead maintains that too many attendants respond to the patients out of fear and they try to control the patients by violence. But if attendants were shown that "insane" people could be "handled" with understanding, their fear would be gone and "with it much of the hell for patients" who have to live under such a regime.[31]

Moreover, the attendants' morale depends, in part, upon their relationships with the physicians; and their morale in turn affects their relationships with the patients. For the attendants find the patients easy marks for their aggressions. When some attendants strive to help the patients, they may find that they are ignored and even rebuffed by the physician, who may view the attendants only in terms of the menial labor they perform.[32] Consequently, they may resent the physicians, but they carry out their resentment on the patients, particularly on those patients whom they dislike.

Intelligence Levels of Attendants. Wittman attempted to evaluate the efficiency of the 412 attendants in the Elgin State Hospital upon the basis of their intelligence.[33] She found that many attend-

[31] Frank Olmstead, "They Asked for a Hard Job," *Fellowship*, November, 1943.
[32] A. H. Eichert, "Morale and the Attendant," *Mental Hygiene*, 1944, 28, pp. 633, 634.
[33] Phyllis Wittman, "An Attempted Evaluation of the Efficiency of State Mental Hospital Attendants," *Elgin State Hospital Papers*, Vol. II, pp. 229-232 (Elgin, Ill.: Department of Public Welfare, 1936).

ants with low intelligence were discharged because of inefficiency. On the other hand, the attendants with mediocre intelligence did better than those in the highest intelligence levels, for the attendants with mediocre intelligence were more content, were more compliant to the orders of authority, and took a greater interest in small details than did attendants with superior intelligence. The attendants with superior intelligence often had personality difficulties which made it difficult for them to adjust to the hospital routine. In brief, Wittman maintained that the "most efficient attendant is one who approaches average intelligence, who likes people, and has a sympathetic regard and a wish to help the patients." [34]

The Attendant and the Psychiatric Aid. An attendant has observed that when he told other people his occupation, they regarded him silently for a moment as if expecting some bizarre behavior. But this attendant was a conscientious objector in World War II and admittedly was very sensitive about his job. He felt that had he been able to refer to himself as a "psychiatric aide" he could have kept his social contacts on a higher level. Of course, most attendants are not so concerned with social status as he was. [35]

But the attendant often has little status in the community. He has little to be proud of in his occupation. Yet, in part, this attendant's feeling that the community discriminates against him is justified, except for the few attendants in the more progressive hospitals. The traditions of the attendants hinder rather than help their effective care or treatment of the patients. If attendants received additional training and were given more status and salary, the patients would benefit because the attendants would get some satisfaction from their work. The conscientious objectors who worked in the hospitals during World War II have attempted to get better care for patients and to dignify the occupation of the attendants. The Mental Health Section of the National Mental Health Assembly recommends that, after proper types of training for psychiatric aides are found, licenses in the states should be granted to qualified attendants. These licenses would eliminate the less qualified and untrained attendants. [36] This program, of course, would

[34] *Ibid.,* pp. 230–231.
[35] Frank Olmstead, "They Asked for a Hard Job," *Fellowship, November,* 1943.
[36] The National Health Assembly, *America's Health,* p. 313 (New York: Harper & Brothers, 1949).

be possible only with higher salaries to attract more competent persons.

Although this type of program is very commendable, its fulfillment seems remote because of the types of attendants now employed. Essentially, the psychiatric aide would be a group leader and counselor, in addition to fulfilling his other duties. One recent incentive for attendants has been the awarding of a prize for the best "attendant of the year." Despite promising projects for the future, meritorious service has only begun to be recognized, and these criteria of merit are not always evaluated by the patients' condition, but by the cleanliness of the ward. Moreover, opportunities for advancement among attendants are few, and salary increases are not always sufficient to enable attendants to regard their work as a career.

Mass Custody and Individual Therapy

Since many state mental hospitals are so large and since the hospital hierarchy is so rigid, the patients become parts of a large anonymous group in which their individuality is lessened. On the one hand, they are virtually divested of initiative and individual decision by remaining completely subservient to the hospital staff; on the other hand, they are supposed to be prepared for participating in a highly competitive and individualistic society. In the hospital, they have little opportunity for exercising individual decision and individual planning. In the outside community, their very adjustment depends upon individual decision and individual planning. The emphasis upon mass custody thus works in opposition to collective therapy.

By collective therapy we mean that individual participation within the hospital society would enable the patients not only to improve and to understand themselves more clearly but also to learn how to participate more effectively with others. The group would then become a therapeutic medium; it would not obscure and hide individuality; it would cultivate the person's favorable characteristics by intensifying his socializing capacities. Presumably, many patients are too fixed in their disorders and are not amenable to collective therapy. But the progressive improvement of these patients would bring greater opportunities for social participation and competitive living. Though many features of state mental hospitals aim at this goal, these features are too haphazard and are not integrated around a central purpose. Based upon diagnostic and prognostic procedures, the hospital can outline a schedule of activities for each patient which, in the process of experiment, will contribute to his maximum improvement. Seemingly, apart from ward assignments, physical therapy, and other adjunct therapies, concerted programs of this type tend to be lacking in most state mental hospitals.

Transition from Custody to Therapy. The orientation among the professional personnel in the state mental hospitals is in the transitional process of changing from diagnosis and custody to diagnosis and treatment. Group psychotherapy and individual psychotherapy are used increasingly in progressive state mental hospitals, if on a research level. Yet research can be conducted in group psychotherapy or in individual psychotherapy for a few patients and can be neglected for the large body of patients. The problem of implementing large-scale group psychotherapy and individual psychotherapy programs as an inevitable part of the patients' treatment remains to be realized in most state mental hospitals.

This practice is not unusual in the social and psychological sciences. That is, the application of knowledge, however feasible theoretically, lags behind the knowledge of social phenomena. This is evident not only in disordered behavior but also in delinquency, crime, prostitution, alcoholism, and other forms of deviant behavior. However, when the feasibility of psychotherapy is recognized widely enough, it may be implemented on a wide enough scale in many state mental hospitals.

State Mental Hospital and Private Mental Hospital. The state mental hospital provides custody to the patients in a relatively simple social environment. It ministers to their physical ills and provides some types of physical therapy. In some progressive state mental hospitals, the beginnings of group therapy and individual psychotherapy are evident, as we have pointed out. But the weight of tradition, as embodied in the fixed attitudes of the hospital personnel, discourages constructive changes such as systematic therapy based upon group dynamics and psychodynamics. By contrast, in some private mental hospitals, milieu or attitude therapy is applied to aid the patients. In this social process the attitudes of the hospital personnel are manipulated for therapeutic ends. Adams has described the following procedure in one private mental hospital:[37]

A systematic attempt to develop a definite plan of attitude therapy was begun at the Menninger Sanitarium 18 years ago. A set of attitudes was developed over the years covering a wide variety of psychodynamic constellations. These attitudes were designed to meet the total needs of the patient both conscious and unconscious. The term, "needs," is not used in the sense of discerning only what the patient wishes, but rather what conditions are necessary in order to restore emotional balance. These attitudes have been defined and explained in a guide booklet that is available to all the professional personnel working in the hospital. When each patient's case is discussed in staff conference, a specific attitude to be maintained by all personnel toward the patient is prescribed. It is written on the orders for the patient and is communicated to all professional personnel, which includes nurses, psychiatric aides, recreational therapists, dietician, and any others who will have important contacts with him.

Consequently, when an attitude of "firm kindness" is ordered for a depressed patient, all the personnel know immediately that assuming such an attitude is for the purpose of helping the patient expiate his irrational guilt feelings. This order indicates they are to insist that he carry out all tasks no matter how much he may complain, in order to enable him to externalize his aggression instead of heaping it all on himself. They know they are not to give in to his pleadings to be left alone to suffer, nor are they to slap him on the back and say "cheer up old boy, life really isn't so bad."

Other private hospitals, such as Chestnut Lodge, have attempted the psychoanalytic therapy of schizophrenics. Fromm-Reichmann has shown the feasibility of these approaches in trying to rehabilitate psychotics.[38] Since psychotic patients are as sensitive as ordered persons, if not more so, and since they cannot always be reached emotionally, this condition requires the kinds of skills which will enable these patients to face their social world.[39] Any display of fear or anxiety which the staff may feel toward patients will obstruct therapeutic efforts. Hence, these attitudes and other subtle

[37] Edward C. Adams, "Problems of Attitude Therapy in a Mental Hospital," *The American Journal of Psychiatry*, December, 1948, 105:6, pp. 456, 457.

[38] Freida Fromm-Reichmann, "Transference Problems in Schizophrenics," *Contemporary Psychopathology*, edited by S. S. Tomkins, pp. 371–380 (Cambridge, Mass.: Harvard University Press, 1947).

[39] Freida Fromm-Reichmann, "Problems of Therapeutic Management in a Psychoanalytic Hospital," *Psychoanalytic Quarterly*, 1947, XVI, pp. 325–356.

attitudes of the personnel of the private hospital have to be controlled in their relations with the patients.

Especially important are the doctor-patient relationships. The doctor orients his behavior to help the patient improve. His dominant position becomes a means for effective treatment. His treatment orientation to the patient requires patience, flexible adaptability, and permission from the hospital. On the other hand, the state-hospital doctor is pressed by too many patients and too many duties. He does not have the time to devote to a particular patient, unless it is for research purposes. Moreover, as we have pointed out, the state mental hospital has so many custodial problems that this type of treatment would be exceptional. Yet the continuing influence of psychotherapy upon psychiatry has begun to make inroads into the more progressive state mental hospitals, and this trend is continuing.

The State Mental Hospital and the Community. The state mental hospital is a subcommunity integrally related to the larger social community. The personnel and practices of the state mental hospital largely reflect the attitudes of conventional society toward it. In the last analysis the mental hospital is the product of the way in which conventional society views and handles the disordered person. The major burden of hospital treatment and care falls upon the state mental hospitals. The private hospitals are so small—usually under 110 beds—and provide care for such a tiny fraction of psychotic patients that any large-scale improvement must take place primarily in the state mental hospital. Despite the aroused interest of citizens since the end of World War II, only a few improvements have been made in the care of the mentally disordered by the state. The changes instituted in some states have been the first in many years. On the one hand, the state mental hospitals are careful to avoid any adverse publicity; on the other hand, the indifference of the public, the political spoils system as a basis for hiring personnel in many states, and the unwillingness of legislators to defray the necessary budget retard the improvement of the state mental hospital.

The emphasis in the state mental hospital is to make the best possible impression upon the community. This is not only apparent from the well-groomed exterior of the hospital; it is more profoundly indicated by the fear of adverse publicity which would reflect mismanagement, corruption, brutality, or poor treatment. The attitudes of the state mental hospital reflect what is believed by the public to be an efficient hospital.

Klapman has suggested that state hospitals maintain a publicity bureau in order to orient the public positively toward the hospital rather than to await the occurrence of disturbing events.[40] The tendency of the layman is to avoid thinking about the mental hospital and to isolate it from the community. Many persons are afraid of disordered behavior and what it connotes, and by avoiding intelligent discussions of the problem, they are reinforced in their ignorance and misconceptions.

Since World War II, however, many informative writings have appeared. Though the state mental hospitals have been criticized, the horror of the mental hospital as an "insane asylum" has been largely removed. Also, the mental-hospital patient has been portrayed more sympathetically as a human being who needs attention, and who can recover, rather than become a "dangerous monster." There are such frank descriptions as *The Snake Pit*, by Mary Jane Ward; *If Man Be Mad*, by Harold Maine; *The World Next Door*, by Fritz Peters; and Albert Deutch's *Shame of the States*.[41] Numerous articles have appeared in widely circulated national magazines such as *Life*, *The Woman's Home Companion*, and other periodicals.[42] Newspaper write-ups and radio sketches have helped the public to understand the plight of the disordered person.[43]

State Mental Hospitals and Politics. The state mental hospital, like other state institutions, is subject to spoils politics in many states. Appointments are made frequently on the bases of party affiliation and political connections instead of on the basis of merit. Superintendents often do not have complete control over appointments. In some state hospitals it is assumed that each employee has some political backer. The state-mental-hospital superintendent, when appointed on considerations other than merit, can lower the

[40] J. W. Klapman, *Group Psychotherapy: Theory and Practice*, pp. 321, 322.

[41] Mary Jane Ward, *The Snake Pit* (New York: Random House, 1946); Harold Maine, *If Man Be Mad* (New York: Doubleday & Company, Inc., 1947); Fritz Peters, *The World Next Door* (New York: Farrar Straus & Young, 1949); Albert Deutch, *Shame of the States* (New York: Harcourt, Brace and Company, Inc., 1948).

[42] Albert Q. Maisel, "Bedlam: 1946: Most U.S. Hospitals Are a Shame and a Disgrace," *Life*, May 6, 1946.

[43] For example, Edan Wright, *Chicago Daily News*, October 24, 1949, p. 1.

whole standard of the state mental hospital. Some superintendents are appointed without the necessary qualifications in psychiatry. Then again, some state-hospital administrations are closely allied with political regimes, and little long-range planning can be realized. Some employees, including executives, think their jobs will last only as long as the particular administration lasts, whether two or four years. This short-range planning cannot lead to significant changes which could be accomplished only by long periods of gradual but continual improvement. Hence, new administrations in many states are usually faced with "emergencies" in hospital care. One constructive means for overcoming this haphazard policy is the introduction of civil service jobs and of making responsible administrative and technical positions nonpolitical. In some states this has been done in large part, but in other states the state mental hospitals remain parts of the "spoils system."

Another political feature which influences the state hospital is the low budget allotted for employees. This is particularly true of salaries for attendants. Hence, the incentives for attracting competent persons are few. The small allotment of funds for salaries means that the types of personnel necessary for furthering therapeutic aspects of the state mental hospital will not be obtained. The reluctance of legislators to appropriate enough funds for welfare agencies is the reason for the prevailing low salaries of employees and hence of the inability to recruit competent personnel.

The typical attitude of many state legislators has been tersely summarized by one hospital superintendent. "For years, the state has followed the unwritten policy that the best institution is the one run at the least per capita cost." [44]

Summary

The state mental hospital can be considered a castelike, relatively isolated, and slow-changing social community. Although the shortage of personnel affects the treatment of the patients, the attitudes of the employees are even more crucial in this respect. The village-like character of the hospital, as shown in its gossip and rumor, tends to type each employee in the eyes of the rest of the personnel and to induce a defensiveness in his personal activities. The formal

[44] Albert Deutch, *Shame of the States*, p. 83 (New York: Harcourt, Brace and Company, Inc., 1948).

hospital organization tends to intensify the sense of status—a condition which fosters petty irritations and controversies over the exercise of authority. These intrastaff tensions, as well as the general orientation, affect their attitudes toward the patients.

The dominant group, the employees, in the castelike structure of the hospital, orient their control of the patients predominantly toward custody. Psychotherapy is given minor consideration. The attitudes of the doctors and other members of the professional staff are primarily diagnostic and medical. These diagnostic procedures in some respects have become ends in themselves rather than means to therapy, particularly for the personality psychoses. The pervasive organic approach to disorders, the many patients per doctor, the resistance of some psychotic disorders to short-term psychotherapy, and the traditions of custody discourage systematic psychotherapy and counseling in the typical state mental hospital.

The attendants who have the most decisive influence upon the patients are usually a marginal, unskilled, and unstable group whose knowledge of the personal disorders and organic disorders is frequently minimal.

Their intent is to see that the patients remain controllable, do not escape, and do their chores. Relations other than those of the commanding and forbidding types are kept to a minimum.

The character of treatment and care in the state mental hospitals is largely a function of the attitudes of the citizenry to the mental hospital. Despite the relative indifference of the public and of many public officials, a number of state mental hospitals are in a state of transition not only with reference to improved custodial conditions and practices but also in encouraging research in psychological as well as physical mediums for facilitating the improvement of the patients.

Selected Readings

Adams, Edward C., "Problems in Attitude Therapy in a Mental Hospital," *The American Journal of Psychiatry*, December, 1948, 105:6, pp. 456–461.

Bateman, J. Fremont, and H. Warren Dunham, "The Mental Hospital as a Specialized Community Experience," *The American Journal of Psychiatry*, December, 1948, 105:6, pp. 445–448.

Bryan, William A., *Administrative Psychiatry* (New York: W. W. Norton & Company, 1936).

Chapman, Ross, "Psychoanalysis in a Psychiatric Hospital," *The American Journal of Psychiatry*, 1935, 91, pp. 1093–1101.

Deutch, Albert, *Shame of the States* (New York: Harcourt, Brace and Company, Inc., 1948).

Eichert, A. H., "Morale and the Attendant," *Mental Hygiene*, 1944, 28, pp. 632–638.

Erickson, Isabel, "The Nursing Problems in the Psychiatric Hospital," *Hospitals*, 1937, 11, pp. 58–62.

Fremont-Smith, F., "New Opportunities for the Improvement of Mental Hospitals," *Mental Hygiene*, 1947, 31, pp. 354–362.

Fromm-Reichmann, Frieda, "Problems of Therapeutic Management in a Psycho-analytic Hospital," *Psychoanalytic Quarterly*, 1947, XVI, pp. 325–356.

Gartland, Ruth, "The Psychiatric Social Worker in a Mental Hospital," *Mental Hygiene*, 1947, 31, pp. 285–295.

Knight, Robert P., "The Plan of Psychoanalytic Therapy in the Mental Hospital," *Current Therapies of Personality Disorders*, edited by Bernard Glueck, pp. 58–69 (New York: Grune & Stratton, Inc., 1946).

Maine, Harold, *If Man Be Mad* (New York: Doubleday & Company, Inc., 1947).

Menninger, William C., "Psychoanalytic Principles Applied to the Treatment of Hospitalized Patients," *Bulletin of the Menninger Clinic*, 1937, I, pp. 35–43.

National Health Assembly, *America's Health* (New York: Harper & Brothers, 1949).

Norman, J. P., "State Hospital Psychiatry," *Mental Hygiene*, July, 1947, 31, pp. 436–448.

Reider, Norman, "Hospital Care of Patients Undergoing Psychoanalysis," *Bulletin of the Menninger Clinic*, 1937, I, pp. 168–175.

"Standards for Psychiatric Hospitals and Out-Patients Clinics Approved by the American Psychiatric Association," *The American Journal of Psychiatry*, 1945, 102, pp. 264–269.

Stanton, Alfred H., and Morris S. Schwartz, "The Management of a Type of Institutional Participation in Mental Illness," *Psychiatry*, February, 1949, XII:1, pp. 3–26.

CHAPTER SEVENTEEN

The State Mental Hospital: The Patients

Once committed to a state mental hospital, the patient forfeits certain rights. His letters are censored; telephone calls are usually forbidden; many of his belongings are temporarily held for him. He is tentatively deprived of civil rights—of voting and of controlling his property. Any initiative he may exercise is considered out of place; sooner or later he becomes aware that his adjustment depends completely upon obeying hospital personnel.

The very agitated or disoriented patients neither comprehend nor care where they are taken. Others, despite their agitation, are oriented enough to resent their commitment. The somewhat oriented patients, generally, are often taken aback by the thought of being committed to a mental hospital. All their prejudices concerning mental patients descend upon them; for now they have become the objects of this stigma. In the words of a patient:[1]

Before I came to this hospital, I was very intolerant of anyone who had any kind of mental illness. I thought they were people to be avoided and if necessary to be watched with caution. I was always on the lookout for peculiar remarks.

On the morning that I came to the hospital, my private doctor had examined me and said he had found nothing wrong with me. I dressed and went downstairs, and thought that some members of my family would be waiting for me. Instead there were two policemen and a policewoman. My doctor then told me there was an unexpected change in plans so I traveled along with them in the automobile quite willingly, wondering what the police were doing in the automobile. As we traveled down Y street, it dawned on me that they were taking me out here to the hospital,

---

[1] Statement in the author's files.

and I couldn't believe it. I had a horror of mental disease. I didn't want
to go there. I hesitated, stammered, wondering whether there was some
mistake. They took me to the doctor at the hospital, a lady doctor. She
asked me questions and I smart-alecked back. Was this all a joke? They
then took me to a ward, and left me, and I knew then that there was no
mistake. I was in a mental hospital. I wanted to call my husband, but I
couldn't. A little suitcase I had was checked for me. I sat down and wrote
a letter, and gave it to the nurse and she said she would see it was mailed.
She told me not to seal the envelope. Then I kept hoping that they were
wrong in the diagnosis of my case.

Some patients are exceptions. They are sufficiently enlightened
to enter the hospital as volunteers. These patients either minimize,
suppress, or disregard the stigma associated with psychotic behavior.

But the hospital also has certain benefits. First, the patient is
removed from his former conflict setting, whether from the family,
from business, or from other associates. Second, by not having to
make many decisions, and by being removed from his former competitive milieu, the patient can get a new perspective toward his
surroundings and toward himself. Third, the patient, despite the
stigma of being disordered, finds himself among other persons in a
like situation who accept him as he is. The shortcomings and merits
of the hospital beyond these features become the bases for evaluating it.

The Commitment Process

Becoming a patient in a state mental hospital—the final step of
a commitment process—varies in different states. In general, the
problem is to safeguard the person's constitutional liberties and yet
to protect the community from any possible danger.

Since an ordered person may be conceivably "railroaded" into
the mental hospital by scheming relatives and a compliant psychiatrist, the state usually requires a court order before a patient can
be committed. Psychiatrists and other persons object to this legal
step because it resembles criminal proceedings and because it
changes a medical case into a legal affair. Other persons, particularly jurists, regard the court proceedings as the proper means to
protect the patients. From the available evidence in mental hospitals, in northern states particularly, it seems that "railroading" is
relatively rare.[2] Depending upon the state, a person can be com-

[2] Albert Deutch, *The Mentally Ill in America*, p. 418 (New York: Columbia
University Press, 1949).

mitted (1) by a court based upon the findings of an "insanity" commission, (2) by a court based upon the findings of one or more medical examiners, (3) by a court following a jury trial, and (4) by an "insanity" commission with lawfully endowed judicial authority.[3]

The specific steps in commitment include: (1) a petition or an application for commitment of the designated "insane" person which is sworn and filed with the recognized authority, (2) a notice which must be served on the person presumed to be disordered, (3) a certificate of insanity signed by one or more physicians, (4) a hearing by a legally designated appropriate body, whether a court of record or a commission, and (5) a commitment order handed down by an appropriate body, which authorizes the admission of the person into a mental hospital of permanent care.[4]

Good intentions, however, do not always fulfill their expected purposes. The open jury trials of disordered persons, especially in small towns, can readily humiliate the person because of the rampant stigma associated with disordered behavior. The legal proceedings can create the impression to the disordered person that he has done something wrong and is being "tried" for it.

Some states have tried to find a middle course for this problem, which would guard the person's constitutional liberties but not subject him to stigmatized humiliation. The psychopathic hospitals, "emergency" commitments, and voluntary admissions are some mediums for this middle course. Persons allegedly psychotic can be committed to the psychopathic hospital or even to some state hospitals for periods not exceeding thirty days in order to be observed. Some states have statutes permitting the temporary commitment of patients of from ten to thirty days when these persons are violent and potentially harmful to themselves or to others. In this way, legal involvements are eliminated, and the patient is treated as a medical case.

Voluntary admissions, which have become more frequent in recent years, are still a relatively small proportion of total commitments. In New York voluntary commitments comprised 7.8 per cent of total commitments. In Illinois, however, the percentage of vol-

---

[3] *Ibid.*, p. 428.
[4] *Ibid.*, pp. 428, 429.

untary commitments increased from 8.3 in 1922 to 27.4 in 1949. This practice is one means of avoiding court procedures, but there are other means besides voluntary commitments or court certification for entering a hospital. In New York, for example, as can be seen from Table 17, 18.7 per cent and 12.9 per cent of the total admissions in 1946 and 1947, respectively, were results in whole or in part of a physician's or health officer's certificate.

TABLE 17

ADMISSIONS TO THE NEW YORK CIVIL STATE HOSPITALS,* CLASSIFIED ACCORDING TO MANNER OF ADMISSION, 1947 AND 1946†

Manner of Admission	1947		1946	
	Number	Per Cent	Number	Per Cent
On court certification	14,144	78.6	12,599	72.7
On voluntary application	1,402	7.8	1,390	8.0
On petition and medical certificate	790	4.4	850	4.9
On health officer's certificate	1,192	6.6	1,368	7.9
On physician's certificate	346	1.9	1,030	5.9
On criminal order	127	0.7	98	0.6
Total	18,001	100.0	17,335	100.0

* Includes patients admitted to Syracuse Psychopathic Hospital on other than an observation basis.

† From *Fifty-Ninth Annual Report of the Department of Mental Hygiene, State of New York for the Year Ended March 31, 1947*, No. 80, p. 73 (Albany, N.Y.: Legislative Document 1947, 1948).

Manner of Commitment and Civil Rights. The manner of the individual's commitment has a direct bearing upon whether or not he retains his civil rights. If he is a voluntary patient he usually retains his civil rights, and he usually can leave at his own request. In Illinois, for example, he merely has to give the superintendent fifteen days' notice of this intent. Moreover, when he leaves the hospital he can resume his activities without the handicap of being deprived of his civil rights. If the patient is committed as in need of mental treatment, instead of as insane, he may also retain his civil rights and have no difficulty in this respect when he leaves the hospital. The chief difficulty for the patient comes when he is committed as insane or mentally ill and is deprived of his civil rights while in the hospital. After his discharge his civil rights usually are restored automatically, but in some instances the restoration of his civil rights is hampered by red tape. A custodian is appointed for the insane person, and this custodian has almost complete charge over the patient.

The Detention Process. Another process which can confuse the patient about his condition is his temporary detention in a jail or prison, although this practice is more prevalent in rural than in urban areas. New York prohibited this practice as far back as 1827, but in 1909 it was estimated that about 18 per cent of all persons admitted to state hospitals were temporarily kept in jails or in similar places. The spread of the psychopathic hospital has diminished the need for detaining the person in jail in urban communities, but in some rural areas it is still prevalent. In 1933, 14 states allowed the detention of persons in jails and 6 other states permitted this practice for violent patients.[5] Indeed, many small communities have no other facilities for keeping the patients. As yet, we do not know what effects this mode of detention has upon the patients. In many cases the persons are dangerous, and their incarceration does remove a potential threat from the community. Also, some agitated patients may not remember these experiences. But in still other cases this mode of incarceration may make a deep impression which can affect the patients' whole outlook and may intensify their agitation, which the parents or friends would attribute to the patients' condition rather than to the situation.

For example, a young lady in a small Middle Western town had an agitated depression. Her mother called the police who placed her temporarily in the town jail until she could be transported to the state mental hospital. In jail, she became increasingly disturbed, screamed, tore her dress, and threw her partial denture on the floor and stepped on it. The mother felt that her daughter's disturbed behavior justified her being placed "behind bars." When the patient later became communicative, she disclosed that the thought of being jailed was so humiliating to her that to register a protest in some way, she reacted in the manner described.

But these practices do not characterize the detention process. The characteristic procedure in urban centers is to send the potential patient to a hospital for temporary care, once he is diagnosed or

[5] *Ibid.,* p. 435.

suspected of being psychotic and in need of treatment or custody. From this hospital, if it is found that the patient requires prolonged care or treatment, he is sent to a mental hospital—usually a state mental hospital. In addition, most patients are not necessarily violent or agitated when they enter the hospital. For example, the behavior classifications of first admissions to the New York state hospitals, shown in Table 18, reveal that the plurality of patients were the "quiet-idle" type. This behavior would preclude the need

TABLE 18

BEHAVIOR CLASSIFICATIONS OF FIRST ADMISSIONS IN NEW YORK CIVIL STATE
MENTAL HOSPITALS, 1947*

Type of Behavior	Total	Per Cent of Ascertained Cases		
		Males	Females	Total
Chronic bedridden	1,669	11.4	14.2	12.9
Acutely ill	285	3.1	1.4	2.2
Feeble	485	4.4	3.1	3.7
Blind	33	0.2	0.3	0.3
Lame	22	0.1	0.2	0.2
Employed	1,078	10.7	6.1	8.3
Quiet-idle	4,530	40.0	30.3	35.0
Depressed	1,093	5.7	10.9	8.4
Suicidal	364	2.2	3.3	2.8
Eloping	23	0.2	0.2	0.2
Resistive to feeding	59	0.3	0.6	0.4
Destructive	135	1.3	0.8	1.0
Soiling and wetting	161	1.4	1.0	1.2
Convulsive	70	0.7	0.4	0.5
Disturbed	2,133	12.9	19.7	16.4
Senile	823	5.2	7.4	6.3
Unascertained	549	0.2		
Total	13,512	100.0	100.0	100.0

* From *Fifty-Ninth Annual Report of the Department of Mental Hygiene, State of New York for the Year Ended March 31, 1947*, No. 80, p. 106 (Albany, N.Y.: Legislative Document 1947, 1948).

for incarceration in jails. But, regardless of the manner of commitment or the condition of the incoming patient, the patient encounters a new and somewhat strange environment when he enters the hospital. Sooner or later, he finds that he must come to terms with this environment.

The Patient's Social World

Despite incapacitating conflicts, the patient usually learns to participate in an established social world in the hospital. From mingling with others he learns to accommodate more readily to his hospital role; learns to soften negative stereotypes concerning "insanity" and acquires practices which operate as defensive mediums, however indirect, to the staff. Some attitudes are common among patients; other attitudes vary in emphasis with different types of patients. But by his social relations with the staff, friends, enemies, and visitors, the incoming patient becomes part of a society; and this society can affect his condition, favorably or adversely.

Attitudes to Their Disorders. Since patients come from the same general society as ordered persons, they, too, resent the stigma of disordered behavior, and such terms as "insane" or "crazy." The private resentment to this stereotype by one patient becomes socialized by being shared with other patients. Moreover, the stereotypes of "insane" or "crazy" are social definitions. These terms do not characterize the personal reactions of the patient. Generally, he is concerned about his symptoms or sometimes about his conflicts; these aspects of his behavior have reality for him. Since these behavior patterns become defined as "crazy" by others, he may accept or reject this social connotation. Depending upon his groups, he may or may not know that he is experiencing a breakdown and may not define his condition as "insane." Consequently, some patients do not picture themselves as "insane" when entering the hospital; others may realize that they are so defined but may resist this definition; a third group, usually the minority, may accept this definition. However they define themselves, the patients already in the hospital tend to suppress this mode of group reference. Hence, the incoming patient will learn that this mode of social reference is not acceptable to, and will be resisted by, other patients.

Some patients may refer to others, particularly those whom they dislike, as "irresponsible," "crazy," or "nutty," but they are often more circumspect about applying such terms to themselves or their friends. Their condition is a result of "nervousness," "overwork," "worry," or "physical illness." Two typical attitudes are the following:

I wasn't ill when I came into the hospital; it was just that my nerves were run down. I was very tired and very tense. I worked too hard, I wanted to get away from everything.

Some have diseases in this hospital and some hear voices. I don't know that I'm insane. An insane man don't know what he's doing, I know what I'm doing and I'm sane. These voices are trying to get me crazy by working on my mind. They are crazy and they work on me.

As we have emphasized, these definitions of their disorders do not result because of lack of insight. Although disoriented patients may have little or no insight into their conditions, the large proportion of patients make these oversights deliberately, as socially defensive reactions, which become reinforced or coerced by the patient milieu.

Attitudes toward the Hospital. Consistent with the disavowal of their disorders, many patients seldom refer to the institution as an "insane asylum." Many patients are usually aware of being in a mental hospital, but they seldom discuss it among themselves. Those who do allude to the hospital usually add that they are not disordered or do not belong in the institution.

One patient remarked:

I know where I'm at. I'm not dumb. I'm ashamed to be here, but it don't help the other patients by reminding them that they're in a mental hospital. I just want to leave this place.

Again:

Patients don't mention they're in a mental hospital, it's too unpleasant.

Some patients who found respite in the hospital from the conflictful situations in the outside society group accept the hospital. But another group, confronted with the stigma of mental disorder, are challenged to improve their condition, so as to become eligible for release.

The Patient and His Hospital Role. In the course of their hospital stay, patients realize that they must conform to hospital rules and must obey the hospital personnel. Regardless of their reactions to the stigma of insanity or of their dread of being in a mental hospital, they realize from their own experiences, or from the experiences of other patients, that they have no alternative but to accept their hospital roles. Some may be reluctant or defiant in complying with this subordinate position; others may do so readily. Regardless of personal differences, the predominant majority of patients conform, at least externally.

When the patients are oriented and in need of activity, they may find this passive hospital role oppressive.

They don't give you a chance to exert your own will. It's always taking orders from a number of people. I have to do exactly what they tell me and when they tell me.

Being locked up in this place gives me the feeling of being helpless and hopeless.

At the other extreme, the long-time or chronic patients often become so accommodated to the hospital situation that they accept it implicitly. These patients who have been returned more than once to the hospital and have more or less given up the project of readjustment to the outside community become completely resigned to their roles.

I have been out twice and couldn't make it. I think I'll stay here for the time. I'm old and can't compete with the younger fellows. I have a sore back and can't work too hard. I may go out and come back worse. I can't take that chance. I'll stay here for the time.

This hospital has been home to me for eleven years. I'm used to it. The work isn't hard and I know how to get along. It wasn't easy the first two years, but after being in and out three times, I can call this home. . . . No complaints.

To understand the process of conformity to the hospital, we must describe the reaction of the personnel to the patients who violate the rules and who remain defiant to the personnel; for the specter of being labelled "disturbed" looms in the background.

"Agitation" and Restraint. The patient's unruliness, disturbance, or defiance is regarded by the hospital personnel as a threat to order and routine. They resolve this problem by labeling the patient "disturbed" and deal with him accordingly. The term "disturbed," however, is defined so broadly by the staff that often it may include any behavior which the particular attendant regards as "disturbed."

It may be the patient's expression of his conflicts. It may be his unwillingness to perform certain chores; his violation of certain rules; his attempt to escape; his indignation at the hospital conditions or at some unjust treatment of himself or at other patients.

One patient said:

As soon as you start holding your own and trying to stand up for yourself, the attendants say you are disturbed and want to put you down on ward 7 [acutely disturbed ward]. It hasn't happened to me but it has to some. I am afraid to say anything, but one has to stand up for oneself on some occasions.

Again:

I've seen patients who stick up for their rights. If a patient passes on an opinion even though he may raise his voice that does not necessarily mean he is disturbed. That business of being disturbed covers an awful lot of territory.

Further:

I've learned to control my emotions. If I want to stay on the best wards I have to control myself. I can't let them see me cry. They might say I'm disturbed.

The person who escapes is automatically placed in a "strong ward" for security reasons, while the person who is agitated because of some inner conflict is also placed in a strong ward or put into restraint. The general tendency by the staff is to respond by punishment or "treatment," whether it be hydrotherapy—"packs"—restraint or placing the patient in a "back" or chronic ward or in an agitated or "strong" ward. Only in very few and isolated cases are exceptions made.[6]

This inflexible reaction by the staff creates an atmosphere of "moral realism" in which the therapeutic concern about the particular reactions of the individual patient becomes secondary to hospital rules. Even the doctors, in time, submit to this arrangement. Though they may prescribe hydrotherapy or "packs" for the patient, which means placing him in wet, tightly bound sheets or placing him in a tub from which he cannot get out, the really disturbed patient comes to regard this as punishment. It means that he has violated a hospital rule and that this restraint is the inevitable punitive result.

One dreadful prospect among many patients who may become "disturbed" is "restraint." Since little effort is made to reason with or to reach the patient emotionally, the need of restraining the patient becomes more necessary. The restraints which are applied

[6] These types include patient functionaries or pseudo-leaders. See section on Chronic Patients, p. 437.

may vary a great deal. Some of them are mild and not feared. The restraint may be just an ankle chain so applied that the patient cannot move beyond a certain distance. It may be "sleeves" in which the patient's hands are tied so that he cannot move them. Or it may be a jacket, which seems to be the most punitive and feared of the "restraints." One patient wrote of his reactions to this last mode of restraint as one of his worst hospital experiences. We quote him:[7]

There were other slow near-deaths, and then the soaring crucifixion at the Fair.

But this had been the worst death of all. It had not been the slow spiral ebbing of blood and feeling into a dark warm dream. It had not been the shuddering resigned death of threatened drowning; nor the quick stroke smashing sleep on the road into almost something deeper; nor the star-shot pinioning against the gate. This had been the death fought in mortal terror, the death grinding and beating and twisting previous life from the tortured body, the unmerciful death that withholds its peace and turns facet after sharp facet of its pain. I do not know words to describe the throttling of my throat and vicious unseeable assault on my body.

I fought all night against the sheet and by daylight I had the top part loose. I don't know how, but I did. I called upon Houdini's spirit. I broke or slipped enough of the knotted tapes from their moorings so that the top of the sheet from behind my head to my waist came free from the underpinnings of the bed and I could sit up. There were still fastenings down my back, but by compressing, contorting one arm I worked it free from its sleeve, though it remained inside the canvas chemise, and the other almost free. With both of them loose I might manage to unfasten the lacings down my back. Once free, I had no program of action. My aim was to demonstrate my unconquerability, to free myself from my unjustly imposed shackles and relieve the torment of lying trussed in one position on my back, which now felt as though the skin had been rubbed off it over every protruding bone.

The door opened and a hospital guard stood there. He was not one of my imprisoners and his regard and tone were mild as he said, "Well, that was quite a trick. I'm sorry, but I'll have to tie you down again."

"Why?" I asked. "Why? If you'd just leave me so I could move I wouldn't try to get out."

"Charge nurse's orders," he said. "You can't get out till he sees you. You're supposed to be in a restraining sheet and if he finds you half out somebody will catch hell."

[7] Carleton Brown, *Brainstorm*, p. 236 (New York: Rinehart & Company, Inc., 1944). By permission. Recently some hospitals have ceased using the more punitive types of restraint.

I protested tiredly as he tied me down again, but I did not fight or curse him. I lay back and tried to come to terms with my pain. But there was no position in which I could hold my body so that it did not ache and burn. I cried soundlessly and abjectly. My tears smarted on my face. I looked up and begged for mercy to fall from whatever source in the universe it might originate.

Perhaps most patients cannot articulate their feelings as fluently as this patient, but the helplessness and futile pain is often there. Enforced physical restraint, then, has an institutional function. It is a traditional medium which is practiced to keep order, and in some hospitals this practice is continued because of a shortage of trained personnel.

We see too from this example that the impersonal rules are so enforced that the individual attendant had little to say about them. He became a cog in an impersonal process who had to obey the commands of his superiors, whether he agreed or disagreed with them.[8] Some doctors, although privately opposed to this mode of handling patients, feel that it would be almost futile to oppose it overtly; for the limited facilities and the lack of qualified attendants in state hospitals preclude care or supervision for those who would be potentially violent. The lack of personnel to supervise agitated patients is, as we have mentioned, necessary to prevent suicide and/or homicide. Some form of restraint, according to sincere psychiatrists, becomes virtually a necessity for some patients.

Erickson maintains that restraint can be used for therapeutic purposes when it meets the patients' needs.[9] Certain patients need something more concrete than their unresolved personal conflicts. The restraint presumably fulfills this need, because "human nature tends to regard a repugnant remedy as effective." [10]

Although the application of restraint may conceivably have some therapeutic value for some patients, this value, even as Erickson points out, at best is on a symptomatic level. Moreover, the majority of hospitals use restraint primarily for administrative and custodial purposes and not for therapeutic purposes. The therapeutic rationale for restraint can easily result in dangerous abuses because of the

[8] Carleton Brown, *Brainstorm*, p. 236. See also Clifford Beers, *A Mind That Found Itself*, p. 129, 130 (New York: Doubleday & Company, Inc., 1924).

[9] Milton H. Erickson, "Psychological Significance of Physical Restraint to Mental Patients," *The American Journal of Psychiatry*, February, 1948, 105:7, pp. 612–614.

[10] *Ibid.*, p. 614.

relative helplessness of the patient with respect to the staff. The policy of trying to understand the viewpoint and elicit the co-operation of the patients is a constructive one. The mild forms of restraint could possibly be used in exceptional cases, but it should be supplemented by other constructive means of quieting the patient once he is communicative. Also, the painful and punitive features of restraint should be eliminated. Most state mental hospitals, however, do not and usually cannot have this approach to restraint for the reason mentioned—lack of qualified personnel.

Conformity as an Only Recourse. The patient's most expedient recourse is to comply. In becoming adjusted to the institution, he knows that the odds are against him, and he willingly or reluctantly reconciles himself to his patient role. It is this accommodation that prevails among the overwhelming number of patients, with the exception, of course, of those in the agitated wards.

Remarks of patients typical of this conformistic attitude are as follows:

I behave myself and obey all the rules because it's the proper thing to do and I don't want to go against that. I'll be happier in the long run and get out that way.

I find it's the best policy to play along with the doctors and attendants. It's simply no percentage in trying to buck them. You don't get anywhere, except in trouble. I want to get out as soon as I can and I'm going to play along.

The patient group also facilitates the adjustment of incoming patients by indirect social pressure. Since all patients on the ward follow a certain routine, this routine indirectly influences the particular patient to do the same. An attendant observed the following changes in certain patients through this process of social emulation:

Following the crowd will help the patient adjust better to the hospital than nagging or threats or attempts at discipline. A restless patient who sees all the other patients going to bed at a certain time usually goes with them. He may not sleep, but he stays in bed. I recall a patient that refused to obey orders. Whatever we did to him he remained stubborn. Then he was transferred from the receiving ward and he noticed the other patients going about their business, washing themselves, getting up on time, bathing, lining up to eat. He was constantly thrown with the group, and soon he was seen to take hold of himself. After that his condition constantly improved. If attendants weren't so impatient, they would get more done with patients. The patients themselves would have the others follow the crowd.

Some patients who were disturbed at the time of admission became more calm after one or two weeks in the hospital. Usually, this altered reaction meant an adjustment to a new situation. Perhaps their agitated responses were defenses to the particular members in the family. In the hospital, their superficial defensive reactions were no longer necessary, and they revised their behavior accordingly.

In brief, the patients learn that it is most expedient to adjust to the patient roles because of the threat of punishment, because of the adjustive techniques acquired from other patients, and because of the indirect social pressure from other patients. Those who do not come to terms with their roles are considered "disturbed" and are removed from the patient milieu or placed in restraint. Only longtime patients who know the ways of evading hospital rules are the conspicuous exceptions. Generally, the patient's role is in such a social groove that personal spontaneity tends to be discouraged. His conforming process also extends to the patient's relationships with the professional staff and with the attendants.

Relations with the Professional Staff. Patients believe that the doctors control their hospital "fate," because they can shorten or prolong their stay in the hospital. Despite limited opportunities, they strive to cultivate favorable relationships with the doctors. These overt reactions signify the "hospitalwise" patients. They realize the detrimental effects of antagonizing the doctors. Nonetheless, they evaluate the doctors but try to conceal their hostility when it is aroused, though not always successfully. Consider the following evaluation of the doctors by a patient.[11]

Confidence between patient and doctor is considered to be the keystone of any attempt at psychotherapy. Neither I nor any of the patients with whom I talked had a scrap of it in Dr. Soup, though a few did in Dr. Mac and more did in a younger doctor who seemed to have entered the field through some genuine interest in it, and sympathy with its subjects. It was perhaps somewhat unfairly that the brunt of our feelings of bad faith fell on Dr. Soup; this came about partly because he was the one who made final decisions as to our movements in this department of the hospital. Thus when I asked Dr. Mac what had happened to the promise that my parents would bring out my typewriter, he told me that the decision rested with Dr. Soup. Dr.

[11] Carleton Brown, *Brainstorm*, p. 249 (New York: Rinehart & Company, Inc., 1944). By permission.

Soup cut short my queries during rounds, and did not give me an interview in his office until after I was transferred to the quiet ward 98 on the floor above, where the balance of my incarceration became a stretch of acute and chafing tedium relieved occasionally by the violent actions of my fellows.

Doctors who are sympathetic, who listen and respond to the patients, usually are esteemed highly. Those physicians who make short shrift of the patients incur their antagonism. These notions are by no means held privately by each patient but are socialized by conversation and gossip. The doctors become typed. Nonetheless, the need for defense creates a disparity between the patients' personal versions and their overt behavior.

The patients curse the doctor all day, but act their best when the doctor appears on the ward. In our ward the patients act different when the doctor isn't around. They become so much nicer when he is on the ward.

Generally the doctors, overburdened by large numbers of patients, have little time to devote to each patient. But the patient seemingly considers his superficial needs fulfilled when he believes the doctor expresses a personal interest in him. In fact, this becomes one of his chief aspirations. He vies with other patients to win the doctor's attention, often approaches him to speak his "piece," and resents the attendants who prevent him from doing so. One patient wrote:[12]

The doctors made their once-daily morning rounds so rapidly that it was necessary to wait watchfully to be sure of catching them. They stopped at most for ten minutes to listen and dismiss all complaints that were brought to them by as many of the twenty or thirty men in the ward as had not yet learned, as they would after one or two such talks, that addressing the water cooler in the bathroom was likely to prove as satisfactory; Kearney and the attendants did their best to forestall and forget all patients' bids for attention, legitimate or not.

But these expressions of feelings and thoughts by the patients may be inhibited by certain factors of the patient culture. They may lead to withholding information which will deter the patient's release. That is, some patients who hallucinate, or some paranoids who retain their delusional systems realize that these symptoms are sources of social disapproval. Hence, they may attempt to minimize or to conceal them. For example, one patient said to another. "Don't tell the doctors that you hear voices. If you do, they'll never

[12] *Ibid.*, p. 246.

let you out." The more appropriate answer which some patients learn is that the "voices were a part of my imagination." This discrepancy between external conformity and symptomatic behavior exists, but it is not known how extensive it may be. Seemingly, it predominates among paranoids.

The doctor makes his morning rounds, asks me how I feel and I say, "Fine." I don't want to tell him what really bothers me or tell him my troubles. It might rub him the wrong way and hurt my chances of getting out. But he's a nice fellow and sometime he's going to play checkers with me.

Nonetheless, by skillful and friendly interviewing, the doctors may detect these symptoms. As we have indicated, the traditions of the hospital impede the doctors from becoming too zealously concerned about their patients. Their conformity is largely a means of practicing specific routines. Some doctors, who feel harassed by their duties, may merely scold or lecture the patients. Usually they do not find out what the patients' problems are, and, at times, leave the patients dissatisfied and frustrated. "My doctor keeps talking and talking. I sit there and have to listen," said one patient. "I should be asked what is on my mind, so that the questions would be like keys to open my mind and have everything to pour out. I have a lot to tell her, but she doesn't give me a chance."

By contrast, consider the following statement of a 19-year-old female manic-depressive who apparently had an intense attachment to her doctor.

If you see Dr. X, you may tell him that I think an awful lot about him. I really adore him. I think he's such a sweet person and he's done so much for me, I could never stop thanking him. I love him with all my heart and I mean every word I've said. I wish he would call me back to examine me. . . . Or I wish Dr. X would call on me soon to care for his kids. I'd love to keep his children and also to meet his sweet wife. If I meet any man who looks like Dr. X my heart will go out to him.

Frequently, patients create definite and very close attachments to the doctors when they feel that the doctors are interested in them and are trying to help them. Because of the character of the relationship, it may become an erotic involvement, as in the illustration cited. But these relationships are usually therapeutic for the patients, because they inspire a positive outlook among patients which contributes to their improvement.

A doctor's interest may reach even an agitated patient. One patient relates the following experiences of a doctor's interest in a patient named Allen and his contribution to the patient's improvement. Though this narrative lacks the finer aspects of a dynamic analysis and may perhaps be one of the hospital legends, it nonetheless reveals the way the patients evaluate the doctor's personal interest and its constructive results. In this sense, this narrative uncovers what some patients ideally expect from doctors.[13]

Speechless, savage, some strange quirk in his mind must have made him believe that he was in a land of animals and that he, too, must choose to be an animal along with the rest. He picked on the gorilla walking in a crouch, his arms almost touching the floor. He let his hair grow long, he growled when people came near him. Here by all laws of chance, he should have stayed and died as did all the others.

Happily, the doctor of the ward took an interest in him. I was assured this was not usually the case. The doctor, surrounded by incurables as he was needing to tend to so many patients, did not often find time in the back hall to do anything but cure physical complaints. In most cases, medical attention was as useful as having a shave before execution.

Whatever the reason, however, the doctor did interest himself in this strange hulk of a man—perhaps because he seemed so much younger than the rest, perhaps because his eyes bore some promise of reason.

He spoke kindly to him, understandingly. Each time he visited a ward, he singled out this wild-looking animal to address some words that might have been to an equal, never receiving a reply, never expecting it. As an animal grows gentle under kind treatment so this patient after some weeks, slunk over to the doctor whenever he put in an appearance in the ward, and waited for a kind word as a dog waits for a pat from his master.

He would still tolerate no one else near him. Guards from time to time beat him to get him to bathe or wash. The doctor did nothing but talk gently to him. Painstakingly he pointed out objects mentioning them by name, repeating them again and again. . . .

Upon the insistence of the doctor, he agreed to have his beard cut off. That too, brought a transformation. His crouch became less pronounced. He began to straighten up, to speak with more and more ease, enunciating clearly, showing greater familiarity with language, making astonishing headway.

The doctor was pleased . . . they could now engage in conversation, each time the doctor came, about simple and unimportant

[13] Lawrence Jayson, *Mania,* pp. 142–145 (New York: Funk & Wagnalls Company, 1937).

things which made the patient friendly and grateful. We must get to the bottom of this, thought the doctor. Now is the time.

So he brought the subject round to personal things. He asked the patient questions about himself, his name, his family, his history. The man answered reluctantly, uneasy as he gave the information, less and less willing to talk. Relentlessly the doctor continued.

"You know you can speak English as well as I do. We are friends. Why not tell me everything. Why do you pretend you can't talk?"

The patient shut up like a clam. From that time on he refused to talk to the doctor. He lapsed back into old ways. The same quiet sullenness. The same animal qualities. Efforts of the doctor to draw him out again were unavailing. He was forced to admit defeat.

But the patient had given him some facts, and the doctor still interested, was able to seek out Allen's frantic family, who, for months had been looking for the boy. A wealthy, intelligent family, they spared no efforts to get him into Druryville, where he was admitted a year ago still in his growling state. Here the same patient process was repeated, this time to bring him finally on the permanent road to recovery.

"It's funny what talking it out can do for a guy," said Eddie, after having finished Allen's story, his broad face aglow. "Something loosens up inside of you and that great lump of tightness disappears as you get the right person to tell it to. That's the way it was with me." That's what happened to Allen, he got the person who could listen to him, who could understand him.

In time, patients become resigned to the slight attention from the physicians and expect little from them. Many chronic patients blame the doctors for their continued detention in the hospital. They feel that, were the doctors willing, they would be released.

On the other hand, since many patients are lonely and isolated, they desperately seek some person to whom they can confide. When encouraged, they readily become dependent upon the doctors. In fact, some doctors claim that some patients become so dependent upon them that they have to create a social distance. Yet these supportive relationships usually help sustain the patients and in some extreme cases help the doctors.[14]

When some doctors to whom patients become attached are transferred to other wards or leave the hospital, the patients tend to go

[14] The isolated doctors who have no personal relationships in their extra-professional life find the patients convenient outlets for their aggressions and prejudices. Also, the patients' attachment, as well as their submission, may readily enhance the doctors' self-esteem, which they do not seemingly derive from any social source.

through an emotional crisis. Yet these doctors who have awakened the confidence of the patients can reach and influence their behavior more readily. Consequently, the transfers may interfere with a therapeutic relationship.

For example, one patient in a back ward who became attached to the doctors, and who improved as a result, was transferred to a "hopeful" ward. In the new ward she initiated new relationships with another doctor, to whom she took a dislike, and became worse. In brief, doctor-patient relationships are not always or necessarily regarded as therapeutic in many state hospitals, but these relationships may facilitate or impede the patient's improvement. Although some hospitals recognize increasingly the social psychological aspects of the therapeutic process, many other hospitals tend to ignore this fact.

Attendant-Patient Relationships. Patients can be vitally affected by their relationships with attendants. Yet these relationships are at best custodial and at worst repressive. Since attendants aspire primarily to control the patients, they frown upon social intimacy or informality with patients because they feel that familiarity may relax their effective control. But, by and large, the patients regard the attendants as distant custodians who neither harm nor help them, but who keep the ward in order and keep unruly patients quiet.

The patients try to adjust to these relationships. They do not dispute the dominance of the attendants but strive to get along with them. Though the degree of compliance seemingly may vary with the individual patient, this mode of behavior, too, is an acquired form of hospital adjustment. "Hospitalwise" patients tend to comply with the attendants' demands, regardless of what they think privately or tell other trusted patients. For the most part, they realize their relative helplessness with respect to the attendants, and that their comfort or discomfort depends upon them.

The patients then try to discover who are the friendly and unfriendly attendants. Their requests and general behavior to the attendants are largely influenced by this collective appraisal. If an attendant is friendly, they become very attached to him, may make requests to him, and try to become informal. When the attendant is unfriendly, they obey but tend to remain distant. One patient evaluated the attendants as follows:

There's different kinds of attendants. Some I don't like. I wouldn't give them any good will. They bawl a man out in front of a bunch of men even when the man is in the right. [Then] there are attendants the men would swear by because they are fair even though they are strict.

The patients who do not get along with some attendants try to get transferred to other wards with friendly attendants. Though many may not succeed, they continue to strive for this change.

Ignorant of the dynamics of disordered behavior and socially distant from the patients, the attendants discourage personal confidences from the patients. Patients who are reconciled to the hospital folkways do not attempt to "open up" to the attendants, unless it concerns some hospital rumor. Other patients may have such pressing conflicts that they may require someone to whom they can confide.

For example, one patient, wracked by attitudes of guilt and self-condemnation, was unable to sleep. She tossed about in bed and started to murmur to herself. When the attendant came into her room to see what was happening, the patient tried to speak with her. The attendant not only refused to listen but thought the patient was disturbed. The patient said:

She gave me a look as if I were crazy, and didn't know what I was doing. She wouldn't bother with me, told me to go to sleep and not make any trouble. I had so much on my mind that I wanted to talk about that I couldn't sleep and keep still. I was so distressed about my husband and children living at home without me and it pressed hard on my mind that I had to try all my might to keep still. I lay awake the whole night, thinking these matters over and over again.

The attendants do not regard this type of counseling as part of their job. As long as they can supervise the ward, they feel they have performed their duty. Since this counseling relationship is necessary for certain cases, it reveals that custodial care is not enough.

Attendants frequently respond to the patients as if they were supposedly rational and ordered. When patients are resistive, many attendants not only consider this behavior as a violation of hospital rules but also as a personal affront. Hence, within their authority, they can call the patient "disturbed" and vindictively attempt to "calm him."

Disoriented patients often do not respond to the attendants as attendants but react in terms of their delusional stereotypes and categorize them as enemies. The punitive retaliation merely confirms the patients' delusions that the attendants are enemies. These patients cannot be reasoned with easily. Attempts to calm them by interviews require time and patience, which are luxuries in the hospital. An attendant in an agitated ward described what he had learned about handling agitated patients:

Distract his attention before you tie him down. Don't hit him where the marks will show or so hard that the patient will become a problem. Humor him if you can and once you get him under control let him stay that way till he quiets down and learns his lesson.

The attendants, who have the lowest status among the employees, can express their aggressions, deliberately or unwittingly, against the patients. Attendants are subject to many rules and must express varied forms of deference to superiors. For example, the charge nurse in one hospital insisted that attendants remain standing when she entered the ward, and that they do exactly as she told them. On the other hand, the doctor felt that the attendants in this ward were under his supervision. The result was that a particular attendant in this ward became disgusted by the dual authority and quit. Before quitting, he became irritated at any recalcitrant move by a patient and became more verbally abusive to the patients than formerly.

Patients are careful to avoid involvement in interstaff controversies. One doctor, who became particularly interested in a patient, found that the attendant resented this interest. The attendant began to tease and humiliate the patient in varied ways. To escape from this difficult position, the patient tried to remain away from the doctor when he visited the ward.

Although attendants maintain a social distance from the patients and concentrate specifically upon their custodial control, they do have "favorites." These "favorites," as in any other social milieu, are often given preferred treatment. These favorites may include the informal "ward leaders," the functionaries, or the "stool pigeons." Generally, the favorites are disliked by the other patients, although the exceptions are those who remain "loyal" to the patients. One such type is "Mr. Peabody" who is described as follows by Rowland:[15]

John Peabody is a paranoid type of schizophrenic about thirty years of age. He is "ward boss" on his ward. He has been in the hospital

[15] Howard Rowland, "Interaction Processes in the State Mental Hospital," *Psychiatry*, August, 1939, 2:3, p. 330.

eight years. He not only tells you he runs the ward, but he actually directs most of the activities and in some measure has the cooperation of the other patients.

Peabody's industrious habits lighten the work which ordinarily falls on the attendant or nurse in charge. Attendants and nurses may come and go, but Peabody is the "oldest resident" who knows the intricate problems of each of the patients on the ward. He organizes the morning clean-up and he cares for the untidy patients. He makes numerous suggestions about occupational assignments. He has a considerable amount of mechanical skill and has fashioned several implements used in the hospital laboratory.

Mr. Peabody's case record states that on one occasion he was badly bruised when another patient became disturbed and struck him. He refused to report the name of the other patient because he was afraid that the man would be sent to the "packs."

It should be noted that this type of patient-attendant relationship is somewhat exceptional in the state mental hospital and is limited to a very few patients who have the confidence of the administrators or superintendent. During and since World War II, the shortage of attendants in many state hospitals has been so great that many of their faults have been overlooked. This problem has been alleviated only slightly during the past year. The usual procedure is to give preference to the employee's rather than to the patient's version of any incident.

Social Structure of the Patients

Patients can be classified roughly by the type of wards to which they are assigned: (1) hopeful, (2) chronic, and (3) agitated. These wards, which have specified meanings for the patients, are named by them accordingly. The hopeful ward is referred to as the "going home," or "open ward," the chronic ward is the "back ward," and the agitated ward is the "strong ward." These different ward classifications usually denote the condition of the patients which, in turn, indicates their status in the hospital and their collective orientation.

Hopeful patients usually are in the hospital a relatively short time, are in an improved and communicative condition, and have favorable prospects for discharge. Chronic patients are usually in the hospital a much longer time, may or may not be communicative, and have unfavorable prospects for discharge. Agitated patients are considered a threat to the hospital or to the community. They are unable to abide by the hospital norms, whether because of their

432 SOCIETY AND PERSONALITY DISORDERS

personal condition or because of their resentment to hospital rules
or conditions.

Hopeful Patients. Hopeful patients regard their stay in the hospital as transient and are mainly concerned with "going home."
With this collective orientation, they regard commitment as an
interruption of their home routine. Since they, more than other
patients, resent the stigma of their commitment, their desire for
leaving the hospital becomes their predominant value. It becomes
socialized by conversation and becomes a competitive basis for
status. The more favorably a patient is considered by the staff for
going home, the more status he may have with the other patients.
Some typical attitudes of hopeful patients are the following:

I want to go home and get away from this place. I don't mind the hospital,
but I'd rather be home. I want to go home as soon as the doctor lets me.

I'm getting fed up. I have to get out of here and soon. I asked my brother
and sister when they were here, when I would leave, and they said that it
was up to the doctor. To think that I even have to be in a place like this.

The discharge or conditional release of some patients accentuates
the desire of others to leave. It is this fact which sharpens the competitive attitudes among the patients and, at times, leads to envy
and hostility.

When a patient is ready to go home, others may gossip: "Oh, she's not as
well as I. How come she's going home so soon. I'm at least as well as she."
The other nods, and says the same thing about herself.

The patients who may want to remain in the hospital for longer
periods incur the hostility, contempt, or pity of the other patients.
Generally, they are considered variants or at least atypical. A few
patients who had experienced hardships on the outside regard the
hospital more favorably. The other patients may tolerate their
claims, but they either avoid them or "feel sorry" for them. One
patient explained her plight in these words:

This is the first vacation I've had in ten years. There is so much work to
do at home, I don't know whether I want to do it. I went home on the
week-end and I felt so tired that the thought of doing it made me sit down.
The girls on the ward say they want to go home, but I don't want to go
home so bad. I want to work this out for myself. They think there's something the matter with me, and that I like it here.

Patients who may want to remain longer do not express their
viewpoints frequently because they discover the resentment of the

other patients. The collective attitude also pertains to the patient's improvement.

Improvement is considered a means to discharge. The "pessimistic" or "complaining" patients who doubt their improvement create a mood which other patients oppose:

C. always talks about how miserable he is, always complaining. Says it's his nerves. He's one to keep away from if you want to get out of here. I want to leave quick and I won't let him get me down.

By stimulating competition for discharge, the hopeful patients indirectly are motivated to improve and recover. Their negative attitude toward the hospital induces a positive attitude toward improvement. The relative simplicity of the hospital environs and the few objectives shared by hopeful patients help their condition, despite the limitations of the hospital facilities. These attitudes apparently have arisen unwittingly. The patients' personalized desires to leave become socialized and reinforced by conversation. This positive indigenous aspect of the hopeful patients' culture has other favorable features in the informal companionships and friendships among the patients. Although friendships exist in almost all types of hospital wards, they appear more significant among hopeful patients as a means to therapy.

Attitudes toward Physical Therapy. Many hopeful patients are required to take electro- and/or insulin shock therapy. As features of hospital living, these activities become topics of discussion among the patients. Consistent with the attitudes of the staff in keeping the patients "in the dark," the staff in some hospitals do not orient the patients to the therapy. Hence, the patients seek information from each other. Their reactions to this process vary. Some feel that they have a right to know what is being done to them; others accept the patient role implicitly and feel it is a matter of concern to the staff only.

If I go to a dentist and he fixes my teeth, he tells me what is wrong and what he is going to do. I can understand some things. Why don't they tell us . . . those of us who can understand . . . what is being done to us. We'll have more confidence in what to believe and in what not to believe.

I don't know whether they have their degrees or not but I don't want to be submitted to any more of these treatments. They line you up regularly; it is a hard and fast rule to take treatments. Are there no human rights at all? They make you feel so helpless when they hold you on the table. Some don't mind it, and I didn't. But for some it was really rough.

The whole arrangement of electroshock therapy presents an apprehensive picture to new patients, particularly women. Patients in one typical hospital who were last in line could hear the first patients awakening from the coma and screaming as if in pain, and their fears became intensified.

You don't know what it is to sit in the room near by and hear the screams and think that you're next. When I first went to shock I heard such screaming I asked the nurse, "What are you doing to them." I couldn't imagine why they would want to yell like that.

Personal Effects of Electric Shock. The shock treatments, which are taken in the morning and three times weekly, range from twelve to twenty-four treatments, although the number is flexible. The immediate effects of the shock are to make the patients hazy and apathetic until well on into the afternoon.[16] Their apprehension concerning the shock persists, and they attribute to it a variety of ailments and difficulties, loss of weight, slowed heartbeats, memory defects, and blunted feelings in varied parts of the anatomy.

They have given me that electricity eleven times. I am losing weight with it all the time. I am down from one hundred and fifty pounds to one hundred and nineteen pounds. Now my toes don't feel as they once did. I dread that machine and I won't have it. I sure would like to tell the person who brought me in here.

I must have lost my memory. The shock treatments I took at the sanatarium were responsible. I forget everything after those shock treatments.

Why did the patients object so strenuously to shock therapy, particularly to electroshock therapy? Were these reactions inevitable outgrowths of the treatment or were they external to the treatment process itself? Although the mysterious and disagreeable setting of the shock may have frightened patients, these fears seldom were allayed by the staff, because the staff were usually indifferent to, and sometimes unaware of, the patients' reactions. Individual fears, in the process of being shared with others, became magnified by many, although not by all, patients. Some patients simply would not enter into or become influenced by the discussions. But the magnified fears were usually cultural emergents of a social process rather than a direct outgrowth of the shock experience.[17]

[16] Some hospitals made these patients return to work within an hour after electroshock therapy.

[17] For example, this pervasive shared fear of shock is not so intense in the better-organized private hospitals.

Psychoanalysts contend that the so-called "death fear" of electric shock may instill in the patients a more intense desire to live and a more positive interest in the surroundings.[18] Also, it has been said that the fears directed to electric shock distracted the patients from their problems. Some patients evidently did regard the electric shock almost as a symbol of a death ritual.

Although no precise data are available, it seems that the manifestly fearful patients did not improve more quickly or in larger numbers than those who were not overtly afraid. It appeared in some instances that the reverse was true. Nonetheless, the socially induced fears were extraneous to the shock therapy per se, and merely reflected the indifference of the professional staff to the reactions of the patients.

In affecting recovery, the electric shock seems to show definite success. Of the 380 patients in one particular hospital who submitted to the electric shock during a one-half-year period, 64.8 per cent were improved or recovered, and 35.2 per cent were unimproved. This compares rather well with other studies made of electroshock therapy in other state mental hospitals.

Insulin Therapy. Insulin therapy is used frequently for those patients who have completed electroshock therapy. It is also used for paranoids and other schizophrenics some of whom are not given electroshock therapy. The favorable effects of this mode of physical therapy for disordered persons were reported by Sakel in 1936. Within the last ten or fifteen years it has been introduced and has spread as a therapeutic device in the state mental hospitals. Many claims have been made for this type of therapy regarding its influence upon improvement.

This treatment is usually administered intravenously, after which the patient goes into a coma. After coming out of the coma, a glucose substance, such as orange juice, is given to the patient to counteract the hypoglycemic—depletion of sugar—body condition. Though the schedule as to the number of shocks administered to the patients varies with their needs, the modal number ranges from forty to sixty shocks on a five-day-week schedule. In some cases, a

---

[18] Fenichel maintains that the patients seem to have a magical experience of "death and rebirth" from the electric shock treatments, but that these reactions do not reveal anything about the biological changes "that may occur within the organism." Otto Fenichel, *The Psychoanalytic Theory of Neuroses*, p. 568 (New York: W. W. Norton & Company, 1945).

certain number of insulin and electric shocks are given alternately rather than successively.

Personal Effects. This treatment is not so vigorous as electroshock therapy, but its temporary effects are more prolonged. Extensive research has been done on the physiological and psychological effects of insulin, and on the basis of these results the routine of administering the insulin has been used by the state hospitals. As in electroshock therapy, the psychological reactions of the patients are largely ignored. Usually, the patients do not fear this treatment as intensely as electric shock, although many dislike it. Since the immediate effects wear off slowly, some claimed they did not feel alert until the week ends, when the treatments were interrupted.

During the treatments the patients feel sluggish and, at times, confused. Because of the glucose imbibed after the treatments, many gain weight and many become amused by their changed appearance. One female patient jokingly remarked: "If my husband sees me this way, he'll disown me."

The Temporary State Hospital Commission studied 1,128 insulin-treated and 876 nontreated schizophrenics. Of the insulin-treated group 79.5 per cent were able to leave the hospital, and of the nontreated group 58.8 per cent were able to leave.[19] Of the subtypes the greatest difference was evident among the paranoids; 70.4 per cent of the treated group were able to leave the hospital, in contrast to 52 per cent of the nontreated group who were able to leave.[20]

Appraisal. The effects of shock therapy upon many patients are regarded as beneficial. At the time of their introduction in the state mental hospitals, these instruments of shock therapy lent themselves to the mass treatment of patients and sometimes were hailed as the solution for the problem of treating personal disorders. Claims in this direction have become more modest with more research. First,

[19] *Insulin Shock Therapy* (New York: Temporary Commission on State Hospital Problems, 1944).

[20] Gralnick found that, of 554 insulin-treated schizophrenics, 75 per cent could be considered failures, if the nonparoled and the returned patients are included. This study pertained to a six years' range. See Alexander Gralnick, "A Seven Years' Survey of Insulin Treatment in Schizophrenia," *The American Journal of Psychiatry*, January, 1945, 101:4, p. 450.

some patients, especially schizophrenics, do not improve necessarily with this mode of treatment. Second, the improvement of some patients is not sustained, particularly when they leave the hospital. There is no definitive evidence as to the long-time effects of shock therapy. Third, the patients who improve through psychotherapeutic means tend to sustain their improvement longer than do those who have been treated by shock methods.

Chronic Patients. Unlike hopeful patients, who are considered objects of therapy, chronic patients are regarded primarily as objects of custody. Of less concern to the doctors and less subject to the varied therapies which might be administered, they are in large part the permanent residents of the hospital. Indeed, some chronic patients have been in the hospital during the major portion of their lives. In one state hospital 44.9 per cent of the patients had been in the hospital for ten or more years, and 66.7 per cent had spent five or more years in the hospital. The hospital had 19 out of 39 wards designated "chronic." Although a few chronic patients became sufficiently improved to be released, their proportion was far fewer than in the hopeful wards.[21]

Because of their disordered condition, hospital position, and routine, chronic patients view the hospital differently than do hopeful patients. Hopeful patients, despite conformity to their hospital roles, are not reconciled to them. Their interest is in discharge and in the outside community. The chronic or long-time patients are either resigned to or accept their hospital positions. Though many want to leave, their prospects of release have dimmed with the years. Their relations with family and friends have become less frequent; some patients have no families and are isolated from the outside community. Many are out of touch with recent events. Their interests and topics of conversation are focused upon such intra-hospital affairs as other patients, jobs, the attendants, doctors, church, deaths, and new arrivals. The problem of discharge recedes into the distance, and the outside community becomes an almost unreal world. The intention of long-time patients is to make hospital

[21] The longer the patient remains in the hospital, the fewer are his chances of release. The majority of patients leave the hospital within the first two years. See Eugene F. Bogen, "Effects of Long Hospitalization on Psychotic Patients," *Mental Hygiene*, October, 1936, 20:4, pp. 566–578.

living tolerable, comfortable, and acceptable. By accepting their role, the chronic patients exemplify the patients' attitudes to the mental hospital.[22]

In aspiring for optimum hospital adjustment, they become concerned with rules to obey or evade, the favored jobs, the types of attendants, and the avoidance of conflict with other patients. In effect, the long-time patients are concerned with easing the deadly hospital monotony and with using facilities at the hospitals for self-expression.

In terms of adjustment, chronic patients are of two types—workers and nonworkers. The workers are occupied most of the day, whether in the kitchen, the laundry, the dining room, the farm, or with cleaning apartments. These workers are oriented enough to function in the relatively simple hospital environment. Their work is a relief from the hospital monotony. In addition, they have "privileges," which include free movement over the hospital grounds during their off hours.

Some patients who work eight or more hours oppose this arrangement. They feel that if they are considered well enough to work eight hours in the hospital they can work outside and also have their "freedom." One patient stated:

I have to work in this booby-hatch eight hours a day. If I can work that long, here, I can do it on the outside. You have nothing to say about yourself. They put you to work and you work, whether it does you any good or not. They say they know what's best for me. Can they tell me what benefit I'm getting from working eight hours shelling peas? It doesn't change any of my ideas. I have the same ideas about people as the time I came in. I said people are enemies and they take advantage of you when they can. That is what is happening here too.

Rowland regards the "institutional cures" as the elite of the chronic patients.[23] These individuals can adjust to the mental hospital but are unable to adjust in the outside community. They have the most favored work and the most privileges. Among this group are those whose psychoses have become "settled" and whose conflicts seemingly have "burned out." He states:[24]

[22] An indication of the doctor's progressively fewer inquiries to the chronic patient is revealed by progress notes; the longer the patient is in the hospital, the less frequent become the progress notes.

[23] Howard Rowland, "The Interaction Processes in the State Mental Hospital," Psychiatry, August, 1939, 2:3, pp. 323–337.

[24] Ibid., p. 328.

Those individuals, largely schizophrenic, who have made a long time adjustment to this environment have lost the emotional extravagance which we ordinarily associate with insanity. Social relationships in this group are made possible because the morbid spread of meaning is withdrawn from the hospital environment. These individuals have approached a "normal" adjustment to their environment.

The nonworkers have a different routine. Though they help in the ward, they are unoccupied most of the day. This type of inactivity seems to coincide with the apathetic, "settled" schizophrenics, but it does not provide even them with fitting modes of self-expression. These long-time patients are the chief custodial problems of the mental hospital. The enforced idleness and boredom of many chronic patients are among the most backward features of the state mental hospital.

One long-time patient said:

It's very heavy during the day, just sit and sit and be quiet. The same thing day in and day out. I tried to read a little then got tired of it, and then there's nothing to do but sit around. The men don't get enough exercise. They sit on those hard chairs and keep sitting until they get sores.

A recreational director said the following:

I gave some chronic women patients in the back wards cloth to tear into strips. We use these strips for rug making. These women would sit there by the hour and rip and rip the cloth. It looked to me that all of their aggressions went out in tearing those sheets. They felt much better than sitting on those hard chairs with nothing to do but twiddle their thumbs.

The outlets for their monotony come in the little episodes of the day: in going to and from meals, in seeing an occasional motion picture, in asking a fellow patient for a light, in gossip and teasing patients. At times, the hostility between some working and non-working patients becomes intense because the "workers" have full or partial privileges. One female patient recalled:

Some are jealous because you work and have privileges and they don't have privileges. They think they should have privileges and not work. But you couldn't trust them to be alone. Some start a conversation and then get personal about you or somebody else. There are nice girls here but you have to be careful of those cats.

Though interpatient conflicts seem more prevalent among the women than the men patients, these conflicts often arise because the nonworking patients have nothing to do and have less status and fewer privileges than the workers.

To avoid these quarrels, many patients tend to select their companions and to avoid other patients who might create difficulties for them with the attendants or with the doctors. Since many patients have occupied the same ward for years, and often had little to do, the need for some social distance among them at times becomes essential.

Agitated Patients. Agitated patients are a miscellany of types who reflect the hospital's definition of "disturbed." The majority are disturbed because of their aberrant condition; others are considered "disturbed" because they have violated hospital rules. "Agitated patients" are confined to the ward continually, even for meals, and are segregated completely from other patients.

Based upon the severity and persistence of their agitated condition, as well as upon their communicative capacity, three types of agitated patients can be discerned: (1) the "isolates," (2) the intermittently disturbed, and (3) the "situationally disturbed." From the modes of interaction among these types, distinct and common "cultural" patterns emerge.

The "isolates" are incapable of sustained symbolic communication, because of their persistently agitated, and/or deteriorated condition. Their modes of interaction are very simple. Some will become increasingly disturbed when others manifest agitation. Some will respond to simple requests, such as moving out of the way or granting a light from a cigarette. These patients, encased in their private worlds, are preoccupied with expressing their conflicts rather than with attempting to share the perspectives and attitudes of others. In one state hospital these patients were usually segregated on the porch rather than allowed on the ward proper. A characteristic scene on the porch of a disturbed female ward is the following:

The majority were seated and were somehow eager for the attention of the visitors. They were disheveled, dressed in wide loose dresses. One elderly woman strutted out semi-nude, her arms folded as if in assertive defiance. A piercing shriek mingled with cursing was heard from the far corner of the porch. A large Negro woman started a vigorous effort to disengage herself from the leather chain about her ankle. She shouted in violent rage and banged her hands on the bench. Her shouting caused waves of excitement to sweep over the patients, some of them mumbled more quickly and more audibly to themselves. Others persisted in their impassive apathy.

When this shrieking subsided, a constant flow of verbal gibberish, of manneristic gestures, of childish smiling was apparent. There were no sustained conversations among the patients, but they did not molest each other. Each seemed aware and yet indifferent to her neighbors. Meaningful interchanges if they could be called such were limited to brief requests and responses.

The "isolates" usually have divested themselves of their capacity for self-control, are unable to retrospect concerning themselves, and are usually unable to communicate.[25]

The intermittently agitated patients experience oriented as well as disturbed episodes. Their impending disturbances become personal problems which they strive to resolve. For example, one manic-depressive patient was coherent, efficient, and had some insight during her oriented periods. Her disturbances, during which she became impulsive, destructive, and scattered in her thinking, left her completely disoriented. When she improved, she regretted her activity but felt helpless to do anything except to retire to her room. She stated:

I try my utmost to keep from getting depressed and upset. I wish someone would help me. I know when these moods are coming on and I try to get out of the way. I stay in my room. I don't know what it could be. I believed the electric shocks would help me, but they didn't. Now I just stay here and know these moods will come over me. . . . I used to feel sorry for the patients and try to help them, but I came to the conclusion that I must concentrate on my own case if I want to get out. I worried too much before and now. I hope I can solve my problems and get down to earth. . . . I remember once on the ward, I got disturbed while I was eating. I threw my tray on the floor. It was forced on me. I couldn't help myself. I was sorry the minute after I did it. I don't trust myself. I don't have much to do with the others—just stay by myself and try to solve this mood.

These patients generally accommodate themselves to the others by tending to withdraw from social participation during their disturbed episodes. The other patients, unwilling to become embroiled in a fight, let them work out their conflicts. For example, one paranoid schizophrenic, who assisted with the cooking on the ward, had periods of sullen moodiness when he would retire to a corner and cease mingling with the other patients. The patients who knew him were aware of these episodes and avoided him. One said:

[25] The chronic and violently agitated are usually segregated from the other patients.

"When he's not around we know what to expect. He must be off in some corner sitting and brooding by himself. Best not to fool with him. He flies off the handle."

The third type compose the "situationally disturbed," who have been segregated into disturbed wards for defying or for disobeying some employee, for attempting to escape, for fighting, or for having potentially homicidal tendencies. These persons are usually oriented, do interact symbolically, and do share common attitudes concerning the hospital and themselves. Like hopeful patients, they want to leave the hospital and want to leave the ward. Because of their confinement and relative neglect, they tend to be more hostile to the hospital employees than are any other patient groups. This shared hostility constitutes their collective orientation to the hospital. The doctors, attendants, the hospital policy, and the inadequate facilities are vigorously condemned. Some typical reactions are:

I'm on this ward for three years and haven't had a doctor as much as inquire and examine me.

The doctors could be better. If you're here a short while it's all right. You may get some attention and get out. If you're here a long time, they take you for granted. That's how they are.

I asked the doctor how long I was going to stay here and he said, as long as it was necessary. O.K. If that's the way they want it, if the state wants to feed me, keep me in tobacco and I have not to do a lick of work, that's all right with me.

All attendants do is drive you. They should help you not drive you, but they do not know any better.

The truth or lack of truth of these statements is not so important as the hostility of the patients which the statements reflect. Nonetheless, certain features in the agitated ward, at least the acutely agitated ward, seem to be common to the modes of interaction among the patients. These features include mutual "tolerance" combined with pervasive suspicion.

Because of the prevalent idiosyncrasies among the patients, each patient has to tolerate the activities of the others in order to get along. The mannerisms, the responses to hallucinations, the peculiar rituals usually are overlooked by other patients, unless these activities interfere with their own privacy and routines. This group tolerance necessarily allows each patient to express his eccentricities without upsetting the ward routine.

On the other hand, the patients tend to suspect each other— more so than in other wards. Even "situationally disturbed" patients feel that the others who are in the ward must have something wrong with them, else why would they be there. Except for the alcoholics, who often group together, each patient tends to be suspicious and to disdain the other patients.

Interaction and Conceptions of the Types of Patients. Social positions of the patients are not fixed. A hopeful patient may relapse or become disturbed and may be removed to a chronic ward or to a disturbed ward. A chronic patient may improve, and a disturbed patient may become calm, and both may be shifted to a hopeful ward. Though mobility exists among the patients, it is not widespread, and it does not change the generalized conceptions which the patients have of their social positions.

Hopeful patients, because of their "going home" orientation and their contacts with persons outside the hospital, regard themselves as different from chronic and agitated patients. They consider their stay in the hospital as transient, and identify themselves with persons in the outer community. They regard the chronic patients as the real residents of the mental hospital and the agitated patients as the really "crazy ones." The writer tried to present a chronic patient to a hopeful patient; the latter appeared very disdainful of the chronic patient. She felt that anybody who was in the hospital more than two years was "off," otherwise he would have left within that time. A hopeful patient, when asked about an agitated patient, remarked that the latter should be removed as quickly as possible from the ward because the others could be so easily disturbed. A hopeful patient who is about to be transferred to a chronic ward is aware that his hospital position is worsened and reacts accordingly. Hopeful patients generally tend to be less tolerant of aberrant behavior than are chronic or agitated patients.

The chronic patients, on the other hand, who have become resigned to the hospital and have more or less lost touch with the outer community, consider the hopeful patients as "never satisfied," and the ones who get "the breaks." They tend to acknowledge that the hopeful patients are in a most favored social position.

Those who are resigned to the hospital seem to have different values and do not regard the outside community as a goal for which to strive. The other chronic patients who want to leave the hospital, on the other hand, strive to get into the hopeful wards, if at all accessible. On the other hand, they regard agitated patients as atypical, as nonconformists, or as trouble makers, and also as the really disordered persons of the hospital.

Of the agitated patients, those with intermittent disturbances are preoccupied with their own problems and, as a rule, want to adjust to the hospital. They tend to acknowledge that the hopeful patients and the chronic patients are in a more favorable position. But the "situationally disturbed," who tend to be hostile to the hospital personnel and to the other patients, do not necessarily regard either the "hopeful" or "chronic" patients as "better" but rather as having been more favored by the hospital staff. Their aspirations, too, are either to be transferred to other wards or to leave the hospital.

Patient Companionships. Among the positive features in the patients' experiences is cultivation of companionships. As long as patients are able to interact symbolically, it seems that they will seek companions. Hopeful patients and workers particularly had social cliques, and some were fast friends. Generally, these companions were selected by background, occupation, age, and ethnic group, although patients may be attracted to each other by their similar idiosyncracies and by the conflicts inherent in their disorders. Patients often discussed their hallucinations, especially the different types of "wireless" or "X ray," by which the "voices" were transmitted. Rowland "learned that suicides clique together and they derive some pleasure from relating details about their attempts at death." [26]

Some alcoholics who improve rapidly become companions or clique together with the more ordered patients. These companions may work together and spend their leisure together. If they have privileges they walk the grounds together, or go to the store. Their loneliness and hospital monotony are reduced, many of their conflicts become socialized, and mutual encouragement often results.

For example, a business executive met a former employee in the state hospital. Before his admission he had scarcely noticed him.

[26] Howard Rowland, "Friendship Patterns in the State Mental Hospital," *Psychiatry*, August, 1938, 1:3, p. 367.

In the hospital they became friends, interested and loyal each to the other. Though both were psychotic at the time of their admission, their improvement was rapid. They even became identified as a "unity" in the hospital. Both improved at the same time, were presented to staff, and were conditionally released at the same time.[27]

These friendships or in-groups are in part based upon the patients' conditions and status in the hospital. That is, hopeful patients went together; chronic working patients associated with each other; and even agitated patients, despite their deficiencies in communicative capacity, somehow paired up.

Relationships with the Outside Community. The patients' relationships with the outside community have these forms: (1) visits by family and friends in the hospital, (2) trial visits by the patients to their home, and (3) letters.

Visitors. In every hospital, designated hours are set aside for visits. These visits are an integral part of hospital living, especially for hopeful patients, who have usually retained their contacts with the family and friends. The long-time patients see the frequency of visits decline. Some become resigned to their loss of outside contacts; others never do. In a tabulation of ward visits, the hopeful and receiving wards had the most visits, the back wards the least. Recency of hospital admission tends to be a decisive factor. One patient evaluated these visits as follows:

Many patients are thrilled to have visitors. It takes their mind off the drabness of the hospital and off their own thoughts. It brings them closer to the world of which they so anxiously want to be a part. Pleasant conversation with company brings an assurance to patients that they may be treated affectionately and warmly by their family and friends.

An attendant remarked:

The saddest cases seen in the hospital are those where it seems the family has forgotten the patient. No letters ever come and no visits. I remember a patient who on every visiting day would slick up in preparation for some member of the family, but none ever came. This sort of thing can sometimes be heartbreaking to the patient.

Since visits are sources of prestige, many patients eagerly anticipate them. These visits instill hope that the patients have not been left and forgotten in the hospital, relieve the hospital monotony,

[27] *Ibid.*, pp. 363, 364.

and give the patients the feeling of still being wanted. Hence, most patients are affected favorably by these visits.

Many patients, nonetheless, may have ambivalent attitudes toward their families. Resentful for having been committed by them, they need the family in order to be released from the hospital, as well as for the intrinsic pleasure of the visits themselves. Some characteristic latent reactions by the patients to the family are the following:

Assume that I was disturbed. What right have they to put me in here, when I can go and want to go to a private institution. Money is no object. I have all the money I can spend. But coming in here? Going through courts? Being probated? For what? I could have gone away for awhile, but they sent me in here. I try to talk to my wife when she comes, but her mother has control over her. I have to be careful what I say. I can antagonize her. And then where would I be?

Many women patients are angry with their husbands because their husbands brought them here. Almost everyone who's here is disturbed with the person who brought them here. R. A. is the only exception, I know of.

Despite their resentments, the patients favorably anticipate visitors and try to get along with the family. They may try to impress other patients or even the staff, and usually they enjoy the visits:

I mean to talk to my family about taking me out, but I never do. I am so glad to see them, they might not come any more. They bring my nephew with them and I don't like to discuss these things in front of him. My father is worried enough and I don't want to worry him any more than I have to. I want to go out. Yes. But I want to see my family too.

Some patients, however, may be more overtly hostile. These patients become disturbed by the visitors, and this may result in conflict or in a refusal to see them.

My mother and brother came here and my brother said that were it up to him, I'd be here the rest of my life. I told him to shut up and to mind his own business. He gets so mad at me, I shudder when I stand close to him. When he leaves, he makes me cry and curse him. I want to see my mother, but I truly hope my brother never comes here.

Keep my wife away. She nags, teases and gets me angry. I want to swat her. I said to my brother, "Tell that woman not to come here."

Generally, the conflicts in the family constellation, of which the patient is a part, do not cease with the patient's removal to the hospital. These conflicts, in large part, remain latent. In a few cases the relatives may try to take advantage of the patient if he has money. In other instances the family may be ashamed of the patient and may hesitate to release him. For example, a catatonic schizo-phrenic was committed by his brother, who was his only close relative. The patient responded well to electroshock and insulin therapy and became oriented and communicative. During one visit the patient asked his brother when he would be released. The brother replied as soon as the doctor permitted it, implying that he was willing to have him released. During one of the doctor's rounds, the patient asked the doctor about his release. The doctor inferred as soon as his family was ready to take him. This created such an intense conflict in the patient that he relapsed completely, became violent, and refused to eat, even having to be force fed.

Despite these hopes for release, patients usually look forward to visits by the family because they find it such a welcome relief from their hospital routine.

The Trial Visit. Before release, hopeful patients are given tem-porary furloughs for periods of varying lengths—ranging from a few hours to a few weeks. This practice enables the patient to receive experience in the outside community and to become reaccustomed to it. It is an indication to the patient and to the family of their capacity to readjust to each other. There is no set reaction that can be expected from the patient as a result of this temporary departure. Since patients want to leave the hospital, the mere episode of being away from the hospital is enough to create anticipation of leaving permanently. The extent to which the trial visit is beneficial to the patient depends upon his experiences in the family and in the com-munity, particularly upon the attitudes of the family and of persons in the community toward him.

Some patients find their experiences with the family very favor-able and become eager to leave. They feel that the trial visit gives them the confidence to want to return home. In these situations the relationships with the family are usually positive, and the family tries to help the patient readjust.

In other instances the trial visit merely re-creates the conflict situation which the patient experienced previously. As a result, the patient returns to the hospital in a worse condition. The inference often is that the patient is not ready for further trial visits.

In still other instances patients may improve during a week-end stay at home but may relapse after a longer period; that is, the family and the patient, in the interaction process, are able to abate their reciprocal hostility for a short period but are unable to withhold their hostility for a long period.

Letters. Letters are other mediums by which patients can communicate with those outside the hospital. This means of communication is less prevalent and less satisfying than visits. In one state hospital, of 161 visitors questioned at random, 16.7 per cent received letters from patients, and of 159 of the same visitors 18.2 per cent sent letters to patients. This indicates that the sending and the receiving of letters are about the same but that less than 1 out of 5 patients who are visited in the hospital have correspondence.

Since the visitors were concentrated among those patients who had been in the hospital less than five years, as a group they received the most letters. But, it is interesting to note that, of the relatives who visited the patients institutionalized between five and ten years, a greater proportion sent letters. Of the patients who had been inmates ten years or longer, few received or sent mail. In this latter group, many were unable to write coherently and many of their relatives and friends were dispersed, had died, or had forgotten them. In brief, the longer the patients remain in the hospital, especially after five years, the greater is their tendency to become isolated from the outside world.

The "Forgotten Patient." The forgotten patient is the one who either has no relatives or friends or has been forgotten by his family. These persons have no visitors and expect none. Moreover, some are ready to leave the hospital, but because they have no family member to be their custodian, they linger in the hospital despite their improved condition which, under other circumstances, would enable them to be released. In every hospital some forgotten patients can be found. A survey in one hospital revealed 20 such patients; they were ready to leave but were not discharged because they had no relatives or friends.

Summary

Persons committed to the state mental hospital, although deprived of certain rights, have respite from the conflict and competitive situations in the outer community. Patients tend to soften the stigma of "insanity" and to refer to their condition by more acceptable terms.

They find it most expedient to conform to their hospital roles because those who defy or disobey authorities can be labeled "disturbed" and penalized by being placed in a "strong ward" or "back
ward" or put into restraint.

One phase of conformity is expressed in the patients' relationships
with the hospital employees, particularly with the doctors and the
attendants. Doctor-patient relationships are partially therapeutic
for hopeful patients and custodial for chronic patients. Attendant-
patient relations are mainly custodial rather than therapeutic.

The patient milieu can be structured into distinct "classes," including hopeful, chronic, and agitated types. These patients tend
to have different perspectives toward the hospital, toward themselves, and toward each other, because of their hospital positions,
length of stay, and personal conditions.

Hopeful patients are primarily concerned with going home, and
with the outside community. This competitive desire to leave moti-
vates them to improve so as to get released. "Kept in the dark"
about physical therapies as electric shock and insulin, they magnify
their fears to each other and approach this physical therapy with a
negative attitude.

Many chronic patients also want to leave the hospital, but their
long stay in the hospital reduces their contacts with persons outside
the hospital. Gradually, they become reoriented to the hospital and
find it necessary to concentrate their interests upon the hospital personnel, the routine, and the other patients. The long-time patients
who have despaired of readjusting in the outside community exemplify the attitudes of the chronic patients. Agitated patients can
be categorized by the severity and persistence of their disturbance.
The majority lack a sustained communicative capacity but can interact and influence each other in very elemental fashion. Those
intermittently agitated, who are fairly well oriented, regard their
disturbed episodes as personal problems which they try to resolve
or overcome. The "situationally agitated" want to leave the hospital, as do the others, and strive to be transferred from the ward.
This latter group can communicate symbolically and seem to be the
most vigorously antiadministration of all the patients. Because of
the prevalence of idiosyncracies among these patients, greater
mutual "tolerance" is manifested than in the other wards, but more
reciprocal suspicion is also evident than in the other wards.

The indigenous positive facets of patient relations are the acquired friendships among the patients and contacts with the outside community.

Contacts with persons outside the hospital are of three types: (1) visits from family and friends, (2) trial visits, and (3) letters. These contacts usually affect the patients favorably, although instances of conflict are evident. Recency of admission is the most decisive factor in the frequency of visits when computed by ward averages of length of stay.

Selected Readings

Beers, Clifford, *A Mind That Found Itself* (New York: Doubleday & Company, Inc., 1924).

Brown, Carleton, *Brainstorm* (New York: Rinehart & Company, Inc., 1944).

Deutch, Albert, *The Mentally Ill in America* (New York: Columbia University Press, 1938).

Erickson, Milton H., "Psychological Significance of Physical Restraint to Mental Patients," *The American Journal of Psychiatry,* 1948, 105:7, pp. 612–614.

Graves, Albert, *Eclipse of a Mind* (New York: The Medical Journal Press, 1942).

Hamilton, Samuel W., A. A. Kempf, G. C. Scholz, and E. G. Caswell, *A Study of the Public Mental Hospitals of the United States* (Washington, D.C.: U.S. Public Health Service, 1941.

Jayson, Lawrence M., *Mania* (New York: Funk & Wagnalls Company, 1937).

Lief, Alfred (editor), "Treatment of the Insane," *The Common Sense Psychiatry of Dr. Adolph Meyer* (New York: McGraw-Hill Book Company, Inc., 1948).

Peters, Fritz, *The World Next Door* (New York: Farrar, Straus & Young, 1949).

Rowland, Howard, "Interaction Processes in the State Mental Hospital," *Psychiatry,* August, 1938, I:3, pp. 363–373.

———, "Friendship Patterns in the State Mental Hospital," *Psychiatry,* August, 1939, II:3, pp. 323–337.

Slotkin, James S., "Nature and Effects of Interaction among Schizophrenics," *Journal of Abnormal and Social Psychology,* 1942, 37, pp. 345–368.

Ward, Mary Jane, *The Snake Pit* (New York: Random House, 1946).

PART V

Rehabilitation and Prevention

CHAPTER EIGHTEEN

The Patient and the Community

A mental hospital patient may return to the community by one of three general ways. First, he may be entrusted to family care outside the hospital but remain under hospital supervision. Second, he may be conditionally discharged for a specified period. During this period he would have to report periodically to the hospital or to a designated clinic until discharged outright. Third, he may be discharged outright from hospital supervision.

The Family-care System

Family care is a minor form of patient treatment and custody in the United States. It contrasts with "closed institutional care" such as is practiced in hospitals or sanataria. The family-care system may consist of the colony system or the district system. Some European countries, such as Belgium, practice the colony system in contrast to the United States where the district system only is practiced. In the colony system a designated town or hamlet is devoted mainly to the care of the insane. In the district system the patients are entrusted to the custody of families who are within easy access of the hospital. To differentiate between the two systems, first the colony of Gheel, Belgium, then the district system in the United States will be discussed.

Gheel: "The Town of Lunatics." Gheel, the small, quiet town situated near the Albert Canal in Belgium, has been called the "town of lunatics" by derisive outsiders. In Gheel, patients generally go about their affairs unmolested and often unsupervised. In this community the form of care of disordered persons is embedded in the traditions of the city that are lost in legend.

In 1939 there were about 3,750 patients out of an approximate total of 20,000 inhabitants in the community. Before World War II, about every fifth inhabitant was a patient. During the war, and after, the number declined, and during 1944 there were approximately 2,600 patients. At present the number fluctuates around 2,500 patients.[1]

Patients are assigned to families according to their financial means and according to the severity of their disorders. Well-to-do patients live with wealthy families, and patients financed by the state are placed with families of lesser means. Each patient is required to have his own room, and not more than two patients can be placed with one family.

The two-hundred-bed hospital, which is located in the center of the town, is the chief institution of the town. Although patients are seemingly free to come and go, a certain amount of supervision exists, especially for agitated patients who are often forbidden freedom. A certain social structure also is evident. The townspeople who care for the patients are, roughly, in the upper stratum, and the patients are in the lower stratum. This division is further subdivided into socioeconomic strata, as has been indicated.

The modes of care are rooted in religion, which means ostensibly that the patients are treated kindly and humanely. This type of care, however, does not have the explicit rational techniques of "milieu therapy." Yet the patients are helped by being accepted into the community and are away from their former conflict situations; these new relationships may serve to revise their orientation to themselves and to others.

Family Care in the United States. In the United States the district system of family care is practiced, but Table 19 shows that this system·is a very minor form of patient care.[2]

---

[1] See Hester B. Crutcher, *Family Home Care for Mental Patients* (New York: Commonwealth Fund, 1944).

[2] Patients in family care have been defined as follows: "Patients not recovered sufficiently to be paroled or discharged, who have been placed in private families other than their own with remuneration to the family by the hospital." *Patients in Mental Institutions, 1944*, p. 6 (Washington, D.C.: Bureau of the Census, U.S. Department of Commerce, 1947).

TABLE 19

STATES WITH PATIENTS IN FAMILY CARE, 1946*

State	Total	Number of Patients Male	Female	Per Cent of Total Patients in Hospital
New York	1,059	393	666	1.3
Illinois	260	123	137	0.8
Massachusetts	236	37	199	1.0
Maryland	226	92	134	3.1
Rhode Island	220	96	124	7.1
Michigan	163	74	89	0.9
Iowa	1	0	1	

* Data taken from *Patients in Mental Institutions, 1946*, p. 56 (Washington, D.C.: Bureau of the Census, U.S. Department of Commerce, 1948). Patients in other types of extramural care were excluded.

Family care has been advocated for several reasons: (1) It provides room in the hospital for those who need specialized treatment and/or require segregation. (2) It costs less than hospital care. (3) It helps many patients make a satisfactory and relatively permanent adjustment outside the hospital.

Two general types of patients are considered for family care. These are (1) the mild and chronic patients who may need custody but do not require the intensive supervision of the closed institution, and (2) the mild and hopeful patients whose improvement may be facilitated by their staying with a family other than their own. In the first type the chief aim is custodial. In the second type the chief aim is therapeutic.

Families are evaluated by and selected for (1) their facility in coping with the patient, (2) the location of their home, (3) their personality composition, (4) the number of patients they could accommodate, and (5) their financial incentives in keeping patients.[3] Clearly, these criteria are not always satisfied.

Appraisal of Family Care. In the first place, family care is a very minor form of patient care in the United States, including New York State, where it is most prevalent. Second, this form of patient

[3] See N. D. Black and V. R. Barritt, *Study of Family Care in the New York State Hospitals* (New York: Temporary Commission on State Hospital Problems, 1943, mimeographed).

care has been opposed by some psychiatrists and by others in state mental hospitals. Third, there are not enough competent social workers to supervise this program adequately. In fact, not many psychiatric social workers are trained for these particular types of skills.[4] Fourth, there is not enough systematized knowledge about patient placement in families to know definitely how preferable it is to hospital custody. That it is often preferable to the patient's own family when conflict exists has been brought out by studies of individual cases. Fifth, family care has been used frequently to reduce hospital overcrowding rather than as an independent means of patient care or treatment. Sixth, the penny-wise attitudes of administrators often defeat the potential therapeutic and custodial value of such a program by allotting funds for only the minimum essentials of the patients' custody.[5]

The Hospital Patient Returns to the Community

Patients who are discharged, whether conditionally or outright, differ from patients entrusted to family care. The discharged patients usually are considered ready for community participation and for civilian life.

When patients are conditionally discharged or "paroled," they are still under state supervision and sometimes do not have their civil rights restored. In this status they cannot vote, care for their property, or even leave the state without permission from a designated authority. The patients who have been discharged outright have had their civil rights restored and have severed their ties completely with the hospital.

But many patients who leave the hospital have paradoxical experiences. They are pleased to be out in the community once more but are apprehensive about their social acceptance and general readjustment. Some realize the stigma directed to former "mental patients" and try to conceal their hospital stay from their associates and others. Some experience the very situations which contributed to their conflicts and original breakdown; others are more fortunate and meet understanding and sympathy. In consequence, their success or failure in adjusting to the community is contingent not only

[4] *Ibid.*

[5] See Edward L. Koos, *Families in Trouble* (New York: King's Crown Press, 1946).

upon their personal condition but also upon the attitudes of the groups in which they participate.

The young lady in the following case, who had been diagnosed as "schizophrenia—unclassified," had been discharged outright from a state hospital as "recovered." In her efforts to resume her place in the community, she somehow felt left out of the "swing of things." Her fear of being "found out" was aggravated by her family's furtive attitudes to her hospital experiences. She felt lonely and isolated, and yearned for someone in whom to confide.

What a beautiful world it was when my family took me home from the hospital. I'd been locked up since January and now it was July. I wanted to do everything—even ride street cars, just to show myself I was free. But then I felt as if I didn't know how to act in the outside world and that made me anxious. What would I tell my friends and acquaintances? I decided with my dad that I had been visiting my sister in the South.

My dad worked terribly hard to keep my stay in the hospital a secret. He didn't want my sisters even to know about me. And he told my friends that I had been visiting down South with my sister for an indefinite time because I liked it there. When I got out, I felt that I was somehow out of touch with people and I was very lonely. My parents wanted me to stay home so I wouldn't get excited very easily. But I wanted to do things. After a few weeks at home, I got bored and tired of being restrained at home, and I wanted more freedom. I was more elated than I had been before I went to the hospital and my family interpreted that as a sign I was going batty again. My father went to a psychiatrist to inquire about me, and he said that I would go through a poor judgment period before I would level off. That helped a lot. I didn't like psychiatrists who were so mysterious with my parents that they wouldn't explain a thing to them.

My biggest problem was getting back in the swing of society. I didn't know anyone at first. I felt I'd be discriminated against, if it were known where I had been. I felt inferior because everyone was doing something, and I was a useless parasite at home. Then I felt that people were watching me, and it was not my imagination. My mother and dad used to close the door on the sun porch and I just knew from the way they looked at me that they were discussing me, and that hurt me a lot. I became more lonely and when I saw anyone I knew, I began to talk and kept talking until I drove him away. I guess I did that because I was so lonely and by myself all the time.

After a couple of months, I joined the church again to help me socially and get me back in the swing of things. One of the biggest things I had to contend with, was explaining to people I met why I was not working. Everybody was doing something and I had to stay home and do nothing. I started looking for a college to go to. I didn't know that colleges were so crowded. I finally got into a college and took two courses the first semester, and the next semester decided to take a full program. Then I was asked repeatedly why only two courses if I didn't work.

My biggest help has been my attitude. I have stopped blaming myself for everything that went wrong. Thank God, I don't feel that I have to get married as the only alternative right away. The thing that kept haunting me was that people might find out that I had been in the mental hospital, and then to feel the shame as if I had deceived them. I get too much advice from my family and my dad brings up the fact that I had been in a hospital once and might have a breakdown again. That hurts me very much, and makes me feel that I have a past, which I can never really live down and then I get very depressed. I have learned too that I cannot tell my family many things about the way I feel because they wouldn't understand and just worry about me.

Around the corner, there was a lady whom I met through a friend and she was so understanding to me. Her husband was in one of the state hospitals, and she knew all the difficulties one had to experience after being out. She was so very understanding to me, especially when I was at sword's points with my family that I'd see her almost every day and talk to her for hours. I felt better just from talking to her and I would tell her many things about myself that I would not tell my family.

This patient, like so many others, had to reintegrate into a variety of groups and had to get a new conception of her role in society. Perhaps she was more fortunate than some patients who must seek employment soon after discharge, or than other patients who encounter hostility or misunderstanding from the family. On the other hand, she may not have been as confident as other patients. Still, most patients who leave the hospital are uncertain about the attitudes of the family and the community and experience doubts about their eventual reception. In any case, the posthospital adjustment of former patients is almost continuous with their hospital stay and has a significant effect on their personal conditions.

In this section, we will present the following facets of posthospital adjustment: (1) discharges and conditions of discharged patients, (2) the ex-patients and the community, (3) the ex-patient and the family, (4) the ex-patients and industry, (5) the patients who stay out of and patients who go back into the hospital, and (6) programs for ex-patients' adjustment.

Patients Discharged from Mental Hospitals. The number of patients who leave mental hospitals increases yearly. Their discharge creates problems for the patients and for the community. In 1946, 151,165 patients left mental hospitals. This number is an increase of about 25,000 persons over the previous year, as can be seen from Table 20.

TABLE 20

PATIENTS DISCHARGED FROM MENTAL HOSPITALS FOR PERMANENT CARE
IN THE UNITED STATES, 1934 TO 1946*

Year	State	Veteran	County and City	Private	Total	Rate per Patient under Treatment† Total	State
1946	66,098	40,317	1,767	42,983	151,165	207.6	119.5
1945	61,902	26,485	1,842	36,041	126,270	153.2	114.7
1944	63,836	20,428	1,682	28,362	114,308	171.0	118.2
1943	67,377	11,451	1,744	27,523	108,095	165.0	125.1
1942	64,696	8,970	2,048	27,018	102,732	160.4	121.6
1941	61,898	8,658	4,908	22,428	97,892	156.1	120.8
1940	58,596	8,646	4,303	21,916	93,461	152.9	116.9
1939	57,606	8,354	4,117	21,786	91,863	152.9	117.8
1938	56,756	7,480	4,863	21,810	90,909	155.4	120.2
1937	52,377	6,102	5,114	23,856	87,449	153.2	114.1
1936	48,420	5,440	5,059	22,291	81,210	147.4	108.9
1935	46,090	3,426	7,465	20,726	77,707	146.9	107.5
1934	45,867	3,255	7,202	19,099	75,423	147.1	110.1

* *Patients in Mental Institutions, 1946*, p. 13 (Washington, D.C.: Bureau of the Census, U.S. Department of Commerce, 1948); *Patients in Mental Institutions, 1943*, p. 14 (Washington, D.C.: Bureau of the Census, U.S. Department of Commerce, 1946).

† "Patients under treatment" includes resident patients at the end of the year, all discharges during the year, and deaths in the hospital during the year.

Condition on Discharge. But discharged patients are not all in a similar condition. Some patients have recovered and others have improved, and still others are unimproved.[6] From Table 21 we can

[6] "Recovered" is defined as regained normal mental health or in which the "mental condition" is the same as that experienced before the onset of the disorder. "Improved" refers to "any degree of mental gain short of recovery." "Unimproved" refers to "no mental gain." *Patients in Mental Institutions, 1944*, p. 24 (Washington, D.C.: Bureau of the Census, U.S. Department of Commerce, 1947). It appears, however, that the categories of "recovered" and "improved" have different meanings for different hospital clinicians. These disparate meanings obviously affect the rates of the different categories. For example, in Arkansas, out of 1,286 discharged patients, only 3 were regarded as "recovered." In Washington State, out of 1,244 discharged patients, 663 patients were regarded as "recovered." Even considering that Arkansas had 544 nonpsychotic patients

see that 45.1 per cent of the manic depressives and only 18.6 per cent of the schizophrenics were discharged as recovered, and of the neurotics, whose condition is considered less severe than manic depressives, only 28.6 per cent were discharged as recovered.

TABLE 21

CONDITION OF PATIENTS DISCHARGED FROM PUBLIC MENTAL HOSPITALS FOR PERMANENT CARE IN THE UNITED STATES, BY TYPE OF DISORDER, 1946 *

Type of Disorder	Total Discharged			Per Cent of Total		
	Number	Per Cent	Re-covered	Im-proved	Unim-proved	Unclas-sified
All psychoses	55,596	100.0	28.8	58.3	11.3	1.6
Male	26,730	100.0	27.4	57.1	13.6	1.9
Female	28,866	100.0	30.0	59.4	9.1	1.5
Neuroses	3,517	100.0	28.6	58.3	7.9	5.2
Male	1,346	100.0	27.9	57.3	9.2	5.6
Female	2,171	100.0	29.0	59.0	7.1	4.9
Schizophrenia	16,906	100.0	18.6	66.0	14.2	1.2
Male	8,226	100.0	16.0	64.1	18.7	1.2
Female	8,680	100.0	21.2	67.8	10.0	1.0
Manic depres-sion	11,074	100.0	45.1	48.7	5.0	1.2
Male	3,873	100.0	45.1	48.1	5.5	1.3
Female	7,201	100.0	45.0	49.1	4.8	1.1

* *Patients in Mental Institutions, 1946*, p. 24 (Washington, D.C.: Bureau of the Census, U.S. Department of Commerce, 1948).

The extent to which these ex-patients can readjust on the outside depends upon their condition at discharge and upon their relationships with the varied social groups in which they participate.

Except for the manic-depressive psychoses, higher proportions of females than males leave the state mental hospitals in a recovered condition. For example, in 1946, 21.2 per cent of the female schizophrenics and only 16.0 per cent of the male schizophrenics were discharged as recovered.

The Ex-patient and the Community. In the late 1930's an ex-

and Washington had 96 nonpsychotic patients who do not go into the "recovered" column, we still find that the discrepancy seems too great. Unless the two states had totally different modes of therapy, which seems unlikely, the disparity very likely resulted from different definitions of "recovered." *Patients in Mental Institutions, 1946*, pp. 116–118 (Washington, D.C.: Bureau of the Census, U.S. Department of Commerce, 1948).

patient who was interviewed over the radio summarized her experiences in this sentence. "I have recovered my mental health, but the community does not consider me recovered." Some patients are in this predicament, but others are not; some patients who have improved are not accepted as such by the community, but others are partially or completely accepted. Yet, many patients hide their past commitment because they have discovered that an honest declaration of their illness can lead to social ostracism.

Stereotypes of Ex-patients. The stigma foisted upon some ex-patients by the community results from the fixed adverse ideas which so many people have of mental patients. Among many segments of the population, one stereotyped image of the ex-patient is, "once insane, always insane." This notion, in part, has been derived from Kraepelin and has been applied mainly to schizophrenic patients. Some psychiatrists maintain: "Once schizophrenic, always schizophrenic." [7] The recurrence of a disorder among ex-patients who were schizophrenic is considered a relapse.[8] The improvement or recovery is a tentative condition which holds the disorder in abeyance. For Kraepelin, by his very definition of schizophrenia, i.e., dementia praecox, gave it a poor prognosis, or chance for recovery. But many schizophrenics as well as manic depressives improve and recover and sustain their improvement for long periods, even indefinitely. Of course, many psychotics do not recover or improve, and some improve for short periods and then experience a recurrence. But the attitudes of the persons around the ex-patients affect and contribute to their prospective condition.

Another view of the ex-patients is that they are, at best, irresponsible and, at worst, prone to violence. The conventional public who are relatively ignorant of disordered persons do not realize that, as a rule, disordered persons are passive and quiet. Certainly some psychotics are agitated and some are violent and dangerous before and during commitment, but these are the minority. Such characteristic headlines as the following, affect the public: "Seamstress kills

[7] G. Lawson Lowrey, *Psychiatry for Social Workers,* p. 194 (New York: Columbia University Press, 1946).

[8] Cameron points out that the attitudes toward the improvement and "relapse" of schizophrenic patients are similar to the manner in which pulmonary tuberculosis was considered forty years ago. See Norman Cameron, *The Psychology of Behavior Disorders,* p. 459 (Boston: Houghton Mifflin Company, 1947). See Chap. Sixteen.

husband over 'my troubles.' " "He had a queer smile—crazed husband kills four." "Deranged mother kills seven with brother's axe." "Dad lets killer 16 go to asylum." [9] "Girl 16 sent to insane asylum for slaying tailor." Sometimes anyone who commits a heinous crime is considered disordered, and the disorder is considered responsible for the crime. If discreet publicity were given to the many ex-patients who recover and readjust to the community, these preconceptions could, in part, be dispelled. In a competitive society the practice of discouraging a person by considering him "irresponsible" is not infrequent. When directed against a person who is known to have been in a mental hospital, the former patient can become very discouraged.

Some maintain that the legal procedure and court routine by which disordered persons are committed to mental hospitals create the impression that insane persons are punished for some wrongdoing rather than treated for some incapacitating disorder. On the other hand, the court procedure, as we have pointed out, is a means of preventing the patient from being "railroaded" into the hospital. However, this procedure does not receive much publicity and usually does not harm the patient.

A Study of Stereotypes. All segments of our society do not judge ex-patients in the same way. Their reactions differ perhaps by type of education, by experience with disordered persons, perhaps by ethnic group and by experience generally. The impact of World War II has had an educative influence upon the conventional public. Many potential inductees were rejected for psychiatric reasons, and many soldiers were discharged for personality disorders, especially neuroses and psychosomatic ailments. This has brought the problem closer to home in many instances and has shown that disordered persons are "human" after all. Since the war, an extensive re-educative program has been made concerning the deplorable conditions in state mental hospitals and concerning the human qualities of the disordered person. In addition, the psychoanalysts, psychiatrists, mental hygienists, and others have made extensive efforts to re-educate the public about personal disorders. The facts that many people who visit psychiatrists at the present time were so

[9] Albert Deutch, "Testimony," *National Neuropsychiatric Institute Act: S. 1160,* March, 6, 7, 8, pp. 106, 107 (Washington, D.C.: U.S. Government Printing Office, 1946).

reluctant to do so before and that many more people commit relatives to mental hospitals or even enter as voluntary patients are indications of these changed attitudes.

To ascertain somewhat more precisely what one segment of our society thinks about ex-patients, a study was made of the opinions of 506 students in a coeducational college located in Chicago. These verbalized opinions are indices as to how these subjects would actually behave in a specific situation concerning disordered persons. As we have pointed out, the pervasive stereotype of "once insane, always insane" is the scourge of ex-patients. The first question was, "Do you believe the statement 'once insane, always insane' is true or false?" To this question, 87.7 per cent of the group replied, "false," 3.8 per cent said, "true," and 8.5 per cent were "undecided." Among this particular group, it would appear that this particular stereotype is in the process of weakening.

As we have shown in Chapter Two, the probability of schizophrenic persons coming from families in which other members have psychoses is about twenty times that of the normal population. Despite this probability, we have indicated that this does not mean indisputably that the psychoses are hereditary but that the predisposition to a disorder may be hereditary. Consequently, the specific influences leading to the disorder are socially induced rather than biologically transmitted. It was asked, "If one or both parents were mentally ill, would you expect the children to have mental illness in their 'blood'?" To this question, 24.9 per cent said, "yes," 56.9 per cent said "no," and 18.2 per cent were "undecided." In this group it appears that about 3 out of 4 did not believe that mental illness was hereditary.

The next question asked was: "Would you continue to associate with a friend of the same sex, if you had discovered that he or she had been committed to a mental institution?" To this 77 per cent replied that they would, 10 per cent indicated that they would not, and 13 per cent were undecided. When these opinions were computed by racial groups, 83.9 per cent and 74.3 per cent of the Negroes and whites, respectively, claimed that it would not affect the friendship.

To the question asked, "Would you hire or recommend the hiring of a qualified person who had been released from a mental institution?" 78.8 per cent of the subjects answered, "yes," 8.3 per cent said "no," and 10.9 per cent were "undecided." Of the Negro and white groups, 82.8 per cent and 77.4 per cent, respectively, answered "yes."

To the more intimate question, "Would you approve the marriage of a member of your family to one who had been released from a mental institution and pronounced 'recovered'?" 35.8 per cent approved, 34.6 per cent did not approve, and 29.6 per cent were "undecided."

Of the Negro group, 37.3 per cent favored, 30.6 per cent opposed, and 32.1 per cent were undecided. Of the white group, 35.2 per cent approved, 36 per cent opposed, and 28.8 per cent were undecided. When comparing the males and females, we found that 39.9 per cent and 31.5 per cent approved, 33.8 per cent and 35.5 per cent opposed, and 26.3 per cent and 33.0 per cent were undecided, respectively.

On the basis of these opinions it seems that many students in this particular group are not prejudiced against former patients. Yet the opinions of these individuals are merely verbalized indicators of the type of action they might take in a self-involving situation. It is quite evident, however, that the more intimate and the more emotionally involved the relationship with the ex-patient, the greater is the tendency to reject him.

The hereditary influence, the influence of one person upon another, and the pressure of the community comprise the content of the prejudices against ex-patients which seem to impede their social acceptance. But extensive publicity and educational programs have reduced the prejudices associated with disordered persons and in recent years have made them more acceptable to many segments of society. But the extent and direction of this educative influence has not been ascertained. What is needed is an extensive survey and analysis of the opinions of persons over different areas of the country in order to determine the extent and intensity of prejudice toward disordered persons among the conventional public.

In one such survey of the opinions of a sample of persons in Louisville, Ky., Woodward found that these persons are gradually giving up some of their fixed notions concerning psychotics. He also found the following: about one half of the Louisville citizens claimed that they would not hesitate to tell their friends and acquaintances about a family member who was "mentally ill." The majority doubted that "most mental illness is inherited," and they

realized that more hospitals and doctors are needed to care for and
to treat psychotics. They were beginning to recognize the psychiatrist as a resource for dealing with problem cases. The college-edu-
cated group were ahead of the other citizens in adopting "modern
attitudes on mental health." [10]

Experiences of Ex-patients. Since many ex-patients fear prejudice
from the conventional community, they frequently conceal their
hospital episodes. Some ex-patients, however, are unable to hide
these experiences, especially those ex-patients who live in small
towns and those who return to the same neighborhood in larger
cities. In these situations they may encounter embarrassing experiences. For example, an ex-patient complained to the landlord that
her apartment was too cold for her aging sick mother. When the
landlord refused to correct the situation, she warned him that the
health department would be notified. He cautioned her against this
move with the threat that he would call the hospital and claim that
her disorder had recurred. To avert this false charge, she desisted
from any action.

This prejudice can also extend to personal relationships. Unless
the ex-patient has some insight into and defense against the prejudiced person, he can experience intense conflicts. For example, an
ex-patient was in "good health" eight years after being discharged
from the hospital and was making a satisfactory adjustment. About
that time, she met a man who became interested in her and who
hoped their friendship would "ripen into marriage." Since they became so friendly, she told him about her breakdown. Despite her
"good health" during these eight years, he recoiled in horror at her
revelation, and said emphatically, "Never, never under any circumstances tell that to any man with whom you hope to be intimate."
Although embarrassed by his remarks she could have been deeply
distressed had she not realized that his reaction was out of all proportion to the facts of the case. She also discovered that he was an
extremely insecure person and could not bear the thought of marrying anyone who was not very secure emotionally. Realizing this
fact, she was not seriously hurt or angry. Instead she "pitied" him.[11]

Some ex-patients, however, from sheer confidence and/or from

[10] Julian L. Woodward, "Changing Ideas on Mental Illness and Its Treatment,"
American Sociological Review, August, 1951, 16:4, pp. 443–454.

[11] From Anonymous, *Lost and Found*, Vol. II, p. 7 (Chicago: Recovery Inc.,
1940).

the tolerance of their friends and neighbors are able to admit and even to discuss their former breakdown. For example, during his disordered state Beers thought he had disgraced his family. When his brother came to bring him home, he refused with all his feeble strength, thinking "that a man who had disgraced his family should again enter his old home and expect his relatives to treat him as though nothing had changed, was a thought against which my whole nature rebelled." [12] When he recovered he became confident and certain in purpose and he was completely unabashed to discuss his breakdown with his friends, even referring to the experience himself. By his persuasive ability, Beers was able to convert others to his own reassuring viewpoint. Of course, many ex-patients do not have this facility, but in this experience Beers points out in some measure what the self-confidence of ex-patients can accomplish. Indeed, many ex-patients are hindered in their adjustment because of lack of confidence.

The Family. The modes of family relationships in which ex-patients participate can be decisive in making or breaking them. First, family members are usually their guardians and have the power to send them back to the hospital. Second, the family can more readily supervise and reach the ex-patients than can any other social unit. By this social intimacy the family can hurt or emotionally support the returned patients. In considering the configurations of family relationships, we must account for the irrational expressions as well as for the deliberate responses. Unwitting reactions toward the former patients are sometimes more important than conscious attitudes. The family may be unaware of attitudes which come out inadvertently.

Their affected kindness and rationalizations frequently are distrusted and resented by ex-patients. All family members obviously do not react to the patients in the same way, and they, in turn, do not respond to the others with identical favor or disfavor. Conflicts among the family members and sudden crises which are beyond family control, as the loss of a job by a breadwinner or the sudden death of a family member, can affect ex-patients adversely.

The New York Temporary Commission on State Hospital Problems found that the more important factors which, in combination,

[12] Clifford W. Beers, *A Mind That Found Itself*, p. 27 (New York: Doubleday & Company, Inc., 1924).

contributed to the recurrence of disorders among patients were (1) conflicts between the parents, (2) sibling rivalry, (3) financial tensions, (4) excessive demands upon the patient, and (5) critical experiences.[13]

Some families expected too much from the ex-patients. They demanded standards of personal behavior which the patients could not meet, or they insisted upon their contribution to the family's economic support. These families could avenge the ex-patients in gross or in subtle ways. Since ex-patients were in the custody of the family, they had to endure their adverse judgments or be returned to the hospital.

Some families do not understand many of the ex-patients' reactions. They want ex-patients to respond rationally to them. When they do not, the family members become irritated, impatient, and hostile.

In the following instance this ex-patient had been discharged from the hospital and had returned home with his mother. His mother had remarried and lived in Wisconsin. The patient, who was entrusted to her care, resented his stepfather's abuse and escaped to Chicago. The following scene, which is typical of a family's attempts to control the ex-patient, was observed and described by a close friend of the family.

The patient was lying across the bed when his brother and I came into the bedroom. Both of us spoke to him for a few minutes. But when he did not reply, we spoke to each other. We spoke of James' (the brother) schoolwork. James mentioned that the patient had helped him a few nights ago with his schoolwork. When this was mentioned William (the patient) sat up on the edge of the bed away from me, as though I frightened him. James then mentioned a few incidents to help William recall who I was. As the patient slowly recollected and began to identify me as a friend, his bewildered expression changed and he smiled faintly at his brother. He extended his hand to me and slowly greeted me. We then talked about a home-built bookcase which was in the room and about some of the books in the bookcase. During the conversation William appeared quite rational, spoke with well-chosen words, and with some deliberation. In the process of conversing, he rose from the bed, excused himself, then turned his back to me and tucked his shirt into his trousers. Not quite certain yet as to who I was, he asked me again as to whether I was a social worker. When I assured him that I was an old friend, he appeared more satisfied, but remained slightly on guard and had a faintly bewildered expression.

[13] New York Temporary Commission on State Hospital Problems, *Insulin Shock Therapy*, p. 35 (Utica, New York: State Hospitals Press, 1942).

When I told him that he looked well, he replied that he had not been feeling well for some time, but that he was better now and that he would have to get some new clothes because the clothes he wore were much too large for him. He said that had he known company was coming he would have shaved and combed his hair. As he said this, he brushed his hair with his hands. When he mentioned that he had lost weight, I suggested that he could go to a doctor who might help him put on a little weight. Though the patient assented that this was a good idea, he said that he couldn't go, that he "just couldn't go."

As we talked about Wisconsin and other matters to get his mind off himself, his sister came in with a bottle of wine and two glasses. She said to me, "Give him some of this wine, get him drunk, and maybe he'll go with you sooner." His sister then approached the patient, who was lying quietly across the bed, and tried to force some of the wine into his mouth. William tightened his lips and resisted her efforts in a passive but firm way. The sister became very irritated and threatened him: "Back to the crazy house for you. Back to the crazy house." Another brother then entered the room and demanded to know why the patient had not drunk the wine. He scolded the patient, and reminded him that he could beat him up any time he wanted to, if William did not do as they requested. Since this brother, Charles, had been drinking, the mother then came into the room and upon seeing the patient stretched across the bed, she began lamenting in a loud voice: "Poor William. Poor William." When she reached for his hand, he quickly withdrew it, but continued to stare at the ceiling in a passive and remote look.

The mother, who had been concerned about the patient's refusal to eat, took some gelatin which had been standing on the window ledge for two days and tried to feed the patient. But the patient tightened his lips, closed his eyes, and strained every muscle of his body in passive protest. His body became rigid and tense. The mother then threatened William with the "crazy house," if he continued to behave in this manner. When I asked why every one threatened the patient with the "crazy house," the mother said that she was so instructed at the hospital. (This has not been verified.) When the mother's pleas had no effect, she left the room.

I remained in the room while the patient withdrew to what seemed a virtual coma. James, who had left the room temporarily, returned and was quite angry, because he thought the wrong approach had been used with William. He then stood William up, leaned him against the wall, straightened his clothes. He then told his brother, the patient, that he had called the doctor and we were all to go that evening. Although William objected, he reluctantly consented when he was told that he could drive. He was about to leave the room and shave when several policemen appeared at the doorway. At the sight of the policemen, William, who had been submissive and seemingly preoccupied with his own thoughts, changed his expression, offered no resistance, and went to the policemen. On the surface, he appeared happy. Since William had done nothing wrong, and had his parole papers in order, no one knew why they had come. The mother said that they had been instructed by the hospital to take him back. Since the mother could not speak English very well, I suggested perhaps the brothers would want to go along. At first they hesitated, then decided to accompany him.

As we left the house, all the neighbors were gathered and watched with eager curiosity. As William went into the patrol wagon, the small children made funny remarks and the neighbors whispered to each other. As the patrol wagon departed, Charles said that the show was over and that the neighbors could disperse now. As we drove to the psychopathic hospital in Charles' car, he shouted angrily that his mother had called the police to take William away. He said that now the children in the neighborhood would call his daughter crazy for having a crazy uncle. He then condemned his mother for being responsible for all the difficulties which the family experienced.

These social relationships between this patient and his family reveal that when he was treated with some consideration, he became interested in his environment and began to respond favorably. When he was treated as a problem personality and was forced into an undesirable role, he responded by the defenses which he knew best—firm and passive withdrawal.

Another prevalent family reaction is to treat the returned patients as if they are convalescing from a physical illness. They are deterred from any work, from taking any initiative, or from spontaneous behavior. As is apparent in the following case, ex-patients want approval but resent intensified regulation and oversolicitous concern by the family.

From early morning till late evening, the mother released an endless stream of warnings and exhortations. If Joan prepared to write a letter the mother cautioned her to "take it easy." If she offered to help with the cleaning the mother objected on the grounds that a patient who had just returned from the hospital must have lots of rest and must not tire herself. Everything Joan did was supervised. If she went to the kitchen to get herself a glass of water, her mother rushed to watch. If she spent more time in the bathroom than her mother thought suitable, the mother inquired, "Don't you feel well, dearie?" Joan was, of course, forbidden to go out alone, not even in daylight. Before visitors came Joan was carefully taught how to behave in their presence. "The Browns don't know that you were in the hospital. I told them you were out of town. Don't say anything about your breakdown."

In another instance a mother who tried to prevent the recurrence of her son's disorders imposed trivial demands and exhortations which hurt rather than helped him.

Another difficulty with which the ex-patients have to cope is the family's attitudes to heredity. Since many persons believe that psychoses are hereditary, they feel that the disorders may be transmitted to the offspring.

Some ex-patients are almost coerced into the very family roles which they considered so distasteful and so threatening to their self-esteem. In a short time, they lose the gains made in the hospital. Since many family attitudes are subtle and often hard to detect, the recurrence of the disorder is attributed to the personality deficits of the ex-patients. The following case illustrates how a revised situation can contribute to an ex-patient's improvement. When this ex-patient lived with her family, her disorder recurred. But when she lived with her great-aunt and great-uncle, she became well enough to get married and has remained improved three years after her last discharge from the hospital.[14]

Ann was admitted to the Brooklyn State Hospital with a diagnosis of schizophrenia, catatonic type. Two months later she was paroled. She returned to her parents with the understanding that she was to start work as soon as possible. This was the mother's plan and the hospital social service department and Ann agreed. She began work immediately and resumed her social activities. By this time, her elder brother and sister had both married and lived away from home. Nonetheless, the same unfavorable condition remained in the family, and Ann reacted with resentment. To escape these conditions, she threw herself in the social whirl and was always "on the go." Because the mother was so persistently critical, Ann left home. She was picked up by the police, sleeping in a parked car. She was run down physically and was quite bewildered, when she was taken back to the hospital.

In the hospital, Ann became cheerful and satisfied and was a willing and cooperative worker. She responded warmly to the friendliness of the doctors and nurses. When Ann was ready to leave the hospital several weeks later, her brother pointed out that because of the discord in the parental home, he wanted Ann to live with him and his wife. The social service department, apparently impressed by the brother's and sister-in-law's visits, readily consented. But this conditional discharge lasted only three days. Ann, jealous of her sister-in-law, had a fist fight with her, returned to her mother, created a scene, and again required hospitalization. At the hospital, she adjusted well and was eager to leave. Although not disordered enough to be hospitalized, Ann had no favorable home in which she could be placed.

It was found that a great-aunt and great-uncle in a nearby city were interested in Ann and seemed to be stable and friendly people. Ann found,

[14] Adapted from *Insulin Shock Therapy*, pp. 36–39 (New York: Temporary Commission on State Hospital Problems, 1944).

at last, warm and accepting people who did not interfere with her free-dom. Since she always responded well to persons outside the family, she made a good adjustment. Seven months later, Ann returned to visit her doctor with her husband, "the boy who lived next door." Since she was able to entertain him "respectably" in her foster home, she was able to carry on this courtship relationship. Three years later, when Ann and her husband were visited in their apartment, both appeared quite happy and satisfied.

Slightly Improved Ex-patients. Many ex-patients who have im-proved slightly remain very dependent upon the family. Many of these patients stagger or muddle through in their posthospital ad-justment, but they are adjusted enough to keep jobs and to get along with people on a superficial level, and are not returned to the hos-pital. Sometimes their families are aware that they cannot care for themselves independently and that they must be continually helped. The reactions among the family members vary of course, and these reactions require further inquiry. When they disregard the needs of the ex-patients these ex-patients may re-experience a breakdown. When the families protect them, these ex-patients may remain adapted within this supervised setting.

The Limits of Family Influence. Some ex-patients, however, can-not be influenced positively by the family, regardless of its conduct. The family may understand and appreciate their condition but still may be unable to help them. These patients may remain emo-tionally incapacitated because of their personality conflicts and, as such, will not be markedly affected in a positive way by the tolerant and accepting family attitudes. They can, however, be easily influ-enced negatively and, under adverse conditions, can experience another breakdown.

These conflicts are rearoused in part by the return home. An ex-patient has written:[15]

Liberty during those seven weeks at the state hospital had seemed such a precious thing that I would have risked my life to achieve it. But as soon as I got it, I lost all capacity for enjoying it and did not recover that capacity for many months.

That night, when I entered the apartment my mother had taken for us, my spirits took a sudden deep drop. Alma had spent many days of loving effort in getting it ready for my home-coming, making it into the sort of place she thought I would like and that would aid my con-valescence. But although on the ride from the asylum my optimism

[15] Carlton Brown, *Brainstorm*, pp. 288, 289, 298, 299 (New York: Rinehart & Company, Inc., 1944). By permission.

had remained high, as soon as I entered the apartment I became so unutterably depressed that I could scarcely speak. The outside world that, from Spithaven, had looked so limitlessly free, suddenly closed in around me. In tangible, inescapable form, the place seemed to represent all the stifling limitations I have ever felt surrounding me. I had an almost physical sensation of sinking, of being irrevocably trapped.

He added:

All winter long people tried to help me to work and to friendship and to love, but I would not be helped by them, could not be helped. Then, in the spring, little by little, it came to me that I could be and would be helped, because it began to be that I wanted to help myself. Only when it left did I see that the condition I had been in could not be called laziness or moral disintegration or any of the words of reprobation that I had been using. A great many of these words are to be found in the books belonging to the goody-goody, cheer-up school of popularized pseudo-psychiatry: "Snap out of it"; "Look on the bright side"; "Stop committing self-sabotage." Far from being of any use to me, such admonitions only emphasized my feelings of guilt and inadequacy. They were as much to the point as it would be to tell a man with two broken legs that only moral cowardice keeps him from walking. The advice that I did find helpful was, reduced to its simplest terms: "Be as lazy as you like; sleep as late as you like; but try to find out what started to make you like to do whatever you have been blaming yourself for doing; and, if possible, end by blaming no one and seeing the symptoms disappear in the light of knowledge of their roots."

Seemingly, some ex-patients, who have not completely recovered, must work out their conflicts in their own way and at their own pace. The depressive aftermath of this patient could not be dispelled by favorable surroundings, by "pep talks," or even by affection. Somehow, he had to get a different conception of himself before he was amenable to help. The problem of reaching manic-depressive patients of this type is admittedly difficult and sometimes requires the aid of a discerning psychiatrist.

Some families become very guilty when they learn that their behavior may have contributed to the ex-patients' breakdowns. Then they try to compensate for their hostility and cannot do enough for the ex-patients to make amends to them. When they can afford it, they lavish gifts upon them and seemingly do whatever they desire, but the difficulty is that they cannot understand and eradicate their own hostility which emerges from the daily process of living. These family members are thus beset by the conflict of shame for having a

disordered person in the family and extreme guilt for possibly having contributed to this disorder. As yet the effects of the developmental theories of psychoses, when propounded to these relatives of
disordered persons, have not been systematically investigated.

The Ex-patient and Industry. When Clifford Beers was discharged
from the hospital in 1903, he was determined to make his way again
in the outside community. At first he wanted to study art, then he
revived his favorable attitudes toward business and he sought to
re-establish connections with a company where he had worked six
years before. He related his re-employment experiences as follows:[16]

> Though persons discharged from mental hospitals are usually able
> to secure, without much difficulty, work as unskilled laborers, or posi-
> tions where the responsibilities are slight, it is often next to impossible
> for them to secure positions of trust. During the negotiations which
> led to my employment, I was in no suppliant mood. If anything, I was
> quite the reverse; and as I have since learned, I imposed terms with an
> assurance so sublime that any less degree of audacity might have put
> an end to the negotiations then and there. But the man with whom I
> was dealing was not only broadminded, he was sagacious. He recog-
> nized immediately such an ability to take care of my own interests as
> argued an ability to protect those of his firm. But this alone would not
> have induced the average businessman to employ me under the cir-
> cumstances. It was common sense and the rational attitude of my em-
> ployer toward mental illness which determined the issue. This view,
> which is indeed exceptional today, will one day (within a few genera-
> tions, I believe) be too commonplace to deserve special mention. As
> this man tersely expressed it: "When an employee is ill, he's ill, and it
> makes no difference to me whether he goes to a general hospital or a
> hospital for the insane. Should you ever find yourself in need of
> treatment or rest, I want you to feel that you can take it when and
> where you please, and work for us when you are able."

Beers's expectations about the future were perhaps overoptimistic.
Many employers even today are not as tolerant and understanding
as the man who hired Beers. Yet few patients have the self-assurance
and ability which Beers possessed.

Often, patients respond to occupational therapy or can work
proficiently around the hospital, but, when in the outside community, they experience problems other than vocational. They may
lack confidence or become upset by the whole pattern of relation-

[16] Clifford W. Beers, *A Mind That Found Itself*, pp. 209, 210 (New York:
Doubleday & Company, Inc., 1924).

ships of which they are an integral part. These relationships can range from the initial interview when in quest of employment to the competitive "social politics" and gossip within the work situation.

In emotionally supportive situations where the conflicts are held in abeyance, the ex-patients have a better chance to sustain their improvement. For example, John, aged 20, was a cab driver, and was hospitalized after a fellow cab driver had been forced to drive some robbers who were escaping from the police. Very upset by this event, John became restless, irritable, was unable to sleep, and imagined he was one of the thieves. When he threatened suicide he was committed. In time, he improved enough to leave the hospital. To prepare for his return home, the family moved to a more attractive apartment in a less crowded neighborhood. They arranged with a family friend to give him a job. Since other members of the family worked in this factory, John went with them to and from work. His mother allowed him to keep the same hours of retiring and awakening that he had in the hospital because he insisted upon it. His employer, aware of his illness, did not expect too much from him. In a follow-up inquiry, he was doing well, one and a half years later. Not many patients have these supportive relationships. But these relationships apparently helped this patient to readjust.

In seeking work the first difficulty that ex-patients experience is accounting for the time spent in the mental hospital. Some may not know whether it is more expedient to cover up this time or to disclose it. One indecisive patient became so flustered when asked by a prospective employer about this period that he could not answer the questionnaire and did not receive the job. In the state of Illinois a question on the civil service examination was, "Were you an inmate of an institution?" This question irritated so many ex-patients who applied for civil service positions that, after protest, it was reworded to specify, "inmates in penal institutions." [17] It was found, too, that large firms with personnel managers were less hesitant about rehiring former patients than were small businessmen such as grocers or garage owners.

Some ex-patients claim that employers, as part of the general public, discriminate against them because they believe that psy-

[17] *Insulin Shock Therapy*, pp. 54, 55; *Lost and Found*, II:2, p. 20.

chotic disorders are incurable. Some ex-patients, however, are so sensitive when they become rejected by prospective employers that they attribute the rejection to the employer's implicit knowledge that they are "crazy."

When ex-patients can successfully conceal their past commitment, they may not meet any difficulty because no one suspects them of having been in mental hospitals. In fact, the popular misconceptions of psychotic persons work to protect many ex-patients, because many persons would anticipate some queer behavior or angry outbursts. Hence, ex-patients who become swallowed up in industrial life usually are indistinguishable from those who have never experienced breakdowns. Nonetheless, some patients retain anxieties about their "past."

The positions of ex-patients differ with the size of the community. In the small town, ex-patients would find it difficult to hide their past commitment, as we have shown before. But in the large cities, anonymity can engulf the ex-patients effectively so that their "past" remains unknown to their employers.

But even in the city ex-patients who have personality problems experience difficulties. Although improved enough to work, they retain many mannerisms and conflicts which they had before their breakdown. The recall of these experiences is likely to continue. For example, one ex-patient, a paranoid schizophrenic, was worried because he had been involved in so many office clashes before his breakdown and feared that these disagreements would recur. "I was afraid of myself. I could do my work, but I was afraid I wouldn't get along. And that caused me more grief than having been in the mental hospital." Finally he worked as a door-to-door salesman and had to solve many of his difficulties with a private psychiatrist. Since his sales were high his employer didn't care whether he had had a breakdown.

A catatonic schizophrenic patient in a competitive industrial situation had transient notions that others might suspect him of having been hospitalized. He became very tense and was reluctant to mingle freely. He believed that his self-conscious and nervous mannerisms of stroking his hair attracted undue attention from others. For a period he ate in restaurants where the other employees did not go. He was continually on the defensive and, having told another employee of his hospitalization, he often regretted this "slip" for fear the others would find out.

In a study of the vocational experiences of 21 schizophrenic ex-patients, Balinsky found that 6 made good adjustments, 7 fair, and 8 poor adjustments.[18] The 6 patients who made good vocational adjustments had confidence that they could retain their social status, while the 8 who made poor adjustments did not have these positive attitudes. Of the 7 who made a fair adjustment, 6 were hindered by undue fearfulness or uncontrolled behavior, and 1 was hindered by unfavorable family relationships.

The well-adjusted ex-patients firmly decided about their type of work, then sought and obtained employment, and experienced no trouble on the job. Usually, they became attracted to their jobs.

The poorly adjusted ex-patients, on the other hand, were undecided about their type of work, had no real goals, or did not know how to attain their goals.

For example, one poorly adjusted type was quite apprehensive that he would not be accepted for employment. In ten referrals by an employment agency, he was hired only once, because each time he made an unfavorable impression. Later, he was rehospitalized, discharged, then re-experienced the same vocational difficulties. In general, those ex-patients who made a fair adjustment could be helped by the psychiatric social worker. Those ex-patients who made a poor adjustment seemingly did not have the requisite personality structure to adjust to a competitive work situation and required either more intensive psychotherapy or a supporting situation.

Employers' Attitudes to Veteran Patients. It would seem that veterans who had incurred neurotic breakdowns in the armed forces would be more tolerated than civilian ex-patients. First, they were not psychotic, and second, they broke down in the line of patriotic duty. This may be the case, for the available evidence seems to show that the huge majority were accepted in industry.

In a follow-up study of 4,178 veterans with medical discharges, in which the diagnosis of "psychoneurosis" was recorded, it was found that the stereotypes toward them existed among the minority

---

[18] Benjamin Balinsky, "Factors in the Vocational Adjustment of Schizophrenics after Mental Hospital Discharge," *Journal of Clinical Psychology,* October, 1947, III:4, pp. 341–349.

of employers.[19] Of this veteran group, 86.9 per cent were employed or attended school; 33 per cent had returned to their former jobs and about 60 per cent secured new jobs, but about 7 per cent of the latter group were not employed at the time of the inquiry. Of those employed, 73.5 per cent claimed that the owners showed no hesitancy in hiring them, and 22.7 per cent indicated that the employers were reluctant to do so. Of the unemployed group, 59.7 per cent of the veterans felt that the prospective employers showed no hesitancy in hiring them, but 32.5 per cent claimed that the employers were reluctant. Of the employed and unemployed groups, 12.4 and 16.2 per cent, respectively, were not put on the payrolls because of their failure to pass the physical examinations.

Rennie, Burling, and Woodward found that out of 2,653 convalescent or discharged patients only 15 per cent could profit by rehabilitative efforts.[20] Of the others in this group, 35 per cent were satisfactorily employed through their own efforts or with the aid of the social-work staff, 26 per cent were housewives who did not wish other employment, 5 per cent were marginal workers, 8 per cent were unable to work because of age or infirmity, and 11 per cent were too disordered to profit from rehabilitation services. Thus, about 50 per cent of the discharged patients were not considered feasible for rehabilitation.

Many patients who had been successfully employed before being admitted to the mental hospitals had no difficulty in regaining their employment. Their employers regarded their disorders as nervous breakdowns and seemingly had no prejudice in rehiring them. Some employers even visited the employees in the hospital.

Those who needed vocational rehabilitation broke down early in life and did not have time to become established vocationally or even to take adequate vocational training. The huge majority in this category were schizophrenics. This group of individuals, unknown to their potential employers, did encounter the prejudice

[19] Norman Q. Brill, M. C. Tate, and William C. Menninger, "Enlisted Men Discharged from the Army Because of Psychoneuroses—A Follow-up Study," *National Neuro-Psychiatric Institute Act: S 1160*, pp. 148–157 (Washington, D.C.: U.S. Government Printing Office, 1946); also in *Journal of the American Medical Association*, January 30, 1945, 128, pp. 633–637.

[20] Thomas A. C. Rennie, Temple Burling, and Luther E. Woodward, *Vocational Rehabilitation of Psychiatric Patients*, pp. 18–20 (New York: Commonwealth Fund, 1950).

of their employers because the employers expressed the general distrust for them that they have for the insane generally, excepting those whom they have known well. Others who needed vocational rehabilitation (1) had a limited amount of work experience, (2) had moved from job to job without developing any interest in any type of job or without developing any marketable skills, (3) could not impress their prospective employers, and (4) had experienced a decided change in personality.

The rehabilitating vocational process covered five related services: (1) vocational counseling, (2) vocational training, (3) physical restoration, (4) job finding and placement, and (5) personal counseling. In trying to gauge the effectiveness of these rehabilitation services in three states—Connecticut, New York, and Michigan—they found that, of the 215 patients to whom services were given, 166, or 77 per cent, were successfully rehabilitated and were satisfactorily employed; 49, or 23 per cent, were not rehabilitated. Of this latter group some became so ill that they had to be returned to the hospital; others were so unco-operative that they could not be helped; still others tried one job after another without success; and some could not succeed vocationally because of family interference.[21]

Patients Who Stay Out and Patients Who Go Back. The general problem of keeping the patients well after they have left the hospital is pervasive and serious. Were this condition similar among patients with physical illnesses, it would be alarming. Except for a few physical illnesses, such as malaria and tuberculosis, physical patients who leave general hospitals as recovered usually stay that way or have lesser recurrences. On the other hand, many patients who are readmitted to mental hospitals are usually in worse condition than when they entered the first time.

As is evident from Table 23, in 1944 the patients with personality psychoses, i.e., schizophrenia and manic-depression, comprised the majority—53.5 per cent—of the patients readmitted to the state mental hospitals.

Schizophrenia. Rupp and Fletcher, in a five- to ten-year follow-up study of 641 schizophrenic patients—340 males and 301 females—found that during this period 27.5 per cent were in the community, 53.5 per cent were in the hospital, 13.9 per cent were dead, and no

[21] *Ibid.*, pp. 27-31.

adequate information could be found for 5.1 per cent. In following up 608 patients, the authors found that 6.6 per cent were much improved, 15.3 per cent improved, 63.5 per cent unimproved, and 24.6 per cent were dead.[22]

Osborne found, in a study of 491 patients, that 44 per cent im-

TABLE 22

PERCENTAGES OF ADMISSIONS AND READMISSIONS TO MENTAL HOSPITALS, BY TYPE OF HOSPITAL, IN THE UNITED STATES, 1933 TO 1946*

Year	State Hospital		Veterans Hospital		County and City Hospital		Private Hospital	
	First	Readmission	First	Readmission	First	Readmission	First	Readmission
1946	76.4	23.6	62.9	37.1	78.3	21.7	65.9	34.1
1945	77.0	23.0	84.6	15.3	78.6	21.4	66.8	33.1
1944	77.5	22.5	82.6	17.4	83.2	16.8	71.1	28.9
1943	77.5	22.5	76.5	23.5	79.9	20.1	66.4	33.6
1942	77.6	22.2	56.7	43.3			66.2	33.8
1941	71.8	28.2	56.7	43.3	79.7	20.8	66.1	33.9
1940	77.7	22.3	58.3	41.7	78.0	22.1	65.6	34.4
1939	72.8	27.2	62.5	37.5	85.3	14.7	62.1	37.9
1938	79.0	21.0	65.5	34.5	86.5	13.5	68.6	31.4
1937	79.3	20.7	56.9	43.1	84.9	15.1	70.0	30.0
1936	80.4	19.6	56.7	43.3	84.1	15.9	70.1	29.9
1935	80.7	19.3	63.9	36.1	84.6	15.4	69.7	30.3
1934	79.8	20.2	52.4	48.6	81.2	18.8	68.2	31.9
1933	80.3	19.7	59.9	39.2	86.4	13.6	67.1	32.9

* Data compiled from *Patients in Mental Institutions, 1946*, pp. 53, 54 (Washington, D.C.: Bureau of the Census, U.S. Department of Commerce, 1948). Transfers omitted.

proved spontaneously and that a recurrence of the disorder led to a poorer chance of recovery.[23] The longest hospitalization among those readmitted occurred among catatonics, while the shortest occurred among simple schizophrenics. Of the subtypes of schizophrenics, the catatonics generally tended to have the best adjustment for the longest period, the paranoids were next, and the

[22] Charles Rupp and Elizabeth K. Fletcher, "A Five to Ten Year Follow-up Study of 641 Schizophrenic Cases," *The American Journal of Psychiatry*, January, 1940, 96:4, pp. 877–888.

[23] Raymond L. Osborne, "Prognosis in Schizophrenia," *Journal of the American Medical Association*, March 9, 1940, 114, pp. 846, 847.

simple and hebephrenic categories had the worst adjustment. Bellak, however, reports that sometimes the undetermined type of schizophrenics have a better outcome than the catatonics.[24]

In general, the psychiatric follow-up studies are based primarily upon the condition of the patient before and during the disorder.

TABLE 23

PER CENT OF FIRST ADMISSIONS AND READMISSIONS IN STATE MENTAL HOSPITALS
IN THE UNITED STATES BY DIAGNOSTIC TYPES, 1944 *

Disorder	First Admissions 83,723	Readmissions 24,265	Percentage of Increase or Decrease of Readmissions Over First Admissions
Manic depression	8.6	22.3	+13.7
Schizophrenia	20.0	31.2	+11.2
Psychosis with psychopathic personality	0.8	1.7	+0.9
Neuroses	2.8	3.0	+0.2
Paranoia and paranoid condition	1.1	1.3	+0.2
Psychopathic personality	0.9	0.9	
Involutional psychoses	4.1	2.7	−1.4
Paresis	6.9	3.2	−3.7
Senile psychoses	12.9	2.7	−10.2
Cerebral arteriosclerosis	15.9	5.3	−10.6
Other psychoses	18.5	16.8	−1.7
Other Nonpsychoses	7.5	8.7	+1.2
Total	100.0	100.0	

* *Patients in Mental Institutions, 1944*, pp. 19, 24 (Washington, D.C.: Bureau of the Census, U.S. Department of Commerce, 1948).

Little or no consideration is given to the attitudes of the persons in the groups in which the patient participates.

Also, the varied follow-up studies use different criteria of improvement and recovery. For example, some investigators used four criteria: recovered, much improved, improved, and unimproved, but others used three criteria. Whether all investigators meant the same thing by these criteria is questionable. Bellak found that the

[24] Leopold Bellak, *Dementia Praecox*, Chap. XV (New York: Grune & Stratton, Inc., 1948).

rates for over-all improvement of schizophrenics ranged from slight improvement to recovery. In terms of duration of those who improved, about 50 per cent improved within six months, about 35 per cent remained improved after six to eighteen months, and about 20 per cent sustained improvement after eighteen months.[25] This means that about one half of those who have improved after six months have a recurrence about one year later. As yet, no definite knowledge exists as to why this happens.

To get more complete knowledge of the types of outcome, it is necessary to consider the following: the ex-patient's previous background, his mode of breakdown—i.e., sudden or slow—how soon he entered the hospital after breakdown, his length of hospital stay, his condition at the time of discharge, and the types of social situations he encountered in the community, especially in the family. Our chief concern, however, is with the condition of ex-patients who remain outside the hospital after a specified period.

Control of posthospital adjustment: To determine the effects of intensive psychiatric social work upon the patient's posthospital adjustment, Field studied two insulin-treated schizophrenic groups.[26] This study arose because so many insulin-treated patients had been recommitted.[27] The experimental group of 138 patients and their families were given special orientation lectures, while 127 patients of the control group were given the customary social-work assistance. This orientation process began before the patients were discharged.

Although the follow-up study was done less than one year after discharge, some significant differences were noted between the two groups. In the experimental group 23 persons, or 16.7 per cent of the patients, as against 37 persons, or 29.1 per cent of the control patients, were returned to the hospital. Even among the returned patients, the experimental group stayed out of the hospital 32 days longer on the average than did the control group. When the patients' conditions were compared, the experimental group had 71.7 per cent doing as "well or better than before the breakdown," but

[25] *Ibid.*

[26] Minna Field, *Psychiatric Social Work with Insulin Treated Patients* (Utica, N.Y.: State Hospitals Press, 1947).

[27] New York Temporary Commission on State Hospital Problems, *Insulin Shock Therapy* (Utica, N.Y.: State Hospitals Press, 1942).

the control group had 51.1 per cent in this condition. In general, intensive treatment seemed most helpful to those who were amenable to improvement.

Manic-depressive Patients. Manic-depressive patients generally recover more spontaneously than schizophrenics and also seem to have a more lasting recovery. In a long-range study of 1,000 patients who had been discharged from the hospital ten or more years ago, Fuller found that, among the manic-depressive group, 57 per cent were living in the community, 20 per cent were in the hospital, and 23 per cent had died. Of the schizophrenic group, 43 per cent were living in the community, 44 per cent had been returned to the hospital, and 13 per cent had died.[28] Rennie's study of 208 manic depressives showed that 80 per cent of the cases had one or more recurrences: 79 per cent had a second attack and 63.5 per cent had a third attack; 45 per cent eventually recovered completely under planned therapy; only 7 per cent remained chronic cases.[29] This may mean that, though manic depressives are more prone to temporary recurrences than schizophrenics, in the long run they recover more completely.

Programs for Ex-patient Readjustment. In recent years the adjustment of patients is being facilitated by (1) the educative attempts of mental-hygiene organizations, (2) the help of psychiatric social workers, (3) outpatient clinics, (4) family-placement programs, and (5) ex-patient-initiated organizations.

The Mental-hygiene Organizations. One educational aim of mental-hygiene organizations is the attempt to facilitate the adjustment of ex-patients by removing the stigma of disordered behavior. Presumably, a public enlightened about personal disorders will be more considerate to ex-patients in their efforts to readjust to the community. Heretofore, this facet of mental hygiene has not been emphasized as much as have other phases. Yet gradual public re-education about disordered behavior generally—by informative motion pictures such as *The Snake Pit,* by radio programs such as "Shadow of the Mind," and by newspaper articles—has influenced the public favorably toward ex-patients.

[28] Raymond G. Fuller, "What Happens to Mental Patients After Discharge from the Hospital," *Psychiatric Quarterly,* 1940, IX, pp. 95–104.

[29] Thomas A. C. Rennie, "Prognosis in the Manic Depressive Psychoses," *The American Journal of Psychiatry,* May, 1942, 98:6, pp. 801–14.

The Psychiatric Social Worker. The psychiatric social worker has the specific function of helping the patient readjust himself during his conditional discharge. By her home visits she sees the patient in his usual habitat and can obtain a real understanding of the problems with which he has to cope. Frequently, she has to deal with the family and some members of the community, as well as with the patient himself. In effect, she becomes a supporting link between the patient and the persons about him.

The social worker must understand the family constellation of interpersonal relationships, the role of the patient in the family, and his attitudes to the different members, as well as their attitudes to him. Frequently, she must interpret the meaning of the disorder to the family, try to remove their attitudes of guilt and shame which result from the disorder, and remove their pressure upon the ex-patient. She must provide an outlet for the accumulated conflicts of members in the family other than the patient, because these conflicts can affect the patient adversely. And she must be able to distinguish between their rational and unconscious attitudes to the patient. For example, the family members may appear kindly and accepting of the patient on a surface level, but unwittingly they may be devastatingly hostile to him.

In short, the psychiatric social worker must almost reorient the patient to the family and the family to the patient. In this manner she becomes a positive influence which revises the patient's social setting. The skills and techniques involved in this social interplay require a facility for developing the type of rapport and interviewing skills by which the patient will confide his difficulties and problems to the social worker and by which the family will regard the social worker as a professional friend.

Outpatient Clinics. More recently the outpatient clinics have been established to facilitate the ex-patient's adjustment. That is, the ex-patient can report to the outpatient clinic instead of going to the hospital during his conditional discharge. He can seek advice and some kind of mild therapy at these outpatient clinics. As yet, these clinics are concentrated in cities, and even in the cities there is a marked shortage of clinics. Nevertheless, the outpatient clinic is an advantage for the ex-patient because he can disassociate himself from the hospital. So far, there have been no definitive studies of the role of the outpatient clinic in the community and of the effects of these institutions upon ex-patients.

"Recovery Incorporated": an Organization of Former Patients. In November, 1937, "Recovery Incorporated" was founded in Chicago by thirty ex-patients, their relatives, and friends. It was organized to help ex-patients become readjusted to the family and to the community. Its immediate aim was to help the patient overcome the stigma of having been in a mental hospital. The motto of the group was: "Nobody must be held responsible for the kind of disease he contracts." "Recovery Incorporated" was adopted as a "safe" name which would not expose the members to their particular communities when they received mail. Despite its biological orientation to disorders, this organization tried to bolster the confidence of the patients by group discussions of their problems, by disseminating information about the problems which the ex-patients would encounter, and by publishing a bulletin.

Before discharge the patients were oriented about what to expect after leaving the hospital. They were taught to expect that others might be suspicious and could readily seize upon their former breakdowns as a cause for criticizing any behavior which seemed even slightly deviant.

Many families of patients were reoriented and were informed about their mode of behavior, attitudes, moods, and dispositions as the important things to which the patient would respond. They were told that sometimes their behavior would be misjudged by the ex-patient, that presumably friendly intentions would sometimes be misconstrued as hostile by him because of his "distorted" views.

A third important feature which was designed to strengthen the ex-patient's self-confidence was group participation and identification. By "belonging" and participating with others in a common situation, the patient felt less lonely. Hence, this organization sponsored meetings, parties, and other social affairs. Recovered patients tried to assist the new members. In this way the ex-patient's private fears and anxieties became socialized, because he was less hesitant in communicating his experiences to a former patient who had been in the same situation. For instance, Adolph felt himself completely alone because he could not express his deepest fears to anyone about not being accepted. With the aid of two former patients, he was able to confide in them and become relieved of his deepest fears.

Within the structure of the group each new member was assigned to a member to whom he could turn in times of duress.[30] This person listened sympathetically and compared his experiences with those of the new member. When this type of counseling did not clear up the problems, the leader of the local panel was called, and if he could not help, the chairman of the organization, who was the physician, was summoned. If all these persons did not succeed, then the psychiatrist was consulted. Usually the case cleared up before it reached the psychiatrist, and few cases went beyond the first adviser.

This organization tried to help the members in other ways. They opposed the court procedures which were preliminary to commitments. They tried to reorient employers and other groups. Despite the excellent potentialities of this organization, it has not grown. It is not known exactly how many persons were deterred from recurrent breakdowns by the work of this organization. The assumptions upon which this group operates seem to be sound and of definite help to ex-patients.

Summary

Ex-patients are confronted by a variety of adverse and hostile stereotypes to which they must adjust or which they must evade. Many patients are hindered by these prejudices, which are often instrumental in their recurrent breakdowns. The most influential relationships to which ex-patients have to adjust are of the family and the immediate persons in the community. Sometimes, the conflicts which contributed to their disorders arise again.

The gap between the regulated life of the mental hospital and the indifferent, competitive relationships of the outside community is often beyond the scope of the patient's abilities. The simple fact is that about one quarter of the patients discharged are returned to the mental hospital.

Of the different disorders, it appears that the manic depressives tend to have greater proportions of the group hospitalized more than once, but it also seems that the manic depressives have a

[30] Note the similarity of the procedure to that of "Alcoholics Anonymous."

greater number whose improvement is sustained after a ten-year period than is true of the schizophrenics' posthospital improvement. The rational techniques implemented to facilitate the adjustment of the ex-patients are not pervasively used. Generally, ex-patients are left to their own resources after they leave the hospital. Psychiatrists and mental hygiene organizations have succeeded in reducing the intensity of some adverse stereotypes concerning the disordered persons, but this knowledge may be limited to urban groups. Self-help organizations for patients, as "Recovery Incorporated," offer one solution toward easing the readjustment of the patient to other persons, but this organization is far too small.

The many gaps in our knowledge concerning the ex-patient can be filled in by further definitive inquiry, which can be both theoretical and practical.

Selected Readings

Balinsky, Benjamin, "Factors in the Vocational Adjustment of Schizophrenics after Mental Hospital Discharge," *Journal of Clinical Psychology*, October, 1947, 3:4, pp. 341–349.

Crutcher, Hester B., *Family Home Care for Mental Patients* (New York: Commonwealth Fund, 1944).

DeWitt, Henrietta B., "What Hospitalization Means to the Mental Patient, The Community and the Hospital Social Worker," *Mental Hygiene*, 1947, XXXI, pp. 266–278.

Evensen, Hans, "Studies Made of 800 Patients after Their Discharge from Psychiatric Hospital at Gausted during Years 1915 to 1929," *Acta psychiatrica et neurologica*, 1937, XI, pp. 799–816.

Field, Minna, *Psychiatric Social Work with Insulin-Treated Patients* (Utica, N.Y.: State Hospitals Press, 1945).

Fuller, Raymond G., "What Happens to Mental Patients after Discharge from the Hospital," *Psychiatric Quarterly*, 1940, IX, pp. 95–104.

Gartland, Ruth, "The Psychiatric Social Worker in a Mental Hospital," *Mental Hygiene*, 1947, XXXI, pp. 285–295.

Hoffman, Jay L., Ernest H. Parson, and Margaret W. Hagen, "Post Hospital Adaption of Selected Groups of Patients with Dementia Praecox," *Journal of Nervous and Mental Disease*, June, 1941, 93, pp. 705–712.

Jacob, Joseph Simeon, "Prediction of Outcome on Furlough of Dementia Praecox Patients," *Genetic Psychology Monograms*, August, 1940, XXII, pp. 425–453.

Levine, Norman, "The Mental Patient in the Community from the Viewpoint of the Family Agency," *Mental Hygiene*, 1947, XXXI, pp. 278–285.

Rabin, Albert I., "Trends of Vocational Achievement in Mental Disorders," *Scientific Monthly*, September, 1947.

Rennie, Thomas A. C., "Prognosis, Follow-up Study of 500 Patients with Schizophrenia Admitted to Hospital from 1913 to 1923," *Archives of Neurology and Psychiatry*, November, 1939, 42, pp. 877–891.

———, "Prognosis in Manic-Depressive Psychoses," *The American Journal of Psychiatry*, 1942, 98, pp. 801–814.

———, "Psychiatric Rehabilitation Techniques," *Current Therapies of Personality Disorders*, edited by B. Glueck, pp. 242–261 (New York: Grune & Stratton, Inc., 1946).

Rupp, Charles, and Elizabeth K. Fletcher, "A Five to Ten Year Follow-up Study of 641 Schizophrenic Cases," *The American Journal of Psychiatry*, 1940, 96:4.

Stalker, Harry, "Prognosis in Schizophrenia Based on Follow-up Study of 129 Cases Treated by Ordinary Methods," *Journal of Mental Science*, 1939, 85, pp. 1224–1240.

Woodward, Julian L., "Changing Ideas on Mental Illness and Its Treatment," *American Sociological Review*, August, 1951, 16:4, pp. 443–454.

CHAPTER NINETEEN

Prevention: Personal Stability and Society

The Need for Prevention

Year after year new patients in undiminished numbers are admitted into the many mental hospitals. Even if state mental hospitals became markedly better and even if outpatient treatment expanded, the ever-growing parade of new patients would not decline. Clearly, preventive measures must be introduced which will get at the sources of these disorders by striving to develop more stable persons and by striving to treat the disorders in the early stages.

But preventive mental-health programs are difficult to apply: Some disagree about the causes of the varied disorders; some psychotic disorders seem to involve more than one aspect of the personality; many laymen would resist the social changes and the costs which these programs might require. Yet the scope of the problem is wide enough to warrant more attention than has been given to it in the past.

Although estimates of the number of aberrant persons vary and are very difficult to compute, one estimate of all organic and personal disorders in the United States is about 8,500,000.[1] Personality disorders alone comprise the formidable sum of about 4,500,000 persons, including about 422,000 psychotics, about 3,000,000 neurotics, and about 1,134,000 disturbed children. This sum omits the

---

[1] "Statistics Pertinent to Psychiatry in the United States," *Group for the Advancement of Psychiatry*, Report No. 7, March, 1949.

many adults who have mild disorders.[2] Between 30 and 60 per cent of the patients who seek medical care usually have a neurotic or psychosomatic disability.[3] Moreover, people seem to be more preoccupied today with their personal condition than during almost any other period. Books which offer some temporary way out have crowded best-sellers' lists: *Peace of Mind,* by J. L. Leibman; *Peace of Soul,* by Bishop F. Sheen; *Guide to Confident Living,* by N. V. Peale; and *How to Stop Worrying and Start Living,* by D. Carnegie, among others, have this wide audience appeal.[4] One poet, not without cause, has referred to this period as "The Age of Anxiety." [5]

Approaches to Prevention

To get at the roots of personal disorders and of "mental health" involves a variety of approaches to personality. These divergent approaches to preventive mental-health programs assume different hypotheses of causation for the personal disorders. But the personality is a many-sided entity, and these approaches often supplement rather than contradict each other. Some approaches, such as the eugenic and the sociological, show extreme differences; other approaches, for example the psychological and sociological, differ in emphasis rather than in direction. Before concentrating upon the sociological approach to mental health, we will consider the eugenic, constitutional, and psychological viewpoints in preventive mental health.

The Eugenics Approach. Eugenics emphasizes the improvement of the human stock by biological means.[6] Some measures, such as

[2] Because "psychopathy" is used so vaguely, statistics of this behavioral type have not been included.

[3] National Health Assembly, *America's Health,* p. 298 (New York: Harper & Brothers, 1949); also Charles A. Rymer, "Psychiatric Education," *The American Journal of Psychiatry,* January, 1946, pp. 548–551; Franklin S. Ebaugh, *The Care of the Psychiatric Patient in a General Hospital* (Chicago: American Hospital Association, 1940).

[4] Joshua L. Leibman, *Peace of Mind* (New York: Simon and Schuster, Inc., 1946); Fulton J. Sheen, *Peace of Soul* (New York: McGraw-Hill Book Company, Inc., 1949); N. V. Peale, *Guide to Confident Living* (New York: Prentice-Hall, Inc., 1949); Dale Carnegie, *How to Stop Worrying and Start Living* (New York: Simon and Schuster, Inc., 1948).

[5] William H. Auden, *The Age of Anxiety* (New York: Random House, 1947).

[6] See J. M. Nielsen and George N. Thompson, *The Engrammes of Psychiatry,* pp. 278–279 (Springfield, Ill.: Charles C. Thomas, Publisher, 1947). (Despite their

birth control, good embryonic development, and the safe processes of birth, may contribute more positively to a healthier human stock. Sterilization of psychotics can be legally performed in twenty-seven states at state expense. Some find sterilization objectionable for cogent reasons: (1) Even if applied, it would not appreciably reduce the number of schizophrenics and manic depressives. (2) Though the probability of psychotic parents having psychotic children is about twenty times greater than that of the normal population, this disparity may result from improper rearing as well as from innate tendencies. Furthermore, many children born of one psychotic parent do not break down. The processes of heredity, at the most, consist of predisposing tendencies. Hence, subsequent social relationships are crucial in determining whether the child does or does not become psychotic. In addition, some parents who are not psychotic have psychotic children. Because of these recessive characteristics, the procedure of sterilization, if followed to its logical conclusion, would sterilize people who are not psychotic. Also, sterilization implies a defeat for the social order. It means that society cannot so arrange its institutions and its interpersonal relationships to avert the onset of these disorders. (3) Moreover, in terms of society's benefit, it can be pointed out that many creative artists and scientists have been psychotic during some period of their lives—Van Gogh, Beethoven, Newton, and Nijinsky, among many others, have made lasting contributions to art and to science.

Gamble has defended sterilization as a simple operation which differs from castration and which does not change the personality characteristics of the sterilized persons. He states:[7]

> In tubectomy, the modern operation for sterilization in both men and women, nothing is removed from the body. The surgeon simply locates and ties off the small tubes leading from the sex glands, preventing the further passage of the female cell, or ovum, and the sperm cells of the male. These minute cells are then absorbed by the body, and the

classical psychiatric approach, they do not believe sterilization is desirable in the present state of social advance.) Also Abraham Meyerson and R. D. Boyle, "The Incidence of Manic-Depressive Psychosis in Certain Socially Important Families," *The American Journal of Psychiatry*, July–November, 1941, p. 19. Among the advocates of sterilization are Franz J. Kallman, *The Genetics of Schizophrenia* (New York: J. J. Augustin, Inc., 1938) and the Human Betterment League. See Clarence J. Gamble, "Preventive Sterilization in 1948," *Journal of the American Medical Association*, 1948, p. 773.

[7] Clarence J. Gamble, "Why Fear Sterilization," *Hygeia,* January, 1948.

sterilized person can detect no change in appearance, feelings, or desires other than the fact that no children are produced.

Although Gamble believes psychotic disorders can be "cured," he defends sterilization for those who have permanent recurrent disorders, because it would protect children from being born in an adverse environment. Perhaps this measure may possibly be permitted in extreme cases when birth-control methods cannot be taught to chronic psychotics, who are unable to support or to rear many children. Yet, in the main, chronic psychotics usually do not present these problems, because they are segregated and reproduce a minimal number of offsprings.

The Constitutional Approach. Physical health, important for its own sake, is often related to emotional stability. Yet, when physical health only is emphasized, it can easily deflect attention from personal conflicts. Conceivably, some mediums for arresting disorders through physical means may be found, but it is not at all certain that physical techniques only will assure emotional growth. Moreover, excessive fatigue, malnutrition, allergies, infections, glandular changes, illness, and physical handicaps may indirectly affect personal stability and should be considered within the general scope of mental health.[8]

The Psychological Approach. The psychological approach technically refers to the developmental process of the individual, particularly in early life. It follows that prevention concentrates upon early parent-child relationships, in order to develop healthy persons who could tolerate the stresses of later life. The techniques and knowledge of this aspect of development have been invaluable in understanding personality. Yet the knowledge of the inherent conflicts in our culture and the knowledge gained from World War II have demonstrated convincingly that crises in later life can incapacitate even the hardiest person. It is not surprising, then, that some persons who were apparently "normal" in childhood incurred difficulties later in life.[9] An individualistic approach sees the person apart from his social setting and in terms of his own deficits. It does not integrate the person with his groups, and it does not con-

[8] See George S. Stevenson, "The Prevention of Personality Disorders," *Personality and Behavior Disorders,* edited by J. McV. Hunt (New York: The Ronald Press Company, 1944).

[9] See Helen L. Witmer, *Psychiatric Clinics for Children* (New York: Commonwealth Fund, 1940).

sider the contributing social influences which affect him in his daily living. Plant, a psychiatrist, has pointed out that it is not enough to try to change individuals only. This purely psychiatric procedure is not only an inefficient mode of dealing with the problem of mental health but also a rather futile flight from the reality of the task. Constructive steps will have been achieved when "certain pressures of the cultural pattern have been relieved." [10]

Because of practical as well as theoretical considerations, more attention is being devoted to the social settings in which the individual participates. Blackmer, who has observed the mental-health services in England, has stated:[11]

> From a recognition of the influences of how people are reared, work, behave, live, has developed what is now called social medicine, which is an aspect—the medical aspect—of sociology. Preventive psychiatry, together with preventive medicine as a whole, has its roots in sociology.

The Sociological Approach. The sociological approach to personal disorders considers the person a participant in a variety of social groups, each of which contributes to his stability or instability. Consequently, both person and group, as parts of a total continuous process, must be considered and acted upon in preventive mental health. Thus, mental health has three aspects: (1) a set of objectives, (2) a set of techniques, and (3) public support and co-operation.

The Norms of Mental Health. Any scheme for preventing mental illness implies the development of certain kinds of social relationships within the culture to foster stable personalities. In our culture, which is sharply individualistic, the emphasis can be upon maximum personal stability to assure the greatest degree of self-realization. In this personal culture area, Plant's conception of the "individual-centered culture" would seem consistent with the ends of mental health. He states his position as follows:[12]

> An individual-centered philosophy focuses its interest upon the personality, but as it does this, it is led out into the entire cultural pat-

---

[10] James S. Plant, *Personality and the Cultural Pattern,* p. 244 (New York: Commonwealth Fund, 1937).

[11] C. P. Blacker, *Neurosis and the Mental Health Services,* p. 38 (New York: Oxford University Press, 1946).

[12] James S. Plant, *Personality and the Cultural Pattern,* pp. 239, 240 (New York: Commonwealth Fund, 1937).

tern. This is not so much because the personality is discovered to be in a cultural pattern of some sort, as because the cultural pattern is discovered existing in the personality. . . . If the content of the personality is affected by the cultural pattern and if through changes in the pattern we have the easiest approach to changing the personality, certain implications follow. Sectors of the cultural pattern can be changed; they have been and are being changed. This implies a procedure which may be simply set forth, though it might be long and tedious of execution. The first step is to discover . . . what the cultural pattern in its various phases means to the individual and his growth. As more is known of the imprint which these various sectors make upon the personality, the door is open for conscious social alteration. . . .

Techniques. But these ends cannot be achieved without cultivating proper techniques, training adequate personnel, and expanding necessary facilities. Mental-health techniques depend upon basic research and action research. Basic research is the means by which the causes and contributing factors of the varied disorders can be understood. Action research is concerned with understanding and also with changing the attitudes and relationships of persons in different groups. It involves the interaction between hypotheses and deliberate social change, for hypotheses are necessary to blueprint planned revisions, and planned changes are necessary to test and correct hypotheses.

The techniques of mental health may differ for different social units; each social unit requires a particular kind of knowledge of the many problems and tensions with which its members are confronted. It means that the preventive personnel must become intimate with the daily problems and conflicts of the persons in these social units. For example, preventive work in the Army required an intimate knowledge of the soldiers' problems. As Spiegel says:[13]

There are those who argue that a doctor is stepping out of his sphere when he concerns himself with whether or not mail gets to the men, whether or not men are confident in their leaders, whether or not discipline is appropriate, whether or not the folks at home appreciate what the fighters are doing, or whether or not the workers at home are working or the merchants are profiteering. But psychiatric casualties are real—and these are the factors that contribute to anxiety which increase the soldier's vulnerability to mental distortions. Concern about this is no different from the concern of the army doctor who

[13] Herbert X. Spiegel, "Preventive Psychiatry with Combat Troops," *The American Journal of Psychiatry*, November, 1944, 101:3, p. 314.

thoroughly delouses hordes of filthy civilians to avoid a typhus epidemic among the oncoming troops. It is detecting and eliminating the causes of disease, instead of waiting for them to occur, then attempting to treat them.

When prevention techniques are applied to civilian social units, the persons in strategic positions also must be persuaded and convinced that prevention is essential for the welfare and smoother functioning of the group as well as for the benefit of the individual.

Yet the sums allotted annually to the social aspects of personal disorders are a small fraction of the two or three million dollars devoted to psychiatric research.[14] Prevention is one of the chief aims of the National Institute for Mental Health, but during 1948, 8 per cent of the grants-in-aid were allocated for preventive work and 61 per cent for treatment clinics.[15]

Technical Personnel. Despite the high incidence of personal disorders, technical personnel are relatively few. In 1948 the American Psychiatric Association had 4,765 members. Of these members, 1,718 had hospital affiliations and 351 accepted private patients. An estimated 5,000 psychiatrists in this country would mean about 1 psychiatrist per 30,000 population. The psychiatrists required would range from about 15,000 to 19,000.[16]

Training a qualified psychiatrist takes a long time. After medical training, which, until quite recently, included a minimum of psychiatry in the curriculum, the prospective psychiatrist usually has to learn his subject matter almost from scratch. Some psychiatrists are well along in their thirties before they become qualified specialists. Moreover, nearly all psychiatrists are engaged in the treatment and care of disordered behavior, and few are working in the field of prevention.

Psychologists, as part of the clinical team, are growing rapidly in numbers. They should number about 1 per 10,000 people.[17] Although the available number of psychologists has been estimated at about 1,100 for 1948, many more have been turned out since that

[14] The National Health Assembly, *America's Health,* p. 199 (New York: Harper & Brothers, 1949).

[15] *The National Mental Health Program: Progress Report* (Washington: U.S. Government Printing Office, July 15, 1949).

[16] "Statistics Pertinent to Psychiatry in the United States," *Group for the Advancement of Psychiatry,* Report No. 7, March, 1949.

[17] *Ibid.*

time.[18] In addition to specified training, certificates which signify qualified ability are also being required in some states.

Qualified psychiatric social workers number 1,011. The estimated need for public institutions alone is placed at about 6,000.[19] Although there are 5,545 nurses in psychiatric service, few are in the field of mental health. In 1947 there were 21,499 public health nurses, but most of them did not have adequate training in preventive mental-health techniques. From 15,000 to 47,000 psychiatric nurses are required to meet the present needs in hospitals and in public health service. Though some psychiatric training is given to about 67 per cent of all undergraduate nurses, this training is not sufficient. Less than 12 schools of nursing offer postgraduate courses in psychiatry, and less than 50 nurses are equipped to teach and supervise public health techniques.[20]

The shortage of qualified personnel is especially felt in rural areas. Qualified personnel concentrate in urban communities because of better facilities and living conditions. For example, in 1941 New York had 585 psychiatrists, but Nevada had none. Since World War II, the distribution to rural areas has improved slightly. (See Map 5.)

Attitudes of the Public. Effective prevention depends upon the support and co-operation of the community. Public information and education in the principles of mental health, therefore, become essential and in keeping with a democratic framework. Felix states: "If we ever hope to get acceptance of psychiatric services in the community, if we ever hope to get the 'unseen' volume of mental diseases under treatment, we must create understanding on the part of the public." [21]

Co-operative action by the public also becomes vital. Varied interest groups must participate jointly, and a balance must be struck between the experts and the lay groups. On the one hand, if the expert disregards the advice of the group, democratic participation in the group may break down. On the other hand, if the expert overappeases the wishes of enthusiastic but uninformed persons, the program may be diverted from the demonstrable needs of the group.

[18] National Health Assembly, *America's Health,* p. 308.
[19] National Health Assembly, *America's Health,* p. 311.
[20] Robert H. Felix, "Psychiatric Plans of the United States Public Health Service," *Mental Hygiene,* July, 1946, XXX, p. 383.
[21] *Ibid.,* p. 387.

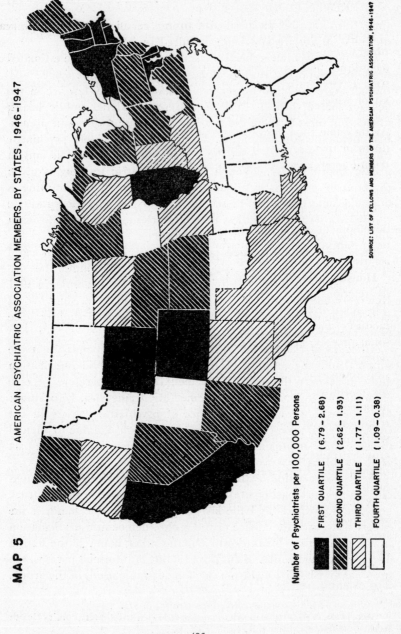

MAP 5

AMERICAN PSYCHIATRIC ASSOCIATION MEMBERS, BY STATES, 1946-1947

SOURCE: LIST OF FELLOWS AND MEMBERS OF THE AMERICAN PSYCHIATRIC ASSOCIATION, 1946-1947

Number of Psychiatrists per 100,000 Persons

FIRST QUARTILE   (6.79 – 2.68)

SECOND QUARTILE (2.62 – 1.93)

THIRD QUARTILE   (1.77 – 1.11)

FOURTH QUARTILE (1.09 – 0.38)

In the sections to follow, we will describe the need for preventive programs in varied social units and assess the types of preventive techniques and programs which are used in specific social units, such as the family, the school, the local community, and industry, all of which are phases of a total social continuum. These focal social units are the areas in which unstable persons can be detected. At the same time, however, the attitudes, relationships, and procedures of these groups frequently require revision in order to contribute more effectively to personal stability.

The Family

Since the influence of the family is so decisive upon personality development, it can be considered the hub of personality stability or instability. In this situation the home setting and the family relationships can be considered parts of an integrated pattern.

Housing and the Family. Insofar as the home setting affects family relationships, it obviously influences personality development. The main difficulties in housing are overcrowdedness, inadequate facilities, and lack of sanitation. Overcrowdedness can destroy personal privacy, make the child calloused to the sexual activities of parents, even induce personal shock. It can irritate and create tension among the family members. Plant pointed out "that the crowding of individuals repeatedly disillusions children." [22] In extreme instances, overcrowded conditions can indirectly or directly contribute to incestuous behavior. In a study of housing and incest, it was found that the homes in which incest occurred were more overcrowded than those for the average population.[23] Moreover, many of these homes were far below the standard necessary for minimum health.

When families double up, tensions multiply, especially in couples who live with their in-laws. Marriages which have ended in divorce because of these inadequate living arrangements have adversely affected the marital partners and their children.

Inadequate facilities in the home can also affect personal growth. For example, in 1940, 78.9 per cent of the rural farm dwellings, 51.2

<hr/>

[22] See James S. Plant, *Personality and the Cultural Pattern*, pp. 214–224 (New York: Commonwealth Fund, 1937).
[23] S. Kirson Weinberg, "Incest Behavior and Family Organization," unpublished Ph.D. thesis, University of Chicago Libraries, 1942.

per cent of the rural nonfarm dwellings, and 8.6 per cent of the urban dwellings had outside toilets.[24] These external factors may have an indirect effect upon personality development. Goldman and Bergman found that outside latrines had some effect in the higher incidence of enuresis among Negroes. The very fact that a child in this situation had to get out of a warm bed and go to a cold latrine could swing the balance in favor of enuresis.[25] We do not know whether rural persons have higher rates of enuresis than urban persons, but perhaps this phenomenon illustrates the relationship between some personality difficulties and dwelling facilities.

Although no definitive studies have shown the direct effects of improved housing upon personal disorders, a time study has been made between improved housing and the rates of juvenile delinquency. In this study of 317 New Haven families, the rate of delinquency was 3.18 for 100 children aged 7 to 17 before they occupied the new dwellings in a local housing authority. After they occupied the new dwellings, the rate was reduced to 1.64 per 100 children. The rate declined in the face of the fact that delinquency actually increased in the city during this period. Thus, improved housing can contribute to the reduction of juvenile delinquency.[26]

Perhaps the reduction of overcrowded, inadequate, and unsanitary housing might lessen existing conflicts within the family and might indirectly contribute to personal stability, at least in some families. As yet, we have no systematic knowledge of the specific correlation of these facts. Attempts to meet the problems and the shortage of housing by some kind of concerted planning, however, have been resisted by vested-interest groups, and at best, these plans are scattered and haphazard rather than concentrated and concerted.

Family Relationships. Since the family is the focal group in personality development, the parents, particularly the mother, often

[24] Sixteenth Census of the United States, 1940, Housing, General Characteristics 2, Part 1, Water Supply, p. 20. Quoted in Ernest W. Burgess and Harvey J. Locke, The Family, p. 103 (New York: American Book Company, 1945).

[25] George S. Goldman ·and Martin S. Bergman, "A Psychiatric and Rorschach Study of Adult Male Enuresis," American Journal of Orthopsychiatry, 1945, XV:1, pp. 160–166.

[26] "National Conference on Prevention and Control of Juvenile Delinquency," Report on Housing and Juvenile Delinquency (Washington, D.C.: U.S. Government Printing Office, 1947). See Walter Reckless, The Crime Problem, p. 511 (New York: Appleton-Century-Crofts, Inc., 1950).

have to be treated as well as the disturbed children. In this respect, the "attitude therapy" of D. Levy has been effective and has been widely accepted. The child is treated by the psychiatrist and the mother by the psychiatric social worker. The workings of this technique can be seen in the following case of Mrs. F.:[27]

It became clear at a certain state in the treatment that no matter what progress was made with her daughter, she would in some way provoke the child to defiant behavior. In the interviews she always asked such questions as: "What would you have done in this case? This is what I did." She would then give an instance of the impudence of her daughter and of her method of punishment. No matter what the social worker replied, she would proceed to defend her own methods and follow with further complaints about the daughter. Using the numerous situations as convincing material, the worker showed the mother how every one of them was a pattern. For example, the daughter, then age fifteen, had lost a hat and had told the mother of her numerous unsuccessful efforts to find it. To the daughter's recitation the mother made no response. This incident occurred in the presence of a neighbor who said to the mother, "I admire your patience." Thereupon the mother, looking angrily at the daughter, said, "If you had a daughter like mine, you'd have to learn patience." To this challenge the daughter responded by telling the mother she needn't get so nasty about it; she really had tried to look for her hat, and it was no fault of hers, etc. The scene finally ended at home with the mother's punishment of the daughter by deprivation of a privilege and a feeling on the latter's part of cruel and unfair treatment.

It was shown that every situation contained the same pattern. With the slightest provocation, the mother set into action a clash of personalities that ended, from the mother's point of view, in merited punishment. It must be added at this point that the mother's willingness to see in these situations a problem in her own attitude is made possible by the release of hostile feelings in recounting numerous incidents related to this pattern. It was important, therefore, that the worker refrain from interrupting such disclosures by rushing to the defense of the daughter, telling the mother how wonderfully she was regarded by the teachers, psychologists, etc. On the contrary, the worker interrupted at one stage only to make possible freer expression of the mother's hostile feelings, knowing that if the mother were put on the defensive, she would be in the position of having to prove how difficult the daughter was, justifying herself for punishing the child to keep her conscience clear. The illustration is used to indicate how the method of giving insight, so that it will be therapeutically effective, be-

[27] David Levy, "Attitude Therapy," *American Journal of Orthopsychiatry*, 1937, VII, pp. 103–113. See also Helen L. Witmer (editor), *Psychiatric Interviews with Children* (New York: Commonwealth Fund, 1946).

comes an integral part of the treatment. Assuming that the mother is convinced that the difficulty with the daughter clearly involved certain difficulties in herself, she is in a position to understand the need of attitude therapy.

Apparently, techniques for changing parental attitudes are known and applied, but these changes should be applied before as well as after a child becomes disturbed. Though the knowledge, the techniques, and some personnel are available, this information is not widespread enough and is not used enough.

Family Guidance. Families are in a stage of transition and confusion, and many need guidance. Urbanization has affected the rising status of women, heightened individuality, affected the marriage bond, and resulted in the declining authority of parents, the greater freedom of children, revisions of the sex mores, and the displacement of some family functions by industry and the state. Obviously, many parents are troubled, and their attitudes are reflected in their own relationships and in their relationships with their children. Blind adherence to family traditions no longer holds; hence, parental guidance becomes essential.

Counseling, which uses scientific techniques, strives to alleviate conflicts among family members—between parents as well as between parents and children. Family counseling centers have been established at many universities and in many large cities, but, family counseling in the rural areas remains a future prospect. Child guidance clinics also have been established in many states, but 25 states have no type of psychiatric clinic.[28] Some clinics not only treat children but also educate parents. For example, in 1935 the New Jersey Division of Maternal and Child Health began to include mental-health efforts in its general health program.

In 1939 the New York Bureau of Mental Hygiene of New York City began an educative program for physicians and nurses who worked in child health stations. Since the staff did not understand many behavior disturbances which occurred, they were supervised in small groups by a pediatrically trained psychiatrist. Occasionally these seminars were supplemented by lectures. In addition, pamphlet materials were issued to mothers who tried to apply the instructions in daily family relationships. Nurses then interviewed

[28] National Health Assembly. *America's Health,* p. 299. Though 600 community clinics exist, the need is for six times that many. *Ibid.,* p. 299.

the mothers to determine the effectiveness of the instructions. By these interviews changes were suggested and incorporated into new instructions.[29]

Though preventive and early treatment measures in the family are necessary for childhood stability, these measures are not enough. Preventive devices must be extended to the school and continued in other social groups.

The School

The Teacher and the School. The school is the first sustained separation of children from their families. This separation requires their reorientation to new persons—schoolmates and teachers. In this new setting the teacher is in a strategic position to detect emotionally disturbed children; and the need for prevention and early treatment is great.

In a study of third- and sixth-grade children from farm, nonfarm, and city dwellings in Miami County, Ohio, Mangus found that about 1 out of 5 children was seriously disturbed in some manner. Of 1,500 children who were tested, he found about 43 per cent were maladjusted in some way, and 19 per cent were very maladjusted. In a follow-up study one year later of 340 children, Mangus found that 80 per cent remained on about the same level of adjustment, 16 per cent improved, and about 4 per cent became worse. In general, this study points to the wide prevalence of disturbed children and to the fact that the family, the school, or both may have contributed to their disturbance.[30]

A mental-health program within the school would require: (1) educating teachers for preventive purposes, (2) recruiting stable teachers, (3) obtaining adequately trained visiting teachers, and (4) enlisting the help of parents.

Teachers can be trained to detect disturbed children, but often they require the co-operation of skilled consultants. The most helpful technical consultants would be acquainted with the special field in which they work. For example, in nursery day centers the most helpful consultants had previous experience in and were familiar

[29] Paul Y. Lemkau, *Mental Hygiene and Public Health* (New York: McGraw-Hill Book Company, Inc., 1949).

[30] Arthur R. Mangus, *Personality Adjustment of School Children* (Columbus, Ohio: F. J. Heer Printing Co., 1949).

with this field; those with inadequate professional training or previous experience were less helpful.[31]

Despite agreement that the teacher's personality is very important for educating children,[32] teachers are still selected primarily on the bases of knowledge of subject matter and formal teaching skills only. Yet studies reveal that as many as 15 per cent of teachers are maladjusted and can be emotionally harmful to the pupils.[33] The National Education Association has emphasized that emotionally unstable teachers can become so harmful to their pupils that they should not be allowed to teach. Such teachers may be very depressed, markedly prejudiced, intolerant, bitingly sarcastic, or extremely irritable, or may habitually scold their pupils. Although such teachers need psychiatric help, they should not teach while they are being helped.[34]

The dilemma of selecting stable and competent teachers is obvious. High standards are expected, and rewards are scant. Only when the incentives are adequate can criteria of personal stability, as well as knowledge of subject matter and training, be considered in the selection of teachers.

In some urban areas, the visiting teacher, formerly called the truant officer, represents the liaison between family and school. Many problems which arise in school result from personal problems in the family and in the community. The visiting teacher, by discovering these problems, can help the parents and the teachers work together for the benefit of the child.

When visiting teachers are adequately skilled and not overloaded with cases and clerical duties, their performances can be very helpful. Many "visiting teachers," however, lack training, are preoccupied with trivial duties, and are really "truant officers" with a new name. On the other hand, many rural communities still have "truant officers" in name as well as in function.

[31] Nina Ridenour, "Mental Hygiene Education," *Orthopsychiatry—1923–1948 —Retrospect and Prospect,* edited by L. G. Lowry and V. Sloane, p. 552 (Menasha, Wis.: American Orthopsychiatric Association, Inc., 1948).

[32] Morris Krugman, "Orthopsychiatry and Education," *Orthopsychiatry—1923– 1948—Retrospect and Prospect,* edited by L. G. Lowry and V. Sloane, pp. 259, 260 (Menasha, Wis.: American Orthopsychiatric Association, Inc., 1948).

[33] M. Ernest Townsend, "Mental Hygiene and Teacher Recruiting," *Mental Hygiene,* 1933, 17, pp. 556–560.

[34] National Education Association, *Health in the Schools,* pp. 138, 139 (Washington, D.C.: American Association of School Administrators, 1942).

The Parent-Teacher Association, which is the most appropriate organization for facilitating the relationship between parents and teachers, provides an opportunity for educating the parents about the emotional problems of their children. But no definitive studies of the effects of these parent-teacher relationships as a mental-health measure have been made.

Mental-health Programs in Elementary Schools. A three-year mental-health study has been in progress at Public School Number 53 in Manhattan, New York City.[35] This school is situated in the poorer and more deteriorated section of the city. The purpose of this study was to understand the varied social groups and the many needs of the children, and to provide them with a "realistic" guidance program by assisting the teachers in understanding the children.

Although this project seems to have a sound approach, results are vague; namely, that most children responded normally to their environment on the basis of their intelligence and personality endowments and that the teachers responded favorably in their daily relationships with students.

Other representative preventive projects in the primary and secondary schools are the "Force Project," the "Ojeman Project," the "Forest Hill Village Project," and the "Bullis Project." [36] We will describe briefly the procedures of the "Bullis Project."

In 1941, the Delaware State Society for Mental Hygiene sponsored weekly sessions in human relations for students in the sixth and seventh grades.[37] These classes lasted ten weeks and consisted of thirty lesson plans, such as "Public Enemies of Good Human Relations," "How Personality Traits Develop," "Our Inner Human Drives," and so on.

[35] Evelyn D. Adlerblum, "A Mental Hygiene Project in a City Public School," *Understanding the Child,* June, 1947, pp. 75–80. Evelyn D. Adlerblum, "Mental Hygiene Begins in School," *Mental Hygiene,* October, 1947, 31, pp. 541–555.

[36] For an evaluation of this program, see Committee on Preventive Psychiatry of the Group for the Advancement of Psychiatry, *Promotion of Mental Health in the Primary and Secondary Schools: An Evaluation of Four Projects,* Report No. 18, January, 1951, pp. 3–6.

[37] H. Edmund Bullis and Emily E. O'Malley, *Human Relations in the Classroom: Course I* (Wilmington, Del.: Delaware Society for Mental Hygiene, 1947); H. Edmund Bullis, *Human Relations in the Classroom: Course II;* Mesrop A. Tarumianz and H. Edmund Bullis, "A Preventive Mental Hygiene Program for Schools," *The American Journal of Psychiatry,* 1942–1943, 103, pp. 398–405.

After the teacher read a story involving certain personality problems, the students were encouraged to discuss the emotional problems, the solutions, and the motivation of the characters in the story, and to relate personal experiences which paralleled those in the story. By verbalizing their problems, the students presumably would gain more insight into them, and would learn that their problems are not unique but common, and generally would discern the importance of emotional reactions, such as worry, in human behavior. This effort as a form of improvised group counseling may be helpful to the students insofar as it possibly can lead to emotional support from their classmates and from the teacher. But whether this actually results can only be determined by further study. At present, human relations classes have been adopted by many schools in other states, so that more than 200,000 students are in these classes annually. This project would require more control of the sessions and a follow-up of disturbed students as well as of other students. The disturbed student who divulges his conflicts may become more miserable, especially when no follow-up interviews would help him solve these conflicts. As a means of detecting disturbed and shy children, however, this classroom technique may have promise. Yet this approach to prevention is based upon the question-and-answer method, in which students raise their hands and are called on by the teacher. Their answers have moral implications insofar as the teacher states whether these answers are right or wrong, and usually regards conformity to the existing mores equivalent to personal happiness. The course in human relations is not integrated with the rest of the curriculum and does not lead to concerted application in daily living.

In general, these programs, with the possible exception of the "Bullis Project," are experimental and somewhat localized but have favorable possibilities. These programs are among the few attempted. Apart from these programs, preventive work in the varied schools remains highly informal and unsystematic. One present trend in community-centered education may lend itself to preventive programs. The obstacles to preventive work, however, are many. Among them are the overcrowded schools, the few incentives for teachers, the tendency to accept emotionally unstable teachers, and the questionable belief that mere discussion of problems will necessarily correct emotional difficulties.

College. Less than 15 universities and colleges have adequate psychiatric counseling services, although the number with psychological counselors is perhaps much greater.[38] Undoubtedly, facilities for caring for disordered persons in colleges are woefully inadequate, and the need is great. Many freshman college students, who have left home for the first time and who have had domineering or overindulgent parents, find the transition difficult. Pressing conflicts can develop. Some may need emotional support to substitute for their family relationships. Also, the problems in the college environment may readily disturb some students. Clearly, a means of detecting those who are disturbed and those who may become disordered becomes rather vital in college.

In 1926 a mental-health project was begun at Yale. During a ten-year period, 1,257 full case studies of students were accumulated.[39] About 47 per cent required more than a few treatment interviews to correct their emotional problems; only 116 cases, or 8 per cent, who were seriously disturbed or psychotic, were regarded as "abnormal." The others were evaluated as "normal" individuals who encountered difficulties which they could not solve themselves and reacted by emotional or physical disturbances.[40]

The personality problems of the students were of two general types. They included distorted relationships with the family and with other persons, and the "school problem," covering social failure, inadequate vocational choice, and scholastic failure.

The aim of the project was to diagnose and to treat personality problems, and, sometimes, to expedite the student's adjustment by environmental manipulation. Students who were rejected by a fraternity or other groups, or who were excessively dependent upon their families, or who were economically handicapped became emotionally disorganized and needed psychiatric attention. By detecting the effects of extra-academic and academic relationships upon student adjustment, the clinicians recognized that students were not merely scholastic creatures limited to college influences but had multiple and contradictory motives. The clinicians not only aimed to treat students in the early stages of their disorders but also strived

[38] National Health Assembly, *America's Health,* p. 299.
[39] Clements C. Fry, *Mental Health in College* (New York: Commonwealth Fund, 1942).
[40] *Ibid.,* p. 31.

to increase personal stability and independence by aiding them to attain "mature self management."

No doubt intensive mental-health programs are necessary in colleges. These programs could enhance the academic performance of some students and redirect the aspirations of other students with lesser abilities to more attainable goals.[41] The Commonwealth Fund, in collaboration with several universities, such as Cornell, Cincinnati, and Harvard, has attempted to implement mental-health clinics in the general health program.[42]

Local Community

The local community is perhaps the most feasible unit for planning preventive programs. Although certain features of disorganization may obtain in all communities, each community has its own peculiar problems. Hence, these conflicts can be understood best when attacked at the local level.

The National Health Assembly has recommended that local communities set up voluntary community councils composed of representative interest groups whose aim would be primarily educational.[43] Assisted by experts, they would uncover the specific personality problems and would propose plans of action to meet these problems.

Community research has been directed mainly to allocating and to ascertaining the extent of personality problems in given communities. Ecological distributions of delinquency have furnished the facts for preventive efforts by pointing out the areas of greatest delinquent concentration.[44] Similarly, the areas of heaviest concentration of schizophrenic and manic-depressive disorders could also be the bases for treatment efforts. In slum residential areas catatonic schizophrenics are often concentrated. In rooming-house areas paranoids are most frequent. These ecological studies, as bases for more intensive social psychological analyses, could provide the knowledge

[41] Portia B. Hume, "Shattered Students in an Atomic Age," *Mental Hygiene,* 1947, XXXI, p. 567.

[42] *Thirtieth Annual Report,* p. 5 (New York: Commonwealth Fund, February, 1949).

[43] National Health Assembly, *America's Health,* pp. 305, 306.

[44] Clifford R. Shaw and Henry D. McKay, *Delinquency and Urban Areas* (Chicago: University of Chicago Press, 1942).

for preventive programs.[45] At the least, the residents could be educated to use the facilities which could handle their problems before their disorders became too serious.

In a study of a predominantly native white population, 96.8 per cent, in a rural and semirural area of Miami County, Ohio, Mangus and Seeley found, by a cautious estimate, that 5,000 to 10,000 persons out of about 52,600 persons, or 10 to 20 per cent, required professional counseling services.[46] They found that about 1 person out of 10 had been rejected for military service and that 109 persons were committed to mental hospitals during the years 1940 to 1945. The rates of rejection for military service were higher among farm than nonfarm persons, and the incidence of personal disorders was higher among farm workers than among persons in other occupational groups. This study shows that farm dwellers are not free of personal difficulties. The farm may be advantageous for younger children; it is less advantageous for older persons. Despite the prevalence of maladjusted persons in many local communities, as these studies show, few preventive programs are in process. We will describe the representative programs.

Community Mental-health Projects. A clinic-centered community mental-health project in Prince Georges County, Maryland, was designed to study methods by which a mental-health program could be made a part of an over-all health program for the county.[47] It strived to demonstrate the importance of psychiatric treatment for existing disorders and to cultivate confidence among the residents in the mental-health principles of the clinic. Each case provided a basis for study of the friction points in the community which contributed to the particular disorders. These friction points revealed where preventive action might have averted the personality disturbance. The functions of the clinic consisted of (1) individual service and treatment, (2) community activities, and (3) demonstration.

From January, 1948, to January, 1949, 423 patients were seen in

[45] H. Warren Dunham, "Ecological Studies of Mental Disorders: Their Significance for Mental Hygiene," *Mental Hygiene,* April, 1940, XXIV, pp. 238–249.

[46] Arthur R. Mangus and John R. Seeley, *Mental Health Needs in a Rural and Semi-Rural Area of Ohio,* Mimeographed Bulletin No. 195 (Columbus, Ohio: Ohio State University, 1947).

[47] Mabel Ross, "Pilot Mental Health Clinic," *Public Health Reports,* June 24, 1949, 2942, pp. 797–801.

the clinic. Of these patients, 281 were under and 142 were over 18 years of age. These patients were referred by physicians, ministers, the probation department, and social agencies, as well as by relatives and friends; some came on their own initiative. Treatment was concentrated upon those persons whose emotional problems interfered with their participation in the family, in the school, or in the work situation. The seriously disturbed persons were referred to other places for more intensive therapy.

The results of this work show an impressive start: 18 patients who might have required institutional care in a general mental hospital were able to participate in the community; 4 persons who attempted suicide were reasonably well adjusted; 5 potential divorces were averted; and 16 families improved their economic status because the patients were either able to accept employment or to change to full-time employment.

The community activities consisted of studying ways of integrating the mental-health program with the general health program of the county, by mothers' discussion groups in prenatal and well-baby clinics, and by conferences with parents. A part-time clinic, held twice monthly, was established in a rural area; greater co-operation was fostered with the schools, and the clinic served as a demonstration center for visitors from other counties and states.

The "Peckham Experiment." As distinguished from the clinic-centered mental-health program, the "Peckham Experiment" in London attempted to integrate the families by a recreation and health center.[48] Though this center provided many recreational facilities and some counseling services, its effectiveness in an encompassing community health program was very limited. At best, it reduced family isolation in an urban community and provided certain satisfactory social outlets for parents and children, but it overlooked the more intricate and subtle facets of family relations which could contribute to disordered conditions.

"Total Approach" to Community Problems. A total approach to community problems has been advocated by the Chicago Back of the Yards Council.[49] Though oriented to delinquency prevention in

[48] Innes H. Pearse and Lucy H. Crocker, *The Peckham Experiment: A Study in the Living Structure of Society* (London: George Allen & Unwin, Ltd., 1943).
[49] Saul D. Alinsky, *Reveille for Radicals* (Chicago: University of Chicago Press, 1946); Saul D. Alinsky, "Community Analysis and Organization," *American Journal of Sociology*, May, 1941, 46, pp. 797–808.

communities of lower income levels, this approach also could pertain to mental-health programs. After the people in the community were organized, these "grass roots" organizations would deal with all social problems and would not be limited to one problem. For example, mental health alone could not be stressed unless poor housing, inadequate schools, lack of recreational facilities, and unemployment were also considered. This approach opposes specialized community councils which do not recognize the integration of all problems, and which do not help the people solve their own problems.

Yet this approach would require an indefinite wait before any results could be achieved. The specific techniques required for solving mental-health problems could be attained by immediate social action. Finally, this approach applies mainly to communities of lower income levels and does not include communities of higher income groups.

Nevertheless, it is hard to deny that an integrated approach to community problems in the family, school, recreational centers, and industry could eliminate needless overlapping of functions among different agencies.

Important Personalities in the Community. The strategic personalities in the community, for instance the doctor and the clergyman, could help detect disordered behavior before it becomes serious.

The Medical Doctor. The doctor can become a significant person in detecting the early stages of personal disorders among his patients when he has some knowledge of the emotional basis of disordered behavior. Generally, the patient seeks relief from his physical disorders and often overlooks his emotional difficulties. The doctor has the unique opportunity to determine when these illnesses are complicated by or are the results of personality disturbances.

The rural practitioner who has a relatively intimate history of his patients is in an especially favorable position to detect these disorders. A working knowledge of psychiatry can become extremely useful, even for treating physical illnesses which are so often admixed with emotional conflicts.

During World War II, thousands of soldier patients were referred to psychiatrists by medical doctors. To offset this tendency, in part, the Army had to prepare a bulletin to instruct the Army doctor about disordered behavior.[50] Doctors who are unaware of the emotional aspects of illness may tend to overexamine the patient in the vain effort to discover a physical cause for the symptoms, may dismiss the patient's complaint with "nothing is the matter," may ignore or neglect the patient, scold or kid him, or express their own annoyance at the patient's lack of improvement.

Apart from referring emotionally disturbed patients to the psychiatrist, the medical practitioner must use his knowledge judiciously, for treatment of emotional difficulties requires a knowledge of psychotherapy and often takes a long time. Yet the doctor may be able to resolve mild family tensions, or he may emotionally support the patient who could then perform his daily routine without aggravating his condition.

The Clergyman and the Church. The clergyman is a crucial person in helping uncover potential and actual disorders among his church members. Often consulted about personal matters, he has a direct and indirect influence upon the members. Frequently, he is close to the family during the critical periods of birth, marriage, and bereavement, and he provides the cultural outlets to these emotional reactions. Moreover, the clergyman can provide the type of religious values which can help to integrate the personality. In 1933 Boisen, recognizing these facts, attempted to acquaint pastors with counseling functions.[51] Since then, pastoral counseling has become widespread among the clergy. In 1941, 18 out of 90 theological schools trained their students in clinical techniques.[52] More recently, about 2,000 clergymen and theological students have had a period of internship in hospitals and clinics. Pastoral counseling is gradually becoming a systematic practice in which the minister can become adept at relieving and resolving personal conflicts or at least in emotionally supporting some of his parishioners.[53] The prestige of the pastor is such that he is a "natural" for counseling. Seeing many

[50] William C. Menninger, *Psychiatry in a Troubled World,* pp. 447–448 (New York: The Macmillan Company, 1948). See "Neuropsychiatry for the General Medical Officer," *Mental Hygiene,* October, 1945, XXIX, pp. 622–643.

[51] See Anton T. Boisen, "Clinical Training for Students of Theology in the Service of the Mentally Ill," *Elgin State Hospital Papers II,* 1936, pp. 154–160.

[52] Seward Hiltner, "Religion and Pastoral Counseling," *American Journal of Orthopsychiatry,* January, 1947, pp. 21–26.

[53] Thomas A. C. Rennie and Luther E. Woodward, *Mental Health and Modern Society,* p. 239 (New York: Commonwealth Fund, 1948).

persons in the throes of personal and familial crises, he is in a position to avert more serious disorders.[54]

Industry

Employees in industry are not merely parts of an economic system; they are parts of a social process which is integrally related with outside social influences. Their interests, productivity, and morale in the particular industry result from their working conditions, from interemployee and employee-supervisor relationships, and from past and present relationships in outside groups. Employees prone to continued absenteeism, to accidents, to excessive fatigue, to psychosomatic ailments, or to nonco-operation have been influenced by one or a combination of these social situations. Yet the sources of these disturbances, when uncovered, reflect the singular personalities involved and also reveal the areas of tension and discontent among employees generally.

Studies by Roethligsberger and Dickson, and others, show that the individual worker cannot be understood apart from his social relationships and from the meanings of his relationships.[55] For example, when employees reacted favorably to rest pauses, they felt that these pauses were for their health rather than for speeding up work. Workers who engaged in repetitive and monotonous tasks offset their brooding by communicating with each other. Innovations in plants which did not consider employees' social interpretations tended to disrupt rather than to facilitate efficient functioning in the factory. Even levels of wages could be best understood in the social context rather than as abstractions.[56]

Studies of the prevalence of the personal disorders in industry are few, and programs of mental health in industry are fewer. None-

[54] See Seward Hiltner, "Religion and Pastoral Counseling," *American Journal of Orthopsychiatry*, January, 1947, pp. 21–24.

[55] John F. Roethligsberger and W. J. Dickson, *Management and the Worker* (Cambridge, Mass.: Harvard University Press, 1943); also John F. Roethligsberger, *Management & Morale* (Cambridge, Mass.: Harvard University Press, 1941); Elton Mayo, *The Human Problems of an Industrial Civilization* (New York: The Macmillan Company, 1935); V. V. Anderson, *Psychiatry in Industry* (New York: Harper & Brothers, 1929); Luther E. Woodward and Thomas A. C. Rennie, *Jobs and the Man* (Springfield, Ill.: Charles C Thomas, Publisher, 1945).

[56] John F. Roethligsberger and W. J. Dickson, *Management and the Worker*.

theless, the need for maintaining the physical and mental health of employees is increasingly recognized.[57]

Preventive Mental Health in Industry. One problem which may have to be overcome in an industrial mental-health program is enlisting the co-operation of management and labor.[58] On the one hand, management would have to be reoriented so that workers are treated as persons and not as labor commodities. On the other hand, the stigma associated with personal disorders would have to be reduced markedly among the workers and supervisors in order to enlist their co-operation to seek treatment when it is necessary. Yet the actual treatment facilities in a factory may necessarily have to be limited to mild disorders.

Preventive measures, apart from actual treatment of mild disorders, require the selection of stable and co-operative personnel, the elimination of tension-inducing conditions, and the resolution of conflicts among employees.[59]

Himmler studied the maladjustments of employees in a factory of 2,200 workers. The plant physician recorded his informal observations of the mental and emotional stability of applicants. About 3 per cent of these applicants were unsuited for factory work because of personal instability and their general social attitudes. To determine the reliability of these observations, he studied the employees who worked in the plant for two or more years. A high proportion of the employees who were unco-operative and who created excessive tension with their co-workers and supervisors were among the 3 per cent of the employees who were considered to have unsuitable personalities, as manifested by arrogance, resentment, distrust, slow mental processes, anxiety, and excitability.[60]

In an attempt to train foremen as counselors, Himmler used lectures, conferences, and direct individual interviews to help foremen recognize problems of maladjustment. He also interviewed

[57] See Russel Fraser, *Incidence of Neurosis among Factory Workers*, p. 14 (London: His Majesty's Stationery Office, 1947); Ernest H. Copel, "Problems of Neurosis in Industry," *Practitioner*, 1942, p. 356.

[58] See Lawrence S. Kubie, "Psychiatry and Industry," *Mental Hygiene*, April, 1945, 29, pp. 201–204.

[59] Christopher Leggo, Stanley G. Law, and Eric K. Clarke, "Industrial Psychiatry in the Community of Oak Ridge," *Industrial Medicine*, April, 1946, XV, pp. 243–254.

[60] L. E. Himmler, "Current Trends in Industrial Psychiatry," *The American Journal of Psychiatry*, 1943, 103, pp. 149–153.

employees in the presence of the foreman in order to give the worker an "impartial" hearing and at the same time to instruct the foreman in interview techniques. The chief tangible result was that the foremen, impressed by the technique, wanted help for their own personal problems.[61] Though foremen might learn to understand their workers more clearly and might detect disturbed workers, it is doubtful whether they could become effective impartial therapists.

Lewin has illustrated how overlapping authority created a persistent conflict in industry among the mechanic, the supervisor, and the operators, and how this conflict was resolved.[62]

Indeed, intensive research in and the application of social dynamics are necessary in industry, but with the joint approval of labor and management. It would be necessary to find the broadly inherent conflicts between labor and management which exaggerate interpersonal conflicts and which confuse the essential issues; the resolution of these conflicts might benefit both groups. Good production tends to heighten morale; low production tends to lower morale.[63]

The reverse can also be true. Roethligsberger has pointed out that the amount of time which subordinates devote to thinking about their superiors, both on and off the job, is tremendous, and that this form of preoccupation has contributed not only to anguish but also to emotional disturbances and disorders. Since the human factor is often omitted from the process of industrial efficiency, the personalized feelings of employees are neglected. As a result, both personal stability and actual efficiency are affected adversely.

By facilitating the communicative process between management and labor, by clarifying the issues of conflict, and by improving the sources of information to the public, much could be done to minimize the broad aspects of industrial conflict. Within this framework, more effective programs of mental health could be achieved. This program of mental health in industry would not only require the advice of a clinical team but would have a productive arrangement

[61] L. E. Himmler, "Psychotherapeutic Aspects of Foremen Contacts," *Mental Hygiene*, 1945, 29, pp. 106–115.
[62] Kurt Lewin, "The Solution of a Chronic Conflict in Industry," *Resolving Social Conflicts*, pp. 125–141 (New York: Harper & Brothers, 1948).
[63] John F. Roethligsberger, *Management and Morale* (Cambridge, Mass.: Harvard University Press, 1944); also see his, "The Foreman—Master and Victim of Double Talk," *Harvard Business Review*, Spring, 1945, 23, pp. 283–299.

which would minimize tensions among the workers and among the supervisors.[64]

"Displaced" Persons: the Unemployed and the Aged

Persons who are economically displaced and handicapped, such as the unemployed and the aged, are especially vulnerable to emotional disturbances. Their limited participation in the economic and social life of the community can create aggravated conflicts and problems which are outgrowths of the social situations in which they find themselves.

The Unemployed. Halliday has pointed out that in the distressed areas of Scotland where unemployment was high, the rates of psychosomatic disorders also increased.[65] Malzberg has shown that schizophrenic and manic-depressive disorders increased during the depression and during unemployment.[66]

The effects of the socioeconomic condition upon the person can be overlooked when the individual's deficiencies alone are stressed. While it is true that disordered persons find it very difficult to participate successfully in economic life, this does not eliminate the fact of the influence of economic adversity upon personal stability. Eisenberg and Lazarsfeld have shown that the unemployed tend to become demoralized, to feel helpless and useless, and that when the unemployment lasts long enough, they tend to narrow their interests and wants, until the self can no longer endure this contraction and a breakdown may occur. Studies of unemployment during the depression by Angell and by Cavan and Rank have arrived at somewhat similar conclusions, although they have shown that different reactions exist among differently classified families.[67]

[64] See David Krech and Richard S. Crutchfield, *Theory and Problems in Social Psychology,* Chap. 14 (New York: McGraw-Hill Book Company, Inc., 1948).

[65] James L. Halliday, *Psychosocial Medicine,* pp. 80–83 (New York: W. W. Norton, Inc., 1948).

[66] Benjamin Malzberg, *Social and Biological Aspects of Mental Disease,* pp. 279–280 (Utica, N.Y.: State Hospitals Press, 1940).

[67] Philip Eisenberg and Paul F. Lazarsfeld, "The Psychological Effects of Unemployment," *Psychological Bulletin,* 1938, XXXV, pp. 358–390; Bohan Zawadski and Paul F. Lazarsfeld, "The Psychological Consequences of Unemployment," *The Journal of Social Psychology,* 1935, VI, pp. 224–250; Robert C. Angell, *The Family Encounters the Depression* (New York: Charles Scribner's Sons, 1936); Ruth S. Cavan and Katherine H. Rank, *The Family and the Depression* (Chicago: University of Chicago Press, 1938).

The Aged. Aged persons, 65 and over, represent one of the most formidable challenges to our society, especially in the field of mental health. The number of aged people has increased to over 11,000,000 for 1950, and continues to increase, but means have not been worked out to care for many of the aged who have been displaced in economic and social life.

Many aged persons are the victims of the smaller family and the smaller home. No longer deferred to as formerly, they become increasingly dependent upon the family for social companionship as well as for economic aid. Differing in their tastes, often rigid and petulant, they find that they cannot fit into the family scheme in a satisfactory manner. Since facilities for their care are few, and since private sanataria are expensive, many families absolve themselves from further responsibility by committing their aged relatives to mental hospitals.

Yet older persons in the higher income brackets have definite social and personal problems, especially with reference to finding new interests and in sustaining new companionships. Those who have been oriented toward an intense work routine find that the transition to a more leisurely life is both irksome and trying for them.

Moreover, the character of our culture is such that the interests and diversions that are emphasized in mass mediums of communication tend toward the likes of the adolescent. Clearly, aged persons are not "older adolescents," and their cultivation of tastes should be in keeping with their more mellow years.

The institutional changes which are necessary to accommodate the needs and tastes of the aged have only begun to be worked out. Although research is being carried out in the psychiatric, psychological, and sociological aspects of aging, the actual institutional needs trail far behind.

A general and concerted program for reorienting the aged to their lives of leisure, coupled with adequate pensions for those who need them, would go far toward instilling purpose and self-reliance among an age group that is still very much neglected in our society.[68]

[68] George A. Lawton, *New Goals for Old Age* (New York: Columbia University Press, 1944).

Cultural Problems in Prevention

Despite some advances in preventive mental health, inherent obstacles in our culture can and do retard this progress.

First, the highly individualistic, competitive, and mobile culture makes conflict and isolation inevitable. The expedient and segmental attitudes among persons in institutional life can lead to tension, hostility, and anxiety. Since persons are evaluated in terms of the norms of a given institution, whether in industry, in school, or in the community, their emotional needs are often overlooked. The total pattern of these impersonal institutions may tend to minimize the personal reactions of people who are in need of help but who have no place to seek it.

Second, the attitudes toward failure are very harsh, and there are few outlets for this predicament. Within our society the aspiring and climbing person has no satisfactory outlets for failure in his career. The function of religion becomes a vital force, and the need for treatment techniques to reorient these persons who have failed are necessary to avert mild and severe breakdowns.

Third, the stigma of personal disorders is still rather widespread, and this may deter the individual from seeking help when it is most needed, so as to avert a more serious disorder. Moreover, the individual who has incurred a breakdown may need the emotional support of the persons about him, rather than their censure, avoidance, or ridicule.

Fourth, the philosophy which opposes constructive social change in any area of personal and social welfare would oppose programs of mental health. The cost would be too forbidding, and the life of the community would involve too much inquiry and perhaps regulation. For this group, the rates of disorders per year would be about as normal and as inevitable as the annual rates of traffic accidents. Yet, if planning were at the local level and would involve the co-operation of the varied agencies and institutions, the voluntary character of the changes in the community would overcome some of these objections.

Fifth, the effects of poverty, such as malnutrition, inadequate housing, and general economic insecurity, can affect personal stability as well as physical health. Though the majority of the persons in the lower socioeconomic strata do not break down, still these factors tend to affect adversely a definite proportion of these groups.

Sixth, the character of impersonal urban living has tended to revise and even to corrode many of the personal relationships which are essential to sustained emotional balance. As a result, many persons are emotionally isolated, families are in a state of transition, and no immediate substitutes for these conditions are accessible in the foreseeable future, except in part by the use of psychotherapy and counseling.

Seventh, along with the urban changes and the increase of leisure time, many adults have been unable to profit by their leisure.[69] Life among the aged, as we have shown, can become boresome and even meaningless. These orientations require extensive programs of re-education.

Summary

Effective programs for preventing personal disorders require the co-operation of many disciplines dealing with personality and the group, the training of technicians, and the co-operation of the society at the local, state and national levels. Since society is a continuum, and one social unit influences another, for practical purposes it is necessary to have a point of departure by which to detect unstable persons and by which to heighten the stability of personalities. Despite the pressing need for preventive programs, few are in operation, and these few are in the beginning stages. The family, school, local community, and industry are the significant social units in which complete or partial preventive programs have been tried.

Displaced persons, such as the unemployed and the aged, are continuing challenges in our culture, and programs of reorientation for both groups must be implemented to avert breakdown. As yet, these programs are slow to come.

Indigenous to our culture are certain obstacles to personal stability. These obstacles include the impersonal and segmental relations in institutions; the few outlets for economic failure and feelings of personal failure; the stigma attached to personal disorders, especially psychotic disorders; the resistance to social change and welfare programs; the prevalence of malnutrition, inadequate housing, and economic insecurity; the personal isolation; and the inability to use leisure time effectively.

[69] See David Reisman, *The Lonely Crowd* (New Haven: Yale University Press, 1950).

Selected Readings

Adlerblum, Evelyn D., "A Mental Hygiene Project in a City Public School," *Understanding the Child,* June, 1947, pp. 75–80.

Bullis, H. Edmund, and Emily E. O'Malley, *Human Relations in the Classroom: Courses* (Wilmington, Del.: Society for Mental Hygiene, 1947).

Burgess, Ernest W., and Harvey J. Locke, "Family Reorganization," *The Family,* Chap. 22 (New York: The American Book Company, 1945).

Felix, Robert H., and Raymond V. Bowers, "Mental Hygiene and Socio-environmental Factors," *The Milbank Memorial Fund Quarterly,* April, 1948, XXVI:2, pp. 125–147.

Fry, Clements C., *Mental Health in College* (New York: Commonwealth Fund, 1942).

Group for the Advancement of Psychiatry, "An Outline for Evaluation of a Community Program in Mental Hygiene," Report No. 8, April, 1949.

———, Committee on Preventive Psychiatry, "Promotion of Mental Health in the Primary and Secondary Schools: An Evaluation of Four Projects," Report No. 18, January, 1951.

Lemkau, Paul V., *Mental Hygiene in Public Health* (New York: McGraw-Hill Book Company, Inc., 1949).

Lewin, Kurt, "The Solution of a Chronic Conflict in Industry," *Resolving Social Conflicts* (New York: Harper & Brothers, 1948).

Mangus, Arthur R., "Personality Adjustment of Rural and Urban Children," *American Sociological Review,* October, 1948, XII:5, pp. 566–575.

Menninger, William C., *Psychiatry in a Troubled World,* Part II (New York: The Macmillan Company, 1948).

Rennie, Thomas A. C., and Luther E. Woodward, *Mental Health and Modern Society* (New York: Commonwealth Fund, 1948).

Roethligsberger, John F., *Management and Morale* (Cambridge, Mass.: Harvard University Press, 1941).

Ross, Mabel, "Pilot Mental Health Clinic," *Public Health Reports,* June 24, 1949, 2942, pp. 797–801.

Snyder, William U., "Recent Investigations of Mental Hygiene in the Schools," *Educational Research Bulletin, Ohio State University* (1945), pp. 178–185.

Stevenson, George S., "The Prevention of Personality Disorders," *Personality and the Behavior Disorders,* edited by J. McV. Hunt, Vol. II, Chap. 35 (New York: The Ronald Press Company, 1944).

Stevenson, George S., and Geddes Smith, *Child Guidance Clinics—A Quarter Century of Development* (New York: Commonwealth Fund, 1935).

The National Health Assembly, *America's Health,* Chap. XII (New York: Harper & Brothers, 1949).

Witmer, Helen L., *Psychiatric Clinics for Children* (New York: Commonwealth Fund, 1940).

Author Index

A

Abel, Theodora, 42
Abeles, M., 159
Abraham, Karl, 258
Abrahams, J., 357
Ackerman, Nathan W., 356, 357
Adams, Edward C., 404, 408
Adler, Alfred, 309
Adler, Herman, 33, 52
Adlerblum, Evelyn D., 503, 518
Aichorn, August, 286, 296
Alexander, Franz, 36, 37, 52, 63, 67, 75, 86, 152, 156, 263, 296, 310, 318, 320, 324, 336, 338.
Alinsky, Saul D., 508
Allen, Frederick H., 302, 304, 328, 338
Allport, Gordon W., 40, 41, 66, 87
Anderson, V. V., 511
Angell, Robert C., 514
Anthonisen, Neils L., 243, 246
Appel, John, 361
Asch, S. E., 25
Auden, William H., 489
Axlinè, Virginia, 328

B

Bain, Read, 58
Baldwin, James M., 40
Bales, Robert F., 355
Balinsky, Benjamin, 476, 486
Barritt, V. R., 455
Bassan, M. E., 106
Bateman, J. Fremont, 408
Bateson, Gregory, 13, 48, 53, 324

Baynes, Cary F., 339
Beaglehole, Ernest, 47, 99, 102, 106, 231
Beck, Samuel J., 239 262
Becker, Howard, 58
Beers, Clifford W., 450, 466, 473
Bellak, Leopold, 211, 212, 233, 368, 480
Bender, Lauretta, 339
Benedict, Ruth, 47, 96, 97, 106
Bennett, E. A., 144
Bentley, Madison, 14, 33, 34, 92
Berg, Charles, 111, 150, 321, 336
Bergman, Martin S., 498
Berman, Harold H., 244
Berrera, S. Eugene, 19, 29
Bettelheim, Bruno, 82
Bierer, J., 354
Black, N. D., 455
Blacker, C. P., 492
Blalock, J. R., 258
Bleuler, Emil, 210
Bleuler, M., 41
Bleuler, R., 41
Block, H., 25
Blumer, Herbert, 43-45, 52
Bogen, Eugene F., 437
Boisen, Anton T., 67, 208, 218, 224, 227, 510
Bonner, Clarence A., 243
Bonney, Merl E., 38
Bowers, Raymond V., 518
Bowman, Karl M., 201, 245
Boyle, Rosalie D., 21, 490
Braceland, Francis J., 217
Brill, A. A., 35, 63, 155, 159, 318
Brill, Norman Q., 477
Bromberg, Walter, 263, 295, 296

519

Subject Index

A

Abnormal behavior
adherence to reality and, 93
as social definition, 91, 94
culture and, 98
defined, 91, 92
disordered behavior and, 94-97
forms of, 88
ideal personal stability and, 89, 90
in American society, 105
institutional outlets and, 94
modal personality stability, 90
personal disorders and, 94-96
universal criteria of, 96
usual behavior and, 89
Acting-out disorders (*see also* Psychopathy)
approaches to, 262, 263
cultural deviant and, 9, 288, 290
defined, 261
delinquency and, 292, 293
drug-addiction and, 293, 294
in Colvin and Needles of Hollow Folk, 100-102
misconceptions of, 260-262
neurosis and, 281-285
self-centered, indulged personality, and, 285-288
society and, 294, 295
types of, 263, 264, 290
Acting-out neurotics (*see also* Acting-out disorders; Neurosis)
defined, 291
development of, 282-285
differences and similarities with the neurotic, 283, 284
dynamics of, 282

Action
as unit of behavior, 60, 61
conflict and, 61-64
frustrated, 62
incompleted, 57, 58
in neurosis, 63
in psychopathy, 64
in psychosis, 64
repeated, 64, 65
simple, 61
threat and, 63
unconscious influences upon, 64-66
Adolescence
anxiety and, 113, 124
manic depression and, 245-248
schizophrenia and, 203-207
Adult behavior
in American society, 91
in Mundugumor society, 91
in Zuñi society, 91
Age
average among patients in mental hospitals, 364
old and mental health, 514, 515
psychosis and, 170, 171
Alcoholics in state mental hospitals, 444, 445
American society
abnormal behavior in, 105, 106
adult behavior in, 91
as competitive and individualistic, 124, 125
disordered behavior in, 105, 106
normal behavior in, 91
psychotherapy and, 325
Amnesia, 141
Anthropology, social, 45-48

526